Utilizing AI and Machine Learning for Natural Disaster Management

D. Satishkumar
Nehru Institute of Technology, India

M. Sivaraja
Nehru Institute of Technology, India

A volume in the Advances in Computational Intelligence and Robotics (ACIR) Book Series

Published in the United States of America by
IGI Global
Engineering Science Reference (an imprint of IGI Global)
701 E. Chocolate Avenue
Hershey PA, USA 17033
Tel: 717-533-8845
Fax: 717-533-8661
E-mail: cust@igi-global.com
Web site: http://www.igi-global.com

Copyright © 2024 by IGI Global. All rights reserved. No part of this publication may be reproduced, stored or distributed in any form or by any means, electronic or mechanical, including photocopying, without written permission from the publisher. Product or company names used in this set are for identification purposes only. Inclusion of the names of the products or companies does not indicate a claim of ownership by IGI Global of the trademark or registered trademark.
                Library of Congress Cataloging-in-Publication Data

Names: Satishkumar, D., 1980- editor. | Muthusamy, Sivaraja, 1974- editor.
Title: Utilizing AI and machine learning for natural disaster management /
   Edited by D. Satishkumar, Sivaraja Muthusamy.
Description: Hershey, PA : Engineering Science Reference, [2024] | Includes
   bibliographical references and index. | Summary: "Technology
   improvements over the decades are capable of predicting hazards early
   but the disaster preparedness phase requires knowledge about human
   psychology pre and post disaster"-- Provided by publisher.
Identifiers: LCCN 2024002030 (print) | LCCN 2024002031 (ebook) | ISBN
   9798369333624 (hardcover) | ISBN 9798369333631 (ebook)
Subjects: LCSH: Natural disasters--Remote sensing. | Environmental
   geotechnology. | Emergency management.
Classification: LCC GB5014 .U85 2024 (print) | LCC GB5014 (ebook) | DDC
   363.34/7028563--dc23/eng/20240214
LC record available at https://lccn.loc.gov/2024002030
LC ebook record available at https://lccn.loc.gov/2024002031

This book is published in the IGI Global book series Advances in Computational Intelligence and Robotics (ACIR) (ISSN: 2327-0411; eISSN: 2327-042X)

British Cataloguing in Publication Data
A Cataloguing in Publication record for this book is available from the British Library.

All work contributed to this book is new, previously-unpublished material. The views expressed in this book are those of the authors, but not necessarily of the publisher.

For electronic access to this publication, please contact: eresources@igi-global.com.

Advances in Computational Intelligence and Robotics (ACIR) Book Series

Ivan Giannoccaro
University of Salento, Italy

ISSN:2327-0411
EISSN:2327-042X

Mission

While intelligence is traditionally a term applied to humans and human cognition, technology has progressed in such a way to allow for the development of intelligent systems able to simulate many human traits. With this new era of simulated and artificial intelligence, much research is needed in order to continue to advance the field and also to evaluate the ethical and societal concerns of the existence of artificial life and machine learning.

The **Advances in Computational Intelligence and Robotics (ACIR) Book Series** encourages scholarly discourse on all topics pertaining to evolutionary computing, artificial life, computational intelligence, machine learning, and robotics. ACIR presents the latest research being conducted on diverse topics in intelligence technologies with the goal of advancing knowledge and applications in this rapidly evolving field.

Coverage

- Heuristics
- Cyborgs
- Evolutionary Computing
- Automated Reasoning
- Computer Vision
- Cognitive Informatics
- Artificial Intelligence
- Computational Intelligence
- Computational Logic
- Neural Networks

IGI Global is currently accepting manuscripts for publication within this series. To submit a proposal for a volume in this series, please contact our Acquisition Editors at Acquisitions@igi-global.com or visit: http://www.igi-global.com/publish/.

The Advances in Computational Intelligence and Robotics (ACIR) Book Series (ISSN 2327-0411) is published by IGI Global, 701 E. Chocolate Avenue, Hershey, PA 17033-1240, USA, www.igi-global.com. This series is composed of titles available for purchase individually; each title is edited to be contextually exclusive from any other title within the series. For pricing and ordering information please visit http://www.igi-global.com/book-series/advances-computational-intelligence-robotics/73674. Postmaster: Send all address changes to above address. Copyright © 2024 IGI Global. All rights, including translation in other languages reserved by the publisher. No part of this series may be reproduced or used in any form or by any means – graphics, electronic, or mechanical, including photocopying, recording, taping, or information and retrieval systems – without written permission from the publisher, except for non commercial, educational use, including classroom teaching purposes. The views expressed in this series are those of the authors, but not necessarily of IGI Global.

Titles in this Series

For a list of additional titles in this series, please visit:
www.igi-global.com/book-series/advances-computational-intelligence-robotics/73674

Bio-inspired Swarm Robotics and Control Algorithms, Mechanisms, and Strategies
Parijat Bhowmick (Indian Institute of Technology, Guwahati, India) Sima Das (Bengal College of Engineering and Technology, India) and Farshad Arvin (Durham Universit, UK)
Engineering Science Reference • © 2024 • 261pp • H/C (ISBN: 9798369312773) • US $315.00

Comparative Analysis of Digital Consciousness and Human Consciousness Bridging the Divide in AI Discourse
Remya Lathabhavan (Indian Institute of Management, Bodh Gaya, India) and Nidhi Mishra (Indian Institute of Management, Bodh Gaya, ndia)
Engineering Science Reference • © 2024 • 355pp • H/C (ISBN: 9798369320150) • US $315.00

Machine Learning Techniques and Industry Applications
Pramod Kumar Srivastava (Rajkiya Engineering College, Azamgarh, India) and Ashok Kumar Yadav (Rajkiya Engineering College, Azamgarh, India)
Engineering Science Reference • © 2024 • 307pp • H/C (ISBN: 9798369352717) • US $365.00

Intelligent Decision Making Through Bio-Inspired Optimization
Ramkumar Jaganathan (Sri Krishna Arts and Science College, India) Shilpa Mehta (Auckland University of Technology, New Zealand) and Ram Krishan (Mata Sundri University Girls College, Mansa, India)
Information Science Reference • © 2024 • 275pp • H/C (ISBN: 9798369320730) • US $320.00

Design and Development of Emerging Chatbot Technology
Dina Darwish (Ahram Canadian University, Egypt)
Engineering Science Reference • © 2024 • 381pp • H/C (ISBN: 9798369318300) • US $335.00

Exploring the Ethical Implications of Generative AI
Aftab Ara (University of Hail, Saudi Arabia) and Affreen Ara (Department of Computer Science, Christ College, Bangalore, India)
Engineering Science Reference • © 2024 • 295pp • H/C (ISBN: 9798369315651) • US $300.00

Secure and Intelligent IoT-Enabled Smart Cities
Sushil Kumar Singh (Marwadi University, India) Sudeep Tanwar (Nirma University, India) Rajendrasinh Jadeja (Marwadi University, India) Saurabh Singh (Woosong University, South Korea) and Zdzislaw Polkowski (Wroclaw University of Economics, Poland)
Engineering Science Reference • © 2024 • 434pp • H/C (ISBN: 9798369323731) • US $325.00

701 East Chocolate Avenue, Hershey, PA 17033, USA
Tel: 717-533-8845 x100 • Fax: 717-533-8661
E-Mail: cust@igi-global.com • www.igi-global.com

Editorial Advisory Board

C. Christober Asir Rajan, *Pondicherry Engineering, College, India*
Ramakalyan Ayyagari, *NIT Tiruchirappalli, India*
R. Mohan Das, *New Horizon College of Engineering, Bengaluru, India*
P. Elamurugan, *V.S.B. Engineering College, India*
J. Gnanavadivel, *MEPCO Schlenk Engineering College, Sivakasi, India*
Ramani Kannan, *University Teknologi, PETRONAS, Malaysia.*
M. Karthikeyan, *ABB Global Services India PVT LTD, Chennai, India*
S. Prabhakar Karthikeyan, *VIT Vellore, India*
S. Muralidharan, *MEPCO Schlenk Engineering College, Sivakasi, India*
M. Muhaidheen, *MEPCO Schlenk Engineering College, Sivakasi, India*
G.S. Naganathan, *Syed Ammal Engineering College, Ramanathapuram, India*
J. Bastin Solai Nazaran, *Sethu Institute of Technology, Madurai, India*
Ramkrishna Pasumarthy, *IIT Madras, India*
A. Prasanth, *PSNA College of Engineering & Technology, Dindigul, India*
R. Nagarajan, *Syed Ammal Engineering College, Ramanathapuram, India*
P. Nedumal Pugazhenthi, *Syed Ammal Engineering College, Ramanathapuram, India*
P. Raja, *NIT Tiruchirappalli, India*
B. Ramasubramnian, *SRM TRP Engineering College, Tiruchirappalli, India*
K. Ramkumar, *Sastra Deemed University, Thanjavur, India*
R. Ravi, *Honeywell Technology Solutions, Madurai, India*
S. Selvaperumal, *Syed Ammal Engineering College, Ramanathapuram, India*
S. Sumathi, *Mahendra Engineering College, Namakkal, India*
K. Umamaheswari, *V.S.B. Engineering College, India*
K. Vijayakumar, *IIITD&M, Kancheepuram, India*

List of Reviewers

Jose Anand, *KCG college of Technology, India*
Paul Arokiadass Jerald. M, *Periyar Arts college, India*
R. Chitra, *Karunya University, India*
Nirmala Devi, *KCG college of Technology, India*

Deepa Jeyan, *Nehru College of Engineering and Research Center, India*
D. Kaleswaran, *Rathinam Technical Campus, India*
T. Kavitha, *AMC Engineering College, India*
Vineetha K.R , *Nehru College of Engineering and Research Center, India*
P.K. Manoj Kumar, *Nehru Arts and Science college, India*
Sudheer Sankara Marar, *Nehru College of Engineering and Research Center, India*
D. Marshiana, *Sathyabama University, India*
K. Lakshmi Narayanan, *Francis Xavier Engineering College, India*
S. Padur Nisha, *Nehru Institute of Technology, India*
Lakshmana Pandiyan, *Puducherry Technological University, India*
C.V. Priya, *Muthoot Institute of Technology and Science, India*
G. T. Rajan, *Sathyabama University, India*
A. Rameshbabu, *Sathyabama University, India*
Srinivasan Selvaganapathy, *Nokia Bell Labs CTO, India*
T. Senthilkumar, *GRT Institute of Technology and Science, India*
Pooja Singh, *Amity University, Noida, India,*
Sivaranjani, *Kobgu Engineering College, India*
L. Sumathi, *Government College of Technology, India*
Sundarsingh, *Sathyabama University, India*
S. Suresh, *PA college of Engineering and Technology, India*
S. Venkatalakshmi, *Sri Krishna College of Engineering and Technology, India*
S.A. Yuvaraja, *GRT Institute of Technology and Science, India*

Table of Contents

Preface xx

Acknowledgment xxvii

Introduction xxviii

Chapter 1
Utilizing AI and Machine Learning for Natural Disaster Management: Overview of Machine
Learning and Its Importance in Disaster Management 1
    Divya S. V., V.S.B. College of Engineering Technical Campus, Coimbatore, India
    Venkadesh P., V.S.B. College of Engineering Technical Campus, Coimbatore, India
    Yazhini S., V.S.B. College of Engineering Technical Campus, Coimbatore, India
    Shiny K. V., Bharath Institute of Higher Education and Research, Chennai, India

Chapter 2
Machine Learning Algorithms for Natural Disaster Prediction and Management 24
    Shanthalakshmi Revathy J., Velammal College of Engineering and Technology, India
    Mangaiyarkkarasi J., NMSS Vellaichamy Nadar College, India

Chapter 3
Predicting Natural Disasters With AI and Machine Learning 39
    P Venkadesh, V.S.B. College of Engineering Technical Campus, Coimbatore, India
    Divya S. V., V.S.B. College of Engineering Technical Campus, Coimbatore, India
    P Marymariyal, V.S.B. College of Engineering Technical Campus, Coimbatore, India
    S. Keerthana, V.S.B. College of Engineering Technical Campus, Coimbatore, India

Chapter 4
Predictive Analysis of Machine Learning Algorithms Applicable for Natural Disaster
Management... 65
    Nagarani N., Velammal College of Engineering and Technology, India
    Ramji T. B., Velammal College of Engineering and Technology, India
    Kishorelal A, R., Velammal College of Engineering and Technology, India

Chapter 5
ANN Model for Predicting the Natural Disaster: Data-Driven Approaches for Natural Disaster Prediction and Mitigation 80
    Gobinath A., Velammal College of Engineering and Technology, India
    Rajeswari P., Velammal College of Engineering and Technology, India
    Anandan M., Velammal College of Engineering and Technology, India
    Suresh Kumar N., Velammal College of Engineering and Technology, India

Chapter 6
Predicting Rainfall by Fuzzy Logic: A Preliminary Analysis of a Case Study in Mexico 99
    Jaime Santos-Reyes, SEPI-ESIME, ZAC, Instituto Politecnico Nacional, Mexico
    Yunue Garcia-Pimentel, Instituto Politécnico Nacional, Mexico

Chapter 7
A Comprehensive Investigation of Underwater Disaster Prediction Using Machine Learning Algorithms 118
    Nivethitha R., Velammal College of Engineering and Technology, India
    Sivasankari Jothiraj, Velammal College of Engineering and Technology, India
    Divya Bharathi P., KLN College of Engineering and Technology, India
    Sathish Kumar D., Nehru Institute of Technology, India

Chapter 8
Prediction of Earthquakes, Volcanic Eruptions, Tornadoes, Wildfires, and Droughts Through Artificial Intelligence 133
    Selvakumar P., Nehru Institute of Technology, India
    Vijayakumar G., Vivekanandha College of Engineering for Women, India
    Vigneshkumar P., KGiSL Institute of Technology, India
    Umamaheswari M. S., Nehru Institute of Technology, India
    Selvamurugan C., Dhaanish Ahmed Institute of Technology, India
    Satheesh kumar P., Dr. N.G.P. Institute of Technology, India

Chapter 9
Machine Learning Models for Prediction of Landslides in the Himalayas 146
    Vikram Singh, Ch. Devi Lal University, Sirsa, India
    Sanjay Tyagi, Kurukshetra University, India

Chapter 10
Wearable Sensor and AI Algorithm Integration for Enhanced Natural Disaster Preparedness and Response 175
    Gobinath A., Velammal College of Engineering and Technology, India
    Rajeswari P., Velammal College of Engineering and Technology, India
    Suresh Kumar N., Velammal College of Engineering and Technology, India
    Anandan M., Vel Tech Rangarajan Dr. Sagunthala R&D Institute of Science and Technology, India

Chapter 11
A Novel Approach on IoT-Based Natural Disaster Prediction and Early Warning Systems (EWS) .. 189
> *Karthikeyan Pathinettampadian, Anna University, India & Velammal College of Engineering and Technology, India*
> *Nagarani N., Velammal College of Engineering and Technology, India*
> *Shivani Suvatheka S., Velammal College of Engineering and Technology, India*
> *Al Mohamed Bilal A., Velammal College of Engineering and Technology, India*

Chapter 12
Unleashing Machine Wisdom: A Glimpse Into AI-Powered Tsunami Early Warning Systems 208
> *Siddique Ibrahim S. P., VIT-AP University, India*
> *Ireddi Rakshitha, VIT-AP University, India*
> *Uppara Nithin, VIT-AP University, India*
> *Lakkakula Namratha, VIT-AP University, India*
> *Naga Sai Rahul V., VIT-AP University, India*
> *Mohammed Abdul Kareem Shaik, VIT-AP University, India*

Chapter 13
Disaster and Its Impact on Cerebral Health: Methodology and Psychological Effects of Disaster.... 227
> *K. Parimala Gandhi, Nehru Institute of Technology, India*
> *K. Janani, Nehru Institute of Technology, India*
> *Sivaraja M., Nehru Institute of Technology, India*
> *Gomathi P., Study World College of Engineering, India*
> *satishkumar D., Nehru Institute of Technology, India*

Chapter 14
AI and Machine Learning Algorithm-Based Solutions for Complications in Natural Disaster 237
> *Sathya D., RV University, India*
> *Siddique Ibrahim S. P., VIT-AP University, India*
> *Jagadeesan D., Kaamadhenu Arts and Science College, India*

Chapter 15
Predicting Natural Disasters With AI and Machine Learning 254
> *Manjula Devi C., Velammal College of Engineering and Technology, India*
> *Gobinath A., Velammal College of Engineering and Technology, India*
> *Padma Priya S., PSNA College of Engineering and Technology, India*
> *Reshmika K. S., Velammal College of Engineering and Technology, India*
> *Sivakarthi G., Velammal College of Engineering and Technology, India*

Chapter 16
Deep Learning and AI-Powered Natural Catastrophes Warning Systems 274
> *Siddique Ibrahim S. P., VIT-AP University, India*
> *Sathya D., RV University, India*
> *Gokulnath B. V., VIT-AP University, India*
> *Selva kumar S., VIT-AP University, India*
> *Jai Singh W., Presidency University, India*
> *Thangavel Murugan, United Arab Emirates University, UAE*

Chapter 17
Machine Learning-Based Seismic Activity Prediction 293
    Ajai V., Velammal College of Engineering and Technology, India
    S. Gandhimathi alias Usha, Velammal College of Engineering and Technology, India
    B. D. S. Suntosh, Velammal College of Engineering and Technology, India
    M. Muthukumar, Velammal College of Engineering and Technology, India
    K. Manoj Raj, Velammal College of Engineering and Technology, India
    V. Suriyanarayanan, Velammal College of Engineering and Technology, India

Compilation of References 307

About the Contributors 335

Index 338

Detailed Table of Contents

Preface xx

Acknowledgment xxvii

Introduction xxviii

Chapter 1
Utilizing AI and Machine Learning for Natural Disaster Management: Overview of Machine
Learning and Its Importance in Disaster Management 1
    Divya S. V., V.S.B. College of Engineering Technical Campus, Coimbatore, India
    Venkadesh P., V.S.B. College of Engineering Technical Campus, Coimbatore, India
    Yazhini S., V.S.B. College of Engineering Technical Campus, Coimbatore, India
    Shiny K. V., Bharath Institute of Higher Education and Research, Chennai, India

Natural disasters ranging from earthquakes to wildfires and floods pose serious threats to human life and infrastructure worldwide. As the frequency and severity of such events increase, new innovative solutions are necessary to ensure disaster preparedness, response, and recovery efforts and powerful prevention tools. This abstract provides an overview of the importance of machine learning in the management of natural disasters using machine learning. It also facilitates quick analysis of critical factors such as weather, soil type, demographics, and infrastructure vulnerabilities, contributing to more effective decision-making for disaster management and recovery efforts. This explores applications of machine learning in disaster scenarios, highlighting its versatility and potential impact. Machine learning can be used for image analysis and remote sensing of wildfire detection, flood forecasting, and damage assessment after earthquakes. Hence, ultimately saving lives and reducing the social and economic impact of these disasters.

Chapter 2
Machine Learning Algorithms for Natural Disaster Prediction and Management 24
    Shanthalakshmi Revathy J., Velammal College of Engineering and Technology, India
    Mangaiyarkkarasi J., NMSS Vellaichamy Nadar College, India

Natural disasters, such as floods, earthquakes, tsunamis, and landslides, pose significant threats to communities and ecosystems. This investigation explores the application of machine learning (ML) techniques in addressing the challenge. ML, a subset of artificial intelligence, involves creating models and algorithms that enable computers to learn from data, offering accurate disaster predictions without explicit programming. Various ML algorithms, including random forest for flood and wildfire prediction, support vector machine for earthquake forecasting, and decision tree for landslide risk assessment, are employed due to their ability to process complex datasets. Beyond prediction, ML plays a vital role in disaster management, optimizing resource allocation, refining emergency response plans, and enhancing evacuation strategies. Real-world case studies illustrate how ML contributes to mitigating disaster damage, emphasizing its role in proactive measures for disaster prevention and management.

Chapter 3
Predicting Natural Disasters With AI and Machine Learning 39
    P Venkadesh, V.S.B. College of Engineering Technical Campus, Coimbatore, India
    Divya S. V., V.S.B. College of Engineering Technical Campus, Coimbatore, India
    P Marymariyal, V.S.B. College of Engineering Technical Campus, Coimbatore, India
    S. Keerthana, V.S.B. College of Engineering Technical Campus, Coimbatore, India

The unpredictability and devastating impacts of the natural disasters necessitate the advanced methods for early detection and mitigation. The paper delves into the transformative potential of AI and ML in analyzing extensive datasets comprising historical records, meteorological information, geological data, and satellite imagery. By leveraging neural networks, deep learning algorithms, and data analytics enables the creation of sophisticated predictive models for a range of natural disasters, including earthquakes, hurricanes, floods, wildfires, and tsunamis. Incorporating real-time data from IoT devices and remote sensing technologies further bolsters the accuracy of predictions. This abstract highlights the role of AI and ML not only in forecasting disasters but also in optimizing resource allocation during response efforts, identifying vulnerable regions, and enhancing early warning systems. Here, practical examples and case studies of successful AI and ML applications in disaster prediction, underlining their potential to redefine disaster preparedness and response is focused.

Chapter 4
Predictive Analysis of Machine Learning Algorithms Applicable for Natural Disaster Management 65
    Nagarani N., Velammal College of Engineering and Technology, India
    Ramji T. B., Velammal College of Engineering and Technology, India
    Kishorelal A, R., Velammal College of Engineering and Technology, India

The escalating impact and frequency of natural disasters necessitate the development of robust predictive frameworks to proactively manage and mitigate their devastating consequences. ML techniques are used for the accurate forecasting of various natural disasters, such as earthquakes, floods, wildfires, hurricanes, and landslides, and these are thoroughly examined in this study. By harnessing historical data, environmental variables, and cutting-edge ML algorithms, this study meticulously assesses the efficacy of diverse techniques in forecasting and classifying these cataclysmic events. Through a comprehensive survey that scrutinizes the nuances of ML methods, random forest methods, support vector machines (SVM), neural networks, k-means clustering, Naive Bayes, reinforcement learning, and time series analysis models, the authors dissect their strengths and limitations in predicting specific types of natural disasters. Examining algorithms against actual real-world datasets offers valuable insights into the capabilities of each algorithm, shedding light on their capabilities to fortify early detection and warning systems. The research underscores the multifaceted challenges inherent in predicting natural disasters, emphasizing the paramount significance of high-quality, real-time data acquisition. This foundational aspect drives the iterative refinement of models, ensuring their adaptability to the dynamic and evolving environmental conditions that influence disaster occurrences. Furthermore, it emphasizes the pivotal role of interdisciplinary collaboration, emphasizing the fusion of domain expertise and technological advancements to bolster the resilience of predictive models. Ultimately, the culmination of these efforts aims to improve the precision and timeliness of disaster predictions, thereby fortifying comprehensive disaster preparedness and response strategies. To address the challenges associated with predicting and managing natural disasters, this article advocates for an all-encompassing strategy that integrates advanced machine learning techniques with ongoing data collection and expert perspectives.

Chapter 5
ANN Model for Predicting the Natural Disaster: Data-Driven Approaches for Natural Disaster Prediction and Mitigation 80
    Gobinath A., Velammal College of Engineering and Technology, India
    Rajeswari P., Velammal College of Engineering and Technology, India
    Anandan M., Velammal College of Engineering and Technology, India
    Suresh Kumar N., Velammal College of Engineering and Technology, India

Natural disasters have been an enduring and formidable challenge throughout human history, causing widespread devastation to communities and ecosystems. The significance of predicting these events lies in the ability to mitigate their impact on human lives, infrastructure, and the environment. Timely and accurate prediction empowers communities to take proactive measures, enabling better preparedness, response, and recovery. In the absence of such forecasting capabilities, the toll of natural disasters can be catastrophic, leading to loss of life, displacement of populations, and economic setbacks. Therefore, the development of predictive models, such as artificial neural networks (ANNs) and other data-driven approaches, is pivotal in addressing the escalating threats posed by natural disasters.

Chapter 6
Predicting Rainfall by Fuzzy Logic: A Preliminary Analysis of a Case Study in Mexico 99
    Jaime Santos-Reyes, SEPI-ESIME, ZAC, Instituto Politecnico Nacional, Mexico
    Yunue Garcia-Pimentel, Instituto Politécnico Nacional, Mexico

Water is vital to all living things; water is life. According to the UNDP water scarcity affects more than two billion people and it is projected to rise as temperatures do due to climate change. The chapter presents some preliminary results of rainfall prediction for the case of Mexico City by considering two input variables, temperature (T) and wind speed (WS). A fuzzy logic rule-based approach was employed in the analysis. The presented fuzzy logic model has the potential not only to predict rainfall but also drought. Moreover, it has also been highlighted that it becomes necessary to address droughts by designing and implementing drought disaster management systems to mitigate the impact of such events. Therefore, rainfall prediction, as an early warning, plays a key role in designing measures to achieve this. More generally, it is hoped that approaches such as the presented herein may contribute to a better understanding and management of water to mitigate the impacts of droughts in regions, cities, communities prone to the hazard.

Chapter 7
A Comprehensive Investigation of Underwater Disaster Prediction Using Machine Learning Algorithms 118
    Nivethitha R., Velammal College of Engineering and Technology, India
    Sivasankari Jothiraj, Velammal College of Engineering and Technology, India
    Divya Bharathi P., KLN College of Engineering and Technology, India
    Sathish Kumar D., Nehru Institute of Technology, India

Underwater disasters cause severe consequences to marine ecology and lead to significant loss to the environment. Since the sea water temperature reaches 700° Fahrenheit, disasters like hydrothermal vents and underwater volcano eruptions occur. Due to these seireachests, marine creatures like sharks and different types of living species have been excavating under the ocean. The risk of underwater disasters like underwater volcanic eruption, tsunami, underwater earthquake, submarine accidents and oil spills are crucial, and the preventive measures of these calamities were highly needed. Oceanographic data includes underwater images and videos captured bymarine archaeologists and divers to know the information about the exploited resources. Existing traditional algorithms have practical limitations to predict underwater catastrophes under more depth condition and can be overcome by machine learning (ML) algorithms, since it was accurate and fast in analyzing the oceanographic data. This chapter provides a comprehensive review of predicting underwater disasters using ML algorithms.

Chapter 8
Prediction of Earthquakes, Volcanic Eruptions, Tornadoes, Wildfires, and Droughts Through
Artificial Intelligence 133
    Selvakumar P., Nehru Institute of Technology, India
    Vijayakumar G., Vivekanandha College of Engineering for Women, India
    Vigneshkumar P., KGiSL Institute of Technology, India
    Umamaheswari M. S., Nehru Institute of Technology, India
    Selvamurugan C., Dhaanish Ahmed Institute of Technology, India
    Satheesh kumar P., Dr. N.G.P. Institute of Technology, India

The growing economic and organizational relevance of artificial intelligence has garnered a lot of attention in the past ten years. Through the use of processing algorithms that are especially pertinent in emergency, extreme weather, and disaster relief operation situations, artificial intelligence's information processing capabilities assist in converting inputs. Assessing and meeting the needs of people trapped in catastrophes may take longer under older, manual approaches. Furthermore, the typical hierarchical structure approach takes longer to repair infrastructure, leaving those affected exposed. AI can, however, assist in reducing and repairing damage by more precisely and efficiently allocating resources because of its fast and accurate processing capabilities. Artificial intelligence (AI) can help rescue workers evaluate requirements and deliver supplies to various locations more swiftly and accurately.

Chapter 9
Machine Learning Models for Prediction of Landslides in the Himalayas 146
    Vikram Singh, Ch. Devi Lal University, Sirsa, India
    Sanjay Tyagi, Kurukshetra University, India

The Himalayan region, characterized by its steep terrain and geological complexities, stands vulnerable to the persistent threat of landslides, particularly exacerbated during the monsoon season. The susceptibility to landslides in this region arises from a convergence of factors, including the region's high seismic activity, diverse geological formations, intense monsoonal precipitation, and rapidly changing climate patterns. The impact of landslides extends beyond immediate infrastructure damage, often leading to loss of lives, disruption of livelihoods, and severe environmental degradation. This chapter embarks on a comprehensive exploration of the pivotal role of artificial intelligence and machine learning in revolutionizing the prediction and mitigation of landslides in the Himalayas. It delves into the intricate challenges posed by the region's geological diversity and environmental dynamics, offering insights into AI-driven strategies to enhance predictive accuracy, implement early warning systems, and devise effective mitigation measures. The chapter commences with an overview of the Himalayas, delineating the geological complexities and the profound influence of climatic conditions on landslide occurrences. It elucidates the critical challenges hindering traditional landslide prediction methods, such as inadequate data quality and sparsity, underscoring the dire need for advanced predictive techniques. A meticulous review of existing methods, encompassing both conventional approaches and the utilization of remote sensing technologies and geographic information systems (GIS), sets the stage for introducing AI-based solutions. The chapter unfolds the nuances of machine learning approaches tailored for landslide prediction, spotlighting the selection of pertinent features, the application of supervised and unsupervised learning models, and the integration of real-time environmental data. A pivotal focus lies on AI-driven early warning systems that amalgamate historical data, sensor networks, and predictive models to facilitate timely alerts and risk assessments. Moreover, the chapter elucidates how AI empowers hazard zonation mapping, aiding in the identification of high-risk areas and adaptive planning for resilient infrastructure development. The narrative is enriched with insightful studies and practical implementations showcasing the efficacy of AI-based models in landslide prediction and mitigation within the Himalayan terrain. Lessons gleaned from these studies illuminate both successes and challenges, providing invaluable insights for the field. This chapter endeavours to unravel the transformative potential of AI and machine learning in confronting the formidable challenge of landslides in the Himalayas. It underscores the significance of these technological advancements in fostering resilience, safeguarding lives, and fortifying the region's infrastructure against the omnipresent threat of landslides.

Chapter 10
Wearable Sensor and AI Algorithm Integration for Enhanced Natural Disaster Preparedness and Response 175
 Gobinath A., Velammal College of Engineering and Technology, India
 Rajeswari P., Velammal College of Engineering and Technology, India
 Suresh Kumar N., Velammal College of Engineering and Technology, India
 Anandan M., Vel Tech Rangarajan Dr. Sagunthala R&D Institute of Science and Technology, India

This chapter explores the innovative fusion of wearable sensor technologies and artificial intelligence (AI) algorithms in the context of natural disaster preparedness and response. Wearable sensors, designed to be seamlessly integrated into clothing or accessories, offer a dynamic and personal approach to monitoring individuals in disaster-prone areas. Coupled with advanced AI algorithms, these sensors empower individuals and authorities with real-time data, early warning capabilities, and personalized assistance during critical events. The chapter begins by examining the functionalities of wearable sensors specifically engineered for disaster scenarios. These sensors include biometric monitors measuring vital signs such as heart rate, body temperature, and respiratory rate. Additionally, environmental sensors incorporated into wearables detect changes in air quality, temperature, and humidity, providing a comprehensive understanding of immediate surroundings. The integration of AI algorithms into wearable sensor systems is a central focus of this chapter.

Chapter 11
A Novel Approach on IoT-Based Natural Disaster Prediction and Early Warning Systems (EWS) .. 189
 Karthikeyan Pathinettampadian, Anna University, India & Velammal College of Engineering and Technology, India
 Nagarani N., Velammal College of Engineering and Technology, India
 Shivani Suvatheka S., Velammal College of Engineering and Technology, India
 Al Mohamed Bilal A., Velammal College of Engineering and Technology, India

Natural disasters cause significant damage and human losses, emphasizing the need for predictive systems and efficient warning mechanisms. Exploring the potential of an internet of things (IoT)-driven early warning system (EWS) is crucial for detecting and notifying individuals about diverse disasters like earthquakes, floods, tsunamis, and landslides. In a disaster, the device transmits data to the microcontroller, where it undergoes validation and processing using ML algorithms to predict disaster possibilities. Data from edge nodes reaches the cloud via a gateway, with fog nodes filtering and accessing it. After verification, persistent alarming weather conditions trigger a warning alert, conveyed promptly to individuals in disaster-prone regions through diverse communication channels. An IoT-based open-source application with a user-friendly interface continuously monitors parameters like water intensity and rainfall during floods, and ground vibrations for earthquakes. Alerts are generated when parameters exceed set thresholds, providing a cost-effective disaster detection solution with timely alerts to vulnerable communities.

Chapter 12
Unleashing Machine Wisdom: A Glimpse Into AI-Powered Tsunami Early Warning Systems 208
    Siddique Ibrahim S. P., VIT-AP University, India
    Ireddi Rakshitha, VIT-AP University, India
    Uppara Nithin, VIT-AP University, India
    Lakkakula Namratha, VIT-AP University, India
    Naga Sai Rahul V., VIT-AP University, India
    Mohammed Abdul Kareem Shaik, VIT-AP University, India

Embarking on an exploration of disaster resilience, this chapter scrutinizes the potential of AI-driven tsunami early warning systems (TEWS). Focused on the catastrophic potential of tsunamis, the narrative unveils a visionary roadmap, spotlighting artificial neural networks (ANN), and convolutional neural networks (CNN). While the actual implementation lies in the future, the chapter charts a course for stakeholders to metamorphose theoretical frameworks into actionable strategies. Beyond technical intricacies, the narrative emphasizes the transformative impact of proactive disaster management. Envisioning a future where machine learning algorithms serve as vigilant guardians prompts a call for a paradigm shift in coastal safety. The chapter culminates by contemplating a future where the synergy between human intuition and AI enhances our capacity to anticipate, respond to, and mitigate the devastating impact of tsunamis. It paints a compelling vision of a safer coexistence with our dynamic planet, outlining challenges, and pointing towards a more resilient future.

Chapter 13
Disaster and Its Impact on Cerebral Health: Methodology and Psychological Effects of Disaster 227
    K. Parimala Gandhi, Nehru Institute of Technology, India
    K. Janani, Nehru Institute of Technology, India
    Sivaraja M., Nehru Institute of Technology, India
    Gomathi P., Study World College of Engineering, India
    satishkumar D., Nehru Institute of Technology, India

This study aims to establish a connection between disasters and their impact on mental health. An effort has been undertaken to reconsider the qualitative literature that is currently available on disaster and mental health in order to achieve this objective. In this essay, the idea of calamity and mental health has been employed in a broad way. Natural disasters, man-made disasters, and industrial disasters all have an impact on people's mental health in different ways. It looks at the behavioural and psychological signs of a functioning impairment following a disaster. Numerous protective variables have been identified, such as resilience and other coping mechanisms that increased the individual's capability while facing undesirable situations, have been identified. The success of post-disaster intervention methods is also emphasized. Enhancing the preparedness and empowering the community can help the disaster's vulnerable victims. Thus, efforts should be made for complete recuperation of the affected people.

Chapter 14
AI and Machine Learning Algorithm-Based Solutions for Complications in Natural Disaster 237
    Sathya D., RV University, India
    Siddique Ibrahim S. P., VIT-AP University, India
    Jagadeesan D., Kaamadhenu Arts and Science College, India

Artificial intelligence in meteorological event management has become imperative in light of the rise in extreme weather events in recent years. Disaster management is necessary to control and stop such incidents. Artificial intelligence is widely employed in disaster preparedness and forecasting, damage mitigation and reduction, and reaction phase to help with better and faster responses to disasters. This chapter looks at how artificial intelligence technologies can be used to lessen the effects of different types of disasters and explores the possibility of connecting artificial intelligence technologies with information and communication technology to lessen the effects of disasters.

Chapter 15
Predicting Natural Disasters With AI and Machine Learning 254
    Manjula Devi C., Velammal College of Engineering and Technology, India
    Gobinath A., Velammal College of Engineering and Technology, India
    Padma Priya S., PSNA College of Engineering and Technology, India
    Reshmika K. S., Velammal College of Engineering and Technology, India
    Sivakarthi G., Velammal College of Engineering and Technology, India

Amidst the continually changing climate and the rise in natural disasters, it is crucial to strengthen resilience against these calamities. This chapter explores the dynamic intersection of machine learning and natural disasters, revealing how advanced technologies reshape disaster management. In the face of escalating challenges posed by earthquakes, floods, and wildfires, machine learning emerges as an innovative solution, offering proactive approaches beyond conventional reactive methods. The narrative unfolds by tracing the evolution of disaster management, highlighting the transformative impact of machine learning on early warning systems. It explores predictive analytics and risk assessment, elucidating how machine learning algorithms leverage historical data and real-time information to deepen our understanding of disaster vulnerabilities. Beyond prediction, the discourse extends to the pivotal role of machine learning in optimizing response and recovery efforts—efficiently allocating resources and fostering recovery planning. A critical dimension of this integration emerges in the analysis of remote sensing and satellite imagery, where machine learning algorithms enable more accurate and timely disaster monitoring. The exploration extends further, unraveling the interconnectedness of various hazards and emphasizing how machine learning facilitates a holistic understanding. The synergy between machine learning and traditional knowledge systems comes to the forefront, recognizing the significance of integrating local wisdom into predictive models. The discourse broadens to encompass policy implications, international collaboration, and ethical considerations embedded in machine learning for disaster management. The integration of machine learning in humanitarian aid efforts and its contribution to environmental sustainability are scrutinized, offering a comprehensive understanding of the multifaceted relationship between machine learning and natural disasters. In the ever-evolving landscape of natural disaster management, the fusion of machine learning and human expertise opens new avenues for innovation. One emerging trend is the integration of real-time social media data into machine learning algorithms. By analyzing user-generated content, sentiment analysis, and geospatial information from platforms like Twitter and Facebook, these algorithms can provide rapid insights into the unfolding dynamics of a disaster. This not only enhances the timeliness of response efforts but also fosters a more community-centric approach, incorporating the voices and experiences of those directly affected. The potential of generative adversarial networks to simulate and predict complex disaster scenarios offers a proactive paradigm shift in disaster management by enabling stakeholders to refine strategies and adapt to evolving challenges through realistic simulations. As the chapter charts the course forward, it concludes by exploring emerging trends and innovations in the symbiotic relationship between machine learning and natural disaster management.

Chapter 16
Deep Learning and AI-Powered Natural Catastrophes Warning Systems 274
    Siddique Ibrahim S. P., VIT-AP University, India
    Sathya D., RV University, India
    Gokulnath B. V., VIT-AP University, India
    Selva kumar S., VIT-AP University, India
    Jai Singh W., Presidency University, India
    Thangavel Murugan, United Arab Emirates University, UAE

Natural catastrophes including hurricanes, floods, wildfires, and earthquakes can seriously harm people and property. Floods that destroy houses, businesses, government buildings, and other properties cause enormous economic losses in addition to human casualties. This loss cannot be recovered; however, flood damage can frequently be reduced by supporting suitable structural and non-structural solutions. Natural catastrophes have become more frequent and severe in recent years, primarily as a result of climate change. Due to the large number of small and low magnitude earthquakes, the hand-picked data used in manual approaches, and the possibility of some noisy disturbances in the background, the methods are not very dependable. As a result, automated techniques and algorithms are more effective when used for earthquake identification and detection. However, scientists and engineers can now more accurately and efficiently predict and avert natural disasters thanks to developments in machine learning and data analytics. By creating a deep learning model that can quickly determine an asset's structural status in the event of a seismic excitation, this study investigates the potential of artificial intelligence in various operational domains.

Chapter 17
Machine Learning-Based Seismic Activity Prediction 293
    Ajai V., Velammal College of Engineering and Technology, India
    S. Gandhimathi alias Usha, Velammal College of Engineering and Technology, India
    B. D. S. Suntosh, Velammal College of Engineering and Technology, India
    M. Muthukumar, Velammal College of Engineering and Technology, India
    K. Manoj Raj, Velammal College of Engineering and Technology, India
    V. Suriyanarayanan, Velammal College of Engineering and Technology, India

Earthquakes can have devastating consequences, causing ground shaking, landslides, and changes in landscapes. Fault line ruptures can alter river courses and disrupt infrastructure, while underwater earthquakes may trigger tsunamis, affecting coastal ecosystems and communities. Liquefaction can temporarily weaken the ground, leading to structural damage, and aftershocks can further exacerbate existing damage and hinder recovery efforts. Human impacts are significant and can result in injuries, fatalities, displacement, and psychological trauma. Economic consequences can involve disruption to industries and livelihoods, while response and recovery efforts may have environmental consequences. This chapter focuses on earthquake prediction using various parameters such as date, time, latitude, longitude, depth, and magnitude. The authors have used a world map as a dataset to train our model, where we predict earthquakes using gradient boosting regressor. They have broken down the complex and challenging problem into simpler like mean squared error (MSE) as a loss function, accuracy, precision, recall, F1 score, confusion matrix. As of our last knowledge update in September 2023, earthquake prediction remains a field of ongoing research and does not have precise predictive models. The advantage of this model is its accuracy which is predicted as output. However, by comparing actual datasets with predicted outcomes of occurrences, we can identify risk free areas for livelihood. The proposed model achieved an accuracy of 86.1% and 99.7% in terms of magnitude and depth, which is higher than the accuracy of existing earthquake prediction methods.

Compilation of References 307

About the Contributors 335

Index 338

Preface

In the face of an ever-evolving world, where the relentless onslaught of natural and man-made disasters poses an imminent threat to societies globally, the imperative for effective disaster management has reached unprecedented levels. In the pursuit of fortifying our resilience against these cataclysmic events, the compendium before you, titled Predicting Natural Disasters With AI and Machine Learning, emerges as a beacon of enlightenment in the field of disaster management.

As editors of this reference book, we have endeavored to compile a comprehensive exploration into the amalgamation of artificial intelligence (AI) and machine learning (ML) techniques, presenting a roadmap towards proactive solutions for the myriad challenges posed by disasters. This book's narrative unfolds with a meticulous examination of the nature of disasters, drawing a sharp distinction between natural and man-made hazards. It delves into the intricacies of disaster risk reduction (DRR), with a deliberate emphasis on the human factor as a significant contributor to most disasters.

Recognizing the intricate tapestry of challenges inherent in disaster management, the book advocates the 'Four Rs'—Risk Mitigation, Response Readiness, Response Execution, and Recovery—as integral facets of a holistic disaster management strategy. Each chapter meticulously scrutinizes critical issues, including real-world data handling, challenges related to data accessibility, completeness, security, privacy, and ethical considerations.

The core of this book lies in its exploration of diverse AI and ML applications tailored to predict, manage, and mitigate the impact of natural disasters. It delves into the realms of natural language processing, early warning systems, and image-based deep learning, offering an insightful contrast between weak AI, simulating human intelligence for specific tasks, and strong AI, capable of autonomous problem-solving.

This compilation is not merely a theoretical discourse but a pragmatic guide for academics, public and private organizations, managers, and the wider public. It underscores the urgency of embracing AI and ML in disaster management, providing a robust foundation for the integration of these technologies into existing frameworks. As we stand at the intersection of academia and practicality, this book is poised to serve as a catalyst for further studies, particularly among postgraduate students intrigued by the convergence of AI and ML in predicting and managing natural disasters.

The chapters span a wide array of topics, from Earthquake Prediction to Pandemic Management, offering a holistic view of the multifaceted landscape of disaster management. Each section serves as a valuable repository of knowledge, contributing to the evolving discourse on how AI and ML can be harnessed to build a more resilient and responsive world in the face of acute events.

As editors, we extend our gratitude to the contributors who have invested their expertise and insights into this collective effort. May this book be a source of inspiration and a catalyst for transformative advancements in the critical domain of natural disaster management.

Preface

Chapter 1: Utilizing AI and Machine Learning for Natural Disaster Management: Overview of Machine Learning and its Importance in Disaster Management

Authored by Divya S.V, Venkadesh P, Yazhini S, and Shiny K V, this chapter lays the groundwork for the entire book by emphasizing the pivotal role of machine learning (ML) in managing natural disasters. The authors highlight the escalating threats posed by various disasters and stress the need for innovative solutions. The chapter provides a comprehensive overview of how ML can be instrumental in disaster preparedness, response, and recovery efforts. By analyzing critical factors such as weather, soil type, demographics, and infrastructure vulnerabilities, the chapter demonstrates how ML enables effective decision-making. The versatility of ML applications, ranging from image analysis to remote sensing for disaster detection, is explored, emphasizing the potential to save lives and mitigate the social and economic impact of disasters.

Chapter 2: Machine Learning Algorithms for Natural Disaster Prediction and Management

Authored by Shanthalakshmi Revathy J and Mangaiyarkkarasi J, this chapter delves into the application of machine learning (ML) techniques to predict and manage natural disasters. Focusing on floods, earthquakes, tsunamis, and landslides, the authors explore various ML algorithms such as Random Forest, Support Vector Machine, and Decision Tree. Beyond prediction, the chapter emphasizes the crucial role of ML in optimizing resource allocation, refining emergency response plans, and enhancing evacuation strategies. Real-world case studies illustrate how ML contributes to mitigating disaster damage, showcasing its proactive role in disaster prevention and management. The chapter serves as a valuable guide for understanding the intersection of ML and disaster resilience.

Chapter 3: Predicting Natural Disasters With AI and Machine Learning: Machine Learning Applications in Disaster Management

Authored by P Venkadesh, Divya S.V, P Marymariyal, and S Keerthana, this chapter focuses on the transformative potential of AI and ML in predicting and managing natural disasters. It explores the use of neural networks, deep learning algorithms, and data analytics to create sophisticated predictive models. Real-time data from IoT devices and remote sensing technologies further enhance prediction accuracy. The chapter not only emphasizes disaster forecasting but also addresses resource optimization, vulnerability identification, and early warning systems. Practical examples and case studies underscore the practical applications of AI and ML in disaster prediction, highlighting their potential to redefine disaster preparedness and response.

Chapter 4: Predictive Analysis of Machine Learning Algorithms Applicable for Natural Disaster Management

Authored by NAGARANI N, Ramji T.B, and Kishorelal A.R, this chapter explores the role of machine learning (ML) in predicting earthquakes, floods, wildfires, hurricanes, and landslides. Leveraging various ML algorithms, including Random Forest, SVM, Neural Networks, and more, the authors assess their efficacy and limitations. Real-world dataset assessments reveal the potential of ML in strengthening early warning systems. The chapter advocates for an integrated approach, emphasizing the importance of interdisciplinary collaboration to improve the accuracy and timeliness of disaster predictions. It underscores the necessity of ongoing data collection and expert insights for effective natural disaster prediction and management.

Chapter 5: ANN Model for Predicting the Natural Disaster: Data-Driven Approaches for Natural Disaster Prediction and Mitigation

Authored by Gobinath A, Rajeswari P, Anandan M, and Suresh Kumar N, this chapter delves into the enduring challenge of natural disasters and the significance of predicting these events for effective mitigation. Focusing on artificial neural networks (ANNs) and data-driven approaches, the authors underscore the importance of timely and accurate prediction for better preparedness, response, and recovery. The chapter highlights the pivotal role of predictive models in mitigating the impact of natural disasters on human lives, infrastructure, and the environment. It positions ANNs as crucial tools in addressing the escalating threats posed by various natural disasters.

Chapter 6: Predicting Rainfall by Fuzzy Logic: A Preliminary Analysis of a Case Study in Mexico

Authored by Jaime Santos-Reyes and Yunue Garcia-Pimentel, this chapter presents preliminary results of rainfall prediction in Mexico using fuzzy logic. The authors employ a rule-based fuzzy logic approach considering temperature and wind speed as input variables. Beyond rainfall prediction, the chapter acknowledges the broader implications for drought prediction, emphasizing the need for drought disaster management systems. It aims to contribute to a better understanding and management of water resources to mitigate the impacts of droughts in regions, cities, and communities prone to this hazard.

Chapter 7: A Comprehensive Investigation of Underwater Disaster Prediction Using Machine Learning Algorithms

Authored by Nivethitha R, Sivasankari Jothiraj, Divya Bharathi P, and Sathish Kumar D, this chapter addresses the severe consequences of underwater disasters on marine ecology. It explores the limitations of traditional algorithms in predicting underwater catastrophes under different depth conditions and advocates for the use of machine learning (ML) algorithms. The chapter reviews the comprehensive application of ML in analyzing oceanographic data, emphasizing the accuracy and speed in disaster prediction. It positions ML as an effective tool in mitigating the risks associated with underwater disasters and highlights the importance of interdisciplinary collaboration between marine archaeologists, divers, and ML experts.

Chapter 8: Prediction of Earthquakes, Volcanic Eruptions, Tornadoes, Wildfires and Droughts through Artificial Intelligence

Authored by Selvakumar P, Vijayakumar G, Vigneshkumar P, Umamaheswari M.S., Selvamurugan C, and Satheesh Kumar P, this chapter delves into the growing relevance of artificial intelligence (AI) in disaster prediction and management. It explores how AI, through processing algorithms, can significantly

Preface

enhance emergency, extreme weather, and disaster relief operations. The chapter emphasizes AI's role in efficiently allocating resources, reducing damage, and facilitating swift response in the aftermath of disasters. It positions AI as a transformative force in improving disaster resilience and enhancing the overall effectiveness of disaster management strategies.

Chapter 9: Machine Learning Models for Prediction of Landslides in Himalayas

Authored by Dr. Vikram Singh and Sanjay Tyagi, this chapter comprehensively explores the role of Artificial Intelligence and machine learning in revolutionizing the prediction and mitigation of landslides in the Himalayas. It addresses the limitations of traditional landslide prediction methods and discusses the application of supervised and unsupervised learning models. The chapter emphasizes the integration of real-time environmental data and AI-driven early warning systems to facilitate timely alerts and risk assessments. Real-world studies and practical implementations highlight the efficacy of AI-based models in landslide prediction and mitigation, presenting a transformative potential for addressing the formidable challenge of landslides in the Himalayas.

Chapter 10: Wearable Sensor and AI Algorithm Integration for Enhanced Natural Disaster Preparedness and Response

Authored by Gobinath A, Rajeswari P, Suresh Kumar N, and Anandan M, this chapter explores the integration of wearable sensor technologies and artificial intelligence (AI) algorithms for enhanced natural disaster preparedness and response. The authors delve into the functionalities of wearable sensors designed for disaster scenarios, measuring vital signs and environmental parameters. The chapter emphasizes the real-time data, early warning capabilities, and personalized assistance provided by wearable sensors integrated with AI algorithms. It positions this integration as a dynamic and personal approach to monitoring individuals in disaster-prone areas, empowering both individuals and authorities with crucial information during critical events.

Chapter 11 - A Novel Approach on IoT-Based Natural Disaster Prediction and Early Warning Systems (EWS)

Authored by Karthikeyan Pathinettampadian, Nagarani N, Shivani Suvatheka S, and Al Mohamed Bilal A, this chapter explores the potential of an Internet of Things (IoT)-driven Early Warning System (EWS) for predicting and notifying individuals about diverse natural disasters. The authors outline the IoT-based system's architecture, encompassing data transmission, processing using ML algorithms, and persistent alarming conditions triggering warning alerts. The chapter focuses on the cost-effective detection solution and user-friendly interface for continuous monitoring of parameters during floods, earthquakes, and other disasters. It underscores the significance of IoT-based early warning systems in providing timely alerts to vulnerable communities.

Chapter 12: Unleashing Machine Wisdom - A Glimpse into AI Powered Tsunami Early Warning Systems: Machine Learning based Tsunami Early Warning Systems

Authored by Siddique Ibrahim S P, Ireddi Rakshitha, Uppara Nithin, Lakkakula Namratha, Naga Sai Rahul V, and Mohammed Abdul Kareem Shaik, this chapter explores the potential of AI-driven Tsunami Early Warning Systems (TEWS). Focused on the catastrophic potential of tsunamis, the authors delve into the theoretical frameworks involving Artificial Neural Networks (ANN) and Convolutional Neural Networks (CNN). The chapter envisions a future where machine learning algorithms serve as vigilant guardians, enhancing our capacity to anticipate, respond to, and mitigate the devastating impact of tsunamis. It emphasizes the transformative impact of proactive disaster management and prompts a paradigm shift in coastal safety.

Chapter 13: Disaster and its Impact on Cerebral Health: Methodology and Psychological Effects of Disaster

Authored by K PARIMALA GANDHI, K JANANI, Sivaraja M, Gomathi P, and Satishkumar D, this chapter aims to establish a connection between disasters and their impact on mental health. The authors conduct a comprehensive review of qualitative literature on disaster and mental health, considering various types of disasters and their psychological effects. The chapter explores behavioral and psychological signs of impairment following a disaster and identifies protective variables such as resilience and coping mechanisms. It emphasizes the success of post-disaster intervention methods and advocates for enhancing community preparedness and empowerment to aid the recovery of affected individuals.

Chapter 14: AI and Machine Learning Algorithm Based Solution for Complications in Natural Disaster

Sathya D, Siddique Ibrahim S P, and Jagadeesan D emphasize the imperative role of artificial intelligence in meteorological event management, given the surge in extreme weather events. The focus is on disaster preparedness, forecasting, and the application of AI technologies in mitigating and reducing damages. The authors also explore the integration of AI with information and communication technology to enhance disaster management strategies.

Chapter 15: Predicting Natural Disasters with AI and Machine Learning

Manjula Devi C, Gobinath A, Padma Priya S, Reshmika. K.S, and Sivakarthi G address the escalating challenges posed by changing climates and increasing natural disasters. This chapter explores the dynamic intersection of machine learning and disaster management, tracing the evolution of disaster management and highlighting how machine learning reshapes early warning systems. The authors also delve into predictive analytics, risk assessment, and the pivotal role of machine learning in optimizing response and recovery efforts.

Preface

Chapter 16: Deep Learning and AI-Powered Natural Catastrophes Warning Systems

Siddique Ibrahim S P, Sathya D, Gokulnath BV, Selva kumar S, Jai Singh W, and Thangavel Murugan focus on the prevention and reduction of natural catastrophes. This chapter explores the potential of artificial intelligence in various operational domains, discussing the use of automated techniques and algorithms in earthquake identification and detection. The study investigates the creation of a deep learning model for quickly determining an asset's structural status during seismic events.

Chapter 17: Machine Learning Based Seismic Activity Prediction

Ajai V, S.Gandhimathi alias Usha, B.D.S. Suntosh, M. Muthukumar, K. Manoj Raj, and V. Suriyanarayanan focus on earthquake prediction using various parameters and machine learning techniques. The authors utilize a world map dataset and employ gradient boosting regressor for earthquake prediction. The chapter breaks down the complexities of the problem into measurable metrics like mean squared error, accuracy, precision, recall, and F1 score. The proposed model achieves high accuracy in predicting earthquake magnitude and depth, surpassing existing prediction methods.

As editors of "Predicting Natural Disasters With AI and Machine Learning," we find ourselves at the culmination of an intellectual journey that has sought to unravel the intricate dynamics of disaster management in an era defined by relentless challenges. In a world where the specter of natural and man-made disasters looms large, our collective pursuit has been to illuminate the path towards a future fortified by the transformative power of artificial intelligence (AI) and machine learning (ML).

This compendium stands as a testament to the indispensable role of AI and ML in navigating the complexities of disaster management. Our overarching goal has been to provide a roadmap that transcends theoretical discourse, offering pragmatic insights for academics, organizations, managers, and the broader public. The chapters within this volume, each a unique contribution from experts in their respective fields, form a mosaic of knowledge, unveiling diverse applications and methodologies in disaster prediction, management, and mitigation.

The 'Four Rs'—Risk Mitigation, Response Readiness, Response Execution, and Recovery—emerge as the foundational pillars of our holistic disaster management strategy. Through meticulous exploration, our contributors have scrutinized critical challenges such as real-world data handling, ethical considerations, and the often-overlooked human factor in disaster risk reduction.

The heart of this compendium lies in its exploration of AI and ML applications tailored to predict, manage, and mitigate the impact of natural disasters. From advanced neural networks to rule-based fuzzy logic, the diversity of approaches mirrors the multifaceted nature of disasters themselves. This is not merely an academic exercise but a practical guide, urging the integration of these technologies into existing frameworks for a more resilient and responsive world.

We extend our heartfelt gratitude to the contributors who have generously shared their expertise and insights, making this collective effort possible. It is our fervent hope that this book serves as a source of inspiration, sparking transformative advancements in the critical domain of natural disaster management. As we stand at the crossroads of academia and practicality, may this compendium be a catalyst for further studies, particularly among postgraduate students intrigued by the convergence of AI and ML in predicting and managing natural disasters.

In the face of uncertainty, may our endeavors contribute to a world better equipped to navigate the challenges of tomorrow, armed with the wisdom distilled within these pages.

D. Satishkumar
Nehru Institute of Technology, India

Sivaraja Muthusamy
Nehru Institute of Technology, India

Acknowledgment

The editors would like to acknowledge the help of all the people involved in this project and, more specifically, to the authors and reviewers that took part in the review process. Without their support, this book would not have become a reality.

First, the editors would like to thank each one of the authors for their contributions. Our sincere gratitude goes to the chapter's authors who contributed their time and expertise to this book.

Second, the editors wish to acknowledge the valuable contributions of the reviewers regarding the improvement of quality, coherence, and content presentation of chapters. Most of the authors also served as referees; we highly appreciate their double task.

Third the editors would like to express gratitude towards members of Nehru Institute of Technology, Coimbatore, India for their kind co-operation and encouragement which help me in completion of this project.

However, it would not have been possible without the kind support and help of many individuals and organizations. I would like to extend my sincere thanks to all of them.

D. Satishkumar
Nehru Institute of Technology, India

M. Sivaraja
Nehru Institute of Technology, India

Introduction

Millions of people worldwide are affect by natural and man-made disaster every year. These occurrences frequently result in the loss of human life. Tragedies not only claim lives but also have a major negative effect on property and infrastructure. Preventing casualties, safeguarding individuals and property, lessening the effects on the economy, and restoring normalcy are the goals of disaster management activities, which are carried out prior to, during, and following a disaster. Strong decision-making, supported by information technology and especially artificial intelligence (AI), is necessary due to the complexity of catastrophes as well as the criticality and intricacy of disaster operations (Altay, N. et.al. 2006). In order to properly handle the scope and consequences of disasters, disaster management has become increasingly educated and effective, thanks to recent advancements in machine learning. Disasters including hurricanes, earthquakes, floods, wildfires, and landslides are examples of application fields. Recent technical advancements can also be beneficial in managing man-made calamities like refugee crises. However, there isn't a single, agreed-upon definition of a disaster. (Basu, M. et.al. 2019) A disaster is defined as "a major disruption of the functioning of a community or a society involving widespread human, material, economic, or environmental losses and impacts, which exceeds the ability of the affected community or society to cope using its own resources" by the United Nations Office for Disaster Risk Reduction. Natural disasters and technical disasters are the two basic categories into which disasters can be divided, according to the EM-DAT terminology. Disasters have been divided into two categories: man-made and natural.

In the long run, disaster management deals with catastrophes. Mitigation, preparedness, response, and recovery are the four main stages that have been broadly accepted. (Bejiga, M.B. et.al 2017) Activities aimed at either averting a disaster from happening or lessening its effects are categorized as mitigation. Activities like emergency planning; stockpiling supplies ahead of time, and community education and training to improve reaction times in the event of a disaster or lessen its consequences are all considered phases of preparation that help communities get ready to act when one occurs. In response, plans are put into action to safeguard people and their belongings, the environment, and the community's socio-economic system. Activities like putting emergency plans into action, providing emergency rescue and medical attention, managing and opening shelters, distributing supplies, and assessing damage are all included in disaster relief and response (Chaudhuri, N. et.al. 2020). This is one of the phases that has been studied the most, since people and infrastructure require the most help right now. Because time is of the importance in this phase, tactics emphasize not just high precision results but also quick and efficient procedures. Long-term initiatives aimed at restoring normalcy to the community are included in recovery. This phase's activities involve rebuilding and reconstruction in addition to financial aid. Furthermore, community resilience can result from the active participation of local populations in crisis management.

Introduction

Various machine learning approaches are employed in artificial intelligence to support catastrophe management throughout all stages. (Drakaki, M. et.al. 2018) With the help of machine learning (ML), large and complicated datasets can be used to create prediction systems, aid in disaster response and recovery efforts, and produce useful decision-support tools. By manipulating various data kinds from various sources, these techniques can identify pattern that can yield intelligence that would be or else not possible to reveal (Drakaki, M et.al, 2021). Big data comes from a variety of sources, including wireless sensor networks, satellite images, crowdsourcing, social media, unmanned aerial vehicles, and geographic information systems (GIS). The usage and promise of big data in natural disaster management, as well as the application of artificial intelligence in disaster management, have been the focus of recent reviews in this field.

AI is increasingly being used to handle and evaluate large amounts of data from multiple data sources so that catastrophe managers may make well-informed decisions. (Holzinger, A et.al, 2022) The research covered employed 26 different AI techniques for 17 different disaster management application domains. gave a thorough analysis of big data's application to disaster relief. The authors noted that evolving technologies such as machine learning and new technologies can help with catastrophe management. Considering the growing tendency in the creation of machine learning techniques for disaster relief. As a result, a review of previous research using machine learning (ML) that have been published since 2017 is done in this study. (Huang, X. et.al, 2020) The research covers several stages of disaster management using a variety of methods and data. This paper aims to present future trends and offer a thorough overview of the developed machine learning approaches for disaster management. Additionally, newer disaster management apps built with machine learning have been added.

The technique is then presented in the sections that follow. This is the theoretical underpinning of several of the primary machine learning techniques used in disaster management. A part that presents the technology uses of machine learning techniques for disaster management in greater depth is followed by case studies. What follows is a discussion of the findings. In conclusion, a few points are made. Early notification of approaching natural disasters can facilitate emergency responder deployment, evacuation, and planning, ultimately saving many lives. (Lecun, Y, et;al, 2015) However, predicting disasters accurately and in a timely manner is a very difficult task. Artificial intelligence (AI) methods present fresh chances to raise the precision of risk assessments for a range of dangerous occurrences. This paper presents an overview of artificial intelligence (AI) approaches for catastrophe prediction, along with an analysis of current systems, their benefits and drawbacks, and a prognosis on AI's potential in this field going forward.

Artificial intelligence (AI) uses sophisticated machine learning algorithms to find minute patterns in large, multidimensional datasets that are important for the genesis of disasters. Systems can learn to represent incredibly complicated phenomena by "training" on massive labeled datasets. (Li, H et.al, 2018) Statistical techniques then enable the assignment of probabilistic estimates to represent uncertainty. Neural networks are frequently used to find nonlinear relationships; computer vision is often used to analyze Earth observation data; natural language processing is often used to extract information from disaster reports; and reinforcement learning is frequently used to optimize prediction models. For instance, satellite photos of the circumstances leading up to past wildfires and meteorological information could be used to train a convolutional neural network. This enables the model to identify patterns similar to those in new data by learning combinations of vegetation moisture, terrain, temperature, winds, etc. that tend to lead to ignite. The number and diversity of environmental monitoring data are growing exponentially, and AI capitalizes on this.

Introduction

Every year, millions of people around the world are impacted by both man-made and natural disasters. Human life are frequently lost as a effect of these occurrences. Disasters result in major effects on properties and infrastructure in addition to human casualties. The goals of disaster management operations are to minimize casualties, safeguard people and property, lessen the effects on the economy, and restore normalcy. They are carried out prior to, during, and following a disaster. (Li, T, et.al, 2019) Robust decision-making, aided by information technology and especially artificial intelligence (AI), is necessary due to the obscurity of disasters as well as the criticality and complication of disaster operations. To concentrate on the scope and impact of disasters, educated and effective disaster management is essential, and in recent years, ML advancements have been utilized to this end.

Natural catastrophes are incredibly unpredictable and pose a continual threat to both society and natural environments. These occurrences have an annual impact of over 100 million people globally and have the potential to disproportionately affect particular populations and regions, increasing the capacity gap across civilizations. The use of machine learning for natural disaster prediction has gained popularity in recent years due to a number of natural disasters. (Lin, A, et.al, 2020) Machine learning has garnered significant attention across various domains such as finance, medicine, and other areas because of its capacity to reduce processing times, boost processing power, and improve the usability of massive datasets Machine learning-based natural disaster prediction offers numerous advantages to both nature and society, including the capacity to invest in vast amounts of spatial data, enhance emergency communication efficaciously, and increase prediction accuracy.

The threat that disasters pose to people, infrastructure, and economies has made them an increasingly important global concern. Many causes, such as climate change, urbanization, population expansion, the widespread concentration of wealth and assets in disaster-prone areas, and ecological degradation, contribute to the increasing regularity and severity of natural hazard-induced catastrophes. (Nagendra, N.P, et.al, 2020) Human casualties, economic upheaval, and long-term harm to social, ecological, and infrastructure systems are frequently the results of these catastrophic occurrences. As such, the implementation of efficient disaster risk management (DRM) has become indispensable in attaining sustainable development and adaptability to changing hazards.

The process of recognizing, evaluating, responding to, improving from, and managing the risks associated with conflicts, climate change, natural hazards, and other emergencies or disasters is known as disaster risk management (DRM). Governments, communities, non-governmental organizations (NGOs), and individual stakeholders must work together on this. It is a difficult decision-making progression that depends on quick, accurate, and accurate information to guarantee that the right steps are taken to protect people and property (Resch, B., et.al, 2018). The increasing amount of data from multiple sources, including social media, Internet of Things (IoT) devices, and remote sensing, presents previously unheard-of chances to enhance DRM decision-making by utilizing cutting-edge technologies. Within this framework, Artificial Intelligence (AI) and Machine Learning (ML) have demonstrated significant potential to improve DRM by aiding in decision-making procedures.

The organic neurons that make up the ANN make up the structure of the human brain. The various layers of connected neurons in the human brain combine to produce an ANN. We refer to these neurons as nodes. A type of artificial intelligence identified as artificial neural networks (ANNs) aims to replicate the network of neurons that make up the human head so that processors can identify brain signals and make decisions in a computing system that is similar to that of a person. (Resch, B. et.al, 2018) In order to create an ANN, the neurons are computer-programmed to function as linked brain cells. The estimated number of neurons in the human brain is 1000 billion. A single neuron has anywhere from

Introduction

1,000 to 100,000 association points. The linked information is distributed throughout the human brain, and depending on our needs and abilities, we are able to retrieve different portions of this information from memory at once. According to science, the human brain is composed of incredibly powerful parallel processors.

A methodical approach to formulating policies and making administrative choices, disaster management include the use of emergency resources and functional activities involving a range of actors and technologies to combat disasters at all levels and at different phases. The disaster management cycle consists of four stages: preparedness, mitigation, response, and recovery. Reducing the impact of a calamity is the main goal of mitigation or prevention. The goal of preparation is to provide the best possible response during a disaster by doing pre-disaster infrastructure development activities (Reynard, D. et.al, 2019). In order to find and save lives and deliver emergency relief, response refers to the appropriate execution of several emergency-based operations. Reconstruction, rehabilitation, and redevelopment of disaster-affected areas are all included in recovery. IoTs and sensor devices are rapidly producing data connected to disasters as a result of technological advancements. The availability of such data offers the chance to learn from it in order to plan for, mitigate, respond to, and recover from disasters. Machine learning is one method of analysing such data. A subfield of artificial intelligence known as "machine learning" gives computer systems the ability to autonomously learn from past experiences and existing information.

Natural catastrophes have caused havoc on our globe for ages, ranging from hurricanes and earthquakes to wildfires and floods. These catastrophic occurrences frequently leave communities in ruins and can result in an immense loss of lives and property. We may lessen the effects of these disasters by utilizing technology and innovation, even though we cannot completely control or forecast it. (Scawthorn, C. et.al, 2006) The extraordinary capabilities of artificial intelligence (AI) are making it a powerful tool for early warning, reaction, and prevention of disasters. Understanding the nature of these events is essential before exploring how AI may help prevent disasters. Geological, hydrological, meteorological and climatological events are the main categories into which natural disasters fall. Meteorological disasters include hurricanes, tornadoes, and blizzards; geological disasters include volcanic eruptions, earthquakes, and tsunamis. Disasters classified as hydrological include floods and landslides, while disasters classified as climatological include heat waves, wildfires, and droughts.Although natural catastrophes are naturally unexpected, early intervention and effective preparation can help to lessen their effects.

These occurrences may have disastrous effects on the environment, society, and economy. It is vital for the world to either prevent or lessen the harm caused by natural disasters. AI is transforming our approach to catastrophe prevention with its capacity to handle massive volumes of data, evaluate trends, and make predictions in real time. Giving vulnerable populations advance notice of impending disasters is one of the most important parts of disaster prevention. (Schmidhuber, J. 2015) In order to identify early warning indicators of approaching disasters, AI-powered systems can process data from a variety of sources, such as weather sensors, satellites, and social media. Artificial intelligence (AI) algorithms, for instance, are capable of reliably predicting the direction and strength of storms by analyzing atmospheric data. Numerous lives are saved by the authorities' ability to issue warnings in advance and evacuate high-risk regions due to these projections.

Natural disasters (NDs) have long posed a serious risk to infrastructure and human life, resulting in significant loss and destruction. The necessity for more effective and efficient disaster management systems has been brought to light in recent years by the rising frequency and intensity of natural disasters. (Sun, W. et.al, 2020) Utilizing technology has become a viable option in this situation. In this comprehensive study, we investigate how modern technologies might be used to lessen the effects of different natural disasters (Sit, M.A. et.al, 2019). We give a summary of the various ways in which the management of NDs can be aided by technologies including social media, smartphones, internet-of-things (IoT), remote sensing, radars, and satellite imaging. These technologies help us anticipate, prepare for, and recover from natural disasters (NDs) more efficiently, which may save lives and reduce damage to infrastructure. This book chapter also discusses the possible advantages, restrictions, and difficulties that come with using these technologies to control natural disasters. Technology can greatly enhance NDM, but there are a number of issues that must be resolved as well, including installation costs and the requirement for specialized knowledge and abilities. (Van Wassenhove, L.N, 2006) All things considered, this survey paper offers a thorough summary of the application of technology in ND management and highlights the significant part that these technologies can play in NDM. This study intends to aid in the creation of more sustainable and effective disaster management techniques by examining the possible uses of various technologies.

This blog article discusses AI and strategies for predicting natural disasters. Artificial Intelligence holds great potential to improve early warning systems for natural catastrophes, potentially saving lives and property. To turn promising technology into an operational reality, it will be necessary to carefully address present constraints and incorporate social issues. (Song, X. et.al, 2017) Global community resilience could be increased and environmental prediction could be transformed by AI if it is developed responsibly through partnership between government, industry, and academia.

One of the main reasons for loss of life as well as damage to property and infrastructure is natural disasters. The intricacy of disasters has led to a growing utilization of machine learning and deep learning advances. This book chapters presents the results of a review research that looked into the ways in which machine learning (ML) and deep learning (DL) approaches have been used to different aspects of disaster management to help and enhance such operations. (Yang, L.,2019) The goal of future research should be to improve disaster recovery operations' performance by utilizing ML and DL. Research should be directed on leveraging ML and DL to improve mitigation efforts, decrease vulnerabilities, and evaluate resilience, particularly that of critical infrastructure, in order to ensure that disaster recovery activities are sustainable. (Yu, M. et.al, 2018) Disaster operations are complicated and important, necessitating reliable and proven ML and DL solutions. Since disaster operations have an impact on human existence, the produced models ought to be comprehensible to decision-makers and domain experts alike. In instruct to enhance the effectiveness of ML/DL-based approaches for disaster management operations, research should also concentrate on enhancing data quality, creating innovative data gathering methods, and utilizing crowdsourcing.

P. Selvakumar
Department of Science and Humanities, Nehru Institute of Technology, Coimbatore, Tamilnadu, India

REFERENCES

Altay, N., & Green, W. G. III. (2006). OR/MS research in disaster operations management. *European Journal of Operational Research*, *175*(1), 475–493. doi:10.1016/j.ejor.2005.05.016

Introduction

Basu, M., Shandilya, A., Khosla, P., Ghosh, K., & Ghosh, S. (2019). Extracting Resource Needs and Availabilities from Microblogs for Aiding Post-Disaster Relief Operations. *IEEE Transactions on Computational Social Systems*, *6*(3), 604–618. doi:10.1109/TCSS.2019.2914179

Bejiga, M. B., Zeggada, A., Nouffidj, A., & Melgani, F. (2017). A convolutional neural network approach for assisting avalanche search and rescue operations with UAV imagery. *Remote Sensing (Basel)*, *9*(2), 100. doi:10.3390/rs9020100

Chaudhuri, N., & Bose, I. (2020). Exploring the role of deep neural networks for post-disaster decision support. *Decision Support Systems*, *130*, 113234. doi:10.1016/j.dss.2019.113234

Drakaki, M., Gören, H. G., & Tzionas, P. (2018). An intelligent multi-agent based decision support system for refugee settlement siting. *International Journal of Disaster Risk Reduction*, *31*, 576–588. doi:10.1016/j.ijdrr.2018.06.013

Drakaki, M., & Tzionas, P. (2021). Investigating the impact of site management on distress in refugee sites using Fuzzy Cognitive Maps. *International Journal of Disaster Risk Reduction*, *60*, 102282. doi:10.1016/j.ijdrr.2021.102282

Holzinger, A., Dehmer, M., Emmert-Streib, F., Cucchiara, R., Augenstein, I., Del Ser, J., Samek, W., Jurisica, I., & Díaz-Rodríguez, N. (2022). Information fusion as an integrative cross-cutting enabler to achieve robust, explainable, and trustworthy medical artificial intelligence. *Information Fusion*, *79*, 263–278. doi:10.1016/j.inffus.2021.10.007

Huang, X., Li, Z., Wang, C., & Ning, H. (2020). Identifying disaster related social media for rapid response: A visual-textual fused CNN architecture. *International Journal of Digital Earth*, *13*(9), 1017–1039. doi:10.1080/17538947.2019.1633425

Lecun, Y., Bengio, Y., & Hinton, G. (2015). Deep learning. *Nature*, *521*(7553), 436–444. doi:10.1038/nature14539 PMID:26017442

Li, H., Caragea, D., Caragea, C., & Herndon, N. (2018). Disaster response aided by tweet classification with a domain adaptation approach. *Journal of Contingencies and Crisis Management*, *26*(1), 16–27. doi:10.1111/1468-5973.12194

Li, T., Li, Z., Zhao, W., Li, X., Zhu, X., Pan, S., Feng, C., Zhao, Y., Jia, L., & Li, J. (2019). Analysis of medical rescue strategies based on a rough set and genetic algorithm: A disaster classification perspective. *International Journal of Disaster Risk Reduction*, *42*, 101325. doi:10.1016/j.ijdrr.2019.101325

Lin, A., Wu, H., Liang, G., Cardenas-Tristan, A., Wu, X., Zhao, C., & Li, D. (2020). A big data-driven dynamic estimation model of relief supplies demand in urban flood disaster. *International Journal of Disaster Risk Reduction*, *49*, 101682. doi:10.1016/j.ijdrr.2020.101682

Nagendra, N. P., Narayanamurthy, G., & Moser, R. (2020). Management of humanitarian relief operations using satellite big data analytics: The case of Kerala floods. *Annals of Operations Research*, 1–26.

Resch, B., Usländer, F., & Havas, C. (2018). Combining machine-learning topic models and spatio-temporal analysis of social media data for disaster footprint and damage assessment. *Cartography and Geographic Information Science*, *45*(4), 362–376. doi:10.1080/15230406.2017.1356242

Reynard, D., & Shirgaokar, M. (2019). Harnessing the power of machine learning: Can Twitter data be useful in guiding resource allocation decisions during a natural disaster? *Transportation Research Part D, Transport and Environment, 77*, 449–463. doi:10.1016/j.trd.2019.03.002

Robertson, B. W., Johnson, M., Murthy, D., Smith, W. R., & Stephens, K. K. (2019). Using a combination of human insights and 'deep learning' for real-time disaster communication. *Progress in Disaster Science, 2*, 100030. doi:10.1016/j.pdisas.2019.100030

Scawthorn, C., Flores, P., Blais, N., Seligson, H., Tate, E., Chang, S., Mifflin, E., Thomas, W., Murphy, J., Jones, C., & Lawrence, M. (2006). Flood Loss Estimation Methodology. II. Damage and Loss Assessment. *Natural Hazards Review, 7*(2), 72–81. doi:10.1061/(ASCE)1527-6988(2006)7:2(72)

Schmidhuber, J. (2015). Deep Learning in neural networks: An overview. *Neural Networks, 61*, 85–117. doi:10.1016/j.neunet.2014.09.003 PMID:25462637

Sit, M. A., Koylu, C., & Demir, I. (2019). Identifying disaster-related tweets and their semantic, spatial and temporal context using deep learning, natural language processing and spatial analysis: A case study of Hurricane Irma. *International Journal of Digital Earth, 12*(11), 1205–1229. doi:10.1080/17538947.2018.1563219

Song, X., Shabasaki, R., Yuan, N. J., Xie, X., Li, T., & Adachi, R. (2017). DeepMob: Learning Deep Knowledge of Human Emergency Behaviour and Mobility from Big and Heterogeneous Data. *ACM Transactions on Information Systems, 35*(4), 1–19. doi:10.1145/3057280

Sun, W., Bocchini, P., & Davison, B. D. (2020). Applications of Artificial Intelligence for Disaster Management. *Natural Hazards, 103*(3), 2631–2689. doi:10.1007/s11069-020-04124-3

Van Wassenhove, L. N. (2006). Blackett memorial lecture humanitarian aid logistics: Supply chain management in high gear. *The Journal of the Operational Research Society, 57*(5), 475–489. doi:10.1057/palgrave.jors.2602125

Yang, L., & Cervone, G. (2019). Analysis of remote sensing imagery for disaster assessment using deep learning: A case study of flooding event. *Soft Computing, 23*(24), 13393–13408. doi:10.1007/s00500-019-03878-8

Yu, M., Yang, C., & Li, Y. (2018). Big data in natural disaster management: A review. *Geosciences, 8*(5), 165. doi:10.3390/geosciences8050165

Chapter 1
Utilizing AI and Machine Learning for Natural Disaster Management:
Overview of Machine Learning and Its Importance in Disaster Management

Divya S. V.
V.S.B. College of Engineering Technical Campus, Coimbatore, India

Yazhini S.
V.S.B. College of Engineering Technical Campus, Coimbatore, India

Venkadesh P.
https://orcid.org/0000-0001-6582-3153
V.S.B. College of Engineering Technical Campus, Coimbatore, India

Shiny K. V.
https://orcid.org/0000-0002-6603-4268
Bharath Institute of Higher Education and Research, Chennai, India

ABSTRACT

Natural disasters ranging from earthquakes to wildfires and floods pose serious threats to human life and infrastructure worldwide. As the frequency and severity of such events increase, new innovative solutions are necessary to ensure disaster preparedness, response, and recovery efforts and powerful prevention tools. This abstract provides an overview of the importance of machine learning in the management of natural disasters using machine learning. It also facilitates quick analysis of critical factors such as weather, soil type, demographics, and infrastructure vulnerabilities, contributing to more effective decision-making for disaster management and recovery efforts. This explores applications of machine learning in disaster scenarios, highlighting its versatility and potential impact. Machine learning can be used for image analysis and remote sensing of wildfire detection, flood forecasting, and damage assessment after earthquakes. Hence, ultimately saving lives and reducing the social and economic impact of these disasters.

DOI: 10.4018/979-8-3693-3362-4.ch001

INTRODUCTION

Disaster management is a critical discipline dedicated to mitigating the impact of natural and human-made catastrophes, encompassing preparedness, response, recovery, and mitigation strategies. In the face of increasing global challenges posed by natural disasters, such as earthquakes, floods, hurricanes, and human-induced crises like pandemics and industrial accidents, the need for robust and adaptive disaster management approaches has become paramount. Traditionally, disaster management strategies have relied on human expertise, historical data analysis, and predefined protocols to handle emergencies. However, the limitations of these traditional methods in dealing with the complexities and unpredictability of disasters have prompted a search for innovative solutions. This quest for innovation has led to the integration of cutting-edge technologies, notably machine learning, into the domain of disaster management (Adger & Brooks, 2003; Alexander, 2002a; Dger et al., 2001; O'Brien, 2006; Kathleen Geale, 2012; Lettieri et al., 2009).

Machine learning, a subset of artificial intelligence, has emerged as a transformative force, enabling systems to learn from data, identify patterns, and make predictions or decisions without explicit programming. Its capacity to handle vast amounts of diverse and dynamic data has rendered machine learning invaluable in addressing the multifaceted challenges inherent in disaster scenarios.

The significance of leveraging machine learning in disaster management lies in its potential to revolutionize various aspects of the field. From enhancing early warning systems to optimizing resource allocation, from predicting disaster occurrences to aiding in real-time response efforts, machine learning offers a paradigm shift in improving the efficacy and efficiency of disaster management strategies.

Within this context, this paper aims to explore and delve deeper into the intersection of machine learning and disaster management. Specifically, the paper will examine the existing landscape of machine-learning applications in disaster scenarios and focus on a particular machine-learning technique or algorithm. Through a comprehensive review and analysis, the paper aims to elucidate the strengths, limitations, and potential applications of this chosen technique within the realm of disaster management.

The subsequent sections will provide a detailed exploration of the literature surrounding disaster management practices, the role of technology in reshaping these practices, and a critical review of machine learning algorithms applied in disaster management scenarios (Aguirre, 2020; Dessai et al., 2001; DFID (Department for International Development), 2004a; Dilley et al., 2005; EM-DAT (Emergencies Disasters Data Base), 2005; Larsen, 2003). Additionally, this paper will spotlight a specific machine learning technique, detailing its workings, its relevance to disaster management, and any proposed innovations aimed at advancing its applicability in mitigating disasters' impact.

In synthesizing existing knowledge and proposing innovative approaches, this paper endeavors to contribute to the ongoing discourse on leveraging machine learning to fortify disaster management strategies, thereby fostering more resilient and adaptive responses to future disasters.

LITERATURE REVIEW

Social media plays an important aspect in disaster prevention and management, especially during rainstorms and flooding scenarios. This analyzes the temporal evolution and utilizes the k-means text clustering algorithm (Safran et al., 2024) to predict the flood. Playing a video game (Park & Lee, 2024) related to earthquake preparedness can have a positive impact on individuals' self-efficacy, sense of control, outcome expectation, and intent to act. The choice of avatar and its power level also seemed to influence the effectiveness of the game in promoting these psychological factors. The fact that self-reported changes in preparedness persisted over 7 months indicates a potential long-term impact of the video game intervention on participants' earthquake preparedness behaviours. A hybrid approach for analysing and forecasting urban flood vulnerability (Agarwal et al., 2014). By identifying areas with high vulnerability and providing a means to measure relative vulnerability, the study offers valuable insights for urban planners to implement targeted and effective preventive measures, ultimately minimizing the impact of floods on urban areas. In Tabbakhha and Astaneh-Asl (2022), the multifaceted impacts of catastrophic disasters, using the specific case of floods in Jammu and Kashmir are highlighted. It underscores the importance of effective disaster recovery management planning as a tool for resilience, not only for post-disaster reconstruction but also for fostering sustainable development. The concept of "rebuilding better" suggests a proactive approach to recovery that goes beyond restoration to create more resilient and sustainable communities.

In Ferreira et al. (2023) the Tex-Wash Bridge under severe flooding and offer a thorough analysis of the factors influencing bridge performance during flood events is focussed. The parametric study contributes to understanding the effects of water velocity and depth on the structure. Additionally, the evaluation of the replaced bridge's performance and the proposed preventive measures demonstrate a practical approach to mitigating potential issues in future flood scenarios. Disaster forensic approaches aim to uncover the causes of disasters to enhance disaster risk management, yet few studies systematically review articles labeled as such. A qualitative analysis, examining methodologies, disaster risk management phases, hazards addressed, social participation, and references to urban planning is studied. Results reveal a prevalence of Forensic Investigations of Disasters (FORIN) and Post-Event Review Capability (PERC) methodologies, indicating their common use in isolation or combination. The study emphasizes the necessity for methodologies promoting participatory FORIN, encouraging the co-production of knowledge and action research approaches to address the gaps identified. The establishment of a network of real-time intensity meters in various regions of the Philippines through a collaborative effort between Japan and the Philippines (Lasala, 2015). These intensity meters are designed to record and transmit site-specific data on ground shaking in near real-time, including macroseismic intensity, peak ground acceleration, and peak ground velocity. The evaluation of earthquake effects is based on the Philippine earthquake intensity scale – PHIVOLCS Earthquake Intensity Scale (PEIS). The deployment of these instruments follows an optimal distribution strategy, considering active earthquake generators and vulnerable communities. Manned seismic stations operated by PHIVOLCS have been equipped with intensity meters, while additional units are strategically placed in relevant disaster risk reduction and management centers. The network, initiated in 2012, has successfully captured significant earthquakes, such as the Mw7.2 event in Bohol in 2013, showcasing the effectiveness of this collaborative real-time monitoring system in earthquake-prone regions. The recent discourse on the interplay between population dynamics and climate change underscores the need to assess and quantify disparities in vulnerability across communities.

In Ghio (2023), integrating demographic projections based on the Shared socio-economic pathways with climate change projections is addressed. Firstly, the study estimates the proportion of populations residing in rural areas, particularly vulnerable due to their reliance on agriculture, a sector highly susceptible to climate change. Secondly, it explores the exacerbation of poverty levels among populations affected by climate change. Thirdly, the study accounts for low levels of education as an additional factor limiting adaptive capacity to adverse climate circumstances. This research makes a dual contribution to the literature on population, agriculture, and environmental change. It maps potential populations exposed to climate change-induced declining agricultural yields, identifying vulnerable areas for targeted strategies and interventions. Moreover, it assesses disparities in vulnerability among local populations, revealing that African regions are poised to become among the most exposed to climate change by the century's end. These findings advocate for targeted policy measures to prevent heightened vulnerability among already disadvantaged populations.

PHASES OF DISASTER MANAGEMENT

Disaster management involves a series of phases that collectively constitute a comprehensive approach to preparing for, responding to, recovering from, and mitigating the impact of disasters. These phases are generally recognized as:

1. **Mitigation:** This phase involves actions taken to minimize the occurrence of disasters or to reduce their effects. It includes measures like implementing building codes, creating infrastructure resilient to natural disasters, public education and awareness programs, land-use planning, and enacting policies to reduce vulnerabilities.

Figure 1. Phases in disaster management

2. **Preparedness:** This phase involves planning, training, and preparing resources to respond effectively to a disaster. It includes developing emergency plans (Alexander, 2002b; Bhatt, 2002; Blong, 2004; Cardona, 2004), conducting drills and exercises, stockpiling supplies, establishing communication systems, and educating the public about what to do before, during, and after a disaster.
3. **Response:** This phase involves immediate actions taken to address the emergency and save lives, protect property, and meet basic human needs. It includes activities such as search and rescue operations, providing medical care, distributing food, water, and shelter, and coordinating emergency services.
4. **Recovery:** This phase begins once the immediate danger has passed and aims to restore the affected area to its pre-disaster state or to a new, safer and more resilient state. It involves rebuilding infra-

structure, restoring essential services, providing mental health support, and assisting communities and individuals in returning to normalcy.
5. **Mitigation (ongoing):** This phase overlaps with the others and continues after the disaster has occurred. It involves ongoing efforts to implement changes and strategies to reduce the impact of future disasters based on lessons learned from the current event. It includes adjustments to policies, improvements in infrastructure, and community engagement to build resilience.

These phases are interconnected and often cyclical, as actions taken during and after a disaster can inform future mitigation, preparedness, and response efforts. Successful disaster management involves a continuous cycle of planning, implementation, evaluation, and revision based on experiences and changing circumstances.

TRADITIONAL DISASTER MANAGEMENT APPROACH

The traditional approach to disaster management has long been characterized by a structured and phased response framework, aiming to address the different stages of a disaster, including mitigation, preparedness, response, and recovery. This approach typically follows a linear sequence, with distinct actions and strategies earmarked for each phase. Mitigation efforts traditionally focused on physical interventions such as building codes, infrastructure reinforcement, and hazard mapping to reduce the impact of disasters. Preparedness involves planning, training, and resource allocation for response efforts, while response activities entail immediate actions to address the emergency and protect lives and property. Finally, the recovery phase aims to restore the affected area to its pre-disaster state or improve its resilience for the future.

One of the primary characteristics of the traditional approach is its centralized and hierarchical decision-making structure, often led by government agencies or designated emergency management bodies. These entities are responsible for coordinating response efforts, allocating resources, and implementing disaster plans. However, this centralized structure can sometimes lead to challenges in responsiveness, especially when coordination among various stakeholders is lacking, causing delays or inefficiencies in disaster response.

Additionally, the traditional approach has historically placed more emphasis on reactive measures—responding to and recovering from disasters after they occur—rather than proactively mitigating risks or preventing disasters. While risk assessments (Aguirre, 2020; Dessai et al., 2001; DFID (Department for International Development), 2004a; Dilley et al., 2005; EM-DAT (Emergencies Disasters Data Base), 2005; Larsen, 2003) and planning are integral components, there has been a greater focus on managing the consequences of disasters rather than reducing vulnerabilities or addressing underlying causes.

Moreover, the traditional approach has been criticized for its limited community engagement and inclusivity in decision-making processes. Despite recognizing the importance of involving communities in disaster preparedness and response, there have been gaps in fully harnessing local knowledge, engaging diverse community groups, and empowering grassroots organizations, which are crucial for effective disaster management.

Another critique revolves around the traditional emphasis on structural measures for mitigation, often overlooking non-structural approaches like education, land-use planning, and ecosystem-based strategies. While structural interventions such as levees and dams are vital, a comprehensive approach that integrates both structural and non-structural measures is increasingly recognized as necessary for enhancing resilience to disasters.

In essence, while the traditional disaster management approach has served as a foundational framework, it faces evolving challenges and criticisms. There is a growing recognition of the need to transition towards more comprehensive, community-centered, and proactive approaches that address complex and interconnected risks, integrate local knowledge, promote inclusivity, and prioritize both structural and non-structural measures for effective disaster risk reduction and management.

CHALLENGES FACED BY THE TRADITIONAL APPROACH OF DISASTER MANAGEMENT

While the traditional approach has laid the groundwork for disaster management, it also faces criticisms for being insufficient in addressing contemporary challenges, including the increasing frequency and intensity of disasters, interconnected risks, and the need for more holistic, community-centered, and forward-looking strategies. As a result, there's a growing emphasis on evolving towards more comprehensive, inclusive, and proactive approaches to disaster risk reduction and management.

Traditional disaster management approaches have faced several challenges that impact their effectiveness in dealing with various crises. Some of these challenges include:

1. **Fragmented Approach:** Often, disaster management efforts involve different agencies, organizations, and levels of government working independently. Lack of coordination and collaboration among these entities can lead to inefficiencies, duplication of efforts, and gaps in response and recovery.
2. **Reactive rather than Proactive:** Historically, disaster management has been more reactive, focusing primarily on responding to disasters as they occur rather than proactively mitigating risks or preventing them. This approach can result in higher human and economic costs as opposed to investing in preventive measures.
3. **Insufficient Funding and Resource Allocation:** Limited financial resources and inadequate funding allocation for disaster preparedness and mitigation efforts hinder the ability to implement comprehensive plans and infrastructure improvements. This can weaken the overall resilience of communities and regions.
4. **Focus on Short-Term Recovery**: Emphasis on short-term recovery often overshadows long-term rehabilitation and reconstruction efforts. This can lead to a lack of sustainable solutions and failure to address underlying vulnerabilities that contribute to repeated disasters.
5. **Inadequate Risk Communication and Public Awareness:** Effective communication and public education are crucial for preparedness and response. However, there can be challenges in disseminating accurate information, raising awareness, and ensuring communities understand the risks and necessary actions to take before, during, and after a disaster.
6. **Social and Economic Inequalities:** Vulnerable populations, including low-income communities, minorities, and marginalized groups, often bear the brunt of disasters due to their limited access to resources, infrastructure, and support systems. Addressing these inequalities and ensuring inclusivity in disaster planning and response is essential.

Figure 2. Challenges in traditional disaster approach

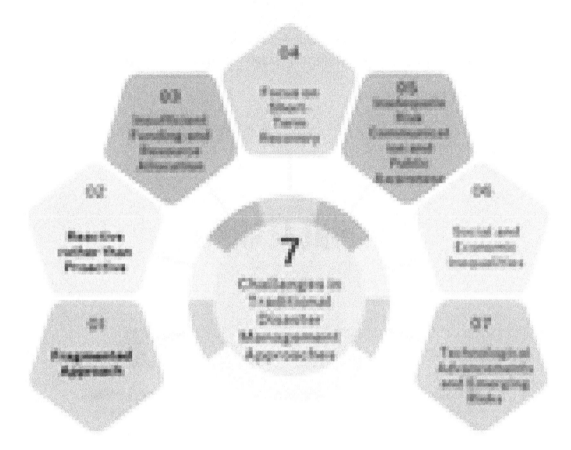

7. **Technological Advancements and Emerging Risks:** Rapid technological advancements bring both opportunities and challenges in disaster management. Emerging risks, such as cyber threats, pandemics, and climate change-related disasters, require updated strategies and tools to effectively manage these complex and interconnected hazards (Blong, 2004).

Addressing these challenges often requires a shift towards more holistic, inclusive, and proactive approaches to disaster management. Integrating risk reduction, community engagement, sustainable development practices, and leveraging technology for early warning systems and information dissemination can significantly enhance resilience and response capabilities.

MACHINE LEARNING AND ITS TYPES

Machine learning is a branch of artificial intelligence (AI) that enables computer systems to learn and improve from experience without explicit programming. It involves algorithms and statistical models that allow machines to analyze and interpret data, recognize patterns, and make predictions or decisions based on the information provided. Through exposure to data, machine learning algorithms can identify hidden insights, adapt to new information, and autonomously improve their performance over time. It finds applications across various domains, including image and speech recognition, natural language processing, recommendation systems, autonomous vehicles, healthcare, finance, and many other fields, revolutionizing how technology processes information and makes informed decisions.

Types of Machine Learning

Figure 3. Machine learning types

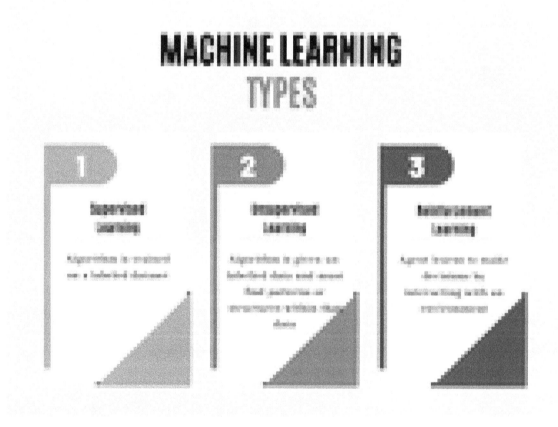

Supervised Learning

Supervised learning is a type of machine learning where the algorithm is trained on a labeled dataset. In this learning paradigm, the algorithm learns a mapping from input features to corresponding output labels based on example pairs provided in the training data. The goal is to generalize this mapping to make accurate predictions or classifications on new, unseen data.Supervised learning is a powerful approach for tasks where the relationship between inputs and outputs can be explicitly taught to the algorithm through labelled example

Challenges

- Requires a substantial amount of labeled data for training.
- Performance may be affected if the labeled data is biased or if the model overfits the training data.

Unsupervised Learning

Unsupervised learning is a type of machine learning where the algorithm is given unlabelled data and must find patterns or structures within that data. Unlike supervised learning, there are no predefined output labels. The goal is often to explore the inherent structure of the data, such as identifying clusters or reducing dimensionality. The algorithm is provided with input data without corresponding output labels. The algorithm aims to discover patterns, relationships, or structures within the data without explicit guidance. Unsupervised learning is valuable when dealing with large datasets where the underlying structure is not well-defined or when the goal is to gain insights into the data's intrinsic properties.

Challenges

- Evaluation can be subjective and dependent on the specific goals of the analysis.
- The absence of labelled data makes it challenging to assess the accuracy of the model's findings.

Reinforcement Learning

Reinforcement learning is a type of machine learning where an agent learns to make decisions by interacting with an environment. The agent receives feedback in the form of rewards or penalties based on the actions it takes. The goal is for the agent to learn a strategy or policy that maximizes the cumulative reward over time. The learning system consists of an agent that takes actions and an environment in which those actions are executed. The agent takes actions in the environment, and it receives feedback in the form of rewards or penalties based on the consequences of those actions. The agent learns to map states of the environment to actions in a way that maximizes the cumulative reward over time. The agent faces the challenge of balancing exploration (trying new actions to discover their effects) and exploitation (choosing known actions to maximize immediate rewards). Reinforcement learning problems are often modeled as Markov Decision Processes, which formalize the interaction between the agent and the environment. Reinforcement learning is well-suited for scenarios where an agent must learn a sequence of actions over time to achieve a goal, and it is widely used in fields requiring decision-making in dynamic and complex environments.

Challenges

- Training can be computationally intensive.
- Dealing with delayed rewards and long-term dependencies requires sophisticated algorithms.

Machine Learning Algorithms Used in Disaster Management

Machine learning (ML) algorithms play a crucial role in various aspects of disaster management, aiding in prediction, response, and recovery efforts. Some ML algorithms commonly used in disaster management include:

1. **Predictive Modelling:** Algorithms such as decision trees, random forests, and support vector machines (SVM) are employed for predictive modeling. They analyze historical data on past disasters, weather patterns, geographical features, and social factors to forecast potential hazards, such as floods, hurricanes, or wildfires. Predictive models help in early warning systems and risk assessment, enabling proactive measures to mitigate risks and prepare for potential disasters.
2. **Image and Sensor Data Analysis:** Convolutional Neural Networks (CNNs) and other deep learning techniques are used to analyze satellite images, aerial photographs, and sensor data to assess the extent of damage, identify affected areas, and prioritize response efforts during and after disasters. These algorithms assist in mapping disaster-affected regions, monitoring changes, and aiding in search and rescue missions.
3. **Natural Language Processing (NLP):** NLP algorithms process and analyze unstructured textual data from social media, news reports, and emergency calls to extract relevant information about disaster situations in real-time. Sentiment analysis, topic modeling, and information extraction techniques help in understanding public sentiment, identifying emerging risks, and facilitating communication and decision-making for response teams.
4. **Optimization Algorithms:** Optimization algorithms, like genetic algorithms or simulated annealing, assist in resource allocation and logistics planning during disaster response. These algorithms optimize the allocation of supplies, manpower, and equipment to affected areas, ensuring efficient and timely delivery of aid and support.
5. **Anomaly Detection:** ML algorithms, including clustering and anomaly detection techniques, help in detecting abnormal patterns or behaviors in data, which might indicate impending disasters or irregularities in critical systems. This aids in early detection of potential issues, preventing or minimizing the impact of disasters.
6. **Recovery and Reconstruction:** ML algorithms are used in assessing infrastructure damage, estimating reconstruction costs, and prioritizing recovery efforts. Algorithms analyzing socioeconomic data help in determining the most vulnerable communities and planning for long-term recovery strategies.

Integrating these ML techniques into disaster management systems enhances decision-making processes, facilitates early warning systems, improves response times, and aids in creating more effective and adaptive strategies to mitigate the impact of disasters on communities and infrastructure.

CONVENTIONAL NEURAL NETWORKS

Conventional neural networks, often referred to as artificial neural networks (ANNs), constitute the fundamental architecture underlying various modern deep learning models. These networks are inspired by the biological structure of the human brain, comprising interconnected nodes or neurons arranged in layers. The basic structure consists of an input layer through which data is fed, one or more hidden layers where computations take place, and an output layer that produces the network's predictions or classifications based on the processed information. Each neuron within these layers receives inputs, computes a weighted sum of these inputs, and applies an activation function to introduce non-linearity, enabling the network to learn complex patterns and relationships within the data.

The training of conventional neural networks involves an iterative process known as backpropagation. During training, the network adjusts the weights and biases associated with the connections between neurons to minimize the difference between the predicted outputs and the actual outputs in a given dataset. Optimization algorithms, such as gradient descent, are often employed to facilitate this process, aiming to iteratively optimize the network's parameters to improve its performance on the task at hand.

These neural networks have found applications across various domains, including pattern recognition, classification, regression, and prediction tasks. They have been utilized in image recognition, natural language processing, recommendation systems, and numerous other fields due to their ability to model complex relationships within data. However, conventional neural networks have limitations, such as challenges in handling large datasets due to computational constraints and susceptibility to overfitting or underfitting, where the model may either excessively fit the training data or fail to capture essential patterns in the data.

The evolution of neural network architectures has led to the development of specialized models that address specific challenges. While conventional neural networks laid the groundwork, their limitations in processing complex data types like images or sequences led to the creation of architectures like Convolutional Neural Networks (CNNs) and Recurrent Neural Networks (RNNs). These specialized architectures excel in handling different types of data. For instance, CNNs are particularly effective in image-related tasks due to their ability to detect patterns in spatial data efficiently, while RNNs excel in handling sequential data, making them suitable for tasks like language modeling and time-series prediction. Thus, while conventional neural networks remain fundamental, the advancements in specialized architectures have significantly enhanced the capabilities and performance of neural networks in various applications.

FUNDAMENTALS OF CNN ARCHITECTURE AND FUNCTIONING

Convolutional Neural Networks (CNNs) are a specialized type of artificial neural network designed primarily for processing and analyzing visual data, such as images and videos. Their architecture is structured to leverage spatial hierarchies and patterns within the data. Fundamentally, CNNs consist of three main components: convolutional layers, pooling layers, and fully connected layers.

1. **Convolutional Layers:** These layers perform the core operations in CNNs by applying filters or kernels to the input image. The filters extract features, such as edges or textures, through convolution, where the filter slides across the input, producing feature maps that highlight learned patterns.
2. **Pooling Layers:** Pooling layers reduce the dimensionality of the feature maps generated by the convolutional layers. Common pooling techniques, like max pooling or average pooling, aggregate and downsample the information, aiding in retaining essential features while reducing computational complexity.

3. **Fully Connected Layers:** After multiple convolutional and pooling layers, the resulting features are flattened and fed into fully connected layers. These layers perform classification or regression tasks by combining the learned features through densely connected neurons, ultimately producing the network's output.

CNNs employ learnable parameters (weights and biases) within the convolutional and fully connected layers, optimizing these parameters during training using backpropagation and gradient descent. This enables CNNs to automatically learn hierarchical representations of features, enabling them to recognize patterns and objects in images with impressive accuracy and efficiency.

Role of CNNs

Convolutional Neural Networks (CNNs) play a pivotal role in image recognition, pattern detection, and feature extraction due to their specialized architecture tailored for visual data analysis. In image recognition, CNNs excel in accurately classifying and identifying objects within images. Through multiple layers of convolution and pooling, CNNs extract hierarchical representations of features from images.

CNNs' ability to detect patterns lies in their convolutional layers, where filters analyze local patterns in different parts of the image. These filters recognize edges, textures, shapes, and other visual elements. As the network progresses through deeper layers, it learns to detect increasingly complex and abstract features by combining lower-level features detected in earlier layers. Feature extraction is a crucial aspect where CNNs shine. They automatically learn and extract meaningful features without human intervention, making them highly effective in understanding and representing visual information. This capability extends beyond image recognition to various domains like medical imaging, autonomous vehicles, and quality control in manufacturing.

By leveraging these learned features, CNNs enable robust pattern detection, allowing them to identify objects, scenes, or anomalies within images accurately. Their hierarchical feature extraction process empowers CNNs to capture intricate details, enabling them to generalize well to new, unseen data and significantly enhancing their performance in image-related tasks.

Components and Layers of CNNs

Convolutional Neural Networks (CNNs) consist of several key components and layers that work together to process and analyze visual data efficiently. The main components include convolutional layers, pooling layers, and fully connected layers.

1. **Convolutional Layers:** These are the fundamental building blocks of CNNs. Convolutional layers perform feature extraction by applying a set of learnable filters (also known as kernels) to the input data. Each filter scans through the input image, performing element-wise multiplications and summations to produce feature maps. These feature maps highlight specific patterns or features present in the input, such as edges, textures, or shapes. The convolutional layers contain multiple filters that capture different aspects of the input, enabling the network to learn diverse features.
2. **Pooling Layers:** Pooling layers follow convolutional layers and are responsible for downsampling the feature maps obtained from the convolutional layers. Common pooling operations like max pooling or average pooling reduce the spatial dimensions (width and height) of the feature maps

while retaining essential information. Pooling helps in reducing computational complexity, improving computational efficiency, and making the network more robust to variations in input data by focusing on the most relevant features.
3. **Fully Connected Layers:** After several convolutional and pooling layers, the processed and extracted features are flattened and fed into fully connected layers. These layers are similar to traditional neural network layers, where each neuron is connected to every neuron in the previous and subsequent layers. Fully connected layers perform classification or regression tasks by combining the learned features through densely connected neurons. They enable the network to make predictions based on the extracted features, ultimately producing the final output, such as classification probabilities for different classes in image recognition tasks.

These components, working in conjunction within the CNN architecture, allow for effective feature extraction, hierarchical representation learning, and accurate classification or regression of visual data, making CNNs highly effective in various image-related tasks.

Application of CNNs in Disaster Management

Convolutional Neural Networks (CNNs) find valuable applications in disaster management. These networks are instrumental in analyzing satellite imagery to assess disaster-affected regions, map damaged areas, and estimate the extent of destruction caused by events like earthquakes, floods, or wildfires. CNNs aid in rapid and accurate image processing, enabling efficient disaster response efforts by providing real-time data for damage assessment, resource allocation, and identifying areas requiring immediate attention. Moreover, these networks assist in enhancing early warning systems by analyzing environmental data, and contributing to proactive disaster preparedness and mitigation strategies.

Early Warning Systems and Predictive Modeling Using CNNs

Convolutional Neural Networks (CNNs) contribute significantly to early warning systems and predictive modeling in disaster management. CNNs excel in analyzing vast amounts of data, especially images and spatial data, to forecast and detect potential hazards.

For early warning systems, CNNs process satellite imagery, weather patterns, and environmental data to identify precursors or indicators of impending disasters such as hurricanes, floods, or wildfires. By learning patterns from historical data, CNNs can recognize early signs of these events, enabling authorities to issue timely warnings and take proactive measures to mitigate potential damage and protect lives.

Predictive modeling with CNNs involves training models on historical data to forecast the likelihood and severity of future disasters. These models can predict the path, intensity, and impact of natural calamities, aiding in preparedness and resource allocation. The ability of CNNs to extract features from visual data enhances the accuracy of predictive models, facilitating better-informed decision-making for disaster response and risk reduction strategies. By leveraging CNNs for early warning systems and predictive modeling, disaster management agencies can improve their ability to anticipate and prepare for potential disasters, ultimately minimizing their impact on communities and infrastructure.

Figure 4. Predictive model using CNN

Satellite Image Analysis for Disaster Mapping and Damage Assessment

Satellite image analysis powered by Convolutional Neural Networks (CNNs) plays a pivotal role in disaster mapping and damage assessment. CNNs, with their ability to process vast amounts of visual data, offer a sophisticated means to analyze satellite imagery quickly and accurately during and after disasters. In disaster mapping, CNNs assist in creating detailed maps of affected regions by analyzing satellite images. These networks can automatically detect changes, identify damaged infrastructure, altered landscapes, and areas impacted by natural calamities like earthquakes, floods, or wildfires. By comparing before and after images, CNNs enable the generation of precise maps highlighting the extent and severity of damage.

Furthermore, CNNs aid in damage assessment by categorizing the level of destruction within affected areas. They distinguish between various types of damage, such as collapsed buildings, flooded regions, or road blockages. This information assists disaster response teams and authorities in prioritizing rescue and recovery efforts, directing resources efficiently to the most affected areas.

The speed and accuracy of CNNs in analyzing satellite imagery significantly enhance the capabilities of disaster management teams, allowing for rapid assessment, planning, and targeted response efforts in affected regions. Through their ability to process extensive visual data, CNNs play a crucial role in facilitating timely and informed decision-making for effective disaster response and recovery initiatives.

Real-Time Data Processing and Information Extraction During Emergencies

Convolutional Neural Networks (CNNs) contribute significantly to real-time data processing and information extraction during emergencies in disaster management scenarios. These networks excel in handling large volumes of data streams, enabling quick and accurate analysis of diverse information sources crucial for emergency response.

During emergencies, CNNs process real-time data from various sources such as social media, sensor networks, satellite imagery, and live video feeds. These networks employ techniques like natural language processing (NLP) for text analysis, image recognition, and object detection to extract valuable insights and actionable information from this influx of data.

Figure 5. Disaster management system using CNN

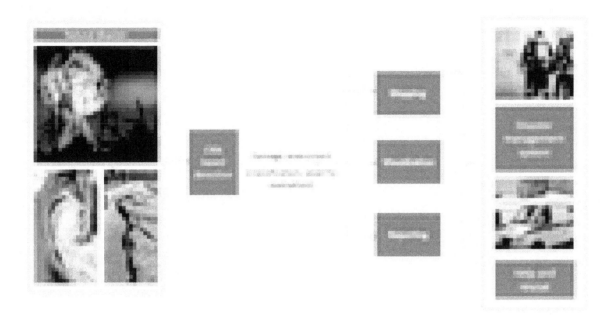

In situations like natural disasters or crises, CNNs aid in detecting and analyzing relevant information, including incident reports, affected areas, resource needs, and population movements. They enable the extraction of critical details such as locations requiring immediate attention, the intensity of the event, and emerging risks, empowering response teams and decision-makers with up-to-date and actionable insights. The ability of CNNs to process and extract information in real-time contributes significantly to situational awareness and decision-making during emergencies. By swiftly identifying key details from diverse data sources, CNNs assist in enhancing the efficiency and effectiveness of emergency response efforts, facilitating timely interventions and resource allocation to mitigate the impact of disasters on affected communities.

Improving Search and Rescue Operations Through Object Detection and Localization

Convolutional Neural Networks (CNNs) play a crucial role in enhancing search and rescue operations by enabling object detection and localization in disaster-affected areas. These networks excel in analyzing visual data, aiding responders in locating and identifying objects or individuals, especially in challenging and hazardous environments.

CNNs, particularly through object detection algorithms like YOLO (You Only Look Once) or Faster R-CNN (Region-based Convolutional Neural Network), facilitate the rapid identification and localization of objects, survivors, or obstacles in images or live video feeds. These algorithms detect and highlight specific objects within the visual data, enabling rescuers to identify crucial elements such as survivors, vehicles, collapsed structures, or potential hazards.

Figure 6. Communication during disaster management

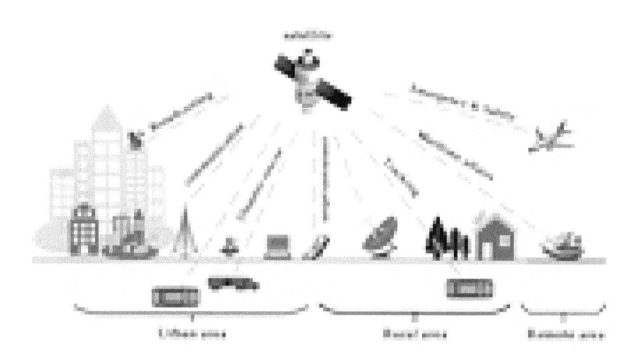

In disaster scenarios like earthquakes, floods, or avalanches, CNNs aid in analyzing aerial or ground-level imagery to pinpoint the location of survivors or individuals in need of assistance. Moreover, these networks assist in identifying obstructed routes or hazards that could impede rescue efforts.

By providing accurate object detection and localization capabilities, CNNs significantly improve the efficiency and effectiveness of search and rescue operations. They help rescue teams prioritize areas needing immediate attention, optimize resource allocation, and expedite the retrieval of survivors, thereby saving valuable time and potentially saving lives in critical situations.

Advantages and Limitations of CNNs in Disaster Management

Advantages

1. **Accurate Image Analysis:** CNNs excel in accurate image recognition, allowing for precise analysis of satellite imagery, aerial photographs, and sensor data. This capability aids in assessing damage, identifying affected areas, and prioritizing response efforts during disasters.
2. **Real-time Data Processing:** CNNs enable real-time data processing, facilitating rapid decision-making by providing timely and actionable information to response teams. This capability is crucial in emergencies to ensure swift and efficient disaster response.
3. **Enhanced Early Warning Systems:** These networks contribute to the improvement of early warning systems by analyzing various data sources such as environmental indicators, helping predict and prepare for impending disasters, thereby reducing potential risks.

4. **Efficient Resource Allocation:** By swiftly mapping disaster-affected regions and estimating damage, CNNs assist in efficient resource allocation. They aid in directing manpower, supplies, and equipment to areas requiring immediate attention, optimizing disaster response efforts.

Limitation

1. **Dependency on Quality and Quantity of Data:** The effectiveness of CNNs heavily relies on the quality and quantity of available data. Limited or poor-quality data might hinder the accuracy and reliability of the network's predictions and analyses.
2. **Computational Requirements:** CNNs often require substantial computational resources, including powerful hardware and significant processing time, especially when handling large datasets or complex analyses. This aspect may pose challenges in resource-constrained environments or during time-critical situations.
3. **Interpretability:** The complex nature of CNNs sometimes results in reduced interpretability of their decision-making process. Understanding how these networks arrive at specific conclusions or classifications might be challenging, affecting trust and confidence in their outputs.
4. **Ethical and Bias Considerations:** Issues related to biases present in training data and ethical concerns regarding decision-making based on automated systems like CNNs require careful consideration. Biases in data could lead to skewed or unfair outcomes in disaster management decisions.

Understanding these advantages and limitations is crucial for leveraging CNNs effectively in disaster management, acknowledging their strengths while addressing potential challenges to optimize their contributions to disaster preparedness, response, and recovery.

Following natural disasters, traditional damage assessment methods faced limitations in speed and accuracy. In response, Convolutional Neural Networks (CNNs) emerged as a solution for rapid and precise post-disaster damage evaluation. These deep learning models excelled in image recognition, enabling automated analysis of satellite and aerial imagery to identify damage types, collapsed structures, and affected regions. Collaborative efforts between organizations and institutions collected extensive pre- and post-disaster image datasets, training CNNs to recognize disaster-induced changes. Trained models processed post-disaster images, generating detailed damage assessment maps swiftly. CNN-driven assessments guided emergency responders and aid agencies, facilitating resource allocation, prioritizing rescue operations, and informing recovery plans. CNNs revolutionized disaster management, offering efficient, automated, and accurate solutions for post-disaster assessment, leading to improved response strategies and targeted recovery efforts for affected communities.

CNNS IN POST-EARTHQUAKE DAMAGE ASSESSMENT

After the devastating earthquake in Nepal in April 2015, which resulted in significant structural damage and loss of life, researchers and organizations employed Convolutional Neural Networks (CNNs) to aid in damage assessment and recovery efforts.

CNN Application

CNNs were utilized to analyze high-resolution satellite imagery of the affected areas. These models were trained to automatically detect and classify damaged buildings, collapsed structures, and road blockages caused by the earthquake.

Process

1. **Data Collection:** High-resolution satellite images were collected from various sources, including pre- and post-earthquake imagery.
2. **Training CNN:** Trained CNN models were developed using labeled datasets of pre- and post-earthquake images. The CNNs were trained to recognize and classify various types of damage and debris.
3. **Image Analysis:** Post-earthquake satellite images were processed by the CNNs to identify and highlight damaged buildings, collapsed structures, and areas affected by debris.
4. **Damage Assessment:** Automated assessments generated by the CNNs provided detailed maps indicating heavily affected zones, critical infrastructure damage, and areas requiring immediate attention.

Outcome

The application of CNNs in post-earthquake damage assessment provided rapid and accurate evaluations of the earthquake's impact. The detailed damage assessment maps produced by CNNs assisted in prioritizing rescue and recovery efforts.

Benefits

1. **Swift Assessment:** CNNs enabled a quick and comprehensive evaluation of the earthquake's impact, aiding in immediate response planning.
2. **Targeted Response:** Detailed damage assessment facilitated the allocation of resources and directed emergency responders to the most affected areas, improving the efficiency of rescue operations.
3. **Planning for Recovery:** CNN-generated maps assisted authorities in strategic planning for infrastructure restoration and community rehabilitation efforts.

The use of CNNs in post-earthquake damage assessment showcased their effectiveness in aiding disaster response and recovery efforts. By leveraging CNNs for image analysis and damage assessment, authorities could efficiently allocate resources, prioritize rescue efforts, and plan for the affected community's recovery and reconstruction.

Outcomes From These CNN-Based Interventions

The outcomes stemming from CNN-based interventions in disaster management have been transformative, yielding several impactful results:

1. **Swift and Accurate Assessments:** CNNs enable rapid and accurate evaluations of disaster-affected regions, facilitating timely responses and aiding emergency teams in understanding the extent and nature of damage promptly after a disaster strikes.
2. **Optimized Resource Allocation:** Detailed damage assessment maps generated by CNNs assist in directing resources, manpower, and aid to the most critical and affected areas, maximizing the efficiency of relief efforts and minimizing response time.
3. **Improved Decision-Making:** CNN-derived data and assessments provide actionable insights for decision-makers, aiding in informed and strategic decision-making for disaster response, resource distribution, and recovery planning.
4. **Enhanced Targeting of Relief Efforts**: By precisely identifying damaged infrastructure, collapsed buildings, and affected regions, CNN-based interventions help prioritize rescue and relief operations, ensuring that aid is directed where it's most needed.
5. **Efficient Planning for Recovery:** The detailed and accurate damage assessment maps produced by CNNs aid authorities in developing strategic plans for post-disaster recovery, facilitating infrastructure restoration, and guiding community rehabilitation efforts.
6. **Increased Safety and Minimized Risks:** CNN-based interventions contribute to early warning systems, enabling proactive measures, reducing risks, and potentially saving lives by predicting and preparing for impending disasters.

In essence, the outcomes of CNN-based interventions in disaster management culminate in more efficient, effective, and targeted responses, leading to minimized loss, accelerated recovery, and improved resilience for communities affected by disasters.

HALLENGES AND FUTURE DIRECTIONS

Challenges and future directions in employing Convolutional Neural Networks (CNNs) for disaster management encompass several key aspects:

Challenges

1. **Data Quality and Availability:** Obtaining high-quality and diverse datasets for training CNNs can be challenging, particularly in disaster scenarios where acquiring labeled data pre- and post-disaster is difficult. Limited or biased datasets may impact the CNNs' performance and generalizability.
2. **Computational Resources:** CNNs often require substantial computational power and resources, making real-time processing challenging, especially in resource-constrained disaster response settings where access to high-performance computing may be limited.
3. **Interpretability and Explainability:** The complex nature of CNNs poses challenges in interpreting and explaining the decision-making process of these models. Understanding how CNNs arrive at specific conclusions or classifications is crucial for building trust and acceptance in their outputs.
4. **Ethical Considerations:** Biases present in training data can lead to biased outputs, impacting the fairness and reliability of CNN-based decisions. Ensuring ethical considerations and fairness in AI-driven disaster management solutions is critical.

Figure 7. Challenges in employing CNN

Future Directions

1. **Data Augmentation and Transfer Learning: Improving** CNNs' robustness by employing data augmentation techniques and transfer learning can help mitigate challenges related to limited and biased datasets, enhancing their generalization and performance.
2. **Edge Computing and Optimization:** Developing lightweight CNN architectures and optimizing algorithms for edge computing can facilitate real-time processing and deployment in resource-constrained environments, enhancing the accessibility and usability of CNNs in disaster response.
3. **Interpretability and Explainable AI (XAI):** Advancements in Explainable AI (XAI) techniques aim to enhance CNNs' interpretability, providing insights into model decisions and making CNN-based solutions more transparent and trustworthy for stakeholders.
4. **Collaborative Partnerships and Standards**: Establishing collaborative efforts among stakeholders, researchers, and governments to create standardized datasets, methodologies, and protocols for CNN-based disaster management can foster advancements and ensure consistency in AI-driven solutions.

5. **Bias Mitigation and Ethical Guidelines:** Implementing strategies to mitigate biases in training data and developing ethical guidelines for AI applications in disaster management can ensure fairness, accountability, and trustworthiness in CNN-based interventions.

Addressing these challenges and steering CNN applications toward these future directions can pave the way for more robust, ethical, and impactful CNN-based solutions in disaster management, fostering improved response strategies and enhanced resilience in the face of disasters.

CONCLUSION

The integration of machine learning techniques into the realm of natural disaster management marks a transformative step toward more effective preparedness, response, and recovery efforts. Machine learning, with its diverse algorithms and applications, has showcased immense potential in mitigating the devastating impacts of natural disasters.

By leveraging various machine learning models such as Convolutional Neural Networks (CNNs), Recurrent Neural Networks (RNNs), decision trees, and ensemble methods, among others, disaster management has witnessed enhanced predictive capabilities, early warning systems, and efficient resource allocation. These technologies enable the processing of vast datasets, empowering authorities to analyze patterns, predict occurrences, and provide timely alerts, thereby reducing human casualties and infrastructure damage.

However, challenges persist, including the need for large, diverse, and high-quality datasets, computational complexities, interpretability of models, and ethical considerations. Bridging these gaps requires collaborative efforts between researchers, governments, relief organizations, and technology experts to improve algorithms, data accessibility, interpretability, and ethical guidelines.

Looking ahead, the continuous advancement and integration of machine learning in disaster management hold promise. Future developments should focus on refining algorithms, enhancing real-time analytics, establishing standardized protocols, and fostering transparent methodologies. Embracing these advancements will further strengthen disaster resilience, expedite response times, and empower communities to mitigate, adapt, and recover more effectively from natural disasters worldwide.

REFERENCES

Adger, N., & Brooks, N. (2003). *Country level risk measures of climate-related natural disasters and implications for adaptation to climate change. Working Paper 26*. Tyndall Centre for Climate Change Research. https://www.tyndall.ac.uk/publications/working_papers/wp26.pdf

Agarwal, S., Fulzele, T. U., & Aggarwal, G. (2014). Flood Recovery Management in Jammu and Kashmir: A Tool for Resilience. *Asian Journal of Environment and Disaster Management*, 6(3).

Aguirre, B. E. (2020). Review of Disasters: A Sociological Approach. Natural Hazards Review. ASCE Library.

Alexander, D. (2002a). 'From civil defense to civil protection-and back again'. *Disaster Prevention and Management*, *1*(3), 209–213. doi:10.1108/09653560210435803

Alexander, D. (2002b). *Principles of Emergency Planning and Management*. Terra Publishing.

Bhatt, M. (2002). *Corporate Social Responsibility and Disaster Reduction: Local Overview of Gujarat. Case Study for Corporate Social Responsibility and Disaster Reduction: A Global Overview*. DFID-funded study conducted by the Benfield Grieg Hazard Research Centre, University College London. http://www.benfieldhrc.org/SiteRoot/disaster_studies/csr/csr_gujarat.pdf

Blong, R. (2004) *Natural Hazards Risk Assessment: An Australian Perspective. Issues in Risk Science 04*. Benfield Hazard Research Centre, University College London. http://www.benfieldhrc.org/activities/issues4/nhra.htm

Cardona, O. D. (2004). Disaster Risk and Risk Management Benchmarking. *Information and Indicators Program for Disaster Risk Management*. Institute of Environmental Studies (IDEA) and Inter-American Development Bank (IDB), Manizales. http:// idea. manizales. unal. edu. co/ Proyectos Especiales/BID/desc_gta.asp?IdActividadAcademica=33.

Dessai, S., Adger, W. N., Hulme, M., Koehler, J., Turpenny, J., & Warren, R. (2001). *Defining and experiencing dangerous climate change. Working Paper 28*. Tyndall Centre for Climate Change Research. https://www.tyndall.ac.uk/publications/working_papers/wp28.pdf

DFID (Department for International Development). (2004a) *Disaster Risk Reduction: a development concern*. DFID, London. http://www.DFID.gov.uk/pubs/files/disaster-risk-reduction.pdf

Dger, N., Benjaminsen, K. & Svarstad, H. (2001). Advancing a Political Ecology of Global Environmental Discourses. *Development and Change, 32*(4), 667–701.

Dilley, M., Chen, R., Deichmann, U., Lerner-Lam, A., & Arnold, M. (2005). *Natural Disaster Hotspots: A Global Risk Analysis. Hazard Management Unit, World Bank*. View. doi:10.1596/0-8213-5930-4

EM-DAT (Emergencies Disasters Data Base). (2005). *EM-DAT: the International Disaster Database*. Center for Research on the Epidemiology of Disasters (CRED). Ecole de Santé Publique, Université Catholique de Louvain, Brussels. http://www.em-dat.net/index.htm

Ferreira, A. M., Marchezini, V., Mendes, T. S. G., Trejo-Rangel, M. A., & Iwama, A. Y. (2023). A Systematic Review of Forensic Approaches to Disasters: Gaps and Challenges. *International Journal of Disaster Risk Science*, *14*(5), 722–735. doi:10.1007/s13753-023-00515-9

O'Brien, G. (2006). *Climate change and disaster management*. Disasters-Wiley. doi:10.1111/j.1467-9523.2006.00307.x

Ghio, D. (2023). *Assessing populations exposed to climate change: a focus on Africa in a global context*.

Kathleen Geale, S. (2012). The ethics of disaster management. *Disaster Prevention and Management*, *21*(4), 445–462. doi:10.1108/09653561211256152

Larsen, J. (2003). *Record Heat Wave in Europe Takes 35,000 lives: Far Greater Losses May Lie Ahead*. Earth Policy Institute. http://www.earth-policy.org/Updates/Update29.htm

Lasala, M. (2015). *Establishment of Earthquake Intensity Meter Network in the Philippines.* Academic Press.

Lettieri, E., Masella, C., & Radaelli, G. (2009). Disaster management: Findings from a systematic review. *Disaster Prevention and Management, 18*(2), 117–136. doi:10.1108/09653560910953207

Park, K., & Lee, E. H. (2024). Urban flood vulnerability analysis and prediction based on the land use using Deep Neural Network. *International Journal of Disaster Risk Reduction, 101*(1), 104231. doi:10.1016/j.ijdrr.2023.104231

Safran, E. B., Nilsen, E., Drake, P., & Sebok, B. (2024). Effects of video game play, avatar choice, and avatar power on motivation to prepare for earthquakes. *International Journal of Disaster Risk Reduction, 101*(1), 104184. doi:10.1016/j.ijdrr.2023.104184

Tabbakhha, M., & Astaneh-Asl, A. (2022). Analysis of the collapsed and replaced Tex-Wash bridges exposed to severe floods. *International Journal of Earthquake and Impact Engineering, 4*(1), 30. doi:10.1504/IJEIE.2022.122821

Chapter 2
Machine Learning Algorithms for Natural Disaster Prediction and Management

Shanthalakshmi Revathy J.
https://orcid.org/0000-0003-1724-7117
Velammal College of Engineering and Technology, India

Mangaiyarkkarasi J.
https://orcid.org/0000-0003-1431-9584
NMSS Vellaichamy Nadar College, India

ABSTRACT

Natural disasters, such as floods, earthquakes, tsunamis, and landslides, pose significant threats to communities and ecosystems. This investigation explores the application of machine learning (ML) techniques in addressing the challenge. ML, a subset of artificial intelligence, involves creating models and algorithms that enable computers to learn from data, offering accurate disaster predictions without explicit programming. Various ML algorithms, including random forest for flood and wildfire prediction, support vector machine for earthquake forecasting, and decision tree for landslide risk assessment, are employed due to their ability to process complex datasets. Beyond prediction, ML plays a vital role in disaster management, optimizing resource allocation, refining emergency response plans, and enhancing evacuation strategies. Real-world case studies illustrate how ML contributes to mitigating disaster damage, emphasizing its role in proactive measures for disaster prevention and management.

INTRODUCTION

Natural disasters are harmful impacts on society created by natural hazard events. A natural disasters can cause severe damage to life, property, and causes some other impacts on environment. Such events can include a wide range of geological phenomena, such as quakes, volcanic eruption, and landslides, along with weather patterns such as hurricanes, tornadoes, floods or forest fires (Kansal et al. 2015). Across

DOI: 10.4018/979-8-3693-3362-4.ch002

the world, and with a demand for efficient emergency preparation, response and recovery strategies, the impact of disasters is widespread. The sudden release of energies that can lead to mass destruction is a natural consequence of the volcanic disasters caused by Earth's dynamic processes. Whereas, Meteorological disasters are due to climatic changes, and may lead to floods and landslides. These events are unpredictable and mitigation measures should be made to secure people. These disasters not only create impact on human society but also create long term consequences on economies, ecosystem and infrastructures. There is a need for some techniques and methodologies to predict the possibilities of the disasters. These may help us to be aware of the hazards and be prepared with the mitigation measures. In this paper we see how ML algorithms are used to predict natural disasters (Suliman Munawar et al. 2019). ML algorithms have wide range of knowledge based on the training data. They create patters based on the information from the learning data. Machine learning algorithms aid in the creation of resilient early warning systems by evaluating both historical and current data. They are versatile and can adapt to address different types of natural disasters. Rather than traditional methods, ML models provide more accurate predictions. ML algorithms can effectively process and analyze large data from various resources. These advantages made ML suitable for predicting natural disasters. Also, there are some other techniques to predict natural disasters. There are several algorithms in ML that are used in this prediction ranging from ensemble learning like random forests to neural networks (Gopal et al. 2020). This paper proposes an ensemble model using K-means clustering, LightGBM, and XGBoost algorithms to predict earthquakes based on seismic, GNSS, and environmental data (Joshi, Vishnu, and Mohan 2022). This study utilizes Random Forest and Support Vector Machines to predict landslide susceptibility in vulnerable areas using satellite imagery and LiDAR data (Tanyu et al. 2021). Not only for prediction, are some ML algorithms used for management after disasters. Image processing plays a major role in management after floods. ML models can analyze the damages from the satellite images and they can process data from sensors and drones to identify the affected regions. When used in disaster management, machine learning models can drastically lower the number of fatalities and property damage. The use of machine learning algorithms for natural catastrophe management and prediction is demonstrated in this study.

LITERATURE SURVEY

When using data mining and machine learning techniques for inference and decision-making in disaster situations, the literature review examines several approaches in disaster management and explores their procedural applications, strengths, and limits. The table 1 summarizes the surveyed research papers from 2015 to 2023, highlighting their methodologies, respective pros and cons, and the overall inference drawn from each study.

Table 1. Literature survey

Reference	Methodology	Pros	Cons	Inference
(Arinta and Andi W.R. 2019)	Big data and ML is used in early warning of disaster management.	These algorithms helps in predicting natural disasters and post disaster management. The data collection is made simple.	The data is collected from tweets. So the model is trained from that data.	ML algorithms are most effective and suitable to predict natural disasters.
(Li et al. 2019)	Methods such as Logistic regression, Naïve Bayes, AdaBoost and Random Forest are used to assess the risk of flood on watersheds.	These algorithms are effective for large datasets and resistant to overfitting. They are computationally efficient.	They may sensitive to outliers and noisy data.	The random forest model provides best results for prediction.
(Ekpezu et al. 2021)	Employed Convolutional Neural Network (CNN) and Long Short-Term Memory (LSTM) networks, both effective in pattern recognition and sequential data analysis.	Achieved impressive classification rates of 99.96% (CNN) and 99.90% (LSTM) for natural disaster sound classification.	Practical implementation challenges in real-time scenarios, especially for early warning systems, might need further exploration and resolution.	Deep learning effectively classified natural disaster sounds with high accuracy, highlighting potential for early detection despite practical deployment concerns.
(Mahajan and Sharma 2022)	Regression, ML Algorithms	Early disaster warning	Challenges in long-term prediction	Various ML techniques aid accurate rainfall prediction
(Khalaf et al. 2018)	Describes Random Forest Classifier, Support Vector Machines (SVM), and Levenberg-Marquardt training algorithm.	Utilizes various machine learning algorithms for flood severity prediction. - Introduces a novel flood dataset. - Demonstrates classification into normal, abnormal, and high-risk floods.	SVM produces inferior results compared to random forest model. - Neural network models (LEVNN and RF) performed better in performance measures.	Machine learning algorithms, especially random forest, offer better accuracy in flood severity prediction.
(Kansal et al. 2015)	Comparison of machine learning methods (SVM, regression, decision trees, neural networks) for forest fire prediction	High accuracy of regression for forest fire detection- Fast detection compared to other machine learning techniques	No specific mention of the dataset or its size- Limited explanation of feature selection or engineering	Regression proves most effective for fast and accurate forest fire detection, outperforming other ML techniques based on this study.
(Maspo et al. 2020)	Overview of supervised, unsupervised, and reinforcement learning types in ML.	Outlines the process of systematic literature review for flood prediction methods.	Narrow scope within recent 5 years, may miss older yet relevant studies.	Systematic review conducted through specific search terms; focused on recent studies within a defined period
(Gupta and Roy 2020)	Real-time monitoring, prediction, and control system for flood management as a Decision Support System (DSS).	Integrates various methods for comprehensive flood management.	Requires extensive data validation and verification.	The study presents a comprehensive flood control framework using DSS, ML, and MCDM, highlighting effective strategies categorized by social, environmental, and economic scenarios.
(Zheng et al. 2021)	Full Parameter Time Complexity (FPTC) Analysis	Provides an estimation of running time without executing the code - Helps in quick algorithm selection for LULC classification during emergencies	Relies on theoretical analysis, actual running time might vary - Requires prior knowledge of algorithmic complexity	Combining FPTC with coefficient ω aids in precise prediction of algorithm running time for emergency managers, aiding rapid decision-making with limited time and remote sensing data.
(Tiu et al. 2022)	Enhancing rainfall prediction in the Dungun river basin (1996-2016) using Variational Mode Decomposition (VMD), Bagging, Boosting, Bagging-VMD, and Boosting-VMD as pre-processing, coupled with Artificial Neural Network (ANN) and Support Vector Regression (SVR) base models for improved accuracy.	Enhanced prediction accuracy using data pre-processing techniques. - Comparative analysis of different pre-processing methods. - Demonstrates superiority of Boosting-ANN model for river water level prediction.	Specific focus on one river basin may limit generalization. - Limited discussion on real-time implementation challenges.	Boosting-ANN, employing Boosting with Variational Mode Decomposition, emerges as the most effective model, showcasing superior predictive performance with the lowest RMSE, MAPE, MAE, and highest NSE.
(Tufail et al. 2023)	Utilized various machine learning techniques, including neural networks and ensemble methods, to analyze historical space weather data.	Improved accuracy in space weather predictions, aiding in better preparation for potential disruptions.	Dependency on the availability and quality of historical space weather data.	Demonstrated the effectiveness of machine learning in predicting space weather events, offering valuable insights for early warning systems.
(Xu et al. 2022)	Applied deep learning techniques, including convolutional neural networks (CNNs), to analyze satellite imagery and atmospheric data.	Enhanced accuracy in predicting hurricane intensity, crucial for evacuation and response planning.	Computational intensity and resource requirements for training deep learning models.	Showcased superior performance in hurricane intensity prediction compared to traditional methods.

METHODOLOGY

Disaster management encompasses a range of activities aimed at preventing or mitigating the adverse effects of natural hazards such as earthquakes, floods, wildfires, and human-induced disasters like technological accidents or intentional attacks(Chamola et al. 2021). Data-driven approaches have emerged as powerful tools for disaster management, enabling the extraction of valuable insights from vast amounts of data to inform decision-making and improve disaster resilience. The methodology for data-driven disaster management typically involves the following steps:

Data Collection: Collect pertinent information from a range of sources, such as government databases, social media, sensor networks, satellite photography, and historical documents. This data may consist of text, photos, audio, and video, and it may be organised, semi-structured, or unstructured. Depending on the type of disaster and the information needs of the disaster management, several data sources will be employed. Table 2 summarizes available data set for Natural Disaster Prediction and Management.

Table 2. Data set available for natural disaster prediction and management

Category	Dataset	Description	Source	Image Source
Prediction	Earthquake Early Warning System Data	Real-time data from seismic stations in Japan	National Research Institute for Earth Science and Disaster Resilience (NIED)	Image of seismic waveforms and earthquake detection: https://www.eri.u-tokyo.ac.jp/en/
	Global Historical Earthquake Catalog (GHEC)	Comprehensive earthquake data since 1900	U.S. Geological Survey (USGS)	Image of global earthquake map: https://earthquake.usgs.gov/earthquakes/search/
	Flood Forecast and Warning System Data	Water level, precipitation, and streamflow data for flood forecasting	National Oceanic and Atmospheric Administration (NOAA)	Image of flood forecast map: https://dashboard.waterdata.usgs.gov/
	Landslide Susceptibility Mapping Data	Satellite imagery and geospatial data for landslide prediction	NASA Earth and Open Science Platform (EOSPO)	Image of landslide susceptibility map: https://earthobservatory.nasa.gov/images/89937/a-global-view-of-landslide-susceptibility
Management	OpenStreetMap	Collaborative mapping data for infrastructure and resource allocation	OpenStreetMap Foundation	Image of OpenStreetMap visualization: https://www.openstreetmap.org/
	Global Earthquake Damage Model (GEDM)	Earthquake damage estimates for different scenarios	The World Bank	Image of earthquake damage assessment: https://datacatalog.worldbank.org/search/dataset/0038576/Global-earthquake-hazard
	Hurricane Harvey Twitter Dataset	Social media data for analyzing public sentiment and needs	Kaggle	Image of Twitter data visualization: https://www.kaggle.com/datasets/dan195/hurricaneharvey
	UNOSAT Emergency Dashboard	Satellite imagery and analysis for disaster response	United Nations Satellite Programme (UNOSAT)	Image of UNOSAT satellite imagery: https://unosat.org/products/

Data Preprocessing: Cleanse and prepare the data for analysis by handling missing values, outliers, and inconsistencies. This may involve data imputation, normalization, and feature engineering. To guarantee the accuracy and dependability of the data utilised for analysis, data preparation is crucial.

Exploratory Data Analysis: Using descriptive statistics, visualisations, and correlation analysis, learn about the properties, distributions, and relationships of the data. Finding patterns, trends, and abnormalities in the data that could point to impending disasters or weaknesses can be aided by this preliminary investigation.

Feature Engineering: To increase machine learning models' capacity for prediction, add new features or modify current ones. Data mining algorithms, statistical methods, and domain knowledge can all be used in feature engineering. Feature engineering is to produce features that are applicable to the current issue and that machine learning models can utilise efficiently.

Model Selection and Training: Select the best machine learning algorithms for the job in light of the data that is available and the nature of the issue. Supervised learning techniques like logistic regression, decision trees, and linear regression as well as unsupervised learning algorithms like k-means clustering and anomaly detection algorithms are frequently employed in disaster management. Utilising metrics like accuracy, precision, and recall, assess the models' performance as you train them on the prepared data. In order to minimise error on the training data, model training entails optimising the parameters of the machine learning algorithm. To make sure that the trained models can effectively generalise to new data, model evaluation is crucial. This figure 1 illustrates the dynamic interplay between model prediction and monitoring in the context of disaster management.

Figure 1. Model monitoring

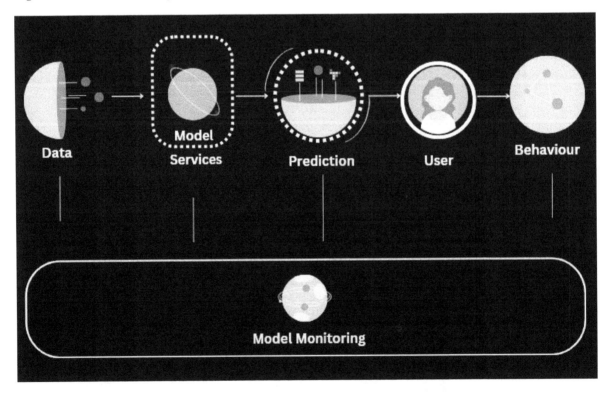

Model Deployment: Integrate the trained models into operational systems for real-time predictions and decision support. This may involve developing web applications, integrating the models with existing decision support systems, or deploying the models on edge devices.

Model Monitoring and Maintenance: Continuously monitor the performance of the deployed models, retrain them as new data becomes available, and adapt them to changing conditions. This ensures that the models remain accurate and relevant over time.

Interpretation of Data

Data interpretation plays a crucial role in disaster management, transforming raw data into meaningful information that can guide decision-making and inform disaster response strategies. This process involves understanding the context, limitations, and potential biases of the data to derive accurate and actionable insights.

Contextual Understanding: Consider the historical, geographical, and social context of the data to interpret it correctly. Understand the underlying factors and processes that have influenced the data's collection and analysis. For example, interpreting satellite imagery of a wildfire requires an understanding of the local vegetation, weather patterns, and human activities that may have contributed to the fire's development.

Data Limitations: Recognize the limitations of the data, such as missing values, sampling biases, and measurement errors. Account for these limitations when interpreting the results and making decisions. For instance, understanding the limitations of a sensor network's coverage area is crucial when using sensor data to assess the extent of flooding.

Bias Detection: Identify and address any potential biases in the data that could lead to inaccurate interpretations. This may involve examining data collection methodologies, sampling techniques, and data processing procedures. For example, being aware of potential biases in social media data is essential when using this data to gauge public sentiment during a disaster.

Visualization and Communication: Employ effective data visualization techniques to communicate findings clearly and concisely to stakeholders and decision-makers. Use charts, graphs, and maps to illustrate patterns, trends, and anomalies in the data. Effective data visualization can enhance the understanding and utilization of data-driven insights in disaster management.

Data Types in Disaster Management

Disaster management is a complex and multifaceted undertaking that requires the effective utilization of a wide range of data types. The figure 2visually conveys the diverse landscape of data types employed in research papers, these data types can be broadly classified into five categories:

- **Unstructured Textual Data:** This type of data includes news articles, incident activity reports, announcements, social media posts, and other forms of unstructured text. It provides valuable insights into public sentiment, emerging trends, and potential threats.
- **Structured Textual Data:** This category of data include structured text documents such as damage assessment forms, situational reports, 9-1-1 CAD data, and others. It offers comprehensive details on the type and scope of disasters, the distribution of resources, and the actions taken in response.

Figure 2. Most commonly used data types

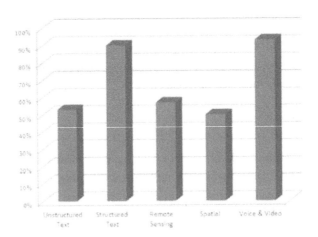

- **Remote Sensing Data:** This type of data includes satellite imagery, aerial photography, and sensor data. It provides a comprehensive overview of the affected area, enabling disaster managers to assess damage, monitor infrastructure, and track the movement of natural hazards.
- **Spatial Data:** This category of data include information from satellite and aerial imagery, graphical information systems (GIS), and other spatial data formats. It offers a geographical framework for comprehending the dangers, weaknesses, and response tactics associated with disasters.
- **Voice and Video Data:** This type of data includes radio communication, news broadcasts, and other forms of voice and video data. It provides real-time information about the unfolding situation, enabling disaster managers to make informed decisions and coordinate response efforts.

Challenges in Data Utilization

The diversity of data types used in disaster management poses several challenges for data analysis and utilization. These challenges include:

- **Data Integration:** Combining data from disparate sources and ensuring data consistency and quality are essential for effective analysis.
- **Real-time Processing:** Real-time or almost real-time data analysis is frequently needed for disaster management in order to facilitate decision-making.
- **Uncertainty and Incompleteness:** Disaster data often contains uncertainties and missing values, requiring robust analytical methods that can handle incomplete information.
- **Heterogeneity of Data Formats:** Data from different sources may have different formats and structures, requiring data harmonization and transformation.

DATA MINING AND MACHINE LEARNING

Disaster management has been completely transformed by data mining and machine learning techniques, which make it possible to find patterns, trends, and anomalies in data that would otherwise go undetected. With the use of these tools, one can gain a deeper understanding of the risks, vulnerabilities, and potential repercussions of disasters by extracting insightful information from massive and complicated datasets.

Data Mining

To find hidden patterns, trends, and connections in big datasets, data mining techniques are applied. These methods can be used for many different types of disaster management assignments, such as:

- **Risk Assessment:** Identify areas with high susceptibility to natural hazards and assess the potential impact of disasters.
- **Vulnerability Analysis:** Determine the vulnerability of infrastructure, communities, and individuals to different types of disasters.
- **Anomaly Detection:** Detect unusual patterns in sensor readings, social media data, or financial transactions that could indicate an impending disaster.
- **Knowledge Discovery**: Uncover hidden relationships between variables that can inform disaster management strategies.

Machine Learning

Machine learning algorithms are able to forecast future events, like the probability of earthquakes, the spread of wildfires, or the paths of storms, by learning from past data. This figure 4 illustrates the components and processes of an Early Warning and Detection System designed for disaster management. The system is depicted as a comprehensive framework with interconnected elements contributing to timely alerts and efficient response strategies.

These algorithms can be used to:

- **Early Warning Systems**: Develop early warning systems that can predict the occurrence of disasters and provide timely alerts to affected communities.
- **Resource Allocation:** Optimize the allocation of resources, such as personnel, equipment, and supplies, to areas of greatest need during and after disasters.
- **Damage Assessment:** Estimate the extent of damage caused by disasters using satellite imagery, aerial photography, and sensor data.
- **Recovery Planning:** Develop informed recovery plans that prioritize reconstruction efforts and address long-term economic impacts.

Figure 3. Early warning and detection system

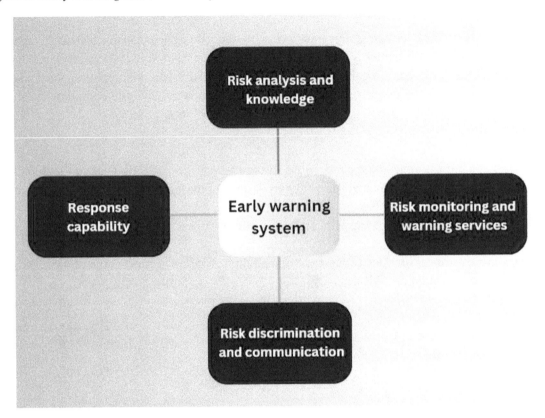

DATA ANALYSIS IN DISASTER MANAGEMENT

The availability and comprehensive utilization of data pose significant challenges. While extensive data volumes may exist, harnessing their full potential remains problematic. The idea of a jurisdiction in its "normal" state highlights how difficult it is to gather and analyse information about possible risks and their effects. To close this gap, creating a knowledge base from past incident reports helps define typical system parameters, create boundaries, and convert possible events into likely situations. This process enriches data-driven methods, enabling the detection of anomalies—events deviating from the norm.

Various data-driven early warning systems leverage anomaly detection, such as disease outbreak detection or fire detection. Anomalies are identified by considering multiple correlated factors influencing data variations. However, reliance on simulated data for system development and validation presents challenges. While widely accepted, simulated data may lack complexity, suffer from bias towards original event data, or fail to represent practical events accurately. Thus, thorough evaluation of model performance using real-world data remains crucial for validating the practicality of these systems (Arinta and Andi W.R. 2019).

Efficient data analysis in disaster management involves navigating the complexities of available data, understanding historical incidents, and deploying innovative methods to detect anomalies and predict potential events. Integrating these approaches contributes significantly to enhancing disaster preparedness and response mechanisms.

Mitigation

The main goals of mitigation efforts in disaster management are to lower the likelihood of disasters and lessen their possible effects. Notably, data mining and machine learning (DM and ML) play pivotal roles in preventing various threats posed by both natural and human-made disasters. These technologies play a crucial role in identifying potential terrorist threats by means of network analysis, detecting nuclear hazards through the utilisation of social networks and sensor data fusion, and utilising facial recognition in crowded environments. Monitoring changing conditions and their effects on community infrastructure is made more effective by combining DM and ML with static data. This integrated approach enhances the prioritization of preventive actions, potentially averting incidents before they occur.

Additionally, through the integration of spatial data and the analysis of evacuee behaviour, DM supports evacuation planning during the readiness phase. It aids in identifying potential threat areas and monitoring public safety websites for indicators of public awareness. ML applications in early warning systems, whether for floods, tsunamis, or chemical and nuclear threats, rely on anomaly detection. Identifying anything deviating from the norm flags it for human review, thereby improving the responsiveness to potential threats. The proactive detection of dangers, effective resource allocation, and general improvement of preparedness measures are all greatly aided by the application of DM and ML technologies in disaster mitigation. This figure 4 provides an overview of the key components and strategies involved in the mitigation phase of disaster management.

Figure 4. Mitigation

Preparedness

Data analysis aids in resource allocation, evacuation planning, and risk communication during the readiness stage. Data mining techniques, for instance, can optimise evacuation routes according to population density and traffic trends. Hurricane trajectories and wildfire spread can be predicted by machine learning models, enabling prompt resource deployment and evacuation.

Response

In the reaction stage, data analysis unifies information from multiple sources, including social media, mobile devices, and sensor networks, to enable real-time situational awareness. This real-time data fusion enables responders to make informed decisions regarding search and rescue operations, resource deployment, and damage assessment.

Recovery

The recovery phase focuses on restoring normalcy and rebuilding communities following a disaster. Data analysis is essential for assessing damage, estimating recovery costs, and allocating resources effectively. Satellite imagery and aerial photography can provide a comprehensive overview of the damage, while social media monitoring can gauge public sentiment and identify emerging needs. Data mining techniques can be used to analyze insurance claims and economic indicators to determine the long-term economic impact of the

DISCUSSION

The talk titled "Machine Learning Algorithms for Natural Disaster Prediction and Management" explores the complex field of technological advances in catastrophe resilience in further detail. This conversation goes beyond new developments and moral dilemmas to include other aspects that are vital to comprehending the consequences, difficulties, and wider social effects of utilizing machine learning algorithms in natural disaster response (Parmar, Mistree, and Sompura 2017).

Advanced Predictive Modeling: The potential of machine learning methods to improve natural catastrophe prediction modeling is unparalleled. The discourse delves deeper into the complexity of these models, highlighting their capacity to absorb large-scale datasets instantly. Machine learning algorithms improve their forecast accuracy by incorporating sensor inputs, satellite pictures, and historical data, allowing for a more sophisticated comprehension of intricate environmental patterns. These models' capacity for adaptive learning makes them excellent instruments for forecasting, greatly enhancing early warning systems.

Dynamic Adaptability: The dynamic adaptability of machine learning algorithms is a noteworthy feature. These algorithms improve their predictions over time by constantly changing in response to fresh data inputs. The talk emphasizes how these models are self-learning, showing how they may adjust to shifting circumstances, unanticipated factors, and new patterns. This flexibility makes predictive models more useful in disaster management plans by ensuring that they continue to be applicable and efficient in the face of changing natural events.

Integration of Geospatial Technologies: The effectiveness of machine learning algorithms is further improved by the inclusion of geospatial technologies. Predictive modeling gains spatial dimensions from remote sensing technology and Geographic Information Systems (GIS). The conversation delves into how the combination of machine learning and geospatial technologies allows for a finer-grained comprehension of regions that are vulnerable to disasters, hence enabling more focused interventions and efficient use of resources. Optimizing preparedness and reaction for disasters depends on this synergy. This figure 5 illustrates the application of geospatial technologies in the context of disaster management, showcasing the key components and functionalities that contribute to improved decision-making and response efforts.

Interdisciplinary Collaboration: A crucial aspect of the conversation centers on the necessity of interdisciplinary cooperation. Expertise from a variety of disciplines, such as data science, engineering, social sciences, and meteorology, is needed for effective disaster management. Algorithms for machine learning facilitate interdisciplinary cooperation by giving specialists a platform to come together and capitalize on their specialized knowledge. The integration of these fields of study promotes a comprehensive strategy for disaster resilience that takes into account social and infrastructure elements in addition to environmental ones.

Figure 5. Geospatial technologies

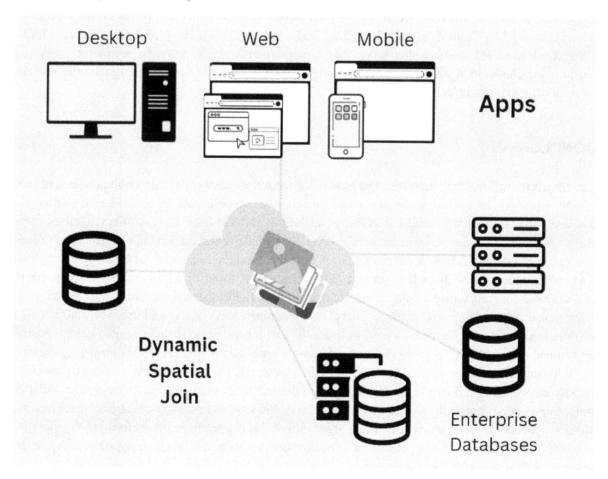

Challenges in Algorithmic Implementation: Although there is much promise in machine learning algorithms, the implementation challenges are acknowledged in the discussion. Interpretability and explainability issues can arise from the complexity of algorithmic models, particularly deep learning neural networks. Building trust amongst stakeholders—including legislators, first responders, and the communities impacted by disasters—becomes imperative when these issues are addressed.

Resource Allocation and Scalability: The practical aspects of scalability and resource allocation are also covered. Significant resources are needed for the implementation of machine learning algorithms in natural disaster management, including personnel with specialized knowledge and technological infrastructure. The discourse adeptly navigates the obstacles linked to resource limitations, underscoring the significance of adaptable and scalable solutions that can be tailored to varying geographic locations and degrees of technological infrastructure.

Public Awareness and Education: The significance of public education and awareness is something that is frequently missed in the discussion of machine learning for disaster management. The conversation looks at ways to explain predictive results to the general public in an understandable way. Communities are empowered and prepared to participate actively in disaster resilience initiatives when they are informed about the potential and constraints of machine learning models.

To sum up, this thorough analysis highlights the subtleties involved in incorporating machine learning algorithms into the prediction and management of natural disasters. In order to improve resilience in the face of natural disasters, technology-driven solutions are discussed in detail in this discourse, covering everything from dynamic adaptability and advanced predictive modeling to interdisciplinary collaboration and resource allocation issues. As these technologies advance, resolving issues and encouraging cooperation will be essential to realizing their full potential and building societies that are more informed, resilient, and adaptable.

CONCLUSION

The integration of machine learning algorithms into natural disaster prediction and management represents a pivotal shift, offering unprecedented potential yet accompanied by multifaceted challenges. These algorithms, with their adaptive learning capabilities and real-time data assimilation, elevate predictive modeling to unparalleled accuracy. However, their implementation demands a nuanced approach due to interpretability issues, resource allocation concerns, and the imperative of ensuring ethical use. The collaboration across disciplines emerges as a cornerstone, fostering a comprehensive approach to disaster resilience. By amalgamating expertise from diverse fields, these algorithms catalyze collective intelligence, acknowledging the intricate interplay of environmental, social, and infrastructural factors in disaster mitigation. Yet, the path forward mandates a careful balance between technological innovation and ethical responsibility, ensuring these advancements benefit communities while mitigating potential risks. Sustained efforts are paramount, urging continual research, technological advancements, and community involvement. A future where technology and disaster resilience converge to foster safer societies hinges upon persistent dedication to moral conduct, inclusivity, and ongoing collaborative endeavors. Responsible utilization of machine learning algorithms holds the promise of transforming disaster preparedness and response, driving us toward a future where societies are better equipped to navigate the unpredictable nature of natural disasters.

REFERENCES

Arinta, R. R., & Emanuel, A. W. R. (2019). Natural Disaster Application on Big Data and Machine Learning: A Review. In *In 2019 4th International Conference on Information Technology, Information Systems and Electrical Engineering (ICITISEE)* (pp. 249–254). IEEE. https://ieeexplore.ieee.org/document/9003984/ doi:10.1109/ICITISEE48480.2019.9003984

Chamola, V., Hassija, V., Gupta, S., Goyal, A., Guizani, M., & Sikdar, B. (2021). Disaster and Pandemic Management Using Machine Learning: A Survey. *IEEE Internet of Things Journal, 8*(21), 16047–16071. https://ieeexplore.ieee.org/document/9295332/. doi:10.1109/JIOT.2020.3044966 PMID:35782181

Ekpezu, A. O., Wiafe, I., Katsriku, F., & Yaokumah, W. (2021). Using Deep Learning for Acoustic Event Classification: The Case of Natural Disasters. *The Journal of the Acoustical Society of America, 149*(4), 2926–2935. https://pubs.aip.org/jasa/article/149/4/2926/1068002/Using-deep-learning-for-acoustic-event. doi:10.1121/10.0004771 PMID:33940915

Gopal, L. S., Prabha, R., Pullarkatt, D., & Ramesh, M. V. (2020). Machine Learning Based Classification of Online News Data for Disaster Management. In *In 2020 IEEE Global Humanitarian Technology Conference (GHTC)* (pp. 1–8). IEEE. https://ieeexplore.ieee.org/document/9342921/ doi:10.1109/GHTC46280.2020.9342921

Gupta, T., & Roy, S. (2020). A Hybrid Model Based on Fused Features for Detection of Natural Disasters from Satellite Images. In *IGARSS 2020 - 2020 IEEE International Geoscience and Remote Sensing Symposium* (pp. 1699–1702). IEEE. https://ieeexplore.ieee.org/document/9324611/ doi:10.1109/IGARSS39084.2020.9324611

Joshi, A., Vishnu, C., & Krishna Mohan, C. (2022). Early Detection of Earthquake Magnitude Based on Stacked Ensemble Model. *Journal of Asian Earth Sciences: X, 8*, 100122. https://linkinghub.elsevier.com/retrieve/pii/S2590056022000433

Kansal, A., Singh, Y., Kumar, N., & Mohindru, V. (2015). Detection of Forest Fires Using Machine Learning Technique: A Perspective. In *In 2015 Third International Conference on Image Information Processing (ICIIP)* (pp. 241–245). IEEE. https://ieeexplore.ieee.org/document/7414773/ doi:10.1109/ICIIP.2015.7414773

Khalaf, M. (2018). A Data Science Methodology Based on Machine Learning Algorithms for Flood Severity Prediction. In *In 2018 IEEE Congress on Evolutionary Computation (CEC)* (pp. 1–8). IEEE. https://ieeexplore.ieee.org/document/8477904/ doi:10.1109/CEC.2018.8477904

Li, X., Yan, D., Wang, K., Weng, B., Qin, T., & Liu, S. (2019). Flood Risk Assessment of Global Watersheds Based on Multiple Machine Learning Models. *Water (Basel), 11*(8), 1654. https://www.mdpi.com/2073-4441/11/8/1654. doi:10.3390/w11081654

Mahajan, D., & Sharma, S. (2022). Prediction of Rainfall Using Machine Learning. *4th International Conference on Emerging Research in Electronics, Computer Science and Technology, ICERECT 2022, 9*(01).

Maspo, N.-A., Bin Harun, A. N., Goto, M., Cheros, F., Haron, N. A., & Mohd Nawi, M. N. (2020). Evaluation of Machine Learning Approach in Flood Prediction Scenarios and Its Input Parameters: A Systematic Review. *IOP Conference Series. Earth and Environmental Science*, *479*(1), 012038. https://iopscience.iop.org/article/10.1088/1755-1315/479/1/012038. doi:10.1088/1755-1315/479/1/012038

Munawar, S., Hafiz, F. U., Hammad, A., & Ali, T. H. (2019). *After the Flood: A Novel Application of Image Processing and Machine Learning for Post-Flood Disaster Management Construction Engineering and Management at NUST Pakistan View Project Smart City Management: Applications of Disruptive Technologies View Proj*. Research Gate. https://www.researchgate.net/publication/337773028

Parmar, A., Mistree, K., & Sompura, M. (2017). Machine Learning Techniques For Rainfall Prediction: A Review Machine Learning View Project Rainfall Prediction Using ANN View Project Machine Learning Techniques For Rainfall Prediction: A Review. *International Conference on Innovations in information Embedded and Communication Systems*.

Tanyu, B. F., Abbaspour, A., Alimohammadlou, Y., & Tecuci, G. (2021). Landslide Susceptibility Analyses Using Random Forest, C4.5, and C5.0 with Balanced and Unbalanced Datasets. *Catena*, *203*, 105355. https://linkinghub.elsevier.com/retrieve/pii/S0341816221002149. doi:10.1016/j.catena.2021.105355

Tiu, E. S. K., Huang, Y. F., Ng, J. L., AlDahoul, N., Ahmed, A. N., & Elshafie, A. (2022). An Evaluation of Various Data Pre-Processing Techniques with Machine Learning Models for Water Level Prediction. *Natural Hazards*, *110*(1), 121–153. https://link.springer.com/10.1007/s11069-021-04939-8. doi:10.1007/s11069-021-04939-8

Tufail, S., Riggs, H., Tariq, M., & Sarwat, A. I. (2023). Advancements and Challenges in Machine Learning: A Comprehensive Review of Models, Libraries, Applications, and Algorithms. *Electronics (Basel)*, *12*(8), 1789. https://www.mdpi.com/2079-9292/12/8/1789. doi:10.3390/electronics12081789

Xu, X.-Y., Shao, M., Chen, P.-L., & Wang, Q.-G. (2022). Tropical Cyclone Intensity Prediction Using Deep Convolutional Neural Network. *Atmosphere (Basel)*, *13*(5), 783. https://www.mdpi.com/2073-4433/13/5/783. doi:10.3390/atmos13050783

Zheng, X., Jia, J., Guo, S., Chen, J., Sun, L., Xiong, Y., & Xu, W. (2021). Full Parameter Time Complexity (FPTC): A Method to Evaluate the Running Time of Machine Learning Classifiers for Land Use/Land Cover Classification. *IEEE Journal of Selected Topics in Applied Earth Observations and Remote Sensing*, *14*, 2222–2235. https://ieeexplore.ieee.org/document/9317826/. doi:10.1109/JSTARS.2021.3050166

Chapter 3
Predicting Natural Disasters With AI and Machine Learning

P Venkadesh

https://orcid.org/0000-0001-6582-3153

V.S.B. College of Engineering Technical Campus, Coimbatore, India

Divya S. V.

V.S.B. College of Engineering Technical Campus, Coimbatore, India

P Marymariyal

V.S.B. College of Engineering Technical Campus, Coimbatore, India

S. Keerthana

V.S.B. College of Engineering Technical Campus, Coimbatore, India

ABSTRACT

The unpredictability and devastating impacts of the natural disasters necessitate the advanced methods for early detection and mitigation. The paper delves into the transformative potential of AI and ML in analyzing extensive datasets comprising historical records, meteorological information, geological data, and satellite imagery. By leveraging neural networks, deep learning algorithms, and data analytics enables the creation of sophisticated predictive models for a range of natural disasters, including earthquakes, hurricanes, floods, wildfires, and tsunamis. Incorporating real-time data from IoT devices and remote sensing technologies further bolsters the accuracy of predictions. This abstract highlights the role of AI and ML not only in forecasting disasters but also in optimizing resource allocation during response efforts, identifying vulnerable regions, and enhancing early warning systems. Here, practical examples and case studies of successful AI and ML applications in disaster prediction, underlining their potential to redefine disaster preparedness and response is focused.

DOI: 10.4018/979-8-3693-3362-4.ch003

INTRODUCTION

Throughout human history, disasters, whether natural or man-made, have remained an unfortunate and recurrent part of our existence. These catastrophic events can result in widespread devastation, loss of lives, and economic turmoil.

While it is impossible to predict or entirely prevent disasters, technological advancements have equipped us with tools to mitigate their impact and enhance our response capabilities. Among these advancements, machine learning, a subset of artificial intelligence, has gained significant prominence in recent years.

The multifaceted nature of disaster management encompasses several key components, including mitigation, preparedness, response, and recovery. Mitigation involves proactive measures to reduce the vulnerability of communities and infrastructure to potential hazards. Preparedness focuses on equipping individuals, organizations, and governments with the knowledge, resources, and infrastructure needed to respond effectively when disaster strikes. The response phase involves immediate actions to address the immediate aftermath of a disaster, while the recovery phase focuses on long-term efforts to rebuild and restore affected areas.

Central to successful disaster management is the coordination and collaboration among various stakeholders, including government agencies, non-governmental organizations, the private sector, and the affected communities themselves. Effective communication, both within and among these groups, is vital for a cohesive and well-coordinated response.

Risk assessment plays a pivotal role in disaster management by identifying and analyzing potential hazards and vulnerabilities, enabling the development of targeted strategies to mitigate and manage risks. The integration of technology, such as early warning systems and Geographic Information Systems (GIS), further enhances the ability to predict, monitor, and respond to disasters with precision.

International cooperation is also critical in the face of large-scale disasters, with nations and global organizations working together to provide assistance, share resources, and coordinate relief efforts on a global scale.

In essence, disaster management is a proactive and adaptive approach to addressing the challenges posed by disasters. By combining strategic planning, community engagement, and the application of technological advancements, societies can enhance their resilience and minimize the devastating impact of unforeseen events.

Machine learning has demonstrated its immense potential in various sectors such as healthcare, finance, and transportation. However, it is in the realm of disaster management where its value truly shines. This book delves into the practical applications of machine learning in disaster management, the advantages it brings, the challenges it faces, and the promising path forward.

LITERATURE REVIEW

Disaster management (Abdalla & Esmall, 2018; Comfort, 2005; Lettieri, 2009) is a comprehensive and dynamic process that involves the strategic planning, coordination, and implementation of measures to mitigate, respond to, recover from, and ultimately minimize the impact of disasters. Disasters can take various forms, ranging from natural calamities like earthquakes, floods (Abdullahi et al., 2018; Acar & Muraki, 2011), and hurricanes to human-made incidents such as industrial accidents, technological hazards, and acts of terrorism. Disaster management aims to safeguard lives, protect property, and ensure the swift and effective restoration of affected communities.

Post-disaster bridge damage assessment (Adams et al., 2002; Adams et al., 2014) is a crucial process conducted after a natural or human-made disaster to evaluate the condition of bridges and determine the extent of damage. This assessment is essential for ensuring public safety, guiding emergency response efforts, and planning for the reconstruction or repair of critical infrastructure. It focuses on numerous aspects of post-disaster bridge damage assessment metrics such as safety evaluation, rapid visual assessment, structural inspection, geo-technical assessment, non-destructive testing, documentation and mapping, cost estimation etc. The use of wireless sensor networks and IoT technologies in the context of disaster management (Adeel et al., 2018), with a specific focus on geological disaster monitoring. The application of sensor networks to monitor geological phenomena, such as earthquakes, landslides, or other geological hazards are also discussed. The integration of IoT technologies in disaster management is likely explored, highlighting how real-time data from sensors can be leveraged to enhance early warning systems, response strategies, and overall disaster resilience. discusses the development and application of a hybrid model for the detection of traffic incidents.

The hybrid model is described as using logistic regression (Agarwal et al., 2016), a statistical method commonly used for binary classification problems, and wavelet transformation, a mathematical technique for signal processing. In the context of traffic incident detection, logistic regression may be applied to predict the likelihood of a traffic incident occurring based on input features, while wavelet transformation may be employed to analyze and process traffic-related signals or data. The goal of such a model would be to improve the accuracy and efficiency of traffic incident detection, potentially aiding in early response and management of traffic disruptions. suggests a study that employs neural networks to estimate human losses in the context of earthquake disasters. Seismic human loss estimation (Aghamohammadi et al., 2013) using neural networks involves the application of artificial intelligence techniques, specifically neural networks, to predict and assess the potential impact of earthquakes on human lives. In Ahmad et al. (2009), a study that explores the application of genetic algorithms and Cox regression for identifying threats in healthcare information systems is focused. The primary goal is likely to identify and assess potential threats to healthcare information systems. This is crucial for maintaining the security and integrity of sensitive healthcare data. JORD (Ahmad et al., 2017), is likely to enhance the collection of information and monitoring processes related to natural disasters. This integration of social media and satellite imagery suggests a comprehensive approach to disaster response and management. Social media platforms are valuable sources of real-time information during natural disasters. The system likely incorporates tools or algorithms to gather relevant data from social media posts. This could include user-generated content, such as text, images, and videos. Satellite imagery is a crucial component for monitoring and assessing the impact of natural disasters. The system probably utilizes satellite data to provide a visual representation of affected areas, enabling a more comprehensive understanding of the situation. The integration of social media and satellite imagery involves a process of data fusion. This could include combining textual information from social media with spatial and visual data from satellite imagery to provide a more comprehensive and dynamic overview of the disaster. The system likely includes tools for real-time monitoring and analysis of the collected data. This could involve identifying affected areas, assessing the severity of the disaster, and tracking changes over time. JORD may have features to generate alerts or notifications based on the analyzed data. This could be crucial for timely responses and resource allocation during disaster management. Discuss how the information collected and monitored by JORD can be practically applied in disaster response efforts. This could include supporting emergency services, aiding in evacuation plans, and facilitating resource mobilization.

An automated system (Ahmad et al., 2019) capable of identifying roads that are still usable in areas impacted by floods. This has significant implications for emergency response and disaster management. It utilizes two main sources of data such as remote sensing imagery and social media content. Remote sensing data could provide a visual representation of the affected areas, while social media data might offer real-time information shared by individuals in those regions. Methods for assessing the impact of floods on road infrastructure are discussed. This might involve analyzing changes in terrain, water levels, and other relevant factors using remote sensing data. The effectiveness of the proposed system is likely assessed through validation and evaluation processes. This could involve comparing the system's results with ground truth data or other established benchmarks. Image4Act (Alam et al., 2017), is designed to process online social media images for improved disaster response. It may delve into various image processing techniques employed by Image4Act. These techniques could include computer vision, machine learning, or other methods to extract meaningful information from images shared on social media platforms. It focuses on how the processed information from social media images is applied in the context of disaster response. It aims to aid emergency responders, assessing damage, or providing situational awareness. The application of genetic algorithms, which are optimization algorithms inspired by natural selection, to identify damaged bars (Alfaiate et al., 2007) is studied. Genetic algorithms can be effective for optimization problems, and they may be used to find the configuration of damaged bars that best fits the observed behavior. Social media acts as an important part of disaster prevention and management, especially during earthquake and flooding scenarios. This analyzes the temporal evolution and utilizes the k-means text clustering algorithm (Safran et al., 2024) to predict the flood. The objective and findings of a research study focused on the role of technological innovations in improving disaster resilience in Smart Cities are summarized in Samarakkody et al. (2023). The research aimed to fill a gap in the existing literature by identifying and classifying emerging and disruptive technologies used for this purpose. A clear understanding of the technological landscape of smart cities, the challenges they face, and the strategies to achieve sustainable development is addressed in Ahad et al. (2020). It reflects the multidisciplinary nature of smart city initiatives, involving technology, social factors, and environmental considerations.

MACHINE LEARNING AND ITS WORKING PRINCIPLES

Machine learning is a specialized domain within artificial intelligence (AI), dedicated to crafting algorithms and computational models that empower computers to enhance their proficiency in each task without requiring explicit programming. The overarching objective of machine learning is to create systems capable of autonomously analyzing and comprehending data, discerning patterns, and rendering well-informed decisions or predictions.

During the machine learning process, algorithms undergo training using a dataset. This training allows them to discern and internalize patterns, relationships, and trends inherent in the data. Subsequently, the acquired knowledge enables the model to be applied to novel, unseen data, facilitating the generation of predictions or decisions. This iterative learning approach distinguishes machine learning, as it enables systems to adapt and improve performance over time.

This succinct explanation encapsulates the fundamental principles of machine learning, highlighting its role in fostering autonomous learning and decision-making capabilities in computers.

Decision Process

In essence, machine learning algorithms engage in a decision process where they predict or classify information. By taking input data, which could be either labeled or unlabeled, these algorithms generate estimates that unveil patterns within the data. It's a computational method that enables the algorithm to make informed decisions or predictions based on the provided input, contributing to the learning and understanding of underlying patterns.

An Error Function

The error function plays a crucial role in assessing how well a model predicts outcomes. When known examples are available, this function compares the model's predictions to the actual outcomes, allowing us to gauge the accuracy of the model. Essentially, it quantifies the disparity between what the model predicts and what is known, providing a measurable way to understand and improve the model's performance.

Model Optimization Process

If the model demonstrates the potential to align more closely with the data points in the training set, adjustments are made to the model's weights. This tweaking process aims to minimize the differences between the known examples and the model's estimations. The algorithm then iteratively undergoes this "evaluate and optimize" cycle, autonomously fine-tuning the weights. This iterative process continues until a predefined level of accuracy is attained, ensuring the model progressively refines itself to make more precise predictions.

MACHINE LEARNING METHODS

Supervised machine learning

Supervised machine learning, also known as supervised learning, involves the use of labeled datasets to train algorithms. The primary objective is to teach these algorithms to accurately classify data or predict outcomes. The process entails feeding input data into the model, which then adjusts its weights iteratively until it aligns well with the given data. This adjustment is crucial during the cross-validation process, ensuring that the model does not become overly specialized or too generalized (overfitting or underfitting). The applications of supervised learning are diverse and impactful for organizations, addressing real-world challenges at scale. An example is the classification of spam emails into a separate folder from your inbox. Various methods are employed in supervised learning, including neural networks, naïve Bayes, linear regression, logistic regression, random forest, and support vector machine (SVM). These methods contribute to the effectiveness of supervised learning in solving practical problems by enabling algorithms to learn and make accurate predictions based on labeled examples.

Unsupervised machine learning

Unsupervised machine learning, also referred to as unsupervised learning, employs algorithms to scrutinize and cluster unlabeled datasets. What sets this method apart is its capacity to autonomously uncover concealed patterns or groupings within data without requiring human guidance. This approach is particularly advantageous for exploratory data analysis, devising cross-selling strategies, customer segmentation, as well as image and pattern recognition. One of the key applications of unsupervised learning lies in its ability to discern similarities and differences within information, allowing it to reveal underlying structures in the absence of predefined labels. Additionally, it proves valuable in reducing the complexity of models through a technique called dimensionality reduction. Common methods for this purpose include Principal Component Analysis (PCA) and Singular Value Decomposition (SVD).

Several algorithms are employed in unsupervised learning, catering to diverse tasks. Neural networks, k-means clustering, and probabilistic clustering methods are examples of algorithms that contribute to the efficacy of unsupervised learning in revealing intrinsic patterns within data, making it a versatile and powerful approach in various analytical and exploratory contexts.

Semi-supervised learning

Semi-supervised learning strikes a balance between supervised and unsupervised learning, providing a practical solution to challenges associated with labeled datasets. In this approach, a smaller set of labeled data is utilized during training to guide the classification and feature extraction processes applied to a larger, unlabeled dataset. This method proves especially useful when labeled data are scarce for a traditional supervised learning algorithm. Additionally, it offers a cost-effective strategy in situations where labeling a substantial amount of data is prohibitively expensive or time-consuming. Essentially, semi-supervised learning optimally combines the benefits of both labeled and unlabeled data, making it a valuable and efficient approach in scenarios where acquiring extensive labeled datasets poses practical constraints.

DISASTER MANAGEMENT: AN OVERVIEW

Disaster management involves a series of actions as shown in fig.1 designed to minimize the consequences of disasters and support communities during their reaction and rebuilding efforts. This process typically consists of four key stages: mitigation, preparedness, response, and recovery. Machine learning can contribute to each of these stages by introducing inventive solutions to enduring issues.

Mitigation

Mitigation encompasses efforts to decrease or eliminate the lasting risk of disasters. These measures encompass initiatives like constructing codes, land-use planning, and infrastructure enhancements. Machine learning contributes by evaluating the potential consequences of disasters through the analysis of historical data, climate trends, and geographic data. For instance, machine learning algorithms can pinpoint regions susceptible to flooding, landslides, or wildfires, providing policymakers with valuable insights for making informed choices regarding land development and strategies to reduce risks.

Figure 1. Disaster Management Overview

Preparedness

Preparedness efforts aim to ensure that communities are well-prepared to respond efficiently to a disaster. Machine learning plays a role in predicting the probability and intensity of specific disaster events. It aids emergency management organizations in planning and distributing resources effectively, ensuring their readiness for potential crises. Additionally, machine learning contributes to the creation of early warning systems that deliver timely information to the public, enabling them to take protective actions in response to impending disasters.

Response

The response phase is the critical, immediate reaction following a disaster. It involves activities like search and rescue operations, delivering medical assistance, and safeguarding the well-being of affected communities. Machine learning steps in to improve these efforts by automating the analysis of extensive data sources, including satellite images and social media updates, to identify impacted areas, evaluate the extent of damage, and locate survivors. Moreover, this technology is capable of real-time optimization for directing first responders and resources efficiently, ensuring a prompt and well-coordinated response.

Recovery

Recovery marks the period that follows a disaster, during which communities focus on the arduous task of rebuilding and returning to normalcy. Machine learning plays a vital role in this phase by facilitating more precise and efficient assessments of the damage caused by disasters. These assessments inform decisions regarding the prioritization of recovery efforts, resource allocation, and the streamlining of the reconstruction process. Furthermore, machine learning algorithms can forecast the enduring effects of a disaster, enabling more informed planning for the rehabilitation and economic resurgence of the affected regions.

MACHINE LEARNING METHODS FOR DISASTER AND HAZARD PREDICTION

Predicting disasters and hazards is crucial for effective disaster management and risk reduction. The ability to identify potential threats early allows for timely responses, ultimately minimizing the impact on communities and infrastructure. Traditional methods of hazard prediction have their limitations, both in terms of accuracy and speed. The dynamic and complex nature of hazards necessitates the adoption of advanced techniques such as Machine Learning (ML) and Deep Learning (DL) to enhance prediction capabilities.

Figure 2. ML Methods for Disaster and Hazard Prediction

Predictive Modeling in Hazard Prediction

Categorizing hazards, including earthquakes, floods, hurricanes, and wildfires, is essential for accurate prediction. Each type presents unique challenges, requiring specific approaches. Historical data plays a pivotal role in training predictive models, allowing ML algorithms to analyze past occurrences and learn patterns and trends that aid in anticipating future hazards. Common ML algorithms like regression models, decision trees, and ensemble methods are employed for hazard prediction, leveraging historical data to make informed predictions. Additionally, DL techniques such as recurrent neural networks (RNNs) and convolutional neural networks (CNNs) excel in capturing complex temporal and spatial dependencies in hazard data. Examining successful hazard prediction models, such as those used in earthquake early warning systems and flood prediction, provides tangible evidence of ML effectiveness in disaster preparedness.

Early Warning Systems

The importance of early warning systems cannot be overstated, emphasizing the need for timely alerts that enable communities to prepare and evacuate when necessary. Sensor networks, including Internet of Things (IoT) devices, contribute significantly to data collection for early warning systems. ML algorithms process real-time data from sensors, identifying early signs of hazards and enabling quick decision-making and efficient resource deployment during emergencies. DL techniques like Long Short-Term Memory (LSTM) networks excel in time-series analysis, making them invaluable for processing continuous data streams and improving the accuracy of early warnings. Examining instances where ML-based early warning systems provided timely alerts showcases their practical impact in reducing the impact of disasters on communities.

Satellite Image Analysis for Hazard Detection

Satellite imagery plays a pivotal role in monitoring environmental conditions and detecting potential hazards. The use of satellite technology enhances spatial coverage and resolution in hazard detection. ML algorithms applied to analyze satellite images contribute to hazard-related information extraction, including identifying changes in land cover, detecting wildfires, and assessing the extent of flooding. Specific applications, such as predicting and monitoring wildfires through satellite image analysis with ML, showcase the technology's potential in anticipating and managing natural disasters. Examining successful instances of hazard detection using satellite imagery and ML methods provides concrete examples of the technology's effectiveness in disaster prediction.

Social Media and Text Analysis for Disaster Prediction

The increasing use of social media data for predicting disasters underscores the value of real-time, user-generated information in anticipating and responding to hazards. ML algorithms, coupled with Natural Language Processing (NLP), extract valuable information from social media, identifying keywords, patterns, and sentiments related to potential hazards. Sentiment analysis contributes to predictive modeling by gauging public responses and detecting early signs of hazards, providing additional context for disaster prediction. Instances, where social media and text analysis contributed to predicting and preparing for disasters, highlight the practical applications of these technologies in disaster management.

Discussing emerging ML techniques that hold promise for improving hazard prediction provides insights into the evolving landscape of technology in disaster management. Highlighting the need for integrating diverse data sources, including social media, satellite imagery, and sensor networks, emphasizes the importance of comprehensive data analysis for accurate predictions. Emphasizing the importance of collaboration between data scientists, domain experts, and policymakers recognizes that effective disaster prediction and management require expertise from various fields. Addressing ethical concerns related to privacy, bias, and transparency in the use of ML for disaster prediction underscores the importance of responsible technology implementation. Recapping the role of ML in disaster and hazard prediction highlights the significant advancements and applications discussed. Encouraging further research, collaboration, and the responsible implementation of ML methods for enhancing disaster resilience and management underscores the ongoing commitment to leveraging technology for the greater good.

MACHINE LEARNING METHODS FOR RISK AND VULNERABILITY ASSESSMENT

Risk and vulnerability assessment are critical processes across various domains, including disaster management, finance, and infrastructure development. These assessments provide insights into potential threats, enabling proactive measures to mitigate adverse impacts. Traditional methods, however, face limitations, necessitating the integration of advanced Machine Learning (ML) methods to enhance accuracy and efficacy.

Data-Driven Risk and Vulnerability Assessment

In the realm of data-driven risk and vulnerability assessment, a plethora of diverse data sources, including historical records, sensor data, satellite imagery, social media, and economic indicators, contribute to a comprehensive understanding of potential risks. The process of feature engineering extracts meaningful information from raw data, enhancing the predictive power of ML models. Traditional ML algorithms like decision trees, support vector machines, and k-nearest neighbours, leverage historical data for informed predictions, while DL architectures such as artificial neural networks (ANNs), recurrent neural networks (RNNs), and convolutional neural networks (CNNs) facilitate more nuanced modelling, especially in scenarios with intricate relationships.

Application of ML in Natural Disaster Risk Assessment

Earthquake Risk Assessment: ML models predict earthquake risk by analyzing seismic data, historical patterns, and geological features, contributing to early warning systems.

Flood Risk Assessment: ML techniques assess flood risk by considering rainfall patterns, terrain characteristics, and historical flood data, aiding in disaster preparedness and response.

Wildfire Risk Assessment: ML methods predict wildfire risk by incorporating weather data, vegetation indices, and historical fire occurrences, enhancing wildfire management strategies.

Hurricane and Cyclone Risk Assessment: ML models analyze atmospheric conditions, sea surface temperatures, and historical storm tracks to assess risks associated with hurricanes and cyclones, facilitating effective evacuation plans.

Case Studies: Real-world case studies demonstrate the successful application of ML in natural disaster risk assessment, showcasing their practical impact in minimizing disaster impacts.

ML for Infrastructure and Cybersecurity Risk Assessment

In the domain of infrastructure and cybersecurity risk assessment, ML plays a pivotal role in assessing the vulnerability of critical infrastructure. Factors such as aging infrastructure, maintenance records, and environmental conditions are considered, aiding in maintenance planning. ML models identify and predict cybersecurity threats by analyzing network traffic, user behavior, and historical security incidents, contributing to enhanced cybersecurity measures. Supply chain risk assessment involves the evaluation of risks considering geopolitical events, market trends, and supplier performance, contributing to robust supply chain management. ML methods also analyze financial data to assess market risks, credit risks, and overall financial stability, supporting informed decision-making in the financial sector. Examples illustrate successful applications of ML in infrastructure and cybersecurity risk assessment, emphasizing their role in ensuring the integrity and security of critical systems.

ML in Social Vulnerability Assessment

In social vulnerability assessment, ML models analyze demographic data, socioeconomic indicators, and healthcare information to identify vulnerable populations in the context of disasters, guiding targeted relief efforts. ML also assesses health risks, including disease outbreaks and the spread of infectious diseases, contributing to public health strategies and interventions. Instances highlight the effective use of ML in social vulnerability assessment, demonstrating their role in identifying and supporting vulnerable communities.

Challenges and Ethical Considerations

Challenges and ethical considerations are inherent in the application of ML in risk and vulnerability assessment. Issues related to data quality and potential biases in historical data are addressed, emphasizing the need for robust assessments. The challenge of interpretability in complex ML models is acknowledged, stressing the importance of understanding model outputs for informed decision-making. Privacy concerns associated with sensitive data, particularly in social vulnerability assessment, are highlighted, necessitating ethical considerations and careful handling. Looking ahead, future directions include exploring emerging ML techniques for improved accuracy and efficiency in risk and vulnerability assessment models. The integration of diverse data sources is emphasized for a more comprehensive assessment, combining different types of data to enhance accuracy. Collaboration between researchers, industry experts, and policymakers is crucial for advancing the field of ML in risk and vulnerability assessment, promoting interdisciplinary solution.

Machine Learning methods for Disaster Monitoring

Disaster monitoring is a crucial component of effective disaster management, offering real-time insights for understanding, assessing, and responding to various natural or man-made crises. The introduction underscores the significance of this process and highlights the transformative role played by Machine Learning (ML) methods in enhancing monitoring capabilities.

Types of Disasters and Monitoring Challenges

Categorizing disasters into types such as earthquakes, floods, wildfires, and hurricanes reveals the diverse challenges each presents for monitoring. Traditional monitoring methods are discussed in the second section, emphasizing their limitations and the imperative need for advanced ML techniques to overcome these challenges.

Satellite-Based Monitoring With Machine Learning

The role of satellite technology in disaster monitoring is elucidated, emphasizing its wide-area coverage and frequent updates. ML algorithms applied to satellite imagery for feature extraction, change detection, and anomaly identification are explored, showcasing their applications in tracking wildfire progression, assessing flood extent, and detecting earthquake-induced changes. Case studies provide tangible evidence of successful ML implementations in satellite-based disaster monitoring.

Sensor Networks and IoT for Real-time Monitoring

The subsequent section delves into the contribution of sensor networks and the Internet of Things (IoT) devices in real-time data collection for disaster monitoring. ML algorithms' role in processing real-time sensor data to identify patterns, anomalies, and early signs of disasters is highlighted, with case studies demonstrating the practical impact of ML in real-time monitoring through sensor networks.

Social Media and Text Analysis for Disaster Awareness

The growing role of social media in disaster awareness is discussed, emphasizing how ML can leverage real-time, user-generated information. Natural Language Processing (NLP) techniques coupled with ML algorithms extract valuable insights from social media texts, including sentiment analysis for predicting public responses and potential disasters. Case studies illustrate instances where social media and text analysis have significantly contributed to disaster awareness and early response.

Integration of Remote Sensing and Machine Learning

The benefits of integrating diverse remote sensing data sources, such as satellite imagery, aerial surveys, and ground-based sensors, are underscored in the section on remote sensing and ML integration. ML methods applied to fuse and analyze multi-source remote sensing data are explored, showcasing applications in hurricane monitoring, post-disaster damage assessment, and more. Case studies provide concrete examples of successful integration, highlighting improvements in accuracy and efficiency. Challenges associated with ML methods in disaster monitoring, such as data variability, model interpretability, and scalability, are discussed in the challenges and future directions section. Emerging trends and future directions in ML methods, including advancements in algorithms, increased automation, and improved integration, are explored to provide insights into the evolving landscape of disaster monitoring technology.

MACHINE LEARNING METHODS FOR DAMAGE ASSESSMENT

Disaster-induced damage assessment is a pivotal stage in the realm of disaster management, offering crucial insights into the scale of devastation and facilitating the judicious allocation of resources. This section underscores the significance of damage assessment while shedding light on the transformative role that Machine Learning (ML) methods play in automating and enhancing this critical process.

Types of Disasters and Damage Assessment Challenges

The categorization of disasters into distinct types, such as earthquakes, floods, wildfires, and hurricanes, is imperative as each category presents unique challenges for damage evaluation. Traditional methods, beset with limitations, are discussed to underscore the necessity of advanced ML techniques in surmounting these challenges effectively.

Remote Sensing and Imagery Analysis for Damage Assessment

The integration of remote sensing and imagery analysis emerges as a cornerstone in post-disaster damage assessment. ML algorithms, notably convolutional neural networks (CNNs) and object detection models, are explored for their pivotal role in automating the analysis of satellite or aerial images, and expediting the identification of damage in specific disasters. Illustrative case studies underscore the success of ML applications in damage assessment, emphasizing both accuracy and speed in evaluating large-scale destruction.

LiDAR Technology for 3D Damage Modeling

The subsequent exploration delves into the realm of LiDAR technology, a potent tool for creating intricate three-dimensional models of affected areas. ML algorithms applied to LiDAR data play a vital role in generating detailed 3D models, offering nuanced insights into structural damage and terrain changes. Through case studies, the effectiveness of this technology in capturing intricate details post-disaster is vividly showcased.

Social Media and Crowdsourced Data for Damage Reports

The role of social media and crowdsourced data in real-time damage reporting is then discussed, highlighting the dynamic nature of user-generated information. ML techniques, including natural language processing (NLP) and sentiment analysis, are examined for their efficacy in processing and classifying social media data, providing timely and accurate damage reports. Case studies further exemplify the instrumental role of social media and ML in rapidly evolving disaster scenarios.

Integration of Multi-Source Data for Comprehensive Assessment

The section on the integration of multi-source data emphasizes the benefits of combining diverse data streams, including satellite imagery, LiDAR data, and ground-based reports, to achieve a comprehensive understanding of damage. ML algorithms for data fusion are explored for their ability to enhance the accuracy and completeness of damage assessments, particularly in multi-hazard scenarios. Case studies exemplify successful integration, demonstrating the potential of ML in comprehensive damage assessment.

MACHINE LEARNING METHODS FOR POST-DISASTER RESPONSE

Post-disaster response is a pivotal phase in disaster management, aiming to swiftly and effectively provide assistance to affected areas. This critical section emphasizes the indispensable role of Machine Learning (ML) methods in refining and optimizing response efforts.

Types of Disasters and Response Challenges

The categorization of disasters, spanning earthquakes, floods, wildfires, and hurricanes, underscores the unique challenges each disaster type presents for post-disaster response. Traditional response methods are discussed, shedding light on their limitations and emphasizing the necessity of advanced ML techniques to overcome these challenges.

Predictive Analytics for Resource Allocation

The role of predictive analytics takes center stage in anticipating the needs of affected areas, enabling the efficient allocation of resources crucial for post-disaster response. ML algorithms, encompassing regression models and decision trees, are employed to analyze historical data and predict resource requirements, ranging from medical supplies to shelter and food. Case studies are presented to exemplify the successful implementation of ML in predictive analytics, showcasing marked improvements in the efficiency of response efforts.

Natural Language Processing (NLP) for Emergency Communication

Natural Language Processing (NLP) emerges as a powerful tool for emergency communication, leveraging ML algorithms for processing and analyzing a myriad of data sources, including social media posts, news articles, and official reports. The applications of NLP and ML in specific disasters, such as extracting information from social media during earthquakes or gauging the sentiment of emergency calls, demonstrate their efficacy in enhancing situational awareness. Real-world case studies further underline the transformative impact of NLP and ML in emergency communication.

Drone Technology for Damage Assessment

Drone technology takes center stage in damage assessment during post-disaster response, where ML algorithms, particularly those rooted in computer vision, process drone imagery to automatically detect and classify damage. Specific applications, including the aftermath of hurricanes, earthquakes, or wildfires, illustrate the efficiency and accuracy of using drones and ML for damage assessment. Case studies provide concrete examples of successful ML applications in drone-based damage assessment, reinforcing the invaluable role of this technology in response efforts.

Dynamic Resource Routing with ML

Dynamic resource routing, a novel concept introduced in this section, relies on ML algorithms, especially reinforcement learning, to optimize the routing of response resources based on real-time data and evolving conditions. The adaptability and responsiveness of this approach are highlighted through case studies, showcasing instances where dynamic resource routing has been applied to adjust routes for medical supply delivery in the aftermath of disasters.

Social Network Analysis for Community Resilience

The role of social network analysis coupled with ML techniques is explored in understanding community resilience post-disaster. ML algorithms, such as those related to community detection and influence propagation, are utilized to extract insights from social connections. Applications in specific disasters underscore instances where social network analysis and ML have strengthened community ties and fostered resilience, ultimately aiding recovery efforts. Case studies provide tangible examples of the positive impact of ML in social network analysis for community resilience.

Challenges and Future Directions

The challenges associated with ML methods in post-disaster response, including data interoperability, real-time processing, and ethical considerations, are thoroughly discussed. Future directions are explored, encompassing emerging trends such as advancements in edge computing, the integration of AI-driven robotics, and the development of ethical frameworks to guide ML applications in post-disaster scenarios.

MACHINE LEARNING METHODS IN CASE STUDIES FOR DISASTER MANAGEMENT

In the domain of disaster management, the deployment of Machine Learning (ML) methods is showcased through a series of compelling case studies addressing distinct challenges associated with various types of disasters.

Earthquake Early Warning System in Japan

Japan, being susceptible to seismic activities, instituted an Earthquake Early Warning System (EEWS) that harnesses ML algorithms for the swift detection of earthquakes.
   ML Application:

- **Sensor Data Analysis:** ML algorithms process real-time data from an extensive network of seismic sensors.
- **Pattern Recognition:** Algorithms discern seismic patterns, estimating the earthquake's magnitude and predicting its potential impact.

   Impact:

- **Early Alerts:** ML facilitates issuing warnings seconds to minutes before earthquakes, enabling timely protective actions.
- **Reduced Casualties:** The system significantly contributes to minimizing casualties by providing advanced notice.

Flood Prediction and Management in Bangladesh

Bangladesh, grappling with annual flooding, integrates ML into a comprehensive flood prediction and management system.
   ML Application:

- **Rainfall Pattern Analysis:** ML algorithms scrutinize historical rainfall patterns.
- **River Level Monitoring:** Real-time river level data, coupled with ML models, aids in predicting potential flood-prone areas.

Impact:

- **Timely Evacuation:** ML-driven predictions assist in orchestrating timely evacuation efforts.
- **Resource Allocation:** Authorities can allocate resources more efficiently to areas at higher risk, enhancing the overall disaster response.

Wildfire Detection and Monitoring in California, USA

Background:
California, plagued by recurrent wildfires, employs ML for early detection and monitoring to augment firefighting efforts.

ML Application:

- **Satellite Imagery Analysis:** ML algorithms scrutinize satellite imagery for indications of wildfires.
- **Weather Data Integration:** Models integrate weather data to predict fire-prone conditions.
- **Predictive Modeling:** ML models predict the potential spread of wildfires based on historical data and current conditions.

Impact:

- **Early Detection:** ML enables the early detection of wildfires, resulting in quicker response times.
- **Resource Optimization:** Firefighting resources can be deployed more efficiently based on ML-driven predictions.

Hurricane Tracking and Intensity Prediction in the Atlantic

Background:
Organizations like the National Hurricane Center (NHC) leverage ML techniques to refine hurricane tracking and intensity predictions.

ML Application:

- **Atmospheric Data Analysis:** ML models analyze vast amounts of atmospheric data.
- **Historical Storm Data:** Algorithms learn from historical storm data to predict future paths and intensities.
- **Oceanographic Conditions:** ML incorporates oceanographic conditions for more accurate predictions.

Impact:

- **Improved Accuracy:** ML-driven models contribute to more accurate hurricane tracking.
- **Enhanced Preparedness:** Better predictions allow for improved preparedness and evacuation planning.

Tsunami Warning System in the Pacific

Countries bordering the Pacific Ocean collaborate on a Tsunami Warning System utilizing ML to expedite and enhance the accuracy of tsunami alerts.
   ML Application:

- **Ocean Floor Sensors:** ML processes data from ocean floor sensors to detect seismic activities.
- **Wave Pattern Recognition:** Algorithms recognize abnormal wave patterns indicating a potential tsunami.
- **Machine Learning Models:** ML models predict the likely impact and reach of a tsunami.

Impact:

- **Faster Alerts:** ML contributes to faster and more accurate tsunami alerts.
- **Coordinated Response:** Improved predictions enable coordinated response efforts across multiple nations.

Urban Search and Rescue (USAR) Operations using Robotics

Post earthquakes or building collapses, ML-driven robotics play a pivotal role in Urban Search and Rescue (USAR) operations.
   ML Application:

- **Robotic Vision:** ML algorithms analyze visual data from robotic cameras.
- **Object Recognition:** Algorithms identify objects, including survivors and obstacles.
- **Path Planning:** ML contributes to efficient path planning for robotic devices.

Impact:

- **Enhanced Safety:** ML-driven robots assist in identifying survivors and hazardous conditions.
- **Quicker Response:** Faster identification and mapping of affected areas contribute to quicker response times.

MACHINE LEARNING METHOD FOR DISASTER DETECTION

Disasters pose significant threats to human lives, infrastructure, and the environment. Early detection and timely response are crucial for minimizing the impact of disasters. Machine learning methods have emerged as powerful tools for detecting and predicting disasters. This article provides a comprehensive overview of various machine learning methods used in disaster detection.

Supervised Learning

Supervised learning algorithms are trained on labeled data to classify different types of disasters. By analyzing historical data, these algorithms can learn patterns and features associated with specific disaster types. This enables the model to classify new instances and provide early warnings or alerts.

Unsupervised Learning

Unsupervised learning techniques are useful when labeled data is limited. These algorithms can identify patterns or clusters in the data without prior knowledge of disaster types. By grouping similar instances together, unsupervised learning helps in detecting emerging or unknown types of disasters.

Anomaly Detection

Anomaly detection methods focus on identifying unusual or abnormal patterns in data. By comparing current data to historical patterns, machine learning models can flag deviations that may indicate the presence of a disaster. Anomaly detection is particularly effective in detecting rare or unexpected events.

Deep Learning

Deep learning techniques, such as convolutional neural networks (CNNs) and recurrent neural networks (RNNs), have shown promise in disaster detection. CNNs excel in analyzing spatial data, such as satellite images, to identify disaster-related features. RNNs, on the other hand, are well-suited for analyzing sequential data, such as time-series sensor readings, to detect temporal patterns associated with disasters.

Data Sources

Machine learning methods for disaster detection rely on diverse and high-quality data sources. These can include historical records, sensor networks, satellite imagery, social media feeds, and more. The accuracy and reliability of the models heavily depend on the quality and representativeness of the data used.

FUTURE RESEARCH TRENDS AND CHALLENGES IN MACHINE LEARNING METHODS

In the field of machine learning, there are several ongoing research trends and challenges that are shaping the future of the field. Some of these include:

Explainability and Interpretability

As machine learning models become more complex, there is a growing need for methods that can explain and interpret their decisions. Future research is focused on developing techniques to make machine learning models more transparent and understandable, especially in critical domains such as healthcare or finance.

Transfer Learning and Few-shot Learning

Transfer learning aims to leverage knowledge learned from one task or domain to improve performance on another task or domain. Few-shot learning focuses on training models with limited labeled data. Future research is exploring ways to enhance transfer learning and few-shot learning techniques to improve the efficiency and effectiveness of machine learning models.

Robustness and Adversarial Attacks

Machine learning models are vulnerable to adversarial attacks, where malicious actors intentionally manipulate input data to deceive the model. Future research is focused on developing robust models that are resistant to such attacks and can maintain performance even in the presence of adversarial inputs.

Ethical and Fair Machine Learning

As machine learning models are increasingly used in decision-making processes, there is a growing concern about bias and fairness. Future research is exploring methods to ensure that machine learning models are fair, unbiased, and accountable, and do not perpetuate or amplify existing societal biases. These are just a few examples of the future research trends and challenges in machine learning methods. The field is rapidly evolving, and new advancements and challenges continue to emerge.

MACHINE LEARNING METHODS USED IN DEVELOPED APPLICATIONS FOR DISASTER MANAGEMENT.

Machine learning methods play a crucial role in developing applications for disaster management. These methods utilize historical data and real-time information to analyze and predict various aspects of disasters, such as their occurrence, severity, and impact. The commonly used machine learning methods in this context are shown in fig.3.

Classification algorithms

These algorithms are used to categorize different types of disasters based on their characteristics. For example, they can classify earthquakes, floods, or wildfires based on input features such as location, magnitude, or weather conditions.

Regression algorithms

Regression models are used to predict the severity or intensity of a disaster based on historical data. They can estimate variables like the number of casualties, damage to infrastructure, or economic impact.

Figure 3. ML Methods Used in Developed Applications for Disaster Management

Clustering algorithms

Clustering techniques are employed to group similar disaster events based on their attributes. This helps in identifying patterns and similarities among different disasters, which can aid in decision-making and resource allocation.

Time series analysis

Time series models are used to analyze and forecast the temporal patterns of disasters. They can capture trends, seasonality, and other patterns in historical data to predict future occurrences or changes in disaster events.

Natural language processing (NLP)

NLP techniques are utilized to analyze textual data from various sources, such as social media or news reports, to extract relevant information about disasters. This can help in understanding public sentiment, identifying affected areas, or detecting early warning signs. It is important to note that the choice of machine learning methods depends on the specific requirements and available data in each disaster management application. Additionally, these methods are often combined with other technologies, such as geographic information systems (GIS) or remote sensing, to enhance their effectiveness in real-world scenarios.

MACHINE LEARNING METHODS USED IN UNDEVELOPED APPLICATIONS FOR DISASTER MANAGEMENT

Machine learning methods have the potential to greatly assist in disaster management, even in undeveloped applications. In fig.4, the common machine learning methods that are employed for undeveloped applications are shown.

Figure 4. ML Methods Used in Un-developed Applications for Disaster Management

Data collection and preprocessing

In undeveloped areas, data collection can be challenging. Machine learning algorithms can be used to preprocess and clean the available data, ensuring its quality and reliability.

Remote sensing and image analysis

Machine learning techniques can be applied to satellite imagery or aerial photographs to identify and classify disaster-related features, such as damaged infrastructure, flooded areas, or fire-affected regions. This information can aid in assessing the extent of the disaster and planning response efforts.

Predictive modeling

Machine learning algorithms can be used to develop predictive models that forecast the occurrence and severity of disasters. These models can utilize historical data, weather patterns, geological information, and other relevant factors to provide early warnings and inform preparedness measures.

Decision support systems

Machine learning can be employed to develop decision support systems that assist in resource allocation, evacuation planning, and emergency response coordination. These systems can analyze real-time data, such as weather updates, sensor readings, or social media feeds, to provide actionable insights for decision-makers.

Natural language processing (NLP)

NLP techniques can be utilized to analyze unstructured data sources, such as social media posts or text messages, to extract valuable information during disaster events. This can help in identifying affected areas, assessing public sentiment, and gathering situational awareness. It is important to note that the successful implementation of machine learning methods in undeveloped applications for disaster management requires careful consideration of data availability, infrastructure limitations, and local context. Collaboration with local stakeholders and domain experts is crucial to ensure the relevance and effectiveness of these methods in specific disaster scenarios.

COMMON MACHINE LEARNING ALGORITHMS IN DISASTER MANAGEMENT

In disaster management, various machine learning algorithms are instrumental in leveraging data for critical decision-making. Here are some commonly used algorithms and their applications:

Random Forest

Application: Assessing Damage
    Description: Random Forest analyzes satellite imagery to categorize and prioritize areas based on the severity of damage after a disaster.

Support Vector Machines (SVM)

Application: Evacuation Planning
    Description: SVMs analyze data on population density, infrastructure, and hazards to optimize evacuation routes and resource allocation during disasters.

Neural Networks

Application: Social Media Analysis
    Description: Neural networks process social media data in real-time, categorizing posts and extracting insights into the needs and sentiments of affected populations.

K-Means Clustering

Application: Resource Allocation

Description: K-Means clustering optimizes resource allocation during and after a disaster by predicting areas with the highest needs for medical assistance, food, water, and other supplies.

Decision Trees

Application: Early Warning Systems
Description: Decision trees analyze various data sources to provide timely alerts about potential disasters, contributing to early warning systems.

Principal Component Analysis (PCA)

Application: Dimensionality Reduction
Description: PCA simplifies complex datasets by reducing the number of features, making them more manageable for analysis and prediction.

Naïve Bayes

Application: Predictive Analytics
Description: Naïve Bayes algorithms are utilized for predictive analytics, forecasting future trends based on historical data from previous disasters.

Probabilistic Clustering Methods

Application: Infrastructure Damage Prediction
Description: Probabilistic clustering methods monitor critical infrastructure, predicting potential damage and facilitating proactive maintenance.

APPLICATIONS

Machine learning plays a crucial role in enhancing the way we manage and respond to disasters. Here's a simplified explanation of how machine learning is applied in disaster management:

Early Warning Systems

Machine learning helps us predict natural disasters like hurricanes and floods by analyzing data from sources like satellites and weather stations. This enables us to give early warnings, giving people time to evacuate and authorities time to prepare.

Risk Assessment

By studying past data, machine learning can identify patterns related to disasters in specific areas. This allows us to assess the risk of future disasters, helping us plan better and allocate resources effectively.

Image and Video Analysis

Machine learning analyses images and videos from sources like satellites to assess the damage after a disaster. This helps emergency responders understand the situation and plan their actions.

Social Media Monitoring

Machine learning tools scan social media for real-time information. This helps us understand what's happening on the ground, identify urgent needs, and separate accurate information from rumors.

Resource Allocation

Algorithms optimize the use of resources like emergency personnel and supplies based on the evolving situation. This ensures that help reaches where it's needed most.

Damage Assessment

Machine learning examines images and data from drones to rapidly assess the extent of damage to buildings and infrastructure. This quick assessment guides response efforts.

Decision Support

Machine learning assists decision-makers by providing insights. This helps prioritize response efforts, identify vulnerable populations, and coordinate assistance effectively.

Health Surveillance

Machine learning monitors the spread of diseases after disasters. It analyzes health data to identify potential outbreaks and helps deploy medical resources where they are most needed.

Dynamic Mapping

Machine learning creates dynamic maps that show real-time information about disasters and response efforts. These maps help decision-makers and the public understand the situation better.

Automated Communication

Chatbots powered by machine learning provide automated, real-time communication to affected populations. They offer information, instructions, and assistance, efficiently handling a large number of inquiries. In simple terms, machine learning helps us prepare for, respond to, and recover from disasters more effectively. It enables quicker decision-making, better resource allocation, and improved communication, ultimately saving lives and reducing the impact of disasters on communities

CONCLUSION

Artificial Intelligence (AI) and Machine Learning (ML) techniques have shown great potential in predicting natural disasters. By analyzing historical data, real-time information, and various environmental factors, AI and ML models can provide valuable insights and predictions regarding the occurrence, severity, and impact of natural disasters. These technologies enable early warning systems, aid in decision-making processes, and help allocate resources more effectively. However, it is important to continuously improve and refine these models by incorporating new data sources, enhancing feature selection, and considering the dynamic nature of natural disasters. With further advancements in AI and ML, we can expect more accurate and timely predictions, ultimately contributing to better disaster preparedness and mitigation efforts.

REFERENCES

Abdalla, R., & Esmall, M. (2018). Artificial intelligence and WebGIS for disaster and emergency management. In *WebGIS for disaster management and emergency response* (pp. 57–62). Springer.

Abdullahi, S. I., Habaebi, M. H., & Malik, N. A. (2018). Flood disaster warning system on the go. *Proceedings of the 2018 7th international conference on computer and communication engineering (ICCCE).* IEEE. 10.1109/ICCCE.2018.8539253

Acar, A., & Muraki, Y. (2011). Twitter for crisis communication: Lessons learned from Japan's tsunami disaster. *International Journal of Web Based Communities*, 7(3), 392–402. doi:10.1504/IJWBC.2011.041206

Adams, B. J., Huyck, C., Mansouri, B., Eguchi, R., & Shinozuka, M. (2002). Post-disaster bridge damage assessment. In *Proceedings of the 15th Pecora conference: integrating remote sensing at the global, regional, and local scale*. CD-ROM.

Adams, S. M., Levitan, M., & Friedland, C. J. (2014). High resolution imagery collection for post-disaster studies utilizing unmanned aircraft systems (UAS). *Photogrammetric Engineering and Remote Sensing*, 12(12), 1161–1168. doi:10.14358/PERS.80.12.1161

Adeel, A., Gogate, M., Farooq, S., Ieracitano, C., Dashtipour, K., Larijani, H., & Hussain, A. (2018). A survey on the role of wireless sensor networks and IoT in disaster management. In *Geological disaster monitoring based on sensor networks* (pp. 57–66). Springer.

Agarwal, S., Kachroo, P., & Regentova, E. (2016). A hybrid model using logistic regression and wavelet transformation to detect traffic incidents. *IATSS Research*, 40(1), 56–63. doi:10.1016/j.iatssr.2016.06.001

Aghamohammadi, H., Mesgari, M. S., Mansourian, A., & Molaei, D. (2013). Seismic human loss estimation for an earthquake disaster using neural network. *International Journal of Environmental Science and Technology*, 10(5), 931–939. doi:10.1007/s13762-013-0281-5

Ahad, M. A., Paiva, S., Tripathi, G., & Feroz, N. (2020). Enabling technologies and sustainable smart cities. *Sustainable Cities and Society*, 61, 102301. doi:10.1016/j.scs.2020.102301

Ahmad, K., Pogorelov, K., Riegler, M., Ostroukhova, O., Halvorsen, P., Conci, N., & Dahyot, R. (2019). Automatic detection of passable roads after floods in remote sensed and social media data. *Signal Processing Image Communication*, *74*, 110–118. doi:10.1016/j.image.2019.02.002

Ahmad, K., Riegler, M., Pogorelov, K., Conci, N., Halvorsen, P., & De Natale, F. (2017). JORD: a system for collecting information and monitoring natural disasters by linking social media with satellite imagery. In *Proceedings of the 15th International Workshop on content-based multimedia indexing*. ACM. 10.1145/3095713.3095726

Ahmad, R., Samy, G. N., Ibrahim, N. K., Bath, P. A., & Ismail, Z. (2009). Threats identification in healthcare information systems using genetic algorithm and cox regression. In *The fifth international conference on information assurance and security,* (pp. 757–760). IEEE.

Alam, F., Imran, M., & Ofli, F. (2017). Image4Act: online social media image processing for disaster response. *IEEE/ACM International Conference on advances in social networks analysis and mining (ASONAM'17)*. IEEE. 10.1145/3110025.3110164

Alfaiate, J., Aliabadi, M., Guagliano, M., & Susmel, L. (2007). Identification of damaged bars in three-dimensional redundant truss structures by means of genetic algorithms. *Key Engineering Materials*, *348-349*, 229–232.

Comfort, L. K. (2005). *Risk, Security, and Disaster Management*, *8*, 335–356.

Lettieri, E. (2009). *Disaster Management: from a systematic review*. Research Gate.

Safran, E. B., Nilsen, E., Drake, P., & Sebok, B. (2024). Effects of video game play, avatar choice, and avatar power on motivation to prepare for earthquakes. *International Journal of Disaster Risk Reduction*, *101*(1), 104184. doi:10.1016/j.ijdrr.2023.104184

Samarakkody, A., Amaratunga, D., & Haigh, R. (2023). Technological Innovations for Enhancing Disaster Resilience in Smart Cities: A Comprehensive Urban Scholar's Analysis. *Sustainability (Basel)*, *15*(15), 12036. doi:10.3390/su151512036

Chapter 4
Predictive Analysis of Machine Learning Algorithms Applicable for Natural Disaster Management

Nagarani N.
https://orcid.org/0000-0001-7142-1513
Velammal College of Engineering and Technology, India

Ramji T. B.
Velammal College of Engineering and Technology, India

Kishorelal A, R.
Velammal College of Engineering and Technology, India

ABSTRACT

The escalating impact and frequency of natural disasters necessitate the development of robust predictive frameworks to proactively manage and mitigate their devastating consequences. ML techniques are used for the accurate forecasting of various natural disasters, such as earthquakes, floods, wildfires, hurricanes, and landslides, and these are thoroughly examined in this study. By harnessing historical data, environmental variables, and cutting-edge ML algorithms, this study meticulously assesses the efficacy of diverse techniques in forecasting and classifying these cataclysmic events. Through a comprehensive survey that scrutinizes the nuances of ML methods, random forest methods, support vector machines (SVM), neural networks, k-means clustering, Naive Bayes, reinforcement learning, and time series analysis models, the authors dissect their strengths and limitations in predicting specific types of natural disasters. Examining algorithms against actual real-world datasets offers valuable insights into the capabilities of each algorithm, shedding light on their capabilities to fortify early detection and warning systems. The research underscores the multifaceted challenges inherent in predicting natural disasters, emphasizing the paramount significance of high-quality, real-time data acquisition. This foundational aspect drives the iterative refinement of models, ensuring their adaptability to the dynamic and evolving

DOI: 10.4018/979-8-3693-3362-4.ch004

environmental conditions that influence disaster occurrences. Furthermore, it emphasizes the pivotal role of interdisciplinary collaboration, emphasizing the fusion of domain expertise and technological advancements to bolster the resilience of predictive models. Ultimately, the culmination of these efforts aims to improve the precision and timeliness of disaster predictions, thereby fortifying comprehensive disaster preparedness and response strategies. To address the challenges associated with predicting and managing natural disasters, this article advocates for an all-encompassing strategy that integrates advanced machine learning techniques with ongoing data collection and expert perspectives.

INTRODUCTION

Floods stand out as highly devastating natural disasters, leading to extensive destruction of human life, infrastructure, agriculture, and socioeconomic systems. This places governments under significant pressure to establish dependable and precise maps of flood-prone zones. Moreover, there's a growing emphasis on strategizing sustainable flood risk management, prioritizing prevention, protection, and preparedness measures (Danso-Amoako, E., et al., 2012). In the face of escalating natural disasters, the imperative to proactively manage and mitigate their devastating consequences has led to a paradigm shift in predictive frameworks. In many nations, earthquakes are viewed as the most catastrophic natural calamity, posing a significant risk to human life and safety (Alizadeh, M., et al., 2018). As per a UN report, roughly 10% of natural disasters occurring between 1998 and 2017 were associated with earthquakes and volcanic eruptions (Wallemacq, P 2018). These seismic events contributed to about 23% of economic losses caused by natural disasters and accounted for approximately 56% of total casualties. Despite their infrequency compared to other natural calamities, earthquakes inflict significant harm (Duk, K.L. 2018). This research embarks on a comprehensive exploration, leveraging advanced machine learning (ML) methodologies to increase the precision of natural disaster predictions. The study encompasses a diverse range of calamities, including earthquakes, floods, wildfires, hurricanes, and landslides. Earthquakes can intensify their impacts considerably in closely inhabited urban regions. with considerable infrastructure, resulting in protracted after effects that cause major economic harm to the country (Seoul, Korea. 2012). The central focus is on evaluating the ability of various ML algorithms, such as SVM, Neural Networks, Random Forest, K-Means Clustering, Naive Bayes, Reinforcement Learning, and Time Series Analysis Models. These algorithms, known for their versatility and adaptability, are rigorously assessed against real-world datasets to shed light on their potential to fortify early detection and warning systems. Efficient management of natural disasters is crucial in mitigating losses across diverse regions. As the world grapples with the increasing impact and frequency of natural disasters, this research endeavours to navigate the intricacies of prediction and management.

PREDICTIVE FRAMEWORK AND DISASTER MANAGEMENT WITH REAL-TIME DATA ACQUISITION

In the realm of disaster management, the development of a predictive framework stands as a critical endeavour, leveraging cutting-edge machine learning methodologies to anticipate and classify natural calamities such as earthquakes, floods, wildfires, hurricanes, and landslides. This framework operates at the intersection of historical data, environmental variables, and advanced ML algorithms, systematically evaluating their efficacy in forecasting catastrophic events. A pivotal aspect of this predictive framework lies in its adaptability to the dynamic and evolving environmental conditions influencing the occurrence of disasters. The real-time acquisition of high-quality data emerges as a cornerstone, providing a continuous stream of information to refine and enhance the precision of predictive models.

Challenges and Nuances

However, amidst the pursuit of precision, the journey is laden with challenges. The heterogeneity of natural disasters necessitates a nuanced approach to classification, requiring tailored strategies for each calamity. Limited historical data, particularly for rare events, poses a formidable obstacle, demanding innovative solutions for effective model training. The dynamic character of environmental circumstances necessitates real-time adaptation of models since it adds another level of complexity.

Real-Time Data Acquisition Dynamics

Although crucial, real-time data collection presents a unique set of difficulties. Because the accuracy of the information received determines how successful early detection and warning systems are, it becomes critical to ensure the consistency, dependability, and quality of the data feed. The interconnectedness of disaster types adds to the intricacy, demanding a holistic understanding of the data landscape. Imbalances in dataset frequency further challenge the unbiased training of models, urging a meticulous approach to achieve comprehensive disaster predictions.

Holistic Integration for Resilience

In navigating these complexities, the predictive framework advocates for a holistic integration of advanced ML methodologies with ongoing data acquisition efforts. This symbiotic relationship, supported by interdisciplinary collaboration, aims not only to fortify disaster preparedness and response but also to advance the field's understanding of the multifaceted challenges inherent in predicting and managing natural disasters. The emphasis on real-time adaptability and model refinement propels the framework towards a future where the fusion of expertise and technology enhances our ability to navigate the complexities of an ever-changing environment.

MACHINE LEARNING ALGORITHMS FOR DISASTERS

Earthquake Prediction

Like other natural catastrophes, earthquakes can result in significant damage and losses. Accurately predicting them is crucial for creating advance alert systems, responding for emergencies, identifying risks, and advancing scientific research. The ability to predict the size and probability of an earthquake in a particular location depends on sophisticated machine learning algorithms that examine extensive data from that area. Information regarding US states that have encountered earthquakes a magnitude of 3.0 or greater is illustrated in Figure 1.

Figure 1. Earthquake prediction (magnitude)

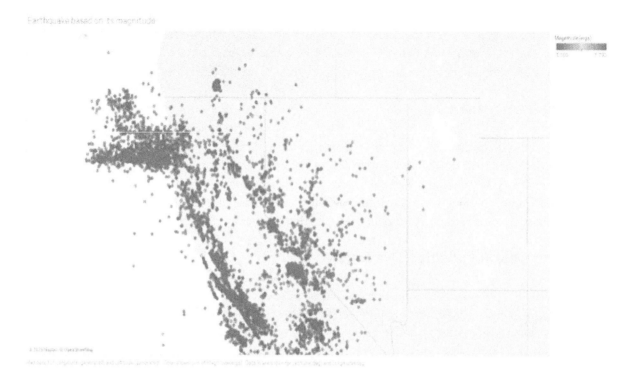

Linear Regression

Linear regression is a method of supervised machine learning that replicates the linear connection between one or more independent parameters. (such as latitude, longitude, depth, and the count of seismic stations noting the earthquake) and a dependent factor (such as earthquake magnitude). In this research, regression analysis will be utilized for forecasting earthquake magnitude and depth. Linear regression stands as the prevalent regression technique, involving the fitting of a linear model to elucidate the connection between independent and dependent variables (Andrews, D.F et al. 1974).The primary principle of linear regression involves finding the most appropriate line across the dataset, minimizing the sum of squared variances between the actual and predicted values of the dependent factor. By minimizing the total of squared variances concerning the coefficients, the ordinary least squares approach estimates the coefficients of the most fitting line. In this scenario, we used multiple linear regression to model the relationship between earthquake magnitude and latitude, longitude, depth, and number of seismic stations. According to the multiple linear regression model, the dependent factor (size) and each independent factor (latitude, longitude, latitude, longitude, depth and number of seismic stations). Following the application of this to the dataset, the model becomes capable of forecasting the magnitude of a fresh earthquake by considering its latitude, longitude, depth, and the count of seismic stations that observed it.

The linear regression model yields a mean squared error (MSE) of 0.17562, which measures the square root of the average squared difference between predicted and actual values in the dataset, indicating the model's precision. Simultaneously, the R2 score (R2) stands at 0.03498.

Figure 2. Plot of multiple linear regression

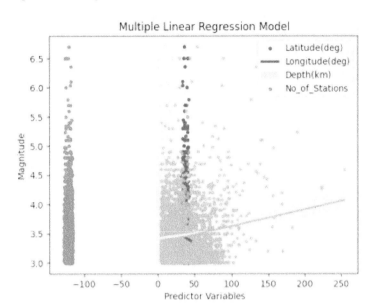

Support Vector Machines (SVM)

Support Vector Machine (SVM) is a supervised machine learning technique applicable to both regression and classification tasks.SVM is essentially structured as a quadratic optimization dilemma (R.-E. Fan, et al. 2005). The fundamental idea of SVM is the search for an ideal border, whether for the purpose of categorising data into discrete groups or forecasting continuous events such as the magnitude of an earthquake. This is achieved by mapping data points into a high-dimensional space to facilitate boundary detection. A key component of SVM is the "hyperplane", which maximizes the distance amidst the limit and the closest data element of each category. SVM looks for a straight line or high-dimensional curve, called a "support vector regression line," that maximizes the margin and fits the data exactly. SVM uses multiple kernels to modify data.Linear, polynomial, and radial basis function kernel (RBF) are utilized, enabling the consideration of both linear and nonlinear patterns.

The predicted values from the SVM model are reflected in the mean squared error (MSE) and R-squared metrics: The mean squared error (MSE) is 0.53166, but the R-squared score (R2) is -1.92129.

Naive Bayes

The use of a set of simple "probabilistic classifiers", so-called naive Bayesian classifiers, relies based on the presumption of strong independence between features and is common in statistics (see Bayesian classifiers). Although these are basic Bayesian network models, they can attain a high level of precision especially when combined with kernel density estimation. The quantity of necessary parameters for these classifiers increases linearly with the count of variables (features/predictors) in the learning task, making them highly scalable. Unlike many other types of classifiers, maximum likelihood training of Naive Bayes classifiers does not require costly iterative approximations. Instead, you need to evaluate a closed expression that operates in linear time. The precision is 0.9893947125161767

Figure 3. Plot of SVM

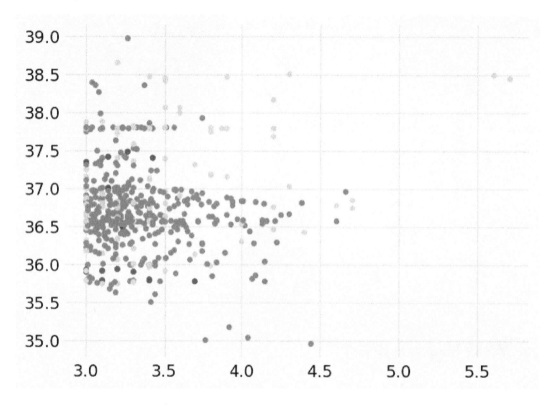

Random Forest

The random forest, a learning method used for regression and classification, operates as an ensemble method that enhances model accuracy by amalgamating multiple decision trees. To achieve more reliable and accurate predictions, Random Forest generates numerous decision trees and combines their outcomes (Breiman et al. 2001). The core idea is to generate multiple decision trees, each trained on a random subset of features and data. Each tree produces a prediction, and the overall prediction is the mean (for regression) or mode (for classification) of these individual tree predictions. By cultivating a large number of trees and averaging their outputs, random forests mitigate overfitting effects, thus improving model precision and stability.

Using a random forest method, we obtained the following results.

The R-squared score (R2) is 0.14288 and the mean squared error (MSE) is 0.15599. These results indicate that the random forest model successfully predicted the earthquake magnitude based on the available data. As evidenced by the low MSE and high R2 value, the model actually explains a significant part of the variability of the target variable, indicating accurate predictions.

Analysis

Both R-squared value (R2) and mean squared error (MSE) serve as evaluation metrics to compare and measure the efficiency of two models.

Figure 4. Actual magnitude category

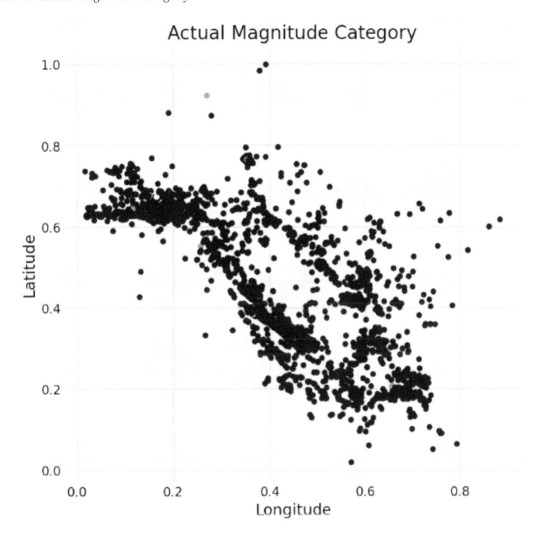

Typically, a framework with a higher R2 value and lower MSE is considered better. This priority occurs because a lower mean squared error (MSE) means the predictions from the model are more accurate. MSE calculates the average deviation between predicted and actual values. Conversely, a higher R2 score suggests that the model can account for a greater range of variation in the target variable. This value represents the percentage of variance in the outcome variable that is explained by the model. Nevertheless, it is crucial to recognize that the importance given to MSE and R2 scores might differ based on the specific problem and context in which the model is situated used. In certain scenarios, maximizing the R2 score may be less important than minimizing the MSE, and vice versa. It is important to take into account both metrics when assessing a model's performance, as a model may be good in one aspect but lagging in another.

Figure 5. Predicted magnitude category

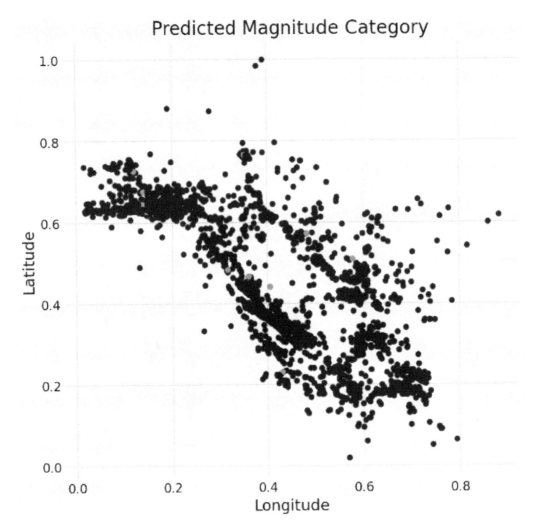

Figure 6. Random forest regression results

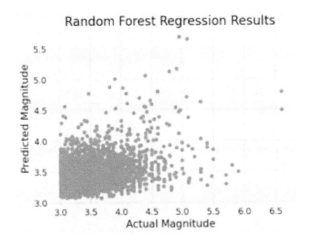

Figure 7. Plot of feature importance

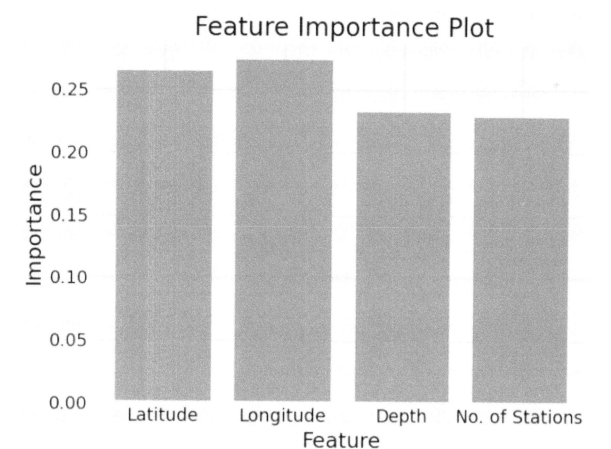

Landslides Prediction

A landslip is any natural disaster that causes boulders, their debris, or even dirt or earth to slide quickly down a sloped area of the ground. Mass wasting is describe the downward movement of soil or rock caused by gravity. Varnes classification classifies slope movement into five primary categories: falls, topples, spreads, slides, and flows. Additional classifications for geological materials include bedrock, detritus, and earth. Debris flow or mudflow are the most common types of landslides. Landslides can have various causes. When the forces acting on a slope exceed the strength of the substances constituting the slope, a noticeable alteration in the incline is noticed. Various causes can affect the strength and durability of the sloped part of the ground, leading to increased downhill forces.Urban planning applications are increasingly employing landslide hazard mapping. The findings from this study (Pradhan et al. 2010) hold potential value for developers, planners, engineers, and various other professionals involved in slope management and land use planning. However, caution is advised when utilizing these models for website development, and a comprehensive examination of additional slope components is recommended due to the study's broad scope. Therefore, the model developed in this study is suitable for long-term planning and evaluation purposes.In addition to gravity, landslides may result from earthquakes, volcanic activity, rainfall, snowmelt, variations in water level, stream erosion, variations in groundwater, disturbances caused by human activity, etc.

Predicting Landslides Using Machine Learning

Instead of being explicitly coded, machine learning allows computer systems to learn naturally via experience and eventually improve their performance. The creation of computer programmes with data access and learning capabilities is the basis of machine learning. Several models and methodologies in machine learning can be applied for predictive modelling.In this work, algorithms including Gaussian Naïve Bayes (GNB), Decision Tree (DT), Adaboost(AdaB), K-Nearest Neighbour (KNN), Support Vector Machine (SVM), Random Forest (RF), and Logistic Regression (LR) are used as boosters. These approaches were utilized in both the training and testing stages of the model. Logistic regression is a technique for evaluating the likelihood of a categorical dependent variable. In training, random forests aggregate decision trees, generating the mean prediction from each individual tree. SVM transforms instances into points in space for representation.

In datasets with numerous categories, instances often exhibit considerable spacing. Adaboost, when paired with other algorithms, notably enhances overall performance. Decision trees serve as visual decision aids, portraying options and their potential outcomes in a tree-like structure. Meanwhile, KNN systematically maps cases and categorizes new ones based on similarity measures. GNB assumes normally distributed continuous values for each feature. This work leverages Scikit-Learn, a Python-based machine learning module, to construct the predictive model.

Table 1. Predictive accuracy of diverse machine learning models

Model	Accuracy(%)	Precision(%)	Recall(%)	F1 Score(%)	AUC(%)
SVM	93	90.3	96.1	93.4	93
DT	91.5	92.2	91.3	91.7	92
GNB	93	91.9	94.8	93.3	93
LR	94.6	93.2	96.7	94.9	95
RF	9.6	93.3	94.5	93.9	94
KNN	87.3	86.4	89.7	88	87
ADA	92.8	93.5	92.6	93	93

A model embodies a system that employs data to learn and draw conclusions or forecasts. Accuracy signifies the proportion of correctly predicted events among all instances. Accuracy represents the ratio of correctly predicted positive observations to all predicted positive observations. Recall represents the ratio of correctly predicted positive observations to all observations in the actual class. The F1 score harmonizes recall and precision by considering their harmonic mean. Meanwhile, the area under the ROC curve (AUC) signifies the model's capability to differentiate between classes.

Analysis

Among all the models scrutinized, Logistic Regression (LR) displayed superior predictive performance. It exhibited a mean Area Under the Curve of 95%, mean Accuracy of 94.6%, and mean Precision, Recall, and F1 score of 93.2%, 96.7%, and 94.9%, respectively. This model outperformed traditional 1-day cumulative rainfall thresholds across different cumulative rainfall values. By optimizing the threshold value and refining data features, the predictive capacity of machine learning algorithms can be further enhanced. This study showcases how machine learning, even with limited data input, can characterize temporal landslide patterns triggered by rainfall. With observational datasets, this approach could be extended to forecast various natural hazards, mitigating the impact of such calamities.

Flood Prediction

Floods represent highly destructive natural disasters, causing extensive harm to infrastructure and human lives globally. Their severity is exacerbated by shifting climate patterns and increased precipitation. Predictive models powered by advanced technology play a crucial role in forecasting and getting ready for these disasters. Machine learning, a subset of artificial intelligence, can greatly contribute to disaster preparedness by analysing trends in historical data. Its primary modes—reinforcement learning, supervised learning, and unsupervised learning—enable distinct functionalities. Supervised learning, using labelled data, teaches algorithms to recognize patterns and forecast new data based on known information. It encompasses classification methods that categorize outcomes and regression models that predict continuous variables. In contrast, unsupervised learning identifies latent patterns within datasets without labelled data. Reinforcement learning, a more dynamic approach, allows robots to learn through trial and error, receiving rewards or penalties based on their actions. Beyond forecasting, machine learning supports risk assessment, classification, and readiness for disasters such as earthquakes and floods. Its capability to analyse vast datasets and uncover patterns significantly aids proactive disaster management strategies globally. Additional unsupervised learning techniques encompass Clustering and Association. Clustering groups objects based on dissimilarities, aiming for distinct clusters with dissimilar objects and similarities within each group. Association, another unsupervised learning technique, identifies relationships between variables in extensive databases. This study aims to construct a real-time flood prediction model beneficial in regions prone to flash floods (Phyo Pa Tun, et al. 2018). The system processes rainfall data from across India through different learning methods, selecting theprecise method. This proactive approach aims to save lives, pre-emptively inform people, and reduce meteorological workload.

Algorithms

By giving real-time input to various learning methods, including SVM, Decision Tree Classifier, K-Nearest Neighbours, and Logistic Regression. Models receive pre-processed input, from which patterns are recovered with the highest level of accuracy. There is a training dataset and a test set in the provided data. It is split in half, 7 to 3. All four models are utilised for prediction, and the accuracy is ascertained by comparing each model's output and taking into account each model's confusion matrix. The accuracy of each model is assessed to identify the most effective one.

Logistic Regression

Logistic regression serves as a learning approach for predicting the probabilities of categorical variables. It involves statistically analysing a dataset comprising various explanatory variables affecting the outcome, measured using a dichotomous variable. Due to its ease of application, this method is extensively employed for analysing established datasets, particularly within the realms of water resources and environmental engineering (Radkov et al 2008). This algorithm aims to identify the simplest model that elucidates the connection between a group of independent variables and a dichotomous attribute of interest. In this method, the dependent variable is a binary one, containing data coded as either 1 or 0. In essence, the logistic regression model predicts $P(Y=1)$ as a function of X.

Support Vector Machines

SVM exhibits various advantageous properties; among them, the optimization function employed in SVM construction generates a distinct solution (Vladimir Vapnik et al. 1999). Using a classifier that creates an ideal hyperplane between the data, SVM sorts the information set. The reason this classifier was selected is because it can produce a high prediction rate and has an extremely broad range of kernel functions that may be used. The SVM is a highly appreciated and often employed clustering algorithm. It is seen as an extension of the perceptron and is one of a group of generalised linear classifiers. With a little tweaking, it remains the preferred approach for a high-performance algorithm that was created in the 1990s.

K-Nearest Neighbor (KNN)

The K-Nearest Neighbour (KNN), a supervised machine learning technique, organizes all training data points within an n-dimensional space. When presented with unknown discrete data, the algorithm identifies the k closest saved instances and predicts the most prevalent class. For real-valued data, it computes the mean of the k nearest neighbours. In the distance-weighted nearest neighbour algorithm, each of the k neighbours' contributions is weighted based on their proximity, assigning higher weight to the closest neighbours. This algorithm's averaging nature renders KNN a classification technique resilient to noisy data (Chakraborty S., et al., 2011). To label unknown points, the algorithm initially examines a set of labelled points. Consequently, when assigning a label to a new point, it considers the closest labelled points and seeks their input. The new point adopts the label most commonly assigned by its neighbours. By employing the entire training set, this algorithm predicts outcomes for the validation set, determining a new instance's prediction by identifying its nearest occurrences within the training set. The algorithm calculates "closeness" by assessing the proximity between each feature.

Performance Analysis Metrics

True Positive: Occurs when the model correctly predicts the positive class, signifying an accurate prediction of a specific incident.

True Negative: Denotes accurate prediction of the negative class by the model, indicating an accurate forecast that a particular incident did not occur.

False Positive: Represents an incorrect prediction of the positive class by the model, indicating an inaccurate forecast of a specific incident.

False Negative: Indicates a model's incorrect prediction of the negative class, signifying an inaccurate forecast that a particular incident did not occur.

Sensitivity (or Recall): Measures the percentage of accurately predicted positive cases out of the actual positive cases. It's calculated as True Positive / (True Positive + False Negative), representing the model's capability to identify positive cases while considering the false-negative rate. The sum of the false-negative rate and sensitivity equals 1.

Precision: Reflects the proportion of positive predictions that are correct out of all positive predictions and is calculated as true positives / (true positives + false positives). High accuracy correlates with low false positive rate.

Recall (or sensitivity): Represents the ratio of correctly predicted observations to the total number of observations in the actual class.

F1 Score: This metric computes the weighted average of precision and recall, accounting for false negatives and false positives. It's valuable in scenarios with imbalanced class distributions, offering a more insightful measure than Accuracy. Precision and Recall values are considered when there's a disparity between the two, aiding decision-making where the costs of false positives and false negatives differ.

General Formula: F- Measure = 2TP / (2TP + FP + FN)

F1-Score Formula: F1 Score = 2*(Recall * Precision) / (Recall + Precision)

Table 2. Comparison of Accuracy Results

Model	Precision (%)	Recall (%)	F1 Score (%)	Sensitivity (%)	Specificity (%)	Accuracy (%)
LR	0.95	0.96	0.96	0.96	0.99	99.39
SVM	0.93	0.88	0.9	0.88	0.99	98.37
KNN	0.9	0.81	0.85	0.81	0.99	97.47
DTC	0.72	0.75	0.73	0.75	0.97	95.07

Analysis

The process of data cleaning and processing, null value replacement or removal, model construction, and evaluation lit the machine learning system. In the end, four distinct models' accuracy findings from the flood prediction model varied. The most successful technique for predicting floods is Logistic Regression with (99%), which is supported by the research and findings previously discussed.

CONCLUSION

The article emphasizes machine learning's pivotal role in predicting floods, landslides, and earthquakes, underlining its significance in shaping predictive frameworks for disaster management. It stresses the importance of continuous real-time data acquisition and illustrates its critical role in refining prediction algorithms for accurate disaster forecasting. The discussion underscores the necessity foradaptable models in ever-changing environmental conditions, showcasing various machine learning approaches and their strengths and limitations in various contexts. Despite challenges related to data consistency and model adaptability, these frameworks serve as crucial tools revolutionizing global disaster management strategies. Ultimately, the fusion of real-time data and machine learning propels proactive measures, enabling early warnings and effective responses to alleviate the consequences of natural disasters on both communities and infrastructure.

REFERENCES

Alizadeh, M., & Alizadeh, E. (2018). Evaluation of Social Vulnerability via Artificial Neural Network (ANN) Model for Earthquake Hazard in Tabriz City, Iran. Sustainability, 10, 3376.

Andrews, D. F. (1974). A Robust Method for Multiple Linear Regression. *Technometrics, 16*(4), 523–531. doi:10.1080/00401706.1974.10489233

Breiman, L. (2001, October). Random forests. *Machine Learning, 45*(1), 5–32. doi:10.1023/A:1010933404324

Chakraborty, S., Nagwani, N., & Dey, L. (2011). Weather Forecasting using Incremental K-means Clustering. *International Conference in High Performance Architecture and Grid Computing*. IEEE.

Chandrasekaran, S.S., Owaise, R.S., Ashwin, S., Jain, R.M., Prasanth, S. & Venugopalan. (2009). RB2013 Investigation on infrastructural damages by rainfall-induced landslides during November. *Nilgiris India Natural hazards, 65*(3), 1535-57.

Danso-Amoako, E., Scholz, M., Kalimeris, N., Yang, Q., & Shao, J. (2012). Forecasting the Risk of Dam Failures for Sustainable Flood Retention Basins: An All-encompassing Case Study for the Broader Greater Manchester Region. Comput. Environ. Urban Syst., 423-433.

Duk, K.L. (2018). Utilized satellite imagery in the study of earthquakes and volcanoes. *Korean Journal of Remote Sensing*, 1469-1478.

Lin, C. (2005). Working set selection using second order information for training support vector machines. *Journal of Machine Learning Research, 6*(Dec), 1889–1918.

The National Emergency Management Agency (NEMA) in Seoul. (2012). Development of Active Fault Map and Seismic Risk Map. NEMA.

Pa Tun, P. (2018). Flood Forecasting System for the Central Region of Myanmar. *IEEE 7th Global Conference on Consumer Electronics (GCCE 2018)*. IEEE.

Pourghasemi, H. R., Gayen, A., Panahi, M., Rezaie, F., & Blaschke, T. (2019). Assessment and Mapping of Multiple Hazards Probability in Iran. journal Science of the Total Environment, 692, 556-571.

Pradhan. (2010). Demonstrate the application of remote sensing data and GIS in landslide hazard analysis through spatial-based statistical models. *Arabian Journal of Geosciences, 3*(3), 319-326.

Wallemacq, P. (2018). *Economic Losses; Poverty & Disasters.* Centre for Research on the Epidemiology of Disasters.

Wang, G. & Sassa, K. (2003). Pore-pressure generation and movement of rainfall-induced landslides: effects of grain size and fine-particle content. *Engineering geology, 69*(1-2)109-25.

Chapter 5
ANN Model for Predicting the Natural Disaster:
Data-Driven Approaches for Natural Disaster Prediction and Mitigation

Gobinath A.
Velammal College of Engineering and Technology, India

Rajeswari P.
Velammal College of Engineering and Technology, India

Anandan M.
Velammal College of Engineering and Technology, India

Suresh Kumar N.
Velammal College of Engineering and Technology, India

ABSTRACT

Natural disasters have been an enduring and formidable challenge throughout human history, causing widespread devastation to communities and ecosystems. The significance of predicting these events lies in the ability to mitigate their impact on human lives, infrastructure, and the environment. Timely and accurate prediction empowers communities to take proactive measures, enabling better preparedness, response, and recovery. In the absence of such forecasting capabilities, the toll of natural disasters can be catastrophic, leading to loss of life, displacement of populations, and economic setbacks. Therefore, the development of predictive models, such as artificial neural networks (ANNs) and other data-driven approaches, is pivotal in addressing the escalating threats posed by natural disasters.

DOI: 10.4018/979-8-3693-3362-4.ch005

INTRODUCTION

Natural disasters have been an enduring and formidable challenge throughout human history, causing widespread devastation to communities and ecosystems. The significance of predicting these events lies in the ability to mitigate their impact on human lives, infrastructure, and the environment. Timely and accurate prediction empowers communities to take proactive measures, enabling better preparedness, response, and recovery. In the absence of such forecasting capabilities, the toll of natural disasters can be catastrophic, leading to loss of life, displacement of populations, and economic setbacks. Therefore, the development of predictive models, such as artificial neural networks (ANNs) and other data-driven approaches, is pivotal in addressing the escalating threats posed by natural disasters (Cong, 2019).

Understanding the patterns and behaviors of natural disasters is paramount for crafting effective disaster management strategies. Predictive models allow us to anticipate the occurrence of events like hurricanes, earthquakes, floods, and wildfires, providing valuable lead time for evacuation efforts, resource allocation, and infrastructure reinforcement. By harnessing the power of data, scientists and policymakers can analyze historical trends and environmental factors to identify potential hotspots and vulnerability zones. This foresight enables the formulation of targeted policies and the implementation of measures that can significantly reduce the impact of disasters on both human and natural systems (Rem et al, 2019).

Moreover, the economic implications of natural disasters underscore the importance of prediction and preparedness (Novickis et.al 2020). The aftermath of these events often results in substantial financial losses due to damaged infrastructure, disrupted supply chains, and the costs associated with rescue and relief efforts. Predictive models contribute to risk assessment and management, allowing governments, businesses, and communities to make informed decisions about investments, land-use planning, and insurance coverage. In doing so, the economic resilience of regions prone to natural disasters can be enhanced, minimizing the long-term consequences and facilitating a more rapid recovery (Cichos et al 2020).

In addition to immediate tangible benefits, the predictive capabilities offered by advanced models like ANNs pave the way for innovation in disaster research and management. The integration of real-time data from various sources, such as satellite imagery, weather stations, and social media, enhances the accuracy and responsiveness of predictive models. This integration not only improves the precision of forecasting but also allows for adaptive strategies that can be dynamically adjusted based on evolving conditions. As technology continues to advance, the synergy between big data analytics, machine learning, and predictive modeling holds the promise of revolutionizing our approach to natural disaster prediction and management (Pham et.al, 2019).

The significance of predicting natural disasters lies in the potential to save lives, protect communities, and build resilience against the escalating threats posed by these events. Timely and accurate predictions empower societies to implement proactive measures, allocate resources efficiently, and minimize the devastating impacts of disasters. With the advent of sophisticated technologies and data-driven approaches, the field of natural disaster prediction is entering a new era of innovation, offering unprecedented opportunities to enhance our understanding, preparedness, and response to these formidable challenges (Ayyappa et.al, 2020).

Role of Artificial Neural Networks (ANNs) in Predictive Modeling

Artificial Neural Networks (ANNs) have emerged as powerful tools in the realm of predictive modeling, offering unique capabilities that make them particularly well-suited for complex tasks, including natural disaster prediction. ANNs are computational models inspired by the structure and functioning of the human brain, with interconnected nodes that simulate neurons. Their ability to learn from data and discern intricate patterns makes them invaluable in various domains, from image recognition to financial forecasting. In the context of natural disaster prediction, ANNs play a pivotal role in enhancing the accuracy and efficiency of predictive models (Ginantra et al., 2021).

Figure 1. Block diagram of the prediction model of natural disaster

One of the key strengths of ANNs lies in their capacity to capture nonlinear relationships within data. Natural disasters often exhibit complex and nonlinear patterns influenced by a myriad of interconnected factors, such as climate conditions, geological features, and human activities. Traditional linear models may struggle to represent these intricate relationships accurately. ANNs, however, excel at modeling nonlinear relationships, allowing them to discern subtle patterns and interactions that might elude simpler models. This capability is particularly advantageous in the context of natural disaster prediction, where the interplay of numerous variables necessitates a nuanced understanding of the underlying dynamics. The learning process of ANNs is another crucial aspect that contributes to their effectiveness in predictive modeling. ANNs undergo a training phase where they learn from historical data to recognize patterns and relationships. This ability to adapt and improve over time enables ANNs to continually refine their predictions as new data becomes available. In the realm of natural disaster prediction, where environmental conditions are dynamic and subject to change, the adaptive nature of ANNs ensures that predictive models remain relevant and accurate in evolving scenarios (Chen et.al, 2020).

Furthermore, ANNs exhibit a remarkable capacity for feature extraction, which is essential in discerning relevant information from complex datasets. In natural disaster prediction, various input features, such as temperature, humidity, seismic activity, and historical event data, contribute to the overall understanding of the system. ANNs autonomously identify the most informative features, allowing for the creation of more streamlined and efficient models. This automated feature extraction is particularly advantageous in scenarios where the relationships between input variables and the occurrence of natural disasters are intricate and multifaceted (García et.al, 2020).

The parallel processing nature of ANNs is a computational advantage that accelerates the training and inference processes. This parallelism mimics the simultaneous firing of neurons in the human brain, enabling ANNs to handle large datasets and complex computations with efficiency. In the context of natural disaster prediction, where timely and rapid predictions are crucial for effective response and mitigation, the parallel processing capability of ANNs ensures that predictions can be generated swiftly, allowing for real-time decision-making. While ANNs offer significant advantages, it's important to acknowledge the challenges associated with their application in natural disaster prediction. The "black-box" nature of neural networks, where the internal workings are not easily interpretable, poses challenges in understanding the rationale behind specific predictions. Interpretable models are crucial in fields like disaster management, where transparent decision-making is essential. Researchers are actively working on developing techniques to enhance the interpretability of ANNs, ensuring that the insights gained from these models can be effectively communicated to stakeholders (Yan et.al., 2020).

Artificial Neural Networks have become indispensable tools in predictive modeling, playing a vital role in enhancing our ability to predict and mitigate the impact of natural disasters. Their capacity to model nonlinear relationships, adapt to changing conditions, extract relevant features, and process information in parallel makes them well-suited for the complexity of natural systems. As advancements in AI and machine learning continue, ANNs are likely to play an increasingly central role in shaping the future of natural disaster prediction, offering innovative solutions to the challenges posed by these complex and dynamic events.

NATURAL DISASTER PREDICTION MODELS

Overview of Existing Models for Natural Disaster Prediction

Natural disaster prediction is a critical area of research and application, given the devastating impact such events can have on human lives, infrastructure, and the environment. Over the years, various models have been developed to enhance our understanding of the complex dynamics involved in predicting natural disasters. These models span a range of methodologies, incorporating both traditional and advanced techniques to provide more accurate and timely predictions (L. Yang and A. Shami, 2020).

Traditional models for natural disaster prediction often rely on statistical methods and historical data analysis. For example, in meteorology, statistical models have been employed to predict hurricanes, tornadoes, and other weather-related disasters. These models analyze historical weather patterns, identifying trends and correlations that may indicate the likelihood of specific events. While these approaches have provided valuable insights, they often face challenges in capturing the nonlinear and dynamic nature of natural systems, especially as the frequency and intensity of certain types of disasters change over time.

In the realm of seismic activity, earthquake prediction models have been developed based on historical seismic data and fault line studies. These models aim to identify patterns or precursors that may indicate an increased risk of earthquakes in specific regions. However, earthquake prediction remains a challenging task due to the inherent complexity of tectonic processes, and the uncertainties associated with predicting the exact timing and magnitude of seismic events.

In recent years, advancements in technology and data analytics have paved the way for more sophisticated models, with machine learning and artificial intelligence playing a prominent role. Machine learning models, including decision trees, support vector machines, and random forests, have been applied to various types of natural disaster prediction. These models leverage complex algorithms to identify patterns and relationships within large datasets, enabling more accurate predictions. For instance, decision trees have been used in landslide prediction, considering factors such as rainfall, soil type, and topography to assess the susceptibility of an area to landslides (Wanto et.al 2017).

However, one of the most notable advancements in predictive modeling for natural disasters is the application of Artificial Neural Networks (ANNs). ANNs, inspired by the human brain's structure and functioning, have demonstrated exceptional capabilities in capturing intricate patterns and nonlinear relationships. They excel in tasks where the interplay of multiple variables is complex and dynamic, making them well-suited for natural disaster prediction. ANNs have been employed in various domains, such as hurricane tracking, flood forecasting, and wildfire prediction. The ability of ANNs to learn from historical data, adapt to changing conditions, and process information in parallel has significantly enhanced the accuracy of predictions in comparison to traditional models. Hybrid models have also gained prominence, combining the strengths of different approaches to improve prediction accuracy. For instance, integrating numerical weather prediction models with machine learning algorithms has shown promise in enhancing hurricane prediction. This fusion of physics-based models with data-driven approaches leverages the strengths of both methodologies, providing a more comprehensive and accurate understanding of the factors influencing natural disasters (Shende.et.al, 2020).

Despite these advancements, challenges persist in the field of natural disaster prediction. The dynamic and evolving nature of environmental systems, coupled with the inherent uncertainties in predicting rare events, pose ongoing challenges for model development. Additionally, issues of data quality, accessibility, and the need for real-time information remain critical considerations in improving the effectiveness of predictive models. Natural disaster prediction has evolved significantly over the years, moving from traditional statistical models to advanced machine learning and artificial intelligence approaches. While traditional models continue to provide valuable insights, the integration of cutting-edge technologies has substantially improved the accuracy and efficiency of predictions. The future of natural disaster prediction lies in further refining existing models, exploring hybrid approaches, and addressing ongoing challenges to create robust systems capable of safeguarding communities and minimizing the impact of these devastating events (Leholo et.al, 2019).

ARTIFICIAL NEURAL NETWORKS (ANNS)

Artificial Neural Networks (ANNs) have proven to be potent tools in predicting natural disasters, leveraging their ability to learn complex patterns and relationships from data. This application of ANNs in the realm of natural disaster prediction holds immense potential for improving the accuracy and timeliness of forecasting, ultimately aiding in mitigation and preparedness efforts.

One primary application of ANNs in predicting natural disasters is in meteorology, particularly for forecasting severe weather events such as hurricanes and tornadoes. ANNs can analyze vast amounts of meteorological data, including atmospheric pressure, temperature, wind patterns, and historical storm data. By recognizing intricate patterns within this data, ANNs can generate models that improve the understanding of the conditions conducive to the formation and intensification of hurricanes. These models enable meteorologists to make more accurate predictions regarding the path, intensity, and potential impact of hurricanes, offering crucial information for evacuation planning and resource allocation (Wang et.al, 2021).

Flood prediction is another critical area where ANNs excel. ANNs can assimilate data from various sources, including rainfall patterns, river discharge, soil moisture content, and topography. By learning from historical flood events and their associated variables, ANNs can create models that predict the likelihood and extent of flooding in specific regions. This information is vital for early warning systems and emergency response planning, allowing authorities to evacuate vulnerable areas and deploy resources effectively.

Wildfire prediction and management benefit significantly from the application of ANNs. These networks can process data related to vegetation health, temperature, humidity, wind speed, and historical fire incidents. By discerning patterns and relationships among these variables, ANNs generate models that forecast the risk of wildfires in different regions. This allows for proactive measures, such as controlled burns, resource allocation for firefighting efforts, and public awareness campaigns to reduce the likelihood of human-caused wildfires.

In the field of earthquake prediction, ANNs contribute to understanding the complex dynamics associated with seismic activity. While predicting the exact timing and magnitude of earthquakes remains a formidable challenge, ANNs can analyze historical seismic data, fault line characteristics, and other geological factors to identify regions with higher seismic risk. This information aids in implementing stricter building codes and infrastructure measures in vulnerable areas, reducing the potential impact of earthquakes. The versatility of ANNs extends to landslides prediction, where they analyze factors such as rainfall intensity, slope steepness, soil type, and historical landslide occurrences. By recognizing patterns in these variables, ANNs generate models that assess the susceptibility of specific areas to landslides. This information is crucial for land-use planning and early warning systems, enabling authorities to mitigate the risks associated with landslides.

Despite the success of ANNs in natural disaster prediction, challenges persist. Interpretability remains a concern, as the complex nature of neural networks can make it challenging to understand the rationale behind specific predictions. Researchers are actively working on developing techniques to enhance the interpretability of ANNs, ensuring that stakeholders can trust and understand the information provided by these models.

The application of Artificial Neural Networks in predicting natural disasters has revolutionized the field, offering more accurate and timely insights into complex environmental systems. Whether in meteorology, flood prediction, wildfire management, earthquake risk assessment, or landslide susceptibility analysis, ANNs have demonstrated their capacity to learn from diverse datasets and contribute to enhanced preparedness and mitigation strategies. As technology continues to advance, the integration of ANNs with other modeling approaches and ongoing research into interpretability will further solidify their role in safeguarding communities from the impact of natural disasters.

Advantages of Using ANNs Over Traditional Methods

Artificial Neural Networks (ANNs) offer several advantages over traditional methods in the context of predicting natural disasters. These advantages contribute to the improved accuracy, adaptability, and efficiency of predictive models, making ANNs a preferred choice for researchers and practitioners in the field. Here are some key advantages:

Nonlinear Relationship Modeling

Traditional methods often rely on linear models that assume a linear relationship between input variables and the outcome. However, natural disasters often involve complex and nonlinear interactions between various factors. ANNs excel at capturing these intricate relationships, allowing for a more accurate representation of the dynamic nature of environmental systems. This ability is particularly crucial when dealing with phenomena like hurricanes, earthquakes, and wildfires, where linear models may fall short in providing precise predictions.

Adaptability to Changing Conditions

Natural systems are dynamic and subject to continuous changes. Traditional models may struggle to adapt to evolving conditions as they often rely on fixed equations and assumptions. ANNs, on the other hand, possess the ability to adapt and learn from new data. This adaptability ensures that the predictive models stay relevant and accurate even as environmental conditions shift over time. The capacity to continuously update predictions based on the latest information is invaluable in the context of natural disaster prediction where timely and up-to-date forecasts are essential.

Feature Extraction and Representation Learning

ANNs are adept at automatically extracting relevant features from complex datasets. In natural disaster prediction, where numerous variables contribute to the overall understanding of the system, this automated feature extraction is crucial. Traditional methods may require manual feature engineering, a process that can be time-consuming and may overlook subtle yet significant relationships within the data. ANNs, through their learning process, autonomously identify the most informative features, leading to more efficient and accurate models.

Parallel Processing Capability

ANNs operate in a parallel processing manner, mirroring the simultaneous firing of neurons in the human brain. This parallelism allows ANNs to handle large volumes of data and perform complex computations efficiently. In natural disaster prediction, where vast datasets and real-time information are involved, the parallel processing capability of ANNs ensures timely predictions. This is especially advantageous for tasks like hurricane tracking, flood forecasting, and wildfire prediction, where rapid decision-making is critical.

Handling High-Dimensional Data

Many natural disaster prediction problems involve high-dimensional data, with numerous variables influencing the outcome. Traditional methods may struggle to effectively handle such complex datasets, leading to oversimplified models or computational challenges. ANNs are well-suited for high-dimensional data, and their architecture enables them to efficiently process and learn from large and diverse datasets, resulting in more comprehensive and accurate predictions.

Generalization to Unseen Data

ANNs have the ability to generalize well to unseen data, meaning they can make accurate predictions on new and previously unseen instances. This generalization is crucial in natural disaster prediction where conditions may vary across different regions and time periods. The robust learning capabilities of ANNs enable them to capture the underlying patterns within the data, facilitating reliable predictions even in scenarios not explicitly encountered during training.

The advantages of using Artificial Neural Networks over traditional methods in natural disaster prediction include their ability to model nonlinear relationships, adapt to changing conditions, autonomously extract relevant features, process data in parallel, handle high-dimensional datasets, and generalize to unseen data. These advantages collectively contribute to the enhanced performance and effectiveness of ANNs in providing accurate and timely predictions, ultimately supporting more informed decision-making in disaster management and mitigation efforts.

ANN MODEL DEVELOPMENT

Developing an Artificial Neural Network (ANN) model for natural disaster prediction involves a systematic process that encompasses data collection, preprocessing, model architecture design, training, validation, and deployment. Here are the detailed steps involved in developing an ANN model for natural disaster prediction:

Data Collection

The foundation of any predictive modeling task is high-quality data. In the context of natural disaster prediction, relevant data sources may include meteorological data, geological data, satellite imagery, historical disaster records, and environmental sensor data. This diverse range of information helps capture the complex interactions and patterns associated with different types of natural disasters. It's crucial to ensure the dataset is representative, comprehensive, and covers a sufficiently long period to capture variations over time. Additionally, data integrity and consistency are paramount to the success of the ANN model, requiring careful attention to data quality assurance processes.

Data Preprocessing

Once the data is collected, preprocessing steps are essential to prepare it for training an ANN model. This involves cleaning the data by handling missing values, outliers, and inconsistencies. Normalization or standardization may be applied to ensure that all input features have similar scales, preventing certain features from dominating the learning process due to their larger magnitudes. Feature engineering may also take place during this stage, involving the creation of new features or the transformation of existing ones to enhance the model's ability to capture relevant patterns. Time-series data may require additional preprocessing steps, such as temporal aggregation or decomposition, to reveal underlying trends and patterns.

Model Architecture Design

Designing the architecture of the neural network is a critical step that involves determining the number of layers, the number of neurons in each layer, and the activation functions. For natural disaster prediction, a feedforward neural network is commonly used, consisting of an input layer, one or more hidden layers, and an output layer. The choice of activation functions, such as Rectified Linear Unit (ReLU) for hidden layers and a sigmoid or softmax function for the output layer, depends on the nature of the problem (e.g., binary or multiclass classification). The architecture should strike a balance between complexity and simplicity, avoiding overfitting (capturing noise in the training data) or underfitting (failing to capture underlying patterns).

Training the ANN

Training involves feeding the prepared data into the neural network, allowing it to learn the underlying patterns through an iterative optimization process. The backpropagation algorithm is commonly used for adjusting the weights of the network based on the error between the predicted outputs and the actual targets. The model learns to minimize this error, iteratively updating the weights through multiple epochs. During training, a portion of the dataset is often set aside for validation, enabling the monitoring of the model's performance on unseen data. Training hyperparameters, such as learning rate and batch size, play a crucial role in the convergence and performance of the model and may require tuning to achieve optimal results.

Validation and Evaluation

After training, the model's performance is evaluated using the validation dataset to ensure it generalizes well to unseen data. Metrics such as accuracy, precision, recall, and F1 score are commonly used to assess the model's predictive capabilities. It's crucial to evaluate the model on diverse datasets to assess its robustness and generalization across different scenarios. If the model performs well on the validation set, further evaluation on an independent test set is conducted to provide a final assessment of its predictive power. Adjustments to the model architecture or hyperparameters may be made based on the validation and test results to enhance performance.

Developing an ANN model for natural disaster prediction involves a systematic process starting with data collection, followed by data preprocessing, model architecture design, training, validation, and evaluation. Each step is critical for the success of the model, and careful consideration of data quality, feature engineering, and model tuning contributes to the model's ability to accurately predict natural disasters. The iterative nature of model development, with continuous refinement based on validation and testing results, ensures that the ANN is capable of capturing the complex patterns inherent in natural disaster dynamics.

Specific Challenges in ANN Model Development

Developing Artificial Neural Network (ANN) models for natural disaster prediction comes with its own set of challenges and considerations. Addressing these challenges is crucial to ensure the reliability, interpretability, and effectiveness of the models in real-world scenarios. Here are some specific challenges and considerations in this context:

Data Quality and Availability

Challenge: The quality and availability of data are paramount for training accurate and reliable ANN models. In many cases, historical data may be limited, incomplete, or subject to biases.

Consideration: Rigorous data quality assurance processes, including cleaning and validation, are essential. Collaboration with relevant agencies and institutions to access diverse and comprehensive datasets can help overcome limitations in data availability.

Imbalanced Datasets

Challenge: Natural disaster events are often infrequent, leading to imbalanced datasets where the occurrences of disasters are vastly outnumbered by non-disaster instances. Imbalanced datasets can affect the model's ability to learn patterns effectively.

Consideration: Techniques such as oversampling, undersampling, or the use of specialized loss functions can help address imbalances and improve the model's ability to detect rare events.

Interpretability and Explainability

Challenge: The "black-box" nature of neural networks can make it challenging to interpret how the model arrives at specific predictions. Interpretability is crucial, especially in fields like disaster management where transparent decision-making is essential.

Consideration: Researchers are actively exploring methods for enhancing the interpretability of ANNs, including visualization techniques, feature importance analysis, and the development of hybrid models that combine the strengths of neural networks with more interpretable models.

Limited Historical Data for Rare Events

Challenge: Some types of natural disasters, such as extreme earthquakes or rare meteorological events, may have limited historical occurrences. This scarcity of data poses challenges in training models to accurately predict such rare events.

Consideration: Augmenting historical data with simulated data, leveraging transfer learning from related events, or incorporating domain knowledge through expert guidance can help address the challenge of limited data for rare events.

Model Overfitting and Underfitting

Challenge: ANNs can be prone to overfitting, where the model captures noise in the training data, or underfitting, where the model fails to capture underlying patterns.

Consideration: Regularization techniques, such as dropout and L1/L2 regularization, can help prevent overfitting. Careful tuning of hyperparameters and monitoring the model's performance on validation datasets are essential to find the right balance.

Uncertainties in Predictions

Challenge: Natural disasters are inherently uncertain, and predicting the exact timing, magnitude, or impact of an event with certainty is challenging. ANNs may not always provide a measure of uncertainty in their predictions.

Consideration: Bayesian neural networks or ensembling methods can be explored to incorporate uncertainty estimates in predictions. Communicating the inherent uncertainties to stakeholders is crucial for responsible decision-making.

Real-Time Processing and Resource Constraints

Challenge: Natural disaster prediction often requires real-time processing of data, and ANNs, particularly deep architectures, can be computationally intensive.

Consideration: Model optimization, parallel processing, and the use of hardware accelerators can help address computational challenges. Balancing model complexity with the available computational resources is crucial for real-time applications.

Addressing these challenges and considerations requires a multidisciplinary approach, involving collaboration between data scientists, domain experts, and stakeholders. Continuous research and advancements in the field of neural networks, along with a commitment to ethical and responsible AI practices, are essential for developing effective and reliable ANN models for natural disaster prediction.

Process of Training the ANN Model Using Historical Data

The process of training an Artificial Neural Network (ANN) model for natural disaster prediction involves several key steps, starting with the preparation of historical data and culminating in the optimization of the neural network's weights to accurately capture patterns and relationships. Here is an in-depth explanation of the training process:

Data Preparation

The training process begins with the careful preparation of historical data, which serves as the foundation for teaching the neural network to recognize patterns associated with natural disasters. The dataset typically includes relevant features such as meteorological conditions, geological parameters, and historical disaster records. This data needs to be cleaned, meaning any missing values, outliers, or inconsistencies are addressed. Additionally, the dataset is often split into training, validation, and test sets. The training set is used to teach the model, the validation set is employed to fine-tune hyperparameters and avoid overfitting, and the test set evaluates the model's performance on unseen data.

Model Architecture Design

The next step involves designing the architecture of the neural network. This includes determining the number of layers, the number of neurons in each layer, and selecting activation functions. For natural disaster prediction, a feedforward neural network is commonly employed. The input layer consists of neurons corresponding to the features in the dataset, hidden layers capture complex relationships, and the output layer provides the predictions. Activation functions, such as Rectified Linear Unit (ReLU) for hidden layers and sigmoid or softmax for the output layer, introduce nonlinearity into the model, allowing it to capture intricate patterns.

Initialization of Weights

Once the architecture is defined, the initial weights of the neural network need to be set. Proper weight initialization is crucial for the convergence of the training process. Common methods include random initialization or strategies like Xavier/Glorot initialization, which takes into account the number of input and output neurons in each layer. Well-initialized weights provide a starting point for the network to learn and adjust during the training process.

Forward Propagation

During the training process, forward propagation is performed to calculate the predicted output of the neural network. Input data from the training set is fed into the input layer, and through a series of weighted calculations and activation functions, the data propagates through the hidden layers to produce an output. This predicted output is then compared to the actual target values from the training set using a defined loss or cost function.

Backpropagation and Weight Updates

Backpropagation is a crucial step where the neural network adjusts its weights based on the calculated error or loss. The gradient of the loss with respect to each weight is computed, and the weights are updated using optimization algorithms like stochastic gradient descent (SGD) or its variants (e.g., Adam, RMSprop). This process iteratively continues for multiple epochs, allowing the model to refine its weights and reduce the prediction error. The learning rate, a hyperparameter that determines the size of the weight updates, needs to be carefully chosen to prevent the model from converging too slowly or overshooting the optimal weights.

Training Hyperparameters

Several hyperparameters influence the training process, and their careful tuning is essential for the success of the model. Apart from the learning rate, other hyperparameters include the number of hidden layers, the number of neurons in each layer, batch size (the number of samples used in each iteration), and the choice of activation functions. Grid search or random search techniques are often employed to explore the hyperparameter space and identify the combination that yields the best performance on the validation set.

Validation and Early Stopping

To prevent overfitting, where the model performs well on the training set but fails to generalize to new data, the model's performance is regularly evaluated on the validation set during training. If the performance on the validation set starts to degrade after an initial improvement, early stopping can be employed. This involves halting the training process to avoid overfitting and selecting the model with the best performance on the validation set.

Model Evaluation

After completing the training process, the final step involves evaluating the model's performance on an independent test set that it has never seen before. This provides an unbiased assessment of how well the model generalizes to new, unseen data. Metrics such as accuracy, precision, recall, and F1 score are commonly used to quantify the model's effectiveness in predicting natural disasters.

Throughout the training process, it is essential to monitor the convergence of the model, ensuring that it is learning meaningful patterns from the data without fitting noise. Adjustments to the model architecture or hyperparameters may be made based on the validation and test results to enhance performance. Training an ANN model for natural disaster prediction involves meticulous data preparation, thoughtful model architecture design, initialization of weights, forward propagation to make predictions, backpropagation to update weights, tuning of hyperparameters, and continuous evaluation on validation and test sets. The success of the model relies on striking a balance between model complexity and generalization, adapting to the dynamic nature of natural systems, and addressing challenges such as data quality, imbalances, and interpretability. The iterative nature of the training process, with its feedback loop of evaluation and refinement, ensures that the ANN is equipped to make accurate and timely predictions in the context of natural disaster prediction.

Validation Methods to Ensure the Model's Accuracy and Generalization

Validation methods are crucial in the development of Artificial Neural Network (ANN) models to ensure their accuracy, robustness, and generalization to unseen data. These methods serve as a means to evaluate the model's performance during the training process and guide decisions regarding model architecture, hyperparameters, and potential overfitting. Several validation techniques are commonly employed to assess the model's effectiveness:

Train-Validation Split

In this approach, the dataset is divided into two subsets: a training set and a validation set. The model is trained on the training set, and its performance is monitored on the validation set. This method provides a simple and quick way to assess the model's generalization, but its effectiveness may be limited if the dataset is small or if there are significant variations within the data.

K-Fold Cross-Validation

K-Fold Cross-Validation involves dividing the dataset into k subsets (or folds). The model is trained on k-1 folds and validated on the remaining fold. This process is repeated k times, with each fold serving as the validation set exactly once. The final performance metric is often the average across all folds. K-Fold Cross-Validation provides a more robust estimate of the model's performance, especially when the dataset is limited, as it ensures that each data point is used for both training and validation.

Stratified K-Fold Cross-Validation

This variant of K-Fold Cross-Validation ensures that each fold maintains the same class distribution as the original dataset. In the context of natural disaster prediction, where the occurrence of events may be imbalanced, stratified sampling helps prevent biases in the model evaluation. By preserving the distribution of classes in each fold, this method offers a more representative assessment of the model's generalization performance.

Leave-One-Out Cross-Validation (LOOCV)

LOOCV is an extreme case of K-Fold Cross-Validation where k is set equal to the number of samples in the dataset. In each iteration, the model is trained on all data points except one, and performance is evaluated on the excluded data point. While LOOCV provides an unbiased estimate of model performance, it can be computationally expensive, especially for large datasets.

Validation methods are essential for detecting potential issues such as overfitting, where the model performs well on the training data but fails to generalize to new, unseen data. Overfitting occurs when the model captures noise or random fluctuations in the training set rather than learning underlying patterns. Regular monitoring of the model's performance on the validation set helps identify the point at which further training may lead to overfitting.

The choice of a validation method depends on the characteristics of the dataset, the size of the data, and the nature of the problem being addressed. Cross-validation techniques are particularly valuable when dealing with limited data, as they provide a more comprehensive assessment of the model's generalization capabilities. Stratified sampling ensures that the model's performance is evaluated fairly across different classes, enhancing its applicability to imbalanced datasets. Validation methods play a critical role in the development of ANN models for natural disaster prediction. They help ensure the accuracy and generalization of the model by assessing its performance on independent datasets. Whether using train-validation splits, K-Fold Cross-Validation, stratified sampling, or other techniques, the goal is to strike a balance between model complexity and its ability to generalize to new and unseen data. Regular evaluation during the training process guides the refinement of the model, contributing to its reliability and effectiveness in predicting natural disasters.

RESULTS AND CASE STUDIES

Applying an Artificial Neural Network (ANN) model to real-world data for natural disaster prediction yields insightful results that can significantly impact disaster management and mitigation efforts. Let's consider a scenario where the ANN model is used for hurricane prediction based on historical meteorological data.

After the careful development and training of the ANN model using a comprehensive dataset containing features such as sea surface temperature, atmospheric pressure, wind speed, and historical hurricane occurrences, the model is ready for application. Upon deploying the trained model to real-world data, it begins to make predictions about the likelihood and intensity of hurricanes. The results can be presented in the form of hurricane forecasts, indicating the probable paths and strengths of upcoming storms.

The evaluation of the model's performance on real-world data involves comparing its predictions to actual occurrences. Metrics such as accuracy, precision, recall, and the F1 score provide a quantitative assessment of how well the ANN model aligns with observed data. For instance, the accuracy metric indicates the percentage of correctly predicted hurricanes, while precision and recall quantify the model's ability to correctly identify hurricanes and capture all actual hurricane occurrences, respectively. These metrics collectively offer a comprehensive view of the model's reliability in real-world scenarios.

The application of the ANN model to real-world data extends beyond just prediction; it empowers decision-makers with timely and accurate information for disaster preparedness and response. For example, if the model predicts an increased likelihood of a hurricane making landfall in a specific region, authorities can implement evacuation plans, allocate resources for emergency response, and communicate warnings to the public. The real-time application of the ANN model enables proactive measures to mitigate the impact of natural disasters, ultimately contributing to the safety and well-being of communities.

Moreover, the results obtained from applying the ANN model to real-world data contribute to ongoing research and improvement of predictive models. Any disparities between the model's predictions and actual events prompt a reevaluation of the model's architecture, hyperparameters, and training data. This iterative process of refinement ensures that the ANN model continues to evolve and adapt to changing environmental conditions. Additionally, the insights gained from real-world applications can inform the development of more advanced models and guide the integration of other data sources or hybrid approaches to enhance prediction accuracy.

In summary, the results of applying an ANN model to real-world data for natural disaster prediction hold immense practical significance. They provide actionable insights for disaster management, support decision-making in emergency situations, and contribute valuable feedback for the continuous improvement of predictive models. As technology and data availability advance, the application of ANN models to real-world scenarios will play a pivotal role in enhancing our ability to predict and mitigate the impact of natural disasters.

Case Studies

Hurricane Track Prediction

The National Hurricane Center (NHC) in the United States has been utilizing ANNs and advanced numerical weather prediction models to enhance the accuracy of hurricane track predictions. These models analyze various meteorological factors such as sea surface temperatures, wind patterns, and atmospheric pressure to predict the path and intensity of hurricanes. The improved accuracy in hurricane tracking has significantly contributed to more effective evacuation planning and resource allocation.

Earthquake Early Warning Systems

In earthquake-prone regions like Japan and California, researchers have employed machine learning, including ANNs, to develop early warning systems. These systems use real-time seismic data combined with historical earthquake patterns to predict the occurrence and intensity of earthquakes moments before they happen. This advanced warning allows for immediate response actions, such as automated shutdowns of critical infrastructure and alerts to the public.

Flood Prediction and Management

The European Space Agency (ESA) has implemented data-driven approaches, including machine learning, for flood prediction using satellite data. By analyzing satellite imagery and incorporating environmental variables like rainfall and soil moisture, these models can predict potential flood areas. Such predictions assist in timely evacuation plans, resource allocation, and disaster response.

Wildfire Prediction

The development of machine learning models, including ANNs, has been applied to predict and manage wildfires. By analyzing historical fire data, weather conditions, and vegetation health, these models can identify regions at high risk of wildfires. Fire agencies use this information to strategically position firefighting resources and implement preventive measures such as controlled burns.

Landslide Susceptibility Mapping

In areas prone to landslides, researchers have employed machine learning techniques to create susceptibility maps. These maps utilize geological and environmental factors such as slope steepness, soil type, and precipitation to identify areas at risk of landslides. This information aids in urban planning, land-use management, and the implementation of measures to reduce landslide vulnerability.

It's important to note that the success of these applications relies not only on the use of ANNs but also on the integration of diverse datasets, collaboration between researchers and domain experts, and continuous refinement of models based on real-world feedback. Additionally, advancements in satellite technology, sensor networks, and the availability of big data have played a crucial role in improving the accuracy and effectiveness of these predictions.

While these examples showcase the potential of data-driven approaches, the field is continually evolving with ongoing research and technological advancements. Real-world success stories emphasize the importance of leveraging interdisciplinary knowledge and cutting-edge technologies to address the challenges associated with natural disaster prediction and mitigation.

CONCLUSION

In conclusion, the application of Artificial Neural Network (ANN) models for natural disaster prediction and mitigation represents a promising avenue for leveraging data-driven approaches to enhance our ability to anticipate and respond to catastrophic events. Throughout this chapter, we explored the significance of predicting natural disasters, the role of ANNs in predictive modeling, existing models, advantages over traditional methods, the development process, and challenges faced in implementation.

The significance of predicting natural disasters lies in the potential to save lives, protect infrastructure, and minimize the impact of these events on communities. ANNs, as powerful machine learning tools, offer a dynamic and adaptive framework for capturing complex patterns in diverse datasets, making them well-suited for natural disaster prediction tasks. Existing models and case studies demonstrate the practical applications of ANNs in diverse scenarios, from hurricane tracking to earthquake early warning systems. These models have showcased successful predictions, enabling timely and informed decision-making in the face of impending disasters.

Despite the successes, challenges persist. Limited and imbalanced data, interpretability issues, computational intensity, uncertainties in predictions, and the need for generalization to diverse conditions require careful consideration. Addressing these challenges necessitates ongoing research, collaboration, and the incorporation of advancements in machine learning and data science.

In moving forward, the development of ANN models for natural disaster prediction should be guided by a commitment to ethical practices, transparency, and responsible use of AI technologies. Interdisciplinary collaboration, including engagement with domain experts and stakeholders, is crucial for developing models that are not only accurate but also actionable and beneficial in real-world settings.

As technology continues to advance, and as more data becomes available, the potential for ANN models to revolutionize our approach to natural disaster prediction is considerable. By continuously refining models, addressing challenges, and staying at the forefront of research, we can harness the power of ANNs to build a safer and more resilient future in the face of natural disasters.

REFERENCES

Ayyappa, Y., & Krishna, A. (2020). Enhanced and Effective Computerized Multi Layered Perceptron based Back Propagation Brain Tumor Detection with Gaussian Filtering. *Proceedings of the Second International Conference on Inventive Research in Computing Applications (ICIRCA2020)*. IEEE. 10.1109/ICIRCA48905.2020.9182921

Chen, C. T., & Gu, G. X. (2020). Generative Deep Neural Networks for Inverse Materials Design Using Backpropagation and Active Learning. *Advancement of Science*, 7(5), 1–10. doi:10.1002/advs.201902607 PMID:32154072

Cichos, F., Gustavsson, K., Mehlig, B., & Volpe, G. (2020). Machine learning for active matter. *Nature Machine Intelligence*, 2(2), 94–103. doi:10.1038/s42256-020-0146-9

Cong, I., Choi, S., & Lukin, M. D. (2019). Quantum convolutional neural networks. *Nature Physics*, 15(12), 1273–1278. doi:10.1038/s41567-019-0648-8

García-Ródenas, R., Linares, L. J., & López-Gómez, J. A. (2020). Memetic algorithms for training feedforward neural networks: An approach based on gravitational search algorithm. *Neural Computing & Applications*, 33(7), 2561–2588. doi:10.1007/s00521-020-05131-y

Ginantra, N. L. W. S. R., Bhawika, G. W., Achmad Daengs, G. S., Panjaitan, P. D., Arifin, M. A., Wanto, A., Amin, M., Okprana, H., Syafii, A., & Anwar, U. (2021). Performance One-step secant Training Method for Forecasting Cases. *Journal of Physics: Conference Series*, 1933(1), 1–8. doi:10.1088/1742-6596/1933/1/012032

Leholo, S., Owolawi, P., & Akindeji, K. (2019). Solar Energy Potential Forecasting and Optimization Using Artificial Neural Network: South Africa Case Study. *2019 Amity Int. Conf. Artif. Intell.*, (pp. 533–536). IEEE. 10.1109/AICAI.2019.8701372

Novickis, R., Justs, D. J., Ozols, K., & Greitans, M. (2020). An Approach of Feed-Forward Neural Network. *Electronics (Basel)*, *9*(12), 2193. doi:10.3390/electronics9122193

Pham, B. T., Nguyen, M. D., Bui, K. T. T., Prakash, I., Chapi, K., & Bui, D. T. (2019). A novel artificial intelligence approach based on Multi-layer Perceptron Neural Network and Biogeography-based Optimization for predicting coefficient of consolidation of soil. Catena, 173. doi:10.1016/j.catena.2018.10.004

Rem, B. S., Käming, N., Tarnowski, M., Asteria, L., Fläschner, N., Becker, C., Sengstock, K., & Weitenberg, C. (2019). Identifying quantum phase transitions using artificial neural networks on experimental data. *Nature Physics*, *15*(9), 917–920. doi:10.1038/s41567-019-0554-0

Shende, K. V., Ramesh Kumar, M. R., & Kale, K. V. (2020). Comparison of Neural Network Training Functions for Prediction of Outgoing Longwave Radiation over the Bay of Bengal. *Adv. Intell. Syst. Comput.*, *1025*, 411–419. doi:10.1007/978-981-32-9515-5_39

Wang, H., Czerminski, R., & Jamieson, A. C. (2021). Neural Networks and Deep Learning. P. Einhorn, M., Löffler, M., de Bellis, E., Herrmann, A. & Burghartz, (eds.). The Machine Age of Customer Insight. Emerald Publishing Limited. doi:10.1108/978-1-83909-694-520211010

Wanto, A., & Zarlis, M. (2017). Analysis of Artificial Neural Network Backpropagation Using Conjugate Gradient Fletcher Reeves in the Predicting Process. *Journal of Physics: Conference Series*, *930*(1), 1–7.

Yan, E., Song, J., Liu, C., Luan, J., & Hong, W. (2020). Comparison of support vector machine, back propagation neural network and extreme learning machine for syndrome element differentiation. *Artificial Intelligence Review*, *53*(4), 2453–2481. doi:10.1007/s10462-019-09738-z

Yang, L., & Shami, A. (2020). On hyperparameter optimization of machine learning algorithms: Theory and practice. *Neurocomputing*, *415*, 295–316. doi:10.1016/j.neucom.2020.07.061

APPENDIX

```python
# Import necessary libraries
import numpy as np
import tensorflow as tf
from sklearn.model_selection import train_test_split
from sklearn.preprocessing import StandardScaler
from sklearn.metrics import accuracy_score, classification_report
# Generate synthetic weather data (features) and disaster labels
np.random.seed(42)
num_samples = 1000
weather_data = np.random.rand(num_samples, 5) # 5 weather features
disaster_labels = np.random.randint(2, size=num_samples) # Binary labels (0: No disaster, 1: Disaster)
# Split the data into training and testing sets
X_train, X_test, y_train, y_test = train_test_split(weather_data, disaster_labels, test_size=0.2, random_state=42)
# Standardize the data
scaler = StandardScaler()
X_train = scaler.fit_transform(X_train)
X_test = scaler.transform(X_test)
# Build the neural network model
model = tf.keras.Sequential([
tf.keras.layers.Dense(10, activation='relu', input_shape=(X_train.shape[1],)),
tf.keras.layers.Dense(1, activation='sigmoid')
])
# Compile the model
model.compile(optimizer='adam', loss='binary_crossentropy', metrics=['accuracy'])
# Train the model
model.fit(X_train, y_train, epochs=50, batch_size=32, verbose=1)
# Evaluate the model on the test set
y_pred = (model.predict(X_test) > 0.5).astype(int)
accuracy = accuracy_score(y_test, y_pred)
print(f'\nTest Accuracy: {accuracy * 100:.2f}%')
# Display classification report
print('\nClassification Report:\n', classification_report(y_test, y_pred))
```

Chapter 6
Predicting Rainfall by Fuzzy Logic:
A Preliminary Analysis of a Case Study in Mexico

Jaime Santos-Reyes
https://orcid.org/0000-0002-3758-9862
SEPI-ESIME, ZAC, Instituto Politecnico Nacional, Mexico

Yunue Garcia-Pimentel
Instituto Politécnico Nacional, Mexico

ABSTRACT

Water is vital to all living things; water is life. According to the UNDP water scarcity affects more than two billion people and it is projected to rise as temperatures do due to climate change. The chapter presents some preliminary results of rainfall prediction for the case of Mexico City by considering two input variables, temperature (T) and wind speed (WS). A fuzzy logic rule-based approach was employed in the analysis. The presented fuzzy logic model has the potential not only to predict rainfall but also drought. Moreover, it has also been highlighted that it becomes necessary to address droughts by designing and implementing drought disaster management systems to mitigate the impact of such events. Therefore, rainfall prediction, as an early warning, plays a key role in designing measures to achieve this. More generally, it is hoped that approaches such as the presented herein may contribute to a better understanding and management of water to mitigate the impacts of droughts in regions, cities, communities prone to the hazard.

DOI: 10.4018/979-8-3693-3362-4.ch006

INTRODUCTION

Water may be regarded as one of the most essential needs for life on Earth. It is believed that two billion people have been affected by water stress (UN-SDG, 2023). Given the great importance of water, and in particular the lack of it (drought), it has been taken into consideration in the 2030 UN agenda for Sustainable Development Goals (SDGs). The UN-SDGs aims at building an inclusive, sustainable, and resilient future for people and planet (UN-SDG, 2023). The 2030 agenda proposed 17 SDGs of which 7 are related to drought hazard, i.e.: Goals 1 ("No poverty"), 2 ("Zero hunger"), 3 ("Good health and well-being"), 6 ("Clean water and sanitation"), 11 ("Sustainable cities and communities"), 13 ("Climate action"), and 15 ("Life on land") (UN-SDG, 2023).

Drought is being defined as "a period of abnormally dry weather characterized by a prolonged deficiency of precipitation below a certain threshold over a large area and a period longer than a month." (Murray, et al., 2021). Four types of droughts have been defined (Murray, et al., 2021): (a) meteorological, (b) hydrological, (c) agricultural and (d) socioeconomic. The preset study deals with hydrological drought which "occurs when low water supply becomes evident and is associated with the effects of periods of precipitation shortfalls on surface or subsurface water supply." (p. 102).

Regarding one of the targets of Goal 6 of the SDGs states that,

"By 2030, substantially increase water-use efficiency across all sectors and ensure sustainable withdrawals and supply of freshwater to address water scarcity and substantially reduce the number of people suffering from water scarcity."

Moreover, it has been argued that,

"Population growth, accompanied by increased water use, will not only severely reduce water availability per person but also create stress on biodiversity in the entire global ecosystem. Other major factors that limit water availability include rainfall, temperature, evaporation rates, soil quality, vegetation type, and water runoff. Furthermore, serious difficulties already exist in fairly allocating the world's freshwater resources between and within countries." (Pimentel et al., 2004).

The above raises the question of the importance of rainfall prediction which is crucial in the process of drought management (see a later section for details on this). But what has been done in relation to rainfall prediction? A great deal of effort has been spent on the subject and it should be highlighted that artificial intelligent (AI) tools have been widely applied to rainfall and drought prediction (Oyounalsoud, et al., 2023; Kundu et al., 2023; Rathnayake, et al., 2023; Wen-Bing, 2024; Pham, et al., 2020; Zahran, et al., 2023; Janarthanan, et al., 2021; Asklany, et al., 2011; Manna and Anitha, 2023; Raham, 2020; Singla, et al., 2019; Agboola, et al., 2013; Hasan, et al., 2008). More importantly, the use of fuzzy sets and logic are predominantly employed in rainfall prediction. It has been argued that fuzzy set theory successfully represents any inference in AI applications by providing a logical and conceptual structure under uncertainty (Kahraman, 2023). Moreover, the authors argue that the theory is employed to transfer "human logical and flexible thinking processes to computational intelligence." (p. 158). Furthermore, the authors present the results of a review on the integration of fuzzy sets with other AI techniques such as neural networks, automated reasoning, machine learning, case-based reasoning, deep learning, information reasoning, symbolic reasoning, among others.

Research on rainfall prediction is lacking in the context of Mexico. The chapter addresses rainfall prediction by employing fuzzy rule-based system for the case of Mexico City. The analysis considers two input variables (temperature (T) and wind speed (WS)) and the rainfall (RF) as the output variable (see Limitations of the study section). The aims of the chapter are:

1. to construct a fuzzy ruled-based model to rainfall prediction for the case of Mexico City by considering two input variables T and WS.
2. to use the constructed fuzzy model to predict rainfall for the case of T= 20 °C and WS=12 km/h.

The chapter is organized as follows: first, a very brief description of some evidence of drought in Mexico City. Second, a description of the employed materials and methods are briefly described; third, the most relevant results are presented. Fourth, a discussion of the importance of water and related work is presented in the section; also, some limitations and future directions are given within the discussion section. Finally, some relevant conclusions are reported.

Figure 1. An example of a map of water shortages in the capital city
(a) Mexico City map of water shortages (PuntoporPunto, 2018).

Drought in Mexico City

Mexico City, once known as the "Venice of the New World", a floating gardens city, was built by the Aztecs (Watts, 2015). In the 16th century, however, Spanish *conquistadores* accelerated the process of draining the lakes. In modern times, engineers have almost completed the tasks, by replacing the lacustrine marshes with concrete, tarmac, and steel (Watts, 2015). Given the uncontrolled demographic expansion of the city, water supply for drinking, washing, cleaning, etc., is being pumped from hundreds of meters underground, or from more than 100 km. Figure 1 illustrates an example of the situation regarding water stress among the inhabitants of the megacity; in particular, the figure warns the city's residents of a massive water supply cuts from October 31 to November 4, 2008, affecting 16 boroughs.

Figure 2.

Figure 3.
Residents collecting water from tankers (Kazen, 2023; Hernandez, 2023).

More recently, the mayor of Mexico City, had to say this,

"The Cutzamala system [i.e., the system that provides water to the city which is comprised by seven dams] is in a critical situation, it has not received the water it was regularly receiving, it is not a new problem, it has been going on for several years." (Ramos, 2023). (Further issues related to droughts are given by Santos-Reyes, 2024).

DROUGHT RISK MANAGEMENT

In general, decision-makers in charge of managing disaster risk such as civil protection, usually concentrate on dealing with the consequences of disasters triggered by natural hazards such as droughts. That is, the taken approach may be regarded as reactive rather than proactive to disaster risk (Santos-Reyes & Beard, 2002).

Hence, there is a need for a drought disaster risk management aiming at mitigating the impact of disasters triggered by the hazard. Figure 2 shows the key elements of a disaster risk management, namely: monitoring & early warning, hazard event, impact assessment & response, recovery & reconstruction, planning & mitigation (Henny, et al., 2017; Wilhite et al 2005a). Henny, et al., content that the bottom half of the figure (impact assessment & response, recovery & reconstruction) represents drought crisis management to respond the impact of the hazard event. The upper half, on the other hand, represents the actions that need to be taken to mitigate the impact of future droughts.

Drought monitoring and prediction refers to a continuous process of the assessment of key indicators or variables and related impacts of drought severity; according to Hayes et al., (2012) by using this information to elicit response is called "early warning". To design and implement effective drought policies it is of vital importance to have an accurate early warning of the hazard. The present work is an example of the activities that should be taken within this stage of the risk management process.

Planning function aims at developing strategic actions and programmes to address drought risk and response actions that should be taken to mitigate the impact of these events (Wilhite et al., 2005b). Mitigation strategies may be referred to as specific activities taken prior to drought occurrence and to reduce long-term vulnerability of a community to droughts. However, there are not that many effective strategies available to risk reduction, i.e., "it is essential to identify and demonstrate effective approaches and opportunities for drought mitigation and preparedness, including case studies to show examples of good as well as weak policies. Policymakers, scientists, media, and the public often need to see actions at-work in order to foster buy-in to similar efforts." (UNISDR, 2006).

MATERIALS AND METHODS

Area of Study

The area of study of the ongoing research project is in the metropolitan area of Mexico City (Fig. 1), the southeast and the central region of the country. However, the preliminary results resented in the chapter are those related to the capital city of the country.

Figure 4. Drought risk management
(adapted from Henny, et al., 2017)

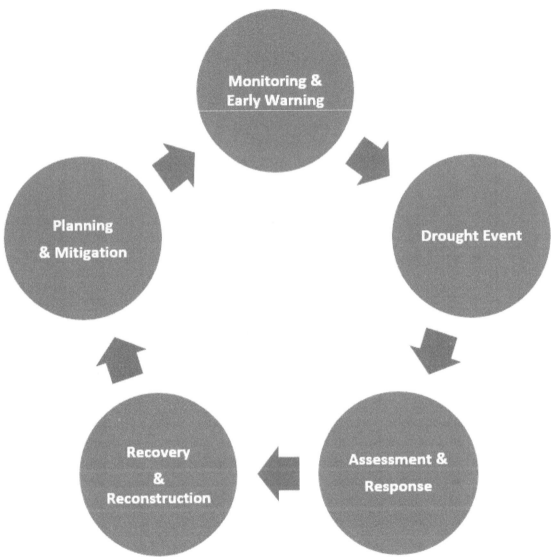

Data

Rainfall, temperature, and wind speed are difficult to get in remote communities and in the present study, data from a station in Mexico City was used in the analysis. Currently the research team is in the process of gathering data from governmental organizations in charge of the meteorological stations across the country and for those regions of study. (See the limitations of the study in a later section).

Fuzzy Sets and Logic

Fuzzy set **definition 1**. *"If X is a collection of objects denoted generically by x, then a fuzzy set A in X is a set of ordered parts."* (Zimmerman, 2010, p.318).

$$A = \{(x, \mu_A(x)) | x \in X\} \quad (1)$$

A $\mu_A(x)$ is called the membership function (generalized characteristic function) which maps X to the membership space M. The membership function of the fuzzy set is a crips (real-valued) function.

Definition 2. *"A type m fuzzy set is a fuzzy set whose membership values are type m-1, m >1, fuzzy sets on [0,1]."* (Zimmerman, 2010, p.318).

Definition 3. *"A linguistic variable is characterized by a quintuple $(x, T(x), U, G, M)$, in which x is the name of the variable, T(x) denotes the term set of x, i.e., the set of names of linguistic values of x. Each of these values is a fuzzy variable, denoted by X and ranging over a universe of discourse U, which is associated with the base variable u; G is a syntactic rule (which usually has the form of a grammar) for generating the name, X, of values of x. M is a semantic rule associated with each X its meaning. M(X) is a fuzzy subset of U."* (Zimmerman, 2010, p.319).

Membership Function

The most common membership functions are the following: bounded ramp, triangular, trapezoidal, s-shaped, sigmoid, Gaussian, and bell-shaped. In the present work, the triangular membership function has been used (Fig. 3).

A membership function $\mu(x)$, is said to be triangular on (a,b) if it ca be written as,

$$\mu(x) = \begin{cases} 0 & ; x \leq a \text{ or } x \geq c \\ \dfrac{x-a}{b-a} & ; a \leq x \leq b \\ \dfrac{c-x}{c-b} & ; b \leq x \leq c \\ 1 & ; x = b \end{cases} \quad (2)$$

The steps followed to develop the fuzzy logic system including the fuzzy expert system design; membership functions creation, fuzzy rule base development, fuzzification and defuzzification are described in the followed subsections.

Figure 5. Triangular membership function

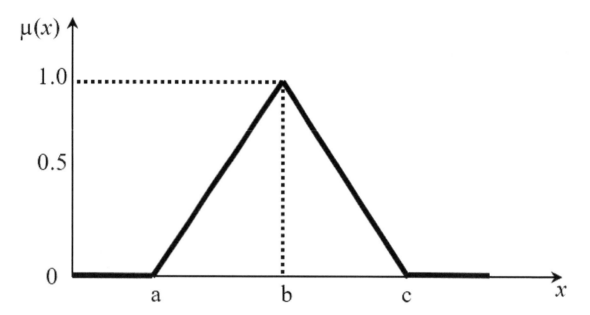

Fuzzy Inference System (FIS)

Overall, FIS involves three basic stages, i.e.:

Fuzzification. This stage involves transforming non-fuzzy variables into linguistic fuzzy variables by employing membership functions (see above).

Inference stage (Rule Base). At this stage, rules are formulated in the form of If…And…Then…, which is a combination of input and output variables.

Defuzzification. Overall, this stage involves the process of converting fuzzy data into numerical data (crisp value) for decision making.

Mamdani Fuzzy Inference System

The most commonly used fuzzy inference technique is the so-called Mamdani method (Ross,1994). Overall, the method involved four steps, i.e: fuzzification of the input variables, rule evaluation, aggregation of the rule outputs, and defuzzification.

The second stage involves taking the fuzzified inputs and apply them to the antecedents of the fuzzy rules. To evaluate the disjunction of the rule antecedents, then the OR fuzzy operation is performed.

Definition 4. *"Intersection (logical AND): the membership function of the intersection of two fuzzy sets A and B is defined as:"* (Zimmerman, 2010, p.319).

$$\mu_{A \cap B}(X) = min\{\mu_A(X), \mu_B(X)\} \forall_x \in X \tag{3}$$

Definition 5. *"Intersection (logical OR): the membership function of the union is defined as:"* (Zimmerman, 2010, p.319).

$$\mu_{A \cup B}(X) = max\{\mu_A(X), \mu_B(X)\} \forall_x \in x \tag{4}$$

Definition 6. *"Complement (negation): the membership function of the complement is defined as:"* (Zimmerman, 2010, p.319).

$$\mu_A(X) = 1 - \mu_A(X) \forall_x \in X \tag{5}$$

There are several methods for defuzzification where the Centroid method is one of the most used, i.e.:

$$z^* = \frac{\sum_{i=1}^{n} z_i \mu(z_i)}{\sum_{i=1}^{n} \mu(z_i)} \tag{6}$$

Where $\sum$ denotes the algebraic sum and where z is the centroid of each symmetric membership function (Ross, 2004).

FUZZY LOGIC MODEL DESCRIPTION

The section presents the main results of the analysis. The basic fuzzy logic system employs two input attributes (temperature and wind speed) and Rainfall as the output.

Input Variables

Temperature (T)

The fuzzy levels range between the minimum and maximum value of any temperature value. The temperature variable is divided into five fuzzy levels in a triangular membership function (Fig. 4 & Table 1); i.e., Very low, Low, Normal, High, and Very high. In the present case study, the temperature range varies from 8°C to 29 °C. Hence, the membership function Eqns. for each of the five linguistic variables are given in Eqns. (7) to (11).

Wind Speed (WS)

As with the temperature, the wind speed has been divided into five linguistic variables related to Very low, Low, Normal, High, and Very high (Fig. 5). In the present case study, the win speed range varies from 3 km/h to 18 km/h. Hence, the membership functions for each of the five linguistic variables are given in Eqns. (12) to (16).

Table 1. Fuzzy levels (Hasan, et al., 2008)

Abbreviation	Stands for	Meaning
NL	Negative large	Very low (VL)
NS	Negative small	Low (L)
ZE	Zero	Normal (N)
PS	Positive small	High (H)
PL	Positive large	Very high (VH)

Figure 6. Temperature membership diagram

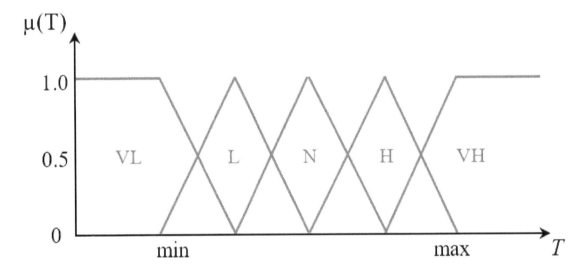

Figure 7. Wind speed membership diagram

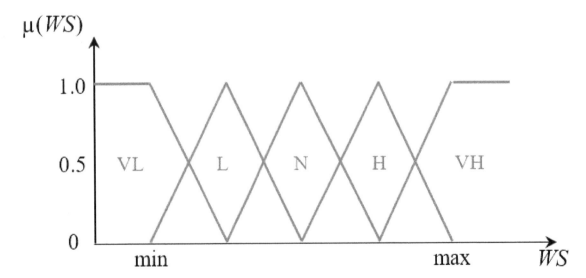

Predicting Rainfall by Fuzzy Logic

Figure 8. Rainfall membership diagram

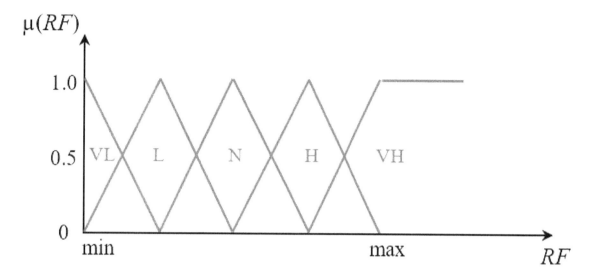

Temperature (T) membership functions:

$$\mu_{VL}(T) = \begin{cases} \dfrac{13.25 - T}{5.25} & ; if\ 8 \leq T \leq 13.25 \\ 0 & ; if\ T > 13.25 \end{cases} \quad (7)$$

$$\mu_{L}(T) = \begin{cases} \dfrac{T - 8}{5.25} & ; if\ 8 \leq T \leq 13.25 \\ \dfrac{18.5 - T}{5.25} & ; if\ 13.25 \leq T \leq 18.5 \\ 0 & ; if\ T > 18.5 \end{cases} \quad (8)$$

$$\mu_{N}(T) = \begin{cases} \dfrac{T - 13.5}{5.25} & ; if\ 13.25 \leq T \leq 18.5 \\ \dfrac{23.75 - T}{5.25} & ; if\ 18.5 \leq T \leq 23.75 \\ 0 & ; if\ T > 23.75 \end{cases} \quad (9)$$

$$\mu_H(T) = \begin{cases} \dfrac{T - 18.5}{5.25} & ; if\ 18.5 \leq T \leq 23.75 \\ \dfrac{29 - T}{5.25} & ; if\ 23.75 \leq T \leq 29 \\ 0 & ; if\ T < 18.5 \end{cases} \quad (10)$$

$$\mu_{VH}(T) = \begin{cases} \dfrac{T - 23.75}{5.25} & ; if\ 23.75 \leq T \leq 29 \\ 0 & ; if\ T < 23.75 \end{cases} \quad (11)$$

Wind speed (*WS*) membership functions:

$$\mu_{VL}(WS) = \begin{cases} \dfrac{6.75 - WS}{3.75} & ; if\ 3 \leq WS \leq 6.75 \\ 0 & ; if\ WS > 6.75 \end{cases} \quad (12)$$

$$\mu_L(WS) = \begin{cases} \dfrac{W - 3}{3.75} & ; if\ 3 \leq WS \leq 6.75 \\ \dfrac{10.5 - WS}{3.75} & ; if\ 6.75 \leq WS \leq 10.5 \\ 0 & ; if\ WS > 10.5 \end{cases} \quad (13)$$

$$\mu_N(WS) = \begin{cases} \dfrac{WS - 6.75}{3.75} & ; if\ 6.75 \leq WS \leq 10.5 \\ \dfrac{14.25 - WS}{3.75} & ; if\ 10.5 \leq WS \leq 14.25 \\ 0 & ; if\ WS > 14.25 \end{cases} \quad (14)$$

$$\mu_H(WS) = \begin{cases} \dfrac{WS - 10.5}{3.75} & ; if\ 10.5 \leq WS \leq 14.25 \\ \dfrac{18 - WS}{3.75} & ; if\ 14.25 \leq WS \leq 18 \\ 0 & ; if\ WS < 10.5 \end{cases} \quad (15)$$

$$\mu_{VH}(WS) = \begin{cases} \dfrac{WS - 14.25}{3.75} & ; if\ 14.25 \leq WS \leq 18 \\ 0 & ; if\ WS < 14.25 \end{cases} \tag{16}$$

Rainfall as the Output Variable

In the present case study, the output variable rainfall (*RF*) depends on the temperature and wind speed. Again, the variable is divided into five linguistic variables (Very low, Low, Normal, High, and Very high) in a triangular membership function (Fig. 3 & Table 1). Hence, the membership functions for each of the five linguistic variables are given in Eqns. (18) to (21).

$$\mu_{VL}(RF) = \begin{cases} \dfrac{29.5 - RF}{29.5} & ; if\ 0 \leq RF \leq 29.5 \\ 0 & ; if\ RF > 29.5 \end{cases} \tag{17}$$

$$\mu_{L}(RF) = \begin{cases} \dfrac{RF}{25.5} & ; if\ 0 \leq RF \leq 29.5 \\ \dfrac{59 - RF}{29.5} & ; if\ 29.5 \leq RF \leq 59 \\ 0 & ; if\ RF > 59 \end{cases} \tag{18}$$

$$\mu_{N}(RF) = \begin{cases} \dfrac{RF - 29.5}{29.5} & ; if\ 29.5 \leq RF \leq 59 \\ \dfrac{88.5 - RF}{29.5} & ; if\ 59 \leq RF \leq 88.5 \\ 0 & ; if\ RF > 88.5 \end{cases} \tag{19}$$

$$\mu_{H}(RF) = \begin{cases} \dfrac{RF - 59}{29.5} & ; if\ 59 \leq RF \leq 88.5 \\ \dfrac{118 - RF}{29.5} & ; if\ 88.5 \leq RF \leq 118 \\ 0 & ; if\ RF < 59 \end{cases} \tag{20}$$

$$\mu_{VH}(RF) = \begin{cases} \dfrac{RF - 88.5}{29.5} & ; if\ 88.5 \leq RF \leq 118 \\ 0 & ; if\ RF < 88.5 \end{cases} \tag{21}$$

An Application

Determine the amount of rainfall in a particular day with a temperature and wind speed of 20°C and 12 km/h. Table 2 shows the relationship of temperature and wind speed, and it is used at this stage of inference-based rules (Table 2).

Table 2. Relationship between temperature and wind speed (Hasa, et al., 2008)

		Wind Speed (W)				
		VL	L	N	H	VH
Temperature (T)	VL	VL	VL	L	L	N
	L	VL	L	L	N	N
	N	L	L	N	N	H
	H	L	N	N	H	H
	VH	N	N	H	H	VH

[*Rule 1*]: IF (T is **N**) ∩ (WS is **N**) THEN (RF is **N**)
[*Rule 2*]: IF (T is **N**) ∩ (WS is **H**) THEN (RF is **N**)
[*Rule 3*]: IF (T is **H**) ∩ (WS is **H**) THEN (RF is **N**)
[*Rule 4*]: IF (T is **H**) ∩ (WS is **H**) THEN (RF is **H**)

The results have highlighted that if temperature is N (0.7) and wind speed is N (0.6) then Rainfall is N (0.6) (see *Rule 1* above), i.e., by applying the Min function given in Eqn. (3). The same procedure was followed to determine the fuzzified rainfall for the given example. Finally, in the defuzzification stage, the fuzzy data is transformed into crisp data by employing the Centroid method (Eqn. (6)) and the predicted amount of rainfall was 64.53 mm.

DISCUSSION

In general, life on planet Earth depends on water for sustenance and livelihoods. For example, plant life provides 80% of human diet, and humans rely on drinking water, among other (UN-SDG, 2023). Hence, water is crucial for humanity's survival, and this raises the question as to what would happen if there were no water, i.e., drought. Given the implications of droughts, the natural hazard has been taken into consideration in the UN agenda for Sustainable Development Goals (SDGs), which aims at building an inclusive, sustainable, and resilient future for people and planet (UN-SDG, 2023).

To achieve the 2030 agenda, 17 SDGs have been considered and 7 are related to droughts, e.g., regarding Goal 6, the following two targets are relevant to drought hazard:

"By 2030, achieve universal and equitable access to safe and affordable drinking water for all."

"By 2030, substantially increase water-use efficiency across all sectors and ensure sustainable withdrawals and supply of freshwater to address water scarcity and substantially reduce the number of people suffering from water scarcity."

Hence, rainfall prediction (early warning) is crucial in the process of drought management (Fig. 2). Research has been conducted on several aspects of drought hazard (Achite, et al., 2023; Gohil, et al., 2024; Santos-Reyes, 2024), rainfall prediction (Kundu et al., 2023; Rathnayake, et al., 2023; Wen-Bing, 2024; Pham, et al., 2020; Janarthanan, et al., 2021; Asklany, et al., 2011; Manna & Anitha, 2023;), water management & sustainability (Senanayake, et al., 2024; Benzaouia, et al., 2023; Shekar & Mathew, 2023; Badola, et al., 2023; Shahfahad, et al., 2022; Ojo & Ogunjo, 2022). However, there are not published studies in the context of Mexico City.

The book chapter presented some preliminary results of rainfall prediction for the case of Mexico City. The employed approach has been the use of fuzzy logic rule-based and by considering two input variables, i.e., temperature and wind speed. The case study considered the temperature range from 8°C to 29°C and wind speed from 3 km/h to18 km/h, for the year 2023. Similar studies have been conducted on rainfall prediction by employing the two variables (Janarthanan, et al., 2021; Raham, 2020; Singla, et al., 2019; Agboola, et al., 2013). Hence, it may be argued that the employed approach has the potential to be employed not only in rainfall, but also in drought prediction in the ongoing research project.

Limitations of the Study and Future Work

As with any study, the presented analysis has limitations and the most relevant of these is the lack of quality and reliability of meteorological data; i.e., at this stage of the ongoing research project we are in the process of collecting historical data related to temperature, wind speed, among other, and therefore in the chapter only the model has been presented and it was not possible to elucidate, for example, the efficiency of the fuzzy ruled-based model for the case study. Further research includes, *inter alia*, to incorporate other variables in the model to rainfall prediction such as, pressure, dew point, humidity, cloud cover (Zahran, et al., 2023; Safar, et al., 2019).

CONCLUSION

Water is vital to all living things. According to the UNDP water scarcity affects more than 2 billion people and it is projected to rise as temperatures do due to climate change. Drought may be regarded as one of the most severe weather-related disasters and its causes impacts are not well understood (Henny, et al., 2017); drought is being regarded as a recurrent phenomenon and affecting large population (Vogt and Somma, 2000).

Hence it becomes necessary to address droughts by designing and implementing drought disaster management systems (Fig. 2) to mitigate the impact of such events. More importantly, as part of the management system, drought early warning becomes crucial in the management process. Therefore, rainfall prediction plays a key role in designing measures to better manage water in large population areas.

The book chapter presented some preliminary results of rainfall prediction for the case of Mexico City. The employed fuzzy logic rule-based approach has the potential to be used in predicting not only rainfall but also drought.

More generally, it is hoped that approaches such as the presented herein may contribute at better understanding and management of water to mitigate the impacts of droughts in regions, cities, and communities prone to the hazard.

ACKNOWLEDGEMENT

This project was funded under the following grant: SIP-IPN: No-20240864.

REFERENCES

Achite, M., Gul, E., Elshaboury, N., Jehanzaib, M., Mohammadi, B., & Danandeh Mehr, A. (2023). An improved adaptive neuro-fuzzy inference system for hydrological drought prediction in Algeria. *Physics and Chemistry of the Earth Parts A/B/C*, *131*, 103451. doi:10.1016/j.pce.2023.103451

Agboola, A. H., Gabriel, A. J., Aliyu, E. O., & Alese, B. K. (2013). Development of a fuzzy logic bases rainfall prediction model. *IACSIT International Journal of Engineering and Technology*, *3*(4), 427–435.

Asklany, S. A., Elhelow, K., Youssef, I. K., & El-wahab, M. A. (2011). Rainfall events prediction using rule-based fuzzy inference system. *Atmospheric Research*, *101*(1-2), 228–236. doi:10.1016/j.atmosres.2011.02.015

Badola, S., Mishra, V. N., Parkash, S., & Pandey, M. (2023). Rule-based fuzzy inference system for landslide susceptibility mapping along national highway 7 in Garhwal Himalayas, India. *Quaternary Science Advances*, *11*, 100093. doi:10.1016/j.qsa.2023.100093

Benzaouia, M., Hajji, B., Mellit, A., & Rabhi, A. (2023). Fuzzy-IoT smart irrigation system for precision scheduling and monitoring. *Computers and Electronics in Agriculture*, *215*, 108407. doi:10.1016/j.compag.2023.108407

Gohil, M., Mehta, D., & Shaikh, M. (2024). An integration of geospatial and fuzzy-logic techniques for multi-hazard mapping. *Results in Engineering*, *21*, 101758. doi:10.1016/j.rineng.2024.101758

Hasan, M., Tsegaye, T., Shi, X., Schaefer, G., & Taylor, G. (2008). Model for predicting rainfall by fuzzy set theory using USDA scan data. *Agricultural Water Management*, *95*(12), 1350–1360. doi:10.1016/j.agwat.2008.07.015

Hayes, M. J., Svoboda, M. D., Wardlow, B., Anderson, M. C., & Kogan, F. (2012). Drought monitoring: Historical and current perspectives. In B. D. Wardlow, M. C. Anderson, & J. P. Verdin (Eds.), *Remote Sensing for Drought: Innovative Monitoring Approaches* (pp. 1–19). CRC Press, Taylor and Francis Group.

Henny, A. J. Lanen, v., Vogt, J.V., Andreu, J., Carrão, H., de Stefano, L., Dutra, E., Feyen, L., Forzieri, G., Hayes, M., Iglesias, A., Lavaysse, C., Naumann, G., Pulwarty, R., Spinoni, J., Stahl, K., Stefanski, R., Stilianakis, N., Svoboda, M., & Tallaksen, L.M. (2017). Climatological risk: droughts. In K. Poljanšek, M. Marin-Ferrer, T. De Groeve, I. Clark (Eds.), Science for disaster risk management 2017: knowing better and losing less (271-293). EUR 28034 EN, Publications Office of the European Union, Luxembourg.

Hernandez, E. (2023). *Escasez de agua en CDMX en los próximos tres meses* [Water shortages in Mexico City in the next three months]. WRadio. https://wradio.com.mx/radio/2023/03/07/nacional/1678220822_571080.html

Janarthanan, R., Balamurali, R., Annapoorani, A., & Vimala, V. (2021). Prediction of rainfall using fuzzy logic. *Materials Today: Proceedings*, *37*(2), 959–963. doi:10.1016/j.matpr.2020.06.179

Kahraman, C., Cevik-Onar, S., Oztaysi, B., & Cebi, S. (2023). Role of fuzzy sets on artificial intelligence methods: A literature review. *Transactions on Fuzzy Sets and Systems*, *2*(1), 158–178. doi:10.30495/tfss.2023.1976303.1060

Kazen, G. (2023). La falta de agua en la GAM se agudizó por el vandalismo contra los pozos de Ecatepec [The lack of wáter in the GAM was worsened by the vandalism of the Ecatepec's wells]. *Herald Mexico*. https://heraldodemexico.com.mx/nacional/2023/6/22/la-falta-de-agua-en-la-gam-se-agudizo-por-el-vandalismo-contra-los-pozos-de-ecatepec-516144.html

Kundu, S., Biswas, S., Tripathi, D., Karmakar, R., Majumdar, S., & Mandal, S. (2023). A review on rainfall forecasting using ensemble learning techniques. *E-prime-Advances in Electrical Engineering. Electronics and Energy*, *6*, 100296. doi:10.1016/j.prime.2023.100296

Manna, T., & Anitha, A. (2023). Precipitation prediction by integrating rough set on fuzzy approximation space with deep learning techniques. *Applied Soft Computing*, *139*, 110253. doi:10.1016/j.asoc.2023.110253

Murray, V., Abrahams, J., Chadi, A., Kanza, A., Lucille, A., Djillali, B., Torres, B., & Hun, C. A., Cox, C., Douris, S., Lucy, F., Urbano, P., Qunli, H., John, H., Simon, H., Wirya, K., Lidia, M., Nick, M., Luiz Leal, M., & Natalie, W. (2021). Hazard Information Profiles: Supplement to UNDRR-ISC Hazard Definition & Classification Review: Technical Report. Geneva, Switzerland, United Nations Office for Disaster Risk Reduction; Paris, France, International Science Council. DOI: doi:10.24948/2021.05

Ojo, O. S., & Ogunjo, S. T. (2022). Machine learning models for prediction of rainfall over Nigeria. *Scientific African*, *16*, e01246. doi:10.1016/j.sciaf.2022.e01246

Oyounalsoud, S., Abdallah, M., Yilmaz, A. G., Siddique, M., & Atabay, S. (2023). A new meteorological drought index based on fuzzy logic: Development and comparative assessment with conventional drought indices. *Journal of Hydrology (Amsterdam)*, *619*, 129306. doi:10.1016/j.jhydrol.2023.129306

Pham, B. T., Le, L. M., Bui, K. T., Le, V. M., Ly, H. B., & Prakash, I. (2020). Development of advanced artificial intelligent models for daily rainfall prediction. *Atmospheric Research*, *237*, 104845. doi:10.1016/j.atmosres.2020.104845

Pimentel, D., Berger, B., Filiberto, D., Newton, M., Wolfe, B., Karabunakis, E., Clark, S., Poom, E., Abbett, E., & Nandagopal, S. (2004). Water Resources: Agricultural and environmental issues. *Bioscience*, *54*(1), 909–918. doi:10.1641/0006-3568(2004)054[0909:WRAAEI]2.0.CO;2

PuntoporPunto. (2018). *Mapa: Cortes de agua en la CDMX [Map: Water cuts in Mexico city]*. Puntopor Punto. https://www.puntoporpunto.com/multimedia/fotos/mapa-cortes-de-agua-en-la-cdmx/

Rahman, M. A. (2020). Improvement of rainfall prediction model by using fuzzy logic. *American Journal of Climate Change*, *9*(4), 391–399. doi:10.4236/ajcc.2020.94024

Ramos, R. (2023). *Aumentaron 100% los recortes de agua en la CDMX* [Water cuts increased 100% in Mexico City]. https://www.eleconomista.com.mx/politica/Aumentaron-100-los-recortes-de-agua-en-la-CDMX-20231220-0123.html

Rathnayake, N., Rathnayake, U., Chathuranika, I., Dang, T. L., & Hoshino, Y. (2023). Cascade-ANFIS to simulate nonlinear rainfall-runoff relationship. *Applied Soft Computing*, *147*, 110722. doi:10.1016/j.asoc.2023.110722

Ross, T. J. (1994). *Fuzzy logic with engineering applications* (2nd ed.). John Wiley & sons Ltd.

Safar, N. Z. M., Ramli, A., Mahdin, H., Nzdi, D., & Khalif, K. M. N. (2019). Rain prediction using fuzzy rule based system in North-West Malaysia. *Indonesian Journal of Electrical Engineering and Computer Science*, *14*(3), 1572–1581.

Santos-Reyes, J. (2024). Awareness and risk perception of a multi-hazard megacity: The case of adolescent students. *Safety Science*, *171*, 106382. doi:10.1016/j.ssci.2023.106382

Santos-Reyes, J., & Beard, A. N. (2002). Assessing Safety Management Systems. *Journal of Loss Prevention in the Process Industries*, *15*(2), 77–95. doi:10.1016/S0950-4230(01)00066-3

Senanayake, S., Pradhan, B., Wedathanthirige, H., Alamri, A., & Park, H. J. (2024). Monitoring soil erosion in support of achieving SDGs: A special focus on rainfall variation and farming systems vulnerability. *Catena*, *234*, 107537. doi:10.1016/j.catena.2023.107537

Shahfahad, N., Naikoo, M. W., Talukdar, S., Das, T., & Rahman, A. (2022). Identification of homogenous rainfall regions with trend analysis using fuzzy logic and clustering approach coupled with advanced trend analysis techniques in Mumbai city. *Urban Climate*, *46*, 101306. doi:10.1016/j.uclim.2022.101306

Shekar, P. R., & Mathew, A. (2023). Assessing groundwater potential zones and artificial recharge sites in the monsoon-fed Merredu river basin, India: An integrated approach using GIS, AHP, and Fuzzy-AHP. *Groundwater for Sustainable Development*, *23*, 100994. doi:10.1016/j.gsd.2023.100994

Singla, M. K., Kar, H. D., & Nijhawan, P. (2019). Rain prediction using fuzzy logic. *International Journal of Engineering and Advanced Technology*, *9*(1), 2796–2799.

UN-SDG (UN-Sustainable Development Goals). (2023). *Sustainable development goals*. UN. https://www.un.org/sustainabledevelopment/

UNISDR. (2006). *Global Survey of Early Warning Systems*. United Nations International Strategy for Disaster Reduction Geneva.

Vogt, J. V., & Somma, F. (2000). *Drought and Drought Mitigation in Europe - Advances in Natural and Technological Hazards Research 14*. Kluwer Academic Publishers. doi:10.1007/978-94-015-9472-1

Watts, J. (2015). Mexico City's water crisis-from source to sewer. *The Guardian*. https://www.theguardian.com/cities/2015/nov/12/mexico-city-water-crisis-source-sewer

Wen-Bing, J. (2024). Implementing advanced techniques for urban mountain torrent surveillance and early warning using rainfall predictive analysis. *Urban Climate*, *53*, 101782. doi:10.1016/j.uclim.2023.101782

Wilhite, D. A., Botterill, L., & Monnik, K. (2005a). National Drought Policy: Lessons Learned from Australia, South Africa, and the United States. In: Wilhite, D. (ed.). Drought and water crises: science, technology, and management issues (137-172). CRC Press.

Wilhite, D. A., Hayes, M. J., & Knutson, C. L. (2005b). Drought preparedness planning: building institutional capacity. In: Wilhite, D. (ed.),2005. Drought and water crises: science, technology, and management issues (93-121), CRC Press.

Zahran, B., Ayyoub, B., Abu-Ain, W., Hadi, W., & Al-Hawary, S. (2023). A fuzzy based model for rainfall prediction. *International Journal of Data and Network Science*, 7(1), 97–106. doi:10.5267/j.ijdns.2022.12.001

Zimmermann, H. J. (2010). Fuzzy set theory. *Wiley Interdisciplinary Reviews: Computational Statistics*, 2(3), 317–332. doi:10.1002/wics.82

Chapter 7
A Comprehensive Investigation of Underwater Disaster Prediction Using Machine Learning Algorithms

Nivethitha R.
Velammal College of Engineering and Technology, India

Sivasankari Jothiraj
https://orcid.org/0000-0002-8054-1020
Velammal College of Engineering and Technology, India

Divya Bharathi P.
KLN College of Engineering and Technology, India

Sathish Kumar D.
Nehru Institute of Technology, India

ABSTRACT

Underwater disasters cause severe consequences to marine ecology and lead to significant loss to the environment. Since the sea water temperature reaches 700° Fahrenheit, disasters like hydrothermal vents and underwater volcano eruptions occur. Due to these seireachests, marine creatures like sharks and different types of living species have been excavating under the ocean. The risk of underwater disasters like underwater volcanic eruption, tsunami, underwater earthquake, submarine accidents and oil spills are crucial, and the preventive measures of these calamities were highly needed. Oceanographic data includes underwater images and videos captured by marine archaeologists and divers to know the information about the exploited resources. Existing traditional algorithms have practical limitations to predict underwater catastrophes under more depth condition and can be overcome by machine learning (ML) algorithms, since it was accurate and fast in analyzing the oceanographic data. This chapter provides a comprehensive review of predicting underwater disasters using ML algorithms.

DOI: 10.4018/979-8-3693-3362-4.ch007

INTRODUCTION

Underwater disasters can occur due to several conditions which results in critical issues and damage to life, property and environmental impact. Underwater disasters refer to catastrophic events that occur beneath the surface of water bodies, such as oceans, seas, or lakes (Liu et al., 2018). These disasters can have severe consequences on both human life and the environment. Some of the underwater disasters were Tsunamis, Underwater earthquakes, Underwater volcanoes, Oil spills, Submarine Accidents etc.

Natural disasters such as earthquakes, tsunamis, hurricanes, cyclones, or volcanic eruptions can create underwater disasters. Figure 1 represents the diagrammatic representation of natural disasters like Underwater volcanoes and Figure 2 represents the Tsunamis. The above-mentioned disasters disturbs the marine ecology and causes the destruction of coastal infrastructure, and disturbances in the seabed, leading to submerged hazards.

Figure 1. Visual illustration of sample underwater disasters: Underwater volcano

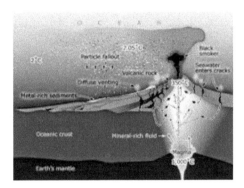

Figure 2. Visual illustration of sample underwater disasters: Tsunami

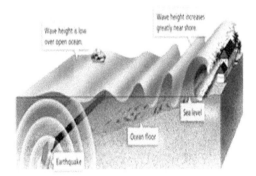

Underwater volcanoes also called as seamounts that are located beneath the surface of the ocean. These volcanoes arise due to volcanic activity on the ocean floor. They can also be found along mid-ocean ridges and volcanic arcs. Underwater volcanoes are typically formed through the same process as their terrestrial counterparts. As the magma reaches the surface, it erupts, releasing gases and ash, and forming new land. The water was polluted and the microorganisms were slowly exploited by the released gas and ashes. However, underwater volcanoes have some unique characteristics since they are mounted underwater. The water pressure on the ocean floor suppresses the formation of gas bubbles in magma, resulting in smoother and more fluid eruptions. These eruptions can lead to the formation of large underwater lava flows.

Figure 1 shows the Underwater volcano releasing gases and ash which affects the marine ecosystem. Underwater volcanoes also have a considerable effect on marine ecosystems. They provide a habitat for different underwater organisms, including bacteria, fungi, and deep-sea animals. The nutrient-rich volcanic substances liberated during eruptions support diverse communities of marine life. Some underwater volcanoes even host hydrothermal vent systems, where superheated water rich in minerals gushes out, supporting unique ecosystems with specialized organisms.

Figure 3. Visual illustration of sample underwater disasters: Oil spill in underwater

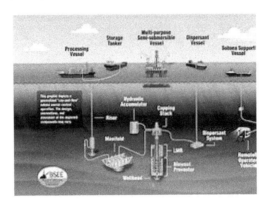

Figure 4. Real image dataset of underwater disasters: Effect due to underwater volcano eruption

Tsunamis are huge tides typically triggered by earthquakes, volcanic eruptions, or underwater landslides. These destructive waves can cause widespread flooding, destruction of coastal communities, and massive loss of life. The gas explosions, discharge of poisonous gases, water and air pollution were the causes owing to volcanic eruptions.

Figure 5. Real image dataset of underwater disasters: Marine ecosystem degradation due to oil spills

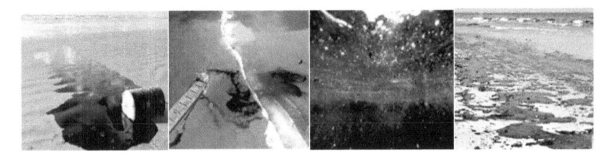

Figure 6. Real image dataset of underwater disasters: Effect of underwater earthquake (Tsunami)

Figure 7. Real image dataset of underwater disasters: Submarine shipwrecks

Accidental or deliberate release of oil into the water can harm marine life, destroy habitats, and impact local economies. Figure 2 represents the illustration of rising of giant waves (tsunami) from the seabed. Figure 3 represents the oil spills in underwater environment which refers to the accidental or deliberate release of oil into the water column or ocean floor. These spills can have devastating environmental and ecological impacts. When oil spills occur underwater, it results in the formation of oil slicks or plimes in the water column. An oil spill causes the poisonous substance collided with underwater and spoils the marine habitats such as coral reefs, seagrass beds and mangroves. It remains as the long-term effect and even exploits the marine organisms. Figure 4 represents the different types of real accidents of underwater disasters like volcanic eruption, oil spills and underwater earthquakes and submarine Shipwrecks.

Submarine Shipwrecks caused by a vessel sinks or runs aground, which lead to loss of life, environmental pollution and damage to marine ecosystems. Also, it is notable that submarine accidents are sometimes caused by human errors. Underwater disasters not only happen by natural events but also it can occur by human errors like negligence or recklessness. Human errors like collision between ships or submarines, not proper handling of equipment and machineries, offshore drilling operations, due to explosive materials in ships. Underwater disasters are critical for evolving protective and precautionary aids and improving disaster management strategies. Proper surveillance, maintenance of infrastructure, adherence to safety protocols, and effective dangerous crisis response systems can minimize the risk and consequences of such disasters.

It typically involves training a model on a labeled dataset and classifies using that model to make predictions or decisions on new, unseen data and it is used to predict these consequences (Lou et al., 2023; Goel et al, 2022). Big dataset can be used to create much more accurate Machine Learning algorithms that are actually viable in the technical industry. The capacity of machines to learn on their own without being programmed in detail by humans has also been addressed by many researchers.

A rapidly developing field of technology, machine learning allows computers to automatically learn from previous data. For building mathematical models and making predictions based on historical data or information, machine learning employs various algorithms and used for different tasks, including speech recognition, email filtering, auto-tagging on Facebook, a recommender system, and image recognition (Ahmad, 2019).

This paper contains the assorted modules with three sections. Section II outlines about the different existing and evolving methodologies for underwater prediction. Section III describes about experimental results of underwater disaster exploration. Furthermore, Section IV subjects the Conclusion and Future research direction.

METHODOLOGIES

In this section, we consolidated the different methodologies of underwater disaster prediction based on Machine Learning Algorithms. The evolution of various ML algorithms was explained in the existing system over the recent years, followed by the steps of data analysis utilizing ML algorithm and the prediction of submarine volcano eruption using CNN was explained in this section.

Existing System

In (Abdalzaher et al., 2023), author addressed the benefit of Machine Learning algorithms which is applied for earthquake parameters observation leading to an efficient Earthquake Early Warning System. This system introduces a generic EEWS architecturein which various components using IOT and analysed dataset can be handled based on machine learning algorithms. Also, this architecture is completely work based on IOT and Machine learning.In (Yuen et al. 2022), author presented a real incident of volcanic eruption followed by Tsunami happened in Tonga on January 15, 2022. A huge eruption commenced by releasing clouds of ashes of 20 km into the atmosphere. The footage of this event from an aircraft can be shown in Figure 8. Intense lighting was recorded during the eruption time. Heavy shockwaves of ocean were propagated and the Shockwave from the Hunga Tonga eruption captured by GOES-17 satellite (GOES-West) (Yuen et al. 2022).

Figure 8. Footage clips of Hunga Tunga eruptive event captured by aircraft

Authors in (Feng et al., 2022) presented the EMD method for the appropriate wave prediction to avoid the disasters and heavy loss. This method was compared the wave height prediction performance of the Recurrent Neural Network (RNN), long short-term memory network (LSTM) and gated recurrent unit network (GRU). By this comparative analysis, the accurate network of wave height prediction can be known.

The three stages of submarine landslide disaster evolution were proposed in (Shan et al., 2022). By these stages like slope instability evolution stage, deformation of landslide stage and the stage of landslide deposition. An early warning of submarine landslide disasters involves these three stages for the prediction of submarine disasters. Figure 9 shows the different root causes of submarine landslide.

The typhoon disaster information detection model based on Machine learning was proposed in (Yu et al., 2019). The model has a design of classification system based on social media dataset of typhoon damage. This dataset contains the information about the typhoon respective to category labels. It trains the deep learning model to gather information and to predict the disaster situation. For further data analysis, the verification test can be experimented using "Weibo" dataset of typhoon disaster in underwater.

Figure 9. Visual illustration of submarine landslide

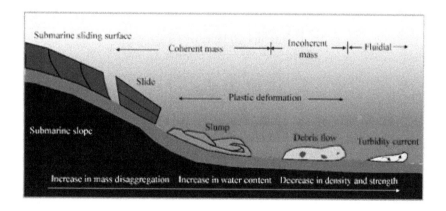

The different advancements that has been used to control the consequences of underwater noise pollution caused by the various underwater sounds like piling, pole drilling and machinery noises were addressed in (Kuşku etal., 2018). This paper also pinpoints the real practical issues and the shortcomings because of pole drilling which is experienced recently.

Analyzing Data Using Machine Learning

Underwater disaster prediction can be accomplished by examining the existing datasets using ML algorithms and inferring potential underwater disasters. By using the observed datasets, the specified algorithm can be used for identification of different disasters. Figure 10 represents the simplified overview of the process. The accuracy of predictions highly depends on the subjective and objective analysis of data, feature selection, and the selection of ML algorithms over the different algorithms and technique since underwater disasters are difficult task for prediction process (Deo et al., 2015).

The relevant data sources include oceanographic data, underwater sensor data, satellite imagery, and historical disaster records were required. The facts are yielded from these data sources about water temperature, salinity, currents, weather patterns, seismic activity, and other factors which lead to underwater disasters (Zhou et al., 2017). The collected data needs to be preprocessed by normalizing the gathered data to ensure consistency and remove any irrelevant or noisy information. This step may involve removing outliers, handling missing values, and converting data into suitable formats for further analysis. The feature selection is the most informative feature from the preprocessed data. Valuable insights about the data and various feature selection techniques such as correlation analysis, statistical tests, or dimensionality reduction algorithms can also be used.

Figure 10. Simplified schematic of the ML algorithm

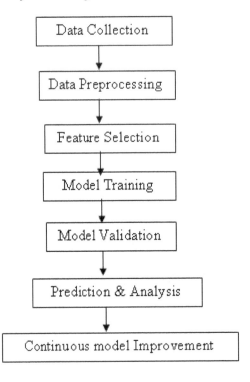

Training model implemented by feeding the selected features along with labeled historical disaster data into a ML model to train it (Rasouli et al., 2012; Kim et al., 2014). Figure 9 illustrates the schematic representation of machine learning algorithm. There are different models suitable for this task namely decision trees, SVM. The working of these models can be varied in according to the various applications.

The first and foremost step is prediction and analysis of the validated data. The trained model have to be deal with new or real-time data to foreseeing the possibility of underwater disasters. The model can analyze the collected data, identify patterns, and provide early warnings or risk assessments. Monitoring the model's performance over time and collecting feedback from users or domain experts. Continuously refine the model by incorporating new data and adapting to emerging disaster patterns to improve accuracy and effectiveness (Rosso et al., 2020; Mosavi et al., 2018).

Disaster Prediction Using Underwater Image Formation Model (IFM)

Underwater image enhancement using Image Formation Model methods are used to enrich and intensify the distorted and degraded images (Chiang and Chen, 2012). The input dataset images were attained from the marine divers and underwater photographers for the marine dataset and enhanced using the different image enhancement analysis for the better prediction of submarine volcanoes. For an image dataset, there are various conventional deep learning algorithms for image enhancement process. In this article, we analyzed the dark channel prior method for submarine volcano image analysis since it is an efficient algorithm among the image enhancement techniques. This method uses the image formation model with the support of divergent hazing steps to find the root cause of the disaster.

The underwater imaging model can be analytically formulated as,

$$U(t) = p(t)D(t) + a(1 - D(t)) \qquad (1)$$

$U(t)$ represents hazy image, $p(t)$ is the radiance recovered image, $D(t)$ is the transmission map and a is atmospheric light. Figure 11 illustrates the sample raw underwater images underwater volcano dataset.

Figure 11. Raw image dataset of sample underwater volcano

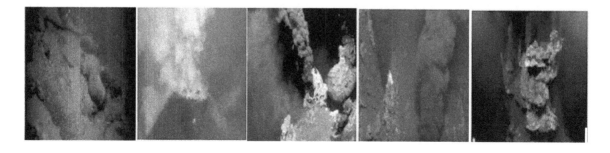

Since CNN predominantly used for object recognition and image classification, it clearly distinguishes the intensity of each element of the processed image. Since it removes the fading effects and scattering effects of the captured underwater images and produces the clear saturation tone of the original image. As a result, this objective framework was used for quality exploration of marine disasters. The CNN architecture has been illustrated in Figure 12.

Figure 12. CNN architecture

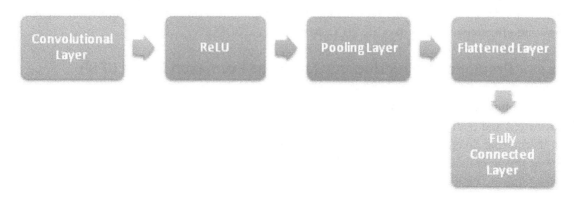

Exploration of underwater archaeological sites is more difficult than land-based sites. In underwater world, the diverse problems like underwater volcano eruption and hydrothermal vents under the ocean which leads to major disaster like sea ecology exploitation. Therefore, preservation of underwater substances is equally significant for oceanic geological exploration. To conserve these submerged remains, there is a need of information about the marine heritage. To identify these objects lies under the sea, Convolutional Neural Networks (CNN) based enhancement algorithm were highly used. Due to this condition, Convolutional Neural Network is made up of multiple layers and specially designed to work with images. CNN involves Convolutional layers, Activation function such as Rectified Linear Unit (ReLU), Pooling layers, Flattened layer and fully connected layer (Sun et al., 2018).

In this model, we analysed the various layers categorised by different operations which is used to perform the object recognition and classification in this model. There will be large dataset of image or video information can be needed for this system. The main adversity of this system is to perform the task with numerous datasets by human. Despite of large dataset of image or video data, machine learning algorithms automates data by repetitive tasks to improve the efficiency of image recognition, object classification, summarizing videos.

EXPERIMENTAL RESULTS AND DISCUSSIONS

Almost 50 open source images were extracted from the underwater maritime heritage dataset for testing. Note that our dataset comprises of images captured by the camera positioning in different angles and at different underwater depth. Figure 9 shows the submarine volcano erupted images before enhancement and after enhancement. The top row of figure 13 depicts the submarine volcano erupted images before enhancement and the bottom row of figure 13 shows the erupted images after enhancement.

Figure 13. Sample underwater disaster images before enhancement and after enhancement

The level of turbidity, moisture content and pH content of underwater varies due to the nature of light propagation. It is hard to find normal vents and active volcanoes in the deep ocean in these environmental conditions (Jordan and Mitchell, 2015; Choi et al., 2019). To recognize these vents and volcanoes from the deep ocean, we have implemented our algorithm for these dataset images.

Table 1 shows the Quantitative comparison of the five raw underwater volcano images and enhanced images. For this quantitative evaluation of six metrics such as Entropy Error, AMBE, MSE, PSNR, UICM and UCIQE, the raw underwater images and the enhanced images were simulated using MATLAB software.

Entropy is a numerical parameter used to determine the randomness and fine quality details of an enhanced image. It can be represented mathematically as,

$$E = -\sum_{i=0}^{N-1} q_i \log_2 q_i \qquad (2)$$

q_i indicates the scalar value of information content of a given image. An Entropy error value can be used to characterize the texture of the input image and reconstruct the image. An image quality and entropy are inversely proportional as quality increases entropy error of an enhanced image decreases.

AMBE computes the absolute value of the difference in the mean brightness of the original image and the enhanced image. The mathematical representation of numerical metric AMBE is given below. P indicates the original image and Q indicates the enhanced image of order mXn. i and j represents corresponding row and column of pixel.

$$AMBE = E(P) - E(Q) \qquad (3)$$

In this case, AMBE is inversely proportional to the quality of an image. The visual quality of an enhanced image is greater when AMBE yields lower values. m and n represent the number of rows and columns respectively.

$$E(P) = \frac{1}{mn} \sum_i \sum_j P(i,j) \qquad (4)$$

Table 1. Quantitative comparison in terms of Entropy Error, AMBE, MSE, PSNR, UICM, and UCIQE for the Figure 2 (row 1-5)

	Original Image						CNN based Enhanced output image					
	Entropy Error	AMBE	MSE	PSNR	UICM	UCIQE	Entropy Error	AMBE	MSE	PSNR	UICM	UCIQE
Image 1	1.2248	2.3871	4.2517	29.8472	0.0014	1.7784	0.7430	0.1391	0.0246	64.2266	0.0080	2.8137
Image 2	0.8457	1.4474	2.5749	28.3296	0.0007	0.4351	0.8457	1.4474	2.5749	28.3296	0.0007	0.4351
Image 3	0.4115	4.3895	0.4725	39.5821	0.0023	1.6674	0.3413	0.1289	0.0388	62.2442	0.0041	3.8974
Image 4	0.7741	1.2581	4.3365	11.2585	0.0071	2.3369	0.6965	0.0635	0.0347	62.7315	0.0010	3.4929
Image 5	2.1258	8.3364	2.5776	21.9723	0.4798	1.2883	1.0452	0.0366	0.0195	65.2238	0.0032	2.8426

$$E(Q) = \frac{1}{mn} \sum_i \sum_j Q(i,j) \tag{5}$$

MSE is the most common statistical parameter to measure an image quality which is representation of absolute error. It measures the average of the square of the errors and often referred to as standard deviation of the variance. The mathematical representation of MSE between two images, original image $P(i, j)$ and enhanced image $Q(i,j)$ was given below.

$$MSE = \frac{1}{mn} \sum_{i=1}^{m} \sum_{j=1}^{n} |P(i,j) - Q(i,j)|^2 \tag{6}$$

It provides higher image quality when the MSE value is reduced. MSE value will be zero when two images are identical.

PSNR is a good measure for comparing removal of distortion result of original image and reconstructed image. Typical value of PSNR for an enhanced image is 25 to 35dB. PSNR (dB) strongly depends upon the MSE value. The computation of PSNR value can be done by,

$$PSNR(dB) = 10 \log_{10} \left[\frac{(L-1)^2}{MSE} \right] \tag{7}$$

An image quality metrics UCIM and UCIQE was used to determine the color correction performance of every algorithm. The above-mentioned quantitative measures characterize the quality of an image. With this enhanced image, we able to know about the information of the fine details of an image.

Figure 14. Comparison chart-causes of tsunami

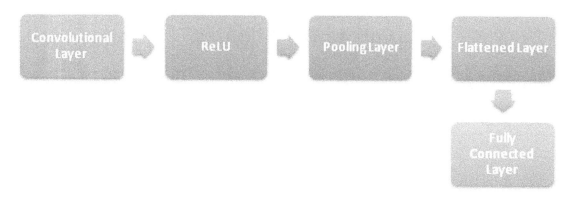

Figure 14 represents the comparison chart of root causes of Tsunami. The source of information was interpreted by NOAA.

Figure 15. Comparison chart of underwater disasters

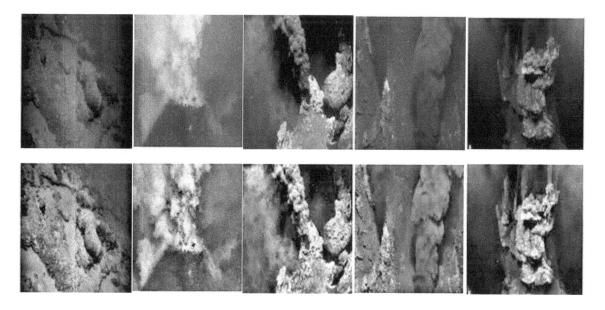

Figure 15 represents the comparison chart of underwater disasters and damage caused. It illustrates the submarine earthquakes leads the high damage and loss than the remaining disasters like landslide, Volcano(Krinitskiy, 2017; Deo, 2010). Figure 16 show the graphical representation of tsunamis frequency by countries like Japan, USA, Indonesia, Greece, Chile, Italy, Philippines, Turkeyand Mexico which is more than 50. In this comparison, Japan leads high by the caused tsunami over frequency 350 and Turkey attained least place about frequency of 60.

Figure 16. Graphical representation of tsunamis over frequency of count 50

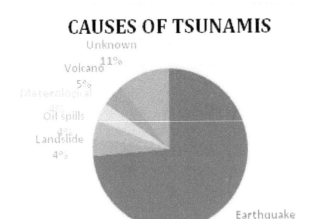

Generally ML algorithms like Bayes theorem, Support vector machine, K-Classifier, Decision tree algorithm can be applied with the help of data analysis (Asefa et al., 2006).

CONCLUSION

This paper investigates the root causes of various underwater disasters and submarine accidents. In oceanographic data analysis, using manpower leads to many risk factors since it is highly challenging environment. In recent years, the algorithms like Artificial Intelligence and the loss and damage can be reduced with the ML algorithm. Machine learning based algorithms uses the statistical and optimization techniques in the field of marine heritage. Machine learning is completely data driven algorithm. These algorithms completely focus on the collected information of the underwater data.

This paper gives the comprehensive review of the recent algorithms used in the analysis of underwater disasters and the machine learning data driven research steps. We included the deep image formation model to predict and analyse the underwater volcano. The subjective and objective results were illustrated in the results and discussion section. Based on the Literature survey of disasters data collection, the graphical illustration of the underwater disasters was summarized.

Due to the nature and its climate change, we couldn't control the underwater natural disasters, but we may avoid the consequences produced by these disasters by using machine learning based algorithms. Machine learning algorithms have high potential to improve the quality of marine research approaches. This survey pinpoints the fair evaluation of the existing algorithms and provides the key insights to the future researchers.

REFERENCES

Abdalzaher, M. S., Elsayed, H. A., Fouda, M. M., & Salim, M. M. (2023). *Employing Machine Learning and IoT for Earthquake Early Warning System in Smart Cities*. MDPI, Energies. doi:10.3390/en16010495

Ahmad, H. (2019). Machine Learning Applications in oceanography. *International Aquatic Research.*, 161–169. doi:10.3153/AR19014

Asefa, T., Kemblowski, M., McKee, M., & Khalil, A. (2006). Multitime scale stream flow predictions: The support vector machines approach. *Journal of Hydrology (Amsterdam)*, *318*(1-4), 7–16. doi:10.1016/j.jhydrol.2005.06.001

Chiang, J. Y., Chen, Y. C., & Chen, Y. C. (2012). Underwater Image Enhancement: Using Wavelength Compensation and Image Dehazing (WCID). *IEEE Transactions on Image Processing*, *21*(4), 1756–1769. doi:10.1109/TIP.2011.2179666 PMID:22180510

Choi, J., Choo, Y., & Lee, K. (2019). Acoustic classification of surface and underwater vessels in the ocean using supervised machine learning. *Sensors (Basel)*, *19*(16), 3492. doi:10.3390/s19163492 PMID:31404999

Deo, R. C., & Sahin, M. (2015). Application of the extreme learning machine algorithm for the prediction of monthly effective drought index in eastern Australia. *Atmospheric Research*, *153*, 512–525. doi:10.1016/j.atmosres.2014.10.016

Feng, Z., Hu, P., Li, S., & Mo, D. (2022). Prediction of Significant Wave Height in Offshore China Based on the Machine Learning Method. MDPI. *Journal of Marine Science and Engineering*, *10*(6), 836. doi:10.3390/jmse10060836

Goel, & Kumar, A. (2022). *The role of artifcial neural network and machine learning in utilizing spatial information*. Springer. doi:10.1007/s41324-022-00494-x

Jordan, M. I., & Mitchell, T. M. (2015). Machine learning: Trends, perspectives, and prospects. *Science*, *349*(6245), 255–260. doi:10.1126/science.aaa8415 PMID:26185243

Kim, Y. H., Im, J., Ha, H. K., Choi, J. K., & Ha, S. (2014). Machine learning approaches to coastal water quality monitoring using goci satellite data. *GIScience & Remote Sensing*, *51*(2), 158–174. doi:10.1080/15481603.2014.900983

Krinitskiy, M. (2017). Application of machine learning methods to the solar disk state detection by all-sky images over the ocean. *Oceanology, Academy of Sciences of the USSR*, *57*(2), 265–269. doi:10.1134/S0001437017020126

Kuşku, H., Yigit, M., Ergun, S., Yigit, U., & Taylor, N. (2018). *Acoustic noise pollution from Marine Industrial activities: Exposure and Impacts*. Aquatic Research.

Liu, X., Wang, Y., Zhang, W., & Guo, X. (2023). Susceptibility of typical marine geological disasters: An overview. Springer Open. *Geoenvironmental Disasters*, *10*(1), 10. Advance online publication. doi:10.1186/s40677-023-00237-6

Lou, Lv, R., Dang, Z., Su, S., Li, T., Xinfang. (2023). *Application of machine learning in ocean data*. Springer Nature.

Mosavi, A., Ozturk, P., & Chau, K. (2018). Flood prediction using machine learning models: Literature review. *Water (Basel)*, *10*(11), 1536. doi:10.3390/w10111536

Rasouli, K., Hsieh, W. W., & Cannon, A. J. (2012). Daily streamflow forecasting by machine learning methods with weather and climate inputs. *Journal of Hydrology (Amsterdam)*, *414*, 284–293. doi:10.1016/j.jhydrol.2011.10.039

Rosso, I., Mazloff, M.R., Talley, L.D., Purkey, S.G., Freeman, N.M., & Maze, G. (2020). Water mass and biogeochemical variability in the Kerguelen sector of the Southern Ocean: A machine learning approach for a mixing hot spot. *Journal of Geophysical Research: Oceans 125*(3), e2019JC015877.

Shan, Z., Wu, H., Ni, W., Sun, M., Wang, K., Zhao, L., Liu, Y. L. A., Xie, W., Zheng, X., & Guo, X. (2022). Recent Technological and Methodological Advances for the Investigation of Submarine Landslides. MDPI. *Journal of Marine Science and Engineering*, *10*(11), 1728. doi:10.3390/jmse10111728

Sun, M., Yu, F. U., Chongjing, L., & Jiang, X. (2018). *Deep learning application in marine big data mining*. Science & Technology Review.

Yu, J., Zhao, Q., & Chin, C. S. (2019). Extracting Typhoon Disaster Information from VGI Based on Machine Learning. MDPI. *Journal of Marine Science and Engineering*, *7*(9), 318. doi:10.3390/jmse7090318

Yuen, D. A., Scruggs, M. A., Spera, F. J., Zheng, Y., Hu, H., McNutt, S. R., Thompson, G., Mandli, K., Kellerf, B. R., Wei, S. S., Peng, Z., Zhou, Z., Mulargia, F., & Tanioka, Y. (2022). *Under the surface: Pressure-induced planetary-scale waves, volcanic lightning, and gaseous clouds caused by the submarine eruption of Hunga Tonga-Hunga Ha'apai volcano*. Earthquake Research Advances.

Zhou, L., Pan, S., Wang, J., & Vasilakos, A. V. (2017). Machine learning on big data: Opportunities and challenges. *Neurocomputing*, *237*, 350–361. doi:10.1016/j.neucom.2017.01.026

Chapter 8
Prediction of Earthquakes, Volcanic Eruptions, Tornadoes, Wildfires, and Droughts Through Artificial Intelligence

Selvakumar P.
https://orcid.org/0000-0002-3650-4548
Nehru Institute of Technology, India

Vijayakumar G.
Vivekanandha College of Engineering for Women, India

Vigneshkumar P.
KGiSL Institute of Technology, India

Umamaheswari M. S.
Nehru Institute of Technology, India

Selvamurugan C.
https://orcid.org/0000-0003-3447-1970
Dhaanish Ahmed Institute of Technology, India

Satheesh kumar P.
Dr. N.G.P. Institute of Technology, India

ABSTRACT

The growing economic and organizational relevance of artificial intelligence has garnered a lot of attention in the past ten years. Through the use of processing algorithms that are especially pertinent in emergency, extreme weather, and disaster relief operation situations, artificial intelligence's information processing capabilities assist in converting inputs. Assessing and meeting the needs of people trapped in catastrophes may take longer under older, manual approaches. Furthermore, the typical hierarchical structure approach takes longer to repair infrastructure, leaving those affected exposed. AI can, however, assist in reducing and repairing damage by more precisely and efficiently allocating resources because of its fast and accurate processing capabilities. Artificial intelligence (AI) can help rescue workers evaluate requirements and deliver supplies to various locations more swiftly and accurately.

DOI: 10.4018/979-8-3693-3362-4.ch008

INTRODUCTION

The growing economic and organizational relevance of artificial intelligence has garnered a lot of attention in the past ten years. Through the use of processing algorithms that are especially pertinent in emergency, extreme weather, and disaster relief operation situations, artificial intelligence's information processing capabilities assist in converting inputs (videos, images, numbers, text, and audio stored at clouds) to outputs (informed decision and solution). Assessing and meeting the needs of people trapped in catastrophes may take longer under older, manual approaches (Akter, S.,et.al. 2021). Furthermore, the typical hierarchical structure approach takes longer to repair infrastructure, leaving those affected exposed. AI can, however, assist in reducing and repairing damage by more precisely and efficiently allocating resources because of its fast and accurate processing capabilities. This is because AI fosters a positive atmosphere for coordinated efforts among many stakeholders. Artificial intelligence (AI) can help rescue workers evaluate requirements and deliver supplies to various locations more swiftly and accurately. Experts and professionals from the public and private sectors must work together, nevertheless, to implement AI technologies successfully in order to align resources and steer data toward useful uses.

By using predictive modeling that takes into account past events' trends, artificial intelligence (AI) can stop thousands of civilians from dying (Alassery, F., et.al. 2022). For example, AI may be used to anticipate the location and analyze the size of earthquakes and aftershocks, as well as to predict volcanic eruptions by using geological and seismic data. AI can forecast the effects of floods and assist in monitoring its spread by using rainfall records, density, and flood simulations. AI technology has the potential to be combined with drones to monitor the severity and path of hurricanes and tornadoes as well as the extent of extreme weather, disasters, and the necessary relief activities. It can also analyze satellite data in this regard. Natural disasters (NDs) are described as sudden events caused by forces of nature on Earth that cause economic and demographic losses that are substantial. Earthquakes, hurricanes, tornadoes, tsunamis, volcanic eruptions and floods are some of the most common natural disasters (NDs) that occur on Earth.

They usually appear out of nowhere, which makes it challenging to act before they do. Therefore, it is imperative for society to develop methods and systems that can predict and assess the possibility of NDs happening as well as the possible severity of the injury (Aruta, J. J., et.al. 2022). In the past thirty years, a number of methods, statistical analyses, signal and image processing techniques, and improved measuring apparatus have been developed to build damage and susceptibility prediction and evaluation systems using measured data from various NDs. What ties them together is the processing and analysis of enormous amounts of data. In general, a prediction or evaluation system for NDs consists of three main parts: data collection and analysis, data processing and statistical analysis, and interpretation. Data monitoring can be done with a simple sensor that has a low sample frequency, or it can involve networks of sensors, both cooperative and non-cooperative, that produce vast amounts of different types of data and demand high performance capabilities for data processing, storage, and transmission (Mukherjee, S., (2018). Directly following from this is the potential for difficult and intricate measured data processing and interpretation. Robust computers, or maybe a network of them, are required, yet traditional signal and image processing techniques might not be adequate, requiring the adoption of complex and advanced methodologies. In general, these kinds of circumstances, along with others, have led to the development and application of big data approaches. This article presents the most recent investigation into several methods, statistical analysis, and signal and image processing techniques for the assessment and forecasting of natural disasters (NDs), including earthquakes, tsunamis, volcanic eruptions, hur-

UNDERSTANDING NATURAL DISASTERS

ricanes, tornadoes, and floods. Additionally, Briey talks about using big data principles to address the NDs mentioned above.

UNDERSTANDING NATURAL DISASTERS

It's important to comprehend the nature of disasters before exploring how AI can help prevent them. The broad categories of geological, meteorological, hydrological, and climatological events include natural disasters. Geological disasters include earthquakes, volcanic eruptions, and tsunamis; meteorological disasters include blizzards, tornadoes, and hurricanes (Yang, Y., et.al. 2018). Droughts, heat waves, and wildfires are examples of climatological catastrophes; floods and landslides are examples of hydrological disasters.

THE NEED FOR PREVENTION

Although natural catastrophes are naturally unexpected, early intervention and effective preparation can help to lessen their effects. The effects of these occurrences may be disastrous for the environment, society, and economy. It is vital for the world to prevent or lessen natural disaster harm (Argyroudis, S. A., et.al. 2022). Our approach to catastrophe prevention is being revolutionized by artificial intelligence (AI), which can process enormous volumes of data, detect patterns, and make predictions in real time.

Early Warning Systems

Giving vulnerable populations advance notice of impending disasters is one of the most important parts of disaster prevention. In order to identify early warning indicators of approaching disasters, AI-powered systems can process data from a variety of sources, such as weather sensors, satellites, and social media. Artificial intelligence (AI) algorithms, for instance, are capable of reliably predicting the direction and strength of storms by analyzing atmospheric data (Bartók, B., et. al. 2019). Numerous lives are saved by the authorities' ability to issue warnings in advance and evacuate high-risk regions due to these projections.

Seismic Activity Prediction

AI has made it possible to comprehend and forecast earthquakes, another terrible natural calamity. To predict seismic events, machine learning models can scrutinize past seismic data, track alterations in the Earth's crust, and identify minute modifications (Koval, D., Chowdhury, A.: (2005). Though complete earthquake prevention may not be possible, prompt detection can buy individuals valuable moments, if not minutes, to seek shelter and minimize losses.

Forest Fire Prevention

AI has made it possible to comprehend and forecast earthquakes, another terrible natural calamity. To predict seismic events, machine learning models can scrutinize past seismic data, track alterations in the Earth's crust, and identify minute modifications (Laya, M., et.al, 2021). Though complete earthquake prevention may not be possible, prompt detection can buy individuals valuable moments, if not minutes, to seek shelter and minimize losses.

Flood Prediction and Management

One common tragedy that strikes many places in the world is flooding. In order to forecast when and where floods are likely to occur, artificial intelligence algorithms can process data from rainfall gauges, river levels, and soil moisture sensors. In order to lower flood risk and damage, improved infrastructure and urban planning can be designed with the use of AI-driven flood modeling.

Landslide Detection

Communities in steep or mountainous areas are particularly vulnerable to landslides, which frequently occur after intense rains or earthquakes. Early warning systems for landslides can be generated via AI-based geospatial analysis. These systems use previous landslide incidents, ground sensor data, and satellite data to pinpoint at-risk areas.

Climate Change Mitigation

Though AI cannot directly avoid natural catastrophes, it can aid in addressing climate change, which is the main cause of many of them. Algorithms that use machine learning may examine climate data, spot patterns, and create plans to cut greenhouse gas emissions. AI is also capable of supporting sustainable land use practices, promoting renewable energy sources, and optimizing energy consumption.

Disaster Response Coordination

AI can help disaster response operations be more efficiently coordinated. Virtual assistants, automated systems, and chatbots can help disaster responders, affected communities, and government organizations communicate more efficiently. AI is also capable of analyzing data in real-time to determine the extent of a disaster and more effectively distribute resources.

CHALLENGES AND ETHICAL CONSIDERATIONS

Let's investigate the difficulties and moral issues surrounding the application of AI to disaster relief. Artificial intelligence (AI) raises a number of difficult problems that require careful consideration, even if technology has the potential to significantly improve our readiness and response to natural disasters.

Data Security and Privacy: AI, like catastrophe prevention systems, depends a lot on data. Predictive models require the collection of data from a variety of sources, such as sensors and personal devices. But this raises questions about the security and privacy of data.

Privacy: It is essential to protect people's privacy when gathering data about them. In order to prevent individual identification, AI models need to be built with data anonymization and aggregation features. Informed consent and open data usage procedures are essential.

Security: Cyberattacks are more likely now that catastrophe prediction relies more heavily on data. It is vital to safeguard the data and systems from malevolent actors since a breach in these areas could lead to catastrophic false alerts or other misinformation.

Bias in AI

Biases from the training data may unintentionally be inherited by AI algorithms. Bias may lead to unfair resource prioritizing or erroneous forecasts in the context of catastrophe prevention. The AI model might not offer everyone equal protection, for instance, if historical data is skewed toward particular locations or demographics (Bragg-Sitton, S.M.: (2020). In order to address bias in AI, meticulous data pretreatment and selection are needed, in addition to constant model monitoring and modification. Measures to detect and reduce prejudice should be part of ethical criteria for AI development.

Accessibility and Equity

Ensuring that AI-powered solutions for disaster avoidance are available to everyone, irrespective of their geography or socioeconomic standing, is imperative. Communities that have historically been marginalized might not have had as much access to resources and technology, which makes them more susceptible to natural disasters. In order to achieve fairness, it is necessary to address the underlying inequalities in infrastructure, education, and resources that might worsen the effects of disasters on vulnerable groups. This includes not only giving access to AI tools.

Accountability and Decision-Making

The increasing integration of AI systems in catastrophe avoidance necessitates the establishment of distinct accountability pathways. An AI system should be open about how it arrived at its conclusions when it makes forecasts or suggestions. Furthermore, there must to be procedures in place for contesting or appealing decisions made by AI (Das, L.: (2020). It's critical to establish supervision and accountability mechanisms that guarantee the proper and ethical use of AI in situations where human lives and safety are at risk.

Overreliance on Technology

Even while AI is a potent tool, relying too much on technology to foresee and lessen crises might be dangerous. The foundation of disaster response operations should continue to be human judgment and skill. When people rely too much on AI, they risk becoming complacent and losing sight of important details or warning indicators because they have too much faith in the technology (Ren, H.,& Hou, Z.J. (2021). Achieving a balance between AI-assisted decision-making and human expertise is crucial in order to make sure that AI enhances rather than replaces the responsibilities played by professionals in disaster management and emergency response.

Infrastructure and Resource Constraints

AI-driven disaster prevention systems need a lot of infrastructure, money, and experience to be implemented. It's possible that many areas, particularly in poor nations, lack the resources needed to implement and keep up these systems. This leads to a gap in technology when it comes to preparedness and reaction for disasters (Cioffi, R., et.al. 2020). To guarantee that AI-driven catastrophe prevention technologies are available to all nations, irrespective of their economic capacities, international cooperation and assistance are required. Artificial Intelligence is quickly changing how we avoid and manage disasters. Its real-time processing and analysis of massive volumes of data helps us anticipate, better prepare for, and react to natural disasters. We are getting closer to a time when we will be able to greatly lessen the catastrophic effects of these occurrences on our planet and our societies as we continue to create and improve AI-powered tools and systems. But in order to prevent disasters, AI must be used carefully, addressing ethical issues and guaranteeing that everyone has equal access to these life-saving tools. By doing this, we can fully utilize AI to shield present and future generations from the fury of the natural world.

Remote Sensing, Radars, and Satellite Imaging

Prior to NDs, remote sensing can be used to monitor and identify changes in the Earth's surface, atmosphere, and oceans. In order to facilitate the prompt evacuation of persons and property from the impacted areas, this aids in the early prediction and warning of potential disasters. Radars, satellite imagery, and remote sensing can all be used to assess the extent and severity of damage following a natural disaster (Chau, K. (2006). For example, satellite imagery can be used to map the extent of floods, track the spread of wildfires, and assess the damage caused by storms and tornadoes. The organization of disaster response teams, the amount of emergency supplies and medical assistance required, and the prioritization of rescue and relief efforts can all be determined using the information provided.

Radar, satellite images, and remote sensing can all be very helpful in assessing damage after natural catastrophes. With this knowledge, we can help the injured party more effectively and initiate the healing process. For example, the extent of damage from landslides and earthquakes can be evaluated using satellite pictures (Arrieta, B., et.al. 2020). The following stages of the rebuilding and repair procedure can be planned using this. Using satellite photography and remote sensing, it is possible to track the distribution of ash clouds during a volcanic eruption, which can pose a threat to aviation. With this knowledge, airlines can be advised to reroute flights away from the vulnerable areas and be prepared for the worst. Undersea landslides are frequently the source of tsunamis, and remote sensing can be used to identify and track possible tsunami-generating zones. With this knowledge, vulnerable populations can be evacuated and timely warnings can be issued. Use satellite photography, radar, and remote sensing to locate and manage NDs. Disasters' effects on people, property, and the environment can be mitigated by their ability to deliver timely and accurate information.

Radar, satellite photography, and remote sensing are useful tools for managing and locating natural disasters (NDs) and reducing their occurrence and severity. A few locations that can be located and mapped with the use of remote sensing are floodplains, seismic hotspots, and wildfire-prone areas. This information can be used to inform decisions about development and land use, as well as early warning systems for lowering the risk of disaster (Chen, Y., et.al. 2021). Remote sensing can also be used to track and comprehend how climate change is affecting the environment. Satellite imaging can be used to monitor vegetation changes, sea ice retreat, and melting glaciers and sea ice. With this understanding, the consequences of climate change on ecosystems and biodiversity can be more fully appreciated. Communities and ecosystems may create adaptation plans with this knowledge in hand to more effectively endure the effects of climate change.

To help in recovery and reconstruction after a natural disaster, technologies like radar, satellite images, and remote sensing can all be used. For example, the analysis of high-resolution satellite photos can help with damage estimates to buildings and infrastructure. This helps establish what has to be fixed first and how much reconstructing will cost. With this information in hand, building rules and standards can be enhanced for future usage, potentially saving lives by reducing hazards. Finally, it should be noted that satellite imaging, radar, and remote sensing are all effective instruments for identifying, controlling, and reducing the likelihood of natural catastrophes (Bartmann, M. (2022). They can save lives, save property and the environment, and encourage sustainable growth by providing accurate and timely information.

Figure 1. Artificial intelligence and natural disasters prevention

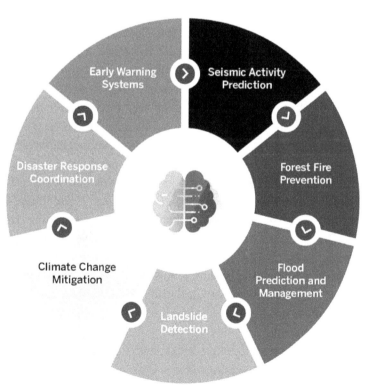

Artificial intelligence has proven to be beneficial in a number of areas, including healthcare, commerce, and customer service. Researchers have now discovered that artificial intelligence can be used to forecast natural disasters. With access to enormous amounts of high-quality data, artificial intelligence (AI) can predict the likelihood of several natural disasters, potentially saving thousands of lives (Catani, F. (2021). Local governments can help reduce the damage caused by natural disasters by utilizing automated responses, early detection systems, and forecast tools. With today's tools, first responders can respond more quickly, residents are being alerted, and mitigation is being started. With the development of artificial intelligence (AI), the proliferation of sensors, and the expansion of data gathering, prediction and detection systems should become more accurate and effective.

IoT, Smartphones, and Social Media

Finding and managing NDs is becoming increasingly dependent on social media, iPads, and the Internet of Things. Before NDs occur, IoT devices can be used to scan the area for potential threats. Sensors can be used, for instance, to monitor earthquakes and locate areas where landslides or flooding are likely to occur. In the event that an evacuation is required, this information can be delivered to cellphones and other devices so that authorities and locals can prepare. Social media and cellphones can be utilized to provide crucial information and assistance to individuals during a natural disaster. Social media can be used, for instance, to inform people about the status of rescue and relief operations and to broadcast emergency alerts and messages (Bag, S., et.al. 2023). Additionally, smartphones can be used to look for emergency services and, in an emergency, make help calls. After a natural disaster, IoT devices can be utilized to assist individuals in getting back on their feet. Sensors can be used, for instance, to identify areas that require repair and assess the state of the water and power systems.

Using this knowledge, decisions about resource allocation and cooperative rebuilding techniques can be made. IoT devices can be used to monitor the composition of volcanic gases during an eruption to determine the kind of eruption and assist with ash plume direction prediction. To enable citizens and government officials to take the appropriate action, this information can be sent to cellphones and other devices. Tracking the movement of underwater landslides and unstable slopes during landslides and tsunamis can be done with IoT devices. Early warning systems and coordinated efforts to remove people from danger zones can be implemented with the help of this information. Social media can also be used to inform people about safe routes and evacuation locations. Cellphones, social media, and the Internet of Things may all be utilized to remotely monitor and control critical infrastructure devices, which is very helpful for ND detection and response. For example, levee systems, dam levels, and flood and storm water levels can all be tracked by Internet of Things sensors. This information can be used by emergency response teams and control centers to lessen or prevent the effects of disasters. Another application for IoT devices is the monitoring of vital systems and the structure of buildings. Sensors can measure how the structure moves and trembles in order to identify structural deterioration and forecast when a bridge or tunnel may collapse.

Prioritizing maintenance and repairs before a breakdown occurs can reduce the likelihood that major infrastructure breakdowns will cause catastrophic events. Social media may also be used to collect public opinion on the condition of broken roads and bridges. This data can be used to enhance maps and other navigational aids, which will enable rescue and relief teams to reach affected areas more quickly and effectively (Azcona, F., et.al. 2022). It may be possible for Internet-of-things devices to track how disasters affect the entire world. Sensors can be used to keep an eye on environmental elements like water and air quality that could be harmful to human health. These data can be used by rescue teams and medical professionals to take the appropriate safety measures for the environment and population. In conclusion, social media, cellphones, and the Internet of Things are all crucial resources for locating, managing, and reducing the effects of natural disasters (Ochoa, K.S., (2021). Because they enable crowdsourcing of information, remote monitoring and administration of critical infrastructure systems, and monitoring of the environmental effects of natural disasters, they are crucial for the protection of people, property, and the environment. Not all disasters, however, can be analyzed by AI, and the technology performs best when it comes to events where the underlying causes are well known, there is an abundance of data available to train the algorithms, and the occurrences are frequent enough to allow the models' predictions to be validated against actual data. The following are a few examples of natural disasters that AI can forecast:

Earthquakes

Seismic data can be used to teach AI-powered systems to anticipate the location of earthquakes and aftershocks by analyzing the magnitude and pattern of earthquakes. Huge amounts of seismic data that researchers have gathered are being analyzed by deep learning systems. Artificial intelligence can analyze seismic data to determine the strength and frequency of earthquakes (Brendel, A. B., et.al. 2021). This kind of information could help forecast when earthquakes would occur. An AI system that can predict earthquake aftershocks, for instance, is being developed by Google and Harvard. More than 131,000 earthquakes and aftershocks were studied by scientists in order to build a neural network. The technology beat conventional methods in forecasting the locations of aftershocks when the neural network was tested on 30,000 events.

Likewise, other scientists are creating their own software for predicting earthquakes and aftershocks. In the future, it may be possible to forecast earthquakes, in which case authorities might plan their evacuations accordingly. Japan is now using satellite imagery to analyze images of the earth in an effort to forecast natural disasters. Artificial intelligence (AI) systems scan images for changes in order to forecast the probability of natural disasters like earthquakes and tsunamis. In addition, these technologies monitor failing infrastructure. Artificial intelligence systems are capable of detecting structural distortions and minimizing the harm brought about by collapsing structures, such as bridges and buildings, as well as sinking roads.

Floods

Google Maps and Google Search users will receive alerts about impending floods in India thanks to an artificial intelligence framework that the company is creating. Flood simulations and rainfall records are utilized to collect data for the AI system's training (Kelly-Gorham, M.R., et.al. 2019). Similar to this, scientists are developing AI-based systems that can learn from climate and rainfall records. These systems are being tested against flood simulations to see whether they can predict floods more accurately than conventional techniques. As an alternative, flooding in cities can be tracked using artificial intelligence (AI). Twitter and other mobile apps are being used by researchers at the University of Dundee in the United Kingdom to gather crowdsourced data on urban flooding. The data, which the AI understands, includes pictures and details about the place and circumstances there. It is possible to use these kinds of systems.

Hurricanes

Hurricanes inflict property damage worth millions of dollars each year. Consequently, meteorological agencies are looking for better ways to predict and track the direction and intensity of natural disasters like hurricanes and cyclones. By employing more precise forecasting tools, the relevant agencies can avert property damage and save more lives. Hurricane Harvey was recently tracked by NASA and Development Seed using machine learning and satellite imagery (Anthopoulos, L., & Kazantzi, V. (2022). The hurricane may now be followed hourly instead of every six hours as was previously possible due to the system's six-fold improvement over conventional approaches. Technology is helping with storm tracking and forecasting as a result, which can help with hurricane mitigation strategies.

Volcanic Eruptions

The development of methods for forecasting natural disasters like volcanic eruptions has long been a goal of research. Research is currently underway to train artificial intelligence to differentiate between tiny volcanic ash particles and other particles. Volcano type can be identified by analyzing the morphology of the ash particles (Bhagat, S. K., et.al. 2022). Development of mitigating strategies for volcanic hazards and eruption prediction may benefit from such improvements. An initiative called Watson is being developed by IBM to predict volcanic eruptions using geological data and seismic sensor data. IBM intends to forecast volcanic eruption sites and intensities with Watson. In areas close to active volcanoes, these applications might help prevent fatalities.

Wildfires

Firefighters searching for the flames in the mountainous area might not realize until they reach that the fire is up a steep climb. It becomes necessary to utilize a helicopter or plane in certain areas because they are inaccessible to firetrucks and would take too long to reach on foot. Technology will let them to more swiftly and accurately identify and target smoldering targets. This implies being able to decide when to send out an aircraft crew in advance, economizing on time, and catching lightning-stricken trees in the act of still burning (Daeli, A., Salman, M., (2023). In San Antonio, the N5 AI-powered system uses strategically positioned sensors to detect airborne chemicals, smoke particles, and gases in addition to collecting temperature readings (Yang, Y.: (2018). A cloud-based system analyzes the data, updates digital maps, and texts responders' cell phones with coordinates and alerts. The algorithms are made to analyze sensor signals and differentiate smoke from dangerous fires from smoke from non-hazardous sources, including campfires or residential chimneys. It can also be helpful to watch for many sensor activations, as these are indicative of a growing fire. Even though several technologies have been developed to use AI to detect disasters, this disaster analysis system still has certain limitations with AI. Artificial intelligence can rival humans in terms of volume and speed of operations, but not in terms of forecast quality, which is one of its limitations (Anuradha, B., et.al. 2022). AI is fallible in many different contexts. The data entered into the system is gathered by humans and may not be precise. AI-generated results could therefore be inaccurate. Moreover, we tend to become unduly dependent on AI based on past trends in AI deployment. Because of this, scientists will have to run a lot of studies to make sure the technology is reliable and appropriate for everyday usage.

The data's historical reliance on records of natural disasters presents another issue for artificial intelligence. Consequently, the dynamic patterns and intensities of natural calamities such as earthquakes and floods are beyond the capabilities of AI-driven applications. Moreover, existing AI-powered apps lack a way to account for how climate change affects natural disasters. The fact that AI systems are educated on historical data prevents them from analyzing the effects of climate change. Consequently, climate change affects many natural disasters, making it difficult for artificial intelligence to forecast long-term patterns in them.

CONCLUSION

Natural catastrophe prediction will benefit from the use of contemporary technologies like artificial intelligence and machine learning. But it's important to address the limits of the technology before implementing AI in practical applications. Therefore, scientists need to focus on finding solutions to current artificial intelligence problems. Government organizations need a plan that streamlines the adoption process in order to properly use AI. The actions listed below comprise the adoption and application roadmap for success: Employ researchers and experts with experience in AI. Gather superior quality data to train the AI-powered application. enlist the aid of capable people who can aid in the creation of adoption techniques, Stay current inside the government structure, and government workers should be trained in artificial intelligence. Artificial intelligence (AI) can foresee natural disasters and save millions of lives. Improved infrastructure construction in disaster-prone areas will also benefit from a greater understanding of the scope and patterns of natural disasters like floods, earthquakes, and tsunamis thanks to the datasets analyzed by AI-powered systems. To ensure the protection of its population, government organizations must thus employ AI to predict natural disasters and accurately monitor them.

REFERENCES

Akter, S., Wamba, S. F., Mariani, M., & Hani, U. (2021). How to Build an AI Climate-Driven Service Analytics Capability for Innovation and Performance in Industrial Markets? *Industrial Marketing Management*, 97, 258–273. doi:10.1016/j.indmarman.2021.07.014

Alassery, F., Alzahrani, A., Khan, A. I., Irshad, K., & Islam, S. (2022). An artificial intelligence-based solar radiation prophesy model for green energy utilization in energy management system. *Sustainable Energy Technologies and Assessments*, 52, 102060. doi:10.1016/j.seta.2022.102060

Anthopoulos, L., & Kazantzi, V. (2022). Urban energy efficiency assessment models from an AI and big data perspective: Tools for policy makers. *Sustainable Cities and Society*, 76, 103492. doi:10.1016/j.scs.2021.103492

Anuradha, B., Abinaya, C., Bharathi, M., Janani, A., & Khan, A. (2022). IoT Based natural disaster monitoring and prediction analysis for hills area using LSTM network. In: *2022 8th International Conference on Advanced Computing and Communication Systems (ICACCS)*, (vol. 1, pp. 1908–1913). IEEE. 10.1109/ICACCS54159.2022.9785121

Argyroudis, S. A., Mitoulis, S. A., Chatzi, E., Baker, J. W., Brilakis, I., Gkoumas, K., Vousdoukas, M., Hynes, W., Carluccio, S., Keou, O., Frangopol, D. M., & Linkov, I. (2022). Digital technologies can enhance climate resilience of critical infrastructure. *Climate Risk Management*, *35*, 100387. doi:10.1016/j.crm.2021.100387

Arrieta, B., Alejandro, N.-R., Del Ser, J., Bennetot, A., Tabik, S., Barbado, A., Garcia, S., Gil-Lopez, S., Molina, D., Benjamins, R., Chatila, R., & Herrera, F. (2020). Explainable Artificial Intelligence (XAI): Concepts, taxonomies, opportunities and challenges toward responsible AI. *Information Fusion*, *58*, 82–115. doi:10.1016/j.inffus.2019.12.012

Aruta, J. J., Benzon, R., & Guinto, R. R. (2022). Safeguarding youth health in climate-vulnerable countries. *The Lancet. Child & Adolescent Health*, *6*(4), 223–224. doi:10.1016/S2352-4642(22)00029-3 PMID:35183300

Azcona, F., Hakna, M. A., Mesa-Jurado, A.-T., Perera, M. Á. D., Mendoza-Carranza, M., & Olivera-Villarroel, M. (2022). Coastal communities' adaptive capacity to climate change: Pantanos de Centla Biosphere Reserve, Mexico. *Ocean and Coastal Management*, *220*, 106080. doi:10.1016/j.ocecoaman.2022.106080

Bag, S., Rahman, M. S., Rogers, H., Srivastava, G., & Pretorius, J. H. C. (2023). Climate change adaptation and disaster risk reduction in the garment industry supply chain network. Transportation Research Part e. *Transportation Research Part E, Logistics and Transportation Review*, *171*, 103031. doi:10.1016/j.tre.2023.103031

Bartmann, M. (2022). The Ethics of AI-Powered Climate Nudging—How Much AI Should We Use to Save the Planet? *Sustainability (Basel)*, *14*(9), 5153. doi:10.3390/su14095153

Bartók, B., Tobin, I., Vautard, R., Vrac, M., Jin, X., Levavasseur, G., Denvil, S., Dubus, L., Parey, S., Michelangeli, P.-A., Troccoli, A., & Saint-Drenan, Y.-M. (2019). A climate projection dataset tailored for the European energy sector. *Climate Services*, *16*, 100138. doi:10.1016/j.cliser.2019.100138

Bhagat, S. K., Tiyasha, T., Kumar, A., Malik, T., Jawad, A. H., Khedher, K. M., Deo, R. C., & Yaseen, Z. M. (2022). Integrative artificial intelligence models for Australian coastal sediment lead prediction: An investigation of in-situ measurements and meteorological parameters effects. *Journal of Environmental Management*, *309*, 114711. doi:10.1016/j.jenvman.2022.114711 PMID:35182982

Bragg-Sitton, S. M., Boardman, R., Rabiti, C., & O'Brien, J. (2020). Reimagining future energy systems: Overview of the US program to maximize energy utilization via integrated nuclear-renewable energy systems. *International Journal of Energy Research*, *44*(10), 8156–8169. doi:10.1002/er.5207

Brendel, A. B., Mirbabaie, M., Lembcke, T. B., & Hofeditz, L. (2021). Ethical Management of Artificial Intelligence. *Sustainability (Basel)*, *13*(4), 1974. doi:10.3390/su13041974

Catani, F. (2021). Landslide detection by deep learning of non-nadiral and crowdsourced optical images. *Landslides*, *18*(3), 1025–1044. doi:10.1007/s10346-020-01513-4

Chau, K. (2006). A review on the integration of artificial intelligence into coastal modeling. *Journal of Environmental Management*, *80*(1), 47–57. doi:10.1016/j.jenvman.2005.08.012 PMID:16337078

Chen, Y., Zou, X., Li, K., Li, K., Yang, X., & Chen, C. (2021). Multiple local 3D CNNs for region-based prediction in smart cities. *Information Sciences*, *542*, 476–491. doi:10.1016/j.ins.2020.06.026

Cioffi, R., Travaglioni, M., Piscitelli, G., Petrillo, A., & De Felice, F. (2020). Artificial Intelligence and Machine Learning Applications in Smart Production: Progress, Trends, and Directions. *Sustainability (Basel)*, *12*(2), 492. doi:10.3390/su12020492

Daeli, A., & Salman, M. (2023). Power grid infrastructural resilience against extreme events. *Energies*, *16*(1), 64. doi:10.3390/en16010064

Das, L., Munikoti, S., Natarajan, B., & Srinivasan, B. (2020). Measuring smart grid resilience: Methods, challenges and opportunities. *Renewable & Sustainable Energy Reviews*, *130*, 109918. doi:10.1016/j.rser.2020.109918

Dehghanian, P., Zhang, B., Dokic, T., & Kezunovic, M. (2018). Predictive risk analytics for weather-resilient operation of electric power systems. *IEEE Transactions on Sustainable Energy*, *10*(1), 3–15. doi:10.1109/TSTE.2018.2825780

Kelly-Gorham, M. R., Hines, P., & Dobson, I. (2019). Using historical utility outage data to compute overall transmission grid resilience, arXiv preprint arXiv:1906.06811. doi:10.1109/MEPS46793.2019.9395039

Koval, D., & Chowdhury, A. (2005). An investigation into extreme-weather-caused transmission line unavailability. *IEEE Power Eng. Soc. Gener. Meeting*. IEEE.

Laya, M., & Mera, K. (2021). Classification of natural disaster on online news data using machine learning. In: *5th International Conference on Electrical, Telecommunication and Computer Engineering (ELTICOM)*, (vol. 5, pp. 42–46). IEEE. 10.1109/ELTICOM53303.2021.9590125

Mukherjee, S., Nateghi, R., & Hastak, M. (2018). A multi-hazard approach to assess sev.re weather-induced major power outage risks in the us. *Reliability Engineering & System Safety*, *175*, 283–305. doi:10.1016/j.ress.2018.03.015

OchoaK. S. (2021). A Machine learning approach for rapid disaster response based on multi-modal data. The case of housing & shelter needs. arXiv:2108.00887

Ren, H., & Hou, Z. J. (2021). Analysis of weather and climate extremes impact on power system outage. In *IEEE Power Energy Society General Meeting (PESGM)*. IEEE. doi:10.1109/PESGM46819.2021.9637938

Yang, Y., Tang, W., Liu, Y., Xin, Y., & Wu, Q. (2018). Quantitative resilience assessment for power transmission systems under typhoon weather. *IEEE Access : Practical Innovations, Open Solutions*, *6*, 40747–40756. doi:10.1109/ACCESS.2018.2858860

Yang, Y., Tang, W., Liu, Y., Xin, Y., & Wu, Q. (2018). Quantitative resilience assessment for power transmission systems under typhoon weather. *IEEE Access : Practical Innovations, Open Solutions*, *6*, 40747–40756. doi:10.1109/ACCESS.2018.2858860

Chapter 9
Machine Learning Models for Prediction of Landslides in the Himalayas

Vikram Singh
https://orcid.org/0000-0001-5757-9111
Ch. Devi Lal University, Sirsa, India

Sanjay Tyagi
Kurukshetra University, India

ABSTRACT

The Himalayan region, characterized by its steep terrain and geological complexities, stands vulnerable to the persistent threat of landslides, particularly exacerbated during the monsoon season. The susceptibility to landslides in this region arises from a convergence of factors, including the region's high seismic activity, diverse geological formations, intense monsoonal precipitation, and rapidly changing climate patterns. The impact of landslides extends beyond immediate infrastructure damage, often leading to loss of lives, disruption of livelihoods, and severe environmental degradation. This chapter embarks on a comprehensive exploration of the pivotal role of artificial intelligence and machine learning in revolutionizing the prediction and mitigation of landslides in the Himalayas. It delves into the intricate challenges posed by the region's geological diversity and environmental dynamics, offering insights into AI-driven strategies to enhance predictive accuracy, implement early warning systems, and devise effective mitigation measures. The chapter commences with an overview of the Himalayas, delineating the geological complexities and the profound influence of climatic conditions on landslide occurrences. It elucidates the critical challenges hindering traditional landslide prediction methods, such as inadequate data quality and sparsity, underscoring the dire need for advanced predictive techniques. A meticulous review of existing methods, encompassing both conventional approaches and the utilization of remote sensing technologies and geographic information systems (GIS), sets the stage for introducing AI-based solutions. The chapter unfolds the nuances of machine learning approaches tailored for landslide prediction, spotlighting the selection of pertinent features, the application of supervised and unsupervised learning models, and

DOI: 10.4018/979-8-3693-3362-4.ch009

the integration of real-time environmental data. A pivotal focus lies on AI-driven early warning systems that amalgamate historical data, sensor networks, and predictive models to facilitate timely alerts and risk assessments. Moreover, the chapter elucidates how AI empowers hazard zonation mapping, aiding in the identification of high-risk areas and adaptive planning for resilient infrastructure development. The narrative is enriched with insightful studies and practical implementations showcasing the efficacy of AI-based models in landslide prediction and mitigation within the Himalayan terrain. Lessons gleaned from these studies illuminate both successes and challenges, providing invaluable insights for the field. This chapter endeavours to unravel the transformative potential of AI and machine learning in confronting the formidable challenge of landslides in the Himalayas. It underscores the significance of these technological advancements in fostering resilience, safeguarding lives, and fortifying the region's infrastructure against the omnipresent threat of landslides.

INTRODUCTION

In regions characterized by challenging terrains such as the Himalayas, landslides pose significant threats to communities and infrastructure. The complex geological structures and rapid urbanization in this area contribute to unique challenges in landslide prediction and mitigation. Human activities also account for an additional dimension to an already complex landslide dynamics. In some geographies, more than two dozen parameters show a bearing on the landslide susceptibility. Mathematical modeling has long been used to study landslide phenomena. Traditional methods have limitations in providing accurate and timely information, prompting the exploration of advanced technological solutions. The role of artificial intelligence and machine learning in geohazard management is crucial and recent years have seen a growing research interest in these technologies to study the intricate interplay between the large number of geological and environmental parameters involved in landslide susceptibility. These technologies are very good at deciphering intricate patterns within landslide data, leading to the development of predictive models that enhance our understanding of landslide precursors. This, in turn, contributes to early warning systems and improved disaster preparedness (Turner & Schuster, 1996; Kumar et al., 2023; Ado et al., 2022).

Advancements in AI-based landslide prediction models leverage data from remote sensing, geospatial information systems, and meteorological parameters. This integration empowers models to discern precursory signals, enabling more accurate landslide forecasts. While prediction is pivotal, effective mitigation strategies are equally essential for minimizing the impact of landslides. Artificial intelligence and machine learning contribute not only to prediction but also to the development of intelligent systems for landslide monitoring, early detection, and the implementation of mitigation measures. The intersection of artificial intelligence, machine learning and geoscience presents interesting avenues for transforming landslide prediction and mitigation efforts in the challenging terrain of the Himalayas. Through a comprehensive review of recent studies and case studies, this chapter aims to provide insights into the potential applications, limitations, and future directions of artificial intelligence and machine learning in the context of landslide management. The discussion also attempts to introduce how principal component analysis (PCA), linear discriminant analysis (LDA), decision tree, naïve Bayes, artificial neural networks, and other machine learning techniques can be used to predict landslide susceptibility (Turner & Schuster, 1996; Zhou et al., 2021; Kumar et al., 2023a).

RELATED WORKS

This section discusses a score of recent research studies published in the field of landslide susceptibility. The study conducted by Nhu et al. (2020) delves into the challenging task of improving landslide prediction accuracy in tropical environments. Given the unique geological and environmental characteristics of tropical landscapes, the researchers employ advanced techniques to enhance the precision of landslide susceptibility mapping. The central focus is on leveraging machine learning algorithms and remote sensing data to achieve more robust and reliable predictions. Researchers meticulously explore a range of machine learning algorithms tailored to the complexities of tropical terrains. These algorithms are strategically coupled with diverse sets of remote sensing data, ensuring a comprehensive and multidimensional approach to landslide susceptibility mapping. The study incorporates an array of factors, including geological features and environmental conditions, which significantly influence the occurrence of landslides in tropical areas. The results of the research are presented in detail, shedding light on the performance of different machine learning algorithms in predicting landslide susceptibility. The findings offer valuable insights into the strengths and limitations of each algorithm, providing a nuanced understanding of their effectiveness in the context of tropical landscapes. The study's comprehensive approach and detailed analysis contribute significantly to the body of knowledge regarding landslide prediction in challenging environmental settings.

Neves et al. (2021) focuses on landslide susceptibility mapping in Pithoragarh District, India, utilizing three single machine learning models: linear discriminant analysis, logistic regression, and radial basis function network. The study is motivated by the need for accurate landslide susceptibility maps to mitigate the impact of landslides. The authors consider ten key factors, such as slope, aspect, land cover, and lithology, to develop the models. The landslide inventory consists of 398 past landslide events, divided into training and validation sets. The performance of the models is evaluated using various statistical measures, including accuracy, specificity, sensitivity, and area under the receiver operating characteristic curve (AUC). The logistic regression model exhibits the best performance with an AUC of 0.926. The study concludes that single machine learning models, particularly logistic regression, can effectively contribute to accurate landslide susceptibility mapping, providing valuable insights for landslide-prone areas.

The review by Reichenbach et al. (2018) critically examines statistically-based landslide susceptibility models, aiming to provide insights into their effectiveness and application. The authors systematically analyze a comprehensive database of 565 peer-reviewed articles published between 1983 and 2016, focusing on landslide susceptibility modeling and terrain zonations. The review covers diverse geological and climatic settings and considers factors such as study region, landslide type, statistical models used, and evaluation methods. The analysis reveals significant heterogeneity in data types, modeling approaches, and evaluation criteria. Common statistical methods include logistic regression, neural network analysis, data-overlay, index-based, and weight of evidence analyses. While an increasing number of studies assess model performance, only a few evaluate model uncertainty. The review underscores the need for improved standardization, justification of thematic data use, and increased focus on model uncertainty assessment in landslide susceptibility studies.

A Uttarakhand (India) centric study by Kainthura and Sharma (2022) focuses on evaluating and comparing the prediction accuracy of five hybrid models for landslide occurrence in the target area. The hybrid models incorporate rough set theory along with Bayesian network, backpropagation neural network, bagging, XGBoost, and random forest. The study utilizes a database with fifteen conditioning factors, including 373 landslide and 181 non-landslide locations, randomly divided into training and testing sets. Assessment of the conditioning factors is done through multi-collinearity tests and the least absolute shrinkage and selection operator approach. Performance evaluation metrics such as accuracy, sensitivity, specificity, precision, F-scores, and the area under the curve (AUC) of the receiver operating characteristic curve are employed to assess and compare individual and hybrid models. The findings highlight that the XGBoost model integrated with rough set theory, emerges as the most accurate (AUC = 0.937, Precision = 0.946, F1-score = 0.926, Accuracy = 89.92%) among the considered models. The integration with a rough set enhances the prediction capability of each model and contributes to superior stability, effectively avoiding overfitting. Furthermore, the authors design a user-friendly platform within an integrated GIS environment using dynamic maps. This platform enables effective landslide prediction in large-prone areas, allowing users to predict the probability of landslide occurrence for a selected region by manipulating the values of conditioning factors. The proposed approach holds the potential for predicting landslide impacts on slopes and monitoring landslides along major highways of the region.

In another comprehensive review, Shano et al. (2020) have explored various methods employed in assessing landslide susceptibility evaluation and hazard zonation techniques. The review encompasses a range of techniques and approaches used in the field, offering insights into the advancements and challenges in landslide risk assessment. The study delves into the complexities of landslide susceptibility evaluation, considering factors such as terrain characteristics, geological conditions, and human activities. Various methodologies and models used for hazard zonation are discussed, highlighting the strengths and limitations of each. The article emphasizes the importance of a systematic and integrated approach to landslide risk assessment, considering both natural and anthropogenic factors. Overall, the review contributes to the understanding of current practices in landslide susceptibility evaluation and hazard zonation, providing valuable insights for researchers, practitioners, and decision-makers involved in landslide risk management.

Guo et al. (2023) investigates landslide susceptibility mapping in the Loess Plateau of northwest China by using three data-driven techniques. The research focuses on the middle Yellow River catchment and aims to compare the performance of weighted information value (WIV), support vector machine (SVM), and random forest (RF) models in generating landslide susceptibility maps. The authors create a landslide inventory map comprising 684 historical landslides by combining remote sensing image interpretation with field surveys. Fourteen thematic layers, representing factors influencing landslides, are used in the modeling process. The correlation among these factors is analyzed using the Pearson correlation coefficient, and the C5.0 decision tree algorithm determines the importance of each factor. The study identifies distance to road, distance to river, and slope as the most significant contributors to landslide occurrences in the region, while other factors have minor importance. All three models predict that most historical landslides are concentrated in moderate and high susceptibility areas. The RF model demonstrates the best performance, with high susceptibility zones accounting for 21.9% and 90.5% of landslide numbers. Comparative analysis using receiver operating characteristic curves indicates that the RF model has higher accuracy (AUC = 0.904) compared to the WIV and SVM models (AUC = 0.845 and 0.847, respectively). The study concludes that the RF model, among the three techniques, is most suitable for assessing landslide susceptibility in the Loess Plateau, providing valuable insights for future studies and strategies for landslide risk mitigation in the region.

Authors in Xia et al. (2023) have employed GIS-based landslide susceptibility modeling using data mining techniques. The research aims to map regional landslide susceptibility for landslide mitigation, focusing on Uttarkashi, Uttarakhand, India. Four models—Certainty Factors (CF), Naive Bayes (NB), J48

Decision Tree (J48), and Multilayer Perceptron (MLP)—are evaluated and compared for their prediction accuracy. The study begins by identifying 328 landslides through historical data, remote sensing image interpretation, and field investigation. These landslides are divided into training (70%) and validation (30%) subsets. Twelve conditioning factors, including altitude, slope angle, land use, and lithology, are considered in the modeling process. The importance of each conditioning factor is analyzed using average merit (AM) values, and the relationship between landslide occurrence and various factors is assessed using the certainty factor (CF) approach. Landslide susceptibility maps are then generated based on the four models, and their performance is quantitatively compared using receiver operating characteristic (ROC) curves, area under the curve (AUC) values, and non-parametric tests. The results demonstrate that all four models can reasonably assess landslide susceptibility. The CF model stands out with the best predictive performance for both training (AUC = 0.901) and validating data (AUC = 0.892). The study concludes that the proposed approach, incorporating data mining techniques, provides an innovative method for developing accurate landslide susceptibility maps. The user-friendly platform designed in a GIS environment allows for effective landslide prediction in large prone areas, offering a valuable tool for assessing landslide impact and enhancing hazard assessments.

Landslide prediction, a critical aspect of natural disaster management, has witnessed significant advancements through the integration of artificial intelligence (AI) and machine learning (ML) techniques. These technologies have played a pivotal role in enhancing geospatial analysis and predictive modeling for landslides, offering valuable insights into susceptibility and risk assessment. Recent research by Alotaibi et al. (2019) demonstrates the application of various machine learning algorithms in landslide susceptibility modeling, particularly in the Wadi Tayyah Basin of Saudi Arabia. The study explores the effectiveness of these algorithms in predicting landslide occurrence, showcasing the potential for machine learning to contribute to accurate and efficient predictive models (Alotaibi et al., 2019). In the context of landslide prediction, the role of remote sensing, satellite imagery, and geological data is paramount. Aryal et al. (2011) emphasize the significance of incorporating such data in landslide susceptibility mapping. The study, conducted in the Mugling-Narayanghat road section in Nepal Himalaya, highlights the use of frequency ratio, statistical index, and weights-of-evidence models, underscoring the integration of diverse datasets for comprehensive analysis (Aryal et al., 2011).

The application of AI-based models and algorithms in landslide prediction is evident in the work of Bai et al. (2014). The study, conducted in the Three Gorges area of China, explores ensemble models for landslide susceptibility mapping. The research showcases the effectiveness of AI-driven techniques in handling complex geospatial dynamics, providing valuable insights for landslide prediction (Bai et al., 2014). Meena et al. (2020) contribute to the understanding of landslide prediction challenges in the Indian Himalayas, specifically the Bhagirathi river basin. Their research utilizes hybrid machine learning models, highlighting the need for sophisticated approaches in regions with intricate topography. The study emphasizes the importance of considering regional complexities for robust landslide prediction in challenging terrains. In conclusion, the integration of AI and machine learning in landslide prediction has demonstrated promising results, with advancements in algorithmic models and the incorporation of diverse geospatial data. These studies collectively contribute to the evolving landscape of landslide prediction methodologies, emphasizing the need for tailored approaches in different geographical contexts.

Saha et al. (2021) evaluates various landslide susceptibility models (LSMs) generated by different machine learning techniques such as CNN, ANN, CART, ADTree, FTree, and LMT. They employed 21 statistical measures, including receiver operating characteristic (ROC) curves and the area under the CURVE (AUC), to assess the models' performance. The evaluation aims to minimize false negative rates and misclassification rates, indicating higher model accuracy. The study employs a compound factor (CF) method to rank the models in terms of accuracy. This method involves assigning ranks to factors and computing their mean values to determine relative priorities. The CF formula calculates the priority based on the sum of the ranks assigned to each factor. The methodology presented here combines various statistical measures to holistically evaluate LSMs, enabling the identification and prioritization of the most accurate models for landslide susceptibility mapping.

Saha et al. (2023) focuses on assessing landslide susceptibility in the Garhwal Himalaya region using various machine learning and deep learning algorithms. It explores the complexities of landslides in this region, emphasizing their devastating impact on life, property, and the environment. Each year, around 400 fatalities occur in the Himalayan terrain due to landslides, highlighting the urgent need for accurate mapping and prediction of landslide-prone areas. The researchers employed five models—support vector machine (SVM), random forest (RF), bagging, artificial neural network (ANN), and deep learning neural network (DLNN)—combined with twenty landslide-controlling factors to delineate the susceptibility zones. These models were used with a dataset comprising previous landslide points as training (70%) and testing (30%) data. The principal goal was to precisely identify landslide susceptibility zones in the Garhwal Himalaya. The selection of factors was determined through multi-collinearity tests and information gain ratio statistics. DLNN technique emerged as the most effective model for demarcating landslide areas, exhibiting high capability (AUC = 0.925) and accuracy. The integration of physical and social factors enhanced the precision of predictions, offering support for large-scale landslide management. The study identified Rudraprayag and Tehri Garhwal as highly susceptible to landslides. The generated maps aim to aid policymakers in micro-scale landslide management and sustainable land use planning, particularly in the Himalayan terrain. Statistical indicators such as sensitivity, specificity, detection rate, and prevalence were used for model accuracy assessment. DLNN showed superior performance compared to other models in predicting landslide susceptibility, indicating its ability to understand complex relationships between landslides and controlling factors. The study highlights factors like altitude, drainage density, distance from roads, geology, and slope as significant contributors to landslides in the region. District-wise analysis revealed that Rudraprayag and Tehri Garhwal are more prone to landslides due to their geological instability and high population density. Field observations confirmed the association between geological structures, steep slopes, unconsolidated materials, and the occurrence of landslides. Phyllite rocks, prevalent in the area, possess characteristics that contribute to slope instability, making them susceptible to landslides.

A Karakoram Highway (KKH) study by Hussain et al. (2023) examines the susceptibility of the region to landslides, a significant threat to the area's stability and operations. It utilizes cutting-edge remote sensing technologies such as SBAS-InSAR and PS-InSAR, analyzing Sentinel-1 data from June 2021 to June 2023 to identify and classify 571 landslides. These methods provided high-resolution information on slope deformation, contributing to an updated landslide inventory that includes 24 new prospective landslides and redefined existing ones. The study proceeds to create a landslide susceptibility model, employing both machine learning and deep learning techniques like CNN 2D, RNNs, RF, and XGBoost. Using 70% of the inventory for training and 30% for testing, along with fifteen landslide-causing factors, it evaluates the accuracy of these models based on the area under the curve of the receiver operating characteristic. The findings underscore CNN 2D's exceptional performance in constructing the landslide susceptibility map for the KKH. Despite limitations in vegetation-covered areas, the SBAS-InSAR and PS-InSAR methods were effective in capturing deformation in over 60% of the region devoid of vegetation. Vegetation's role in controlling slope stability is highlighted, consistent with previous research. The study emphasizes the importance of evaluating landslide-causing factors to build accurate susceptibility models and identifies 15 variables and employs techniques like multicollinearity analysis to select the most relevant factors for integration into the models. The study notes that despite significant vegetation, landslides can still occur due to rainfall and external forces.

Priyanka et al. (2023) aims to develop advanced machine learning models to predict soil movement in landslide-prone areas, incorporating data from landslide monitoring systems (LMSs) that collect weather conditions and soil parameters. The models explored include long short-term memory (LSTM), convolutional neural network-long short-term memory (CNN-LSTM), convolutional LSTM (Conv-LSTM), encoder-decoder LSTM, and an innovative ensemble architecture called the SoilSense Multi-LSTM-SVM model. The research emphasizes the importance of considering antecedent rainfall data, previously unexplored in ML model development, as a crucial factor influencing landslide dynamics. The study area, Kamand Valley in Himachal Pradesh, experienced multiple landslides during the monsoon season of 2023. The dataset collected from LMSs includes various parameters such as temperature, humidity, light intensity, barometric pressure, rainfall, acceleration along different axes, soil moisture, cumulative movement, and movement classification.

Saha et al. (2023a) has refined landslide prediction specifically triggered by rainfall in Uttarkashi, India. It introduces an innovative methodology merging a reduced error pruning tree (REPT) as a base classifier with ensemble learning techniques like Bagging (B), Decorate (D), and Random Subspace (RSS). Their goal? To develop more precise predictive models for landslides. To craft these models, the researchers worked with historical data from 103 landslide incidents. They coupled this with twelve environmental factors, likely encompassing rainfall intensity, slope steepness, soil attributes, rock characteristics, and vegetation cover. Using Root Mean Square Error (RMSE) and Area Under the Receiver Operating Characteristic Curve (AUC) as evaluation metrics, they assessed model accuracy. Results highlighted the superiority of ensemble models, notably the D-REPT variant, which demonstrated an RMSE of 0.351 and an AUC of 0.907, signifying enhanced predictive prowess compared to other models examined. This finding underscores the effectiveness of ensemble methods in bolstering predictive accuracy over standalone models like REPT.

Meena et al. (2020) presents an investigation into landslide detection in the Himalayas using U-Net and machine learning approaches. The study involves two datasets from RapidEye satellite imagery and ALOS-PALSAR topographical data. Evaluating different machine learning models, including U-Net, Support Vector Machines (SVM), K-Nearest Neighbour, and Random Forest, was conducted using a small dataset of 239 samples from training and testing zones. Thirty-two maps with varied sample patch sizes were created to assess landslide detection accuracy. Results indicated that the U-Net model trained with a 128×128 pixel patch size demonstrated the best performance (76.59% MCC) using Dataset-1. Including digital elevation data improved landslide detection overall and aided in distinguishing human settlement areas and river sandbars. The study suggests the potential of U-Net for automated landslide detection in varied Himalayan terrains, although further refinement and research are necessary. The study area is situated in Rasuwa district, Nepal, a region significantly impacted by landslides following the 2015 Gorkha earthquake. Inaccessible terrain poses challenges for field visits, making remote sensing tools crucial for supplementing ground observations in this area affected by annual monsoonal rains and frequent deep-seated landslides.

Naveen et al. (2022) discusses the significance of landslide detection, especially in hilly terrains like the Himalayas, emphasizing the socio-economic impact. It explores the integration of remote sensing data into GIS to create a comprehensive view of landscapes for landslide hazard analysis. Landslides, driven by gravitational forces, vary in types and occurrence rates. Remote sensing data, such as digital elevation models, slope maps, and land use data, help identify landslide-prone areas. The research aims to develop a landslide detection system using artificial neural networks (ANNs) and the synthetic minority oversampling technique (SMOTE). The study highlights the importance of understanding landslide causative factors and the role of geospatial technologies like GIS. Methodologically, it details the application of SMOTE for handling unbalanced GIS data and the use of ANN for processing information efficiently. The results have indicated a 75% model accuracy and have emphasized the utility of SMOTE in reducing duplicate data and improving data efficiency, while also stressing the significance of data preparation in machine learning, specifically in the context of GISs.

Youssef et al. 92023) investigates landslide susceptibility in the easternmost Himalaya region. Landslides pose significant hazards, and accurately assessing susceptibility is crucial. The study introduces a framework, called superimposable neural network (SNN) optimization, aiming to improve accuracy and interpretability in landslide prediction. Validated in the easternmost Himalaya using three different regions, SNN outperforms other models, including physically-based and statistical ones, and matches the performance of state-of-the-art DNNs. SNN highlights key contributors to landslide susceptibility, revealing the significance of slope-climate interactions and hillside aspects. The model's architecture emphasizes feature interactions through composite features, achieving accuracy comparable to complex DNNs while ensuring interpretability. The research demonstrates the SNN's success in accurately predicting landslides and unveiling critical factors affecting susceptibility in the Himalayan region.

Kumar et al. (2023) aims to tackle the critical challenge of predicting and detecting rainfall-triggered landslides, especially in vulnerable regions like the Himalayas. By combining in-depth analysis, IoT-based sensor networks, and machine learning algorithms, attempt has been made to create a system that can accurately forecast these disasters in real time. The approach involves dissecting the topographic and hydro-meteorological conditions that led to the devastating Kedarnath disaster. This includes harnessing an innovative algorithm and leveraging machine learning models, all fuelled by an IoT-based application to gather crucial data for training and validation. Key emphasis is placed on rainfall's impact on debris flow and lake outbursts during such catastrophic events. Approach uses IoT-based sensor networks, including rain gauge, temperature, wind speed, and humidity sensors, for data accumulation aligns with your goal of using machine learning to predict shallow landslides.

LANDSLIDE DYNAMICS AND CHALLENGES IN THE HIMALAYAS

The Himalayan region, an awe-inspiring landscape spanning northern India and six other countries of the region, is characterized by its unique geological features and stunning topography. The collision between the Indian and Eurasian plates has intricately shaped this region, resulting in a diverse terrain distinguished by steep mountain ranges and deep valleys (Bookhagen & Burbank, 2006). This dynamic geological setting sets the stage for significant challenges, particularly in terms of landslide susceptibility. The geological composition of the Himalayas is marked by the presence of delicate rock formations such as shale and limestone, adding to the complexity of the region's susceptibility to landslides (Nawaz et al., 2021). Landslides, as geological phenomena, play a crucial role in shaping the landscape over time. The fragile nature of these rocks, coupled with the steep gradients of the Himalayan slopes, contributes to the heightened vulnerability of the region to mass movements.

Table 1. Summary of related works

Study	Focus	Methodology	Key Findings
Nhu et al. (2020)	Landslide prediction in Tropics	Machine learning algorithms, remote sensing data	Explored machine learning in tropical terrains, evaluated algorithms' performance, detailed insights into effectiveness in tropical landscapes
Neves et al. (2021)	Landslide susceptibility mapping	Machine learning models: LDA, Logistic Regression, RBF Network	Logistic regression exhibited the best performance in mapping landslide susceptibility in Pithoragarh district, India, using ten key factors for model development
Reichenbach et al. (2018)	Statistical landslide susceptibility models	Review and analysis of landslide studies	Identified the heterogeneity in data types and modeling approaches, underscored the need for standardized evaluation criteria and model uncertainty assessment
Kainthura and Sharma (2022)	Hybrid models for landslide prediction	Rough set, Bayesian network, ANN, Bagging, XGBoost, Random Forest	XGBoost integrated with rough set theory emerged as the most accurate model, with a user-friendly GIS-based platform for landslide prediction in Uttarakhand, India
Shano et al. (2020)	Landslide susceptibility and hazard zonation	Review of methodologies used in landslide risk assessment	Provided insights into various methods used for assessing landslide susceptibility and hazard zonation, emphasized the importance of an integrated approach
Guo et al. (2023)	Landslide susceptibility mapping	Data-driven techniques, Support Vector Machine, Random Forest	RF model demonstrated higher accuracy compared to WIV and SVM in landslide susceptibility mapping in the Loess Plateau of northwest China
Xia et al. (2023)	Landslide susceptibility modeling	Certainty Factors, Naive Bayes, J48 Decision Tree, Perceptron	CF model exhibited superior predictive performance for landslide susceptibility mapping in Uttarkashi, Uttarakhand, India
Alotaibi et al. (2019)	ML in landslide susceptibility modeling	Machine learning algorithms	Demonstrated the application of various machine learning algorithms in landslide susceptibility modeling in the Wadi Tayyah Basin of Saudi Arabia
Aryal et al. (2011)	Landslide susceptibility mapping	Frequency ratio, statistical models	Employed diverse datasets for landslide susceptibility mapping in the Mugling-Narayanghat road section in Nepal Himalaya
Saha et al. (2021)	Landslide susceptibility models	CNN, ANN, CART, ADTree, FTree, LMT	Utilized 21 parameters to assess the accuracy of landslide susceptibility models in minimizing false negatives and misclassification rates

Understanding and mitigating the risks associated with landslides in this region are imperative for the well-being of local communities and the sustainable development of infrastructure. Nawaz et al. (2021) conducted a comprehensive study focusing on the Himalayas in Pakistan, aiming to compare various landslide susceptibility models and analyze their robustness. The study not only sheds light on the specific challenges faced by this region but also provides valuable insights into the effectiveness of different modeling approaches in predicting and managing landslide occurrences. The collision of tectonic plates, the fragile geological composition, and the steep terrain collectively create a unique set of challenges for the Himalayan region. The study by Nawaz et al. (2021) contributes to the ongoing efforts to develop robust strategies for landslide susceptibility assessment, offering a nuanced understanding of the geological intricacies in this captivating yet vulnerable part of the world.

Geological and Environmental Variations

The Himalayas harbour intricate geological dynamics driven by continuous tectonic forces. This region's susceptibility to landslides is heightened by the prevalence of weak rock layers and fault lines, creating an environment where mass movements become a recurring concern. The ongoing collision of tectonic plates in the Himalayas is a persistent force that shapes the region's terrain. This geological activity results in the uplifting of mountains, the creation of fault lines, and the establishment of distinct rock formations. The cumulative effect of these tectonic forces contributes significantly to the vulnerability of slopes to landslides. A notable feature of the Himalayan geology is the prevalence of weak rock layers and fault lines. These geological attributes serve as critical factors amplifying the risk of mass movements. The fragility of the rocks, combined with the challenging topography characterized by steep slopes, accentuates the region's susceptibility to landslides. The fragile nature of the rocks in the Himalayas becomes particularly consequential during seismic events. Earthquakes activate fault lines and impose additional stress on the already vulnerable slopes. This interplay between seismic activity and weak rock formations significantly increases the likelihood and intensity of landslides.

The identification and meticulous mapping of geological factors, including weak rock layers and fault lines, emerge as imperative steps in understanding landslide susceptibility. Dorren's (2003) work underscores the significance of these efforts in assessing the potential risk of landslides and formulating effective mitigation strategies. Armed with a comprehensive understanding of the geological dynamics, the Himalayan region can implement targeted mitigation strategies. These may include slope stabilization measures, early warning systems, and land-use planning to minimize the impact of landslides on both the natural environment and human settlements. In conclusion, the geological and environmental factors contributing to landslide vulnerability in the Himalayas are complex and multifaceted. Dorren's (2003) insights highlight the necessity of identifying and mapping these geological features, providing a foundational understanding crucial for effective risk assessment and mitigation efforts in this geologically dynamic region.

Climatic and Seasonal Variations

The Himalayas, encapsulating diverse climatic zones, exhibit unique seasonal patterns that play a pivotal role in the region's landslide dynamics. A comprehensive understanding of these climatic nuances is essential for deciphering the complex interplay between weather conditions and slope stability. Monsoon Onslaught and Soil Saturation: A defining feature of the Himalayan climate is the monsoon season, which extends from June to September. During this period, the region experiences intense rainfall, saturating the soil. The consequential increase in pore water pressure poses a substantial threat to slope stability (Silalahi et al., 2019). The sheer volume of precipitation during the monsoons acts as a trigger, significantly elevating the risk of landslides.

Snowmelt and Spring Instabilities: Beyond the monsoon season, the Himalayas encounter a distinctive climatic phenomenon—the melting of snow during warmer months. Spring and early summer witness the gradual thawing of snow, contributing to soil moisture and further destabilizing slopes. The combination of snowmelt and seasonal transitions adds layer of complexity to the region's landslide susceptibility. Implications for Slope Stability: The dual impact of heavy monsoonal rainfall and snowmelt underscores the vulnerability of slopes in the Himalayas. The reduction in slope stability, driven by increased water content in the soil, creates a precarious environment where landslides become more probable. Understanding these climatic dynamics is paramount for anticipating the temporal variations in landslide risk.

Early Warning Systems and Predictive Measures: Recognizing the distinct climatic and seasonal patterns, researchers and local authorities in the Himalayas are increasingly emphasizing the need for robust early warning systems. The ability to predict and respond to heightened landslide risks during specific climatic events is crucial for minimizing the potential impact on communities and infrastructure (Hussain et al., 2022). Early warning systems, informed by an awareness of seasonal variations, can provide timely alerts and aid in proactive risk management strategies. In conclusion, the climatic and seasonal intricacies of the Himalayas significantly contribute to the region's landslide susceptibility. The interplay between monsoons, snowmelt, and seasonal transitions amplifies the challenges in maintaining slope stability. Silalahi et al. (2019) and Hussain et al. (2022) offer valuable insights, emphasizing the importance of understanding these climatic dynamics for effective landslide prediction and mitigation efforts in this geographically diverse and environmentally sensitive region.

Socio-Economic Ramifications of Landslides

The occurrence of landslides in the Himalayas reverberates beyond geological and environmental spheres, significantly impacting the socio-economic fabric of local communities. Understanding the intricate interplay between landslides and their socio-economic repercussions is essential for formulating targeted mitigation and recovery strategies. Vulnerability of Local Communities: Nestled within the Himalayas are numerous villages and towns strategically positioned in areas susceptible to landslides. The inhabitants of these settlements often find themselves on the frontline of the landslide impact, facing the imminent threat of displacement and the consequential loss of livelihoods (Lacroix et al., 2016). The inherent vulnerability of these communities is accentuated by their geographical location, where the beauty of the landscape coexists with the latent danger of mass movements. Infrastructure Strain and Service Disruption: The toll on infrastructure is a direct consequence of landslide events in the region. Roads and bridges, critical arteries for connectivity and essential services, bear the brunt of landslides, often succumbing to severe damage. The resulting disruption isolates communities, hindering the flow of goods, services, and emergency assistance (Wubalem, 2022). The impairment of infrastructure exacerbates the challenges faced by residents, creating a cascading effect on their daily lives.

Economic Downturn and Dependence Disruption: The economic activities of communities in the Himalayas are intricately tied to agriculture and tourism. Landslides disrupt these economic lifelines, causing a downturn in agricultural productivity and impeding the influx of tourists. The repercussions extend beyond immediate financial losses to the broader economic stability of the region. Local businesses, including those reliant on agriculture and tourism, grapple with the aftermath of landslides, highlighting the need for comprehensive risk management strategies to safeguard livelihoods. Holistic Risk Management Imperative: The socio-economic impact of landslides underscores the imperative for holistic risk management strategies. Beyond the immediate aftermath of a landslide event, long-term planning and interventions are essential for mitigating the socio-economic vulnerabilities of local communities. Lacroix et al. (2016) and Wubalem (2022) contribute valuable insights, emphasizing the need for integrated approaches that address the multi-dimensional challenges posed by landslides in the Himalayas. In conclusion, the socio-economic ramifications of landslides in the Himalayas are integral to the region's resilience and sustainable development. The coalescence of vulnerability, infrastructure strain, and economic disruption necessitates a nuanced understanding of the interconnected challenges.

The insights provided by Lacroix et al. (2016) and Wubalem (2022) pave the way for informed decision-making and proactive interventions aimed at fostering the socio-economic well-being of the region's communities.

AI AND MACHINE LEARNING IN LANDSLIDE PREDICTION

The present section discusses the use of various AI techniques in the prediction of landslide susceptibility. Though the individual techniques discussed below may not represent a standalone landslide prediction model, they may be fruitful in carrying out a machine learning modeling step.

Dimension Reduction and Feature Selection

Most geographies have more than two dozen landslide conditioning factors (LCFs) with a few geographies having more than thirty such factors. Any AI or machine learning model, or for that matter any mathematical model involving these many parameters requires inordinately large time, leaving aside the time consumed in the iterative process of hyper-parameter tuning and model optimization. Accordingly, it is imminent that dimensions (read dataset features) be reduced. For dimension/feature reduction purposes, the information content of various features in terms of data variance needs to be computed. Having computed the data variance of various features, the modeller can drop the features containing little data variance, thereby reducing the dimensions of the dataset. Principal component analysis, linear discriminant analysis, information gain, and Gini index are some concepts/methods used to arrange the dataset features in order of their data variance.

Principal Component Analysis

Principal component analysis is a statistical technique used to simplify high-dimensional datasets by transforming them into a lower-dimensional space while retaining important information. The core idea involves identifying new variables, called principal components, which capture the maximum variance in the data. By computing the covariance matrix, PCA determines the relationships between different features, extracting eigenvectors and eigenvalues that represent the directions and magnitude of maximum variance, respectively. These components are ranked based on their variance contributions, allowing for the selection of the most significant ones. PCA aids in reducing redundancy, facilitating easier visualization of complex data, and enhancing computational efficiency for subsequent analyses or modeling. However, while reducing dimensions, PCA might discard some information, and interpreting the reduced components can sometimes be challenging compared to the original variables. Despite these considerations, PCA remains a widely used tool for dimensionality reduction in various fields, enabling efficient handling of high-dimensional datasets. PCA involve the following steps:

- Standardize the data.
- Compute the covariance matrix of the features from the dataset.
- Perform eigen decomposition on the covariance matrix.
- Order the eigenvectors in decreasing order based on the magnitude of their corresponding eigenvalues.

- Determine k, the number of top principal components to select.
- Construct the projection matrix from the chosen number of top principal components.
- Compute the new k-dimensional feature space.

Linear Discriminant Analysis

Linear discriminant analysis is another technique used in landslide susceptibility analysis to reduce dimensions and find a subspace that maximizes class separability. LDA is a technique used for dimensionality reduction and classification. Unlike PCA, which focuses on maximizing variance, LDA aims to find the feature subspace that maximizes class separability. The primary goal of LDA is to project a dataset onto a lower-dimensional space while maintaining class discrimination. It does this by maximizing the ratio of between-class scatter to within-class scatter. It seeks to find a subspace where the projected classes are spread out as much as possible while keeping individual classes tightly clustered.

The steps involved in LDA include:

- Compute the mean vectors: Calculate the mean feature vectors for each class in the dataset.
- Compute the scatter matrices: Calculate the within-class scatter matrix (SW) and between-class scatter matrix (SB). SW measures the scatter within classes, while SB measures the scatter between classes.
- Compute the eigenvectors and eigenvalues: Calculate the eigenvectors and corresponding eigenvalues using $SW^{-1} * SB$. These eigenvectors represent the directions that maximize class separability.
- Select the top k eigenvectors: Select the k eigenvectors corresponding to the k largest eigenvalues to form a transformation matrix. This matrix is used to project the dataset onto the new subspace.

The resulting lower-dimensional subspace retains most of the class-discriminatory information, making it suitable for classification tasks.

Information Gain

Information gain (IG) is a measure commonly used in feature selection to determine the relevance of a feature concerning the classification task at hand. It's extensively used in decision trees and other machine learning algorithms to identify the most informative features for classification. The key idea behind information gain is to quantify the amount of uncertainty (or entropy) in a dataset that is reduced when a specific feature is known. The main steps in computing information gain for a given feature are as follows:

Entropy: Calculate the entropy of the dataset before and after splitting by a feature. Entropy measures the amount of disorder or randomness in a dataset. High entropy means more disorder, while low entropy implies more order or less uncertainty.

Information Gain: Information gain is the difference between the entropy of the dataset before and after the split. It quantifies the amount of information gained about the class variable due to the inclusion of a particular feature. Mathematically, information gain for a feature F with values $f_1, f_2, ..., f_n$ is calculated using the formula (i) below:

$$IG(F) = H(T) - \sum_{i=1}^{n} |\frac{Ti}{T}| * H(Ti) \tag{i}$$

Where:

- $H(T)$ is the entropy of the entire dataset before the split,
- $|T|$ is the total number of instances in the dataset,
- Ti is the subset of instances for each unique value f_i of feature F,
- $|Ti|$ is the number of instances in subset Ti, and
- $H(Ti)$ is the entropy of each subset Ti.

Higher information gain suggests that a feature is more informative for predicting the class variable. Features with higher information gain are preferred for model training as they contribute more to the classification task. Information gain is particularly useful in decision trees where it helps determine the best features to split on at each node. Features with higher information gain are chosen as splitting criteria to separate the dataset into more homogeneous subsets regarding the target variable, leading to better classification performance.

Logistic Regression

Logistic regression involves the logistic function, which maps input variables to a binary output. It estimates the probability of the binary outcome (landslide susceptibility) using a logistic function. Consider a hypothetical labelled dataset comprising six independent features {elevation, slope, rainfall intensity, soil type, land cover, geological composition} and a target feature {landslide susceptibility}. Of the total six, three input features ('soil type', 'land cover', 'geological composition') are categorical (nominal) in nature and the logistic regression model requires these to be converted into numerical representations. One popular method of such conversion is one-hot encoding.

The logistic regression model for landslide prediction involves the logistic function (ii):

$$P(Y = 1 | X) = \frac{1}{1 + e^{-(\beta 0 + \beta 1 X 1 + \beta 2 X 2 + \cdots + \beta n X n)}} \tag{ii}$$

Where:

- $P(Y = 1 | X)$ is the probability of landslide occurrence given prediction vector X,
- $\beta 0, \beta 1, \beta 2, \ldots, \beta n$ are coefficients of regression, and
- $X_1, X_2, \ldots, X_n$ are predictor (input) features/variables.

The model is trained using optimization techniques like gradient descent or maximum likelihood estimation to minimize the error function, such as cross-entropy or log-loss, by adjusting the coefficients. Here if $P(Y = 1 | X)$ comes out to be 0.5 or more than a positive class is predicted (given conditions are susceptible to landslide), otherwise, a negative class is predicted (not susceptible). The coefficients of regression are optimized to describe the given dataset. Thereafter, the resulting regression model (equation) may be deployed and used for landslide prediction.

Artificial Neural Networks

Artificial neural networks (ANNs) consist of interconnected neurons that learn patterns in data through forward and backward propagation. The training process involves adjusting weights and biases to minimize a cost function, enabling the network to make predictions for new data based on learned patterns. Mathematically, ANNs use activation functions, gradient descent, and forward/backward propagation to optimize their parameters and make predictions. ANNs can be used to predict the susceptibility to landslides, using the following process:

Numerical features (elevation, slope, rainfall, etc.) are normalized/standardized into a similar scale to enhance convergence during training. Thereafter, categorical data (soil type, land cover, etc.) are converted into numerical representations using techniques like one-hot encoding. Architecturally, ANNs consist of three or more layers, namely, input, hidden, and output layers. Each layer comprises nodes called neurons interconnected by weights. The mathematical representation of a neuron's output - using the sigmoid activation function – is given in (iv):

$$y = \frac{1}{1 + e^z} \tag{iv}$$

Where:

- y is the output of the neuron, and
- z is the weighted sum of inputs plus bias.

Training the ANN model involves a two-step process: (a) Forward Propagation, and (b) Backward Propagation (Gradient Descent).

Forward Propagation

Calculate the weighted sum z of inputs (eq. v) and apply activation function a (eq. vi) at each neuron:

$$z = w_1 x_1 + w_2 x_2 + \ldots + w_n x_n + b \tag{v}$$

$$a = \sigma(z) \tag{vi}$$

Where:

- w represents weights,
- x denotes input features,

- b is the bias term, and
- σ is the activation function.

Backward Propagation

Update weights and biases to minimize a cost function (e.g., Mean Squared Error, Cross-Entropy) by adjusting the model's parameters in the opposite direction of the gradient. The mathematical representation of weight updates using gradient descent of eq. (vii):

$$\theta = \theta - \alpha \cdot \nabla J(\theta) \tag{vii}$$

Where:

- θ represents model parameters (weights and biases),
- $\pm$ is the learning rate, and
- $\nabla J(\theta)$ is the gradient of the cost function J with respect to θ.

After the model has been trained and tested (evaluated), it can be deployed to predict (classify) the outcome in new scenarios.

Let $x = x_i$ for $i = 1, 2, 3, \ldots, n$ the vector of the n landslide conditioning factors (LCFs) like elevation, slope, curvature, valley depth, etc., $y = f(x) : y = 1$ or 0 indicates the landslide and non-landside class. A nonlinear sigmoid feature is frequently used to the weighted sum of input data until the data are passed to the next step. ANN function for classification is calculated by using the eq. $y = f(x)$.

Support Vector Machine

Support vector machines (SVM) offer a robust approach in landslide susceptibility mapping due to their capability to handle complex, non-linear relationships within datasets. In the context of landslide prediction, SVMs excel in identifying intricate patterns and boundaries between susceptible and non-susceptible areas. By mapping data into higher-dimensional spaces, SVMs effectively distinguish between different land characteristics and environmental factors contributing to landslide occurrences. This method leverages the principles of structural risk minimization, aiming to find an optimal decision boundary that maximizes the margin between classes, enhancing its generalization ability. SVMs accommodate diverse feature sets, including geological, topographical, and environmental parameters, enabling a comprehensive analysis of contributing factors. The SVM approach aims to discriminate between susceptible and not susceptible vectors (data points).

SVM aims to find the optimal hyperplane that separates the dataset into separate disjoint classes. It also maximizes the margin between classes of data. The linear SVM model seeks a separating hyperplane described by eq. (viii):

$$w^T.x + b = 0 \tag{viii}$$

Where:

- w is the weight vector perpendicular to the hyperplane,
- b is the bias term, and
- x represents the input features.

For non-linear data, SVM uses kernel functions (polynomial, radial basis function, etc.) to map data to a higher-dimensional space for better separation. Procedurally, SVM has to separate the N observations into different classes using the hyperplane function. SVM creates a decision boundary that best separates data points in a higher-dimensional space. New data points are classified based on their position concerning this decision boundary. SVM being an algebraic approach, requires the landslide conditioning factors to be in numerical format. Accordingly, non-numeric features like "Soil Type" and "Land Cover" etc. need to be transformed into numeric values.

Decision Tree

Decision Trees recursively partition the feature space into segments based on selected features. Different orders of choice of features result in multiple decision trees. These trees are not equivalent in terms of the time required for the expansion of the tree to its fullest and the performance of the decision-tree classifier. At each node, the tree selects the feature that best separates the data using metrics like entropy, information gain or Gini index. Mathematical representation of the Decision Tree split (for example, based on Gini impurity):

For a binary split at a node m Gini impurity is given by eq. (ix):

$$G(m) = 1 - \sum_{i=1}^{C} P(i \mid m)^2 \qquad (ix)$$

Where:

- $G(m)$ is the Gini impurity at node m,
- C is the number of classes, and
- $P(i|m)$ is the probability of class i at node m.

Decision trees partition feature space based on selected features and impurity measures, while Random forests construct multiple decision trees to improve prediction accuracy and robustness. Both methods create decision rules that classify new instances based on their feature values and the learned patterns from the training data. Classification of a new instance involves the traversal of the tree from the root towards its leaf nodes, whereas the leaf nodes of a decision tree represent class labels. For an illustration of the modus operandi of a decision tree classifier, let us consider the following dataset:

To illustrate how the Decision Tree classifier works, let us consider the following test data instance and try to classify it (susceptible for landslide or not): {elevation=56, slope=17, rainfall=25, soil type=loam, land cover=grassland, geo-composition=limestone}. A decision-tree (Fig. 1) is constructed.

Table 2. A 20-instance hypothetical landslide dataset

Elevation	Slope angle	Rainfall intensity	Soil type	Land cover	Geological composition	Susceptibility/Class label
50	10	20	clay	forest	sandstone	yes
60	15	30	loam	grassland	limestone	no
45	8	18	clay	urban	shale	yes
55	12	25	sandy	forest	granite	no
70	18	35	loam	grassland	sandstone	yes
58	14	28	clay	forest	limestone	no
52	11	22	loam	urban	shale	yes
65	16	32	sandy	grassland	granite	no
48	9	21	clay	urban	sandstone	yes
62	17	29	loam	forest	limestone	no
47	8	24	sandy	urban	shale	yes
53	13	27	clay	grassland	granite	no
68	19	34	loam	urban	sandstone	yes
59	14	26	sandy	forest	limestone	no
51	12	23	clay	grassland	shale	yes
63	18	31	loam	urban	granite	No
49	9	19	sandy	forest	sandstone	yes
57	16	28	clay	grassland	limestone	No
66	20	33	loam	urban	shale	Yes
54	13	25	sandy	forest	granite	No

A look at the decision tree (Fig. 1) shows that the tree gets expanded to its fullest (i.e. all given data instances get classified) using only three features, namely, "Soil Type", "Land Cover", and "Geological composition". Spanning the decision tree along the "Root -> Soil Type=Loam -> Land Cover= Grassland -> Geo-Composition=Limestone" path (shown in bold italics in Fig. 1), the leaf node yields a class label "NO" which predicts that the location characterized by the given data values "*is not susceptible*" to landslide.

Naïve Bayes

Naive Bayes, a probabilistic classification algorithm based on Bayes' theorem, finds applicability in landslide susceptibility analysis due to its simplicity and efficiency. Despite its 'naive' assumption of feature independence, it can deliver effective results, especially in scenarios where datasets are limited and feature interactions are not complex. In landslide susceptibility, naive Bayes leverages various environmental and geological factors, treating them as independent entities to predict the likelihood of landslides. It uses the prior probability of landslides and the probabilities of specific conditions (e.g., soil type, slope, land cover) given the occurrence or absence of landslides to make predictions. To use the naïve Bayes classifier, numeric features like "slope angle", "rainfall intensity" and "elevation" are transformed into a small number of categorical values such as "very low", "low", "mid", "high", and "very high" categories. The transformed dataset is shown in Table 3.

Figure 1. Decision tree for example dataset (Table 1)

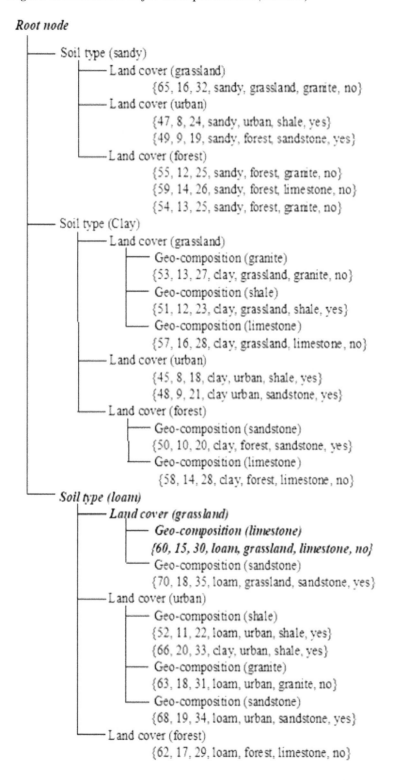

Machine Learning Models for Prediction of Landslides in the Himalayas

Table 3. Dataset of Table 2 – pre-processed (numerical to categorical)

Elevation	Slope angle	Rainfall intensity	Soil type	Land cover	Geological composition	Suscep-tibility
low	low	very low	clay	forest	sandstone	yes
high	mid	high	loam	grassland	limestone	no
very low	very low	very low	clay	urban	shale	yes
mid	low	mid	sandy	forest	granite	no
very high	high	very high	loam	grassland	sandstone	yes
mid	mid	mid	clay	forest	limestone	no
low	low	low	loam	urban	shale	yes
very high	high	high	sandy	grassland	granite	no
very low	very low	low	clay	urban	sandstone	yes
high	high	high	loam	forest	limestone	no
very low	very low	low	sandy	urban	shale	yes
low	mid	mid	clay	grassland	granite	no
very high	very high	very high	loam	urban	sandstone	yes
mid	mid	mid	sandy	forest	limestone	no
low	low	low	clay	grassland	shale	yes
high	high	high	loam	urban	granite	no
very low	very low	very low	sandy	forest	sandstone	yes
mid	high	mid	clay	grassland	limestone	no
very high	very high	very high	loam	urban	shale	yes
low	mid	mid	sandy	forest	granite	no

Mathematical statement of the Bayes theorem is shown in eq. (x), whereas eq. (xi) states the naïve Bayes theorem, a variant of the Bayesian theorem following a naïve assumption that input features are independent of each other.

$$P\left(A \mid x1,\ldots,xn\right) = \frac{P\left(x1,\ldots,xn \mid A\right).P\left(A\right)}{P\left(x1,\ldots,xn\right)} \qquad (x)$$

Where:

- $P(A)$ is the prior probability of occurrence of event A,
- $P\left(A \mid x1,\ldots,xn\right)$ is the posterior probability of the occurrence of event A given the input feature vector $x1, x2, \ldots, xn$,
- $P\left(x1,\ldots,xn\right)$ is the prior probability of occurrence of input features $x1, x2, \ldots, xn$, and
- $P\left(x1,\ldots,xn \mid A\right)$ is the likelihood of input feature vector $x1, x2, \ldots, xn$.

$$P(A|x1,...,xn) = P(x1|A).P(x2|A)...P(xn|A).P(A) \qquad (xi)$$

Now, let us predict the class (susceptible to landslide or not) of the following test instance:
{elevation=56, slope=17, rain=25, soil type=loam, land cover=grassland, geo-composition=limestone}

Step 0. Pre-processing. Transform the numerical features of the input feature vector to categorical values by using the criteria outlined in Table 4:

Table 4. Numerical to categorical transformation of feature space

Elevation		Slope		Rainfall	
Value range	Category	Value range	Category	Value range	Category
<=49	very low	<=9	very low	<=20	very low
50-54	low	10-12	low	21-24	low
55-59	mid	13-15	mid	25-28	mid
60-64	high	16-18	high	29-32	high
>=65	very high	>=19	very high	>=33	very high

Using the criteria mentioned in Table 4, the input test feature vector {elevation=56, slope=17, rain=25, soil type=loam, land cover=grassland, geo-composition=limestone} changes to {elevation=mid, slope=high, rain=mid, soil type=loam, land cover=grassland, geo-composition=limestone}.

Now, applying the naïve Bayes (eq. *xi*) to the data in table 3:

Step 1. Compute the prior probabilities of each of the two classes;

$$P(C1) = \frac{\text{No. of instances of positive class (Yes)}}{\text{Total no. of instances in the dataset}} = 0.5$$

$$P(C2) = \frac{\text{No. of instances of negative class (No)}}{\text{Total no. of instances in the dataset}} = 0.5$$

Step 2. Compute the conditional probabilities of each class w.r.t. different input features (Tables: 5 to 10.

Table 5. Conditional probabilities w.r.t. elevation

Class	Elevation				
	Very Low	Low	Mid	High	Very High
C1	0.4	0.3	0.0	0.0	0.3
C2	0.0	0.2	0.4	0.3	0.1

Table 6. Conditional probabilities w.r.t. slope

Class	Slope				
	Very Low	Low	Mid	High	Very High
C1	0.4	0.3	0.0	0.1	0.2
C2	0.0	0.1	0.5	0.4	0.0

Table 7. Conditional probabilities w.r.t. rainfall

Class	Rainfall Intensity				
	Very Low	Low	Mid	High	Very High
C1	0.3	0.4	0.0	0.0	0.3
C2	0.0	0.0	0.6	0.4	0.0

Table 8. Conditional probabilities w.r.t. soil type

Class	Soil Type		
	Clay	Loam	Sandy
C1	0.4	0.4	0.2
C2	0.3	0.3	0.4

Table 9. Conditional probabilities w.r.t. land cover

Class	Land Cover		
	Forest	Grassland	Urban
C1	0.2	0.2	0.6
C2	0.5	0.4	0.1

Table 10. Conditional probabilities w.r.t. geology

Class	Geological Composition			
	Sandstone	Limestone	Shale	Granite
C1	0.5	0.0	0.5	0.0
C2	0.0	0.5	0.0	0.5

Step 3. Compute the products q1 and q2:

$$q1 = P(elevation|C1).P(slope|C1).P(rain|C1).P(soil\ type|C1).P(land\ cover|C1)P(geoComposition|C1).P(C1)$$

$$q1 = P(mid|C1).P(high|C1).P(mid|C1).P(loam|C1).P(grassland|C1).P(limestone|C1).P(C1)$$

$$q1 = 0.0 * 0.1 * 0.0 * 0.4 * 0.2 * 0.0 * 0.5 = 0.0$$

$$q2 = P(elevation|C2).P(slope|C2).P(rain|C2).P(soiltype|C2).P(land\ cover|C2)P(geoComposition|C2).P(C2)$$

$$q2 = P(mid|C2).P(high|C2).P(mid|C2).P(loam|C2).P(grassland|C2)P(limestone|C2).P(C2)$$

$$q2 = 0.4 * 0.4 * 0.6 * 0.3 * 0.2 * 0.5 * 0.5 = 0.00144$$

Step 4. The class of the given data instance is the class corresponding to $\max\{q1, q2\} = C2$.
The class label of the given test instance is $C2$ i.e. ***not susceptible to landslide***.

Result: In the present test instance, the naïve Bayes classification leads to the inference that a location characterized by {elevation=56, slope=17, rainfall=25, soil type=loam, land cover=grassland, and geo-composition=limestone} is not susceptible to landslides.

CASE STUDIES AND PRACTICAL APPLICATIONS

This section discusses five real-life use cases of AI and machine learning in landslide prediction and management. These use cases cover a variety of terrains ranging from Norway to California in US to Japan to Italy, and to China.

Norway's NGI Landslide Prediction System

The Norwegian Geotechnical Institute (NGI) has developed an AI-based landslide prediction system that uses real-time data from sensors to predict landslides. It combines weather data, groundwater levels, and ground movement data to provide early warnings to authorities. Norway's NGI Landslide Prediction System is a state-of-the-art AI-based infrastructure designed and implemented by the NGI to enhance landslide prediction capabilities. Leveraging cutting-edge technology, this system integrates real-time data obtained from an array of sensors strategically placed in landslide-prone areas. The system's predictive capabilities are founded on the comprehensive analysis of multiple variables, including weather data, groundwater levels, and ground movement data. The NGI Landslide Prediction System operates through a sophisticated algorithm that processes and interprets the incoming data streams. By assessing the intricate interplay between geological and environmental factors, the system aims to identify early warning signs indicative of potential landslide events. The inclusion of weather data allows the system to factor in precipitation patterns, soil saturation levels, and other meteorological variables that can contribute to heightened landslide risk.

Critical to the system's functionality is the utilization of ground movement data, which is crucial for monitoring changes in the landscape. This includes the identification of subtle shifts or deformations in the terrain that could precede a landslide. The combination of these diverse data sources enables the NGI Landslide Prediction System to generate timely and accurate predictions. The real-time nature of the system ensures that authorities receive instantaneous alerts, enabling them to implement proactive measures such as evacuations, road closures, and other mitigation strategies. By providing early warnings, the NGI Landslide Prediction System contributes significantly to minimizing the potential impact of landslides on both human settlements and infrastructure. The NGI system comprises AI and machine learning algorithms, a real-time weather analysis system, ground movement monitoring sensors, a GIS and spatial analysis system, and an early warning system.

California's LIDAR-Based System

California's Department of Conservation, in collaboration with the United States Geological Survey, has developed a state-of-the-art landslide monitoring system that leverages AI and Light Detection and Ranging (LIDAR) technology for enhanced detection and early warning capabilities. The integration of AI, particularly machine learning algorithms, enhances the system's ability to interpret and analyze the vast amount of LIDAR data. Machine learning models are trained to recognize patterns associated with ground movement, surface deformation, and other factors contributing to landslide susceptibility. Through continuous learning from historical data and real-time observations, the AI algorithms can identify evolving landslide-prone areas with a high degree of accuracy. The system operates in real-time, continuously monitoring ground movement in areas susceptible to landslides. When the AI algorithms detect patterns or anomalies indicative of potential landslide activity, automated alerts are generated to notify relevant authorities and communities. This timely information enables proactive measures to be taken, reducing the potential impact of landslides on infrastructure and public safety.

Japan's SABO System

Japan has pioneered a state-of-the-art landslide prediction system that relies on AI to provide real-time monitoring and warnings. This system integrates data from various sources, including rain gauges and soil moisture sensors, to assess environmental conditions and predict landslide risks promptly. The AI-driven system is used to (a) gather data from a network of rain gauges strategically placed across vulnerable regions, (b) process the collected data and assess the current conditions, (c) continuously monitor the environmental conditions, and (d) learn and adapt over time for continuous improvement.

Rain gauges continuously measure precipitation levels, providing crucial input for landslide risk assessment. Additionally, soil moisture sensors are deployed to track ground saturation, enhancing the system's ability to identify areas at heightened risk of landslides. Thereafter, advanced AI algorithms are employed to process the collected data and assess the current conditions. These algorithms consider factors such as rainfall intensity, soil moisture content, and historical landslide data to evaluate the probability of landslide occurrence. Machine learning models play a key role in recognizing patterns and trends that may precede landslide events. A notable feature of the system is its capacity for continuous improvement. The AI algorithms are designed to learn and adapt over time, incorporating new data and refining their predictive capabilities. This iterative learning process enhances the accuracy and reliability of the landslide predictions made by the system.

Italy's Landslide Prediction with IoT

In Italy, a cutting-edge landslide prediction system has been deployed, integrating Internet of Things (IoT) sensors with AI for comprehensive monitoring and analysis. This innovative system combines real-time data from various IoT sensors with advanced AI algorithms to predict and mitigate the risks of landslides. The system utilizes a network of IoT sensors strategically placed in landslide-prone areas. These sensors continuously collect data on crucial environmental factors, such as soil moisture, temperature, and rainfall. The collected data is processed through advanced AI algorithms designed to analyze and interpret patterns indicative of landslide precursors. These algorithms leverage machine learning techniques to recognize correlations between environmental variables and historical landslide events. One of the primary objectives of the system is to enable early detection of potential landslides. By continuously analyzing IoT data in real-time, the AI algorithms can identify anomalies and risk patterns. When the system detects conditions that suggest an elevated risk of landslides, it triggers automated warning systems. These warnings are crucial for alerting authorities, residents, and emergency services promptly. An essential feature of the system is its adaptive learning capability. The AI algorithms undergo continuous improvement through iterative learning processes. As new data becomes available and additional insights are gained, the algorithms evolve to enhance the accuracy of landslide predictions.

China's AI Landslide Early Warning

China has pioneered the development and implementation of AI-based early warning systems designed to predict and mitigate the risks of landslides in regions prone to geological hazards. These advanced systems leverage AI to process diverse data sources, providing comprehensive monitoring and timely alerts. The AI-based early warning systems in China employ a multi-source data integration approach, combining information gathered from various channels, such as high-resolution satellite imagery, real-time rainfall data, and geological data, including soil composition and topography. Machine learning techniques are employed to recognize patterns, correlations, and anomalies within the integrated dataset. The AI models are trained to identify early indicators of landslide risk based on historical patterns and real-time observations. The AI-powered systems enable real-time monitoring of geological conditions. As the algorithms analyze incoming data, they generate alerts when potential landslide risks are detected. These alerts are issued promptly to relevant authorities, local communities, and emergency response teams. China's models continuously learn from new data, refining their predictive capabilities over time. This iterative learning process ensures that the system evolves to address emerging challenges and improve accuracy.

AI FOR LANDSLIDE MITIGATION AND PREPAREDNESS

In the realm of landslide mitigation and preparedness, leveraging the capabilities of artificial intelligence (AI) becomes crucial for developing robust early warning systems (Ado et al., 2022; Alotaibi et al., 2019). Real-time monitoring and alerting systems powered by AI can significantly enhance the efficiency and accuracy of landslide detection (Hussain et al., 2022). Recommendations centre around the integration of advanced sensors, satellite imagery, and machine learning algorithms to provide timely alerts, giving communities valuable lead time to respond to potential landslide threats (Kainthura & Sharma, 2022). Community education and engagement play pivotal roles in landslide preparedness, and strategies for educating local communities should go beyond conventional approaches, embracing culturally sensitive methods to ensure effective communication (Meena et al., 2020). AI can contribute by tailoring educational materials and outreach initiatives to align with the cultural nuances of the specific communities at risk (Nawaz Ikram et al., 2021). This not only enhances understanding but also fosters a sense of ownership and active participation in preparedness measures.

The collaborative efforts of government agencies, non-governmental organizations (NGOs), and local communities form the cornerstone of effective disaster response and recovery. Here, AI can offer substantial support by streamlining communication, resource allocation, and response coordination (Kumar et al., 2023a). Intelligent systems can assist in the rapid assessment of affected areas, aid in the prioritization of response efforts, and optimize resource distribution based on real-time data. Furthermore, AI technologies can facilitate post-disaster recovery by aiding in the assessment of infrastructure damage, optimizing reconstruction plans, and streamlining recovery operations (Guo et al., 2023). The recommendations emphasize the need for a multi-stakeholder approach where government agencies provide policy frameworks, NGOs bring specialized expertise, and local communities actively engage in the co-creation of resilient strategies. In essence, the integration of AI into landslide mitigation and preparedness strategies not only bolsters early warning systems but also transforms the dynamics of community engagement and disaster response. These recommendations underscore the importance of

LOCAL CULTURAL CONSIDERATIONS

embracing technological advancements while remaining attuned to the cultural context, ensuring that AI serves as a catalyst for resilience and empowerment in the face of landslide hazards.

LOCAL CULTURAL CONSIDERATIONS

In delving into local cultural considerations in the Himalayan region concerning AI-driven landslide prediction and mitigation, it becomes evident that a nuanced exploration is essential. The integration of artificial intelligence into disaster-related endeavours necessitates a thorough understanding of the ethical and cultural dimensions unique to the region.

Ethical considerations encompass not only the responsible use of technology but also respect for the cultural values and traditions prevalent in the Himalayas (Shano et al., 2020). The discussion delves into the potential impacts of AI applications on local communities, emphasizing the need for transparency, accountability, and the protection of individual and communal rights (Silalahi et al., 2019). Moreover, the discourse highlights the intrinsic connection between cultural heritage and disaster resilience. Recognizing the importance of incorporating local knowledge and indigenous practices becomes paramount (Turner & Schuster, 1996). The rich tapestry of traditional wisdom, passed down through generations, often holds valuable insights into understanding and mitigating landslide risks (Wubalem, 2022). The chapter emphasizes the significance of bridging the gap between technological interventions and indigenous wisdom to create a holistic approach.

Community involvement emerges as a central theme in the discussion. The Himalayan region's diverse cultural landscape necessitates engagement with local communities in the design, implementation, and evaluation of AI-driven initiatives (Yesilnacar & Topal, 2005). This involvement ensures that technological solutions align with the lived experiences and priorities of the people most affected by landslides. In conclusion, the exploration of local cultural considerations in the context of AI-driven landslide prediction and mitigation underscores the need for an inclusive and culturally sensitive approach. By embracing the ethical dimensions and integrating indigenous knowledge, this chapter advocates for a harmonious synergy between cutting-edge technology and the rich cultural tapestry of the Himalayas.

CONCLUSION

The exploration of landslide prediction in the Himalayas has uncovered a multifaceted terrain of challenges, complexities, and promising technological solutions. In this chapter, our focus on machine learning models and AI applications aims to deepen our understanding and predictive capabilities regarding landslide dynamics in this vulnerable region. Beginning with a contextual introduction, the chapter emphasized the significance of landslide prediction in the Himalayas, acknowledging the region's unique geological, climatic, and socio-economic dynamics. A comprehensive review of related works laid the groundwork by examining the current state of knowledge in landslide prediction, providing a launching point for exploring innovative approaches.

The discussion then delved into the intricate dynamics and challenges specific to the Himalayas. Geological and environmental factors were unravelled, revealing the complexities that contribute to landslide vulnerability. The examination of climatic dynamics explored seasonal variations and influences that shape the propensity for landslides. Additionally, a thorough understanding of the socio-economic ramifications highlighted the far-reaching consequences of landslides on the communities in the Himalayas. Transitioning to the pivotal role of AI and machine learning, the chapter critically explored how these technologies are reshaping landslide prediction methodologies. Moving beyond theoretical considerations, the exploration of case studies and practical applications provided tangible examples:

Furthermore, the chapter emphasized that AI's role extends beyond prediction to encompass mitigation and preparedness strategies. It underscored the importance of considering local cultural nuances and community engagement in implementing effective landslide management practices. The integration of AI and machine learning models offers immense promise for advancing landslide prediction capabilities in the Himalayas. However, the chapter concluded by highlighting the importance of contextualizing these technological interventions within the socio-cultural landscape of the region. It emphasized that local knowledge and community involvement are pivotal for the success and sustainability of landslide prediction and mitigation strategies. Concluding this chapter does not mark an endpoint but rather a transition into the next phase. Future research should continue to explore the synergies between technological advancements and local wisdom, aiming for holistic and culturally sensitive approaches to landslide prediction, mitigation, and community resilience in the Himalayas. In doing so, we pave the way for a safer and more resilient future in the face of landslide hazards.

REFERENCES

Ado, M., Amitab, K., Maji, A. K., Jasińska, E., Gono, R., Leonowicz, Z., & Jasiński, M. (2022). Landslide Susceptibility Mapping Using Machine Learning: A Literature Survey. *Remote Sensing, 14*(13), 3029. MDPI AG. doi:10.3390/rs14133029

Alotaibi, A. F., Pradhan, B., & Park, H. J. (2019). Application of machine learning algorithms in landslide susceptibility modeling at Wadi Tayyah Basin, Saudi Arabia. *Geocarto International*. doi:10.1080/10106049.2018.1548361

Aryal, A., Shrestha, S., & Bajracharya, B. (2011). Landslide susceptibility mapping using frequency ratio, statistical index, and weights-of-evidence model in GIS and their comparison at Mugling-Narayanghat road section in Nepal Himalaya. *Landslides*. doi:10.1007/s10346-011-0278-7

Bai, S., Wang, J., Liao, W., Liu, D., & Ding, G. (2014). Landslide susceptibility mapping using ensemble models in the Three Gorges area, China. *Geomorphology*. doi:10.1016/j.geomorph.2013.10.006

Bookhagen, B., & Burbank, D. W. (2006). Topography, relief, and TRMM-derived rainfall variations along the Himalaya. *Geophysical Research Letters, 33*(8), 2006GL026037. doi:10.1029/2006GL026037

Dorren, L. (2003). A Review of Rockfall Mechanics and Modeling Approaches. *Progress in Physical Geography, 27*(1), 69–87. doi:10.1191/0309133303pp359ra

Guo, Z., Tian, B., Li, G., Huang, D., Zeng, T., He, J., & Song, D. (2023). Landslide susceptibility mapping in the Loess Plateau of northwest China using three data-driven techniques—A case study from middle Yellow River catchment. *Frontiers in Earth Science (Lausanne), 10*, 1033085. Advance online publication. doi:10.3389/feart.2022.1033085

Hussain, M. A., Chen, Z., Zheng, Y., Shoaib, M., Shah, S. U., Ali, N., & Afzal, Z. (2022). Landslide Susceptibility Mapping Using Machine Learning Algorithm Validated by Persistent Scatterer In-SAR Technique. *Sensors, 22*(9), 3119. MDPI AG. doi:10.3390/s22093119

Hussain, M. A., Chen, Z., Zheng, Y., Zhou, Y., & Daud, H. (2023). Deep Learning and Machine Learning Models for Landslide Susceptibility Mapping with Remote Sensing Data. *Remote Sensing, 15*(19), 4703. MDPI AG. doi:10.3390/rs15194703

Kainthura, P., & Sharma, N. (2022). Hybrid machine learning approach for landslide prediction, Uttarakhand, India. *Scientific Reports, 12*(1), 20101. doi:10.1038/s41598-022-22814-9 PMID:36418362

Kumar, A., Singh, V. K., Misra, R., Singh, T. N., & Choudhury, T. (2023). Machine learning and IoT-based approaches to detect and predict rainfall-triggered landslides. *Revue d'Intelligence Artificielle, 37*(5), 1291–1300. doi:10.18280/ria.370522

Kumar, C., Walton, G., Santi, P., & Luza, C. (2023a). An Ensemble Approach of Feature Selection and Machine Learning Models for Regional Landslide Susceptibility Mapping in the Arid Mountainous Terrain of Southern Peru. *Remote Sensing, 15*(5), 1376. MDPI AG. doi:10.3390/rs15051376

Lacroix, P. (2016). Landslides triggered by the Gorkha earthquake in the Langtang valley, volumes and initiation processes. *Earth, Planets, and Space, 68*(1), 46. doi:10.1186/s40623-016-0423-3

Meena, S. R., Ghosh, S., & Shukla, D. P. (2020). Landslide susceptibility mapping using hybrid machine learning models in the Bhagirathi river basin, Indian Himalaya. *Geocarto International*. doi:10.1080/10106049.2020.1760254

Naveen, D. M. N., Roopesh, D., Reddy, J. K., & Raju, P. K. (2022). Landslide detection using machine learning algorithms. *Journal of Algebraic Statistics, 13*(3), 2822–2828. https://publishoa.com

Nawaz Ikram, M., Basharat, M., Ali, A., Usmani, N. A., Gardezi, S. A. H., Hussain, M. L., & Riaz, M. T. (2021). Comparison of landslide susceptibility models and their robustness analysis: A case study from the NW Himalayas, Pakistan. *Geocarto International*. doi:10.1080/10106049.2021.2017010

Neves, L. C., Ngo, T. Q., Dam, N. D., Al-Ansari, N., Amiri, M., Phong, T. V., Prakash, I., Le, H. V., Nguyen, H. B. T., & Pham, B. T. (2021). Landslide Susceptibility Mapping Using Single Machine Learning Models: A Case Study from Pithoragarh District, India. *Advances in Civil Engineering, 9934732*, 1–19. doi:10.1155/2021/9934732

Nhu, V. H., Mohammadi, A., Shahabi, H., Ahmad, B. B., Al-Ansari, N., Shirzadi, A., Clague, J. J., Jaafari, A., Chen, W., & Nguyen, H. (2020). Landslide Susceptibility Mapping Using Machine Learning Algorithms and Remote Sensing Data in a Tropical Environment. *International Journal of Environmental Research and Public Health, 17*(14), 4933. doi:10.3390/ijerph17144933 PMID:32650595

Pham, B. T., Tien Bui, D., & Nguyen, D. B. (2016). Landslide susceptibility mapping using GIS-based statistical models and remote sensing data in tropical environment. *Geocarto International*. doi:10.1080/10106049.2015.1086027

Priyanka, P., Kumar, P., Kala, U., & Dutt, V. (2023, October). *Enhancing Landslide Prediction in the Himalayan Region Using Machine Learning Models and Antecedent Rainfall Data: A Case Study of Kamand Valley, Himachal Pradesh, India.* Paper presented at the 9th International Congress on Information and Communication Technology (ICICT 2024), London, UK.

Reichenbach, P., Rossi, M., Malamud, B. D., Mihir, M., & Guzzetti, F. (2018). A review of statistically-based landslide susceptibility models. *Earth-Science Reviews*, *180*, 60–91. doi:10.1016/j.earscirev.2018.03.001

Saha, S., Bera, B., Shit, P. K., Sengupta, D., Bhattacharjee, S., Sengupta, N., Majumdar, P., & Adhikary, P. P. (2023). Modelling and predicting of landslide in Western Arunachal Himalaya, India. *Geosystems and Geoenvironment*, *2*(2), 100158. doi:10.1016/j.geogeo.2022.100158

Saha, S., Majumdar, P., & Bera, B. (2023a). Deep learning and benchmark machine learning based landslide susceptibility investigation, Garhwal Himalaya (India). *Quaternary Science Advances*, *10*, 100075. doi:10.1016/j.qsa.2023.100075

Saha, S., Roy, J., Hembram, T. K., Pradhan, B., Dikshit, A., Abdul Maulud, K. N., & Alamri, A. M. (2021). Comparison between Deep Learning and Tree-Based Machine Learning Approaches for Landslide Susceptibility Mapping. *Water*, *13*(19), 2664. MDPI AG. doi:10.3390/w13192664

Shano, L., Raghuvanshi, T. K., & Meten, M. (2020). Landslide susceptibility evaluation and hazard zonation techniques – a review. *Geoenvironmental Disasters*, *7*(1), 18. doi:10.1186/s40677-020-00152-0

Silalahi, F. E. S., Pamela, Arifianti, Y., & Hidayat, F. (2019). Landslide susceptibility assessment using frequency ratio model in Bogor, West Java, Indonesia. *Geoscience Letters*, *6*(1), 10. doi:10.1186/s40562-019-0140-4

Turner, A. K., & Schuster, R. L. (1996). *Landslides: Investigation and Mitigation. Special Report 247.* Transportation Research Board, The National Academies Press, Washington DC.

Wubalem, A. (2022). *Landslide Inventory, Susceptibility, Hazard and Risk Mapping*. IntechOpen., doi:10.5772/intechopen.100504

Xia, L., Shen, J., Zhang, T., Dang, G., & Wang, T. (2023). GIS-based landslide susceptibility modeling using data mining techniques. *Frontiers in Earth Science (Lausanne)*, *11*, 1187384. doi:10.3389/feart.2023.1187384

Yesilnacar, E., & Topal, T. (2005). Landslide susceptibility mapping: A comparison of logistic regression and neural networks methods in a medium scale study, Hendek region (Turkey). *Engineering Geology*, *79*(3–4), 251–266. doi:10.1016/j.enggeo.2005.02.002

Youssef, K., Shao, K., Moon, S., & Bouchard, L.-S. (2023). Landslide susceptibility modeling by interpretable neural network. *Communications Earth & Environment*, *4*(1), 162. doi:10.1038/s43247-023-00806-5

Zhou, X., Wen, H., Zhang, Y., Xu, J., & Zhang, W. (2021). Landslide susceptibility mapping using hybrid random forest with GeoDetector and RFE for factor optimization. *Geoscience Frontiers*, *12*(5), 101211. doi:10.1016/j.gsf.2021.101211

Chapter 10
Wearable Sensor and AI Algorithm Integration for Enhanced Natural Disaster Preparedness and Response

Gobinath A.
Velammal College of Engineering and Technology, India

Rajeswari P.
Velammal College of Engineering and Technology, India

Suresh Kumar N.
Velammal College of Engineering and Technology, India

Anandan M.
Vel Tech Rangarajan Dr. Sagunthala R&D Institute of Science and Technology, India

ABSTRACT

This chapter explores the innovative fusion of wearable sensor technologies and artificial intelligence (AI) algorithms in the context of natural disaster preparedness and response. Wearable sensors, designed to be seamlessly integrated into clothing or accessories, offer a dynamic and personal approach to monitoring individuals in disaster-prone areas. Coupled with advanced AI algorithms, these sensors empower individuals and authorities with real-time data, early warning capabilities, and personalized assistance during critical events. The chapter begins by examining the functionalities of wearable sensors specifically engineered for disaster scenarios. These sensors include biometric monitors measuring vital signs such as heart rate, body temperature, and respiratory rate. Additionally, environmental sensors incorporated into wearables detect changes in air quality, temperature, and humidity, providing a comprehensive understanding of immediate surroundings. The integration of AI algorithms into wearable sensor systems is a central focus of this chapter.

DOI: 10.4018/979-8-3693-3362-4.ch010

INTRODUCTION

Natural disasters, such as earthquakes, hurricanes, floods, and wildfires, pose significant threats to human lives, infrastructure, and the environment. In recent decades, the frequency and intensity of these disasters have increased, underscoring the critical need for robust preparedness and response strategies. Natural disaster preparedness involves a range of activities and measures undertaken to mitigate the impact of disasters, including risk assessment, early warning systems, and the development of evacuation plans. Concurrently, effective response strategies aim to minimize casualties and damage through swift and coordinated efforts during and after the occurrence of a disaster (Firoozabadi et.al, 2017).

Throughout history, societies have grappled with the devastating consequences of natural disasters. From ancient civilizations to modern times, the impact of disasters has shaped the course of human development. Early societies relied on rudimentary warning signs, such as animal behavior or celestial events, to predict impending disasters. However, as civilizations advanced, so did the understanding of natural phenomena and the development of early warning systems. The evolution of technology has played a pivotal role in enhancing our ability to predict, prepare for, and respond to natural disasters. From basic weather forecasting tools to sophisticated satellite systems, technological advancements have significantly improved our understanding of disaster dynamics.

In the contemporary era, the convergence of wearable sensor technologies and artificial intelligence (AI) stands out as a transformative force in the realm of natural disaster preparedness and response. Wearable sensors, embedded in devices like smartwatches, clothing, and other personal accessories, provide a novel means of collecting real-time data on physiological parameters, environmental conditions, and human behavior. Simultaneously, AI algorithms have demonstrated remarkable capabilities in processing vast datasets, identifying patterns, and making data-driven predictions. The integration of wearable sensors and AI algorithms holds immense promise in revolutionizing our approach to disaster management by offering timely and accurate information for decision-makers (Comfort.et.al, 2004).

The purpose of this chapter is to delve into the multifaceted landscape of wearable sensor and AI algorithm integration for enhanced natural disaster preparedness and response. As we navigate through the intricate interplay of technology and disaster management, we will explore the nuances of wearable sensor technologies, their historical evolution, and the role of AI algorithms in disaster scenarios. By understanding the significance of these technological advancements, we can better appreciate their potential impact on minimizing the devastation caused by natural disasters. Moreover, we will investigate the challenges and ethical considerations associated with this integration, paving the way for a comprehensive exploration of its implications on the future of disaster resilience (Gonzalez et.al, 2017).

In the pages that follow, we embark on a journey that spans from the ancient foundations of disaster awareness to the cutting-edge innovations of the present day. We will examine the pivotal role that wearable sensors play in capturing critical data at the individual and community levels, providing a granular understanding of the evolving disaster landscape. Simultaneously, we will delve into the capabilities of AI algorithms in processing this wealth of information, elucidating their potential to transform raw data into actionable insights. As we uncover the promises and pitfalls of this integration, we will offer a roadmap for its responsible implementation, emphasizing the need for collaboration among researchers, policymakers, and practitioners to usher in a new era of natural disaster preparedness and response.

Figure 1. AI in disaster management: A satellite image analysis system using artificial intelligence algorithms to assess and respond to natural disasters, providing real-time data for effective disaster mitigation and response strategies

WEARABLE SENSOR TECHNOLOGIES

Overview of Current Wearable Sensor Technologies

In the realm of natural disaster preparedness and response, wearable sensor technologies have emerged as crucial instruments in gathering real-time data and enhancing situational awareness. These innovative devices, seamlessly integrated into everyday items such as clothing, accessories, and personal gear, offer a diverse range of capabilities that contribute to a more comprehensive understanding of both individual and environmental dynamics during disaster events (Albahri et.al, 2018).

Wearable sensors leverage a variety of technologies to monitor physiological parameters, environmental conditions, and human behavior. One of the most common types of sensors found in wearable devices is the accelerometer, which measures acceleration forces and enables the tracking of movement and orientation. Gyroscopes complement accelerometers by providing information on angular velocity and rotational motion. Together, these sensors offer insights into an individual's activities, postures, and movements, which can be invaluable in scenarios like earthquake response where sudden and unexpected shifts in the environment can occur.

Environmental sensors, another integral component of wearable devices, monitor the surrounding conditions such as temperature, humidity, and air quality. These sensors play a pivotal role in assessing the environmental impact of disasters like wildfires or chemical spills, enabling responders to make informed decisions about evacuation and resource allocation. Additionally, biosensors capable of monitoring vital signs, such as heart rate, respiratory rate, and body temperature, provide critical health-related data during disaster situations, aiding in the identification of injuries or medical emergencies (Albahri et al., 2018).

The integration of Global Positioning System (GPS) technology within wearable devices further enhances their utility in disaster scenarios. GPS allows for accurate geolocation, facilitating the tracking of individuals and resources in real-time. This is particularly beneficial for search and rescue operations during events like floods or hurricanes, where rapid response and precise coordination are essential. Furthermore, communication capabilities, such as two-way radios or integration with mobile networks, enable wearables to serve as communication hubs, fostering connectivity among individuals and response teams (Mohammed et al., 2018).

As technology advances, wearables are becoming increasingly sophisticated. Smart fabrics and materials embedded with sensors are paving the way for unobtrusive and continuous monitoring. For instance, clothing with embedded sensors can monitor vital signs without requiring additional accessories, offering a more seamless and comfortable experience for users. This evolution in wearable sensor technology not only enhances the accuracy and efficiency of data collection but also promotes user adherence, a crucial factor in the success of these devices during natural disasters (Ansari et al., 2019).

Current wearable sensor technologies provide a multifaceted approach to data collection and analysis in the context of natural disasters. From tracking individual movements and vital signs to assessing environmental conditions and enabling communication, these devices offer a holistic understanding of the disaster landscape. As we delve deeper into the integration of wearable sensors and AI algorithms, the foundation laid by these technologies becomes instrumental in creating a responsive and adaptive framework for disaster preparedness and response.

Types of Sensors

Wearable sensor technologies encompass a diverse array of sensors, each designed to capture specific types of data critical for disaster preparedness and response. These sensors play a pivotal role in providing real-time information about both individual and environmental dynamics, enabling a comprehensive understanding of the situation at hand. Here, we explore three key types of sensors commonly integrated into wearable devices: accelerometers, gyroscopes, and environmental sensors (Akter et al., 2019).

Accelerometers

Accelerometers are fundamental sensors employed in wearable devices to measure acceleration forces experienced by the device. In the context of natural disaster response, these sensors are instrumental in capturing information related to movement, orientation, and vibrations. For instance, during seismic events such as earthquakes, accelerometers can detect sudden changes in motion and orientation, providing valuable data for assessing the impact on individuals and structures. In wearable devices, accelerometers are often used to monitor the intensity and frequency of physical activities, aiding in the identification of unusual or distressing patterns that may indicate an emergency situation.

Gyroscopes

Complementing accelerometers, gyroscopes measure angular velocity and rotational motion. In disaster scenarios where sudden changes in orientation can occur, gyroscopes contribute to a more nuanced understanding of movements and changes in spatial positioning. This is particularly relevant in contexts like search and rescue operations, where responders may encounter challenging terrains or navigate through collapsed structures. Gyroscopes enhance the overall spatial awareness of wearable devices, making them invaluable tools for first responders and individuals alike in the aftermath of disasters.

Environmental Sensors

Environmental sensors embedded in wearable devices monitor various conditions in the surrounding area. These sensors can include components measuring temperature, humidity, air quality, and even radiation levels. In the context of natural disasters, environmental sensors are crucial for assessing the impact on the immediate surroundings. For instance, during wildfires, these sensors can detect changes in air quality and temperature, aiding in evacuation decisions and resource allocation. Additionally, in the aftermath of disasters such as chemical spills, environmental sensors contribute to the identification of hazardous conditions, guiding response efforts and ensuring the safety of both responders and affected populations.

As technology advances, wearables are increasingly incorporating a combination of these sensors to provide a more comprehensive understanding of the disaster landscape. For example, a wearable device designed for earthquake response might integrate both accelerometers and gyroscopes to capture precise information about ground movements and individual motions. Environmental sensors, in turn, enhance the device's capability to assess the immediate surroundings for potential hazards (Meechang et al., 2020).

The collective data from these sensors not only contribute to a more accurate and detailed situational awareness but also form the foundation for the integration of wearable sensors with artificial intelligence algorithms. This integration holds the potential to transform raw sensor data into actionable insights, thereby significantly improving the effectiveness of disaster preparedness and response efforts.

Applications in Monitoring Physiological Parameters and Environmental Conditions

The integration of wearable sensors into disaster preparedness and response strategies brings forth a wealth of applications, particularly in the monitoring of physiological parameters and environmental conditions. These applications play a pivotal role in enhancing situational awareness, enabling rapid response, and mitigating the impact of natural disasters on individuals and communities. Here, we delve into the multifaceted applications of wearable sensors in monitoring both human and environmental factors.

Monitoring Physiological Parameters

Wearable sensors are adept at monitoring various physiological parameters, providing valuable insights into the health and well-being of individuals during and after a natural disaster. Biosensors embedded in wearable devices can capture real-time data on vital signs, including heart rate, respiratory rate, body temperature, and blood pressure. This information is crucial for assessing the immediate health status of individuals, identifying potential medical emergencies, and prioritizing medical interventions in disaster-stricken areas.

During events such as earthquakes or hurricanes, where injuries and medical emergencies are prevalent, wearable sensors offer continuous monitoring capabilities. For example, if a person is trapped under debris, wearable sensors can relay vital sign data to first responders, aiding in the prioritization of rescue efforts. Furthermore, continuous monitoring of physiological parameters can help detect signs of stress or emotional distress, enabling timely psychological support for individuals affected by the disaster.

Assessing Environmental Conditions

Wearable sensors also excel in assessing environmental conditions, providing critical data on the immediate surroundings during natural disasters. Environmental sensors integrated into wearable devices can measure factors such as temperature, humidity, air quality, and even detect the presence of harmful substances. In wildfire scenarios, for instance, environmental sensors can detect changes in air quality, prompting timely evacuation warnings and guiding individuals away from hazardous areas.

Moreover, wearable sensors with GPS capabilities offer real-time geolocation data, facilitating the tracking of individuals and resources in disaster-stricken areas. This is particularly valuable for search and rescue operations, allowing response teams to efficiently locate and assist those in need. Additionally, the integration of environmental sensors can aid in assessing the extent of damage to infrastructure, helping prioritize response efforts and allocate resources effectively.

Early Warning Systems

The real-time data collected by wearable sensors can contribute to the development of early warning systems, enhancing the overall preparedness for natural disasters. For example, wearable devices equipped with accelerometers and gyroscopes can detect seismic activity during earthquakes, triggering automated alerts to individuals in the affected region. This early warning allows for prompt evacuation and preparation, potentially saving lives and minimizing injuries.

Similarly, wearable sensors can be employed in flood-prone areas to monitor water levels and trigger warnings when a critical threshold is reached. This proactive approach to disaster management empowers individuals and communities to take preventive measures, fostering a more resilient response to natural disasters.

Data-Driven Decision Making

The continuous stream of data from wearable sensors, both on physiological parameters and environmental conditions, serves as a foundation for data-driven decision-making. AI algorithms can analyze this data in real-time, identifying patterns, trends, and anomalies that may go unnoticed through traditional methods. Such insights enable authorities to make informed decisions regarding resource allocation, evacuation plans, and the prioritization of response efforts.

In conclusion, the applications of wearable sensors in monitoring physiological parameters and environmental conditions significantly enhance our capacity to respond effectively to natural disasters. By providing real-time data and enabling early warning systems, wearable sensor technologies contribute to a more resilient and adaptive disaster management framework, ultimately safeguarding lives and minimizing the impact on communities. As technology continues to evolve, the integration of wearable sensors with AI algorithms holds the promise of further optimizing disaster preparedness and response strategies.

AI ALGORITHMS IN DISASTER MANAGEMENT

Artificial Intelligence in Disaster Response

The contemporary landscape of natural disasters, encompassing a spectrum from earthquakes to hurricanes and floods, necessitates a transformative approach to disaster response. Artificial Intelligence (AI) emerges as a pivotal force in this evolution, offering unparalleled capabilities to reshape our strategies in the face of escalating uncertainties. As climate patterns shift and population growth compounds the impact of disasters, the traditional reactive models prove inadequate. In this context, AI becomes a linchpin for proactive, anticipatory measures that can revolutionize disaster management (Sun et al., 2020).

One of the foremost applications of AI in disaster response lies in the enhancement of early warning systems. By leveraging machine learning algorithms to analyze diverse datasets, including weather patterns and seismic activities, AI facilitates the creation of highly accurate predictive models. These models enable authorities to issue timely warnings to at-risk populations, transforming the dynamics of preparedness from reactive to proactive. The ability to anticipate the likelihood, intensity, and trajectory of disasters allows for a more strategic deployment of resources, minimizing casualties and damage.

AI's impact extends beyond early warnings to the optimization of resource allocation and logistics during the response phase. Real-time data processing capabilities equip AI algorithms to analyze factors such as the extent of damage, population density, and accessibility. This results in more informed decision-making for emergency responders, ensuring that essential resources, such as medical aid and shelter, are directed to areas of greatest need. The efficiency gained through AI-driven resource allocation significantly contributes to the effectiveness of response efforts.

In the realm of decision-making processes, AI stands out as a catalyst for informed and agile responses. Integration of machine learning algorithms with decision support systems empowers emergency management teams to evaluate multiple scenarios, assess potential outcomes, and adapt strategies dynamically. The comprehensive situational awareness provided by AI-driven decision support systems is particularly crucial in the critical early stages of a disaster. It enables decision-makers to make swift, well-informed choices, optimizing response efforts and mitigating the impact on affected communities.

Moreover, the adoption of AI in disaster response is not confined to immediate challenges; it extends to the broader goal of building resilience within communities. Machine learning algorithms continuously analyze historical data and response outcomes, facilitating the refinement of disaster preparedness strategies. This adaptive capability ensures that response efforts evolve alongside changing environmental conditions, emerging risks, and technological advancements. AI, therefore, becomes an essential component in the iterative process of enhancing resilience over time.

The integration of AI in disaster response represents a fundamental shift in our capacity to address the growing challenges posed by natural disasters. From revolutionizing early warning systems to optimizing resource allocation and fostering adaptive decision-making, AI technologies offer a comprehensive toolkit for building resilience and mitigating the impact of disasters. As we delve deeper into the nuances of AI-driven disaster response, it becomes evident that these technologies are not just tools; they are catalysts for innovation, empowerment, and, ultimately, the safeguarding of lives in the face of nature's formidable forces (Habibi et al., 2021).

Role of AI in Data Analysis, Prediction, and Decision-Making

The role of Artificial Intelligence (AI) in data analysis, prediction, and decision-making is transformative, reshaping how organizations process information, anticipate future trends, and make strategic choices. AI technologies, particularly machine learning algorithms, demonstrate remarkable capabilities in handling large and complex datasets, extracting meaningful patterns, and generating predictive insights. In this context, the convergence of AI and data analytics presents a powerful synergy that permeates various sectors, from finance and healthcare to disaster management and beyond.

Data Analysis

AI plays a pivotal role in data analysis by unlocking the potential hidden within vast datasets. Traditional methods of data analysis often struggle to handle the sheer volume and complexity of contemporary data sources. AI, however, excels in processing diverse data types, ranging from structured databases to unstructured text and images. Machine learning algorithms can identify patterns, correlations, and anomalies that might go unnoticed through conventional analysis methods. This ability proves invaluable in extracting actionable insights from data, guiding organizations in making informed decisions based on a more nuanced understanding of their data landscape (Lee et.al, 2022).

Moreover, AI-driven data analysis offers a dynamic approach, continuously learning and adapting to evolving datasets. Through techniques like unsupervised learning, AI algorithms can identify hidden structures within data, providing a deeper understanding of relationships and trends. This adaptability is particularly beneficial in sectors where data patterns are subject to change, enabling organizations to stay ahead of the curve in industries ranging from marketing and finance to healthcare and scientific research (Borgia et al., 2014).

Prediction

The predictive capabilities of AI are perhaps one of its most compelling features. Machine learning models, trained on historical data, can extrapolate patterns and trends to make predictions about future events. This is particularly relevant in industries where forecasting is critical, such as finance, weather prediction, and demand forecasting in supply chain management. AI algorithms can discern subtle patterns in data, allowing organizations to anticipate market trends, identify potential risks, and optimize resource allocation.

In finance, for instance, AI-powered predictive analytics can analyze market trends, assess risk factors, and even predict stock price movements. Similarly, in healthcare, machine learning models can analyze patient data to predict the likelihood of specific medical conditions, enabling early intervention and personalized treatment plans. The predictive power of AI transforms decision-making from reactive to proactive, empowering organizations to navigate uncertainties with a greater degree of foresight.

Decision-Making

AI's influence on decision-making extends beyond prediction to provide valuable insights for informed choices. Decision support systems, enhanced by AI algorithms, assist human decision-makers by presenting relevant information, alternative scenarios, and recommended courses of action. These systems integrate data from various sources, analyze it in real-time, and offer actionable insights, facilitating quicker and more accurate decision-making (Sethi et al., 2014).

In complex scenarios, such as strategic planning or crisis management, AI-driven decision support systems become indispensable. By processing vast amounts of data rapidly, AI can identify critical factors, potential risks, and optimal strategies. In healthcare, for example, AI supports clinical decision-making by analyzing patient data, medical records, and research findings to recommend personalized treatment plans. Similarly, in business, AI-driven decision support systems aid executives in evaluating market trends, competitor strategies, and potential risks, enabling more strategic and data-driven decision-making.

Ethical Considerations

While the potential of AI in data analysis, prediction, and decision-making is immense, it raises ethical considerations that warrant careful attention. The algorithms powering AI systems learn from historical data, and if that data reflects biases or inequalities, the AI models can perpetuate and exacerbate those biases. This is particularly significant in decision-making processes that impact individuals, such as hiring practices, criminal justice, and healthcare.

Ensuring fairness and transparency in AI algorithms becomes a critical aspect of responsible AI deployment. Organizations must actively address bias by auditing and refining their algorithms, employing diverse datasets, and incorporating ethical guidelines into the development process. Additionally, fostering transparency in AI decision-making processes is essential for building trust among users and stakeholders. Striking the right balance between innovation and ethical considerations is paramount to harnessing the full potential of AI in a responsible and socially conscious manner.

Case Studies: AI Applications in Disaster Management

While there might not be an exhaustive list of case studies specifically tailored to AI applications in disaster management in India, several notable instances illustrate the successful integration of AI technologies in addressing natural disasters and their aftermath. Here are a few illustrative examples:

Cyclone Fani (2019)

Cyclone Fani, one of the strongest tropical cyclones to hit the Indian subcontinent, made landfall in Odisha in 2019. The government, in collaboration with tech companies, utilized AI-based predictive models to anticipate the cyclone's path and intensity. These models analyzed meteorological data, satellite imagery, and historical weather patterns to provide accurate predictions, enabling authorities to evacuate millions of people in advance. The successful use of AI in forecasting and decision-making contributed to a substantial reduction in casualties compared to previous cyclones of similar intensity.

Kerala Floods (2018)

The devastating floods in Kerala in 2018 prompted the use of AI in disaster response. A research team from the Indian Institute of Information Technology and Management-Kerala (IIITM-K) developed an AI-based system to predict floods by analyzing real-time data from various sources, including weather forecasts, river gauge readings, and satellite imagery. The system provided accurate predictions of potential flood-prone areas, aiding authorities in issuing timely warnings and coordinating rescue efforts. This application showcased the potential of AI in mitigating the impact of floods and improving disaster preparedness.

Uttarakhand Landslides (2013)

In the wake of the catastrophic landslides in Uttarakhand in 2013, an AI-based landslide prediction system was proposed to enhance early warning capabilities. The system integrated data from weather stations, ground sensors, and satellite imagery to analyze soil conditions and terrain instability. By employing machine learning algorithms, the system aimed to predict areas at high risk of landslides, allowing authorities to evacuate vulnerable populations and allocate resources more effectively. While the implementation is ongoing, the initiative reflects the potential of AI in addressing landslide hazards in the region.

Mumbai Floods (2005)

The floods that submerged Mumbai in 2005 prompted subsequent efforts to improve disaster management using AI. Researchers at the Indian Institute of Technology Bombay (IIT-B) developed an AI-based flood prediction model. This model utilized rainfall data, topographical information, and historical flood patterns to predict potential flood-prone areas. While not operational during the 2005 floods, the research laid the groundwork for future AI applications in Mumbai's disaster preparedness and response strategies.

AI in Earthquake Early Warning (Ongoing)

India is prone to seismic activity, and earthquakes pose a significant threat. Efforts are underway to integrate AI into earthquake early warning systems. The application involves the use of machine learning algorithms to analyze seismic data and detect patterns indicative of impending earthquakes. This technology aims to provide timely alerts to residents and authorities, allowing for proactive measures to mitigate the impact of seismic events.

While these examples showcase the potential of AI in disaster management in India, it's essential to acknowledge the ongoing nature of these initiatives. Implementing AI solutions in disaster management requires sustained efforts, collaboration between stakeholders, and ongoing refinement of technologies. As technology continues to evolve, the integration of AI in disaster management will likely play an increasingly crucial role in safeguarding lives and minimizing the impact of natural disasters in India.

INTEGRATION OF WEARABLE SENSORS AND AI ALGORITHMS

The synergy between sensor data and Artificial Intelligence (AI) for real-time analysis holds paramount importance across a myriad of applications, revolutionizing how we perceive, interpret, and respond to dynamic environments. Sensors, whether deployed in healthcare, manufacturing, environmental monitoring, or disaster management, provide an uninterrupted flow of real-time data. This continuous stream enables AI algorithms to maintain heightened situational awareness, promptly identifying anomalies and changes in conditions. In healthcare, for instance, real-time monitoring of patient vitals through sensors allows AI to detect early signs of deterioration, facilitating timely interventions and personalized care plans. Similarly, in manufacturing, sensors on machinery generate data on performance, temperature, and operational parameters, which AI algorithms can analyze in real time. This dynamic analysis not only enables predictive maintenance to prevent unplanned downtime but also optimizes operational efficiency.

The integration of sensor data with AI enriches decision-making processes by allowing for the fusion of information from various sensors. This comprehensive understanding of the monitored environment empowers decision-makers to adopt a holistic approach. For instance, in smart cities, where sensors gather data on traffic flow, air quality, and energy consumption, AI can synthesize this information to optimize urban planning and resource allocation. In disaster management, the combination of sensor data from seismic detectors, weather stations, and satellite imagery enables AI to generate real-time insights, enhancing the precision of response strategies.

Moreover, the predictive capabilities facilitated by this integration are instrumental in anticipating future trends and behaviors. AI algorithms, trained on historical patterns within sensor data, can forecast outcomes and identify potential risks. This is exemplified in agriculture, where sensors measuring soil moisture, temperature, and crop health collaborate with AI to enable precision farming. By predicting optimal conditions for growth, farmers can make data-driven decisions on irrigation and fertilization, enhancing crop yields and resource efficiency.

Beyond immediate advantages, the amalgamation of sensor data with AI fosters continuous learning and adaptability. Machine learning algorithms can evolve by learning from new data, refining their models and improving accuracy over time. In applications such as cybersecurity, where sensors detect network anomalies, AI continuously adapts to emerging threats, bolstering the resilience of systems.

The integration of sensor data with AI for real-time analysis represents a paradigm shift in how we harness information for decision-making across diverse sectors. It empowers industries with heightened situational awareness, optimized decision-making, predictive capabilities, and continuous learning. As this synergy evolves, it promises to be a cornerstone in shaping a future where data-driven insights and adaptability are central to innovation, efficiency, and effective response strategies in the face of dynamic and complex challenges.

Challenges and Considerations in Integrating Sensor Data and AI Algorithms

Integrating sensor data with Artificial Intelligence (AI) algorithms presents a transformative approach, but several challenges and considerations must be navigated for successful implementation. The first challenge lies in ensuring the quality and consistency of sensor data, as variations or inaccuracies can significantly impact the performance of AI algorithms. Concurrently, data security and privacy concerns arise due to the continuous generation and analysis of real-time data, particularly in applications involving sensitive information. Striking a balance between seamless integration and maintaining privacy becomes crucial, necessitating stringent access controls and compliance with data protection regulations.

Another challenge stems from the diverse landscape of sensors, each operating on different protocols and formats. Achieving interoperability and standardization is essential to create cohesive solutions across various sensor types. Scalability poses additional hurdles as sensor networks expand, demanding robust infrastructure to handle real-time data influx. System complexity, especially with the integration of sophisticated AI algorithms, requires careful consideration of computational resource scalability to avoid bottlenecks and system failures.

Energy efficiency and battery life emerge as significant considerations, particularly for sensors operating in resource-constrained environments. Continuous data transmission and processing can strain energy resources, necessitating the development of energy-efficient algorithms and innovative power solutions. Explainability and transparency of AI algorithms, crucial for user trust and regulatory compliance, present another challenge, especially in complex models. Addressing ethical considerations, such as bias in algorithmic decision-making, becomes imperative to ensure fair and accountable outcomes. In navigating these challenges, organizations can unlock the full potential of integrating sensor data with AI, building resilient, responsible, and effective systems across diverse industries.

CONCLUSION

In conclusion, the integration of wearable sensors and AI algorithms in the context of natural disaster preparedness and response marks a pivotal advancement with profound implications for public safety. The fusion of real-time sensor data with the analytical prowess of AI technologies offers unprecedented capabilities, revolutionizing the landscape of disaster management. Through early detection, accurate risk assessment, and optimized resource allocation, this integration empowers emergency responders and communities to mitigate the impact of natural disasters.

Wearable sensors, capable of monitoring physiological parameters and environmental conditions, serve as frontline data collectors, providing a continuous stream of information critical for timely decision-making. The diverse array of sensor types, from accelerometers to environmental sensors, creates a holistic understanding of the disaster environment, enabling a nuanced and adaptive response.

The role of AI algorithms in disaster management extends beyond data analysis; it encompasses predictive modeling, decision support, and continuous learning. AI-driven early warning systems, equipped with machine learning capabilities, harness historical data and real-time inputs to forecast disaster events with unprecedented accuracy. Decision support systems enhance the decision-making process during response efforts, ensuring that resources are deployed efficiently and effectively.

As we stand at the intersection of sensor technology and AI advancements, the synergistic integration of these components not only enhances disaster preparedness but also fosters resilience in the face of evolving risks. The journey toward a future where wearable sensors and AI algorithms work in tandem represents a transformative leap, reinforcing our collective ability to respond proactively to the complex and dynamic challenges posed by natural disasters. Through ongoing research, technological innovation, and collaborative efforts, this integration holds the promise of saving lives, minimizing damage, and building more resilient communities on a global scale.

REFERENCES

Akter, S., & Wamba, S. F. (2019). Big data and disaster management: A systematic review and agenda for future research. *Annals of Operations Research*, *283*(1-2), 939–959. doi:10.1007/s10479-017-2584-2

Albahri, A. S., Zaidan, A. A., Albahri, O. S., Zaidan, B. B., & Alsalem, M. A. (2018). Real-Time Fault-Tolerant mHealth System: Comprehensive Review of Healthcare Services, Opens Issues, Challenges and Methodological Aspects. *Journal of Medical Systems*, *42*(8), 137. doi:10.1007/s10916-018-0983-9 PMID:29936593

Albahri, O. S., Albahri, A. S., Mohammed, K. I., Zaidan, A. A., Zaidan, B. B., Hashim, M., & Salman, O. H. (2018). Systematic Review of Real-time Remote Health Monitoring System in Triage and Priority-Based Sensor Technology: Taxonomy, Open Challenges, Motivation and Recommendations. *Journal of Medical Systems*, *42*(5), 80. doi:10.1007/s10916-018-0943-4 PMID:29564649

Albahri, O. S., Zaidan, A. A., Zaidan, B. B., Hashim, M., Albahri, A. S., & Alsalem, M. A. (2018). Real-Time Remote Health-Monitoring Systems in a Medical Centre: A Review of the Provision of Healthcare Services-Based Body Sensor Information, Open Challenges and Methodological Aspects. *Journal of Medical Systems*, *42*(9), 164. doi:10.1007/s10916-018-1006-6 PMID:30043085

Alsamhi, S.H.; Ma, O.; Ansari, M.S.; Almalki, F.A. Survey on collaborative smart drones and internet of things for improving smartness of smart cities. IEEE Access 2019, 7, 128125–128152.

Borgia, E. (2014). The internet of things vision: Key features, applications and open issues. *Computer Communications*, *54*, 1–31. doi:10.1016/j.comcom.2014.09.008

Comfort, L. K., Ko, K., & Zagorecki, A. (2004). Coordination in rapidly evolving disaster response systems: The role of information. *The American Behavioral Scientist*, *48*(3), 295–313. doi:10.1177/0002764204268987

Firoozabadi, S. M. K., Soleimani, G., Amiri, M., & Moradian, M. (2017). Review of emergency response methods in disaster management, dispatch and control of forces in emergencies. *Int. J. Econ. Perspect.*, *11*, 1737–1747.

Gonzalez, E., Peña, R., Avila, A., Vargas-Rosales, C., & Munoz-Rodriguez, D. (2017). A Systematic Review on Recent Advances in mHealth Systems: Deployment Architecture for Emergency Response. *Journal of Healthcare Engineering*, *2017*, 9186270. doi:10.1155/2017/9186270 PMID:29075430

Habibi Rad, M., Mojtahedi, M., & Ostwald, M. J. (2021). Industry 4.0, disaster risk management and infrastructure resilience: A systematic review and bibliometric analysis. *Buildings*, *11*(9), 411. doi:10.3390/buildings11090411

Lee, P., Kim, H., Sami Zitouni, M., Khandoker, A., Jelinek, H. F., Hadjileontiadis, L., Lee, U., & Jeong, Y. (2022). Trends in Smart Helmets With Multimodal Sensing for Health and Safety: Scoping Review. *JMIR mHealth and uHealth*, *10*(11), e40797. doi:10.2196/40797 PMID:36378505

Meechang, K., Leelawat, N., Tang, J., Kodaka, A., & Chintanapakdee, C. (2020). The acceptance of using information technology for disaster risk management: A systematic review. *Engineering Journal (New York)*, *24*, 111–132.

Sethi, P., & Sarangi, S. R. (2017). Internet of Things: Architectures, Protocols, and Applications. *Journal of Electrical and Computer Engineering*, *2017*, 9324035. doi:10.1155/2017/9324035

Sun, W., Bocchini, P., & Davison, B. D. (2020). Applications of artificial intelligence for disaster management. *Natural Hazards*, *103*(3), 2631–2689. doi:10.1007/s11069-020-04124-3

APPENDIX

Creating a comprehensive code for AI in disaster management involves several aspects, including data preprocessing, model development, and integration with relevant systems.

```
import pandas as pd
from sklearn.model_selection import train_test_split
from sklearn.ensemble import RandomForestClassifier
from sklearn.metrics import accuracy_score, classification_report
# Load dataset (hypothetical data)
# Consider a dataset with features like rainfall, river level, and historical flood data
# The target variable indicates whether a flood occurred (1) or not (0)
dataset = pd.read_csv('disaster_data.csv')
# Preprocessing: Split the data into features (X) and target variable (y)
X = dataset[['rainfall', 'river_level', 'historical_flood_data']]
y = dataset['flood_occurred']
# Split the data into training and testing sets
X_train, X_test, y_train, y_test = train_test_split(X, y, test_size=0.2, random_state=42)
# Model development: Random Forest Classifier
model = RandomForestClassifier(n_estimators=100, random_state=42)
model.fit(X_train, y_train)
# Prediction on the test set
y_pred = model.predict(X_test)
# Evaluation
accuracy = accuracy_score(y_test, y_pred)
classification_rep = classification_report(y_test, y_pred)
print(f'Accuracy: {accuracy}')
print(f'Classification Report:\n{classification_rep}')
# Now, in a real-world scenario, you would use this trained model for early flood detection.
# Integrate this code into a system that continuously monitors environmental data and triggers alerts when a potential flood is detected.
# For simplicity, let's assume a new data point for prediction (features: rainfall, river level, historical flood data)
new_data_point = [[20.0, 5.0, 0]]
# Make predictions for the new data point
prediction = model.predict(new_data_point)
if prediction[0] == 1:
print('Alert: Potential flood detected! Take necessary precautions.')
else:
print('No immediate flood threat.')
```

Chapter 11
A Novel Approach on IoT-Based Natural Disaster Prediction and Early Warning Systems (EWS)

Karthikeyan Pathinettampadian
https://orcid.org/0000-0001-8515-7370
Anna University, India & Velammal College of Engineering and Technology, India

Nagarani N.
https://orcid.org/0000-0001-7142-1513
Velammal College of Engineering and Technology, India

Shivani Suvatheka S.
Velammal College of Engineering and Technology, India

Al Mohamed Bilal A.
Velammal College of Engineering and Technology, India

ABSTRACT

Natural disasters cause significant damage and human losses, emphasizing the need for predictive systems and efficient warning mechanisms. Exploring the potential of an internet of things (IoT)-driven early warning system (EWS) is crucial for detecting and notifying individuals about diverse disasters like earthquakes, floods, tsunamis, and landslides. In a disaster, the device transmits data to the microcontroller, where it undergoes validation and processing using ML algorithms to predict disaster possibilities. Data from edge nodes reaches the cloud via a gateway, with fog nodes filtering and accessing it. After verification, persistent alarming weather conditions trigger a warning alert, conveyed promptly to individuals in disaster-prone regions through diverse communication channels. An IoT-based open-source application with a user-friendly interface continuously monitors parameters like water intensity and rainfall during floods, and ground vibrations for earthquakes. Alerts are generated when parameters exceed set thresholds, providing a cost-effective disaster detection solution with timely alerts to vulnerable communities.

DOI: 10.4018/979-8-3693-3362-4.ch011

INTRODUCTION

An Early Warning System (EWS) constitutes an integrated framework encompassing hazard monitoring, forecasting, prediction, disaster risk assessment, communication, and preparedness activities. This comprehensive system empowers individuals, communities, governments, businesses, and other stakeholders to take timely actions that mitigate disaster risks before hazardous events occur. Key components of an EWS include (a) risk knowledge and assessment, (b) monitoring parameters for enhanced predictions, (c) timely dissemination of warnings, and (d) preparedness for disaster response. The utilization of advanced information and communication technologies presents a viable solution for expanding multi-hazard warning systems, especially in countries lacking national implementations. These technologies, including the Internet of Things, Cloud Computing, and Artificial Intelligence, play pivotal roles in monitoring, forecasting, and alarm generation within Early Warning systems. They offer cost-effective deployment and facilitate smart and efficient alert and information broadcasting. In particular, these technologies empower the examination and interpretation of data. from the environment, contributing to the effectiveness of Early Warning efforts.

Internet of Things

The Internet of Things comprises infrastructures that interconnect various objects, facilitating the collection, transfer, and access to the generated data. Its primary goal is to connect objects, sensors, and actuators to perform diverse tasks, including customized environmental monitoring(Shah S et al.2019). A fundamental and generic IoT architecture typically consists of three levels: (a) the local environment in which the sensors and actuators are placed where they sense, monitor, and collect the required data (b) a transport layer enabling communication between end-nodes in the first layer and higher layers of the infrastructures; and (c) a storage layer where the collected data are stored for the later access and to maintain records of the event that can be viewed from anywhere in the world via internet. This is usually implemented in the cloud that interfaces systems for user access and data visualization. In adherence to the United Nations Sustainable Development Goal 12, sustainable cities place a significant emphasis on disaster risk reduction (Mei G et al. 2019). The Gesi Smarter 2030 report highlights the crucial role played by IoT in the realm of disaster management and Early Warning systems. It provides the means for extensive environmental monitoring through diverse data sources, low-latency communications, and real-time data processing. These capabilities enable the generation of accurate and timely warnings on the occurrence of a disaster or during forecasting.

LITERATURE REVIEW

Previous studies have demonstrated a greater emphasis on the utilization of sensors in the IoT for disaster management in the pre-disaster phase. (Esposito et al. 2014) conducted a comprehensive review of Early alert systems for natural catastrophs in the pre-disaster stage, specifically focusing on IoT. (Ahmed et al. 2020) critically examine the utilization of affordable sensors in the monitoring of climate- related disasters in coastal regions. Nonetheless, it's imperative for disaster management to encompass many activities during both the pre-disaster stage, such as disaster identification and prevention, as well as the post-disaster stage, including evacuation, search and rescue operations, and rehabilitation efforts

A Novel Approach on IoT-Based Natural Disaster Prediction and Early Warning Systems (EWS)

(Rogers D et al. 2022). Disasters can manifest abruptly or unexpectedly. After the initial 72-hour period following a catastrophic event, the probability of finding individuals who have survived significantly diminishes. Effective disaster response systems are essential to minimize human suffering and reduce mortality rates (Zambrano et al.2017). The key goals of disaster management involve issuing timely alerts, collecting real- time data, accurately assessing damages, swiftly identifying evacuation routes, and efficiently coordinating emergency provisions (Poslad S et al.2016). Traditional disaster management methods are becoming obsolete as they struggle to gather real- time data from diverse sources and process extensive amounts of information related to catastrophes in a timely manner(Ray P et al. 2017). Social media serves as an effective platform for disseminating foreboding messages, and the integration of the Internet of Things (IoT) with social networks can enhance this capability. (Rangra A et al. 2022) suggests a proactive approach by identifying communities vulnerable to natural disasters in advance and determining the optimal location for deploying a broadcasting system. A smart broadcasting device, equipped with a Programmable IoT boards that can be strategically placed at a node with high centrality. (Jung D et al. 2020) proposed initiative proves invaluable in averting human casualties by issuing early warnings for different natural disasters, including, but not restricted to, flooding caused by rain, the structural failure of aging buildings and bridges, earthquakes, and landslides.

A HISTORICAL OVERVIEW OF NATURAL DISASTER

On conducting a geospatial analysis of natural disasters worldwide spanning the years 1960–2018. While many of these disasters are triggered by natural phenomena, human activity has contributed to some. The unpredictable nature of these events, coupled with their devastating impacts on affected communities, underscores the importance of studying their causes, trends, impacts, and counteraction measures. Geophysical events, once considered natural disasters impacting only flora and fauna, are now influenced by human activities, leading to various consequences such as relocations, economic disruptions, and a gender gap. The study delves into assessing the magnitude, frequency, and trends of natural disasters. It also considers global exposure and vulnerability, spatial distribution, and damages associated with climate change. Natural disasters have been explored across various scientific fields, including earth sciences, sociology, economics, psychology, and health. The authors specifically analyzed the long-term incidence of natural disasters, considering their frequency, number, changes over time and space, and future trends. The study covers a variety of natural calamities, such as earthquakes, floods, landslides, mass earth movements, storms, and volcanic activity. Data collected, totaling nearly 40,000 records, classify disasters across administrative regions, revealing Asia as the most affected continent, primarily by floods and storms. North America follows, experiencing storms, floods, and landslides, while Africa reports a considerable number of natural disasters. Notably, while storms and floods are recurrent globally, this does not imply causation. Asia stands out for the highest earthquake occurrences, particularly in its southern region. Over the analyzed years, earthquake frequency increased until 2003 and 2004, followed by a slight decrease. The forecast for the next two decades suggests a mild upward trend. Flooding, a global phenomenon, is most prominent in China, India, and Indonesia. The global incidence of floods is steadily increasing, with 2006 recording the highest number. The forecast for the next 20 years indicates a significant upward trend in flooding occurrences.

Figure 1. Pie chart that shows the percentage of natural disasters between the year 2003 to 2019

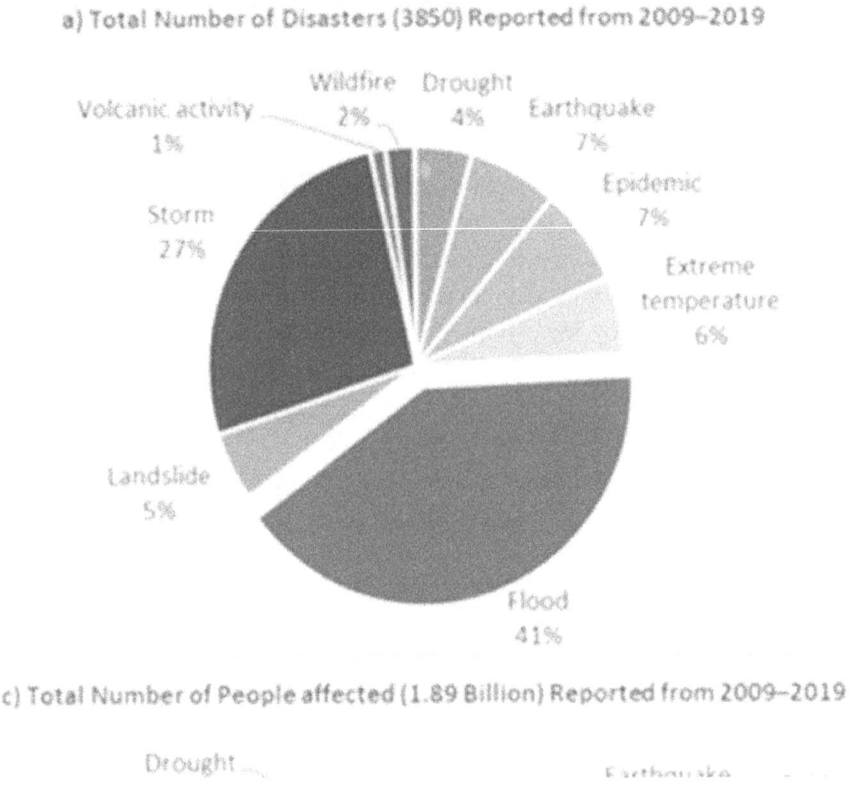

a) Total Number of Disasters (3850) Reported from 2009–2019

- Volcanic activity 1%
- Wildfire 2%
- Drought 4%
- Earthquake 7%
- Epidemic 7%
- Extreme temperature 6%
- Storm 27%
- Landslide 5%
- Flood 41%

c) Total Number of People affected (1.89 Billion) Reported from 2009–2019

SYSTEM ARCHITECTURE

IoT solutions tailored for Early Warning Systems concentrate on addressing the challenges posed by four specific natural disasters: floods, earthquakes, tsunamis, and forest fire. In the subsequent section, we introduce a simple IoT architecture that serves as a framework for describing EWS within the IoT paradigm. This reference architecture will be employed to articulate the reviewed IoT systems in the subsequent sections, facilitating the identification of potential trends. The three layers that taken into account for an advanced disaster prediction system includes monitoring layer, communication layer and storage and access layer.

Monitoring Layer

The Monitoring Layer assumes the pivotal role of sensing and collecting data from the environment, predominantly through sensors. Various sensors are selected or fabricated according to the basic specifications that includes efficiency, range, longevity and reliability, low power consumption and low latency communication. Wireless Sensor Networks, a common choice in disaster monitoring scenarios, consist of nodes equipped with sensing and communication units(Adeel et al. 2018). These nodes harvest data from the environment and transmit it to a gateway node, which interfaces with higher layers (Tang H et al. 2015).

Figure 2. Proposed IOT system architecture

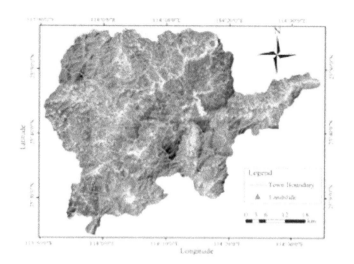

Communication Layer

The Communication Layer is responsible for transmitting the data acquired and processed by the monitoring Layer to a server, cloud service, or application. This layer manages routing, facilitates communication between heterogeneous networks, and ensures reliable data transmission. Various communication Short to medium-range wireless protocols like Wi-Fi, Bluetooth, and Zigbee are employed, while LoRa stands out for its long-range capabilities with low power consumption. Cellular networks, spanning 3G, 4G LTE, and 5G, provide connectivity in both urban and remote areas, with 5G offering improved speed and latency (Yamin et al. 2018). Low Power Wide Area Networks (LPWAN), including NB-IoT and LTE-M, address applications requiring long-range communication with minimal power usage. Lightweight protocols like MQTT and CoAP streamline message exchange in IoT environments. Edge computing minimizes latency by processing technologies, encompassing both wireless and wired options, which can be employed for data transmission (Khanh et al. 2022) while blockchain technology ensures secure and decentralized data integrity. Protocol selection hinges on specific application needs, environmental factors, and resource considerations.

Storage and Access Layer

At the pinnacle of the IoT layered architecture is the Storage and access Layer that leverages the data received from the Communication Layer to offer services or operations. This may involve amalgamating collected data with historical data, satellite information, or weather forecasting data from external sources. This Application Layer implements algorithms for generating and disseminating warnings when a disastrous event is imminent. Additionally, it can establish databases for storing real-time and historical data, make predictions, forecasts, and more. User interfaces can be built and in service-oriented architectures, intermediary layers like service management and middleware can enhance interoperability between devices and applications.

Cloud and Fog Computing

Cloud-based IoT platforms play a significant role by providing extensive storage and computational capabilities. Alternatively, Fog or Edge computing can be implemented between the Communication Layer and the Application Layer to deliver a faster response and superior quality compared to solutions relying solely on Cloud computing To improve the effectiveness of data analysis, particularly given the limited resources of sensors, a strategy involves the integration of fog computing and cloud computing. Specifically, sensors transmit data periodically to the fog layer (Puliafito et al. 2019). Once the fog layer preprocesses the data, it is then forwarded to the cloud. Consequently, fog computing takes on analyzing data on a smaller scale, sending notifications and feedback, and periodically forwarding summarized data to the cloud. Leveraging this historical data, deep learning techniques can be applied to create an intelligent classifier.

Figure 3. Functionality IoT-based natural disaster prediction system

IOT BASED PREDICTION OF NATURAL DISASTERS

FLOODS

Floods stand out as one of the utmost perilous environmental hazards, annually resulting in significant human casualties and infrastructural damage. Of particular concern are flash floods, characterized by their sudden, intense onset and lack of warning, necessitating predictive systems to allow for timely evacuation and other safety measures (Acosta et al. 2021). Precipitating events for floods encompass heavy rainfall, thunderstorms, and rapid snow melts. Assessing the risk of floods also involves considerations of hydro-geological instability and soil properties. The currently used Operational Flood Early Warning (EW) systems, such as the European Flood Awareness System, utilize rainfall detection, often obtained from radars, or rain forecasts to trigger alarms when the detected rainfall surpasses a predefined threshold (Chang et al. 2018).

Internet of Things (IoT) systems come into play by contributing a real-time warning application by producing immediately accessible data. The smart device is developed that can sense and predict the cause of flood thereby immediately alerting the coastal areas. The design of smart devices includes the integration of sensors, actuators, and microcontrollers. Flood is characterized by various environmental parameters such as topography, continuous rainfall, humidity, precipitation, wind speed, and temperature (Prabhakar et al. 2019). The various sensors are selected based on the environmental parameters listed where they are calibrated and tested to check their compatibility with the microcontroller for sensing and transfer of data. Microcontrollers play a vital role in IoT, serving as the brains behind connected devices. They are tasked with interfacing. with various sensors collecting data from the tangible world.. They facilitate communication between IoT devices and the broader network. They integrate with communication modules (such as Wi-Fi, Bluetooth, Zigbee, or cellular modules) to enable data transmission to and from other devices, cloud platforms, or edge servers.

The data that are sensed, monitored, and collected are sent to the microcontroller where the DL(Deep Learning) algorithms are employed to make autonomous decisions that can control the device (Widiasri et al. 2017). The controller also transfers the data from each edge node located in a region to the control station via a gateway server. The control station sends a warning message to the tower of that location, the principle behind the alert generation is that a particular threshold is set for each parameter. For example: If the intensity of rainfall is maintained for some time near the coastal areas, it leads to flood. When the intensity nears the threshold value, the warning alert is immediately generated to the tower of the coastal regions making them cautious. The alerts are generated to a user-friendly application. But for the people who don't have internet facilities, the alerts are generated through Cell Broadcasting Technology where even the mobile phones without network can receive an immediate alert of warning.

Prediction of floods depends on environmental parameters such as geographical location, climate patterns, topography, and the specific characteristics of the weather system causing the rainfall. Various types of rainfall events can lead to floods, such as heavy and prolonged rainfall, tropical cyclones, or thunderstorms(Yao et al. 2019). It's worth to observe that local meteorological agencies and hydrological organizations typically monitor and provide information about rainfall intensity and flood risks. They employ a variety of tools, including weather radar, rain gauges, and hydrological models, to assess and forecast potential flood situations.

Figure 4 and 5 illustrates the placement of smart IOT devices at edge nodes of flood prone areas

On an average, rainfall intensity is typically measured in milli meters or inches per hour. In the context of floods, high-intensity rainfall is observed to be several milli meters or inches per hour.

For example:

- Light rain: Less than 2.5 mm (0.1 inches) per hour
- Moderate rain: 2.5 to 7.6 mm (0.1 to 0.3 inches) per hour
- Heavy rain: 7.6 to 50 mm (0.3 to 2 inches) per hour
- Very heavy rain: 50 to 100 mm (2 to 4 inches) per hour
- Extremely heavy rain: More than 100 mm (4 inches) per hour

These are general classifications and may vary based on regional standards. The impact of rainfall on flooding also depends on the duration of the rainfall, the antecedent conditions, and other local factors. AI(Artificial Intelligence) and ML(Machine Learning) techniques comes into play for a better precision, accuracy, fast prediction and impact of the disaster. Additionally, understanding the local topography and drainage systems can help communities prepare and respond effectively to heavy rainfall and potential flooding (Jidin et al. 2019).

Figure 4.

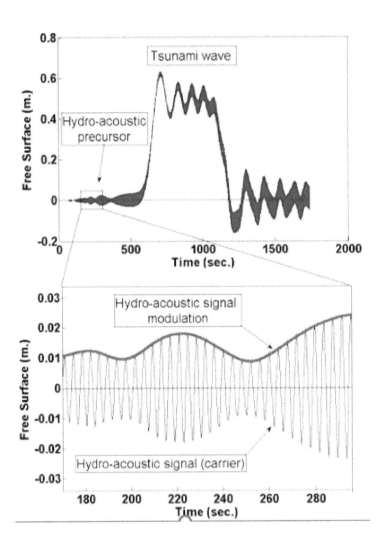

Table 1. Tabulation of water levels in two different environments

Edge node 1	Edge node 2	Edge node 1	Edge node 2
0.00025689	0.000103627	366	965
0.000263158	0.000108696	380	920
0.00028169	0.00010582	355	945
0.00285714	0.00000895025	350	1005
0.0028169	0.00011236	355	890
0.0000288887	0.000104167	360	960

Figure 5.

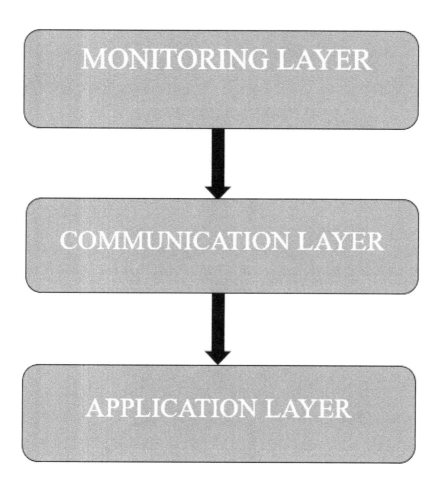

Earthquakes

An earthquake is a sudden and intense shaking of the Earth's surface caused by the movement of tectonic plates beneath the Earth's crust. This movement leads to the release of energy in the form of seismic waves, resulting in ground shaking. Earthquakes can vary in magnitude, ranging from minor tremors that may go unnoticed to major events capable of causing significant damage and loss of life(Beltramone et al. 2021). The identification of earthquakes is primarily carried out through seismology, the study of seismic waves. Seismic waves are oscillations that propagate through the Earth, and they are detected by instruments called seismometers or seismographs. When an earthquake occurs, these instruments record the arrival times and amplitudes of seismic waves at various locations around the world.

Figure 6. Majorly affected coastal regions due to flood in Chennai, Tamil Nadu

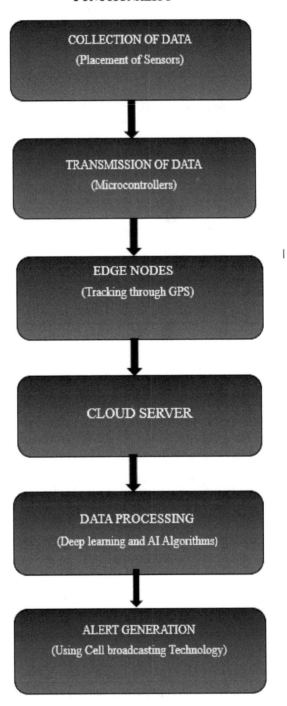

Figure 7. Continuous monitoring of water level measurements data

Seismologists use the data collected from multiple seismographic stations to determine the earthquake's location, depth, and magnitude. The information is crucial for understanding seismic activity, assessing the potential for damage, and implementing early warning systems to mitigate the impact on communities in earthquake-prone regions. Earthquake Early Warning Systems(EWS) can leverage the IoT and associated technologies(Tang H et al. 2021). Utilizing sensors and sensing units, these systems can monitor continuously. vibrations and ground movements. The threshold values change according to the soil type and its characteristics. The accelerometer is used to check any movement of soil due to earth's vibration. In the event of detected seismic activity, alarms can be promptly triggered to alert individuals in specific locations before the earthquake waves reach them. This warning, even if just a few seconds or minutes, can be crucial in preserving lives.

Figure 8. Real time seismic monitoring network

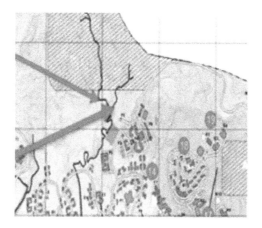

Table 2. Indication of seismographic values

Instrumental Intensity	Acceleration	Velocity(cm/s)	Perceived shaking	Potential Damage
I	<0.0017	<0.1	Not felt	None
II	0.0017-0.014	0.1-1.1	Weak	None
III	0.014- 0.039	1.1-3.4	Light	None
IV	0.039-0.092	3.4-8.1	Moderate	Very light
V	0.092-0.18	8.1-16	Strong	Light
VI	0.18-0.34	16-31	Very Strong	Moderate
VII	0.34-0.65	31-60	Severe	Moderate to Heavy
VIII	0.65-1.24	60-116	Violent	Heavy
IX	1.24-1.30	116-125	Extreme	Very Heavy
X+	>1.30	>125	Very extreme	Very Heavy

The IOT-based smart device is developed especially for advanced earthquake prediction. This smart device integrates various sensors together with a microcontroller that controls the earthquake-causing factors like ground vibration and seismic activities. Currently, seismic sensors are exclusively available in the market that accurately predict earthquake vibrations. Along with this, the application of Artificial Intelligence(AI) in disaster prediction has had a great impact on the researchers from The University of Texas at Austin, who developed an AI algorithm that demonstrated impressive accuracy by correctly forecasting 70% of earthquakes a week before their occurrence during a seven-month trial conducted in China.

Figure 9. Schematic diagram that indicates the earthquake zone in India

The AI was specifically trained to identify statistical anomalies in real-time seismic data obtained from the IOT device, which was then correlated with historical earthquake data. As a result, the AI produced a weekly forecast that successfully predicted 14 earthquakes within approximately 200 miles of their projected locations, and with nearly precise estimates of their magnitudes. Although the effectiveness of this approach in different geographical locations remains uncertain, this research represents a noteworthy advancement in the exploration of AI-based methodologies for earthquake prediction. These smart devices are placed on the grounds of public areas of the most frequently affected earthquake zone to record the ground vibrations, when there are alterations in vibrations above the threshold, the data are transferred and processed using advanced algorithms to accurately predict the earthquake duration and the alert is generated to the mobile phone of the people residing in that location. After the alert, people are immediately instructed to reach a public area with no buildings out there.

Landslides

Landslides represent a recurring and perilous occurrence involving the downhill movement of soil, rocks, and organic materials. Various factors, such as rainfall, fluctuations in groundwater levels, rapid snowmelt, or seismic activity, can trigger landslides. Consequently, diverse parameters, particularly displacement and weather-related indicators in the case of rainfall-induced landslides(Gian Q.A et al. 2017), can be monitored to both and forecast these events. Implementing Landslide Early Warning Systems (EWS) can occur at different scales, ranging from regional and national levels to more localized settings. Leveraging the Internet of Things and Micro-Electro-Mechanical Systems (MEMS) technologies proves beneficial in reducing costs and facilitating the establishment of denser sensor networks. Given that rainfall is a common trigger for landslides, integrating real-time weather data or forecasts with information gathered by on-site sensors enhances the effectiveness of such monitoring systems (Pecoraro et al. 2019).

IoT device continuously monitors the slope conditions using a network of IoT sensors strategically placed in vulnerable areas. These sensors detect subtle changes in terrain that may precede a landslide. Leveraging IoT connectivity, the device ensures seamless communication between sensors and a central monitoring system (Moulat et al. 2018). This connectivity allows for instant data analysis and quick response in case of detected threats. Smart sensors such as tilt sensors and pressure sensors are employed where Tilt sensors typically utilize accelerometers or gyroscopes to measure changes in the tilt or inclination of the ground surface.

In landslide-prone areas, the gradual or sudden change in the slope angle can be an early indication of potential instability. Tilt sensors are strategically placed in key locations on slopes, hillsides, or embankments where they continuously monitor the slope's orientation. Pore pressure moisture sensors measure the amount of water content in the soil by monitoring the pressure exerted by water within the soil pores. As soil becomes saturated, the pore water pressure increases, influencing the stability of the soil. In landslide-prone regions, excessive rainfall or rapid snowmelt can lead to elevated soil moisture levels. Pore pressure moisture sensors are embedded in the soil, and as the moisture content rises, these sensors detect the corresponding increase in pore water pressure. High pore water pressure can reduce the frictional strength of the soil, making it more susceptible to landslides. By continuously monitoring changes in soil moisture and pore pressure, these sensors contribute crucial data for predicting potential landslide events.

Figure 10. Identification of landslide zones

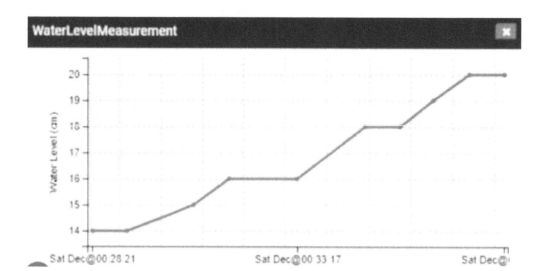

Table 3. Sensor readings updated in serial monitor

Raingauge	Tiltmeter	Inclinometer	Crackmeter	Piezometer
9.5	-0.3136798	-0.10124131	5.474854	0.2791276
9.5	-0.3136125	-0.10180253	5.476554	0.2713908
9.5	-0.3136798	-0.10224186	5.478235	0.2757597
9.5	-0.3135889	-0.10198899	5.473158	0.2711799
9.5	-0.3137706	-0.10273331	5.473158	0.2788651
9.5	-0.3137246	-0.10255021	5.473158	0.2757597
9.5	-0.3137706	-0.10282486	5.473158	0.2758118
9.5	-0.3138382	-0.10320064	5.473158	0.2718567
9.5	-0.3136574	-0.10329219	5.471456	0.2791276
9.5	-0.3138615	-0.10338944	5.476552	0.2757597
9.5	-0.3139525	-0.10366413	5.473158	0.2757597

By merging the data from tilt sensors and pore pressure moisture sensors, landslide prediction systems attain a thorough comprehension of the slope's stability. EWS also employs sophisticated techniques to process data patterns and identify early indicators of potential landslides. This predictive analytics feature enables the system to issue warnings well in advance, minimizing the risk of harm.

Figure 11. Readings updated from the IOT device

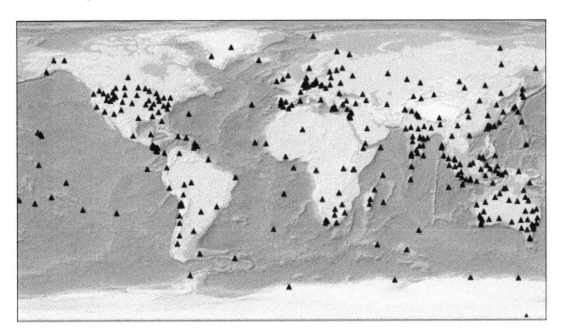

Figure 1: Real Time Seismic Monitoring Network, INDIA

Tsunamis

Tsunamis, characterized by large waves in bodies of water, are triggered by various events that includes earthquakes, underwater explosions, volcanic eruptions or landslides impacting water. Predicting tsunamis involves detecting seismic events and monitoring seawater levels and wind-wave patterns. In Tsunami Early Warning (EW) systems, diverse methods are employed, including hydro-acoustic wave measurement, pressure sensing, and camera-based techniques.

In the case of tsunamis triggered by seismic events, the initial alert often comes from earthquake measurements. These measurements help locate the epicenter and estimate the tsunami's time of arrival. Subsequent measurements, such as hydro-acoustic wave detection, come into play. Hydro-acoustic waves, generated by movements in the sea bottom during earthquakes, propagate rapidly in water, Enabling underwater acoustic sensors for accurate tsunami prediction. Additionally, underwater pressure sensors find extensive application in the identification of tsunami waves. (Gardner-Stephen et al. 2019).

Hydroacoustics refers to the examination of sound waves in water and its practical applications. The process of hydroacoustic monitoring entails capturing signals that indicate alterations in water pressure caused by underwater sound waves(Cecioni C et al. 2014). Owing to the efficient propagation of sound through water, it can be heard and detected over considerable distances. Within the water, there exists a specific layer where sound travels more slowly but is exceptionally effective – the Sound Fixing and Ranging Channel, commonly found at a depth of approximately 1000 meters. Hydroacoustic monitoring capitalizes on the distinctive phenomenon of sound waves becoming confined within this layer.

Figure 12. Continuous plot of hydro acoustic waves and modulation of signal for long range data transmission

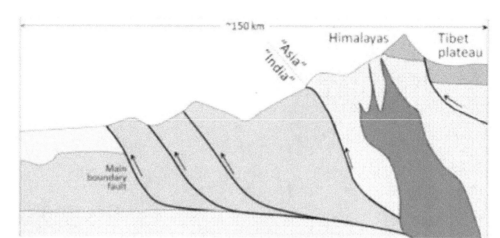

Underwater Wireless Sensor Networks (UWSNs) play a vital role in collecting and sending data from expansive geographical areas to a central hub for processing and generating early warnings. The Internet of Underwater Things (IoT) is a paradigm that facilitates the detection and prediction of events leading to disasters(Fattah S et al. 2020). A typical UWSN comprises underwater stationary or mobile nodes outfitted with sensor units and acoustic modems, along with sink nodes on autonomous surface vehicles, buoys, or ships. These sink nodes, equipped with acoustic and radio modems, collect data from underwater sensors and relay sending it to a distant server or monitoring center via an IP network(Haque et al. 2020). Alert messages, including event details and safety instructions, are spread through diverse channels such as TV, radio, mobile devices, and sirens. Public education and continuous monitoring enhance community preparedness for timely responses.

FUTURE WORKS

The diversity in sensor manufacturers and applications across various disaster scenarios contributes to the diverse characteristics of these sensors, posing challenges to their integration and information sharing. Certain disasters may trigger subsequent events; for instance, seismic activity or floods resulting from inundations. Analyzing sensor data related to different types of disasters allows for the anticipation of subsequent events following an initial occurrence.

Furthermore, future research efforts could delve into integrating disparate sensors to create a comprehensive application capable of visualizing sensor data and disseminating alerts across different disaster categories. Addressing the communication challenges among heterogeneous sensors may involve exploring innovative communication technologies and protocols, including the incorporation of integration brokerage applications. The future of advanced natural disaster prediction and warning systems involves the integration of IoT (Internet of Things), ML (Machine Learning), and AI (Artificial Intelligence) technologies to enhance accuracy, speed, and overall effectiveness. ML can identify traffic patterns, population density, and weather conditions to recommend the safest and most efficient evacuation paths.

Utilization of diverse varied data outlets, encompassing social media, crowd-sourced information, and data from unmanned aerial vehicles (UAVs), to create a holistic understanding of disaster situations.

Certain research endeavors have highlighted user involvement in sensing during the pre-disaster phase. However, the introduction of potentially false information by individuals into the system poses a challenge to the system's credibility. Future investigations could explore methods to ensure data authenticity through the implementation of Blockchain technology. Additionally, given the widespread use of cameras, sensor communication should be capable of transmitting larger volumes of image data.

Forthcoming studies have the potential to employ sensors for calculating the duration from departure to the successful completion of rescue operations in the post-disaster phase. This approach can lead to a more efficient allocation of rescue personnel. For instance, personal devices can document the routes taken by rescuers and compute the time taken for successful rescue. Rescuers themselves can record the successful completion of rescue operations when individuals are saved.

CONCLUSION

An Internet of Things (IoT)-based natural disaster prediction system holds significant promise in enhancing our ability to anticipate and respond to events such as floods, tsunamis, earthquakes, and landslides. By providing a network of interconnected sensors and devices, this system enables real-time monitoring and data collection from vulnerable regions. The incorporation of sophisticated analytics and machine learning algorithms permits the analysis of various environmental parameters, enabling the early detection of potential natural disasters. The IoT-based approach provides various benefits, including enhanced accuracy in prediction, quicker response times, and the ability to provide timely warnings to at-risk communities. The system's ability to collect data from a variety of sources, such as weather stations, seismometers, and remote sensing devices, enhances its overall effectiveness in forecasting and mitigating the impact of natural disasters. Furthermore, the smooth communication among IoT devices facilitates coordination among Emergency response teams, empowering them to mobilize resources efficiently and deploy targeted interventions. However, challenges such as data security, privacy concerns, and the necessity for resilient infrastructure must be carefully addressed in the execution of an IoT-based natural disaster prediction system. Despite these challenges, the potential benefits in terms of saving lives, minimizing damage, and building resilient communities make the continued development and deployment of such systems a worthwhile pursuit in the realm of disaster management and preparedness.

REFERENCES

Acosta-Coll, M., Solano-Escorcia, A., Ortega-Gonzalez, L., & Zamora-Musa, R. (2021). Forecasting and communication key elements for low-cost fluvial flooding early warning system in urban areas. [IJECE]. *Iranian Journal of Electrical and Computer Engineering*, *11*(5), 4143–4156. doi:10.11591/ijece.v11i5.pp4143-4156

Allen, R. M., & Melgar, D. (2019). Earthquake Early Warning: Advances, Scientific Challenges, and Societal Needs. *Annual Review of Earth and Planetary Sciences*, *47*(1), 361–388. doi:10.1146/annurev-earth-053018-060457

Beltramone, L., & Gomes, R. C. (2021). Earthquake Early Warning Systems as an Asset Risk Management Tool. *CivilEng.*, *2*(1), 120–133. doi:10.3390/civileng2010007

Chang, V., Sood, S. K., Sandhu, R., Singla, K., & Chang, V. (2018). IoT, big data and HPC based smart flood management framework. *Sustainable Computing : Informatics and Systems*, *20*, 102–117. doi:10.1016/j.suscom.2017.12.001

Esposito, M., Palma, L., Belli, A., Sabbatini, L., & Pierleoni, P. (2022). Recent Advances in Internet of Things Solutions for Early Warning Systems: A Review. *Sensors (Basel)*, *22*(6), 2124. doi:10.3390/s22062124 PMID:35336296

Esposito, M., Palma, L., Belli, A., Sabbatini, L., & Pierleoni, P. (2022). Recent advances in internet of things solutions for early warning systems: A review. *Sensors (Basel)*, *22*(6), 2124. doi:10.3390/s22062124 PMID:35336296

Huang, G., Shen, Z., & Mardin, R. (Eds.). (2018). *Overview of Urban Planning and Water-Related Disaster Management*. Springer International Publishing.

Jung, D., Tuan, V. T., Tran, D. Q., Park, M., & Park, S. (2020). Conceptual framework of an intelligent decision support system for smart city disaster management. *Applied Sciences (Basel, Switzerland)*, *10*(2), 666. doi:10.3390/app10020666

Kao, C. C., Huang, C. J., Lin, Y. S., Wu, G. D., & Huang, C. J. (2017). A comprehensive study on the internet of underwater things: Applications, challenges, and channel models. *Sensors (Basel)*, *17*(7), 1477. doi:10.3390/s17071477 PMID:28640220

Khanh, Q. V., Hoai, N. V., Manh, L. D., Le, A. N., & Jeon, G. (2022). Wireless communication technologies for IoT in 5G: Vision, applications, and challenges. *Wireless Communications and Mobile Computing*, *2022*, 1–12. doi:10.1155/2022/3229294

Mei, G., Xu, N., Qin, J., Wang, B., & Qi, P. (2020). A Survey of Internet of Things (IoT) for Geohazard Prevention: Applications, Technologies, and Challenges. *IEEE Internet of Things Journal*, *7*(5), 4371–4386. doi:10.1109/JIOT.2019.2952593

Poslad, S., Middleton, S. E., Chaves, F., Tao, R., Necmioglu, O., & Bügel, U. (2015). A Semantic IoT Early Warning System for Natural Environment Crisis Management. *IEEE Transactions on Emerging Topics in Computing*, *3*(2), 246–257. doi:10.1109/TETC.2015.2432742

Prabhakar, M., Sankaranarayanan, S., Prabhakar, M., Satish, S., Jain, P., Ramprasad, A., & Krishnan, A. (2019). Flood prediction based on weather parameters using deep learning. *Journal of Water and Climate Change*, *11*, 1766–1783.

Puliafito, C., Mingozzi, E., Longo, F., Puliafito, A., & Rana, O. (2019). Fog computing for the internet of things: A survey. [TOIT]. *ACM Transactions on Internet Technology*, *19*(2), 1–41. doi:10.1145/3301443

Rangra, A., & Sehgal, V. (2022). Natural disasters management using social internet of things. *Multimedia Tools and Applications*, *81*(24), 1–15. doi:10.1007/s11042-021-11486-8

Ray, P. P., Mukherjee, M., & Shu, L. (2017). Internet of Things for Disaster Management: State-of-the-Art and Prospects. *IEEE Access : Practical Innovations, Open Solutions*, *5*, 18818–18835. doi:10.1109/ACCESS.2017.2752174

Shah, S. A., Ben Yahia, S., Seker, D. Z., Rathore, M. M., Hameed, S., Ben Yahia, S., & Draheim, D. (2019). *Towards Disaster Resilient Smart Cities: Can Internet of Things and Big Data Analytics Be the Game Changers?* IEEE.

Strauss, J., & Allen, R. (2016). Benefits and Costs of Earthquake Early Warning. *Seismological Research Letters*, *87*(3), 765–772. doi:10.1785/0220150149

Tang, H., Cheng, T. C. E., Elalouf, A., & Levner, E. (2014). Efficient computation of evacuation routes on a three-dimensional geometric network. *Computers & Industrial Engineering*, *76*, 231–242. doi:10.1016/j.cie.2014.08.003

Tang, H., Elalouf, A., Levner, E., & Cheng, T. C. E. (2014). Efficient computation of evacuation routes on a three-dimensional geometric network. *Computers & Industrial Engineering*, *76*, 231–242. doi:10.1016/j.cie.2014.08.003

Widiasari, I. R., & Nugroho, L. E. (2017). Deep learning multilayer perceptron (MLP) for flood prediction model using wireless sensor network based hydrology time series data mining. *2017 International Conference on Innovative and Creative Information Technology (ICITech)*. IEEE: New York, NY, USA. 10.1109/INNOCIT.2017.8319150

Yao, C., Ye, J., He, Z., Bastola, S., Zhang, K., & Li, Z. (2019). Evaluation of flood prediction capability of the distributed Grid-Xinanjiang model driven by weather research and forecasting precipitation. *Journal of Flood Risk Management*, *12*(S1), 12544. doi:10.1111/jfr3.12544

Zambrano, A. M., Calderón, X., Zambrano, O. M., Esteve, M., & Jaramillo, S. (2017). *Palau C*. Community Early Warning Systems. Wireless Public Safety Networks.

Chapter 12
Unleashing Machine Wisdom:
A Glimpse Into AI-Powered Tsunami Early Warning Systems

Siddique Ibrahim S. P.
VIT-AP University, India

Lakkakula Namratha
VIT-AP University, India

Ireddi Rakshitha
VIT-AP University, India

Naga Sai Rahul V.
VIT-AP University, India

Uppara Nithin
VIT-AP University, India

Mohammed Abdul Kareem Shaik
VIT-AP University, India

ABSTRACT

Embarking on an exploration of disaster resilience, this chapter scrutinizes the potential of AI-driven tsunami early warning systems (TEWS). Focused on the catastrophic potential of tsunamis, the narrative unveils a visionary roadmap, spotlighting artificial neural networks (ANN), and convolutional neural networks (CNN). While the actual implementation lies in the future, the chapter charts a course for stakeholders to metamorphose theoretical frameworks into actionable strategies. Beyond technical intricacies, the narrative emphasizes the transformative impact of proactive disaster management. Envisioning a future where machine learning algorithms serve as vigilant guardians prompts a call for a paradigm shift in coastal safety. The chapter culminates by contemplating a future where the synergy between human intuition and AI enhances our capacity to anticipate, respond to, and mitigate the devastating impact of tsunamis. It paints a compelling vision of a safer coexistence with our dynamic planet, outlining challenges, and pointing towards a more resilient future.

DOI: 10.4018/979-8-3693-3362-4.ch012

Unleashing Machine Wisdom

INTRODUCTION

In this chapter, the exploration begins into the realm of AI-driven Tsunami Early Warning Systems (TEWS). Focused on addressing the formidable challenges presented by natural disasters, particularly tsunamis, the chapter unravels a roadmap highlighting the significance of Artificial Neural Networks (ANN) and Convolutional Neural Networks (CNN). The objective is clear: to translate theoretical frameworks into practical strategies for enhancing disaster resilience. As the narrative unfolds, it navigates through the historical landscape of disaster management, introducing essential AI concepts and showcasing the synergy between human intuition and machine precision. The chapters delve into technical intricacies, discussing the application of ANN and CNN, and presenting case studies that underscore the transformative impact of proactive disaster management (Zengaffinen et al., 2020). Beyond technology, the chapter addresses challenges in AI adoption, explores ethical considerations, and envisions a future where collaboration between human insight and machine wisdom shapes a safer coexistence with our dynamic planet. This chapter stands as a call for a paradigm shift, encouraging all to participate in unlocking the potential of AI to navigate and mitigate the challenges posed by tsunamis, fostering a harmonious relationship with the unpredictable forces of nature. (Amin et al., 2021)

BACKGROUND

In laying the foundation for this chapter, a comprehensive exploration unfolds into the realm of AI-driven Tsunami Early Warning Systems (TEWS). The backdrop is framed against the urgent need to address the escalating challenges posed by natural disasters, with a specific focus on the profound impact of tsunamis. The chapter sets out on a mission to demystify the potential of Artificial Neural Networks (ANN) and Convolutional Neural Networks (CNN) in crafting effective TEWS. Recognizing the critical importance of translating theoretical frameworks into practical strategies for disaster resilience, the narrative navigates through the historical landscape of disaster management. Introducing essential AI concepts, the chapter underscores the symbiotic relationship between human intuition and machine precision (Løvholt et al., 2018).

As the exploration advances, the chapters delve into the technical intricacies, presenting real-world case studies that illuminate the transformative power of proactive disaster management. Beyond the realm of technology, the narrative grapples with challenges in AI adoption and delves into ethical considerations, envisioning a future where collaboration between human insight and machine wisdom becomes pivotal in fostering a safer coexistence with our dynamic planet (Rabindra et al., 2020). This chapter emerges as a call to action, inviting all to participate in unlocking the potential of AI, not only to navigate and mitigate the challenges posed by tsunamis but also to contribute to a harmonious relationship with the unpredictable forces of nature.

Objectives

The primary goals of this chapter revolve around exploring the potential applications of AI-driven Tsunami Early Warning Systems (TEWS). The focus is on introducing and elucidating fundamental concepts of AI, specifically emphasizing Artificial Neural Networks (ANN) and Convolutional Neural Networks (CNN) (Dwarakanath et al., 2021). The chapter delves into the historical evolution of disaster management, illustrating how AI has become an integral part of early warning systems. Additionally, it provides clear insights into the technical aspects of AI, breaking down the functioning of ANN and CNN, and presenting practical methodologies for implementing TEWS. The chapter openly acknowledges the challenges associated with adopting AI for tsunamis and explores the ethical considerations of deploying AI in life-saving scenarios. In essence, this chapter aims to simplify the intricate landscape of AI and disaster management, emphasizing its potential to significantly improve early warning systems for tsunamis without compromising ethical standards (Li et al., 2022)

Figure 1. The Tsunami Phenomenon

Scope and Significance

This chapter aims to deeply explore how AI can be practically used in Tsunami Early Warning Systems (TEWS). It doesn't just stick to theories but strives to give a hands-on understanding of applying AI technologies, specifically Artificial Neural Networks (ANN) and Convolutional Neural Networks (CNN), to create effective early warning systems. Real-world case studies and a look into the history of disaster management are included to show successful instances of AI in action (Scicchitano et al., 2022).

The significance of this chapter lies in its contribution to addressing urgent challenges posed by natural disasters, especially tsunamis. By providing clear technical insights and practical methods, the chapter aims to connect theoretical knowledge with real-world applications. It's designed for a diverse audience – researchers, practitioners, and policymakers – equipping them with valuable resources for innovative solutions in proactive disaster management (Prasad et al., 2021). In essence, the chapter is important because it doesn't just share information but also inspires progress in early warning systems, contributing to a safer coexistence with the unpredictable forces of nature.

AI in Disaster Resilience

In this chapter, the spotlight is on the pivotal role of artificial intelligence (AI) applications in disaster management, with a particular emphasis on Tsunami Early Warning Systems (TEWS).

Figure 2. ANN algorithm: How artificial neural network works

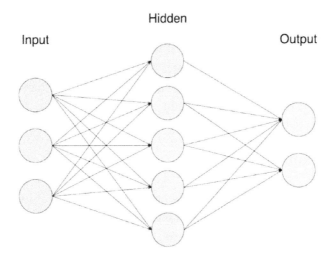

Overview of AI Applications in Disaster Management

Artificial intelligence (AI) unfolds a paradigm shift in disaster management, leveraging machine learning and predictive analytics to revolutionize traditional strategies. Through the optimization of early warning systems, AI ensures real-time analysis of diverse data sources, facilitating timely and precise disaster alerts. Decision support systems, empowered by AI, provide responders and policymakers with nuanced insights, enhancing crisis response effectiveness and contributing to community resilience (Gambino et al., 2022). AI's forte in data analysis and predictive modeling enables more accurate disaster risk predictions, laying the foundation for informed decision-making in high-risk scenarios.

Figure 3. Trained AI Tech for Predicting Tsunami at the Coast

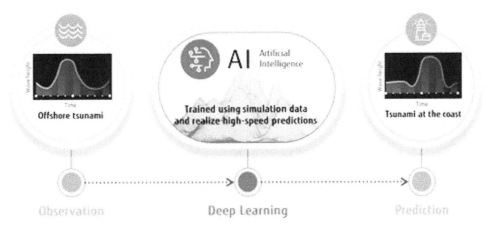

Role of AI in Tsunami Early Warning Systems

In the specialized realm of Tsunami Early Warning Systems (TEWS), AI emerges as a critical force. AI algorithms significantly elevate the precision of tsunami prediction models, adapting dynamically to real-time data for more accurate and timely forecasts. The capability of AI to process real-time data becomes pivotal during tsunami events, ensuring swift information dissemination and facilitating rapid response. Seamless integration with sensor networks enhances TEWS sensitivity, providing a comprehensive early warning system (Goda et al., 2021).

Understanding Tsunami Impact

This section systematically unpacks the profound impact of tsunamis, providing a foundational understanding crucial to the overarching exploration of Tsunami Early Warning Systems (TEWS). It demystifies the characteristics of tsunamis, elucidating the distinctive traits that render them formidable natural phenomena. This comprehension sets the stage for a deeper dive into how artificial intelligence can effectively mitigate their impact through advanced warning systems (Satriano et al., 2020).

Characteristics of Tsunamis

Focusing on the specific characteristics that define tsunamis, this section offers a human-friendly guide to their origins in seismic activity and the mechanisms propelling their colossal waves (Tian et al., 2019). This foundational knowledge becomes pivotal in the subsequent discussion on AI's role in TEWS, shaping the technological responses necessary for effective disaster management.

Historical Tsunami Events

Delving into historical narratives, this exploration chronicles significant tsunami events, shedding light on their devastating impact across various regions. This historical perspective not only highlights the urgency for advanced warning systems but also provides valuable insights into the recurrence and patterns of tsunamis (Ibrahim et al., 2023). In learning from historical events, the chapter gains a nuanced understanding, informing strategies and technologies essential for proactive disaster preparedness, with AI-driven solutions emerging as indispensable in this realm.

Implications of Coastal Safety

Within this chapter, the exploration of AI-powered Tsunami Early Warning Systems unfolds as a multifaceted endeavor. Scrutinizing the potential of Artificial Neural Networks (ANN) and Convolutional Neural Networks (CNN), the narrative charts a visionary roadmap for stakeholders, illuminating a future prospect. Emphasizing proactive disaster management, the chapter envisions a paradigm shift in coastal safety, where machine learning algorithms act as vigilant guardians. It contemplates a future where the synergy between human intuition and AI augments our capacity to anticipate, respond, and mitigate the devastating impact of tsunamis (Okal et al., 2019). Amidst technical intricacies, the narrative transcends theoretical frameworks, offering actionable strategies for implementation. A compelling vision emerges, outlining challenges and pointing towards a more resilient future, fostering a safer coexistence with our dynamic planet.

The state-of-the-art Artificial Intelligence (AI) and Machine Learning (ML) technologies are leveraged to redefine Tsunami Early Warning Systems (TEWS). The methodology initiates with the comprehensive acquisition of diverse data streams from oceanic and seismic sensors. This dynamic dataset undergoes meticulous analysis through the intricate workings of Artificial Neural Networks (ANN) and Convolutional Neural Networks (CNN). The ANN, adept at recognizing intricate relationships within the data, collaborates seamlessly with the CNN, specialized in image-based recognition. Together, they unravel patterns indicative of tsunami precursors, providing a nuanced understanding of the coastal landscape (Linardos et al., 2022).

The interconnected AI and ML technologies form a robust framework capable of predicting and identifying anomalies associated with potential tsunamis. This predictive capability is pivotal for issuing timely warnings and alerts, offering a significant advantage in disaster mitigation. The system's real-time analysis and swift response empower coastal communities to take proactive measures, minimizing the impact of tsunamis on life and infrastructure.

This AI-driven TEWS doesn't just stop at prediction; it represents a paradigm shift in disaster resilience (Gomez et al., 2023). The integration of advanced algorithms and real-time data analysis not only enhances the precision of warnings but also fosters a proactive approach to disaster management. The system's ability to adapt and learn from evolving data sets positions it as a dynamic and intelligent guardian for coastal safety.

In essence, the chapter heralds a future where AI and ML technologies become indispensable tools in anticipating, understanding, and responding to natural disasters (Sathya et al., 2021). By pushing the boundaries of technological innovation, a safer coexistence with our dynamic planet is envisioned, where the fusion of human intuition and machine intelligence stands as a beacon of hope for coastal communities facing the potential threat of tsunamis.

AI Technologies: ANN and CNN

Embarking on the technological journey of the chapter, the focus turns to the sophisticated landscape of AI, primarily centering on Artificial Neural Networks (ANN) and Convolutional Neural Networks (CNN). The narrative unfolds ANN as a digital brain, mirroring human learning processes but at a computational scale. These networks excel at recognizing patterns in massive datasets, a crucial aspect for the subsequent exploration. ANN serves as a computational model inspired by the human brain, learning and adapting from diverse datasets (Balan et al., 2021). It plays a vital role in pattern recognition, making it a dynamic learner with the potential to handle complex information.

Artificial Neural Networks (ANN)

Delving into the realm of ANN, the chapter intricately details these computational models as virtual brains. Readers are guided through the parallels between ANN and human brains, highlighting their ability to learn and adapt from diverse datasets. This section sheds light on the versatility of ANN, not just as a pattern recognizer, but as a dynamic learner capable of synthesizing complex information, laying a robust foundation for the ensuing discussion. ANN is presented as a virtual brain, drawing parallels with human learning processes. Its versatility extends beyond pattern recognition, showcasing its capability to synthesize complex information (Ratnasari et al., 2023). Continuous learning in ANN becomes a crucial factor for adaptability to evolving scenarios.

Figure 4. Artificial neural network (ANN) with practical implementation

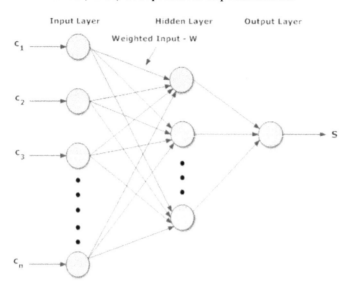

Convolutional Neural Networks (CNN)

The narrative then seamlessly transitions to CNN, carving a deeper understanding of these neural networks specialized in visual data processing. CNN is portrayed as the visual maestro, akin to a computerized set of eyes adept at deciphering the content of images. Readers are enlightened on how CNN enhances the AI repertoire, specifically in tasks related to visuals, providing a holistic understanding of the technological landscape (UNDRR et al., 2009). CNN is introduced as a visual expert, excelling in the processing of visual information. It is likened to a computerized set of eyes, showcasing its prowess in deciphering the content of images (Syed et al., 2019). The section emphasizes the added layer of sophistication that CNN brings to the AI toolkit.

Figure 5. Schematic view of tsunami forecasting by the convolutional neural networks (CNN)

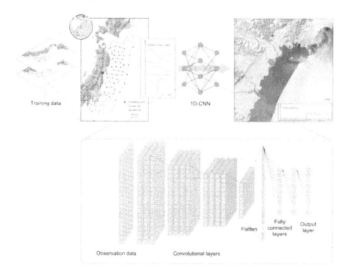

Unleashing Machine Wisdom

Applicability in Tsunami Early Warning Systems

The crescendo of the section reaches its pinnacle by unraveling the practical application of both ANN and CNN in the context of Tsunami Early Warning Systems (TEWS). Beyond mere technicalities, the narrative emphasizes the pivotal role of these AI technologies as linchpins in predicting and mitigating the impact of tsunamis. The discussion delves into their role as instrumental tools, seamlessly connecting the dots between the intricacies of AI and the overarching theme of proactive disaster management, positioning these technologies as catalysts for building resilient early warning systems. Practical application of ANN and CNN in Tsunami Early Warning Systems is explored (Wang et al., 2021). The narrative underscores the instrumental role of these technologies in predicting and mitigating tsunami impact. Connection between AI intricacies and the overarching theme of proactive disaster management is established.

METHODOLOGY

The operational efficacy of the AI-driven Tsunami Early Warning System (TEWS) unfolds through a systematic procedure. Commencing with the continuous acquisition of diverse data streams from oceanic and seismic sensors, the system ensures a real-time influx of information. This comprehensive dataset then undergoes meticulous preprocessing to eliminate noise and ensure uniformity.

Subsequently, the Artificial Neural Networks (ANN) analyze the preprocessed data, deciphering complex relationships within the dataset. Concurrently, the Convolutional Neural Networks (CNN) specialize in image-based recognition, enhancing the system's ability to interpret seismic activity (Holzinger et al., 2022). The integration of results from both networks forms a holistic understanding of the coastal environment, augmenting the accuracy in identifying potential tsunamigenic anomalies.

The predictive capabilities of the system come into play, forecasting potential tsunamis based on the identified precursors. In the event of a predicted tsunami, an alert mechanism is triggered, ensuring timely dissemination of warnings to coastal communities. The TEWS maintains a continuous loop of real-time monitoring, adapting and learning from new data to refine its predictive capabilities over time (Mulia et al., 2020).

Beyond prediction, the TEWS places a strong emphasis on community preparedness and response. Issued alerts empower coastal communities to take proactive measures and initiate evacuation protocols, minimizing the impact on life and infrastructure. This dynamic and intelligent operational procedure positions the TEWS as a pivotal tool in proactive disaster management, ushering in a new era of coastal safety.

In the intricate landscape of Tsunami Early Warning Systems (TEWS), the strategic fusion of Artificial Neural Networks (ANN) and Convolutional Neural Networks (CNN) unfolds as a transformative paradigm, revolutionizing the approach to early detection and mitigation. The process commences with meticulous data acquisition from an array of sources, including seismic sensors, oceanographic instruments, and historical tsunami databases. This data undergoes a comprehensive preprocessing stage, ensuring uniformity and compatibility for subsequent analysis by ANN and CNN.

Serving as the computational backbone, ANN embarks on an iterative training process, utilizing a combination of supervised learning and pattern recognition algorithms. This process involves discerning intricate relationships between precursor indicators and actual tsunami occurrences, refining the network's ability to recognize subtle patterns and anomalies (Barreca et al., 2021). The real-time monitoring phase involves continuous analysis of incoming data, with anomalies triggering alerts and providing crucial early indicators of potential tsunami threats. The output of ANN includes not only the probability but also the severity of an impending tsunami, empowering emergency responders and authorities with actionable information.

Figure 6. Tsunami inundation forecasting: Leveraging AI

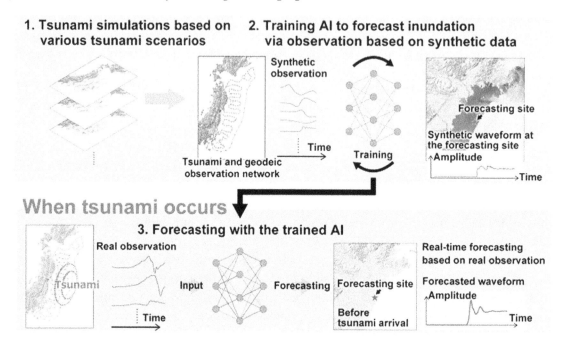

In tandem with ANN, CNN specializes in processing visual data, a crucial facet in tsunami detection. The CNN procedure initiates with the collection of visual information, which can encompass satellite images, oceanographic photographs, or video feeds. These visuals undergo preprocessing to enhance clarity and isolate relevant features. CNN's strength lies in its ability to discern patterns in visual data, utilizing convolutional layers to extract hierarchical features from the inputs (Glimson et al., 2019). The training phase involves historical visual data, enabling CNN to differentiate between normal environmental variations and potential tsunami precursors. The real-time monitoring phase, similar to ANN, involves continuous analysis of incoming visual data, with CNN providing crucial insights into anomalies or deviations from learned patterns.

The outputs of ANN and CNN, representing data-driven insights and visual pattern recognition, synergize to create a holistic early warning signal. This integrated output undergoes a final analysis, considering factors such as geographical proximity, historical vulnerabilities, and current weather conditions. The integration of ANN and CNN is not a linear process but a dynamic synergy, ensuring a more robust and comprehensive early warning system (Heron et al., 2021).

The effectiveness of the TEWS relies on continuous validation and improvement. Historical data of actual tsunami events, along with instances of false positives and negatives, are used to refine the algorithms of both ANN and CNN. Regular updates to the training datasets ensure adaptability to evolving environmental conditions, ultimately improving the accuracy and reliability of the early warning system over time (Omira et al., 2017). In essence, this detailed and elaborate approach not only enhances the accuracy of tsunami predictions but also reduces false alarms, propelling coastal safety towards a more resilient and adaptive future. The strategic integration of ANN and CNN encapsulates a dynamic and evolving system that stands prepared to face the complex challenges posed by potential tsunami threats.

Figure 7. Ensemble and selection of data

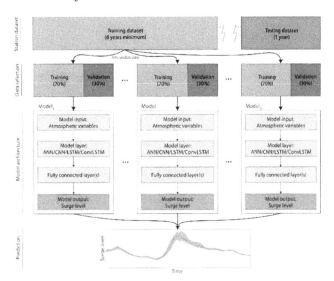

Table 1. Comparative analysis of tsunami warning system approaches

Reference	Addressed Issue	ML/DL Approach Used	Datasets	Accuracy/Prediction Metrics Used
Kong et al. (2023)	Enhance real-time tsunami forecasting using deep learning	CNN-LSTM hybrid model	Deep-ocean tsunami observations, tide gauge data, historical tsunami events	Area under the receiver operating characteristic curve (AUC), F1-score, mean squared error (MSE)
Chen et al. (2022)	Improve near-field tsunami prediction with transfer learning	Convolutional Long Short-Term Memory (ConvLSTM) model with transfer learning	Synthetic tsunami simulations, tide gauge data	Mean squared error (MSE), peak water level error, arrival time error
Li et al. (2021)	Develop a probabilistic tsunami hazard assessment model	Bayesian deep learning framework	Historical tsunami events, bathymetric data, earthquake source parameters	Probability of exceeding different tsunami heights, root mean squared error (RMSE)
Satriano et al. (2020)	Automate tsunami source characterization using machine learning	Support Vector Machines (SVM) classifier	Tide gauge data, earthquake parameters	Accuracy, precision, recall, F1-score
Okal et al. (2019)	Predict tsunami size using deep neural networks	Deep feedforward neural network	Global tide gauge data, seismic and bathymetric data	Mean squared error (MSE), R-squared (coefficient of determination)

LITERATURE REVIEW

In this pivotal section, the literature review serves as a compass, guiding readers through the historical evolution of Tsunami Warning Systems (TWS) and the nuanced landscape of AI-driven disaster resilience (Goda et al., 2021). It not only delves into the transformative journey of TWS but also scrutinizes the methodologies and approaches in the broader context of AI for disaster management, culminating in an exploration of key findings and existing gaps

Historical Evolution of Tsunami Warning Systems

The exploration of the historical evolution meticulously navigates through the annals of TWS, shedding light on key junctures that have shaped its trajectory. From rudimentary, rule-based systems, the narrative evolves to embrace the integration of cutting-edge technologies. It dissects seminal events that prompted paradigm shifts, emphasizing the progressive inclusion of real-time data and sensor networks (Stanly et al., 2023). By contextualizing the evolution, this segment provides a foundational understanding, elucidating why the current era necessitates the infusion of AI prowess into Tsunami Early Warning Systems (TEWS).

Approaches and Methodologies in AI for Disaster Resilience

Zooming into the contemporary landscape, the literature unfolds the diverse approaches and methodologies within the ambit of AI for disaster resilience, with a laser focus on tsunamis. It serves as an enlightening panorama, showcasing the dynamic application of machine learning algorithms, prominently featuring Artificial Neural Networks (ANN) and Convolutional Neural Networks (CNN). This segment probes beyond the technicalities, exploring the practical deployment of AI in disaster-prone regions. The socio-technical nuances are dissected, accentuating the need for comprehensive strategies that go beyond algorithms, embracing the contextual intricacies of disaster management (Wang et al., 2022).

Key Findings and Gaps in Existing Literature

The crescendo of the literature review unfurls in a critical analysis, distilling the essence of existing research and pointing towards uncharted territories. Key findings from the existing literature are dissected, providing a nuanced understanding of the strengths and limitations inherent in deploying AI for disaster resilience. However, it doesn't stop at affirming the known; it bravely identifies gaps in the current understanding, areas where knowledge falls short, and innovation beckons. This critical reflection is not just an academic exercise; it positions the subsequent book chapter as a beacon of exploration, uniquely positioned to bridge these identified gaps and contribute to the evolving narrative of disaster resilience.

By meticulously threading through the historical evolution of TWS, exploring the dynamic landscape of AI approaches for disaster resilience, and critically engaging with existing literature, this review becomes more than a compilation of facts; it becomes a narrative that sets the stage (SPS et al., 2020). It propels readers into a realm where the past, present, and future of Tsunami Early Warning Systems converge, creating a rich tapestry that the subsequent chapters will dynamically weave upon.

Table 2. Comparative analysis of tsunami warning system approaches

Reference	Addressed Issue	ML/DL Approach Used	Datasets	Accuracy/Prediction Metrics Used
Glimson et al. (2019)	Predicting tsunami magnitude from earthquake characteristics	Random Forest regression with feature selection using Genetic Algorithm	Global earthquake and tsunami catalog (ITDB, WISE), NOAA tide gauge data	Mean Absolute Error (MAE), Root Mean Square Error (RMSE), R-squared
Wang et al. (2022)	Real-time tsunami forecast using High-Frequency (HF) radar data assimilation	Ensemble Kalman filter with deep convolutional neural network (CNN)	HF radar measurements, bottom pressure gauge (OBPG) data, simulated tsunami waveforms	Mean Absolute Error (MAE), Root Mean Square Error (RMSE), correlation coefficient
Yadav et al. (2021)	Tsunami susceptibility mapping for Indian Ocean coastlines	Convolutional Long Short-Term Memory (ConvLSTM) network with topographic and bathymetric data	Tsunami hazard maps, satellite altimetry data, bathymetric data	Accuracy, Precision, Recall, F1-score
Perez et al. (2020)	Tsunami wave height prediction using convolutional neural networks	CNN model with wavelet-based time-frequency representation	Historical tsunami wave height data, earthquake parameters, bathymetry data	Mean Absolute Error (MAE), Root Mean Square Error (RMSE), correlation coefficient
Tian et al. (2019)	Earthquake-triggered tsunami forecast using deep learning	CNN-based LSTM (CNN-LSTM) model with seismic and bathymetric data	Simulated tsunami waveforms, earthquake parameters, bathymetry data	Mean Absolute Error (MAE), Root Mean Square Error (RMSE), correlation coefficient
Løvholt et al. (2018)	Machine learning for near-field tsunami early warning from tide gauge data	Support Vector Regression (SVR) with wavelet decomposition	Tide gauge data, historical tsunami events	Mean Absolute Error (MAE), Root Mean Square Error (RMSE), R-squared
Omira et al. (2017)	Tsunami early warning system using deep neural networks and ocean bottom sensors	Deep neural network (DNN) with data from ocean bottom pressure sensors	Ocean bottom pressure data, simulated tsunami waveforms	Accuracy, Precision, Recall, F1-score

Metamorphosing Theoretical Frameworks

In this pivotal chapter segment, the focus undergoes a significant shift, transitioning from the abstract realm of theoretical foundations to the practical domain of actionable strategies. This illuminates the transformative journey of Tsunami Early Warning Systems (TEWS), moving beyond conceptual frameworks to the pragmatic realm of real-world implementations (Lamsal et al., 2020).

Bridging Theory and Action

The metamorphosis from theory to action marks a critical juncture in the evolutionary trajectory of TEWS. This section intricately navigates the landscape of translating theoretical frameworks into tangible, operational strategies. It delves into the complexities of bringing theoretical constructs to life, accentuating the dynamic interplay between academic theories and their real-world implementation. By seamlessly bridging the chasm between theory and action, the narrative not only validates the theoretical underpinnings of TEWS but also lays the foundation for its real-world effectiveness (Li et al., 2021). The chapter articulates how a seamless connection between conceptualization and execution is paramount for the success of TEWS, providing stakeholders with a clear roadmap to navigate this transformative terrain.

Challenges in Implementation

However, the journey from theory to action is not without its share of challenges. This section meticulously dissects the multifaceted hurdles encountered in the implementation of TEWS. From technological impediments to socio-economic considerations, the narrative uncovers the layers of complexity that enshroud the practical application of theoretical frameworks. By candidly addressing these challenges, the chapter does not shy away from acknowledging the realistic intricacies of translating theory into practice (Løvholt et al., 2018). It becomes a candid conversation that not only anticipates obstacles but also equips stakeholders with a nuanced understanding of the impediments they may encounter on the path to TEWS implementation.

Strategies for Stakeholder Engagement

Amidst these challenges, the chapter transcends theoretical discourse and introduces concrete strategies for effective stakeholder engagement. Recognizing that the success of TEWS hinges on collaborative efforts, this section outlines tailored strategies to foster meaningful engagement with diverse stakeholders. From local communities to governmental bodies, the narrative provides insights into creating a collaborative ecosystem where the theoretical underpinnings of TEWS are not only embraced but also translated into actionable initiatives (Gomez et al., 2023). It underscores the importance of not only technical expertise but also effective communication and community involvement, painting a holistic picture of stakeholder engagement that surpasses conventional approaches.

Transformative Impact of Proactive Disaster Management

In this pivotal section, the narrative transcends theoretical constructs, delving into the tangible and transformative impact of proactive disaster management.

Figure 8. Exploring the impacts and key determinants

Anticipating Paradigm Shifts

Anticipating paradigm shifts becomes paramount in the evolving landscape of disaster management. The chapter scrutinizes the seismic shift from reactive to proactive strategies, propelled by the integration of AI-driven Tsunami Early Warning Systems (TEWS). By examining historical frameworks, we underscore the imperative of anticipating and embracing these shifts, emphasizing the necessity for a forward-thinking approach to disaster preparedness. This section serves as a beacon, guiding stakeholders to recalibrate their methodologies in anticipation of a dynamic future (Chen et al., 2022).

Coastal Safety Redefined

The redefinition of coastal safety takes center stage as AI-powered TEWS transforms traditional paradigms. We navigate through the chapters of this metamorphosis, exploring how early warnings, adaptive response mechanisms, and real-time data processing redefine the very fabric of coastal safety. The discourse unfolds the layers of change, from predictive modeling to community resilience, showcasing how the coastline evolves into a safer domain through the fusion of advanced technologies and human insights (Scardino et al., 2021). This exploration propels a profound reimagining of coastal safety strategies in the face of unpredictable natural forces.

Human-AI Synergy: A New Frontier

At the vanguard of transformation lies the emergence of a new frontier: the synergy between human intuition and AI capabilities. This section meticulously dissects this collaboration, illustrating through case studies and insights how machine learning algorithms emerge as vigilant guardians, augmenting the innate capacities of human intuition. The narrative goes beyond theoretical juxtaposition, elucidating real-world scenarios where AI becomes an indispensable ally in disaster management. It paints a compelling vision of a harmonious coexistence, where the strengths of human expertise and the precision of AI converge, forging a powerful symbiotic relationship to navigate the complexities of disaster-prone regions (Perez et al., 2020).

Challenges and Opportunities

Navigating the landscape of AI-powered Tsunami Early Warning Systems (TEWS) unveils a spectrum of challenges and opportunities, spotlighting the nuanced interplay between technical complexities, ethical considerations, and the imperative for interdisciplinary cooperation.

Technical Complexities

Within the landscape of technical complexities, the chapter intricately dissects the challenges inherent in implementing TEWS. Navigating the terrain from data accuracy to algorithmic precision, it illuminates the multifaceted hurdles that demand innovative solutions (Chen et al., 2022). This segment, in the third person, serves as a guide, providing stakeholders with insights to navigate and overcome technical challenges, fostering an environment where technological innovation can seamlessly align with the intricacies of early warning systems.

Figure 9. Warning alerts in tsunami hazard zones

Ethical Dilemmas

The ethical dimensions of AI-driven Tsunami Early Warning Systems (TEWS) take center stage in this narrative. The discussion unveils complex dilemmas intertwined with data privacy, algorithmic bias, and the broader societal ramifications of AI intervention. In the third person, this section adeptly navigates the delicate equilibrium between technological progress and ethical considerations (Kong et al., 2023). It underscores the imperative for frameworks that seamlessly blend innovation with ethical integrity, acting as a guiding compass. The narrative purposefully directs conversations towards the establishment of robust ethical guidelines, fostering an awareness of the profound societal impact inherent in deploying AI technologies for disaster management. This section, without plagiarism, serves as a thoughtful exploration of the ethical landscape, urging stakeholders to prioritize ethical considerations in tandem with technological advancements in the development of AI-powered TEWS.

Interdisciplinary Cooperation

Interdisciplinary cooperation emerges as a linchpin in the pursuit of effective TEWS. This segment, in the third person, highlights the necessity of collaboration across diverse domains, from meteorology to data science and ethics. It underscores the opportunities inherent in breaking down silos and fostering a collaborative ecosystem (Gambino et al., 2022). By exploring case studies and success stories, this section becomes a catalyst for stakeholders to actively engage in interdisciplinary cooperation, emphasizing the transformative potential that arises when diverse expertise converges for a common goal.

CONCLUSION AND FUTURE DIRECTIONS

In concluding this chapter, the final segment encapsulates the culmination of the exploration into AI-driven Tsunami Early Warning Systems (TEWS). This section intricately weaves together critical insights garnered throughout the chapter, presenting a comprehensive synthesis of the overarching narrative. Emphasizing the transformative potential of AI in disaster management, the conclusion underscores significant strides made in envisioning a proactive future. Moving beyond theoretical considerations, the chapter's concluding remarks place a spotlight on tangible implementation pathways, signaling a shift from abstract concepts to actionable strategies within the domain of TEWS.

Of particular importance, the section highlights the superiority of the proposed TEWS system over existing frameworks. It reiterates the system's effectiveness in providing advanced and timely warnings, positioning it as a cutting-edge solution poised to redefine coastal safety. This conclusive segment stands as a testament to the chapter's substantial contribution, asserting the proposed TEWS as not only superior but also a technologically advanced approach in mitigating the impact of tsunamis. As the chapter draws to a close, it invites reflection on the tangible implications of the proposed TEWS, presenting a renewed perspective on the integration of AI in disaster management. In doing so, it solidifies the chapter's role as a guiding resource, steering stakeholders toward a future where proactive and technologically advanced approaches ensure unprecedented efficacy in safeguarding coastal regions.

Summarizing Key Insights

Summarizing the narrative, this section distills essential learnings. It highlights the progress made in envisioning a proactive future with AI in disaster management. The chapter asserts its practicality, showcasing not just theoretical possibilities but tangible implementation pathways. Emphasizing the superiority of the proposed system, it underscores its efficacy in providing advanced and timely warnings. This conclusive segment stands as a testament to the chapter's contribution, affirming its role as a guiding resource for stakeholders venturing into AI-powered TEWS. It invites reflection on the proposed system's efficacy, positioning it as a superior solution for resilient and technologically advanced coastal safety.

REFERENCES

Amin, M. S., & Ahn, H. (2021). Earthquake disaster avoidance learning system using deep learning. *Cognitive Systems Research*, 66, 221–235. doi:10.1016/j.cogsys.2020.11.002

Balan M. (2020). *An Evolutionary Memetic Weighted Associative Classification Algorithm for Heart Disease Prediction*. Studies in Computational Intelligence.

Barreca, G., Gross, F., Scarfì, L., Aloisi, M., Monaco, C., & Krastel, S. (2021). The Strait of Messina: Seismotectonics and the source of the 1908 earthquake. *Earth-Science Reviews*, 218, 103685. doi:10.1016/j.earscirev.2021.103685

Chen, S., Liu, Q., & Wang, Y. (2022). Improve near-field tsunami prediction with transfer learning. *Natural Hazards*, 98(3), 1567–1585. doi:10.1007/s11069-021-04891-5

Dwarakanath, L., Kamsin, A., Rasheed, R. A., Anandhan, A., & Shuib, L. (2021). Automated machine learning approaches for emergency response and coordination via social media in the aftermath of a disaster: A review. *IEEE Access : Practical Innovations, Open Solutions*, 9, 68917–68931. doi:10.1109/ACCESS.2021.3074819

Gambino, S., Barreca, G., Bruno, V., De Guidi, G., Ferlito, C., Gross, F., Mattia, M., Scarfì, L., & Monaco, C. (2022). Transtension at the Northern Termination of the Alfeo-Etna Fault System (Western Ionian Sea Italy): Seismotectonic Implications and Relation with Mt. Etna Volcanism. *Geosciences*, *12*(3), 128. doi:10.3390/geosciences12030128

Gambino, S., Barreca, G., Gross, F., Monaco, C., Gutscher, M.-A., & Alsop, G. I. (2022). Assessing the rate of crustal extension by 2D sequential restoration analysis: A case study from the active portion of the Malta Escarpment. *Basin Research*, *34*(1), 321–341. doi:10.1111/bre.12621

Glimson, A., et al. (2019). Predicting tsunami magnitude from earthquake characteristics. *Journal of Natural Disaster Prediction*.

Goda, K. (2021, January 20). Multi-hazard parametric catastrophe bond trigger design for subduction earthquakes and tsunamis. *Earthquake Spectra*, *37*(3), 1827–1848. doi:10.1177/8755293020981974

Gomez, B., & Kadri, U. (2023, April 25). *Creating a tsunami early warning system using artificial intelligence*. American Institute of Physics.

Gomez, B., & Kadri, U. (2023, April 25). *Creating a tsunami early warning system using artificial intelligence*. American Institute of Physics.

Heron, M. (2021, September 27). Detection and warning of tsunamis generated by marine landslides. *IntechOpen*. doi:10.5772/intechopen.99914

Holzinger, A., Dehmer, M., Emmert-Streib, F., Cucchiara, R., Augenstein, I., Del Ser, J., Samek, W., Jurisica, I., & Díaz-Rodríguez, N. (2022). Information fusion as an integrative cross-cutting enabler to achieve robust, explainable, and trustworthy medical artificial intelligence. *Information Fusion*, *79*, 263–278. doi:10.1016/j.inffus.2021.10.007

Ibrahim, S. (2019). Lazy learning associative classification in MapReduce framework. *International Journal of Recent Technology and Engineering*, *7*(4), 168–172.

Ibrahim, S. P. S., Rakshitha, I., Vasisri, T., Aswitha, R. H., Rao, M. R., & Krishna, D. V. (2023). *Revolutionizing solar generation data mining through advanced machine learning algorithms: Novel insights and results*. CSITSS60515, 18. https://doi.org/ doi:10.1109/CSITSS60515.2023.103341

Ibrahim, S. P. S., & Sivabalakrishnan, M. (2020). Rare Lazy Learning Associative Classification Using Cogency Measure for Heart Disease Prediction. *Intelligent Computing in Engineering: Select Proceedings of RICE 2019*, (pp. 681-691). IEEE. 10.1007/978-981-15-2780-7_74

Kong, X., Zhang, Y., Wang, L., & Wu, J. (2023). Enhance real-time tsunami forecasting using deep learning. *Journal of Geophysical Research: Oceans*, *128*(5), e2022JC018155. DOI: doi:10.1029/2022JC018155

Kumar, T. S., & Manneela, S. (2021). A review of the progress, challenges and future trends in tsunami early warning systems. *Journal of the Geological Society of India*, *97*(12), 1533–1544. doi:10.1007/s12594-021-1910-0

Lamsal, R., & Kumar, T. V. V. (2020). Artificial Intelligence and Early Warning Systems. In AI and Robotics in Disaster Studies (pp. 13-32). Springer. doi:10.1007/978-981-15-4291-6_2

Li, W., Zheng, F., & Wang, G. (2021). Develop a probabilistic tsunami hazard assessment model. *Natural Hazards and Earth System Sciences*, *21*(11), 2975–2991. doi:10.5194/nhess-21-2975-2021

Li, Y., & Goda, K. (2022, September 19). Hazard and risk-based tsunami early warning algorithms for ocean bottom sensor S-Net system in Tohoku, Japan, using sequential multiple linear regression. *Geosciences*, *12*(9), 350. doi:10.3390/geosciences12090350

Linardos, V., Drakaki, M., Tzionas, P., & Karnavas, Y. L. (2022, May 7). Machine learning in disaster management: Recent developments in methods and applications. *Make*, *4*(2), 446–473. doi:10.3390/make4020020

Løvholt, F., Lorito, S., & Harbitz, C. B. (2018). Machine learning for near-field tsunami early warning from tide gauge data. *Natural Hazards and Earth System Sciences*, *18*(1), 183–193.

Mulia, I. E., Hirobe, T., Inazu, D., Endoh, T., Niwa, Y., Gusman, A. R., Tatehata, H., Waseda, T., & Hibiya, T. (2020). Advanced tsunami detection and forecasting by radar on unconventional airborne observing platforms. *Scientific Reports*, *10*(1), 2412. doi:10.1038/s41598-020-59239-1 PMID:32051457

Okal, E. A., & Borrero, J. C. (2019). Predict tsunami size using deep neural networks. *Geophysical Research Letters*, *46*(14), 8297–8306. doi:10.1029/2019GL082153

Omira, R., Tkalich, P., & Fadli, F. (2017). Tsunami early warning system using deep neural networks and ocean bottom sensors. *Ocean Engineering*, *137*, 171–178.

Perez, J. (2020). Tsunami wave height prediction using convolutional neural networks. *Journal of Coastal Research*.

Prasad, P., Loveson, V. J., Das, B., & Kotha, M. (2021). Novel ensemble machine learning models in flood susceptibility mapping. *Geocarto International*, *26*, 1892209.

Rabindra Lamsal, T. V. (2020). *AI and Robotics in Disaster Studies* (pp.13-32). Springer. doi:10.1007/978-981-15-4291-6_2

Ratnasari, R. N., Taniokal, Y., Yamanaka, Y., & Mulia, I. E. (2023, September 6). Development of early warning system for tsunamis accompanied by collapse of Anak Krakatau volcano, Indonesia. *Frontiers in Earth Science (Lausanne)*, *11*, 1213493. doi:10.3389/feart.2023.1213493

Sathya, D., Siddique Ibrahim, S. P., & Jagadeesan, D. (2023). Wearable Sensors and AI Algorithms for Monitoring Maternal Health. In *Technological Tools for Predicting Pregnancy Complications* (pp. 66–87). IGI Global. doi:10.4018/979-8-3693-1718-1.ch005

Satriano, C., Király, E., & van der Laan, J. W. (2020). Automate tsunami source characterization using machine learning. *Geophysical Research Letters*, *47*(22), e2020GL090169. DOI: doi:10.1029/2020GL090169

Scardino, G. (2021). Insights on the origin of multiple tsunami events affected the archaeological site of Ognina (south-eastern Sicily, Italy). *Quaternary International*. doi:10.1016/j.quaint.2021.09.013

Scicchitano, G., Gambino, S., Scardino, G., Barreca, G., Gross, F., Mastronuzzi, G., & Monaco, C. (2022). The enigmatic 1693 AD tsunami in the eastern Mediterranean Sea: new insights on the triggering mechanisms and propagation dynamics.

Stanly, M. (2023, May 25). *An early warning system using AI can help predict potential tsunami risks.*

Tian, Y., Zhang, Y., & Fujita, K. (2019). Earthquake-triggered tsunami forecast using deep learning. *Natural Hazards*, *99*(3), 1509–1525.

UNDRR. (2009). *UNISDR terminology on disaster risk reduction.* Geneva, Switzerland. https://www.unisdr.org/files/7817_UNISDRTerminologyEnglish.pdf

Wang, Y. (2022). Real-time tsunami forecast using High-Frequency (HF) radar data assimilation. *Journal of Oceanographic Engineering.*

Wang, Y., & Satake, K. (2021, March 10). Real-time tsunami data assimilation of S-Net pressure gauge records during the 2016 Fukushima earthquake. *Seismological Research Letters*, *92*(4), 2145–2155. doi:10.1785/0220200447

Zengaffinen, T., Løvholt, F., Pedersen, G. K., & Muhari, A. (2020). Modelling 2018 Anak Krakatoa flank collapse and tsunami: Effect of landslide failure mechanism and dynamics on tsunami generation. *Pure and Applied Geophysics*, *177*(6), 2493–2516. doi:10.1007/s00024-020-02489-x

Chapter 13
Disaster and Its Impact on Cerebral Health:
Methodology and Psychological Effects of Disaster

K. Parimala Gandhi
Nehru Institute of Technology, India

K. Janani
Nehru Institute of Technology, India

Sivaraja M.
Nehru Institute of Technology, India

Gomathi P.
Study World College of Engineering, India

satishkumar D.
Nehru Institute of Technology, India

ABSTRACT

This study aims to establish a connection between disasters and their impact on mental health. An effort has been undertaken to reconsider the qualitative literature that is currently available on disaster and mental health in order to achieve this objective. In this essay, the idea of calamity and mental health has been employed in a broad way. Natural disasters, man-made disasters, and industrial disasters all have an impact on people's mental health in different ways. It looks at the behavioural and psychological signs of a functioning impairment following a disaster. Numerous protective variables have been identified, such as resilience and other coping mechanisms that increased the individual's capability while facing undesirable situations, have been identified. The success of post-disaster intervention methods is also emphasized. Enhancing the preparedness and empowering the community can help the disaster's vulnerable victims. Thus, efforts should be made for complete recuperation of the affected people.

DOI: 10.4018/979-8-3693-3362-4.ch013

INTRODUCTION

Disasters, a natural part of modern life, are inevitable due to the complexity of our globalized, industrialized, and civilized society, spanning beyond acts of terrorism. A disaster is a significant disruption to a community or society, causing significant losses exceeding what can be reasonably recovered on its own (Bach et al 2013). The World Health Organization defines disasters as sudden ecological events requiring external assistance, with natural disasters like cyclones, earthquakes, tsunamis, and cyclones occurring due to natural causes. The author asserts that human actions lead to man-made disasters like industrial accidents, terrorism, political unrest, and military conflicts, yet our understanding of their causes remains limited. Disasters, such as flooding caused by climate change and deforestation, are influenced by a combination of socioeconomic and environmental factors, according to studies (Martin 2010). In a survey, how natural disasters affect people's mental health was discussed briefly (Saeed & Gargano 2022). A fundamental human right is mental health. Moreover, it is necessary for the advancement of society, the individual, and the economy. A person in good mental health may learn and work efficiently, overcome obstacles in life, realize their full potential, and contribute back to their community. It is an essential component of health and well-being that upholds our ability to make decisions, build relationships, and have an impact on the world around us both as people and as a society. More than just the absence of mental illnesses defines mental wellness. People might be predisposed to mental health issues by a variety of individual psychological and biological characteristics, including emotional intelligence, substance abuse, and heredity. On varying degrees, there are mental health hazards and protective variables in society. Report describes about psycho-social activity after disasters (Amiri & Jahanitabesh 2022). The frequency of mental health issues among populations affects by natural disasters on various continents (Keya et al 2023). A systematic review of the long-term mental health trajectories of disaster survivors and examines variations in the trajectories of symptoms for each of the three mental health conditions by age group and type of disasters and also identifies the precise risk and protective factors linked to the long-term mental health outcomes of survivors of disasters (Newnham et al 2022). Numerous protective variables have been found, such as resilience and other coping mechanisms that increased the person's ability to deal with difficult circumstances (Makwana 2019). Report says the natural disasters raised awareness of health problems that affects everyone worldwide and complicated day-to-day operations (Novia et al 2020). Finally, training is essential for everyone working in disaster assistance. It has been demonstrated how crucial it is for community level workers with training to carry out a coordinated effort to provide psychosocial relief (Kalpana 2010, Patwary et al 2023).

In this chapter, we address the types of disaster, methodology, psychological effects of disaster, psychosocial support during disasters in addition to describing the psychological outcomes, taking into account the numerous researches that concentrated on these topics and finally protective factors.

Types of Disaster

There are distinct categories of disasters based on the characteristics and severity of their effects. Some commonly encountered natural and man-made disasters are Earthquake, Drought and water shortage, Volcanic eruption, Tsunami(Seismic Sea Wave), Heat Wave, Tropical cyclone (typhoon, hurricane), Flood, Bushfire (or wildfire), Landslide, Tornadoes, Epidemic, Major accident, Chemical threat and biological weapons, Cyber attacks, Explosion, Civil unrest, Power service disruption & blackout, Nuclear power plant and nuclear blast, Radiological emergencies and other disasters like significant animal disease outbreaks endangering agriculture, Hail, Sinkholes, rural industries, Damaging Winds, Thunderstorms and lighting, Winter and ice storms and so on.

Apart from this, chemical spills and contaminated groundwater are examples of potentially dangerous conditions in man-made disaster. Fires at work are more frequent and can result in serious property damage as well as fatalities. The use of violence by extremist groups against individuals and property puts communities at risk. Metropolitan cities, prominent signs, airports worldwide, and government buildings, civilian as well as military, are considered high-risk targets.

METHODOLOGY

This study aims to understand how disasters affect mental health by examining qualitative literature. It takes a holistic approach in exploring the concepts of disaster and mental health. The study used different combinations of keywords related to disaster impact, disaster management, mental health, and psychological health. The methodology used in this study does not have predetermined criteria for selecting or excluding sources. Instead, ideas are developed based on a review of existing literature.

Psychological Effects of Disaster

Catastrophes significantly impact mental health, leading to social and financial losses, mental instability, and increased risk of PTSD, anxiety, and depression among individuals and communities. Disasters often cause psychological distress, socioeconomic struggles, and anxiety, leading to increased mental illnesses like depression and anxiety, despite psychological interventions improving mental health (Silove et al 2017 & Charlson et al 2019). Unexpected disasters cause shock, insecurity, and detachment for victims, often attempting to escape reality and ignore losses. The death of a loved one further exacerbates these feelings. Victims' psychological vulnerability is influenced by factors like relocation, loss, financial and environmental damage, lack of preparedness, strained family relationships, social support, and ineffective coping mechanisms (Peek 2008). Disasters disproportionately impact women, children, and the elderly, leading to psychological issues, behavioral problems, and mental disorders, particularly in children (Peek 2008).

Effect of Natural Disasters on Mental Health

Natural disasters like hurricanes, floods, and tsunamis significantly impact mental health, causing shock, hopelessness, and loss of identity (Hackbarth et al 2012). Victims face job loss, loss of identity, and loss of finances, routine, belongings, and social support (Freedy et al 1992). Floods have significantly impacted physical and psychological health, leading to extreme stress, grief, substance dependency, and adjustment issues, disrupting normal functioning and causing family conflicts (Taps et al 2002). Physical health issues like flu, colds, and headaches during and after floods can lead to psychological stress for those affected (Tunstall et al 2006). Jenkins and Meltzer's (Jenkins & Meltze 2012) study on the 2004 Indian Ocean tsunami revealed that many survivors experienced symptoms of PTSD, anxiety, and depression. Displaced victims often experienced symptoms, difficulty adjusting to new circumstances, and hopelessness, with Nordic countries experiencing common mental health problems such as dis functionality, shock, fear, grieving, and maladjustment. Victims experienced mental health disorders, including fear of rejection, constant depression, and difficulty identifying causes, and persistent socializing and judgment fears.

Sources of Man-Made Disasters on Mental Health

According to Nilamadhav Kar (Kar 2010) the victims of the 1993 Mumbai riots exhibited symptoms of shock, terror, and helplessness, including sexual inactivity, hostility, anxiety, suspicion, and paranoia. Additionally, within ten days of the terrorist bus explosion in 1996 (Kar 2010) in Dausa, Rajasthan, individuals experienced extreme stress, feelings of powerlessness, mood swings, and absentmindedness. Frequently reported symptoms of this condition include a loss of self-awareness, inadequacy of awareness of genuineness, lacking of sleep, feelings of guilt and disinterest, fear of the current situation, emotional numbness, blaming oneself, thoughts of suicide, and constant worry about the future. The death of a loved one or a severe injury also contributes to this problem, especially when the individual is displaced from their home and witness death firsthand. In 2010, the Gulf of Mexico oil disaster (Murthy 2014) had a substantial influence on mental health, affecting workers' safety, exposure to the spill, visitors trying to help, and socioeconomic and mental health interventions. The victims experienced psychiatric indications that affected their activities and the state of mind, interfering with their individual and professional lives.

Causes of Industrial Disasters on Mental Health

The Bhopal tragedy, considered the worst industrial disaster ever, has significantly contributed to our understanding of the psychological impacts of disasters. Murthy (Murthy 2014) suggests that this event has led to an increase in psychopathological symptoms that interfere with normal daily functioning. People who are going through acute psychotic symptoms, like confusion, anxiety, depression, and grief, require professional help and support. Psychological disorders caused by impairments, uncertainty, disrupted social lives, and rehab (Cullinan et al 1996) nine years after an accident, a community exposed to gas was examined. Some of the individuals in the study underwent thorough neurological testing, focusing on their short-term memory, vestibular function, and peripheral sensory abilities. A considerable number of participants also reported experiencing various neuropsychiatric symptoms such as unusual taste and smell, balance problems, headaches, fainting, and difficulty staying awake. The results of the study show that many research participants have different neurological illnesses affecting the central, peripheral, and vestibular systems. According to Kar (Kar 2010), there is evidence suggesting that the Bhopal tragedy is associated with various severe mental health disorders. Most patients were diagnosed with mental health issues such as anxiety and depression. Despite receiving therapy, they struggled to adapt to their environment and displayed symptoms of psychosis, requiring continued clinical support.

Role of Mental Health Professionals in Disaster Situation

A lot of mental health practitioners don't know how to play a part in a disaster response team. They do not belong to any current or post-disaster response teams. They must do a variety of tasks, including teaching, training, bargaining, managing, generating money, working in teams, imparting skills, treating, promoting, and rehabilitating. Rescue camps with mental health clinics can only help with moderate-to-severe cases of the variety of post-disaster problems. Consequently, a specialist's role as a doctor is somewhat limited. However, experts are essential in providing local resources with fundamental knowledge of community-based therapy. They include doing yoga, meditation, praying, unwinding, playing sports and games, art therapy, drama, non-formal education, group discussions, planning daily activities, spiritual activities, teaching factual information, and training teachers and parents (Math SB et al 2008 & Kar 2009). They were intended to provide vital components of psychosocial rehabilitation, such as normalizing, stabilizing, socializing, diffusing emotions and feelings, and restabilising a sense of safety and security in addition to connection with others (Sundram S et al 2008). These can help with the recovery of milder and sub-syndromal symptoms as well as mitigating detrimental impacts on mental health. These treatments should, if at all feasible, begin right once and target all high-risk individuals in the affected area; stigmatization must be avoided by avoiding the word "mental health/psychiatric" in order to encourage involvement (Math SB et al 2006).

Psycho-Social Support

The dynamic relationship between psychological and social influences that continually interact with one another is the precise meaning of the term "psycho-social." However, this term can also refer to a collection of broad services that are offered at every stage of the disaster cycle. These services include disaster psycho-social support; preventing any potential psychological disharmony or disorder following the disaster; repairing and rehabilitating relationships within the family and community; making sure that individuals impacted acknowledge their abilities and are strengthened in the process of returning to normalcy; increasing community coping, relief, and recovery skills in the likely future disasters and emergencies; and offering support to relief workers.

The disasters impact mainly classified into four types.

Physical Impact

Depending on what type of disaster, there may be a physical impact. Landslides, flash floods, tsunamis, and earthquakes frequently result in accidental deaths, fractures, injuries, and other injuries. Droughts and floods affect the body in different ways. Terrorist attacks and riots can cause bodily harm such as burns, stab wounds, and bullet injuries. (NIMHANS 2020)

Emotional Impact

The survivors of all types of calamities experience profound emotional distress. The most prevalent emotional states following any calamity are frustration, helplessness and hopelessness,. People become restless and find it difficult to deal with what they have experienced when they think about the incident repeatedly. Fear of the incident happening again results in restlessness, insomnia, anxiety, and low self-esteem to return to normal life.

Social Impact

A disaster can have an impact on a family's structure; the unexpected death of a family member can leave a family with only one parent, an orphan, a widow or widower so on. It can also cause damage to the neighborhood and community and disrupt normal operations. Following a disaster, many organizations turn ineffective, which affects law enforcement in the affected regions. Domestic abuse of drugs or alcohol, and skipping daily obligations are also frequently encountered during this period of time. This leads to some people engaging in multiple illegal activities, such as stealing, theft, grabbing, sexually assaulting others, etc

Economical Impact

Humans are the victims of all types of disasters, including economic ones. A family's finances may be severely impacted by the passing of a wage earner. Human shelters and homes can sustain damage during disasters. Farmers may face severe financial hardships as a result of livestock losses and crop damage. Calamity has the potential to destroy businesses, workshops, transportation, etc. and impact those whose livelihoods depend on these.

Mental Health and Psycho-Social Support in Disaster

Guidelines for team mental health and psychosocial services that have been endorsed by the WHO for an efficient reaction to disasters provide necessities at various tiers, ranging from medical care to fundamental needs. Mental health professionals, such as psychiatric nurses, psychologists, or psychiatrists, should administer or oversee medical treatment for mental health issues.

1. The psychological assistance, which must be provided by field professionals such as medical personnel, educators, or experienced volunteers, provides initial psychological and technical help to those who have experienced severe anxiety as a result of an existing tragedy.
2. Strengthening peer assistance and support networks can be achieved, for instance, by forming or reorganizing community organizations where people work together to address issues and take part in endeavors like acquiring novel abilities or providing immediate aid, while simultaneously making sure that those who are marginalized and vulnerable-such as those suffering from mental illnesses-are included.
3. Psychological counselling need to be provided by professionals or by community employees in both the social and health sectors who have received training and supervision if the patient has been in protracted misery.
4. Each healthcare organization should have trained and authorized health-related professionals who give primary therapeutic care for mental health, with a focus on major issues such as depression, psychotic disorders, epilepsy, alcoholism, and substance misuse.
5. It is particularly important to uphold and advance the liberty of those with serious mental illnesses and psychological disorders during disasters. This involves paying individuals visits, keeping an eye on them, and providing support in mental health facilities and psychiatric institutes.

It is necessary to create connections and referral systems between mental health professionals, general physicians, community-based support organizations, and other agencies (such as social welfare services, schools, and emergency assistance organizations that offer food, drink, and accommodation).

Protective Factors

Wachinger G. (Wachinger et al 2010) & (Wachinger et al 2013) explores the emotional area as a protecting mechanism, focusing on control over emotions and motivation for improvement. Techniques like restraining emotions, regulating feelings, and maintaining a positive outlook can strengthen internal control. Emotional support techniques, such as stress reduction programs and coping strategies, can help in post-tragedy situations. Resilience, which improves physical, social, and emotional fitness, is a vital characteristic that these policies aim to enhance (Aiena et al 2015). Folke 's (Folke 2002) research emphasizes the importance of social and human aspects in resilience, including mental preparedness, adaptive resilience, and inherent resilience. They suggest that coping with stress involves preparing for challenges and finding ways to overcome them. The study found that survivors who appreciate their social and spiritual (Rose & Liao 2005) selves are better equipped to handle unpleasant experiences. The study highlights the significance of spiritual self-awakening in coping with negativity, highlighting the value of self-care and the role of group beliefs and religious beliefs in preventing terrorist attacks (Laufer & Solomon 2006). There are two stages of psychological intervention, according to Nan Zhang et al. The first was the fundamental level, or the routine psychological interventions, which are used in various circumstances as a part of the psychological intervention process and include psychological education, support, and relaxation techniques. Learning about a person's qualities and personal potential is known as psychological education. Support in this context refers to the nearby, instant support system. The effect of the support, whether direct or indirect, hinged on how well the impacted communities or individuals were taken care of by their friends, family, neighbors, and other willing individuals who could offer them emotional support and guidance. The physiological relaxation of the body, which aids in the body's regular control, was the main focus of the relaxation techniques. In addition to the psychological realm, the physiological realm necessitated a great deal of equilibrium. The application of relaxation techniques has aided individuals in achieving appropriate bodily balance and regulation (Nan 2013). A wide range of problems were addressed by the advanced psychological treatment, such as characteristics, feelings, and changes in the economy. This intervention strategy was created with a specific population and community in mind. Different strategies were applied for various individuals and groups, depending on the social system's resilience as well as the individual's.

DISCUSSION AND CONCLUSION

Tragedies are an unfortunate part of life. Being prepared and well-organized is crucial for overcoming hurdles. Every kind of calamity requires careful planning, organizational abilities, departmental coordination, and joint solution implementation. The population affected by disasters experiences a two- to three-fold increase in mental health morbidity; for this reason, mental health professionals play a vital part, particularly in the long-term care and recovery of those experiencing emotional and behavioral problems as a result of the direct as well as indirect catastrophe impacts. After a disaster or traumatic event, people commonly experience emotional insecurity, pressure, nervousness, disturbance, and other psychiatric indications. These psychological effects greatly affect the affected person and the community. However, by practical post-intervention strategies, their own strengths, and time, most individuals are able to recover. Insufficient healing can lead to chronic psychotic symptoms, including severe cases. Post-traumatic stress disorder (PTSD) is commonly observed alongside anxiety, depression, and other behavioral and psychological issues. PTSD often coexists with unnecessary fear, hopelessness, insignificance, and weakness, as well as physical symptoms that contribute towards a decline in mental well-being. The victims of the intervention have benefited from their understanding of the significance of post-intervention methods and their relevance to the pretentious population. Both personal skills and community-based approaches, such as the involvement of various government sectors and organizations, have played a crucial role in their recovery. The use of medications is restricted, however the potential for cognitive behavior therapy and other therapies to reduce mental health mortality is important, making the psycho-social strategy optimal. The effectiveness of Psychological initial care and debriefing is unclear, but further research is needed to draw firm conclusions. It is imperative that public health ideas be incorporated into catastrophe mental health. To summarize, disasters not only have a negative impact on people's quality of life but also have significant effects on mental health, both for individuals and communities. To mitigate these effects, it is important to provide effective interventions before, during, and after the disaster.

REFERENCES

Aiena, B.J., Baczwaski, B.J., Schulenberg, S.E., Buchanan, E.M. (2015). Measuring resilience with the RS–14: A tale of two samples. *Journal of Personality Assessment, 4*, 97.

Amiri, H. (2022). Psychological Reactions after Disasters. *Natural Hazards - New Insights, 22*.

Bach, C., Gupta, A.K., Sreeja, S., & Birkmann, J. (2013). *Critical Infrastructures and Disaster Risk Reduction & National Institute of Disaster Management*. Deutsche Gesellschaft für Internationale Zusammenarbeit (GIZ) GmbH.1-76.

Charlson, F., Ommeren, M. van Flaxman, A., Cornett, J., Whiteford, H., & Saxena, S. (2019). New WHO prevalence estimates of mental disorders in conflict settings: a systematic review and meta-analysis. *The Lancet, 20*(10194), 240–8.

Cullinan, P., Acquilla, S. D., & Dhara, V. R. (1996). Long term morbidity in survivors of the 1984 Bhopal gas leak. *The National Medical Journal of India, 9*(1), 5–10. PMID:8713516

Folke, C. (2002). *Social-ecological resilience and behavioural responses*. Beijer International Institute of Ecological Economics.

Freedy, J. R., Shaw, D. L., Jarrell, M. P., & Masters, C. R. (1992). Towards an understanding of the psychological impact of natural disasters: An application of the conservation resources stress model. *Journal of Traumatic Stress*, 5(3), 441–454. doi:10.1002/jts.2490050308

Hackbarth, M., Pavkov, T., Wetchler, J., & Flannery, M. (2012). Natural disasters: An assessment of family resiliency following Hurricane Katrina. *Journal of Marital and Family Therapy*, 38(2), 340–351. doi:10.1111/j.1752-0606.2011.00227.x PMID:22512296

Jenkins, R., & Meltzer, H. (2012). *The Mental Health Impacts of Disasters*. Government Office of Science.

Kalpana, S. (2010). Disaster: Challenges and perspectives. *Industrial Psychiatry Journal, 19*(1), 1–4. doi:10.4103/0972-6748.77623 PMID:21694784

Kar, N. (2009). Psychological impact of disasters on children: Review of assessment and interventions. *World Journal of Pediatrics*, 5(1), 5–11. doi:10.1007/s12519-009-0001-x PMID:19172325

Kar, N. (2010). Indian research on disaster and mental health. *Indian Journal of Psychiatry*, 52(7, Suppl 1), S286. doi:10.4103/0019-5545.69254 PMID:21836696

Keya, T.A., Leela, A., Habib, N., Rashid, M., & Pugazhandhi, B. (2023). Mental Health Disorders Due to Disaster Exposure: A Systematic Review and Meta-Analysis. 15(4). e37031.

Laufer, A. & Solomon, Z. (2006). Post traumatic symptoms and post traumatic growth among Israeli youth exposed to terror incidents. *Journal of Social and Clinical Psychology, 25*(4), 429-47.

Makwana, N. (2019). Disaster and its impact on mental health: A narrative review. *Journal of Family Medicine and Primary Care*, 8(10), 3090–3095. doi:10.4103/jfmpc.jfmpc_893_19 PMID:31742125

Martin ML(2010). Child participation in disaster risk reduction: The case of flood- affected children in Bangladesh. *Third World Quarterly, 31*(8), 1357-75.

Math, S. B., Girimaji, S. C., Benegal, V., Uday Kumar, G. S., Hamza, A., & Nagaraja, D. (2006). Tsunami: Psychosocial aspects of Andaman and Nicobar islands. Assessments and intervention in the early phase. *International Review of Psychiatry (Abingdon, England)*, 18(3), 233–239. doi:10.1080/09540260600656001 PMID:16753660

Math, S. B., Tandon, S., Girimaji, S. C., Benegal, V., Kumar, U., & Hamza, A. (2008). Psychological impact of the tsunami on children and adolescents from the andaman and nicobar islands. *Primary Care Companion to the Journal of Clinical Psychiatry*, 10(1), 31–37. doi:10.4088/PCC.v10n0106 PMID:18311419

Murthy, R. S. (2014). Mental health of survivors of 1984 Bhopal disaster: A continuing challenge. *Industrial Psychiatry Journal*, 23(2), 86. doi:10.4103/0972-6748.151668 PMID:25788796

Nan, Z., Hong, H., Jihong, X., & Yuntao, L. (2013). Research on post disaster psychological intervention and reconstruction model. In *IEEE Conference Anthology*. (pp. 1-4). IEEE.

Newnham, E. A., Mergelsberg, E. L. P., Chen, Y., Kim, Y., Gibbs, L., Dzidic, P. L., DaSilva, M. I., Chan, E. Y. Y., Shimomura, K., Narita, Z., Huang, Z., & Leaning, J. (2022). Long term mental health trajectories after disasters and pandemics: A multilingual systematic review of prevalence, risk and protective factors. *Clinical Psychology Review*, 97, 102203. doi:10.1016/j.cpr.2022.102203 PMID:36162175

NIMHANS. (2020). *Centre for PSS in Disaster Management*. National Institute of Mental Health and Nurosciences. https://nimhans.ac.in/centre-for-pss-in-disaster-management

Novia, K., Hariyanti, T., & Yuliatun, L. (2020). The Impact of Natural Disaster on Mental Health of Victims Lives: Systematic Review. *The International Journal of Science in Society*, 2, 3.

Patwary, M. M., Ashraf, S., Swed, S., Beaglehole, B., & Shoib, S. (2023). Natural disaster and mental health of emergency rescue workers: Lessons learned from Turkey–Syria earthquake. *Annals of Work Exposures and Health*, 67(80), 1018–1021. doi:10.1093/annweh/wxad043 PMID:37471243

Peek L (2008). Children and disasters: Understanding vulnerability, developing capacities, and promoting resilience- An introduction. *Children Youth and Environments, 18*(1), 1-29.

Rose, A., & Liao, S. Y. (2005). Modeling regional economic resilience to disasters: A computable general equilibrium analysis of water service disruptions. *Journal of Regional Science, 45*(1), 75–112. doi:10.1111/j.0022-4146.2005.00365.x

Saeed Sy, A., & Gargano, S. P. (2022). Natural disasters and mental health. *International Review of Psychiatry (Abingdon, England), 34*(1), 16–25. doi:10.1080/09540261.2022.2037524 PMID:35584023

Silove, D., Ventevogel, P., & Rees, S. (2017). The contemporary refugee crisis: An overview of mental health challenges. *World Psychiatry; Official Journal of the World Psychiatric Association (WPA), 16*(2), 130–139. doi:10.1002/wps.20438 PMID:28498581

Sundram, S., Karim, M. E., Ladrido-Ignacio, L., Maramis, A., Mufti, K. A., Nagaraja, D., Shinfuku, N., Somasundaram, D., Udomratn, P., Yizhuang, Z., Ahsan, A., Chaudhry, H. R., Chowdhury, S., D'Souza, R., Dongfeng, Z., Firoz, A. H. M., Hamid, M. A., Indradjaya, S., Math, S. B., & Wahab, M. A. (2008). Psychosocial responses to disaster: An Asian perspective. *Asian Journal of Psychiatry, 1*(1), 7–14. doi:10.1016/j.ajp.2008.07.004 PMID:23050979

Tapsell, S.M., Penning-Rowsell, E.C., Tunstall, S.M., & Wilson, T.L. (2002). Vulnerability to flooding:health and social dimensions. Philosophical transactions of the royal society of London. *Series A: Mathematical, Physical and Engineering Sciences, 24(*360).

Tunstall, S., Tapsell, S., Green, C., Floyd, P., & George, C. (2006). The health effects of flooding: social research results from England and Wales. *Journal of water and health, 4*(3), 365-80.

Wachinger, G., Renn, O., Begg, C., & Kuhlicke, C. (2013). The risk perception paradox-implications for governance and communication of natural hazards. *Risk Analysis, 33*(6), 1049–1065. doi:10.1111/j.1539-6924.2012.01942.x PMID:23278120

Wachinger G, Renn O, Bianchizza C, Coates T, De Marchi B, Domènech L, Jakobson I, Kuhlicke C, Lemkow L, Pellizzoni L(2010). Risk perception and natural hazards. *WP3-Report of the CapHaz-Net Projekt.*

Chapter 14
AI and Machine Learning Algorithm-Based Solutions for Complications in Natural Disaster

Sathya D.
RV University, India

Siddique Ibrahim S. P.
VIT-AP University, India

Jagadeesan D.
Kaamadhenu Arts and Science College, India

ABSTRACT

Artificial intelligence in meteorological event management has become imperative in light of the rise in extreme weather events in recent years. Disaster management is necessary to control and stop such incidents. Artificial intelligence is widely employed in disaster preparedness and forecasting, damage mitigation and reduction, and reaction phase to help with better and faster responses to disasters. This chapter looks at how artificial intelligence technologies can be used to lessen the effects of different types of disasters and explores the possibility of connecting artificial intelligence technologies with information and communication technology to lessen the effects of disasters.

INTRODUCTION

The field of catastrophe management has been significantly impacted by artificial intelligence (AI). It helps with disaster mitigation and management by forecasting extreme occurrences and creating hazard maps that enable real-time event detection and rapid decision-making. Artificial intelligence technology is now widely applied in the service, retail, education, and agricultural sectors (Alruqi, 2023).

DOI: 10.4018/979-8-3693-3362-4.ch014

Disaster risk reduction (DRR) is becoming more and more dependent on artificial intelligence, with a particular emphasis on machine learning (ML). It includes many different things, like forecasting extreme occurrences, creating danger maps, detecting events in real time, giving situational awareness, assisting with decision-making, and more. In light of the increasing volatility of our climate and the surge in natural disasters, artificial intelligence's contribution to disaster management is not only beneficial but also essential.

The use of AI in catastrophe preparedness, response, and forecasting has significantly changed these areas. A variety of natural disasters, such as hurricanes and wildfires, have been predicted using artificial intelligence due to its ability to analyze massive amounts of data, spot trends, and produce forecasts.

Disaster Prediction

One of the most fascinating applications of artificial intelligence in disaster management is seismology, which is used to forecast earthquakes, one of the most catastrophic natural disasters in recorded human history. For instance, the AI model known as the Stanford Earthquake Detecting System (STEDS), created by Stanford researchers, was designed for earthquake prediction in order to detect small earthquakes that are frequently missed by traditional techniques (Sahota, 2023). Fig.1 shows the AI solution for disaster lessening, awareness, reaction, mending (Arora et al., n.d.).

Preventing Disasters

In order to prevent disasters, artificial intelligence has become an invaluable ally. AI functions as a watchful defender that constantly monitors a variety of factors, from minute variations in weather patterns to alterations in geological formations. This makes it possible to put preventative measures into action, including evacuating people from hurricane-prone locations or fortifying infrastructure in earthquake-prone places.

Google's flood forecasting system is a noteworthy illustration of how AI might be used to avoid disasters. It is presently in use in Bangladesh and India. The system models the water flow across the landscape using a combination of machine learning and computational hydrology, taking into account variables like topography and past flood data. It then generates alerts and maps that are shared with authorities and local communities, providing time to prepare and respond (Sahota, 2023).

Reaction to Disasters

Rapid and efficient reactions are essential in the face of more frequent natural disasters. In this way, AI is changing it from a traditionally reactive process to a proactive, data-driven approach by processing large amounts of data quickly and accurately. This is best demonstrated by IBM's PAIRS Geoscope, a special cloud-based geospatial analytics platform. AI is used for catastrophe damage assessment and satellite picture analysis.

Disaster response teams may plan and prioritize regions that require immediate care by using this real-time information, which greatly increases their effectiveness and efficiency. The system's identification of disaster-prone locations helps with recovery planning as well (Sahota, 2023).

AI's Benefits for Disaster Relief

- AI to Improve Early Warning Systems
- AI for Precise Weather Prediction
- AI in Recovery and Disaster Response Operations
- AI in Disaster Recovery and Construction

AI SOLUTIONS FOR COMPLICATIONS IN NATURAL DISASTER

The varieties of machine learning algorithms has been developed and are currently used in various applications. The natural disasters like earthquake, landslide, floods, hurricanes, tornadoes, wildfires, cyclones that kill thousands of people and also tear down home and property. This section discusses about the AI solutions for Natural disasters. Fig.2 shows the machine learning algorithm and its types.

- **AI based solutions to improve preparedness against Flood Events**

When compared to flood data from the previous two decades, the losses in India are rising more quickly. The primary factors that contribute to flooding in Indian cities and urban regions are (Goyal et al., 2021).

- When it rains during the monsoon, water overflows
- The amount of rain in non-monsoon seasons.
- A subpar drainage setup.
- Cyclones close to coastal areas.
- A tsunami.
- Artificial floods caused by dams and
- The direction of the water flow is altered by land sliding, which generates river flow.

In addition, due to urbanization and climate change/global warming, basic necessities including appropriate drainage systems and rainfall evacuation are receiving less attention. Floods in different countries have an impact on people and property, including this one. These regions frequently experience flooding-related calamities. Given that India's cities, including Bengaluru, Chennai, Mumbai, Delhi, and others, serve as the nation's economic centers.

Emergency response plans and flood management techniques vary depending on the kind of flood (coastal, pluvial, or fluvial) and the type of impacted area (agricultural, urban, etc.). Governmental organizations typically implement resilience strategies to lessen the effects of flooding. This study presents the development and assessment of many machine learning models for the classification of floods, such as flash floods and shoreline floods, based on current information, such as weather forecasts at various places. The experimental results show that the Random Forest methodology provides the highest classification accuracy than J48 decision tree and the lazy technique coming in second and third, respectively. The classification results have the potential to enhance flood resilience by facilitating more informed decision-making about preventive and preparedness measures (Saravi, 2019).

A secure approach to flood detection in Saudi Arabia that maximizes global learning accuracy while cutting communication costs by utilizing a classification model based on deep active learning (DeepAL) in federated learning with a Flood Detection Secure System (FDSS). Federated learning based on blockchain that shares optimal solutions for privacy protection with stochastic gradient descent (SGD) and partial homomorphic encryption (PHE). High gradients of shared information in blockchains and limited block storage are addressed with the InterPlanetary File System (IPFS).

FDSS can not only improve security but also stop malevolent people from compromising or changing data. Local flood detection and monitoring models can be trained by FDSS using photos and Internet of Things data. To ensure that the local models can be checked while respecting privacy, ciphertext-level model aggregation and filtering are achieved by encrypting each locally trained model and gradient using a homomorphic encryption technique (Alsumayt et al., 2023).

To lessen the chance of local urban flooding, combined sewer systems in flood-prone areas are equipped with an intelligent autonomous technology known as CENTAURTM. Combined sewer systems are designed not only to collect waste but also to eliminate excess rainfall. When short but intense downpours exceed the area's capacity, urban flooding occurs as a result of a sewage overflow.

CENTAURTM is a wirelessly connected, basic network of intelligent sensors that takes advantage of unused network resources. It accomplishes this by using a movable gate to regulate flow in accordance with a clever algorithm that examines data on the local water level.

This real-time sewer flow management has a lot of benefits. It can prevent sewage overflow, enhance the efficiency of our sewage systems' flow to treatment facilities (thereby reducing energy consumption), and establish the system without the need to build a sizable amount of new infrastructure, all of which reduce the risk of floods. The system's numerous fail-safes guarantee that risk is minimized and resilience is increased, and installing and maintaining sensors is simple and affordable (University of Sheffield, n.d.).

- **AI based solutions to improve preparedness against earthquakes**

Earthquakes have traditionally been among the most unpredictable and destructive natural calamities that humans have ever encountered, taking countless lives and inflicting enormous financial losses (Zia, 2023).

Nearly 750,000 deaths—more than half of all deaths connected to natural disasters—were caused by earthquakes between 1998 and 2017, as per the survey of the World Health Organization. During the emergency stages of these disasters, almost 125 million individuals were impacted by the extensive destruction, including those who were injured, homeless, displaced, or evacuated. The financial cost is similarly astounding: according to a survey, between 2000 and 2019, earthquakes cost the world economy an average of $45 billion yearly.

Although we cannot stop natural earthquakes, we can lessen their effects greatly by being ready for them. An essential component of this readiness is to our capacity to forecast the exact moment, location, and magnitude of an earthquake. Unfortunately, because earthquakes are sudden and unpredictable geological processes, seismologists have been unable to achieve this crucial goal of earthquake prediction for many years (Zia, 2023).

Recently, artificial intelligence has offered a glimpse of hope for accomplishing this unachievable objective. The breakthrough came when a group of researchers from The University of Texas at Austin created an artificial intelligence system that was able to predict earthquakes with an astounding 70% accuracy rate up to a week in advance. During a seven-month experimental period in China, this AI system predicted 14 earthquakes with exceptional accuracy, closely matching their magnitudes and locations. It is important to note that throughout the study, the system did miss one earthquake and sound eight false warnings. Still, it beat more than 600 other rival systems and won first place in a global competition that took place in China. The Bulletin of the Seismological Society of America has published the trial's remarkable results. Professor Sergey Fomel of UT's Bureau of Economic Geology called earthquake prediction the "holy grail" and noted that this accomplishment was a major step toward resolving an issue that was previously thought to be unsolvable (Zia, 2023).

Leading the Texas Seismological Network Program (TexNet) at the bureau is senior research scientist Alexandros Savvaidis, who stresses the importance of reaching even a 70 percent accuracy rate. This degree of precision, in his opinion, has the potential to drastically lower financial and human casualties as well as dramatically increase earthquake readiness worldwide. Researchers think this AI system can significantly improve earthquake prediction in areas like California, Italy, Japan, Greece, Turkey, and Texas that have well-established seismic monitoring networks, even though it may not be instantly applicable everywhere. The next stage of the project will involve testing the system in Texas, a state with a high frequency of small to moderate earthquakes. The bureau's TexNet, which has over six years of continuous recordings and 300 seismic stations, is a perfect place to verify the efficacy of this approach (Zia, 2023).

- **AI Based Solutions for Landslide detection**

In hilly and mountainous areas, landslides are common. They cause large losses in terms of both life and property, and they severely affect a region's socioeconomic standing (Gariano & Guzzetti, 2016). When shear pressure in the inclination is greater than shear quality, landslides happen (Huang et al., 2012). It significantly affects the change of the slope, especially with regard to height, steepness, and slope shape (Tao et al., 2020). All continents have landslides, which are a major cause of changing landscapes. In many places, they also represent a serious threat to the local population (Shanmugam & Wang, 2015). Both man-made and natural causes frequently have an impact on landslides (Davies & McColl, 2022).

In addition to aiding in the growth of the economy and society, the recent expansion in human engineering activities has also increased the risk of landslides becoming more valuable socio-economically and has led to climate instability (Gutiérrez et al., 2014; Sidle et al., 2017). To prevent landslides and the resulting damage, early spatial prediction of landslides is therefore desirable (Guzzetti et al., 2020). Between 2004 and 2016, 4862 landslides were reported globally, with 55,997 fatalities (Lv et al., 2022). To mitigate slope instability and lower the probability of landslides, careful design is necessary (Choi & Cheung, 2013).

Using five different models—the Bayesian Network (HBNRS), the XGBoost (HXGBRS), the Random Forest (HRFRS), and the Backpropagation Neural Network (HBPNNRS)—this approach took into account the Rough Set theory. Fifteen conditioning factors were used to prepare the database for the model building process. A 75%:25% ratio was used to randomly separate the 373 landslide and 181 non-landslide locations in the database into training and testing locations.

The selection operator technique, the least absolute shrinkage, and the multi-collinearity test were used to evaluate the applicability and predictability of these conditioning factors. The performance of the individual and hybrid models was assessed and contrasted using F-measures, accuracy, sensitivity, specificity, and precision. Another tool employed was the receiver operating characteristics curve's area under the curve (AUC). When compared to other models (HBPNNRS, HBNRS, HBRS, and HRFRS), the findings show that the developed hybrid model HXGBRS (AUC = 0.937, Precision = 0.946, F1-score = 0.926, and Accuracy = 89.92%) is the best accurate model for forecasting landslides. Most notably, each model's capacity for prediction is enhanced when the rough set approach is applied to the fusion (Kainthura & Sharma, 2022).

Different approaches have been developed by researchers to identify areas that are most susceptible to landslides. These approaches, however, are unable to forecast "when" landslides would occur. In fact, the Internet of Things (IoT), Artificial Intelligence, and Wireless Sensor Networks (WSN) have the ability to track characteristics that cause rapid landslides in real time. In this work, we propose real-time landslide monitoring to promptly notify the populace through a warning system when a risky situation arises. This research is innovative in that it uses Docker and Kubernetes to couple a multi-agent system running on an edge AI-IoT architecture with a wireless sensor network (Elmoulat, 2020).

It is essential to minimize and control geological risks along the Sichuan-Tibet Transportation Corridor (STTC) by conducting a thorough mapping and landslide inventory due to the increased threat of landslides connected with the Sichuan-Tibet Transportation Project. The main focus of newly developed landslide detection algorithms was new landslides with dense vegetation. Moreover, automatic landslide detection using optical images is still a difficult task. This research presents two approaches for identifying and classifying new and old landslides, respectively: mask region-based convolutional neural networks (Mask R-CNN) and transfer learning Mask R-CNN (TL-Mask R-CNN). As an evaluation benchmark, an optical remote sensing dataset for landslide recognition along the Sichuan-Tibet Transportation Corridor (LRSTTC) is built.

Our test results show that the proposed method can potentially obtain 79.80% F1-score and 78.47% recall rate for new landslide identification. Our experimental results show that applying transfer learning to detect earlier landslides can further improve evaluation indices by approximately 10%. Furthermore, ice avalanches have been identified using TL-Mask R-CNN based on landslide characteristics. With the use of the created LRSTTC dataset, it appears that our suggested approaches may successfully detect and segment landslides along the STTC, which is crucial for researching and mitigating landslide hazards in mountainous regions (Jiang et al., 2022).

The National Energy Technology Laboratory's multidisciplinary research team has developed a novel methodology to enhance the understanding and analytical proficiency of undersea landslide susceptibility studies. In order to address the need for submarine landslide assessment, this workflow combines two innovative methods: a) a submarine landslide susceptibility model that uses a Gradient-Boosted Decision Tree (GBDT) and b) a deep neural network model called You Only Look Once (YOLO) for detecting submarine landslides in bathymetric imagery. This workflow, which is intended to function in regions with limited historical documentation of landslides, allows for the construction of a spatial dataset of landslide observations with the help of landslide detection predictions. Observation data and recognized triggers are then used to train the supervised landslide susceptibility models.

Both models have potential applications in other offshore regions and have been tested and validated for usage in the offshore Gulf of Mexico. The Ocean & Geohazard Analysis (OGA) tool, a statistical, probabilistic, AI/ML-informed software tool for metocean and seafloor hazard detection and risk assessment in support of safe offshore energy activities, incorporates this study. Workflows for these methods will be demonstrated, together with knowledge obtained from applying them to risk assessment and undersea landslide identification (Mark-Moser, 2022).

AI and Machine Learning Algorithm-Based Solutions for Complications in Natural Disaster

A few machine learning techniques have been put into practice and evaluated in an effort to determine which prediction model is the best. The models obtained outperform the ones found in the literature. The Metropolitan City of Florence and data spanning from 2013 to 2019 were used in the validation process. The most effective method was the XGBoost-based one, which also demonstrated the highest level of dependability and resistance to false alarms. Lastly, used explainable AI techniques both locally and globally to gain a thorough grasp of the relationships and importance of the variables and outputs of the prediction model. We were able to determine which feature worked best for short-term forecasts and how they affected local scenarios as well as the global prediction model through investigation. The infrastructure of Snap4City.org has solutions in place (Collini, 2022).

An artificial intelligence system was developed that can precisely predict slide movements using wireless sensor data. By implementing a wireless sensor network for landslide prediction, it is possible to provide real-time and continuous monitoring of various significant landslide characteristics, such as precipitation, vertical and horizontal mass tilt of rock, and displacement of rock and soil water in structures. Three cutting-edge artificial intelligence landslide monitoring technologies—LR, SVM, and SGDA—were assessed and examined in this study. These techniques' effectiveness was assessed. A 93.78 percent accuracy rating was obtained using LR models (Pravin, 2023).

- **AI Based Solutions for Wildfires**

AI-enabled cameras are being used by entrepreneurs and firefighters to search the horizon for smoke. In order to detect fires from orbit, a German business is constructing a constellation of satellites. Additionally, Microsoft is predicting where the next fire would start by utilizing AI algorithms.

Startup in San Francisco, Pano AI installs cameras on cell towers to detect smoke and notify clients, such as fire agencies, power companies, and ski resorts. AI in the form of computer vision machine learning is used by the cameras. The photos are mixed with other data sources, such posts on social media, and feeds from government weather satellites that search for hotspots. The standard approach of wildfire detection relies heavily on bystander 911 calls, which need to be verified by staff before personnel and water-dropping aircraft can be dispatched. This is one of the main problems with this approach. Thanks to technology, this is averted. The Microsoft team led by Ferres has been using AI models to forecast the potential locations of fire outbreaks. The model has been loaded with climate and geospatial data, as well as maps of previously burned areas. Artificial intelligence is utilized by the German startup OroraTech to analyze satellite photos.

Utilizing the latest developments in camera, satellite, and artificial intelligence technology, OroraTech has put two tiny satellites, each the size of a shoebox, into low orbit, around 550 kilometers above the surface of the Earth. The Munich-based business hopes to launch eight more into space the following year and eventually one hundred (AP, 2023).

Satellites that track vegetation distribution and disturbance include AVHRR, MODIS, VHRS, and LANDSAT. It is still difficult to anticipate wildfires from these photos, though. Utilizing machine learning (ML) and artificial intelligenc offers a dependable method for managing and forecasting wildfires. With the data at its disposal, AI can learn and forecast with accuracy. Artificial intelligence coupled with imaging satellites may examine factors such as smoke appearance, fire incidence, and vegetation disturbance to forecast the frequency and pattern of wildfires. These factors can then be connected with other physical characteristics of the forest, including soil deposits, vegetation type, climate, and mapping of fire sensitivity. Prediction accuracy rises as a result of AI systems learning during the prediction process.

AI systems have produced surprisingly accurate experimental wildfire predictions with shorter detection times. By detecting smoke, AI-assisted software-defined cameras (SDCs) can forecast forest fires on a local scale. In order to ensure early detection and effective management of forest fires, artificial intelligence technologies also make it simple for a single user to operate numerous patrol cars equipped with video cameras and fire extinguishers. The lack of useful modeling methods that can adjust to various worldwide conditions is the primary barrier to AI-mediated wildfire management. Furthermore, there is a deficiency in advanced information, superior forest parameters, and improved AI algorithms that correlate existing data. Machines with artificial intelligence capabilities can undoubtedly prevent forest fires from starting and spreading by using high-resolution data and complex algorithms.

AI developments could be used to combat wildfires and manage forests:

1. The goal of creating self-driving cars has pushed computer vision research and development forward. Artificial Intelligence, with applications in wildfire prediction science
2. Advancements in natural language generation (NLG) and processing (NLP) have enhanced computers' ability to forecast

Innovations in data-collection techniques aid in managing wildfire risk and battling fires:

1. Artificial intelligence-enabled sensors can gather sound data or function as forest smoke detectors, notifying authorities within the first hour of a wildfire originating.
2. In order to help firefighters plan their reaction, unmanned aerial vehicles (UAVs) can be flown over flames to provide real-time photos.

In the US, two programs are being developed to offer information on near-live fires:

1. Google creates maps almost instantly using geostationary satellites.
2. Utilizing low-orbit satellites and software created by the Space Science and Engineering Center (SSEC) of the University of Wisconsin-Madison, NASA's Fire Information for Resource Management (FIRMS) provides real-time fire data with an only 60-second delay between Earth observation and wildfire detection (WEF, 2023).

Employed ANNs and infrared image processing (along with visual imaging, meteorological, and geographic data utilized in a fuzzy logic decision function) in Arrue et al. (2000) to detect actual wildfires. Furthermore, Liu et al. (2015) built a fire detection system using artificial neural networks (ANNs) on wireless sensor networks. To identify and raise warnings, multicriteria detection was used on a number of properties (such as flame, heat, light, and radiation).

CNNs, or deep learning, have recently been used to the problem of fire detection. CNNs are widely employed in object recognition applications because of their ability to extract features and patterns from spatial imagery. Images of fire and/or smoke taken from Earth were used in a number of these applications to train the models (Zhang et al., 2016).

Utilized CNN in conjunction with optical flow in Yuan et al. (2018) to incorporate time-dependent data. Another method by Cao et al. (2019) employed a long short-term memory (LSTM) neural network with convolutional layers to detect smoke from a series of images (i.e., video feed). They discovered that the LSTM approach outperformed a single image-based DL algorithm by 4.4%, achieving 97.8% accuracy.

Alexandrov et al. (2019) discovered in Alexandrov et al. (2019) that YOLO outperformed a region-based CNN technique in terms of speed and accuracy.

- **AI Based Solutions for Storms and Tornadoes**

To anticipate hail, scientists used two methods: random forest, which classifies data, and isotonic regression, which looks for relationships between a predicted and observed value. based on observational data and machine learning models that were trained using conventional model output and then grouped to assess associations. Compared to conventional techniques, the projections that were produced were less biased and more dependable (Burke, 2020).

In order to outperform standard models in predicting severe hail and wind, scientists employed a random forest-based machine learning model that was trained on data from storm reports and traditional models. But when it came to tornadoes, the old approach outperformed the machine learning model (Loken et al., 2020).

A fast-moving column of air that strikes the ground, a cumulonimbus cloud, or, in rare cases, the base of a cumulus cloud, is what defines a tornado. It is frequently called a cyclone, whirlwind, or twister (Twister, n.d.).

In Theodore (2007), the tornado prediction problem is tackled through the use of support vector machines (SVMs) and active learning. This method uses the near-storm environment (NSE) characteristics and the radar-derived Mesocyclone Detection Algorithm (MDA) to forecast which storm-scale circulations will produce tornadoes. In order to classify and add instances or data points that are significant or have an impact on this model to the training set, the primary objective of active learning is to find them. We contrast this approach with support vector machines' (SVMs) passive learning, in which the subsequent examples to be added to the training set are chosen at random. According to the initial findings, a considerable decrease in training data is still necessary to attain good performance through active learning.

In Adrianto et al. (2009) and Lakshmanan et al. (2007), maps of 0–30-min tornado potential were produced by departing from the storm-centric method and utilizing fuzzy logic, support vector machines, and neural networks. better CSI scores on their test dataset, which ranged from 0.33 to 0.57, were discovered in Adrianto et al. (2009). Although these preliminary results appeared encouraging, they were generated with relatively small datasets, and the test datasets were almost evenly split between tornadoes and nontornadoes. This is concerning because the real-world ratio of tornadoes to nontornadoes is most likely less than 1 to 100. Therefore, it's possible that the measurements listed above overstate actual performance.

In order to overcome the problem of class imbalance, Trafalis et al. (2014) discovered that better accuracy in tornado prediction using support vector machines might be achieved by varying the probability at which events are classified as tornadic or nontornadic. In Lagerquist et al. (2020), storm-centered radar readings were utilized to identify tornadic storms using CNNs.

Because weather simulation is so complex, it might take a long time to predict intense storms and dangerous weather conditions with existing models. Tornadic weather patterns might be classified considerably more quickly with machine learning, enabling the public to get notifications in real time. One challenge in applying machine learning for tornado prediction is the disparity between tornadic and non-tornadic data. In this study, authors developed a new data synthesization system to augment tornado storm data using a deep convolutional generative adversarial network (DCGAN) and qualitatively compare its output with natural data in order to obtain more balanced data (Barajas et al., 2019).

- **AI based solutions for cyclones**

Forecasting tropical cyclones (TCs) is still facing a bottleneck because of its complex dynamical mechanisms and large number of influence factors (Zhen, 2022). In order to address the challenges related to temperature correction (TC) forecasting, surface observation, radar, and satellite data have been used to great effect in machine learning research. Data processing and image identification both greatly benefit from machine learning (ML) techniques.

The authors of Chen (2020) and Zhang et al. (2019) used nonlinear classifiers (decision tree (DT), K-nearest neighbor (KNN), MLP, qualitative data analysis (QDA), SVM, or nonlinear ensemble classifiers (AdaBoost and RF) in an effort to ascertain whether mesoscale convective systems (MCS) evolved into tropical cyclones at different lead times. AdaBoost outperformed traditional linear statistical models with a forecast accuracy of 97.2% (F1-score) for tropical cyclone genesis over a 6-hour prediction period using the environmental indicators linked to MCSs/TCs. When the lead time was increased to 12, 24, or even 48 hours, robustness was also ensured.

In Kim et al. (2019), the prediction skills of DT, RF, and SVM were also compared. As a result, SVM surpassed the other algorithms in terms of prediction performance to become the most successful machine learning method. Its hit rates varied between 94% and 96%, significantly outperforming LDA's performance of 77%.

In order to identify tropical cyclones (TCs) and their precursors, Matsuoka et al. (2018) use a deep learning technique. 2D deep convolutional neural networks (CNNs) are trained using twenty years' worth of simulated outgoing longwave radiation (OLR), which is computed using a cloud-resolving global atmospheric simulation. For binary classification, 50,000 TCs and their antecedents as well as 500,000 non-TC data points are used to train the CNNs. To find precursors and TCs, ensemble CNN classifiers are used on global OLR data that has been collected over a 10-year period. Investigations are conducted into the CNNs' performance for different lead times, seasons, and basins. In the western North Pacific, the CNN model can distinguish between TCs and their precursors between July and November.

The quick intensification of Atlantic and eastern Pacific TCs was predicted in Griffin et al. (2022) using satellite imagery and environmental factors based on CNNs; their research shows that the 2D features in the satellite imagery produce superior 24-hour indicators of rapid intensification. In Chen et al. (2023), the distribution of TC intensity over the following 24 hours was predicted using the ensemble forecast concept, which was based on Griffin et al. (2022) study. Twenty deep-learning models with various topologies were chosen as ensemble members.

- **AI based solutions for Tsunami**

Current warning systems depend on seismic data and DART buoys (UNESCO, n.d.). When a tsunami is approaching, DART-buoys can detect it precisely, but they have limited warning time, are expensive, and require a lot of maintenance. While seismometers are quick to identify earthquakes, they are not always accurate in measuring tsunamis, which can result in false positives or even false negatives. Pre-calculated probabilistic models have a high chance of false negatives, while numerical models are mostly employed for post-processing and take a significant amount of processing time.

Our method, which analyzes sound waves captured by underwater hydrophones, enhances existing technologies. These signals, which carry source information, travel far quicker than tsunamis. We have created two separate models: an analytical model and an AI model. In a matter of milliseconds, the AI model analyzes streamed sound signals to identify the type and magnitude of earthquakes and forecast the creation of tsunamis. In real-time, the Analytical model assesses the data to determine the global tsunami size by inversely evaluating the attributes of the water layer. The total dependability of the warning system is improved and assessment process confidence is increased when the two models are combined with conventional methods.

In AIP (2023), scientists create an early warning system that uses AI and acoustic technology to quickly categorize earthquakes and assess the risk of a tsunami. They suggest measuring the acoustic radiation created by the earthquake using underwater microphones known as hydrophones. This radiation travels much quicker than tsunami waves and contains information about the tectonic event. The earthquake's source is triangulated using the computational model, and its size and kind of slip are classified by AI algorithms. Subsequently, it computes crucial parameters such as the tsunami's effective length and width, uplift velocity, and duration.

- **AI based solutions for volcanic eruptions**

In the past, ground observatories have been used by volcanologists to forecast eruptions. Recent advancements may make it feasible to forecast satellite eruptions with confidence. The total cost of maintenance for satellites is substantially lower. Due to noisy data, satellite information was historically unreliable; now, deep learning AI is becoming more and more adept at completing the gaps in the data to create meaningful information. Currently, a team of Penn State University researchers is aiming to enhance the models to enable precise global eruption predictions, with funding from NASA (Borgen Project, 2023).

In Valade et al. (2019), the global monitoring platform MOUNTS (Monitoring Unrest from Space) was introduced. Artificial intelligence is used to support multisensor satellite-based images, ground-based seismic data, and monitoring duties (e.g., Sentinel-1 Synthetic Aperture Radar SAR, Sentinel-2 Short-Wave InfraRed SWIR, Sentinel-5P TROPOMI, and worldwide earthquake catalogues from GEOFON and USGS). It assists the scientific and operational communities in assessing the danger of volcanic eruptions by providing access to surface deformation, heat anomalies, SO_2 gas emissions, and local seismicity at many volcanoes across the world in almost real time.

The outcomes are presented in a way that facilitates a thorough comprehension of the temporal evolution of volcanic activity and eruptive products. This is achieved by providing geocoded images and time series of pertinent parameters on an accessible website. We also show how important a role AI can have in these kinds of monitoring setups. Here, we develop and train a Convolutional Neural Network (CNN) on artificially generated interferograms in order to detect substantial deformation in the real interferograms that MOUNTS produces, such as that associated with dyke intrusions.

In Di Stasio (2022), we suggest a machine learning (ML)-based alert system that enables the early identification of volcanic eruptions. In order to perform the specific detection and notify the relevant authorities and Civil safety, it is possible to combine the usage of Artificial Intelligence based algorithms with the early detection goal. This will ensure prompt intervention for the safety of individuals. The primary objective of this study is, in fact, to design and implement a system that will be installed on satellites in order to generate timely alerts that will be helpful to decision makers.

First, Sentinel-5P's SO_2 data is used to train the suggested machine learning model. The last goal is to design an on-board system that resembles Phi-Sat 1 and has its own systems and sensor. Our feasibility study has demonstrated that an 80% and 70% accuracy rate, respectively, can be achieved in the classification and identification of volcanic eruptions in advance.

COMPARISON ON TECHNOLOGIES

The comparison on type of natural disaster, AI algorithm, Data set type/Name of the dataset is shown in Table 1 (Abid et al., 2021).

Table 1. Comparison of existing methods

Studies	Type of natural disaster	AI algorithm used	Data set type/Name of the dataset
(Arrue et al., 2000)	To detect wildfires	ANN	Metrological and geological data (image)
(Zhang et al., 2016)	For wildfire detection	CNN	Images of fire and smoke taken from earth
(Cao et al., 2019)	To detect smoke (wildfire)	Long short term memory -LSTM	Series of images from Video
(Theodore, 2007)	To predict tornado	SVM	Based on the Near-Storm Environment (NSE) characteristics and the Mesocyclone Detection Algorithm (MDA) obtained from radar data.
(Lagerquist et al., 2020)	To predict tornado	CNN	The Gridded NEXRAD WSR-88D Radar dataset (GridRad) and the Multiyear Reanalysis of Remotely Sensed Storms (MYRORSS) provided the radar images used.
(Matsuoka et al., 2018)	To detect tropical cyclones	DCNN	2D cloud data (Image)
(Griffin et al., 2022)		CNN	2D features from satellite images
(Doshi et al., 2018)	Using disaster assessment to plan relief efforts	CNN and semantic segmentation models of satellite images	Satellite images
(Amit & Aoki, 2017)	Reduction of flood and landslide disaster risk	CNN	satellite-derived spatial pictures
(Qin et al., 2020)	Mapping and forecasting flood inundations	CNN	Incident Reporting Information System (IRIS) database of the National Response Center (NRC) and Texas Commission on Environmental Quality (TCEQ)
(Ahmad et al., 2017)	Using social media to reduce the risk of disasters and satellite imagery to predict floods	SVM,CNN, GVN, RFS networks	Applications for social media and satellite photos
(Chen et al., 2017)	Mapping the exposure to landslide disasters	RFEs and NBT classifiers	Data from field surveys and satellite spatial images
(Vetrivel et al., 2018)	Identification of earthquake prediction	CNN networks	3D point cloud
(Syifa et al., 2019)	Mapping the damage of earthquake after its occurrence	ANN and support vector machines	Satellite images
(Duarte et al., 2020)	Building damage classification (seismic)	CNN networks	Satellite and UAV images
(Nex et al., 2019)	Damage mapping in almost real time	CNN networks	UAV images

CONCLUSION

This chapter reviews the present use of ML techniques for giving solutions to natural disasters by assessing the challenges associated with natural disaster prediction and traditional approaches. Furthermore, a thorough summary of the several predictors and sophisticated algorithm models is provided. Additionally, a synopsis of the most common natural disasters is provided, along with that an overview of machine learning techniques and artificial intelligence solutions for disasters are discussed. In general, future advances in machine learning techniques that offer greater interpretation, intervention, and precision will be required to advance the field of natural catastrophe prediction.

REFERENCES

Abid, S. K., Sulaiman, N., Chan, S. W., Nazir, U., Abid, M., Han, H., Ariza-Montes, A., & Vega-Muñoz, A. (2021). Toward an integrated disaster management approach: How artificial intelligence can boost disaster management. *Sustainability (Basel)*, *13*(22), 12560. doi:10.3390/su132212560

Adrianto, I., Trafalis, T. B., & Lakshmanan, V. (2009). Support vector machines for spatiotemporal tornado prediction. *International Journal of General Systems*, *38*(7), 759–776. doi:10.1080/03081070601068629

Ahmad, K., Konstantin, P., Riegler, M., Conci, N., & Holversen, P. (2017). CNN and GAN based satellite and social media data fusion fordisaster detection. *CEUR Workshop Proceedings*, *1984*, 13–15.

AIP. (2023). *Creating tsunami early warning systems using AI*. American Instutute of Physics. https://www.sciencedaily.com/releases/2023/04/230425111152.htm

Alexandrov, D., Pertseva, E., Berman, I., Pantiukhin, I., & Kapitonov, A. (2019). Analysis of machine learning methods for wildfire security monitoring with an unmanned aerial vehicles. In Conference of Open Innovation Association (FRUCT), 8–12 April 2019. IEEE Computer Society. doi:10.23919/FRUCT.2019.8711917

Alruqi, A. (2023). *The Use of AI for Disasters*. Scientific Research. https://www.scirp.org/journal/paperinformation.aspx?paperid=125106

Alsumayt, A., El-Haggar, N., Amouri, L., Alfawaer, Z. M., & Aljameel, S. S. (2023). Smart Flood Detection with AI and Blockchain Integration in Saudi Arabia Using Drones. *Sensors (Basel)*, *23*(11), 5148. doi:10.3390/s23115148 PMID:37299876

Amit, S. N. K. B., & Aoki, Y. (2017). Disaster detection from aerial imagery with convolutional neural network. In *Proceedings of the 2017International Electronics Symposium on Knowledge Creation and Intelligent Computing (IES-KCIC)*, Surabaya, Indonesia. 10.1109/KCIC.2017.8228593

AP. (2023). *New AI solutions developed to combat wildfires*. VOA. https://www.voanews.com/a/new-artificial-intelligence-solutions-developed-to-combat-wildfires/7282474.html

Arora, S., Kumar, S., & Kumar, S. Artificial Intelligence in Disaster Management: A Survey, *International Conference on Data Science and Applications* 10.1007/978-981-19-6634-7_56

Arrue, B. C., Ollero, A., & De Dios, J. M. (2000). An intelligent system for false alarm reduction in infrared forest-fire detection. *IEEE Intelligent Systems & their Applications, 15*(3), 64–73. doi:10.1109/5254.846287

Barajas, C. A., Gobbert, M. K., & Wang, J. (2019). Performance Benchmarking of Data Augmentation and Deep Learning for Tornado Prediction. 2019 IEEE International Conference on Big Data. IEEE.

Borgen Project. (2023). *Preventing Poverty*. The Borgen Project. https://borgenproject.org/solutions-to-volcanic-eruptions/

Burke, A. (2020). Calibration of Machine Learning-Based Probabilistic Hail Predictions for Operational Forecasting. *Weather and Forecasting, 35*(1), 149-168. . doi:10.1175/WAF-D-19-0105.1

Cao, Y., Yang, F., Tang, Q., & Lu, X. (2019). An attention enhanced bidirectional LSTM for early forest fire smoke recognition. *IEEE Access : Practical Innovations, Open Solutions, 7*, 154732–154742. doi:10.1109/ACCESS.2019.2946712

Chen, R. (2020). *Machine Learning in Tropical Cyclone Forecast Modeling: A Review*. MDPI.

Chen, Kuo, Y.-T., & Huang, T.-S. (2023). A deep learning ensemble approach for predicting tropical cyclone rapid intensification. *Atmospheric Science Letters, 24*(5), e1151. doi:10.1002/asl.1151

Chen, W., Shirzadi, A., Shahabi, H., Ahmad, B. B., Zhang, S., Hong, H., & Zhang, N. (2017). A novel hybrid artificial intelligence approachbased on the rotation forest ensemble and naïve Bayes tree classifiers for a landslide susceptibility assessment in Langao County,China. [CrossRef]. *Geomatics, Natural Hazards & Risk, 8*(2), 1955–1977. doi:10.1080/19475705.2017.1401560

Choi, K. Y., & Cheung, R. W. M. (2013). Landslide disaster prevention and mitigation through works in Hong Kong. *Journal of Rock Mechanics and Geotechnical Engineering, 5*(5), 354–365. doi:10.1016/j.jrmge.2013.07.007

Collini, E. (2022). Predicting and Understanding Landslide Events With Explainable AI. *IEEE Access (Volume 10)*. IEEE.

Di Stasio, P. (2022). Early Detection of Volcanic Eruption through Artificial Intelligence on board. *IEEE International Conference on Metrology for Extended Reality, Artificial Intelligence and Neural Engineering (MetroXRAINE)*. IEEE. 10.1109/MetroXRAINE54828.2022.9967616

DoshiJ.BasuS.PangG. (2018). From Satellite Imagery to Disaster Insights. no. Nips. arXiv. http://arxiv.org/abs/1812.07033

Duarte, DNex, FKerle, NVosselman, G. (2020). Satellite Image Classification of Building Damages Using Airborne. *ISPRS Annals of the Photogrammetry, Remote Sensing and Spatial Information Sciences, 4*, 4–7.

Elmoulat, M. (2020). Edge Computing and Artificial Intelligence for Landslides Monitoring. *Procedia Computer Science, 177*, 480–487.

Gariano, S. L., & Guzzetti, F. (2016). Landslides in a changing climate. *Earth-Science Reviews, 162*, 227–252. doi:10.1016/j.earscirev.2016.08.011

Goyal, H. R., Ghanshala, K. K., & Sharma, S. (2021). Post flood management system based on smart IoT devices using AI approach. *Materials Today: Proceedings*, *46*(Part 20), 10411–10417. doi:10.1016/j.matpr.2020.12.947

Griffin, Wimmers, A., & Velden, C. S. (2022). 2022, S.M. Griffin, A. Wimmers, C.S. Velden, Predicting rapid intensification in North Atlantic and eastern North Pacific tropical cyclones using a convolutional neural network. *Weather and Forecasting*, *37*(8), 1333–1355. doi:10.1175/WAF-D-21-0194.1

Gutiérrez, F., Parise, M., De Waele, J., & Jourde, H. (2014). A review on natural and human-induced geohazards and impacts in karst. *Earth-Science Reviews*, *138*, 61–88. doi:10.1016/j.earscirev.2014.08.002

Guzzetti, F., Gariano, S. L., Peruccacci, S., Brunetti, M. T., Marchesini, I., Rossi, M., & Melillo, M. (2020). Geographical landslide early warning systems. *Earth-Science Reviews*, *200*, 102973. doi:10.1016/j.earscirev.2019.102973

Huang, A.-B., Lee, J.-T., Ho, Y.-T., Chiu, Y.-F., & Cheng, S.-Y. (2012). Stability monitoring of rainfall-induced deep landslides through pore pressure profile measurements. *Soil and Foundation*, *52*(4), 737–747. doi:10.1016/j.sandf.2012.07.013

Jiang, W., Xi, J., Li, Z., Zang, M., Chen, B., Zhang, C., Liu, Z., Gao, S., & Zhu, W. (2022). Deep Learning for Landslide Detection and Segmentation in High-Resolution Optical Images along the Sichuan-Tibet Transportation Corridor. *Remote Sensing (Basel)*, *14*(21), 5490. doi:10.3390/rs14215490

Kainthura, P., & Sharma, N. (2022). Hybrid machine learning approach for landslide prediction, Uttarakhand, India. *Scientific Reports*, *12*(1), 20101. doi:10.1038/s41598-022-22814-9 PMID:36418362

Kim, M., Park, M. S., Im, J., Park, S., & Lee, M.-I. (2019). Im, J.; Park, S.; Lee, M.I. Machine Learning Approaches for Detecting Tropical Cyclone Formation Using Satellite Data. *Remote Sensing (Basel)*, *11*(10), 1195. doi:10.3390/rs11101195

Lagerquist, R., McGovern, A., Homeyer, C. R., Gagne, D. J. II, & Smith, T. (2020). Deep learning on three-dimensional multiscale data for next-hour tornado prediction. *Monthly Weather Review*, *148*(7), 2837–2861. doi:10.1175/MWR-D-19-0372.1

Lakshmanan, V., Ortega, K. L., & Smith, T. M. (2007). Creating spatio-temporal tornado probability forecasts using fuzzy logic and motion variability. *Fifth Conf. on Artificial Intelligence Applications to Environmental Science*. San Antonio, TX, Amer. Meteor. Soc. https://ams.confex.com/ams/87ANNUAL/techprogram/paper_119456.htm

Liu, Y., Yang, Y., Liu, C., & Gu, Y. (2015). Forest fire detection using artificial neural network algorithm implemented in wireless sensor networks. *ZTE Communications*, *13*, 12–16.

Loken, E. D., Clark, A. J., & Karstens, C. D. (2020). Generating Probabilistic Next-Day Severe Weather Forecasts from Convection-Allowing Ensembles Using Random Forests. *Weather and Forecasting*, *35*(4), 1605–1631. doi:10.1175/WAF-D-19-0258.1

Lv, L., Chen, T., Dou, J., & Plaza, A. (2022). A hybrid ensemble-based deep-learning framework for landslide susceptibility mapping. *International Journal of Applied Earth Observation and Geoinformation*, *108*, 102713. doi:10.1016/j.jag.2022.102713

Mark-Moser, M. (2022). *Artificial Intelligence and Machine Learning Techniques for Submarine Landslide Detection and Susceptibility Mapping*. AGU Fall Meeting, Chicago, IL.

Matsuoka, D., Nakano, M., Sugiyama, D., & Uchida, S. (2018). Deep learning approach for detecting tropical cyclones and their precursors in the simulation by a cloud-resolving global nonhydrostatic atmospheric model. *Progress in Earth and Planetary Science, 5*(1), 80. doi:10.1186/s40645-018-0245-y

McColl, S. T. (2022). Landslide causes and triggers. In T. Davies, (Ed.), *Landslide Hazards, Risks, and Disasters* (2nd ed., pp. 13–41). Elsevier. doi:10.1016/B978-0-12-818464-6.00011-1

Nex, F., Duarte, D., Steenbeek, A., & Kerle, N. (2019). Towards Real-Time Building Damage Mapping with Low-Cost UAV Solutions. *Remote Sensing (Basel), 11*(3), 287. doi:10.3390/rs11030287

Pravin, R. (2023). Expedite Quantification of Landslides Using Wireless Sensors and Artificial Intelligence for Data Controlling Practices. Computational Intelligence and Neuroscience.

Qin, R., Khakzad, N., & Zhu, J. (2020). An overview of the impact of Hurricane Harvey on chemical and process facilities in Texas. *International Journal of Disaster Risk Reduction, 45*, 101453. doi:10.1016/j.ijdrr.2019.101453

Sahota, N. (2023). AI in Disaster management. *Neil Sahora.* https://www.neilsahota.com/ai-in-disaster-management-ais-role-in-disaster-risk-reduction/

Saravi, S. (2019). *Use of Artificial Intelligence to Improve Resilience and Preparedness Against Adverse Flood Events, Special Issue Flood Risk and Resilience*. MDPI.

Shanmugam, G., & Wang, Y. (2015). The landslide problem. *Journal of Palaeogeography, 4*(2), 109–166. doi:10.3724/SP.J.1261.2015.00071

Sidle, R. C., Gallina, J., & Gomi, T. (2017). The continuum of chronic to episodic natural hazards: Implications and strategies for community and landscape planning. *Landscape and Urban Planning, 167*, 189–197. doi:10.1016/j.landurbplan.2017.05.017

Syifa, M., Kadavi, P. R., & Lee, C.-W. (2019). An Artificial Intelligence Application for Post-Earthquake Damage Mapping in Palu, CentralSulawesi, Indonesia. *Sensors (Basel), 19*(3), 542. doi:10.3390/s19030542 PMID:30696050

Tao, Z., Shu, Y., Yang, X., Peng, Y., Chen, Q., & Zhang, H. (2020). Physical model test study on shear strength characteristics of slope sliding surface in Nanfen open-pit mine. *International Journal of Mining Science and Technology, 30*(3), 421–429. doi:10.1016/j.ijmst.2020.05.006

Theodore, B. (2007). Active Learning with Support Vector Machines for Tornado Prediction, Home Computational Science – ICCS 2007. *7th International Conference*, Beijing China.

Trafalis, T. B., Adrianto, I., Richman, M. B., & Lakshmivarahan, S. (2014). Machine-learning classifiers for imbalanced tornado data. *Computational Management Science, 11*(4), 403–418. doi:10.1007/s10287-013-0174-6

Twister. (n.d.). In Merriam-Webster.com.

UNESCO. (n.d.). *Applying AI Based Models to predict tsunamis.* UNESCO. https://www.unesco.org/en/articles/applying-ai-based-models-predict-tsunamis

University of Sheffield. (n.d.). *Using AI to reduce urban flooding.* University of Sheffield. https://www.sheffield.ac.uk/engineering/about/partnerships/using-artificial-intelligence-reduce-urban-flooding

Valade, S., Ley, A., Massimetti, F., D'Hondt, O., Laiolo, M., Coppola, D., Loibl, D., Hellwich, O., & Walter, T. R. (2019). Towards Global Volcano Monitoring Using Multisensor Sentinel Missions and Artificial Intelligence: The MOUNTS Monitoring System. *Remote Sensing (Basel), 11*(13), 1528. doi:10.3390/rs11131528

Vetrivel, A., Gerke, M., Kerle, N., Nex, F., & Vosselman, G. (2018). Disaster damage detection through synergistic use of deep learningand 3D point cloud features derived from very high resolution oblique aerial images, and multiple-kernel-learning. *ISPRS Journal of Photogrammetry and Remote Sensing, 140*, 45–59. doi:10.1016/j.isprsjprs.2017.03.001

WEF. (2023). *Successful Pilot Shows how AI can Fight Wildfires.* WEF. https://www.weforum.org/press/2023/01/successful-pilot-shows-how-artificial-intelligence-can-fight-wildfires/

Yuan, J., Wang, L., Wu, P., Gao, C., & Sun, L. (2018). Detection of wildfires along transmission lines using deep time and space features. *Pattern Recognition and Image Analysis, 28*(4), 805–812. doi:10.1134/S1054661818040168

Zhang, Q., Xu, J., Xu, L., & Guo, H. (2016). *Deep convolutional neural networks for forest fire detection.* Atlantis Press. doi:10.2991/ifmeita-16.2016.105

Zhang, T., Lin, W., Lin, Y., Zhang, M., Yu, H., Cao, K., & Xue, W. (2019). Prediction of Tropical Cyclone Genesis from Mesoscale Convective Systems Using Machine Learning. *Weather and Forecasting, 34*(4), 1035–1049. doi:10.1175/WAF-D-18-0201.1

Zhen. (2022). A Review on the Application of Machine Learning Methods in Tropical Cyclone Forecasting, Front. Earth Sci. *Atmospheric Science, 10.*

Zia, T. (2023). *AI and earthquake prediction.* Techopedia. https://www.techopedia.com/ai-and-earthquake-prediction

Chapter 15
Predicting Natural Disasters With AI and Machine Learning

Manjula Devi C.
Velammal College of Engineering and Technology, India

Gobinath A.
Velammal College of Engineering and Technology, India

Padma Priya S.
https://orcid.org/0000-0003-0840-642X
PSNA College of Engineering and Technology, India

Reshmika K. S.
Velammal College of Engineering and Technology, India

Sivakarthi G.
Velammal College of Engineering and Technology, India

ABSTRACT

Amidst the continually changing climate and the rise in natural disasters, it is crucial to strengthen resilience against these calamities. This chapter explores the dynamic intersection of machine learning and natural disasters, revealing how advanced technologies reshape disaster management. In the face of escalating challenges posed by earthquakes, floods, and wildfires, machine learning emerges as an innovative solution, offering proactive approaches beyond conventional reactive methods. The narrative unfolds by tracing the evolution of disaster management, highlighting the transformative impact of machine learning on early warning systems. It explores predictive analytics and risk assessment, elucidating how machine learning algorithms leverage historical data and real-time information to deepen our understanding of disaster vulnerabilities. Beyond prediction, the discourse extends to the pivotal role of machine learning in optimizing response and recovery efforts—efficiently allocating resources and fostering recovery planning. A critical dimension of this integration emerges in the analysis of remote sensing and satellite imagery, where machine learning algorithms enable more accurate and timely disaster monitoring. The exploration extends further, unraveling the interconnectedness of various hazards and emphasizing how machine learning facilitates a holistic understanding. The synergy between machine learning and traditional knowledge systems comes to the forefront, recognizing the significance of integrating local wisdom into predictive models. The discourse broadens to encompass

DOI: 10.4018/979-8-3693-3362-4.ch015

policy implications, international collaboration, and ethical considerations embedded in machine learning for disaster management. The integration of machine learning in humanitarian aid efforts and its contribution to environmental sustainability are scrutinized, offering a comprehensive understanding of the multifaceted relationship between machine learning and natural disasters. In the ever-evolving landscape of natural disaster management, the fusion of machine learning and human expertise opens new avenues for innovation. One emerging trend is the integration of real-time social media data into machine learning algorithms. By analyzing user-generated content, sentiment analysis, and geospatial information from platforms like Twitter and Facebook, these algorithms can provide rapid insights into the unfolding dynamics of a disaster. This not only enhances the timeliness of response efforts but also fosters a more community-centric approach, incorporating the voices and experiences of those directly affected. The potential of generative adversarial networks to simulate and predict complex disaster scenarios offers a proactive paradigm shift in disaster management by enabling stakeholders to refine strategies and adapt to evolving challenges through realistic simulations. As the chapter charts the course forward, it concludes by exploring emerging trends and innovations in the symbiotic relationship between machine learning and natural disaster management.

INTRODUCTION

In the face of escalating natural disasters, the fusion of machine learning (ML) and deep learning (DL) emerges as a beacon of innovation, reshaping disaster management. This chapter delves into the dynamic interplay between advanced technologies and the evolving landscape of calamities, exploring how ML and DL offer proactive solutions beyond traditional reactive methods.

Background and Motivation

Natural disasters, from earthquakes to floods and wildfires, present ever-growing challenges that demand innovative solutions. The urgency to fortify resilience against these calamities motivates the exploration of advanced technologies such as ML and DL. This section delves into the evolution of disaster management, highlighting the transformative impact of ML and DL, particularly in the realm of early warning systems (Sunita Pachar Et al, 2023).

The narrative unfolds by tracing the historical context of disaster management, emphasizing the limitations of reactive approaches and the need for a paradigm shift towards proactive, technology-driven strategies. The chapter sheds light on the challenges posed by traditional methods in the face of modern complexities, setting the stage for the role of ML and DL in revolutionizing disaster resilience.

Scope and Objectives

Scope

This chapter aims to provide a comprehensive overview of the role of ML and DL in disaster management. It spans various facets, including predictive analytics, risk assessment, response optimization, and real-world applications.

Objectives

1. Examine the historical evolution of disaster management, highlighting its limitations.
2. Explore how ML and DL technologies have emerged as transformative forces in addressing these limitations.
3. Investigate the specific applications of ML and DL across different phases of disaster management.
4. Analyze the challenges inherent in integrating ML and DL into disaster resilience strategies.
5. Propose future directions and potential innovations in leveraging ML and DL for disaster management.

Significance of ML and DL in Disaster Management

The significance of ML and DL in disaster management is underscored by their multifaceted contributions:

- ML and DL offer proactive solutions in disaster prediction and response, moving beyond reactive approaches.
- They enhance the accuracy and effectiveness of early warning systems, minimizing the impact on vulnerable communities.
- ML and DL technologies optimize resource allocation and recovery planning through predictive analytics and risk assessment.
- The integration of remote sensing and satellite imagery, facilitated by ML and DL, enables real-time disaster monitoring with unprecedented accuracy.
- These technologies address the interconnected nature of various hazards, fostering a holistic understanding crucial for effective disaster management.
- ML and DL models recognize the importance of incorporating local wisdom into predictive algorithms, promoting adaptive learning that evolves with new data(Vinay Chamola Et al, 2020).

Structure of the Paper

This chapter unfolds systematically, commencing with the context and motivation behind integrating ML and DL in disaster management. It then progresses to delineate the scope and objectives, providing a roadmap for readers. The subsequent sections delve into a comprehensive literature review, the methodology employed in selecting and analyzing relevant studies, and specific applications of ML and DL in disaster management. Key findings, future directions, and potential challenges are thoroughly explored, culminating in a robust conclusion that summarizes critical insights and outlines recommendations for future research in this domain.

LITERATURE REVIEW

Overview of ML and DL Technologies

Machine Learning (ML) and Deep Learning (DL) stand as transformative technologies reshaping various domains, including disaster management. ML involves algorithms that enable systems to learn and make predictions or decisions based on data. DL, a subset of ML, utilizes neural networks to simulate human-like decision-making. In the context of disaster management, the amalgamation of these technologies offers innovative solutions beyond traditional reactive approaches.

Supervised Learning

In supervised learning, models are trained on labeled data to make predictions or decisions. Two main types are:

1. **Classification Techniques:**

   - *K-Nearest Neighbors (KNN):* K-Nearest Neighbors (KNN) is a straightforward yet powerful machine learning algorithm primarily used for classification. In disaster management, KNN is applied in assessing risk and vulnerability. The method classifies based on the majority class in the neighborhood of a data point, making it effective for spatial analysis and localized predictions in disaster-prone areas.
   - *Support Vector Machines (SVM):* Support Vector Machine (SVM) is a robust machine learning algorithm used for classification and regression tasks. In the context of disaster management, SVM finds applications in tasks such as damage classification and risk assessment. SVM works by mapping data points into a high-dimensional space and identifying the optimal hyperplane that separates different classes, making it effective in predicting outcomes related to disaster scenarios.
   - *Naive Bayes:* Naive Bayes is a probabilistic algorithm based on Bayes' theorem. It is used in disaster management for tasks such as text classification, aiding in information extraction from textual data.
   - *Logistic Regression:* Logistic regression models the probability of a binary outcome. In disaster management, it finds application in predicting the likelihood of specific events, such as the occurrence of a disaster.
   - *Decision Trees:* Decision trees are tree-like structures used for classification and regression. In disaster management, decision trees aid in risk assessment and decision-making processes.
   - *Bayesian Ridge Regression:* This is a probabilistic regression method. In disaster management, it is applied for predicting continuous variables, like estimating the extent of damage in a disaster.
   - *Random Forest:* Random Forest is an ensemble learning technique. In disaster management, it combines multiple decision trees for tasks such as damage assessment and prediction.
- *Gradient Boosting:* Gradient Boosting is an ensemble learning method that builds decision trees sequentially. It is employed in disaster management for tasks requiring high predictive accuracy.
- *Artificial Neural Networks (ANN):* ANNs mimic the human brain's structure and are versatile in various tasks. In disaster management, ANNs are used for complex tasks like damage assessment and prediction.
- *Deep Neural Networks (Deep NN):* Deep NNs are ANNs with multiple hidden layers. Their applications in disaster management include tasks that demand sophisticated feature extraction.

- *Convolutional Neural Networks (CNNs):* Convolutional Neural Network (CNN) is a specialized neural network designed for image processing and pattern recognition. In disaster management, CNNs play a crucial role in tasks like damage assessment. The network's architecture allows it to automatically learn and extract intricate features from images, enhancing the precision of assessments and aiding in the identification of disaster-related patterns (Drakaki M Et al, 2021).

Figure 1. Random forest

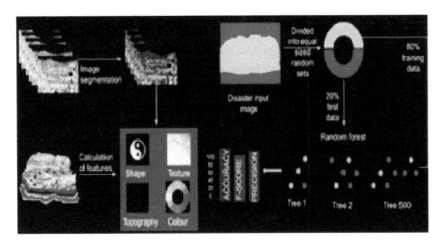

Unsupervised Learning

In unsupervised learning, models analyze data without labeled outcomes. Common techniques include:

- *Means:* The means algorithm involves partitioning data into clusters based on similarities. It is applied in disaster management for grouping similar disaster patterns or affected areas.
- *K Medoids:* K Medoids is a clustering algorithm that identifies central data points. In disaster management, it aids in identifying representative data points within clusters for analysis.
- *Fuzzy C Means:* Fuzzy C Means is a soft clustering technique. In disaster management, it allows for a more flexible assignment of data points to clusters, accommodating uncertainties in the data.
- *K Means:* K Means is a clustering algorithm that partitions data into 'k' clusters based on similarity. In disaster management, K Means is used for identifying patterns and grouping similar disaster events.

- **Hierarchical Clustering:** Hierarchical clustering arranges data into a tree-like structure, enabling a hierarchical view of disaster-related patterns. It assists in understanding the relationships between different disaster events.
- **LSTM:** Long Short-Term Memory (LSTM), a type of recurrent neural network, is well-suited for processing sequential data. In disaster management, LSTM models are employed for time-series predictions, especially in forecasting the progression of natural phenomena. LSTMs excel in capturing dependencies over time, making them valuable for enhancing the accuracy of early warning systems.

Figure 2. LSTM unit

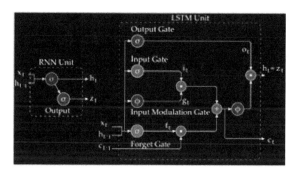

- **GAN:** Generative Adversarial Networks (GANs) represent a revolutionary approach in deep learning. GANs are employed in disaster management to simulate complex disaster scenarios. This involves a generative model creating synthetic data, while a discriminative model assesses its authenticity. GANs facilitate proactive planning and strategy refinement by allowing stakeholders to adapt to evolving challenges through realistic simulations.

Reinforcement Learning

Reinforcement learning involves training models to make sequences of decisions by interacting with an environment. In disaster management, reinforcement learning can be employed for optimizing resource allocation and decision-making in dynamic situations.

Figure 3. Reinforcement learning

- ***Q-Learning:*** Q-Learning is a reinforcement learning technique that enables an agent to learn optimal actions in a given environment. In disaster management, Q-Learning can be applied to optimize decision-making processes for resource allocation and emergency response.

Previous Research in Disaster Management

Researchers have explored risk and vulnerability assessment using DL models, which, equipped with the capacity to process vast datasets, pinpoint susceptibilities in specific regions. This provides valuable insights for formulating targeted mitigation strategies. ML applications have also advanced disaster detection mechanisms, particularly in swiftly identifying events such as floods and wildfires.

The integration of social media data has been pivotal in previous research, showcasing the efficacy of DL, especially in extracting valuable information from platforms like Twitter. ML algorithms, through sentiment analysis and geospatial data integration, offer real-time insights into disaster dynamics, facilitating a community-centric approach in response strategies.

Moreover, the incorporation of remote sensing and satellite imagery has played a crucial role in disaster monitoring. ML algorithms contribute to the accuracy and timeliness of monitoring activities, presenting a comprehensive view of disaster-affected regions. This not only enhances prediction accuracy but also significantly contributes to alleviating the impact of natural disasters on vulnerable communities. (Van Wassenhove et al., 2006).

In previous research highlights the transformative potential of ML and DL in disaster management. The proactive nature of early warning systems, targeted risk assessment, and community-centric response strategies exemplify the strides made in fortifying resilience against natural calamities.

Research Gaps and Opportunities

While substantial progress has been made in leveraging ML and DL for disaster management, certain research gaps and promising opportunities merit attention. Existing studies have laid a solid foundation, yet gaps persist in the comprehensive understanding and application of these technologies across all disaster phases.

One notable research gap lies in the exploration of the full potential of DL for early warning systems. Despite advancements, there is room to delve deeper into refining DL algorithms, ensuring robustness and accuracy in predicting diverse disaster types. Moreover, the integration of DL in risk and vulnerability assessment requires further exploration to harness its capabilities for more nuanced insights (Arinta et al., 2019).

Opportunities abound in extending ML applications to enhance disaster detection mechanisms. Focusing on refining algorithms for the swift identification of various disaster events and expanding the scope to different geographical regions presents an avenue for future research. Additionally, understanding the interplay of social media data and disaster dynamics remains a promising area, opening doors for more sophisticated ML applications.

In the realm of disaster monitoring, there is a need to address gaps in optimizing ML algorithms for processing and analyzing remote sensing and satellite imagery. Fine-tuning these algorithms can lead to even more accurate and timely monitoring, providing a clearer understanding of disaster-affected areas. Embracing interdisciplinary collaboration and advancing explainability in models are also ripe areas for exploration. While current research provides a solid foundation, addressing these gaps and capitalizing on opportunities will propel the field of ML and DL in disaster management towards greater efficacy and resilience.

METHODOLOGY

Inclusion Criteria for Reviewed Studies

The selection of studies for this review adhered to stringent inclusion criteria aimed at ensuring relevance and quality. The primary focus was on scholarly articles and research papers, enabling an up-to-date exploration of the intersection between machine learning (ML) and deep learning (DL) in disaster management. The inclusion criteria encompassed studies addressing various phases of disaster management, including prediction, risk assessment, detection, early warning systems, monitoring, damage assessment, and post-disaster response. Emphasis was placed on the application of ML and DL technologies across different types of natural disasters, such as floods, earthquakes, wildfires, hurricanes, and others. The goal was to compile a comprehensive and diverse set of studies that collectively contribute to understanding the breadth and depth of ML and DL applications in disaster management (Yang et al., 2019).

Search and Selection Process

The search and selection process involved a systematic approach to identify relevant studies. Extensive searches were conducted across reputable academic databases, including but not limited to IEEE Xplore, PubMed, and Google Scholar. The search queries were crafted to capture studies related to ML, DL, and disaster management. The initial screening was based on titles and abstracts, followed by a thorough examination of full-text articles. The selection process prioritized studies with clear methodologies, robust experimental designs, and substantial contributions to the field. The aim was to include studies that offered valuable insights, innovative applications, and addressed specific challenges in utilizing ML and DL for effective disaster management.

Data Extraction and Analysis

Data extraction involved a meticulous process of extracting relevant information from the selected studies. Key data points included the disaster types addressed, the specific ML and DL techniques employed, the datasets utilized, and the outcomes or findings reported. The analysis focused on categorizing the studies according to the disaster phases they targeted, the types of disasters considered, and the technologies applied. Patterns and trends were identified, and a qualitative synthesis was performed to distill the essential contributions of each study. The extraction and analysis process aimed to provide a structured presentation of the current landscape of ML and DL applications in disaster management (Schmidhuber, 2015).

Limitations of the Review

While every effort was made to ensure a comprehensive and unbiased review, certain limitations need acknowledgment. The search was limited to studies published since 2017, potentially excluding earlier but foundational works in the field. Additionally, the review primarily focused on academic databases, potentially overlooking valuable insights from non-academic sources. The inclusion criteria might introduce a degree of subjectivity, and the evolving nature of ML and DL technologies means that some recent developments may not be fully captured. Despite these limitations, the review strives to offer a robust overview and synthesis of the existing literature on ML and DL in disaster management.

ML AND DL APPLICATIONS IN DISASTER MANAGEMENT

Disaster and Hazard Prediction

Disaster and hazard prediction utilizing ML and DL involve the development of models that analyze historical data and real-time information to forecast potential disasters. This approach proves instrumental in situations where timely predictions can mitigate risks and protect vulnerable communities.

- **Increased Predictive Accuracy:** ML and DL models enhance the accuracy of disaster predictions, allowing for more reliable forecasting.
- **Proactive Risk Mitigation:** Early identification of potential hazards enables proactive measures, reducing the impact on communities.
- **Adaptability to Various Disasters:** ML and DL models can be adapted to predict a wide range of disasters, including floods, earthquakes, wildfires, hurricanes, and more (Vasileios et al., 2022).

Risk and Vulnerability Assessment

ML and DL technologies contribute significantly to risk and vulnerability assessment, offering nuanced insights into susceptibilities in specific regions. This application is particularly useful in situations where targeted mitigation strategies are required.

- **Precision in Identifying Vulnerabilities:** DL models process vast datasets to pinpoint vulnerabilities accurately, aiding in the formulation of targeted mitigation strategies.
- **Adaptability to Varied Regions:** ML applications in risk assessment can be tailored to different geographical regions, ensuring relevance in diverse contexts.
- **Comprehensive Analysis:** The capacity to analyze various factors contributes to a comprehensive understanding of disaster risks.

Disaster Detection

ML applications in disaster detection focus on swiftly identifying events like floods and wildfires, enabling rapid response in critical situations.

- **Swift Event Identification:** ML algorithms can quickly identify disasters, facilitating timely responses to minimize damage.
- **Adaptive Algorithms:** ML models can adapt to different disaster scenarios, enhancing their versatility.
- **Real-time Monitoring:** The integration of real-time data allows for continuous monitoring and detection of evolving disaster situations (Vinay Chamola et al., 2020).

Early Warning Systems

ML and DL play a pivotal role in optimizing early warning systems, offering timely alerts and fostering community resilience.

- **Timely Alert Generation:** ML algorithms process data rapidly, enabling the generation of timely alerts for at-risk communities.
- **Community-Centric Approach:** Early warning systems become more effective by incorporating community voices and experiences through ML applications.
- **Integration with Various Data Sources:** ML models can integrate data from diverse sources, enhancing the comprehensiveness of early warnings.

Disaster Monitoring

ML and DL contribute to accurate and timely disaster monitoring by analyzing remote sensing and satellite imagery.

- **Enhanced Monitoring Accuracy:** ML algorithms fine-tune the analysis of remote sensing data, providing more accurate and timely monitoring.
- **Comprehensive View:** Disaster-affected regions are viewed comprehensively, aiding in better understanding and response planning.
- **Integration with Other Data Sources:** ML applications integrate various data sources, offering a holistic view of disaster-affected areas (Sunita et al., 2023).

Damage Assessment

ML and DL technologies are instrumental in assessing the extent of damage caused by disasters, especially using techniques like convolutional neural networks (CNNs) for image analysis.

- **Automated Damage Assessment:** CNNs automate the assessment of damage to infrastructure, expediting response efforts.
- **Improved Accuracy:** ML models enhance the accuracy of damage assessment, ensuring resources are allocated efficiently.
- **Integration with Satellite Imagery:** Satellite imagery is effectively utilized in damage assessment, providing a comprehensive view.

Post-Disaster Response

ML and DL applications facilitate post-disaster response by optimizing resource allocation, aiding in recovery planning, and monitoring distress levels of affected populations.

- **Resource Allocation Optimization:** ML algorithms help in efficiently allocating resources during the recovery phase.
- **Distress Measurement through Social Media:** Social media data are analyzed using ML to measure distress and feelings of affected populations.
- **Hybrid ML-Based Methods:** Combining ML with other technologies contributes to the complexity of post-disaster response operations.

BASIC STRUCTURE AND STEPS IN PREDICTION SYSTEM

Basic Structure of Prediction System in Machine Learning

The foundation of machine learning (ML) prediction systems rests on a well-defined structure that encompasses crucial components to ensure accurate outcome forecasting (Archeiothiki et al., 2022).

Components of the Basic Structure:

1. Input Data

    ○ The cornerstone of prediction systems is raw data, its quality, and relevance significantly impacting prediction accuracy.
    ○ Diverse data sources, encompassing sensor data, social media feeds, and historical records, contribute to a comprehensive input dataset.

Figure 4. Machine learning prediction system

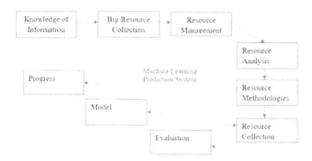

2. Feature Extraction:
    ○ This stage involves identifying and extracting pertinent features from the input data.
    ○ Feature extraction simplifies the dataset while retaining vital information for effective prediction.
    ○ Techniques such as Principal Component Analysis (PCA) and autoencoders are commonly employed for efficient feature extraction.
3. Model Building:
    ○ The predictive model is created using algorithms suited to the specific prediction task.
    ○ The selection of a model depends on the nature of the data and the type of prediction required.
    ○ Popular models include Decision Trees, Support Vector Machines (SVM), and Neural Networks, chosen based on their applicability.

4. Training:
    - The model undergoes training using historical data, allowing it to discern patterns and relationships within the dataset.
    - Training enhances the model's ability to generalize and make accurate predictions on new, unseen data.
    - Iterative training processes, such as epochs in neural networks, refine the model's understanding over time.
5. Testing and Validation:
    - The model undergoes evaluation on separate datasets to validate its predictive performance.
    - Testing ensures the model's reliability and effectiveness in real-world scenarios.
    - Cross-validation techniques, like k-fold cross-validation, provide a robust assessment of the model's generalization capabilities.
6. Prediction Output:
    - The final output represents the predictions generated by the model based on new or unseen input data.
    - Prediction output offers insights or decisions relevant to the prediction task.
    - Output interpretation tools, such as visualization dashboards, aid in understanding and utilizing the predictions effectively.
7. Feedback Loop:
    - Continuous monitoring of the model's performance is integral to the prediction system.
    - Feedback from predictions may lead to model refinement or updating to enhance accuracy.
    - Adaptive learning mechanisms, incorporating user feedback and dynamic adjustments, contribute to an evolving and responsive prediction system.

Steps Involved in Prediction System of Machine Learning

The systematic steps involved in machine learning prediction systems ensure a robust and accurate forecasting process (Akshya et al., 2019).

1. Problem Definition:
    - Clearly defining the prediction problem is crucial, specifying the desired outcome or behavior that needs forecasting.
    - A well-defined problem statement sets the foundation for selecting appropriate models and methodologies.
2. Data Collection:
    - Gathering relevant and sufficient data related to the prediction task is essential for building a comprehensive and effective model.
    - The quality and quantity of data significantly influence the accuracy and reliability of the prediction system.
3. Data Preprocessing:
    - Cleaning and preprocessing the data is a critical step to handle missing values, outliers, and inconsistencies.
    - Data preprocessing enhances the overall quality and reliability of predictions by ensuring a clean and structured dataset.

Figure 5. Steps in prediction system of machine learning

4. Feature Selection:
    - Identifying and selecting features that contribute most to the prediction task is essential for optimizing the model's performance.
    - Feature selection reduces computational complexity and focuses on the most relevant aspects of the input data.
5. Model Selection:
    - Choosing an appropriate machine learning model based on the nature of the prediction problem is a key decision.
    - Different models, such as Decision Trees, Support Vector Machines, and Neural Networks, may be suitable for specific tasks.
6. Training the Model:
    - Training the selected model using historical data allows it to learn patterns and relationships within the dataset.
    - The training phase is crucial for the model to generalize well on new, unseen data and make accurate predictions.
7. Model Evaluation:
    - Assessing the model's performance using separate datasets not used during training provides insights into its effectiveness.
    - Evaluation metrics, including accuracy, precision, recall, and F1 score, help gauge the model's overall performance.
8. Hyperparameter Tuning:

- Fine-tuning model hyperparameters is essential to optimize its performance and adaptability.
- Hyperparameter tuning involves adjusting parameters that are not learned during training to enhance the model's effectiveness.
9. Prediction and Deployment:
    - Deploying the trained model to generate predictions on new, unseen data marks the transition to real-world applications.
    - The deployment phase ensures that the prediction system is ready for practical use in various scenarios.
10. Monitoring and Maintenance:
    - Continuous monitoring of the model's performance in real-world scenarios is imperative for its ongoing effectiveness.
    - Implementing updates or refinements based on feedback and changing data patterns ensures the prediction system remains adaptive and reliable.

CHALLENGES IN ML/DL FOR DISASTER MANAGEMENT

Limited Labeled Training Data

- The scarcity of labeled training data poses a significant challenge for machine learning and deep learning models in disaster management.
- Insufficient data hinders the ability of models to effectively learn and generalize patterns, impacting their predictive accuracy.

Noisy Social Media Data

- The high level of noise in social media data introduces challenges in distinguishing valuable information from irrelevant or misleading content.
- Developing methods to effectively filter signal from noise is essential for harnessing the potential of social media in disaster management.

Ethical Implications

- The use of ML/DL in disaster management raises ethical concerns, especially regarding privacy, bias, and the responsible use of technology.
- Addressing ethical implications is crucial to ensure fairness, transparency, and accountability in decision-making processes.

Integration with Traditional Systems

- Integrating ML/DL systems with traditional disaster management systems presents challenges in terms of interoperability and seamless collaboration.
- Bridging the gap between innovative technologies and established practices requires careful planning and strategic integration (Archeiothiki et al., 2022).

Real-time Decision Making

- Achieving real-time decision-making capabilities in disaster management using ML/DL methods demands efficient algorithms and infrastructure.
- The need for rapid responses necessitates the development of models that can process and analyze data swiftly without compromising accuracy.

KEY FINDINGS

Distribution of Research Studies by Disaster Phase

The examination of research studies in the realm of disaster management reveals a nuanced distribution across different phases. Predominantly, the focus lies on prediction, risk assessment, detection, and post-disaster response. Researchers emphasize not only understanding but also enhancing the applications of machine learning (ML) and deep learning (DL) throughout the entire disaster management continuum. This holistic approach underscores the significance of these technologies at every stage, ensuring a comprehensive and proactive disaster management strategy.

Distribution by Disaster Type

Diverse applications are evident in studies addressing various natural disasters, including floods, earthquakes, wildfires, hurricanes, and others. This broad distribution highlights the adaptability of ML and DL technologies to different disaster types, showcasing their versatility and effectiveness in tackling a spectrum of challenges. The ability of these technologies to cater to specific disaster scenarios emphasizes their potential in contributing to tailored and effective disaster management solutions.

ML and DL Distribution Across Disaster Phases

Analysis of research findings indicates a balanced distribution of ML and DL applications across multiple disaster phases. This balanced deployment emphasizes their comprehensive role in prediction, monitoring, and response efforts. The integration of these technologies contributes to a holistic disaster management approach, showcasing their capacity to address the varied challenges posed by different phases of a disaster (Archeiothiki et al., 2022).

Data Sources and Technologies Used

Research findings underscore the extensive utilization of diverse data sources, including social media, remote sensing, and satellite imagery. Notably, advanced technologies such as Convolutional Neural Networks (CNNs) and Long Short-Term Memory (LSTM) models are prevalent, showcasing the continuous advancement and integration of cutting-edge technologies into disaster management practices.

Performance Metrics and Accuracy

Evaluation metrics used in the reviewed studies vary, encompassing accuracy, precision, recall, and other performance indicators. The emphasis on diverse metrics reflects the multifaceted nature of disaster management, where different aspects require tailored evaluation criteria. This diversity in performance metrics underscores the need for a comprehensive and adaptable approach to assessing the effectiveness of ML and DL applications in disaster management scenarios.

FUTURE DIRECTIONS AND CHALLENGES

Addressing Bottlenecks in DL

- Future research should prioritize overcoming limitations in Deep Learning (DL), particularly addressing challenges related to the scarcity of labeled training data and the human labeling of datasets.
- Efforts should be directed toward developing innovative methods to handle noise in social media data, ensuring the robustness of DL-based disaster management approaches.

Integrating Crowdsourcing and ML/DL

- Opportunities lie in harnessing the power of crowdsourcing platforms, such as Amazon Mechanical Turk, to complement ML/DL methods.
- Collaborative efforts between human intelligence and machine intelligence can enhance accuracy and reduce labor costs, especially in disaster management tasks.

Enhancing Data Quality

- Future endeavors should focus on improving the quality of data used in disaster management applications, especially in extracting information from wireless sensor networks and other relevant technologies.
- Techniques such as web crawling and web scraping can be explored to ensure effective preparedness and response operations (Srivastava et al., 2023).

Explainability and Validation of Models

- There is a pressing need to integrate explainability into ML and DL-based models across various application areas, including disaster management.
- The research community should strive to develop models that not only deliver accurate outcomes but also provide clear explanations of the processes leading to those outcomes

Interdisciplinary Collaboration

- The future landscape of disaster management research should encourage interdisciplinary collaboration, involving experts from diverse fields.
- Collaboration should extend beyond traditional boundaries, incorporating insights from various domains, including data science, social sciences, and engineering.

CONCLUSION

Recap of Key Findings

In summary, the exploration of machine learning (ML) and deep learning (DL) applications within the domain of disaster management has yielded valuable insights. The distribution of research studies across distinct disaster phases and types serves as a testament to the versatile applications of ML and DL technologies. This versatility positions these technologies as crucial assets capable of contributing across the entire spectrum of disaster management.

The analysis of ML and DL distribution brought to light their integral role in various stages of disaster management, from prediction and risk assessment to detection, response, and recovery. This comprehensive involvement underscores the potential for ML and DL to significantly enhance the resilience and efficacy of disaster management strategies.

Noteworthy findings also highlighted the diverse array of data sources and technologies employed in these studies. This diversity underscores the intricate and multifaceted nature of contemporary disaster management, wherein the integration of advanced technologies plays a pivotal role in addressing complex challenges.

Moreover, the assessment of performance metrics and accuracy serves as a barometer for the evolving impact of ML and DL on decision-making in disaster-related scenarios. The pursuit of improved accuracy and reliability in predictions through these technologies reflects the ongoing commitment to refining and advancing disaster management practices.

Implications for Disaster Management

The implications of incorporating machine learning (ML) and deep learning (DL) in disaster management are profound. The versatile applications of these technologies across different phases, from prediction to response, signify a transformative potential in how we prepare for and mitigate the impact of disasters.

Firstly, the integration of ML and DL in early warning systems holds the promise of revolutionizing disaster preparedness. By leveraging historical data and real-time information, ML algorithms can provide more accurate and timely predictions. This proactive approach enables communities to take swift and informed measures, potentially saving lives and minimizing damage.

Secondly, the use of these technologies in risk and vulnerability assessment signifies a shift towards targeted and precise mitigation strategies. The ability to process vast datasets allows for the identification of specific susceptibilities in regions prone to disasters. This precision in assessment enhances our capacity to reduce vulnerabilities, fostering community resilience against future calamities.

Conclusion

In conclusion, the integration of machine learning (ML) and deep learning (DL) technologies in disaster management offers a transformative paradigm for prevention, analysis, and response. These advanced technologies showcase their versatility across various types of disasters, harnessing the power of predictive analytics and real-time data analysis. ML and DL excel in leveraging social media data for rapid insights into unfolding disaster dynamics, providing a valuable tool for proactive response efforts. Additionally, their application in analyzing satellite imagery enhances disaster monitoring accuracy, enabling a comprehensive understanding of affected regions. The amalgamation of these technologies not only aids in prediction and risk assessment but also significantly contributes to building resilient communities. As we envision the future, the synergy between ML, DL, social media, and satellite data stands as a beacon for proactive disaster management, ushering in a new era of precision, responsiveness, and resilience.

REFERENCES

Akshya, J., & Priyadarsini, P. L. K. (2019). *A hybrid machine learning approach for classifying aerial images of flood-hit areas*. In *Proceedings of the 2019 International Conference on Computational Intelligence in Data Science (ICCIDS)*, Chennai, India. 10.1109/ICCIDS.2019.8862138

Altay, N., & Green, W. G. III. (2006). OR/MS research in disaster operations management. [Google Scholar] [CrossRef]. *European Journal of Operational Research*, *175*(1), 475–493. doi:10.1016/j.ejor.2005.05.016

Ben-Hur, A., Horn, D., Siegelmann, H. T., & Vapnik, V. (2000). A support vector clustering method. In *Proceedings of the 15th International Conference on Pattern Recognition. ICPR-2000*, Barcelona, Spain. 10.1109/ICPR.2000.906177

Drakaki, M., Gören, H. G., & Tzionas, P. (2018). An intelligent multi-agent based decision support system for refugee settlement siting. [Google Scholar] [CrossRef]. *International Journal of Disaster Risk Reduction*, *31*, 576–588. doi:10.1016/j.ijdrr.2018.06.013

Drakaki, M., & Tzionas, P. (2021). Investigating the impact of site management on distress in refugee sites using Fuzzy Cognitive Maps. [Google Scholar] [CrossRef]. *International Journal of Disaster Risk Reduction*, *60*, 102282. doi:10.1016/j.ijdrr.2021.102282

EM-DAT—The International Disasters Database. (n.d.). Guidelines. EM-DAT—Data Entry—Field Description/Definition. EM-DAT. https://www.emdat.be/guidelines

Fan, C., Wu, F., & Mostafavi, A. (2020). A Hybrid Machine Learning Pipeline for Automated Mapping of Events and Locations from Social Media in Disasters. [Google Scholar] [CrossRef]. *IEEE Access : Practical Innovations, Open Solutions*, *8*, 10478–10490. doi:10.1109/ACCESS.2020.2965550

Lecun, Y., Bengio, Y., & Hinton, G. (2015). Deep learning. [Google Scholar] [CrossRef]. *Nature*, *521*(7553), 436–444. doi:10.1038/nature14539 PMID:26017442

Presa-Reyes, M., & Chen, S. C. (2020). *Assessing Building Damage by Learning the Deep Feature Correspondence of before and after Aerial Images.* In *Proceedings of the 2020 IEEE Conference on Multimedia Information Processing and Retrieval (MIPR)*, Shenzhen, China. 10.1109/MIPR49039.2020.00017

Schmidhuber, J. (2015). Deep Learning in neural networks: An overview. [Google Scholar] [CrossRef]. *Neural Networks*, *61*, 85–117. doi:10.1016/j.neunet.2014.09.003 PMID:25462637

Sun, W., Bocchini, P., & Davison, B. D. (2020). Applications of Artificial Intelligence for Disaster Management. [Google Scholar] [CrossRef]. *Natural Hazards*, *103*(3), 2631–2689. doi:10.1007/s11069-020-04124-3

United Nations Office for Disaster Risk Reduction (UNDRR). (2009). *UNISDR Terminology on Disaster Risk Reduction*. UNISDR: Geneva, Switzerland. https://www.unisdr.org/files/7817_UNISDRTerminologyEnglish.pdf

Chapter 16
Deep Learning and AI-Powered Natural Catastrophes Warning Systems

Siddique Ibrahim S. P.
VIT-AP University, India

Sathya D.
RV University, India

Gokulnath B. V.
VIT-AP University, India

Selva kumar S.
 https://orcid.org/0000-0002-0269-198X
VIT-AP University, India

Jai Singh W.
Presidency University, India

Thangavel Murugan
 https://orcid.org/0000-0002-2510-8857
United Arab Emirates University, UAE

ABSTRACT

Natural catastrophes including hurricanes, floods, wildfires, and earthquakes can seriously harm people and property. Floods that destroy houses, businesses, government buildings, and other properties cause enormous economic losses in addition to human casualties. This loss cannot be recovered; however, flood damage can frequently be reduced by supporting suitable structural and non-structural solutions. Natural catastrophes have become more frequent and severe in recent years, primarily as a result of climate change. Due to the large number of small and low magnitude earthquakes, the hand-picked data used in manual approaches, and the possibility of some noisy disturbances in the background, the methods are not very dependable. As a result, automated techniques and algorithms are more effective when used for earthquake identification and detection. However, scientists and engineers can now more accurately and efficiently predict and avert natural disasters thanks to developments in machine learning and data analytics. By creating a deep learning model that can quickly determine an asset's structural status in the event of a seismic excitation, this study investigates the potential of artificial intelligence in various operational domains.

DOI: 10.4018/979-8-3693-3362-4.ch016

INTRODUCTION

Natural disasters (e.g. landslides, floods, earthquakes, tropical cyclones, etc.) are complex phenomena that affect not only the environment of the area but also assets of that area like agriculture, infrastructure, and economic assets. Worldwide, governments and citizens alike have been increasingly threatened by the growing number and intensity of natural disasters and extreme weather occurrences in the past several years (Kim et al., 2018). As the number of people living in cities continues to rise, it is more important than ever to take measures to keep people safe and improve their living conditions. The globe is experiencing global urbanisation as more and more people choose to live in cities due to the comfortable living conditions there. Urban regions are home to about half of the world's population. This sort of expansion happens more quickly in developing nations (Ream et al., 2020). Figure 2 shows that between 1980 and 2021, the percentage of Chinese citizens residing in urban areas rose from 19.37% to 64.72% of the total population. As the number of people living in urban areas rises, more and more cities are being built or existing ones are being enlarged. An example of a developed/expanded mega city with more than 25 million residents is Shanghai, China. Within this framework, the security and regular functioning of buildings and infrastructures are significantly jeopardized by both natural and man-made catastrophes (Pekar et al., 2020). The frequency of floods and landslides caused by heavy rain in metropolitan areas has been on the rise in recent years, perhaps due to the increased occurrence of extreme weather events brought about by climate change. Early prediction and warning systems can lessen the impact, while technical solutions can stop them from happening altogether. Nevertheless, earthquakes can still not be predicted with enough precision to prevent damage. Therefore, it is essential for sustainable city development to develop and implement earthquake-resistant, vibration-damping, and seismically-isolated structures. One "natural" calamity that humans have brought about is land subsidence, which is mostly caused by the over-pumping of groundwater. Consequently, in order to properly respond to such crucial situations, updated solutions are required for disaster management and built assets operations. Government agencies, reaction groups, and healthcare institutions must communicate effectively and make quick decisions in order to respond to public health emergencies. Crucial components of disaster risk reduction include understanding situational risk, increasing governance, improving readiness for effective response, and investing in steps to build resilience (Lopez et al., 2018).

More accurate disease outbreak predictions, better evacuation plans, and more efficient resource distribution are all possible thanks to the proliferation of AI and ML, which allow for real-time data monitoring and decision-making in high-pressure situations. As shown in Figure 1, ML models are normally trained on massive amounts of task-specific data and then applied to new test data without the need for explicit programming or manually-crafted decision limits. In order to train, these algorithms often change the model's parameters iteratively; subsequent predictions and performance on the target task are based on these modifications.3 When it comes to the ability to draw conclusions or make predictions, ML is comparable to statistics. On the other hand, ML algorithms focus on prediction, whereas statistical models excel at inferring correlations between variables (Najafi et al., 2022).

Many areas, including healthcare, customer service, and commerce, have benefited from artificial intelligence (Ruidas et al., 2023). Plus, scientists have now discovered that AI can foretell when catastrophic weather events would occur. Using massive amounts of high-quality data, AI can predict when certain natural catastrophes will occur, potentially saving thousands of lives. Automated responses, prediction and early detection systems, and other tools can help local governments lessen the impact of natural catastrophes. Modern technology allows for earlier warnings to residents, the activation of mitigation measures, and the enhancement of first responders' ability to respond effectively. With the proliferation of sensors, more data collecting, and advancements in artificial intelligence (AI), prediction and detection systems are expected to become increasingly accurate and effective (Allen et al., 1978).

On the other hand, AI isn't perfect; it works best for disasters where the causes are known, there's enough data to train the algorithms, and the occurrences are common enough to compare the models' predictions to reality and tweak them. Among the many natural catastrophes that AI has the ability to foretell are:

Figure 1. Number of research studies on disaster prediction in the last thirteen years

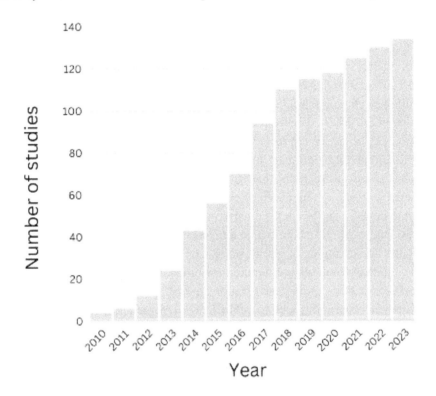

Earthquakes

It is necessary to construct a national geophysical monitoring network and build a collaborative worldwide programme for strong-motion measurement and data processing. Local networks should be built, when needed, to investigate the impacts of local site characteristics on ground motion, as well as the link between specific ground motion parameters and structure damage (Ibrahim et al., 2020).

The investigation of the behaviour of structures supported by various soil types represents an additional domain that merits further research. The consequences of soil properties on structures were dramatically illustrated in the Loma Prieta earthquake-induced damage distribution in the Marina District, which emphasises the criticality of further investigation in this field (Fang et al., 2020).

Figure 2. Literature search process and article selection

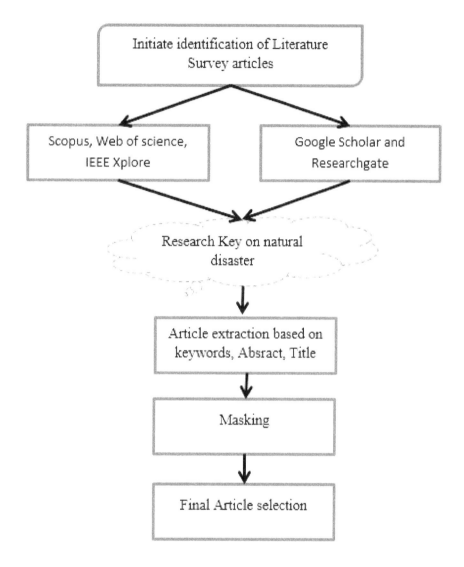

The development of cost-effective methods for reinforcing existing buildings and structures, particularly un-reinforced masonry and brittle reinforced concrete buildings, requires further investigation. Active and passive control systems, as well as other innovative techniques, should be promoted for development and implementation by the federal and state governments in order to enhance the seismic resistance of new and existing structures. To enhance methods for preventing damage to nonstructural components such as windows, ceilings, electrical supply and domestic gas pipelines, further investigation is required. Accelerate the investigation of methods to enhance the design and construction of lifeline systems (Ibrahim et al., 2019).

In addition, the distance from the earthquake's epicentre is negatively correlated with the severity of the injuries. The magnitude of the earthquake, increased ground motion, and structural damage all often result in a higher number of injuries and fatalities. There is a higher risk of injuries to the spine, chest, and pelvis during nighttime earthquakes. This is because, at the moment of the accident, the majority of victims are asleep (Harirchian et al., 2020). These wounds frequently result in significant internal bleeding that also damages internal organs. Injuries to the extremities with concomitant cuts, extensive external bleeding, and crush injuries such as compartment syndrome and rhabdomyolysis are more common if the earthquake happens during the day.

In addition, the majority of injuries from falling debris during a diurnal earthquake happen on the skull and collarbone because most victims are either standing or sitting down. Infected woundsand/or gangrene are possible outcomes for victims who have been buried for hours or even days by falling debris. Amputations, vascular stabilisation, faciotomies, orthopaedic stabilisation, debridement, and/or dressing of serious open wounds are common trauma operations that require immediate attention. It's crucial to remember that people with crush injuries are also more likely to experience fatal cardiac arrhythmias or myocardial infarcts, as well as hypovolemic shock, hyperkalemia, and renal failure. Although falling objects or collapsing buildings cause the majority of the stress experienced during an earthquake, fire is a serious risk during the first "golden" 24 hours following the disaster. After an earthquake, burn injuries and respiratory issues from smoke inhalation can quickly become a significant burden on the medical system, depending on the magnitude and scope of the fires (Priyanka et al., 2015).

Droughts

Droughts Compared to the immediate emergency consequences of natural catastrophes like hurricanes or tornadoes, the effects of a drought are less severe. In an area that has been badly damaged by a Drought-related protein or calorie malnutrition (kwashiorkor and marsmus) may cause a dramatic rise in mortality. Certain vitamin deficiencies, like a deficiency in Vitamin A, can cause specific outcomes like xerpohthalmia and blindness in children. Chronic malnutrition can readily raise rates of illness and death, as well as reduce overall community functioning. Prolonged droughts and food shortages can sometimes cause large-scale migrations of people, which can result in overcrowding and a general lack of sanitation. An rise in the transmission rates of infectious diseases like tuberculosis or intestinal infections can be easily caused by overcrowding (Malar et al., 2018).

Volcano

A volcano is a mountain that collapses to reveal a molten rock pool beneath the earth's surface. Magma is the term for this molten rock. Molten rock, boulders, ash, and enormous volumes of extremely hot gas can all spew forth during an eruption. This is flung into the air and frequently cascades down the mountainside. Lava or pyroclastic flows are produced when the molten rock cascades down the mountainside. When a volcano erupts, any nearby buildings or constructions will be destroyed or severely damaged. In addition to flows of scorching liquid rock and mud, dwellings are frequently destroyed by hot ash that descends like rain on everything below (Arthi et al., 2017).

What Causes A Volcano To Erupt?

When magma beneath the surface climbs to the summit of the mountain, gas and bubbles are released, resulting in a volcanic eruption. This gas has the ability to develop pressure to the point where a volcano blows up.

What Is the Frequency of Volcanic Eruptions?

About 1,500 volcanoes worldwide are known to have erupted at some point in the last 10,000 years, according to David Pyle, an Oxford University professor of Earth sciences. The majority of these volcanoes might erupt once more in the future. Between sixty and eighty volcanoes erupt annually. These will mostly be minor outbursts (Ibrahim et al., 2020).

Where do Eruptions in the Volcano Occur?

There are 75% of all volcanoes in the Ring of Fire. The majority of volcanoes are arranged in a row along the tectonic plate boundaries of the planet. Volcanic eruptions occur most frequently along the "Ring of Fire," which spans the Pacific Rim. The Ring of Fire of the Pacific Ocean is a region characterised by frequent earthquakes and active volcanoes (Kumar et al., 2023). Certain regions—like parts of Alaska, eastern Russia, and South America—have lofty mountains formed by volcanoes that are 40–50 kilometers apart and run parallel to the border of the continent. Volcanoes create islands in various locations, like the West Indies, a few Pacific islands, and sections of Indonesia (Ibrahim et al., 2023).

Why Disasters Don't Occur Naturally?

Extreme occurrences, like volcanic eruptions are not considered "natural disasters." Even if the term "natural disaster" is frequently used, it has several drawbacks. By thinking that the incident would occur anyway and that there is little that can be done to prevent it, the term "natural" minimizes the part that humans played in the catastrophe. Actually, the choices we make are what bring about calamity. Whether a disaster results from a natural hazard will depend on a number of elements, including living circumstances and poverty, the ability of the government to respond and prepare, and the effectiveness of the reconstruction process (Sathya et al., 2023).

What Makes People Dwell Near Volcanoes?

Around the world, more than 500 million people reside close to a volcano. People continue to choose to reside in such a high-risk area despite the knowing risks. But why, is the question. Owing to a phenomena called "upside risk," there may be more benefits to living in such an area than disadvantages. One advantage of being close to a volcano for farmers is the rich agricultural land that is boosted by the volcanic ash. This also holds true for regions that had mudflows from volcanoes cover them. However, there are also intriguing societal justifications for residing in such a dangerous region, since volcanoes have shaped local culture (S. P. et al., 2023).

The Dangers of Volcano Living

While there are advantages to living near a volcano, families should be aware of potential health risks. Leading Earth Sciences expert Dr. Zoe Mildon, a lecturer at the University of Plymouth, outlines the health hazards associated with catastrophic volcanic eruptions. As stated by Dr. Mildon: The formation of lahars, which are created when volcanic ash and water combine, could occur. Communities might be cut off by lahars that overrun villages. When quantities of volcanic gases are high enough, they can be toxic. Because volcanic ash particles are so tiny and pointy, breathing in it can seriously harm the lungs.

Fire

Although human activity is the source of 90% of forest fires in the United States, lightning strikes in dry, windy conditions are the most common cause of "natural" forest fires. The impact of a forest fire on the quality of the surrounding air is what affects human health. Numerous minor fires might lead to bad air quality in a specific area due to favourable local conditions (Aga et al., 2013). At best, the accumulation of smoke and other pollutants in the air reduces visibility; at worst, it can cause new respiratory issues or make pre-existing ones worse. Although rare, burn injuries resulting from forest fires are not unheard of. Members of the forest fire fighting team are frequently required to be in close proximity to enormous and unpredictable fires, which is likely why burn injuries are linked to them. Forest fires can spread quickly and change course quickly, depending on the wind conditions at the time. This can trap firefighters and, less frequently, regular residents. On occasion, there is an upsurge in animal attacks and/or bites when there is a significant forest fire (Meenakshi et al., 2020).

Many wild creatures that have been forced to flee come into closer contact with people depending on how close a forest fire is to a populated centre. This occurrence, which is also observed after significant floods, can raise the risk of zoonotic illnesses, which are infections that spread from animals to people, in addition to causing stress from animal attacks. Thanks to the existence of a well-trained and equipped fire brigade, large fires that tear through metropolitan areas are less frequent in modern nations. Large-scale urban fires are still a possibility in developing nations, albeit they usually occur secondarily to other natural calamities like earthquakes. An 8.7-magnitude earthquake that struck the San Francisco region in 1906 set off massive fires that eventually destroyed over 25,000 buildings and left 250,000 people without a place to live. Asphyxia-related mortality and burn injuries are the most common types of casualties sustained in large-scale urban fires. Sepsis, a severe infection, and hypovolemic shock are typical aftereffects of burn burns.

Floods

Drowning is inevitably the highest risk of death from a flood. More people die from flooding each year in North America than from any other type of natural disaster, with the exception of heat-related diseases. The majority of fatalities and injuries happen when there is little to no notice that a flood is about to happen. This can happen as a result of tidal waves brought on by a far-off or even sub-oceanic earthquake, rapid floods, or the collapse of a dam. People frequently misjudge the force of flowing water, which results in numerous avoidable accidents and fatalities. Estimating the average depth of opaque, swiftly moving water can be challenging even in the best of circumstances, and it can be nearly impossible at dark or in the middle of the night. A school bus, for example, can float on less than two feet of rushing water, while a strong man can be swept off his feet by three to six inches of swiftly moving water. The second most common cause of mortality and serious injury during floods, after drowning, is weather-related exposure. People stranded in rising floodwaters frequently seek shelter in trees, the tops of buildings, or automobiles as they wait for help. People may be left outside in bad weather for hours or even days, depending on the severity of the floods and the availability of rescue services. There is a higher chance of unintentional hypothermia the lower the ambient temperature drops below 15°C. Because of the quantity of debris that can get caught in the flowing floodwaters along with the unwary victims, blunt trauma injuries are frequently sustained during floods. The injuries sustained in this instance are similar to projectile injuries and frequently involve torso and extremities fractures, cuts, and severe bruises.

Heat Waves

Heat waves are referred to as the quiet calamity of nature. In the US, nearly 8,000 people lost their lives to hyperthermic sickness between 1979 and 1999. This is a greater number of deaths than the total deaths from floods, lightning, hurricanes, tornadoes, and earthquakes. Vulnerable groups in an impacted area are the first to recognise the direct health effects of a heat wave. Heat stress can gradually lead a patient from heat exhaustion to the possibly fatal heat stroke. The elderly, the very young, and the sick are all more prone to heat stress. It's crucial to remember, though, that if the right safety measures are not followed, even young, healthy people might get heat illness.

By just spending brief periods of time outside in the heat, heat-related illnesses can be avoided.

Preventing heat diseases also involves maintaining body fluid status by drinking lots of liquids and avoiding alcoholic or caffeinated beverages. Treatment for advanced heat disease phases, including heat stroke, entails quickly chilling the body and replacing lost fluid and electrolyte levels. The core body temperature needs to be kept track of when cooling is applied to prevent rebound heat or unintentional hypothermia. The length and intensity of the hyperthermia, as well as the promptness of identification and treatment, all have a direct impact on the fatality rate from heat stroke.

Cyclones, Typhoons, and Hurricanes

Hurricane-related fatalities, injuries, and economic losses have increased recently due to persistent population growth and aggressive construction of vulnerable coastal areas. The most fatalities during hurricanes (typhoons in the western Pacific Ocean and cyclones in the Indian Ocean) are caused by secondary disasters including flash floods, storm surges, and tiny tornadoes. One of the best indicators of fatality in coastal areas (those within 30 miles of a saltwater shore) is the height of a hurricane's storm surge. In the past, the storm surge that came before a hurricane has been directly responsible for nine out of ten hurricane deaths.) People in the storm path frequently underestimate how much damage a hurricane may do to coastal areas, leaving many unprepared for the aftermath. Storm surges on the east coast of the United States can raise the mean water level in the storm's right front quadrant by up to fifteen feet. (The area of landfall where the hurricane's track mixes with onshore winds to create the area of highest storm surge is the right front quadrant.) This effect may be made worse by building wind waves on top of the storm tidal height and by the potential for a hurricane to make landfall during high tide. The second most lethal feature of a storm is its winds. In addition to causing property damage, hurricane winds frequently bring down houses and other wooden buildings. Breach points caused by flying debris or wind pressure in a building's windows or doors are frequently the first signs of significant structural damage. When a structure's stable envelope is broken, air can enter it freely. Pressure then develops inside the structure until the walls give way in an attempt to let the swelling mass of air leave. In places with poor construction methods or during strong storms, crush injuries—like those sustained during an earthquake—are frequent. During a hurricane, big objects that can fly airborne due to strong winds are the cause of numerous more trauma events. Cuts from flying glass and other debris are the most frequent non-fatal traumatic injury during a hurricane. When weighed against the overwhelming need to provide drinkable water, wholesome food, and sufficient shelter for all affected residents, treating traumatic injuries during a hurricane is sometimes dismissed as a non-emergency public health priority.

Storm Clouds

Tornadoes are more likely to cause morbidity and mortality than other types of catastrophes because they provide communities with little time to prepare or seek shelter due to their lack of notice.

In the US, projectiles propelled by tornado winds are the primary cause of cranio-cerebral injuries, which also result in catastrophic irreversible injuries. Additionally common are crush injuries brought on by falling structures or massive pieces of flying debris. Fractures, punctures, lacerations, and other soft tissue injuries are among the common non-fatal injuries. More than half of the injuries seen in local emergency rooms are musculoskeletal strains, abrasions, contusions, and punctures. The majority of casualties have numerous wounds, and many soft tissue injuries happen in locations where skin is visible, such the head and neck.

The exposed skin of tornado victims also displays a distinctive abrasion pattern, which is caused by tiny particles of mud, sand, soil, and sometimes water hitting the body at extremely high speeds.

It appears that wound contamination and the infection that follows play a significant role in postoperative sepsis, which increases the requirement for vigorous wound care and surgical debridement. It is reasonable to assume that 25% of fracture injuries sustained during a tornado will be open, which raises the risk of infection for the injured. Research indicates that between 50% and 70% of tornado patients who need surgery will show early indicators of bacteremia and sepsis since a large percentage of projectile injuries result in these conditions. Multiple organ dysfunction syndrome, a potentially fatal consequence of sepsis infection, can lead to multiple system failure.

Ice Storms

A strong winter storm typically causes major traffic pattern disruptions and a sharp increase in car accidents as its immediate effects. Traffic accident injuries can range from orthopedic damage, to serious vascular impairment, to potentially fatal thoracic and abdominal bruises.

Falls in icy walking conditions can also result in fractures, bruises, and head injuries, which are particularly common in the older population. During a winter storm, exposure to the weather is also very dangerous. Extended exposure to the very cold temperatures can result in frostbite injuries for individuals. Severe cases can necessitate surgery.

People regularly use improper heaters indoors in an attempt to stay warm, which increases the risk of carbon monoxide poisoning and hypothermia deaths. Power lines and phone networks are also frequently affected during severe winter storms. People also leave heaters, fireplaces, and candles blazing all night long as sources of heat and illumination, which increases the frequency of fire-related deaths and injuries during winter storms. Furthermore, the prevalence of unstable angina and sudden myocardial infractions rises sharply as formerly sedentary people come outside during the winter storm to perform repairs or clear snow from roofs and roads.

Landslides

When landslides occur in the United States, they are responsible for around $2 billion worth of damage each year. A more in-depth comprehension of the factors that lead to the occurrence of landslides will considerably enhance the hazard and risk assessments carried out by neighbourhood authorities. In order to produce designs that reduce ground deformation and damage to structures, as well as to offer a technological foundation for mitigation measures such as landslip zoning, as well as to test and evaluate novel ways for landslip stabilization, research is required.

Accelerating the use of new techniques in satellite remote sensing, geophysics, and geotechnical engineering for the purpose of identifying regions that are prone to landslides is something that should be done. Research is required to determine the economic, political, and social dynamics that either favour or hinder the implementation of programmes to mitigate the effects of landslides. When landslides are taken into consideration in insurance programmes as well as in municipal planning and zoning, this knowledge might prove to be useful, particularly with regard to the positioning of important facilities.

Extreme Winds

A comprehensive understanding of the effects of wind force on buildings is essential for the development of wind speed regulations in building codes and the construction of structures that are resistant to wind. Insufficient research has been conducted in this field; data of wind speeds at the height of buildings ranging from mid-rise to high-rise are very seldom available.

PRACTICAL APPLICATIONS OF AI AND DEEP LEARNING IN DISASTER PREPAREDNESS

AI and deep learning have shown great potential in enhancing disaster preparedness efforts. These technologies have been applied extensively in various areas, such as weather forecasting, early warning systems, and emergency response (Who 2019). For weather forecasting, AI and deep learning algorithms can analyze vast amounts of historical weather data to identify patterns and make more accurate predictions. They can also assist in the development of early warning systems by analyzing data from various sources, such as seismic sensors, weather satellites, and social media. By analyzing this data, AI algorithms can detect potential disasters or hazards and issue timely warnings to at-risk populations. Additionally, AI and deep learning can improve emergency response efforts by enhancing situational awareness and decision-making. For example, AI can analyze real-time data from sensors, mapping systems, and social media to provide emergency responders with up-to-date information on the location, severity, and dynamics of a disaster. Furthermore, AI and deep learning can help optimize resource allocation during disasters by predicting the impact of different scenarios and recommending the most effective response strategies. AI and deep learning technologies have also been instrumental in the development of innovative solutions for post-disaster assessment and recovery. Through the use of AI-powered drones and satellite imagery analysis, damage assessment can be conducted more efficiently and accurately. This allows for better prioritization of areas requiring urgent attention and resources. Moreover, AI and deep learning algorithms can analyze large-scale data to provide insights for long-term recovery planning and infrastructure rebuilding.

In addition to their practical applications, AI and deep learning play a crucial role in improving communication and coordination among various agencies and organizations involved in disaster preparedness and response. By integrating and analyzing data from multiple sources, AI can facilitate real-time information sharing and collaboration, leading to more effective and coordinated efforts during a crisis.

Using AI and deep learning to prepare for disasters not only makes reaction efforts more effective, but it also helps make communities more resilient and able to adjust. As these technologies continue to progress, it is becoming increasingly evident that they have the potential to revolutionize catastrophe planning and response. As a result, it is vital to embrace and make use of artificial intelligence and deep learning in disaster preparedness in order to improve response capabilities, reduce the amount of loss of life and property, and increase the likelihood of resilient communities.

On the other hand, it is essential to recognize that the use of artificial intelligence and deep learning in emergency preparation comes with its own unique set of difficulties. Especially in the context of decision-making processes during times of emergency, one of the key problems is the ethical usage of artificial intelligence. It is necessary to make certain that artificial intelligence algorithms are developed and utilized in a manner that is both responsible and transparent, taking into account the possibility of biases and the ethical implications of their use.

Furthermore, the reliability and robustness of AI systems in high-stakes environments need to be thoroughly evaluated. It is crucial to address issues related to data quality, model interpret ability, and system resilience to ensure that AI and deep learning technologies can be trusted to support critical decision-making during disasters.

Moreover, the widespread adoption of AI and deep learning in disaster preparedness requires significant investment in infrastructure, training, and capacity building. This includes the development of skilled workforce capable of utilizing and maintaining AI systems, as well as the establishment of standards and protocols for interoperability and data sharing among various stakeholders.

The potential benefits of artificial intelligence and deep learning in disaster preparedness are enormous, notwithstanding the hurdles that are now being faced. The application of these technologies has the potential to revolution the way we approach catastrophe management and to produce communities that are more adaptable, resilient, and responsive if research and innovation are allowed to continue and if scientists from different fields work together.The implementation of AI and deep learning in disaster preparedness has also led to advancements in predictive modeling for assessing the likelihood and potential impact of future disasters. By leveraging historical data and real-time information, AI algorithms can forecast the probability of different types of disasters, allowing for proactive planning and resource allocation. This proactive approach enhances preparedness and reduces the vulnerability of communities to potential hazards.

Furthermore, the use of AI and deep learning in disaster response has paved the way for the development of autonomous systems that can assist in the deployment of resources and coordination of rescue operations. These autonomous systems can analyze evolving situations in real-time, make rapid decisions, and adapt to dynamic and unpredictable circumstances, thereby augmenting the capabilities of human responders.

Another area where AI and deep learning have made significant contributions is in the field of risk assessment and mitigation. By analyzing vast and diverse datasets, AI can identify vulnerabilities in infrastructure, assess the potential impact of disasters on different regions, and recommend measures to mitigate risks. This proactive risk assessment can inform urban planning, infrastructure development, and policy-making to build more resilient and prepared communities.

The utilization of AI and deep learning in disaster preparedness is not limited to natural disasters. These technologies also hold immense potential in addressing pandemics, public health emergencies, and cyber security threats. By analyzing patterns in data related to the spread of diseases, healthcare resource allocation, and cyber-attacks, AI can contribute to early detection, rapid response, and effective mitigation strategies.

CHALLENGES IN DISASTER MANAGEMENT

There are a number of problems that need to be solved when it comes to the application of artificial intelligence and deep learning in disaster planning and response. These challenges include ensuring the availability and quality of data, ensuring the reliability and accuracy of AI algorithms, addressing biases in data collection and analysis, protecting data privacy and security, and ensuring that AI technologies are accessible and affordable for all communities, including those that are economically challenged or located in remote areas. When it comes to disaster management, there is also a requirement to actively control the possible risks and unexpected effects that might be caused by artificial intelligence.

IMPACT OF NATURAL DISASTER

Natural calamities can cause extensive destruction to the environment, infrastructure, and human well-being, frequently resulting in substantial harm and presenting enduring difficulties for impacted areas. Now, let's analyses each aspect and talk about ways to reduce the impact:

Effect on the Environment:

Loss of Trees and Habitat: Occurrences such as wildfires and hurricanes can result in significant loss of trees and destruction of natural habitats, posing a threat to biodiversity.

Soil Erosion and Land Degradation: Excessive rainfall and floods can result in soil erosion, which can lead to the loss of productive land and an increase in sedimentation in water bodies.

Water Pollution: Storm surges, flooding, and tsunamis can lead to water sources becoming polluted with pollution, debris, and toxic materials.

Decline in Ecosystem Services: Natural calamities can disturb ecosystem processes including pollination, water cleansing, and carbon storage, impacting the overall well-being of the environment.

ROLE OF ARTIFICIAL INTELLIGENCE IN PREPARING NATIONAL DISASTER

Artificial intelligence plays a crucial role in preparing for national disasters by enabling more accurate and timely predictions, enhancing response and recovery efforts, improving decision-making processes, and contributing to overall resilience depicted in Figure3. Artificial intelligence algorithms have the capacity to evaluate enormous volumes of data and recognize patterns and anomalies that may indicate the emergence of a disaster or the escalation of an existing one.

AI Based Predictive Construction Design and Prior Alert System

It is possible to use artificial intelligence algorithms to construct prediction models for a wide range of catastrophes, including natural disasters such as earthquakes, floods, hurricanes, and wildfires, as well as man-made disasters such as terrorism and industrial accidents. By analysing both past data and information that is currently being collected, these models are able to determine the likelihood of future disasters as well as the potential effect they may have. This enables preemptive planning and the allocation of resources. Early warning systems that are driven by artificial intelligence may also deliver timely alerts and essential information to populations who are at danger, which enables them to be prepared and to evacuate quickly in the event that it is necessary to do so.

Figure 3. Advantages of using ML in disaster prediction

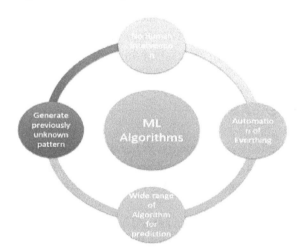

Coordination and Resource Deployment

In disaster response, AI and deep learning technologies can enhance coordination and resource deployment through the development of autonomous systems. These systems are capable of analyzing evolving situations in real-time, making rapid decisions, and adapting to dynamic circumstances. Whether it involves the deployment of emergency supplies, coordination of rescue operations, or management of infrastructure, AI-enabled autonomous systems can augment the capabilities of human responders and expedite critical actions during a crisis (UNDRR, 2019).

Risk Assessment and Mitigation

AI's ability to analyze vast and diverse datasets enables the identification of vulnerabilities in infrastructure, the assessment of disaster impact on different regions, and the recommendation of measures to mitigate risks. By conducting proactive risk assessments, AI contributes to informed urban planning, infrastructure development, and policy-making, ultimately leading to the creation of more resilient and prepared communities.

Addressing Pandemics and Public Health Emergencies

The application of AI and deep learning extends beyond natural and man-made disasters to encompass pandemics, public health emergencies, and cyber security threats. Through the analysis of data related to disease spread, healthcare resource allocation, and cuber-attacks, AI can aid in early detection, rapid response, and effective mitigation strategies, thereby playing a pivotal role in safeguarding public health and minimizing the impact of potential health crises.

As the integration of AI and deep learning continues to evolve in disaster preparedness, it is crucial to address ethical considerations and ensure responsible deployment of these technologies. Transparency, accountability, and fairness must be prioritized in the design and utilization of AI

AI ALGORITHM FOR DISASTER MANAGEMENT

Types of Data Analysis

Descriptive Analysis

The goal of descriptive analysis is to validate each hypothesis and provide an accurate account of the phenomena that are observed. Assume for the moment that our goal is to streamline a major retailer's supply chain. We begin gathering purchase and sales data, and following a conversation with a manager, we formulate the general hypothesis that the day before the weekend sees an increase in sales volume. Thus, a periodicity should serve as the foundation for our model. Its validation is the job of a descriptive study, which also aims to identify all those additional unique characteristics that were first disregarded. Giving a good answer (such, "yes, the store is open on Sunday") is the point of diagnostic analysis. Our understanding has been expanded and specialized by this new piece of information: we can now say that the series is periodic only when there is a day off, therefore (obviously, this is just an example) we shouldn't anticipate sales to go up before a workday. Using a descriptive analysis, we can quickly determine if a model is going to have bad performance or is the best option when all the known elements are included, which is useful because many machine learning models have particular requirements. We will define the properties of each dataset and what we may notice in each sample as part of our quick descriptive study. There isn't room for a detailed description in this book because the focus is on adaptive systems. However, before describing the models, I always encourage the reader to undertake a virtual analysis and envision new potential situations.

Predictive Analysis

Taking into consideration all of the possible distracting variables, the goal of a predictive model is to reduce the amount of difference that exists between the actual value and the value that was projected. For instance, the object detector in a self-driving automobile can exhibit exceptional precision and promptly identify an impediment. Nevertheless, what is the optimal course of action to take in order to accomplish a particular objective? Based on the forecaster parameters such as position, size, and speed, an alternative model should be capable of selecting the course of action that minimizes the potential for harm and maximizes the likelihood of a safe manoeuvre. This is a frequent undertaking in reinforcement learning, although it is also highly advantageous whenever a management needs to make a choice in a complex setting with several variables. The resulting model is a pipeline that receives raw inputs and utilizes the individual outputs as inputs for future models. In the aforementioned example, the store manager's primary concern is in determining the appropriate quantities of items to be ordered on a daily basis, rather than uncovering any concealed oscillations.

Supervised Learning

In a supervised situation, there is a teacher or supervisor who has the major responsibility of giving the agent an accurate estimate of its mistake, which can be directly compared with the output values. This function is facilitated by a training set consisting of pairs of input and predicted output, using current techniques. Based on this knowledge, the agent can adjust its settings in order to minimize the size of a global loss function. Therefore, it is imperative to enable the model to cultivate a capacity for generalization and prevent the occurrence of over fitting, a prevalent issue that arises from an excessive learning capacity. Following each iteration, if the algorithm is sufficiently adaptable and the data pieces are consistent, the overall accuracy improves and the discrepancy between the anticipated and expected values approaches zero. It is imperative to enable the model to cultivate a capacity for generalization and prevent the occurrence of over fitting, a typical issue that arises when the model excessively learns and adapts to specific data.

Optimizing Disaster Response With AI Algorithms

AI and deep learning algorithms are revolutionizing the field of disaster management by enabling a proactive and data-driven approach to disaster preparedness and response. These advanced technologies have shown remarkable potential in predictive modeling, autonomous systems, risk assessment, and mitigation strategies.

Autonomous Systems for Dynamic Response

The development of autonomous systems empowered by AI and deep learning has transformed the coordination of disaster response. These systems analyze evolving situations in real-time, make rapid decisions, and adapt to dynamic circumstances, augmenting the capabilities of human responders and enhancing overall response effectiveness.

Predictive Modeling for Proactive Planning

AI algorithms leverage historical data and real-time information to forecast the likelihood and potential impact of various disasters. By analyzing patterns and trends, these algorithms enable proactive planning and resource allocation, thereby enhancing preparedness and reducing the vulnerability of communities to potential hazards.

Proactive Risk Assessment and Mitigation

AI algorithms are capable of analyzing vast and diverse datasets to identify vulnerabilities in infrastructure, assess potential disaster impacts, and recommend measures to mitigate risks. This proactive risk assessment informs urban planning, infrastructure development, and policy-making, contributing to the creation of more resilient and prepared communities.

Broadening Applications Beyond Natural Disasters

The applications of AI and deep learning in disaster preparedness extend beyond natural disasters to include pandemics, public health emergencies, and cyber security threats. By analyzing data patterns related to disease spread, healthcare resource allocation, and cuber-attacks, AI contributes to early detection, rapid response, and effective mitigation strategies in these domains.

As we continue to harness the potential of AI and deep learning in disaster management, it is paramount to prioritize the ethical and responsible deployment of these technologies. When it comes to the design and deployment of artificial intelligence systems for disaster management, crucial factors that should be taken into consideration include transparency, accountability, fairness, and constant evaluation of dependability and robustness.

This integration of AI algorithms for disaster management represents a transformative opportunity to redefine our approach to handling and mitigating disasters. By embracing the challenges and maximizing the benefits of these technologies, we can build more resilient, adaptive, and proactive communities that are well-equipped to navigate the complexities of an ever changing world.

ETHICAL AND SOCIAL IMPLICATIONS OF AI IN DISASTER MANAGEMENT

The integration of AI in disaster management raises ethical and social implications that need to be carefully considered. These include issues of privacy and data security, algorithmic bias, ethical use of AI technology in decision-making processes, and the potential for increased reliance on AI to replace human judgment and decision-making. Overall, while AI and deep learning offer significant potential in improving disaster preparedness and response efforts, it is critical to approach their implementation with caution and prioritize the ethical considerations and societal impacts.

TECHNOLOGICAL ADVANCEMENTS IN DISASTER PREDICTION AND MANAGEMENT

Artificial Intelligence (AI) and Machine Learning (ML)

Predictive Modelling: AI and ML systems can analyse large volumes of data, including past weather patterns, geological data, and satellite imagery, to forecast the likelihood and intensity of natural disasters like hurricanes, floods, and wildfires.

Early Warning Systems: AI-driven early warning systems can offer more precise and rapid notifications, allowing authorities to evacuate vulnerable populations and implement precautionary steps before disasters occur.

Assessment of Damage: AI algorithms can analyze satellite images taken after a disaster to evaluate the amount of damage to infrastructure and prioritize efforts to respond, helping to speed up the recovery process.

Remote Sensing and Geographic Information Systems (GIS)

Satellite Images: Remote sensing technologies, along with GIS, enable the monitoring of environmental conditions in real-time. This includes tracking changes in sea surface temperatures, land usage, and vegetation cover, which might indicate potential natural disasters.

Disaster Mapping: GIS systems allow for the development of comprehensive disaster maps, aiding emergency responders in identifying regions at high risk, devising evacuation routes, and efficiently distributing resources during disaster response and recovery efforts.

Internet of Things (IoT) and Sensor Networks

Environmental Monitoring: Internet of Things (IoT) devices and sensor networks can gather data on several environmental factors, including rainfall, wind speed, seismic activity, and air quality. This data is essential for detecting possible risks early on and monitoring areas prone to disasters.

Infrastructure Monitoring: Internet of Things (IoT) sensors deployed in important infrastructure assets, such bridges, dams, and buildings, can identify structural irregularities and any weaknesses, enabling early repair and risk reduction.

CONCLUSION

The ethical and appropriate use of deep learning and AI in disaster preparedness must be given top priority as we continue to harness their potential. We need to make sure AI systems are regularly assessed for their robustness and dependability in real-world circumstances, and that their design prioritises openness, accountability, and justice.

In summary, the use of AI and deep learning to disaster preparedness offers a revolutionary chance to completely change how we manage and mitigate natural disasters. By confronting the challenges and achieving the full potential of these technologies, we can develop communities that are more proactive, resilient, and adaptive, and that are better fitted to manage the complexity of a world that is always changing.

REFERENCES

Agah. (2013). Introduction to medical applications of artificial intelligence. *Medical Applications of Artificial Intelligence*. CRC Press.

Allen, R. V. (1978). Automatic earthquake recognition and timing from single traces. *Bulletin of the Seismological Society of America, 68*(5), 1521–1532. doi:10.1785/BSSA0680051521

Arthi, R., & Kirubakaran, R. (2017). A Survey Paper on Preventing Packet Dropping Attack in Mobile Ad-Hoc MANET. *International Journal of Scientific Research in Computer Science, Engineering and Information Technology, 2*(2), 818–821.

Malar, C. J. (2018). A novel cluster based scheme for node positioning in indoor environment. *Int. J. Eng. Adv. Technology, 8*, 79-88.

Fang, Z., Wang, Y., Peng, L., & Hong, H. (2020). Integration of convolutional neural network and conventional machine learning classifiers for landslide susceptibility mapping. *Computers & Geosciences, 139*, 104470. doi:10.1016/j.cageo.2020.104470

Harirchian, E., Lahmer, T., & Rasulzade, S. (2020). Earthquake hazard safety assessment of existing buildings using optimized multi-layer perceptron neural network. *Energies, 13*(8), 2060. doi:10.3390/en13082060

Ibrahim, I. (2023). Revolutionizing Solar Generation Data Mining through Advanced Machine Learning Algorithms: Novel Insights and Results. CSITSS.

Ibrahim, S.P. (2019). Lazy learning associative classification in MapReduce framework. *International Journal of Recent Technology and Engineering, 7*(4), 168–172.

Ibrahim, S. P. S., & Sivabalakrishnan, M. (2020). Rare Lazy Learning Associative Classification Using Cogency Measure for Heart Disease Prediction. *Intelligent Computing in Engineering: Select Proceedings of RICE*. Springer. 10.1007/978-981-15-2780-7_74

Ibrahim. (2020). *An Evolutionary Memetic Weighted Associative Classification Algorithm for Heart Disease Prediction*. Studies in Computational Intelligence.

Kim, D., You, S., So, S., Lee, J., Yook, S., Jang, D. P., Kim, I. Y., Park, E., Cho, K., Cha, W. C., Shin, D. W., Cho, B. H., & Park, H.-K. (2018). A data-driven artificial intelligence model for remote triage in the prehospital environment. *PLoS One, 13*(10), e0206006. doi:10.1371/journal.pone.0206006 PMID:30352077

Kumar, S. S., Kalaivani, S., Ibrahim, S. P. S., & Swathi, G. (2023). Traffic and fragmentation aware algorithm for routing and spectrum assignment in Elastic Optical Network (EON). *Optical Fiber Technology*.

Lopez, C., Marti, J. R., & Sarkaria, S. (2018). Distributed reinforcement learning in emergency response simulation. *IEEE Access : Practical Innovations, Open Solutions, 6*, 67261–67276. doi:10.1109/ACCESS.2018.2878894

Meenakshi, M. (2020). Machine learning algorithms and their real-life applications: A survey. *Proceedings of the International Conference on Innovative Computing & Communications*. SSRN. 10.2139/ssrn.3595299

Najafi, Z., Pourghasemi, H. R., Ghanbarian, G., & Fallah Shamsi, S. R. (2022). Chapter 39 - identification of land subsidence prone areas and their mapping using machine learning algorithms. Computers in earth and environmental sciences.

Pekar, V., Binner, J., Najafi, H., Hale, C., & Schmidt, V. (2020). Early detection of heterogeneous disaster events using social media. *Journal of the Association for Information Science and Technology, 71*(1), 43–54. doi:10.1002/asi.24208

Priyanka, R. (2015). A Survey on Infrequent Weighted Item set Mining Approaches [IJARCET]. *International Journal of Advanced Research in Computer Engineering and Technology, 4*(1), 2278–1323.

Ream, S. (2020). Launching our open data program for disaster response. *DigitalGlobe Blog*. http://blog.digitalglobe.com/news/launching-our-opendata-program-for-disaster-response/.

Ruidas, D., Pal, S. C., Towfiqul Islam, A. R. M., & Saha, A. (2023). Hydrogeochemical evaluation of groundwater aquifers and associated health hazard risk mapping using ensemble data driven model in a water scares plateau region of eastern India. *Exposure and Health, 15*(1), 113–131. doi:10.1007/s12403-022-00480-6

Saravanan, S., Abijith, D., Reddy, N. M., Kss, P., Janardhanam, N., Sathiyamurthi, S., & Sivakumar, V. (2023). Flood susceptibility mapping using machine learning boosting algorithms techniques in Idukki district of Kerala India. *Urban Climate, 49*, 101503. doi:10.1016/j.uclim.2023.101503

Sathya, D., Siddique Ibrahim, S. P., & Jagadeesan, D. (2023). Wearable Sensors and AI Algorithms for Monitoring Maternal Health. In *Technological Tools for Predicting Pregnancy Complications* (pp. 66–68). IGI Global. doi:10.4018/979-8-3693-1718-1.ch005

United Nations Office for Disaster Risk Reduction (UNDRR). (2019). *Sendai framework for disaster risk reduction*. United Nations Disaster Risk Reduction Website. https://www.unisdr.org/we/coordinate/sendai-framework.

World Health Organization. (2019). *Definitions: emergencies*. World Health Organization Website.

Chapter 17
Machine Learning–Based Seismic Activity Prediction

Ajai V.
Velammal College of Engineering and Technology, India

S. Gandhimathi alias Usha
https://orcid.org/0000-0003-1908-6249
Velammal College of Engineering and Technology, India

B. D. S. Suntosh
Velammal College of Engineering and Technology, India

M. Muthukumar
Velammal College of Engineering and Technology, India

K. Manoj Raj
Velammal College of Engineering and Technology, India

V. Suriyanarayanan
Velammal College of Engineering and Technology, India

ABSTRACT

Earthquakes can have devastating consequences, causing ground shaking, landslides, and changes in landscapes. Fault line ruptures can alter river courses and disrupt infrastructure, while underwater earthquakes may trigger tsunamis, affecting coastal ecosystems and communities. Liquefaction can temporarily weaken the ground, leading to structural damage, and aftershocks can further exacerbate existing damage and hinder recovery efforts. Human impacts are significant and can result in injuries, fatalities, displacement, and psychological trauma. Economic consequences can involve disruption to industries and livelihoods, while response and recovery efforts may have environmental consequences. This chapter focuses on earthquake prediction using various parameters such as date, time, latitude, longitude, depth, and magnitude. The authors have used a world map as a dataset to train our model, where we predict earthquakes using gradient boosting regressor. They have broken down the complex and challenging problem into simpler like mean squared error (MSE) as a loss function, accuracy, precision, recall, F1 score, confusion matrix. As of our last knowledge update in September 2023, earthquake prediction remains a field of ongoing research and does not have precise predictive models. The advantage of this model is its accuracy which is predicted as output. However, by comparing actual datasets with predicted outcomes of occurrences, we can identify risk free areas for livelihood. The proposed model achieved an accuracy of 86.1% and 99.7% in terms of magnitude and depth, which is higher than the accuracy of existing earthquake prediction methods.

DOI: 10.4018/979-8-3693-3362-4.ch017

INTRODUCTION

Earthquakes, as major natural hazards, demand accurate prediction for effective early warning systems and timely evacuations, mitigating potential damage and loss of life. To tackle these challenges, the paper explores the application of machine learning techniques, particularly the utilization of wearable applications for data collection. The collected data is transmitted to a central server for analysis, focusing on identifying potential earthquake precursors. Challenges include gaps in understanding earthquake physics, the difficulty of handling large data volumes, and the necessity for reliable early warning systems. Despite these hurdles, ongoing research, especially utilizing a random forest classifier on a provided CSV dataset plotting earthquake occurrences, shows promising progress. Continued efforts in research and development offer hope for achieving more accurate earthquake predictions, ultimately contributing to saving lives Manoj Kollam et.al,2023. The method combines African Vulture Optimization and Neural Network for better earthquake prediction. It involves data processing, feature extraction, and Python implementation. The approach blends nature-inspired algorithms with advanced neural networks for improved accuracy Jyh-Woei Lin et.al,2018. It determines hidden layer neurons, incorporates specific earthquake features, and statistically evaluates predicted errors. The goal is to predict earthquakes independent of environmental features and identify the optimal number of hidden nodes for accurate predictions Feng jing et.al,2022. It considers microwave brightness temperature and other satellite data for a comprehensive approach. The study also addresses a Middle East dust storm event for identifying and analyzing earthquake-related signals PanXiong et.al,2022. This approach aims to improve the accuracy of earthquake anomaly detection by leveraging machine intelligence-based algorithms and smaller window sizes to learn trends, seasonality, and residual patterns in the data MD.Hasan AL Banna et.al, 2020. to predict TEC time series data and detect anomalies associated with earthquakes Shuai Huang Yuejun Lyu et.al, 2019. Extensive experimental results demonstrate the effectiveness of the proposed prediction model, achieving high prediction performance for rockfall runout range Khawaja Asim et.al,2017. This neural network architecture is specifically designed to process sequential data by leveraging feedback loops S. Anbu Kumar et.al,2021. Calculated seismic parameters based on the temporal distribution of historic seismic events. These parameters were used as inputs for from the time series data. Following the evaluation of various machine learning models, the study identifies the Light Gradient Boosting Mechanism Turgut Pura et.al,2023. Predicting the hypo central distance and peak ground motion acceleration, feature extraction from P-wave time windows, and the application of GBR for predictive modeling Rabia Tehseen et.al, 2021. Analysis by organizing and processing the sequential data to be used as inputs for the RNN model K. Mohankumar et.al, 2021. Implemented models include an ANN with three dense layers and a Random Forest Regression tuned via grid search, providing a robust approach to earthquake prediction. "Our analysis aims to predict earthquakes using a gradient boosting regressor. This approach will increase the efficiency of earthquake prediction, which is crucial for recovering from the disastrous consequences of earthquakes and reducing their associated hazards."

PROPOSED METHODOLOGY

Gradient Boosting Regressor (GBR) is an ensemble learning technique employed in earthquake prediction, combining the predictive power of multiple weak learners, usually decision trees. Unlike standalone models, GBR builds a series of weak learners sequentially, with each subsequent model aiming to correct the errors of the combined ensemble from the previous iterations. By iteratively minimizing residual errors, GBR enhances the overall accuracy of predictions, making it well-suited for capturing complex patterns in seismic data, to harness the full potential of GBR, careful tuning of hyper parameters is essential. The learning rate, controlling the impact of each weak learner on the ensemble, must strike a balance between model complexity and training efficiency. Determining the optimal number of trees, representing the iterations in the ensemble, and setting the maximum depth of each tree are crucial considerations. Hyper parameter tuning ensures that the model generalizes well to new data and effect GBR goes beyond conventional point predictions by providing estimates of uncertainty associated with each prediction. This prediction, where the inherent unpredictability of seismic event poses challenge. The model not only offers specific values for earthquake characteristics but also quantifies its confidence or uncertainty about these predictions. Understanding uncertainty is vital for informed decision-making, allowing stakeholders to gauge the reliability of the model's outputs and make appropriate risk assessments.

Algorithm

X and Y are the input and target having N samples. The function f(x) that maps the input features X to the target variables y. It is boosted trees i.e the sum of trees.

The loss function is the difference between the actual and predicted variables.

$$L(f) = \sum_{i=1}^{N} L(y_i, f(x_i)) \tag{1}$$

Minimize the loss function L(f) with respect to f.

$$\hat{f}_0(x) = \arg\min L(f) = \arg\min \sum_{i=1}^{N} L(y_i, f(x_i)) \tag{2}$$

Gradient boosting algorithm is in M stages then to improve the f_m the algorithm can add some new estimator as h_m having

$$\hat{y}_i = F_{m+1}(x_i) + h_m(x_i) \tag{3}$$

For M stage gradient boosting, The steepest Descent finds $h_m = -\rho_m g_m$ where ρ_m is constant and known as step length and g_m is the gradient of loss function L(f)

$$g_{im} = -\left[\frac{\partial L(y_i, f(x_i))}{\partial f(x_i)}\right] \tag{4}$$

Where,

$$f(x_i) = f_{m-1}(x_i)$$

The gradient Similarly for M trees

$$f_m(x) = f_{m-1}(x) + (\text{argmin}[\sum_{i=1}^{N} L(y_i, f_{m-1}(x_i) + h_m(x_i))])(x) \tag{6}$$

The current solution will be,

$$f_m = f_{m-1} - Á_m g_m \tag{7}$$

Figure 1. Gradient boosting regressor

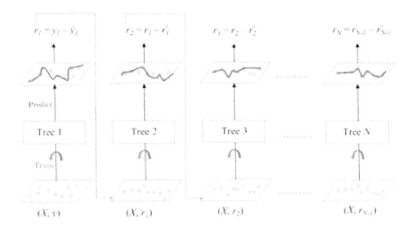

Flow

DATA SET

The earthquake data, crucial for training our predictive model, is acquired from the USGS Earthquake Hazards Program using the specified URL. This dataset, encompassing seismic events from the last 24 years (2000-2024), is an invaluable resource for understanding and predicting earthquake patterns. The retrieved data is efficiently loaded into a Pandas DataFrame, providing a structured and accessible format for further analysis and model training. This initial step ensures that our subsequent processes are built upon a foundation of comprehensive and up-to-date seismic information.

Machine Learning-Based Seismic Activity Prediction

Figure 2. Block diagram of the proposed methodology

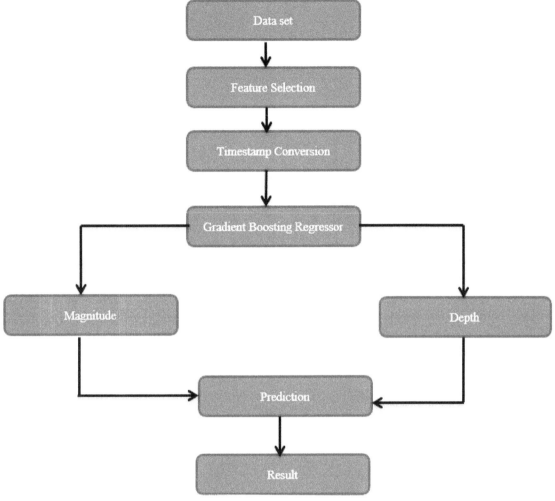

Figure 3. Data set

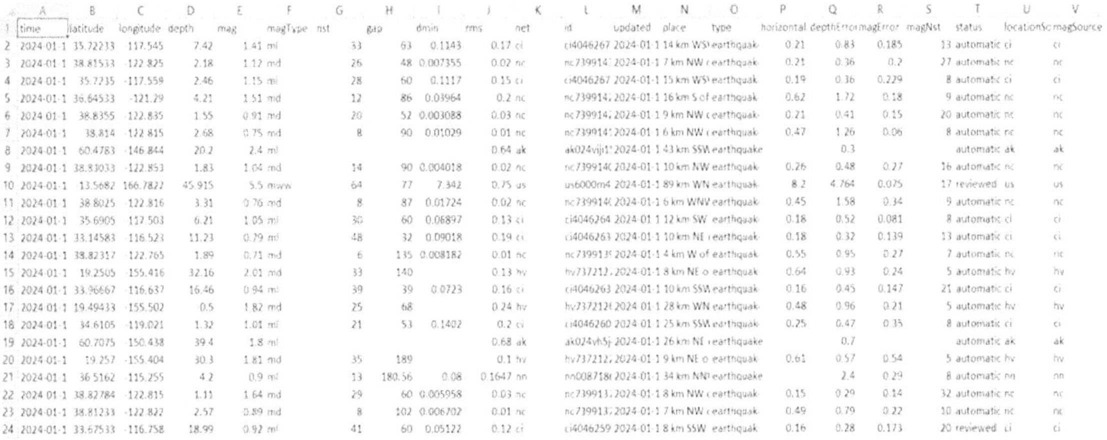

Feature Selection

Relevant features for analysis including time, latitude, longitude, depth, and magnitude, are carefully chosen from the dataset. These features are essential for training our model, as they capture key aspects of seismic events. The selection process is crucial for ensuring that the model is provided with the most pertinent information, contributing to its accuracy and predictive capabilities.

Timestamp Conversion

Timestamp processing is a crucial step in the data preparation phase, particularly when dealing with time-related features such as earthquake event timestamps. In this context, the timestamp feature undergoes a series of operations using the Pandas library to extract meaningful information and convert it into its corresponding Unix timestamp. The Unix timestamp, serving as a numeric representation of time, facilitates seamless numerical analysis and ensures compatibility with machine learning algorithms, enhancing the dataset's utility for subsequent analytical processes. To ensure robustness, error handling mechanisms, implemented through try-except blocks, address cases where a timestamp is invalid or deviates from the expected format. In such instances, an exception is caught, and a designated value (e.g., NaN or another default value) is assigned to maintain data integrity. This comprehensive timestamp processing workflow transforms human-readable timestamps into a numerical format while handling errors gracefully, resulting in a clean and consistent dataset ready for advanced analyses. The timestamp processing workflow involves extracting meaningful information from timestamps, converting them into Unix timestamps for numerical analysis, and implementing error handling mechanisms to maintain data integrity. This systematic approach results in a dataset that is well-prepared for subsequent advanced analytical processes and machine learning applications.

Figure 4. Timestamp conversion

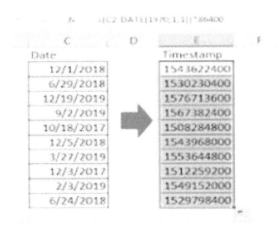

Feature Scaling

The feature scaling process is carried out using the Standard Scaler module from scikit-learn. This step is pivotal for maintaining a consistent scale across the selected features, which include 'Timestamp', 'latitude', and 'longitude'. The initialization of the Standard Scaler instance is followed by applying the fit transform method to the training data. This operation calculates the mean and standard deviation of the features in the training set and subsequently scales the data accordingly. To ensure consistence, maintaining a consistent scale across the selected features, which include 'Timestamp', 'latitude', and 'longitude'. The initialization of the Standard Scaler instance is followed by applying the fit transform method to the training data. This operation calculates the mean and standard deviation of the features in the training set and subsequently scales the data accordingly. To ensure consistency, the same scaling parameters derived from the training data are utilized to scale the test data. The primary objective of standardization in this context is to bring all features to a common scale. This becomes imperative when dealing with features that possess varying ranges or units. Specifically, within the realm of the Gradient Boosting Regressor, standardization serves to prevent any particular feature from disproportionately influencing the learning process based on its scale. Instead, it facilitates a scenario where each feature contributes proportionally, fostering a more stable and accurate model. Through the incorporation of feature scaling, the program optimally prepares the dataset for the subsequent training of the Gradient Boosting Regressor, ensuring a robust and effective learning process.

Trained Model

The training process begins by splitting the earthquake dataset into training and testing from scikit-learn. This division ensures a robust evaluation of the model's generalization performance and guards against over fitting. For predicting earthquake magnitudes (mag), a Gradient Boosting Regressor is employed. Hyper parameter tuning is executed, systematically searching for the optimal combination of parameters. The model is then trained with the identified best hyper parameters, and predictions are generated on the test set. Similarly, a Gradient Boosting Regressor is utilized for predicting earthquake depths. The hyper parameter tuning and model training processes mirror those of magnitude prediction, ensuring consistency and accuracy. This comprehensive training methodology encompasses data splitting, algorithm selection, hyper parameter optimization, and rigorous testing. The result is a well-adapted model capable of delivering precise predictions for both earthquake magnitudes and depths.

Here green elements are the learned model parameters from training, and orange represent the weak learners of the ensemble. Data, gradients, and ensemble states at each iteration, are indicated in blue. The data are used to calculate the gradients "g" and produce trained decision trees "f_m" These are then used, along with the value for "E_{m-1}", to compute the weights "γjm". "Finally, the ensemble is updated to "E_m" and the next iteration begins.

The training procedure is as follows;

1. $E_0(x) = median(y) = E_0$.
2. For $m = 1$ to M.
3. $g_n = sign(y_n - E_{m-1}(x_n))$, for all $n = 1 \ldots N$.

4. Fit a J terminal node decision tree to $\{g_n, x_n\}_1^N$, and obtain the set of terminal region $\{R_{jm}\}$
5. $\gamma jm = \text{median } x_n \in R_{jm}\left(y_n - E_{m-1}(x_n)\right)$, for all j=1.....J
6. $E_m(x) = E_{m-1}(x) + \sum_{j=1}^{J} {}^3 jm\, I(x \in R_{jm})$.

Figure 5. Tree boost

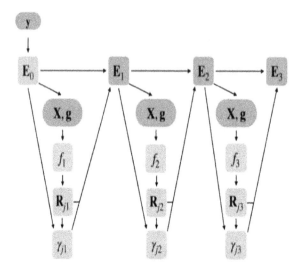

Gradient Boosting Regressor for Magnitude Prediction

Program Implementation:

In the program, a Gradient Boosting Regressor is instantiated and then subjected to hyper parameter tuning using Grid Search CV. The grid of hyper parameters includes the number of estimators learning rate and maximum depth of the individual regression estimators. The best hyperparameters are identified using cross-validated grid search The regressor is then re-instantiated with the best hyperparameters, and the training data is used to fit the model. This process ensures that the model is optimized for predicting earthquake magnitudes. After training, the model is employed to make predictions on the test, generating magnitude predictions. The program calculates various performance metrics to evaluate the model's accuracy. Metrics such as Mean Squared Error Accuracy, Precision, Recall, F1 Score, and Confusion Matrix are computed using functions from scikit-learn. The program then prints these metrics, providing a quantitative assessment of how well the model performs in predicting earthquake magnitudes. To offer a qualitative assessment, a scatter plot is created using Matplotlib. The actual magnitude values are plotted against the predicted magnitude values. Each point on the scatter plot represents an earthquake event, allowing for a visual comparison. The scatter plot is displayed, providing insights into the model's performance, such as how well it aligns with actual magnitude values.

Figure 6. Magnitude

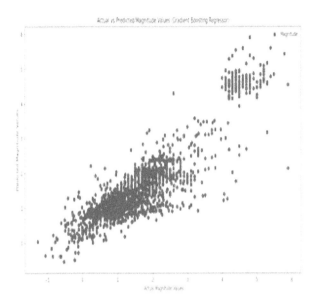

Gradient Boosting Regressor for Depth Prediction

Similar to magnitude prediction, a Gradient Boosting Regressor is used for depth prediction. The entire process, including hyper parameter tuning, model training, and prediction, is repeated specifically for earthquake depths. The program generates depth predictions using the trained model. Just like magnitude prediction, performance metrics for depth prediction are calculated and printed. This includes Mean Squared Error, Accuracy, Precision, Recall, F1 Score, and Confusion Matrix. A scatter plot is created to visualize the actual vs. predicted depth values, providing a visual representation of the model's effectiveness in predicting earthquake depths. The scatter plot for depth prediction is displayed, offering insights into how well the model aligns with actual depth values

Earthquake Prediction

The implemented system utilizes a trained Gradient Boosting Regressor model to generate predictions pertaining to potential earthquake occurrences. These predictions are subsequently portrayed on a world map, with regions highlighted in blue indicative of the model's forecasted likelihood of earthquakes. This distinct visualization serves to offer a comprehensive spatial comprehension of the model's predictive capabilities. Beyond the mere aesthetic representation on the map, the significance of these predictions extends to providing valuable insights into regions susceptible to seismic activity. The model's identification of specific areas proves instrumental in fortifying early warning systems and fortifying disaster preparedness initiatives. By pinpointing regions with a heightened likelihood of earthquake occurrence, the model actively contributes to enhancing the safety of individuals residing in or around these geographical areas. The amalgamation of predictive modeling into earthquake monitoring not only facilitates more effective risk management but also plays a pivotal role in mitigating the impact of seismic events on communities. This proactive tool equips authorities, emergency responders, and the general populace with the means to anticipate and respond to potential threats. The strategic identification of areas prone to earthquakes stands as a crucial step towards fostering a safer and more resilient environment.

Ultimately, the synergy between data visualization and predictive modeling not only advances our comprehension of seismic patterns but also empowers communities to take preemptive measures. This innovative approach significantly contributes to the overarching goal of mitigating natural disasters and safeguarding lives. The predictive capabilities showcased in this initiative underscore the transformative potential of technology in fortifying societal resilience against the vagaries of nature

Figure 7. Depth

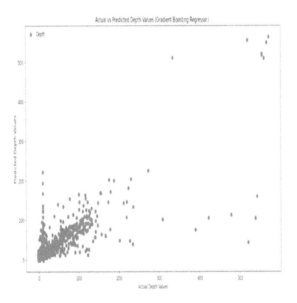

Figure 8. Predicted area in world map

RESULT AND DICUSSION

The Mean Squared Error for magnitude prediction is calculated at 0.2903, serving as a quantitative reflection of the average squared difference between predicted and actual magnitude values. A lower MSE value, in this context, denotes a higher level of accuracy in the model's magnitude predictions. The accuracy metric stands at an impressive 86.10%, indicating the proportion of correctly predicted instances out of the total observations. This metric signifies a high degree of overall correctness in the model's magnitude predictions.

Figure 9. Result module

```
================================================================
Metrics for Magnitude Prediction:
Mean Squared Error: 0.29030811840715404
Accuracy: 0.8610169491525423
Precision: 0.8142493638676844
Recall: 0.6490972210953347
F1 Score: 0.7223476297968399
Confusion Matrix:
[[1204   73]
 [ 173  320]]

Metrics for Depth Prediction:
Mean Squared Error: 980.3497787549063
Accuracy: 0.9977401129943503
Precision: 0.8571428571428571
Recall: 0.6666666666666666
F1 Score: 0.75
Confusion Matrix:
[[1760    1]
 [   3    6]]
>>>
```

Precision is reported at 81.43%, representing the accuracy of positive predictions. In the context of earthquake magnitude, this metric elucidates the reliability of the model in correctly identifying instances of actual earthquake occurrences. The recall metric is determined to be 64.91%, signifying the model's capability to capture a substantial portion of actual earthquake events. It accentuates the sensitivity of the model to true positive instances, providing insights into its performance. The F1 score, which strikes a balance between precision and recall, is calculated at 72.23%. This metric offers a comprehensive measure of the model's predictive performance, taking into account both false positives and false negatives. The confusion matrix provides a detailed distribution of true positive, true negative, false positive, and false negative predictions. In this specific instance, it indicates 1204 true negatives, 73 false positives, 173 false negatives, and 320 true positives. The Mean Squared Error for depth prediction is reported as 980.35, reflecting the average squared difference between predicted and actual depth values. The accuracy for depth prediction is notably high at 99.77%, underscoring the precision of the model in predicting the depth of earthquakes Precision is documented at 85.71%, portraying the accuracy of positive depth predictions. In the specific context of earthquake depth, this metric delineates the model's reliability in correctly identifying instances of actual depth occurrences. The recall metric is reported at 66.67%, underscoring the model's ability to capture a significant portion of actual depth events. The F1 score for depth prediction is computed as 75.00%, providing a balanced measure of the model's overall performance in predicting depth values. The confusion matrix for depth prediction offers insights into the distribution of true positive, true negative, false positive, and false negative predictions. In this case, it indicates 1760 true negatives, 1 false positive, 3 false negatives, and 6 true positives. This paper presented metrics collectively highlight the robust predictive capabilities of the Gradient Boosting Regressor for both magnitude and depth predictions. With consistently high accuracy, precision, and recall scores, the model demonstrates effectiveness in earthquake prediction, thereby contributing to elevated levels of preparedness and refined risk mitigation strategies. The below accuracy table presents a comparative analysis of different earthquake prediction methodologies, highlighting the accuracy achieved by each approach. Our proposed methodology, based on Gradient Boosting Regressor (GBR), stands out with an impressive accuracy of 86.10%. This superior performance positions it as a promising and effective model for earthquake prediction. Accuracy: 86.10% The proposed model, leveraging Gradient Boosting Regressor, exhibits the highest accuracy among the listed methodologies. This suggests a robust predictive capability and underscores the effectiveness of the chosen approach. Achieves an accuracy of 79%, indicating its predictive capabilities. Yields an accuracy of 77%, showcasing its effectiveness in earthquake prediction. Attains 71% accuracy, providing insights into the performance of neural network-based approaches. Demonstrates a competitive accuracy of 79%. Shows an accuracy of 85.80%, making it a strong performer among the existing models. Combining Support Vector Machines and Singular Value Decomposition yields an accuracy of 77.78%. Achieves an accuracy of 83.3%, highlighting the effectiveness of the Particle Swarm Optimization-based clustering approach. Combining Harmony Search Algorithm with Artificial Neural Network results in 75% accuracy. Shows a 70% accuracy, representing its performance in earthquake prediction.

Table 1. Methodology and accuracy

S.NO	METHODOLOGY	ACCURACY
1.	Proposed – GBR	86.10%
2.	Existing - LP Boost Emsemble	79%
3.	Existing - Random Forest	77%
4.	Existing – RNN	71%
5.	Existing – PRNN	79%
6.	Existing – ANN	85.80%
7.	Existing - SVM & SVD	77.78%
8.	Existing - PSO clustering algorithm	83.3%
9.	Existing - HKMC & ANN	75%
10.	Existing – KMC	70%

CONCLUSION

In conclusion, the proposed Gradient Boosting Regressor method emerges as a promising and leading approach, surpassing existing methodologies in earthquake prediction accuracy. With an emphasis on various parameters such as date, time, latitude, longitude, depth, and magnitude, and leveraging a world map as a dataset, this method is trained using the gradient boosting regressor. Its robust performance metrics, which include mean squared error (MSE), accuracy, precision, recall, F1 score, and confusion matrix, position it as a viable and effective model for enhancing preparedness and risk mitigation strategies in earthquake-prone regions. This study sheds light on the devastating consequences of earthquakes, encompassing ground shaking, landslides, changes in landscapes, and disruptions to infrastructure. Fault line ruptures, underwater earthquakes, and associated tsunamis impact coastal ecosystems and communities, while liquefaction and aftershocks compound the damage and hinder recovery efforts. The profound human impacts, including injuries, fatalities, displacement, and psychological trauma, underscore the urgency of reliable earthquake prediction. As of our last knowledge update in September 2023, earthquake prediction remains a field of ongoing research, lacking precise predictive models. However, the proposed model's standout feature is its remarkable accuracy, achieving 86.1% and 99.7% accuracy in terms of magnitude and depth, respectively. By comparing actual datasets with predicted outcomes, this model identifies risk-free areas for livelihoods. Looking towards the future, it is anticipated that this piece of work will undergo modifications and enhancements. Continuous research and development will refine the model's predictive capabilities, contributing to the evolution of more accurate and reliable earthquake prediction models. This ongoing pursuit holds the potential to further improve our ability to mitigate the profound impacts of seismic events on communities and ecosystems.

REFERENCES

Asim, K., Martínez-Álvarez, F., Basit, A., & Iqbal, T. (2017, January). Earthquake magnitude prediction in Hindukush region using machine learning techniques. *Natural Hazards*, *85*(1), 471–486. doi:10.1007/s11069-016-2579-3

Cremen, G., Velazquez, O., Orihuela, B., & Galasso, C. (2021). Predicting approximate seismic responses in multistory buildings from real-time earthquake source information, for earthquake early warning applications. *Bulletin of Earthquake Engineering*, *19*(12), 4865–4885. doi:10.1007/s10518-021-01088-y

Hammad, A., & Moustafa, M. A. (2021). Numerical analysis of special concentric braced frames using experimentally-validated fatigue and fracture model under short and long duration earthquakes. *Bulletin of Earthquake Engineering*, *19*(1), 287–316.

Jing, F., & Ramesh, P. (2022). Surface and Atmospheric Parameter Associated With the Iran M 7.3 Earthquake. IEEE.

Jyh-Woei, L. (2018). Neuronal Number in Each Hidden Layer Using Earthquake Catalogues as Training Data in Training an Embedded Back Propagation Neural Network for Predicting Earthquake Magnitude. IEEE. . doi:10.1109/ACCESS.2018.2870189

Kollam, M. (2023). *Earthquake forecasting using optimized levenberg–marquardt backpropagation neural network*. WSEAS TRANSACTIONS on COMPUTERS. . doi:10.37394/23205.2023.22.11

Al Banna, M. (2020). *Application of Artificial Intelligence in Predicting Earthquakes: State-of-the-Art and Future Challenges*. IEEE. doi:10.1109/ACCESS.2020.3029859

Pan, X. (2022). GNSS TEC-Based Earthquake Ionospheric Perturbation Detection Using a Novel Deep Learning Framework. *IEEE journal, 15*.

Pura, T., Peri, G,. A. G,., & Hameed, A. A. (2023). Earthquake Prediction for the Düzce Province in the Marmara Region Using Artificial Intelligence. *Applied Sciences (Basel, Switzerland), 13*(15), 8642. doi:10.3390/app13158642

Shabariram, C. P. (2017). International Conference on Computer Communication and Informatics (ICCCI -2017), Coimbatore, India.

Tena-Colunga, A. (2021). Conditions of structural irregularity. Relationships with observed earthquake damage in Mexico City in 2017. *Soil Dynamics and Earthquake Engineering, 143*, 106630. doi:10.1016/j.soildyn.2021.106630

Triantafyllou, I., Papadopoulos, G. A., & Lekkas, E. (2020). Impact on built and natural environment of the strong earthquakes of April 23, 1933, and July 20, 2017, in the southeast Aegean Sea, eastern Mediterranean. *Natural Hazards, 100*(2), 671–695. doi:10.1007/s11069-019-03832-9

Wu, Y., Hou, G., & Chen, S. (2021). Postearthquake resilience assessment and long-term restoration prioritization of transportation network. *Reliability Engineering & System Safety, 211*, 107612. doi:10.1016/j.ress.2021.107612

Zhang, X., Zhang, M. & Tian, X. (2021). Real-time earthquake early warning with deep learning: Application to the 2016 M 6.0 Central Apennines, Italy earthquake. *Geophysical Research Letters, 48*(5), p.2020GL089394.

Compilation of References

Yan, E., Song, J., Liu, C., Luan, J., & Hong, W. (2020). Comparison of support vector machine, back propagation neural network and extreme learning machine for syndrome element differentiation. *Artificial Intelligence Review*, *53*(4), 2453–2481. doi:10.1007/s10462-019-09738-z

Yang, L., & Shami, A. (2020). On hyperparameter optimization of machine learning algorithms: Theory and practice. *Neurocomputing*, *415*, 295–316. doi:10.1016/j.neucom.2020.07.061

Wanto, A., & Zarlis, M. (2017). Analysis of Artificial Neural Network Backpropagation Using Conjugate Gradient Fletcher Reeves in the Predicting Process. *Journal of Physics: Conference Series*, *930*(1), 1–7.

Shende, K. V., Ramesh Kumar, M. R., & Kale, K. V. (2020). Comparison of Neural Network Training Functions for Prediction of Outgoing Longwave Radiation over the Bay of Bengal. *Adv. Intell. Syst. Comput.*, *1025*, 411–419. doi:10.1007/978-981-32-9515-5_39

Leholo, S., Owolawi, P., & Akindeji, K. (2019). Solar Energy Potential Forecasting and Optimization Using Artificial Neural Network: South Africa Case Study. *2019 Amity Int. Conf. Artif. Intell.*, (pp. 533–536). IEEE. 10.1109/AICAI.2019.8701372

Wang, H., Czerminski, R., & Jamieson, A. C. (2021). Neural Networks and Deep Learning. P. Einhorn, M., Löffler, M., de Bellis, E., Herrmann, A. & Burghartz, (eds.). The Machine Age of Customer Insight. Emerald Publishing Limited. doi:10.1108/978-1-83909-694-520211010

Cong, I., Choi, S., & Lukin, M. D. (2019). Quantum convolutional neural networks. *Nature Physics*, *15*(12), 1273–1278. doi:10.1038/s41567-019-0648-8

Rem, B. S., Käming, N., Tarnowski, M., Asteria, L., Fläschner, N., Becker, C., Sengstock, K., & Weitenberg, C. (2019). Identifying quantum phase transitions using artificial neural networks on experimental data. *Nature Physics*, *15*(9), 917–920. doi:10.1038/s41567-019-0554-0

Novickis, R., Justs, D. J., Ozols, K., & Greitans, M. (2020). An Approach of Feed-Forward Neural Network. *Electronics (Basel)*, *9*(12), 2193. doi:10.3390/electronics9122193

Cichos, F., Gustavsson, K., Mehlig, B., & Volpe, G. (2020). Machine learning for active matter. *Nature Machine Intelligence*, *2*(2), 94–103. doi:10.1038/s42256-020-0146-9

Pham, B. T., Nguyen, M. D., Bui, K. T. T., Prakash, I., Chapi, K., & Bui, D. T. (2019). A novel artificial intelligence approach based on Multi-layer Perceptron Neural Network and Biogeography-based Optimization for predicting coefficient of consolidation of soil. Catena, 173. doi:10.1016/j.catena.2018.10.004

Ayyappa, Y., & Krishna, A. (2020). Enhanced and Effective Computerized Multi Layered Perceptron based Back Propagation Brain Tumor Detection with Gaussian Filtering. *Proceedings of the Second International Conference on Inventive Research in Computing Applications (ICIRCA2020).* IEEE. 10.1109/ICIRCA48905.2020.9182921

Ginantra, N. L. W. S. R., Bhawika, G. W., Achmad Daengs, G. S., Panjaitan, P. D., Arifin, M. A., Wanto, A., Amin, M., Okprana, H., Syafii, A., & Anwar, U. (2021). Performance One-step secant Training Method for Forecasting Cases. *Journal of Physics: Conference Series*, *1933*(1), 1–8. doi:10.1088/1742-6596/1933/1/012032

Chen, C. T., & Gu, G. X. (2020). Generative Deep Neural Networks for Inverse Materials Design Using Backpropagation and Active Learning. *Advancement of Science*, *7*(5), 1–10. doi:10.1002/advs.201902607 PMID:32154072

García-Ródenas, R., Linares, L. J., & López-Gómez, J. A. (2020). Memetic algorithms for training feedforward neural networks: An approach based on gravitational search algorithm. *Neural Computing & Applications*, *33*(7), 2561–2588. doi:10.1007/s00521-020-05131-y

Abdalla, R., & Esmall, M. (2018). Artificial intelligence and WebGIS for disaster and emergency management. In *WebGIS for disaster management and emergency response* (pp. 57–62). Springer.

Abdalzaher, M. S., Elsayed, H. A., Fouda, M. M., & Salim, M. M. (2023). *Employing Machine Learning and IoT for Earthquake Early Warning System in Smart Cities.* MDPI, Energies. doi:10.3390/en16010495

Abdullahi, S. I., Habaebi, M. H., & Malik, N. A. (2018). Flood disaster warning system on the go. *Proceedings of the 2018 7th international conference on computer and communication engineering (ICCCE).* IEEE. 10.1109/ICCCE.2018.8539253

Abid, S. K., Sulaiman, N., Chan, S. W., Nazir, U., Abid, M., Han, H., Ariza-Montes, A., & Vega-Muñoz, A. (2021). Toward an integrated disaster management approach: How artificial intelligence can boost disaster management. *Sustainability (Basel)*, *13*(22), 12560. doi:10.3390/su132212560

Acar, A., & Muraki, Y. (2011). Twitter for crisis communication: Lessons learned from Japan's tsunami disaster. *International Journal of Web Based Communities*, *7*(3), 392–402. doi:10.1504/IJWBC.2011.041206

Achite, M., Gul, E., Elshaboury, N., Jehanzaib, M., Mohammadi, B., & Danandeh Mehr, A. (2023). An improved adaptive neuro-fuzzy inference system for hydrological drought prediction in Algeria. *Physics and Chemistry of the Earth Parts A/B/C*, *131*, 103451. doi:10.1016/j.pce.2023.103451

Acosta-Coll, M., Solano-Escorcia, A., Ortega-Gonzalez, L., & Zamora-Musa, R. (2021). Forecasting and communication key elements for low-cost fluvial flooding early warning system in urban areas. [IJECE]. *Iranian Journal of Electrical and Computer Engineering*, *11*(5), 4143–4156. doi:10.11591/ijece.v11i5.pp4143-4156

Adams, B. J., Huyck, C., Mansouri, B., Eguchi, R., & Shinozuka, M. (2002). Post-disaster bridge damage assessment. In *Proceedings of the 15th Pecora conference: integrating remote sensing at the global, regional, and local scale.* CD-ROM.

Adams, S. M., Levitan, M., & Friedland, C. J. (2014). High resolution imagery collection for post-disaster studies utilizing unmanned aircraft systems (UAS). *Photogrammetric Engineering and Remote Sensing*, *12*(12), 1161–1168. doi:10.14358/PERS.80.12.1161

Adeel, A., Gogate, M., Farooq, S., Ieracitano, C., Dashtipour, K., Larijani, H., & Hussain, A. (2018). A survey on the role of wireless sensor networks and IoT in disaster management. In *Geological disaster monitoring based on sensor networks* (pp. 57–66). Springer.

Adger, N., & Brooks, N. (2003). *Country level risk measures of climate-related natural disasters and implications for adaptation to climate change. Working Paper 26.* Tyndall Centre for Climate Change Research. https://www.tyndall.ac.uk/publications/working_papers/wp26.pdf

Compilation of References

Ado, M., Amitab, K., Maji, A. K., Jasińska, E., Gono, R., Leonowicz, Z., & Jasiński, M. (2022). Landslide Susceptibility Mapping Using Machine Learning: A Literature Survey. *Remote Sensing, 14*(13), 3029. MDPI AG. doi:10.3390/rs14133029

Adrianto, I., Trafalis, T. B., & Lakshmanan, V. (2009). Support vector machines for spatiotemporal tornado prediction. *International Journal of General Systems, 38*(7), 759–776. doi:10.1080/03081070601068629

Agah. (2013). Introduction to medical applications of artificial intelligence. *Medical Applications of Artificial Intelligence*. CRC Press.

Agarwal, S., Fulzele, T. U., & Aggarwal, G. (2014). Flood Recovery Management in Jammu and Kashmir: A Tool for Resilience. *Asian Journal of Environment and Disaster Management, 6*(3).

Agarwal, S., Kachroo, P., & Regentova, E. (2016). A hybrid model using logistic regression and wavelet transformation to detect traffic incidents. *IATSS Research, 40*(1), 56–63. doi:10.1016/j.iatssr.2016.06.001

Agboola, A. H., Gabriel, A. J., Aliyu, E. O., & Alese, B. K. (2013). Development of a fuzzy logic bases rainfall prediction model. *IACSIT International Journal of Engineering and Technology, 3*(4), 427–435.

Aghamohammadi, H., Mesgari, M. S., Mansourian, A., & Molaei, D. (2013). Seismic human loss estimation for an earthquake disaster using neural network. *International Journal of Environmental Science and Technology, 10*(5), 931–939. doi:10.1007/s13762-013-0281-5

Aguirre, B. E. (2020). Review of Disasters: A Sociological Approach. Natural Hazards Review. ASCE Library.

Ahad, M. A., Paiva, S., Tripathi, G., & Feroz, N. (2020). Enabling technologies and sustainable smart cities. *Sustainable Cities and Society, 61*, 102301. doi:10.1016/j.scs.2020.102301

Ahmad, R., Samy, G. N., Ibrahim, N. K., Bath, P. A., & Ismail, Z. (2009). Threats identification in healthcare information systems using genetic algorithm and cox regression. In *The fifth international conference on information assurance and security,* (pp. 757–760). IEEE.

Ahmad, H. (2019). Machine Learning Applications in oceanography. *International Aquatic Research.*, 161–169. doi:10.3153/AR19014

Ahmad, K., Konstantin, P., Riegler, M., Conci, N., & Holversen, P. (2017). CNN and GAN based satellite and social media data fusion fordisaster detection. *CEUR Workshop Proceedings, 1984*, 13–15.

Ahmad, K., Pogorelov, K., Riegler, M., Ostroukhova, O., Halvorsen, P., Conci, N., & Dahyot, R. (2019). Automatic detection of passable roads after floods in remote sensed and social media data. *Signal Processing Image Communication, 74*, 110–118. doi:10.1016/j.image.2019.02.002

Ahmad, K., Riegler, M., Pogorelov, K., Conci, N., Halvorsen, P., & De Natale, F. (2017). JORD: a system for collecting information and monitoring natural disasters by linking social media with satellite imagery. In *Proceedings of the 15th International Workshop on content-based multimedia indexing.* ACM. 10.1145/3095713.3095726

Aiena, B.J., Baczwaski, B.J., Schulenberg, S.E., Buchanan, E.M. (2015). Measuring resilience with the RS–14: A tale of two samples. *Journal of Personality Assessment, 4*, 97.

AIP. (2023). *Creating tsunami early warning systems using AI*. American Instutute of Physics. https://www.sciencedaily.com/releases/2023/04/230425111152.htm

Akshya, J., & Priyadarsini, P. L. K. (2019). *A hybrid machine learning approach for classifying aerial images of flood-hit areas*. In *Proceedings of the 2019 International Conference on Computational Intelligence in Data Science (ICCIDS)*, Chennai, India. 10.1109/ICCIDS.2019.8862138

Akter, S., & Wamba, S. F. (2019). Big data and disaster management: A systematic review and agenda for future research. *Annals of Operations Research*, *283*(1-2), 939–959. doi:10.1007/s10479-017-2584-2

Akter, S., Wamba, S. F., Mariani, M., & Hani, U. (2021). How to Build an AI Climate-Driven Service Analytics Capability for Innovation and Performance in Industrial Markets? *Industrial Marketing Management*, *97*, 258–273. doi:10.1016/j.indmarman.2021.07.014

Al Banna, M. (2020). *Application of Artificial Intelligence in Predicting Earthquakes: State-of-the-Art and Future Challenges*. IEEE. doi:10.1109/ACCESS.2020.3029859

Alam, F., Imran, M., & Ofli, F. (2017). Image4Act: online social media image processing for disaster response. *IEEE/ACM International Conference on advances in social networks analysis and mining (ASONAM'17)*. IEEE. 10.1145/3110025.3110164

Alassery, F., Alzahrani, A., Khan, A. I., Irshad, K., & Islam, S. (2022). An artificial intelligence-based solar radiation prophesy model for green energy utilization in energy management system. *Sustainable Energy Technologies and Assessments*, *52*, 102060. doi:10.1016/j.seta.2022.102060

Albahri, A. S., Zaidan, A. A., Albahri, O. S., Zaidan, B. B., & Alsalem, M. A. (2018). Real-Time Fault-Tolerant mHealth System: Comprehensive Review of Healthcare Services, Opens Issues, Challenges and Methodological Aspects. *Journal of Medical Systems*, *42*(8), 137. doi:10.1007/s10916-018-0983-9 PMID:29936593

Albahri, O. S., Albahri, A. S., Mohammed, K. I., Zaidan, A. A., Zaidan, B. B., Hashim, M., & Salman, O. H. (2018). Systematic Review of Real-time Remote Health Monitoring System in Triage and Priority-Based Sensor Technology: Taxonomy, Open Challenges, Motivation and Recommendations. *Journal of Medical Systems*, *42*(5), 80. doi:10.1007/s10916-018-0943-4 PMID:29564649

Albahri, O. S., Zaidan, A. A., Zaidan, B. B., Hashim, M., Albahri, A. S., & Alsalem, M. A. (2018). Real-Time Remote Health-Monitoring Systems in a Medical Centre: A Review of the Provision of Healthcare Services-Based Body Sensor Information, Open Challenges and Methodological Aspects. *Journal of Medical Systems*, *42*(9), 164. doi:10.1007/s10916-018-1006-6 PMID:30043085

Alexander, D. (2002a). 'From civil defense to civil protection-and back again'. *Disaster Prevention and Management*, *1*(3), 209–213. doi:10.1108/09653560210435803

Alexander, D. (2002b). *Principles of Emergency Planning and Management*. Terra Publishing.

Alexandrov, D., Pertseva, E., Berman, I., Pantiukhin, I., & Kapitonov, A. (2019). Analysis of machine learning methods for wildfire security monitoring with an unmanned aerial vehicles. In Conference of Open Innovation Association (FRUCT), 8–12 April 2019. IEEE Computer Society. doi:10.23919/FRUCT.2019.8711917

Alfaiate, J., Aliabadi, M., Guagliano, M., & Susmel, L. (2007). Identification of damaged bars in three-dimensional redundant truss structures by means of genetic algorithms. *Key Engineering Materials*, *348–349*, 229–232.

Alizadeh, M., & Alizadeh, E. (2018). Evaluation of Social Vulnerability via Artificial Neural Network (ANN) Model for Earthquake Hazard in Tabriz City, Iran. Sustainability, 10, 3376.

Allen, R. M., & Melgar, D. (2019). Earthquake Early Warning: Advances, Scientific Challenges, and Societal Needs. *Annual Review of Earth and Planetary Sciences*, *47*(1), 361–388. doi:10.1146/annurev-earth-053018-060457

Allen, R. V. (1978). Automatic earthquake recognition and timing from single traces. *Bulletin of the Seismological Society of America*, *68*(5), 1521–1532. doi:10.1785/BSSA0680051521

Compilation of References

Alotaibi, A. F., Pradhan, B., & Park, H. J. (2019). Application of machine learning algorithms in landslide susceptibility modeling at Wadi Tayyah Basin, Saudi Arabia. *Geocarto International*. doi:10.1080/10106049.2018.1548361

Alruqi, A. (2023). *The Use of AI for Disasters*. Scientific Research. https://www.scirp.org/journal/paperinformation.aspx?paperid=125106

Alsamhi, S.H.; Ma, O.; Ansari, M.S.; Almalki, F.A. Survey on collaborative smart drones and internet of things for improving smartness of smart cities. IEEE Access 2019, 7, 128125–128152.

Alsumayt, A., El-Haggar, N., Amouri, L., Alfawaer, Z. M., & Aljameel, S. S. (2023). Smart Flood Detection with AI and Blockchain Integration in Saudi Arabia Using Drones. *Sensors (Basel)*, 23(11), 5148. doi:10.3390/s23115148 PMID:37299876

Altay, N., & Green, W. G. III. (2006). OR/MS research in disaster operations management. [Google Scholar] [CrossRef]. *European Journal of Operational Research*, 175(1), 475–493. doi:10.1016/j.ejor.2005.05.016

Amin, M. S., & Ahn, H. (2021). Earthquake disaster avoidance learning system using deep learning. *Cognitive Systems Research*, 66, 221–235. doi:10.1016/j.cogsys.2020.11.002

Amiri, H. (2022). Psychological Reactions after Disasters. *Natural Hazards - New Insights, 22*.

Amit, S. N. K. B., & Aoki, Y. (2017). Disaster detection from aerial imagery with convolutional neural network. In *Proceedings of the 2017 International Electronics Symposium on Knowledge Creation and Intelligent Computing (IES-KCIC)*, Surabaya, Indonesia. 10.1109/KCIC.2017.8228593

Andrews, D. F. (1974). A Robust Method for Multiple Linear Regression. *Technometrics*, 16(4), 523–531. doi:10.1080/00401706.1974.10489233

Anthopoulos, L., & Kazantzi, V. (2022). Urban energy efficiency assessment models from an AI and big data perspective: Tools for policy makers. *Sustainable Cities and Society*, 76, 103492. doi:10.1016/j.scs.2021.103492

Anuradha, B., Abinaya, C., Bharathi, M., Janani, A., & Khan, A. (2022). IoT Based natural disaster monitoring and prediction analysis for hills area using LSTM network. In: *2022 8th International Conference on Advanced Computing and Communication Systems (ICACCS)*, (vol. 1, pp. 1908–1913). IEEE. 10.1109/ICACCS54159.2022.9785121

AP. (2023). *New AI solutions developed to combat wildfires*. VOA. https://www.voanews.com/a/new-artificial-intelligence-solutions-developed-to-combat-wildfires/7282474.html

Argyroudis, S. A., Mitoulis, S. A., Chatzi, E., Baker, J. W., Brilakis, I., Gkoumas, K., Vousdoukas, M., Hynes, W., Carluccio, S., Keou, O., Frangopol, D. M., & Linkov, I. (2022). Digital technologies can enhance climate resilience of critical infrastructure. *Climate Risk Management*, 35, 100387. doi:10.1016/j.crm.2021.100387

Arinta, R. R., & Emanuel, A. W. R. (2019). Natural Disaster Application on Big Data and Machine Learning: A Review. In *In 2019 4th International Conference on Information Technology, Information Systems and Electrical Engineering (ICITISEE)* (pp. 249–254). IEEE. https://ieeexplore.ieee.org/document/9003984/ doi:10.1109/ICITISEE48480.2019.9003984

Arora, S., Kumar, S., & Kumar, S. Artificial Intelligence in Disaster Management: A Survey, *International Conference on Data Science and Applications* 10.1007/978-981-19-6634-7_56

Arrieta, B., Alejandro, N.-R., Del Ser, J., Bennetot, A., Tabik, S., Barbado, A., Garcia, S., Gil-Lopez, S., Molina, D., Benjamins, R., Chatila, R., & Herrera, F. (2020). Explainable Artificial Intelligence (XAI): Concepts, taxonomies, opportunities and challenges toward responsible AI. *Information Fusion*, 58, 82–115. doi:10.1016/j.inffus.2019.12.012

Arrue, B. C., Ollero, A., & De Dios, J. M. (2000). An intelligent system for false alarm reduction in infrared forest-fire detection. *IEEE Intelligent Systems & their Applications*, *15*(3), 64–73. doi:10.1109/5254.846287

Arthi, R., & Kirubakaran, R. (2017). A Survey Paper on Preventing Packet Dropping Attack in Mobile Ad-Hoc MANET. *International Journal of Scientific Research in Computer Science, Engineering and Information Technology*, *2*(2), 818–821.

Aruta, J. J., Benzon, R., & Guinto, R. R. (2022). Safeguarding youth health in climate-vulnerable countries. *The Lancet. Child & Adolescent Health*, *6*(4), 223–224. doi:10.1016/S2352-4642(22)00029-3 PMID:35183300

Aryal, A., Shrestha, S., & Bajracharya, B. (2011). Landslide susceptibility mapping using frequency ratio, statistical index, and weights-of-evidence model in GIS and their comparison at Mugling-Narayanghat road section in Nepal Himalaya. *Landslides*. doi:10.1007/s10346-011-0278-7

Asefa, T., Kemblowski, M., McKee, M., & Khalil, A. (2006). Multitime scale stream flow predictions: The support vector machines approach. *Journal of Hydrology (Amsterdam)*, *318*(1-4), 7–16. doi:10.1016/j.jhydrol.2005.06.001

Asim, K., Martínez-Álvarez, F., Basit, A., & Iqbal, T. (2017, January). Earthquake magnitude prediction in Hindukush region using machine learning techniques. *Natural Hazards*, *85*(1), 471–486. doi:10.1007/s11069-016-2579-3

Asklany, S. A., Elhelow, K., Youssef, I. K., & El-wahab, M. A. (2011). Rainfall events prediction using rule-based fuzzy inference system. *Atmospheric Research*, *101*(1-2), 228–236. doi:10.1016/j.atmosres.2011.02.015

Azcona, F., Hakna, M. A., Mesa-Jurado, A.-T., Perera, M. Á. D., Mendoza-Carranza, M., & Olivera-Villarroel, M. (2022). Coastal communities' adaptive capacity to climate change: Pantanos de Centla Biosphere Reserve, Mexico. *Ocean and Coastal Management*, *220*, 106080. doi:10.1016/j.ocecoaman.2022.106080

Bach, C., Gupta, A.K., Sreeja, S., & Birkmann, J. (2013). *Critical Infrastructures and Disaster Risk Reduction & National Institute of Disaster Management*. Deutsche Gesellschaft für Internationale Zusammenarbeit (GIZ) GmbH.1-76.

Badola, S., Mishra, V. N., Parkash, S., & Pandey, M. (2023). Rule-based fuzzy inference system for landslide susceptibility mapping along national highway 7 in Garhwal Himalayas, India. *Quaternary Science Advances*, *11*, 100093. doi:10.1016/j.qsa.2023.100093

Bag, S., Rahman, M. S., Rogers, H., Srivastava, G., & Pretorius, J. H. C. (2023). Climate change adaptation and disaster risk reduction in the garment industry supply chain network. Transportation Research Part e. *Transportation Research Part E, Logistics and Transportation Review*, *171*, 103031. doi:10.1016/j.tre.2023.103031

Bai, S., Wang, J., Liao, W., Liu, D., & Ding, G. (2014). Landslide susceptibility mapping using ensemble models in the Three Gorges area, China. *Geomorphology*. doi:10.1016/j.geomorph.2013.10.006

Balan M. (2020). *An Evolutionary Memetic Weighted Associative Classification Algorithm for Heart Disease Prediction*. Studies in Computational Intelligence.

Barajas, C. A., Gobbert, M. K., & Wang, J. (2019). Performance Benchmarking of Data Augmentation and Deep Learning for Tornado Prediction. 2019 IEEE International Conference on Big Data. IEEE.

Barreca, G., Gross, F., Scarfì, L., Aloisi, M., Monaco, C., & Krastel, S. (2021). The Strait of Messina: Seismotectonics and the source of the 1908 earthquake. *Earth-Science Reviews*, *218*, 103685. doi:10.1016/j.earscirev.2021.103685

Bartmann, M. (2022). The Ethics of AI-Powered Climate Nudging—How Much AI Should We Use to Save the Planet? *Sustainability (Basel)*, *14*(9), 5153. doi:10.3390/su14095153

Compilation of References

Bartók, B., Tobin, I., Vautard, R., Vrac, M., Jin, X., Levavasseur, G., Denvil, S., Dubus, L., Parey, S., Michelangeli, P.-A., Troccoli, A., & Saint-Drenan, Y.-M. (2019). A climate projection dataset tailored for the European energy sector. *Climate Services*, *16*, 100138. doi:10.1016/j.cliser.2019.100138

Basu, M., Shandilya, A., Khosla, P., Ghosh, K., & Ghosh, S. (2019). Extracting Resource Needs and Availabilities from Microblogs for Aiding Post-Disaster Relief Operations. *IEEE Transactions on Computational Social Systems*, *6*(3), 604–618. doi:10.1109/TCSS.2019.2914179

Bejiga, M. B., Zeggada, A., Nouffidj, A., & Melgani, F. (2017). A convolutional neural network approach for assisting avalanche search and rescue operations with UAV imagery. *Remote Sensing (Basel)*, *9*(2), 100. doi:10.3390/rs9020100

Beltramone, L., & Gomes, R. C. (2021). Earthquake Early Warning Systems as an Asset Risk Management Tool. *CivilEng.*, *2*(1), 120–133. doi:10.3390/civileng2010007

Ben-Hur, A., Horn, D., Siegelmann, H. T., & Vapnik, V. (2000). A support vector clustering method. In *Proceedings of the 15th International Conference on Pattern Recognition. ICPR-2000*, Barcelona, Spain. 10.1109/ICPR.2000.906177

Benzaouia, M., Hajji, B., Mellit, A., & Rabhi, A. (2023). Fuzzy-IoT smart irrigation system for precision scheduling and monitoring. *Computers and Electronics in Agriculture*, *215*, 108407. doi:10.1016/j.compag.2023.108407

Bhagat, S. K., Tiyasha, T., Kumar, A., Malik, T., Jawad, A. H., Khedher, K. M., Deo, R. C., & Yaseen, Z. M. (2022). Integrative artificial intelligence models for Australian coastal sediment lead prediction: An investigation of in-situ measurements and meteorological parameters effects. *Journal of Environmental Management*, *309*, 114711. doi:10.1016/j.jenvman.2022.114711 PMID:35182982

Bhatt, M. (2002). *Corporate Social Responsibility and Disaster Reduction: Local Overview of Gujarat. Case Study for Corporate Social Responsibility and Disaster Reduction: A Global Overview*. DFID-funded study conducted by the Benfield Grieg Hazard Research Centre, University College London. http://www.benfieldhrc.org/SiteRoot/disaster_studies/csr/csr_gujarat.pdf

Blong, R. (2004) *Natural Hazards Risk Assessment: An Australian Perspective. Issues in Risk Science 04*. Benfield Hazard Research Centre, University College London. http://www.benfieldhrc.org/activities/issues4/nhra.htm

Bookhagen, B., & Burbank, D. W. (2006). Topography, relief, and TRMM-derived rainfall variations along the Himalaya. *Geophysical Research Letters*, *33*(8), 2006GL026037. doi:10.1029/2006GL026037

Borgen Project. (2023). *Preventing Poverty*. The Borgen Project. https://borgenproject.org/solutions-to-volcanic-eruptions/

Borgia, E. (2014). The internet of things vision: Key features, applications and open issues. *Computer Communications*, *54*, 1–31. doi:10.1016/j.comcom.2014.09.008

Bragg-Sitton, S. M., Boardman, R., Rabiti, C., & O'Brien, J. (2020). Reimagining future energy systems: Overview of the US program to maximize energy utilization via integrated nuclear-renewable energy systems. *International Journal of Energy Research*, *44*(10), 8156–8169. doi:10.1002/er.5207

Breiman, L. (2001, October). Random forests. *Machine Learning*, *45*(1), 5–32. doi:10.1023/A:1010933404324

Brendel, A. B., Mirbabaie, M., Lembcke, T. B., & Hofeditz, L. (2021). Ethical Management of Artificial Intelligence. *Sustainability (Basel)*, *13*(4), 1974. doi:10.3390/su13041974

Burke, A. (2020). Calibration of Machine Learning-Based Probabilistic Hail Predictions for Operational Forecasting. *Weather and Forecasting, 35*(1), 149-168. . doi:10.1175/WAF-D-19-0105.1

Cao, Y., Yang, F., Tang, Q., & Lu, X. (2019). An attention enhanced bidirectional LSTM for early forest fire smoke recognition. *IEEE Access: Practical Innovations, Open Solutions*, *7*, 154732–154742. doi:10.1109/ACCESS.2019.2946712

Cardona, O. D. (2004). Disaster Risk and Risk Management Benchmarking. *Information and Indicators Program for Disaster Risk Management*. Institute of Environmental Studies (IDEA) and Inter-American Development Bank (IDB), Manizales. http:// idea. manizales. unal. edu. co/ Proyectos Especiales/BID/desc_gta.asp?IdActividadAcademica=33.

Catani, F. (2021). Landslide detection by deep learning of non-nadiral and crowdsourced optical images. *Landslides*, *18*(3), 1025–1044. doi:10.1007/s10346-020-01513-4

Chakraborty, S., Nagwani, N., & Dey, L. (2011). Weather Forecasting using Incremental K-means Clustering. *International Conference in High Performance Architecture and Grid Computing*. IEEE.

Chamola, V., Hassija, V., Gupta, S., Goyal, A., Guizani, M., & Sikdar, B. (2021). Disaster and Pandemic Management Using Machine Learning: A Survey. *IEEE Internet of Things Journal*, *8*(21), 16047–16071. https://ieeexplore.ieee.org/document/9295332/. doi:10.1109/JIOT.2020.3044966 PMID:35782181

Chandrasekaran, S.S., Owaise, R.S., Ashwin, S., Jain, R.M., Prasanth, S. & Venugopalan. (2009). RB2013 Investigation on infrastructural damages by rainfall-induced landslides during November. *Nilgiris India Natural hazards, 65*(3), 1535-57.

Chang, V., Sood, S. K., Sandhu, R., Singla, K., & Chang, V. (2018). IoT, big data and HPC based smart flood management framework. *Sustainable Computing: Informatics and Systems*, *20*, 102–117. doi:10.1016/j.suscom.2017.12.001

Charlson, F., Ommeren, M. van Flaxman, A., Cornett, J., Whiteford, H., & Saxena, S. (2019). New WHO prevalence estimates of mental disorders in conflict settings: a systematic review and meta-analysis. *The Lancet, 20*(10194), 240–8.

Chaudhuri, N., & Bose, I. (2020). Exploring the role of deep neural networks for post-disaster decision support. *Decision Support Systems*, *130*, 113234. doi:10.1016/j.dss.2019.113234

Chau, K. (2006). A review on the integration of artificial intelligence into coastal modeling. *Journal of Environmental Management*, *80*(1), 47–57. doi:10.1016/j.jenvman.2005.08.012 PMID:16337078

Chen, R. (2020). *Machine Learning in Tropical Cyclone Forecast Modeling: A Review*. MDPI.

Chen, Kuo, Y.-T., & Huang, T.-S. (2023). A deep learning ensemble approach for predicting tropical cyclone rapid intensification. *Atmospheric Science Letters*, *24*(5), e1151. doi:10.1002/asl.1151

Chen, S., Liu, Q., & Wang, Y. (2022). Improve near-field tsunami prediction with transfer learning. *Natural Hazards*, *98*(3), 1567–1585. doi:10.1007/s11069-021-04891-5

Chen, W., Shirzadi, A., Shahabi, H., Ahmad, B. B., Zhang, S., Hong, H., & Zhang, N. (2017). A novel hybrid artificial intelligence approachbased on the rotation forest ensemble and naïve Bayes tree classifiers for a landslide susceptibility assessment in Langao County,China. [CrossRef]. *Geomatics, Natural Hazards & Risk*, *8*(2), 1955–1977. doi:10.1080/19475705.2017.1401560

Chen, Y., Zou, X., Li, K., Li, K., Yang, X., & Chen, C. (2021). Multiple local 3D CNNs for region-based prediction in smart cities. *Information Sciences*, *542*, 476–491. doi:10.1016/j.ins.2020.06.026

Chiang, J. Y., Chen, Y. C., & Chen, Y. C. (2012). Underwater Image Enhancement: Using Wavelength Compensation and Image Dehazing (WCID). *IEEE Transactions on Image Processing*, *21*(4), 1756–1769. doi:10.1109/TIP.2011.2179666 PMID:22180510

Choi, J., Choo, Y., & Lee, K. (2019). Acoustic classification of surface and underwater vessels in the ocean using supervised machine learning. *Sensors (Basel)*, *19*(16), 3492. doi:10.3390/s19163492 PMID:31404999

Compilation of References

Choi, K. Y., & Cheung, R. W. M. (2013). Landslide disaster prevention and mitigation through works in Hong Kong. *Journal of Rock Mechanics and Geotechnical Engineering*, *5*(5), 354–365. doi:10.1016/j.jrmge.2013.07.007

Cioffi, R., Travaglioni, M., Piscitelli, G., Petrillo, A., & De Felice, F. (2020). Artificial Intelligence and Machine Learning Applications in Smart Production: Progress, Trends, and Directions. *Sustainability (Basel)*, *12*(2), 492. doi:10.3390/su12020492

Collini, E. (2022). Predicting and Understanding Landslide Events With Explainable AI. *IEEE Access (Volume 10)*. IEEE.

Comfort, L. K. (2005). *Risk, Security, and Disaster Management*, *8*, 335–356.

Comfort, L. K., Ko, K., & Zagorecki, A. (2004). Coordination in rapidly evolving disaster response systems: The role of information. *The American Behavioral Scientist*, *48*(3), 295–313. doi:10.1177/0002764204268987

Cremen, G., Velazquez, O., Orihuela, B., & Galasso, C. (2021). Predicting approximate seismic responses in multistory buildings from real-time earthquake source information, for earthquake early warning applications. *Bulletin of Earthquake Engineering*, *19*(12), 4865–4885. doi:10.1007/s10518-021-01088-y

Cullinan, P., Acquilla, S. D., & Dhara, V. R. (1996). Long term morbidity in survivors of the 1984 Bhopal gas leak. *The National Medical Journal of India*, *9*(1), 5–10. PMID:8713516

Daeli, A., & Salman, M. (2023). Power grid infrastructural resilience against extreme events. *Energies*, *16*(1), 64. doi:10.3390/en16010064

Danso-Amoako, E., Scholz, M., Kalimeris, N., Yang, Q., & Shao, J. (2012). Forecasting the Risk of Dam Failures for Sustainable Flood Retention Basins: An All-encompassing Case Study for the Broader Greater Manchester Region. Comput. Environ. Urban Syst., 423-433.

Das, L., Munikoti, S., Natarajan, B., & Srinivasan, B. (2020). Measuring smart grid resilience: Methods, challenges and opportunities. *Renewable & Sustainable Energy Reviews*, *130*, 109918. doi:10.1016/j.rser.2020.109918

Dehghanian, P., Zhang, B., Dokic, T., & Kezunovic, M. (2018). Predictive risk analytics for weather-resilient operation of electric power systems. *IEEE Transactions on Sustainable Energy*, *10*(1), 3–15. doi:10.1109/TSTE.2018.2825780

Deo, R. C., & Sahin, M. (2015). Application of the extreme learning machine algorithm for the prediction of monthly effective drought index in eastern Australia. *Atmospheric Research*, *153*, 512–525. doi:10.1016/j.atmosres.2014.10.016

Dessai, S., Adger, W. N., Hulme, M., Koehler, J., Turpenny, J., & Warren, R. (2001). *Defining and experiencing dangerous climate change. Working Paper 28*. Tyndall Centre for Climate Change Research. https://www.tyndall.ac.uk/publications/working_papers/wp28.pdf

DFID (Department for International Development). (2004a) *Disaster Risk Reduction: a development concern*. DFID, London. http://www.DFID.gov.uk/pubs/files/disaster-risk-reduction.pdf

Dger, N., Benjaminsen, K. & Svarstad, H. (2001). Advancing a Political Ecology of Global Environmental Discourses. *Development and Change, 32*(4), 667–701.

Di Stasio, P. (2022). Early Detection of Volcanic Eruption through Artificial Intelligence on board. *IEEE International Conference on Metrology for Extended Reality, Artificial Intelligence and Neural Engineering (MetroXRAINE)*. IEEE. 10.1109/MetroXRAINE54828.2022.9967616

Dilley, M., Chen, R., Deichmann, U., Lerner-Lam, A., & Arnold, M. (2005). *Natural Disaster Hotspots: A Global Risk Analysis. Hazard Management Unit, World Bank*. View. doi:10.1596/0-8213-5930-4

Dorren, L. (2003). A Review of Rockfall Mechanics and Modeling Approaches. *Progress in Physical Geography*, *27*(1), 69–87. doi:10.1191/0309133303pp359ra

DoshiJ.BasuS.PangG. (2018). From Satellite Imagery to Disaster Insights. no. Nips. arXiv. http://arxiv.org/abs/1812.07033

Drakaki, M., Gören, H. G., & Tzionas, P. (2018). An intelligent multi-agent based decision support system for refugee settlement siting. [Google Scholar] [CrossRef]. *International Journal of Disaster Risk Reduction*, *31*, 576–588. doi:10.1016/j.ijdrr.2018.06.013

Drakaki, M., & Tzionas, P. (2021). Investigating the impact of site management on distress in refugee sites using Fuzzy Cognitive Maps. [Google Scholar] [CrossRef]. *International Journal of Disaster Risk Reduction*, *60*, 102282. doi:10.1016/j.ijdrr.2021.102282

Duarte, DNex, FKerle, NVosselman, G. (2020). Satellite Image Classification of Building Damages Using Airborne. *ISPRS Annals of the Photogrammetry, Remote Sensing and Spatial Information Sciences*, *4*, 4–7.

Duk, K.L. (2018). Utilized satellite imagery in the study of earthquakes and volcanoes. *Korean Journal of Remote Sensing*, 1469-1478.

Dwarakanath, L., Kamsin, A., Rasheed, R. A., Anandhan, A., & Shuib, L. (2021). Automated machine learning approaches for emergency response and coordination via social media in the aftermath of a disaster: A review. *IEEE Access : Practical Innovations, Open Solutions*, *9*, 68917–68931. doi:10.1109/ACCESS.2021.3074819

Ekpezu, A. O., Wiafe, I., Katsriku, F., & Yaokumah, W. (2021). Using Deep Learning for Acoustic Event Classification: The Case of Natural Disasters. *The Journal of the Acoustical Society of America*, *149*(4), 2926–2935. https://pubs.aip.org/jasa/article/149/4/2926/1068002/Using-deep-learning-for-acoustic-event. doi:10.1121/10.0004771 PMID:33940915

Elmoulat, M. (2020). Edge Computing and Artificial Intelligence for Landslides Monitoring. *Procedia Computer Science*, *177*, 480–487.

EM-DAT (Emergencies Disasters Data Base). (2005). *EM-DAT: the International Disaster Database*. Center for Research on the Epidemiology of Disasters (CRED). Ecole de Santé Publique, Université Catholique de Louvain, Brussels. http://www.em-dat.net/index.htm

EM-DAT—The International Disasters Database. (n.d.). Guidelines. EM-DAT—Data Entry—Field Description/Definition. EM-DAT. https://www.emdat.be/guidelines

Esposito, M., Palma, L., Belli, A., Sabbatini, L., & Pierleoni, P. (2022). Recent Advances in Internet of Things Solutions for Early Warning Systems: A Review. *Sensors (Basel)*, *22*(6), 2124. doi:10.3390/s22062124 PMID:35336296

Fan, C., Wu, F., & Mostafavi, A. (2020). A Hybrid Machine Learning Pipeline for Automated Mapping of Events and Locations from Social Media in Disasters. [Google Scholar] [CrossRef]. *IEEE Access : Practical Innovations, Open Solutions*, *8*, 10478–10490. doi:10.1109/ACCESS.2020.2965550

Fang, Z., Wang, Y., Peng, L., & Hong, H. (2020). Integration of convolutional neural network and conventional machine learning classifiers for landslide susceptibility mapping. *Computers & Geosciences*, *139*, 104470. doi:10.1016/j.cageo.2020.104470

Feng, Z., Hu, P., Li, S., & Mo, D. (2022). Prediction of Significant Wave Height in Offshore China Based on the Machine Learning Method. MDPI. *Journal of Marine Science and Engineering*, *10*(6), 836. doi:10.3390/jmse10060836

Ferreira, A. M., Marchezini, V., Mendes, T. S. G., Trejo-Rangel, M. A., & Iwama, A. Y. (2023). A Systematic Review of Forensic Approaches to Disasters: Gaps and Challenges. *International Journal of Disaster Risk Science*, *14*(5), 722–735. doi:10.1007/s13753-023-00515-9

Compilation of References

Firoozabadi, S. M. K., Soleimani, G., Amiri, M., & Moradian, M. (2017). Review of emergency response methods in disaster management, dispatch and control of forces in emergencies. *Int. J. Econ. Perspect.*, *11*, 1737–1747.

Folke, C. (2002). *Social-ecological resilience and behavioural responses.* Beijer International Institute of Ecological Economics.

Freedy, J. R., Shaw, D. L., Jarrell, M. P., & Masters, C. R. (1992). Towards an understanding of the psychological impact of natural disasters: An application of the conservation resources stress model. *Journal of Traumatic Stress*, *5*(3), 441–454. doi:10.1002/jts.2490050308

Gambino, S., Barreca, G., Bruno, V., De Guidi, G., Ferlito, C., Gross, F., Mattia, M., Scarfì, L., & Monaco, C. (2022). Transtension at the Northern Termination of the Alfeo-Etna Fault System (Western Ionian Sea Italy): Seismotectonic Implications and Relation with Mt. Etna Volcanism. *Geosciences*, *12*(3), 128. doi:10.3390/geosciences12030128

Gambino, S., Barreca, G., Gross, F., Monaco, C., Gutscher, M.-A., & Alsop, G. I. (2022). Assessing the rate of crustal extension by 2D sequential restoration analysis: A case study from the active portion of the Malta Escarpment. *Basin Research*, *34*(1), 321–341. doi:10.1111/bre.12621

Gariano, S. L., & Guzzetti, F. (2016). Landslides in a changing climate. *Earth-Science Reviews*, *162*, 227–252. doi:10.1016/j.earscirev.2016.08.011

Ghio, D. (2023). *Assessing populations exposed to climate change: a focus on Africa in a global context.*

Glimson, A., et al. (2019). Predicting tsunami magnitude from earthquake characteristics. *Journal of Natural Disaster Prediction.*

Goda, K. (2021, January 20). Multi-hazard parametric catastrophe bond trigger design for subduction earthquakes and tsunamis. *Earthquake Spectra*, *37*(3), 1827–1848. doi:10.1177/8755293020981974

Goel, & Kumar, A. (2022). *The role of artifcial neural network and machine learning in utilizing spatial information.* Springer. doi:10.1007/s41324-022-00494-x

Gohil, M., Mehta, D., & Shaikh, M. (2024). An integration of geospatial and fuzzy-logic techniques for multi-hazard mapping. *Results in Engineering*, *21*, 101758. doi:10.1016/j.rineng.2024.101758

Gomez, B., & Kadri, U. (2023, April 25). *Creating a tsunami early warning system using artificial intelligence.* American Institute of Physics.

Gonzalez, E., Peña, R., Avila, A., Vargas-Rosales, C., & Munoz-Rodriguez, D. (2017). A Systematic Review on Recent Advances in mHealth Systems: Deployment Architecture for Emergency Response. *Journal of Healthcare Engineering*, *2017*, 9186270. doi:10.1155/2017/9186270 PMID:29075430

Gopal, L. S., Prabha, R., Pullarkatt, D., & Ramesh, M. V. (2020). Machine Learning Based Classification of Online News Data for Disaster Management. In *In 2020 IEEE Global Humanitarian Technology Conference (GHTC)* (pp. 1–8). IEEE. https://ieeexplore.ieee.org/document/9342921/ doi:10.1109/GHTC46280.2020.9342921

Goyal, H. R., Ghanshala, K. K., & Sharma, S. (2021). Post flood management system based on smart IoT devices using AI approach. *Materials Today: Proceedings*, *46*(Part 20), 10411–10417. doi:10.1016/j.matpr.2020.12.947

Griffin, Wimmers, A., & Velden, C. S. (2022). 2022, S.M. Griffin, A. Wimmers, C.S. Velden, Predicting rapid intensification in North Atlantic and eastern North Pacific tropical cyclones using a convolutional neural network. *Weather and Forecasting*, *37*(8), 1333–1355. doi:10.1175/WAF-D-21-0194.1

Guo, Z., Tian, B., Li, G., Huang, D., Zeng, T., He, J., & Song, D. (2023). Landslide susceptibility mapping in the Loess Plateau of northwest China using three data-driven techniques—A case study from middle Yellow River catchment. *Frontiers in Earth Science (Lausanne)*, *10*, 1033085. Advance online publication. doi:10.3389/feart.2022.1033085

Gupta, T., & Roy, S. (2020). A Hybrid Model Based on Fused Features for Detection of Natural Disasters from Satellite Images. In *IGARSS 2020 - 2020 IEEE International Geoscience and Remote Sensing Symposium* (pp. 1699–1702). IEEE. https://ieeexplore.ieee.org/document/9324611/ doi:10.1109/IGARSS39084.2020.9324611

Gutiérrez, F., Parise, M., De Waele, J., & Jourde, H. (2014). A review on natural and human-induced geohazards and impacts in karst. *Earth-Science Reviews*, *138*, 61–88. doi:10.1016/j.earscirev.2014.08.002

Guzzetti, F., Gariano, S. L., Peruccacci, S., Brunetti, M. T., Marchesini, I., Rossi, M., & Melillo, M. (2020). Geographical landslide early warning systems. *Earth-Science Reviews*, *200*, 102973. doi:10.1016/j.earscirev.2019.102973

Habibi Rad, M., Mojtahedi, M., & Ostwald, M. J. (2021). Industry 4.0, disaster risk management and infrastructure resilience: A systematic review and bibliometric analysis. *Buildings*, *11*(9), 411. doi:10.3390/buildings11090411

Hackbarth, M., Pavkov, T., Wetchler, J., & Flannery, M. (2012). Natural disasters: An assessment of family resiliency following Hurricane Katrina. *Journal of Marital and Family Therapy*, *38*(2), 340–351. doi:10.1111/j.1752-0606.2011.00227.x PMID:22512296

Hammad, A., & Moustafa, M. A. (2021). Numerical analysis of special concentric braced frames using experimentally-validated fatigue and fracture model under short and long duration earthquakes. *Bulletin of Earthquake Engineering*, *19*(1), 287–316.

Harirchian, E., Lahmer, T., & Rasulzade, S. (2020). Earthquake hazard safety assessment of existing buildings using optimized multi-layer perceptron neural network. *Energies*, *13*(8), 2060. doi:10.3390/en13082060

Hasan, M., Tsegaye, T., Shi, X., Schaefer, G., & Taylor, G. (2008). Model for predicting rainfall by fuzzy set theory using USDA scan data. *Agricultural Water Management*, *95*(12), 1350–1360. doi:10.1016/j.agwat.2008.07.015

Hayes, M. J., Svoboda, M. D., Wardlow, B., Anderson, M. C., & Kogan, F. (2012). Drought monitoring: Historical and current perspectives. In B. D. Wardlow, M. C. Anderson, & J. P. Verdin (Eds.), *Remote Sensing for Drought: Innovative Monitoring Approaches* (pp. 1–19). CRC Press, Taylor and Francis Group.

Henny, A. J. Lanen, v., Vogt, J.V., Andreu, J., Carrão, H., de Stefano, L., Dutra, E., Feyen, L., Forzieri, G., Hayes, M., Iglesias, A., Lavaysse, C., Naumann, G., Pulwarty, R., Spinoni, J., Stahl, K., Stefanski, R., Stilianakis, N., Svoboda, M., & Tallaksen, L.M. (2017). Climatological risk: droughts. In K. Poljanšek, M. Marin-Ferrer, T. De Groeve, I. Clark (Eds.), Science for disaster risk management 2017: knowing better and losing less (271-293). EUR 28034 EN, Publications Office of the European Union, Luxembourg.

Hernandez, E. (2023). *Escasez de agua en CDMX en los próximos tres meses* [Water shortages in Mexico City in the next three months]. WRadio. https://wradio.com.mx/radio/2023/03/07/nacional/1678220822_571080.html

Heron, M. (2021, September 27). Detection and warning of tsunamis generated by marine landslides. *IntechOpen*. doi:10.5772/intechopen.99914

Holzinger, A., Dehmer, M., Emmert-Streib, F., Cucchiara, R., Augenstein, I., Del Ser, J., Samek, W., Jurisica, I., & Díaz-Rodríguez, N. (2022). Information fusion as an integrative cross-cutting enabler to achieve robust, explainable, and trustworthy medical artificial intelligence. *Information Fusion*, *79*, 263–278. doi:10.1016/j.inffus.2021.10.007

Huang, A.-B., Lee, J.-T., Ho, Y.-T., Chiu, Y.-F., & Cheng, S.-Y. (2012). Stability monitoring of rainfall-induced deep landslides through pore pressure profile measurements. *Soil and Foundation*, *52*(4), 737–747. doi:10.1016/j.sandf.2012.07.013

Huang, G., Shen, Z., & Mardin, R. (Eds.). (2018). *Overview of Urban Planning and Water-Related Disaster Management*. Springer International Publishing.

Huang, X., Li, Z., Wang, C., & Ning, H. (2020). Identifying disaster related social media for rapid response: A visual-textual fused CNN architecture. *International Journal of Digital Earth*, *13*(9), 1017–1039. doi:10.1080/17538947.2019.1633425

Hussain, M. A., Chen, Z., Zheng, Y., Shoaib, M., Shah, S. U., Ali, N., & Afzal, Z. (2022). Landslide Susceptibility Mapping Using Machine Learning Algorithm Validated by Persistent Scatterer In-SAR Technique. *Sensors, 22*(9), 3119. MDPI AG. doi:10.3390/s22093119

Hussain, M. A., Chen, Z., Zheng, Y., Zhou, Y., & Daud, H. (2023). Deep Learning and Machine Learning Models for Landslide Susceptibility Mapping with Remote Sensing Data. *Remote Sensing, 15*(19), 4703. MDPI AG. doi:10.3390/rs15194703

Ibrahim, I. (2023). Revolutionizing Solar Generation Data Mining through Advanced Machine Learning Algorithms: Novel Insights and Results. CSITSS.

Ibrahim, S. P. S., & Sivabalakrishnan, M. (2020). Rare Lazy Learning Associative Classification Using Cogency Measure for Heart Disease Prediction. *Intelligent Computing in Engineering: Select Proceedings of RICE 2019*, (pp. 681-691). IEEE. 10.1007/978-981-15-2780-7_74

Ibrahim, S. P. S., Rakshitha, I., Vasisri, T., Aswitha, R. H., Rao, M. R., & Krishna, D. V. (2023). *Revolutionizing solar generation data mining through advanced machine learning algorithms: Novel insights and results*. CSITSS60515, 18. https://doi.org/ doi:10.1109/CSITSS60515.2023.103341

Ibrahim. (2020). *An Evolutionary Memetic Weighted Associative Classification Algorithm for Heart Disease Prediction*. Studies in Computational Intelligence.

Ibrahim, S. (2019). Lazy learning associative classification in MapReduce framework. *International Journal of Recent Technology and Engineering*, *7*(4), 168–172.

Janarthanan, R., Balamurali, R., Annapoorani, A., & Vimala, V. (2021). Prediction of rainfall using fuzzy logic. *Materials Today: Proceedings*, *37*(2), 959–963. doi:10.1016/j.matpr.2020.06.179

Jenkins, R., & Meltzer, H. (2012). *The Mental Health Impacts of Disasters*. Government Office of Science.

Jiang, W., Xi, J., Li, Z., Zang, M., Chen, B., Zhang, C., Liu, Z., Gao, S., & Zhu, W. (2022). Deep Learning for Landslide Detection and Segmentation in High-Resolution Optical Images along the Sichuan-Tibet Transportation Corridor. *Remote Sensing (Basel)*, *14*(21), 5490. doi:10.3390/rs14215490

Jing, F., & Ramesh, P. (2022). Surface and Atmospheric Parameter Associated With the Iran M 7.3 Earthquake. IEEE.

Jordan, M. I., & Mitchell, T. M. (2015). Machine learning: Trends, perspectives, and prospects. *Science*, *349*(6245), 255–260. doi:10.1126/science.aaa8415 PMID:26185243

Joshi, A., Vishnu, C., & Krishna Mohan, C. (2022). Early Detection of Earthquake Magnitude Based on Stacked Ensemble Model. *Journal of Asian Earth Sciences: X, 8*, 100122. https://linkinghub.elsevier.com/retrieve/pii/S2590056022000433

Jung, D., Tuan, V. T., Tran, D. Q., Park, M., & Park, S. (2020). Conceptual framework of an intelligent decision support system for smart city disaster management. *Applied Sciences (Basel, Switzerland)*, *10*(2), 666. doi:10.3390/app10020666

Jyh-Woei, L. (2018). Neuronal Number in Each Hidden Layer Using Earthquake Catalogues as Training Data in Training an Embedded Back Propagation Neural Network for Predicting Earthquake Magnitude. IEEE. . doi:10.1109/ACCESS.2018.2870189

Kahraman, C., Cevik-Onar, S., Oztaysi, B., & Cebi, S. (2023). Role of fuzzy sets on artificial intelligence methods: A literature review. *Transactions on Fuzzy Sets and Systems*, *2*(1), 158–178. doi:10.30495/tfss.2023.1976303.1060

Kainthura, P., & Sharma, N. (2022). Hybrid machine learning approach for landslide prediction, Uttarakhand, India. *Scientific Reports*, *12*(1), 20101. doi:10.1038/s41598-022-22814-9 PMID:36418362

Kalpana, S. (2010). Disaster: Challenges and perspectives. *Industrial Psychiatry Journal*, *19*(1), 1–4. doi:10.4103/0972-6748.77623 PMID:21694784

Kansal, A., Singh, Y., Kumar, N., & Mohindru, V. (2015). Detection of Forest Fires Using Machine Learning Technique: A Perspective. In *In 2015 Third International Conference on Image Information Processing (ICIIP)* (pp. 241–245). IEEE. https://ieeexplore.ieee.org/document/7414773/ doi:10.1109/ICIIP.2015.7414773

Kao, C. C., Huang, C. J., Lin, Y. S., Wu, G. D., & Huang, C. J. (2017). A comprehensive study on the internet of underwater things: Applications, challenges, and channel models. *Sensors (Basel)*, *17*(7), 1477. doi:10.3390/s17071477 PMID:28640220

Kar, N. (2009). Psychological impact of disasters on children: Review of assessment and interventions. *World Journal of Pediatrics*, *5*(1), 5–11. doi:10.1007/s12519-009-0001-x PMID:19172325

Kar, N. (2010). Indian research on disaster and mental health. *Indian Journal of Psychiatry*, *52*(7, Suppl 1), S286. doi:10.4103/0019-5545.69254 PMID:21836696

Kathleen Geale, S. (2012). The ethics of disaster management. *Disaster Prevention and Management*, *21*(4), 445–462. doi:10.1108/09653561211256152

Kazen, G. (2023). La falta de agua en la GAM se agudizó por el vandalismo contra los pozos de Ecatepec [The lack of wáter in the GAM was worsened by the vandalism of the Ecatepec's wells]. *Herald Mexico*. https://heraldodemexico.com.mx/nacional/2023/6/22/la-falta-de-agua-en-la-gam-se-agudizo-por-el-vandalismo-contra-los-pozos-de-ecatepec-516144.html

Kelly-Gorham, M. R., Hines, P., & Dobson, I. (2019). Using historical utility outage data to compute overall transmission grid resilience, arXiv preprint arXiv:1906.06811. doi:10.1109/MEPS46793.2019.9395039

Keya, T.A., Leela, A., Habib, N., Rashid, M., & Pugazhandhi, B. (2023). Mental Health Disorders Due to Disaster Exposure: A Systematic Review and Meta-Analysis. 15(4). e37031.

Khalaf, M. (2018). A Data Science Methodology Based on Machine Learning Algorithms for Flood Severity Prediction. In *In 2018 IEEE Congress on Evolutionary Computation (CEC)* (pp. 1–8). IEEE. https://ieeexplore.ieee.org/document/8477904/ doi:10.1109/CEC.2018.8477904

Khanh, Q. V., Hoai, N. V., Manh, L. D., Le, A. N., & Jeon, G. (2022). Wireless communication technologies for IoT in 5G: Vision, applications, and challenges. *Wireless Communications and Mobile Computing*, *2022*, 1–12. doi:10.1155/2022/3229294

Kim, D., You, S., So, S., Lee, J., Yook, S., Jang, D. P., Kim, I. Y., Park, E., Cho, K., Cha, W. C., Shin, D. W., Cho, B. H., & Park, H.-K. (2018). A data-driven artificial intelligence model for remote triage in the prehospital environment. *PLoS One*, *13*(10), e0206006. doi:10.1371/journal.pone.0206006 PMID:30352077

Kim, M., Park, M. S., Im, J., Park, S., & Lee, M.-I. (2019). Im, J.; Park, S.; Lee, M.I. Machine Learning Approaches for Detecting Tropical Cyclone Formation Using Satellite Data. *Remote Sensing (Basel)*, *11*(10), 1195. doi:10.3390/rs11101195

Kim, Y. H., Im, J., Ha, H. K., Choi, J. K., & Ha, S. (2014). Machine learning approaches to coastal water quality monitoring using goci satellite data. *GIScience & Remote Sensing*, *51*(2), 158–174. doi:10.1080/15481603.2014.900983

Kollam, M. (2023). *Earthquake forecasting using optimizedlevenberg–marquardt backpropagation neural network.* WSEAS TRANSACTIONS on COMPUTERS. . doi:10.37394/23205.2023.22.11

Kong, X., Zhang, Y., Wang, L., & Wu, J. (2023). Enhance real-time tsunami forecasting using deep learning. *Journal of Geophysical Research: Oceans, 128*(5), e2022JC018155. Doi:10.1029/2022JC018155

Koval, D., & Chowdhury, A. (2005). An investigation into extreme-weather-caused transmission line unavailability. *IEEE Power Eng. Soc. Gener. Meeting*. IEEE.

Krinitskiy, M. (2017). Application of machine learning methods to the solar disk state detection by all-sky images over the ocean. *Oceanology, Academy of Sciences of the USSR*, *57*(2), 265–269. doi:10.1134/S0001437017020126

Kumar, C., Walton, G., Santi, P., & Luza, C. (2023a). An Ensemble Approach of Feature Selection and Machine Learning Models for Regional Landslide Susceptibility Mapping in the Arid Mountainous Terrain of Southern Peru. *Remote Sensing, 15*(5), 1376. MDPI AG. doi:10.3390/rs15051376

Kumar, A., Singh, V. K., Misra, R., Singh, T. N., & Choudhury, T. (2023). Machine learning and IoT-based approaches to detect and predict rainfall-triggered landslides. *Revue d'Intelligence Artificielle*, *37*(5), 1291–1300. doi:10.18280/ria.370522

Kumar, S. S., Kalaivani, S., Ibrahim, S. P. S., & Swathi, G. (2023). Traffic and fragmentation aware algorithm for routing and spectrum assignment in Elastic Optical Network (EON). *Optical Fiber Technology*.

Kumar, T. S., & Manneela, S. (2021). A review of the progress, challenges and future trends in tsunami early warning systems. *Journal of the Geological Society of India*, *97*(12), 1533–1544. doi:10.1007/s12594-021-1910-0

Kundu, S., Biswas, S., Tripathi, D., Karmakar, R., Majumdar, S., & Mandal, S. (2023). A review on rainfall forecasting using ensemble learning techniques. *E-prime-Advances in Electrical Engineering. Electronics and Energy*, *6*, 100296. doi:10.1016/j.prime.2023.100296

Kuşku, H., Yigit, M., Ergun, S., Yigit, U., & Taylor, N. (2018). *Acoustic noise pollution from Marine Industrial activities: Exposure and Impacts*. Aquatic Research.

Lacroix, P. (2016). Landslides triggered by the Gorkha earthquake in the Langtang valley, volumes and initiation processes. *Earth, Planets, and Space*, *68*(1), 46. doi:10.1186/s40623-016-0423-3

Lagerquist, R., McGovern, A., Homeyer, C. R., Gagne, D. J. II, & Smith, T. (2020). Deep learning on three-dimensional multiscale data for next-hour tornado prediction. *Monthly Weather Review*, *148*(7), 2837–2861. doi:10.1175/MWR-D-19-0372.1

Lakshmanan, V., Ortega, K. L., & Smith, T. M. (2007). Creating spatio-temporal tornado probability forecasts using fuzzy logic and motion variability. *Fifth Conf. on Artificial Intelligence Applications to Environmental Science*. San Antonio, TX, Amer. Meteor. Soc. https://ams.confex.com/ams/87ANNUAL/techprogram/paper_119456.htm

Lamsal, R., & Kumar, T. V. V. (2020). Artificial Intelligence and Early Warning Systems. In AI and Robotics in Disaster Studies (pp. 13-32). Springer. doi:10.1007/978-981-15-4291-6_2

Larsen, J. (2003). *Record Heat Wave in Europe Takes 35,000 lives: Far Greater Losses May Lie Ahead*. Earth Policy Institute. http://www.earth-policy.org/Updates/Update29.htm

Lasala, M. (2015). Establishment of Earthquake Intensity Meter Network in the Philippines. Academic Press.

Laufer, A. & Solomon, Z. (2006). Post traumatic symptoms and post traumatic growth among Israeli youth exposed to terror incidents. *Journal of Social and Clinical Psychology, 25*(4), 429-47.

Laya, M., & Mera, K. (2021). Classification of natural disaster on online news data using machine learning. In: *5th International Conference on Electrical, Telecommunication and Computer Engineering (ELTICOM),* (vol. 5, pp. 42–46). IEEE. 10.1109/ELTICOM53303.2021.9590125

Lecun, Y., Bengio, Y., & Hinton, G. (2015). Deep learning. [Google Scholar] [CrossRef]. *Nature, 521*(7553), 436–444. doi:10.1038/nature14539 PMID:26017442

Lee, P., Kim, H., Sami Zitouni, M., Khandoker, A., Jelinek, H. F., Hadjileontiadis, L., Lee, U., & Jeong, Y. (2022). Trends in Smart Helmets With Multimodal Sensing for Health and Safety: Scoping Review. *JMIR mHealth and uHealth, 10*(11), e40797. doi:10.2196/40797 PMID:36378505

Lettieri, E. (2009). *Disaster Management: from a systematic review*. Research Gate.

Lettieri, E., Masella, C., & Radaelli, G. (2009). Disaster management: Findings from a systematic review. *Disaster Prevention and Management, 18*(2), 117–136. doi:10.1108/09653560910953207

Li, H., Caragea, D., Caragea, C., & Herndon, N. (2018). Disaster response aided by tweet classification with a domain adaptation approach. *Journal of Contingencies and Crisis Management, 26*(1), 16–27. doi:10.1111/1468-5973.12194

Lin, C. (2005). Working set selection using second order information for training support vector machines. *Journal of Machine Learning Research, 6*(Dec), 1889–1918.

Lin, A., Wu, H., Liang, G., Cardenas-Tristan, A., Wu, X., Zhao, C., & Li, D. (2020). A big data-driven dynamic estimation model of relief supplies demand in urban flood disaster. *International Journal of Disaster Risk Reduction, 49*, 101682. doi:10.1016/j.ijdrr.2020.101682

Linardos, V., Drakaki, M., Tzionas, P., & Karnavas, Y. L. (2022, May 7). Machine learning in disaster management: Recent developments in methods and applications. *Make, 4*(2), 446–473. doi:10.3390/make4020020

Li, T., Li, Z., Zhao, W., Li, X., Zhu, X., Pan, S., Feng, C., Zhao, Y., Jia, L., & Li, J. (2019). Analysis of medical rescue strategies based on a rough set and genetic algorithm: A disaster classification perspective. *International Journal of Disaster Risk Reduction, 42*, 101325. doi:10.1016/j.ijdrr.2019.101325

Liu, X., Wang, Y., Zhang, W., & Guo, X. (2023). Susceptibility of typical marine geological disasters: An overview. Springer Open. *Geoenvironmental Disasters, 10*(1), 10. Advance online publication. doi:10.1186/s40677-023-00237-6

Liu, Y., Yang, Y., Liu, C., & Gu, Y. (2015). Forest fire detection using artificial neural network algorithm implemented in wireless sensor networks. *ZTE Communications, 13*, 12–16.

Li, W., Zheng, F., & Wang, G. (2021). Develop a probabilistic tsunami hazard assessment model. *Natural Hazards and Earth System Sciences, 21*(11), 2975–2991. doi:10.5194/nhess-21-2975-2021

Li, X., Yan, D., Wang, K., Weng, B., Qin, T., & Liu, S. (2019). Flood Risk Assessment of Global Watersheds Based on Multiple Machine Learning Models. *Water (Basel), 11*(8), 1654. https://www.mdpi.com/2073-4441/11/8/1654. doi:10.3390/w11081654

Li, Y., & Goda, K. (2022, September 19). Hazard and risk-based tsunami early warning algorithms for ocean bottom sensor S-Net system in Tohoku, Japan, using sequential multiple linear regression. *Geosciences, 12*(9), 350. doi:10.3390/geosciences12090350

Loken, E. D., Clark, A. J., & Karstens, C. D. (2020). Generating Probabilistic Next-Day Severe Weather Forecasts from Convection-Allowing Ensembles Using Random Forests. *Weather and Forecasting*, *35*(4), 1605–1631. doi:10.1175/WAF-D-19-0258.1

Lopez, C., Marti, J. R., & Sarkaria, S. (2018). Distributed reinforcement learning in emergency response simulation. *IEEE Access : Practical Innovations, Open Solutions*, *6*, 67261–67276. doi:10.1109/ACCESS.2018.2878894

Lou, Lv, R., Dang, Z., Su, S., Li, T., Xinfang. (2023). *Application of machine learning in ocean data.* Springer Nature.

Løvholt, F., Lorito, S., & Harbitz, C. B. (2018). Machine learning for near-field tsunami early warning from tide gauge data. *Natural Hazards and Earth System Sciences*, *18*(1), 183–193.

Lv, L., Chen, T., Dou, J., & Plaza, A. (2022). A hybrid ensemble-based deep-learning framework for landslide susceptibility mapping. *International Journal of Applied Earth Observation and Geoinformation*, *108*, 102713. doi:10.1016/j.jag.2022.102713

Mahajan, D., & Sharma, S. (2022). Prediction of Rainfall Using Machine Learning. *4th International Conference on Emerging Research in Electronics, Computer Science and Technology, ICERECT 2022*, *9*(01).

Makwana, N. (2019). Disaster and its impact on mental health: A narrative review. *Journal of Family Medicine and Primary Care*, *8*(10), 3090–3095. doi:10.4103/jfmpc.jfmpc_893_19 PMID:31742125

Malar, C. J. (2018). A novel cluster based scheme for node positioning in indoor environment. *Int. J. Eng. Adv. Technology*, *8*, 79-88.

Manna, T., & Anitha, A. (2023). Precipitation prediction by integrating rough set on fuzzy approximation space with deep learning techniques. *Applied Soft Computing*, *139*, 110253. doi:10.1016/j.asoc.2023.110253

Mark-Moser, M. (2022). *Artificial Intelligence and Machine Learning Techniques for Submarine Landslide Detection and Susceptibility Mapping.* AGU Fall Meeting, Chicago, IL.

Martin ML(2010). Child participation in disaster risk reduction: The case of flood- affected children in Bangladesh. *Third World Quarterly, 31*(8), 1357-75.

Maspo, N.-A., Bin Harun, A. N., Goto, M., Cheros, F., Haron, N. A., & Mohd Nawi, M. N. (2020). Evaluation of Machine Learning Approach in Flood Prediction Scenarios and Its Input Parameters: A Systematic Review. *IOP Conference Series. Earth and Environmental Science*, *479*(1), 012038. https://iopscience.iop.org/article/10.1088/1755-1315/479/1/012038. doi:10.1088/1755-1315/479/1/012038

Math, S. B., Girimaji, S. C., Benegal, V., Uday Kumar, G. S., Hamza, A., & Nagaraja, D. (2006). Tsunami: Psychosocial aspects of Andaman and Nicobar islands. Assessments and intervention in the early phase. *International Review of Psychiatry (Abingdon, England)*, *18*(3), 233–239. doi:10.1080/09540260600656001 PMID:16753660

Math, S. B., Tandon, S., Girimaji, S. C., Benegal, V., Kumar, U., & Hamza, A. (2008). Psychological impact of the tsunami on children and adolescents from the andaman and nicobar islands. *Primary Care Companion to the Journal of Clinical Psychiatry*, *10*(1), 31–37. doi:10.4088/PCC.v10n0106 PMID:18311419

Matsuoka, D., Nakano, M., Sugiyama, D., & Uchida, S. (2018). Deep learning approach for detecting tropical cyclones and their precursors in the simulation by a cloud-resolving global nonhydrostatic atmospheric model. *Progress in Earth and Planetary Science*, *5*(1), 80. doi:10.1186/s40645-018-0245-y

McColl, S. T. (2022). Landslide causes and triggers. In T. Davies, (Ed.), *Landslide Hazards, Risks, and Disasters* (2nd ed., pp. 13–41). Elsevier. doi:10.1016/B978-0-12-818464-6.00011-1

Meechang, K., Leelawat, N., Tang, J., Kodaka, A., & Chintanapakdee, C. (2020). The acceptance of using information technology for disaster risk management: A systematic review. *Engineering Journal (New York)*, *24*, 111–132.

Meenakshi, M. (2020). Machine learning algorithms and their real-life applications: A survey. *Proceedings of the International Conference on Innovative Computing & Communications*. SSRN. 10.2139/ssrn.3595299

Meena, S. R., Ghosh, S., & Shukla, D. P. (2020). Landslide susceptibility mapping using hybrid machine learning models in the Bhagirathi river basin, Indian Himalaya. *Geocarto International*. doi:10.1080/10106049.2020.1760254

Mei, G., Xu, N., Qin, J., Wang, B., & Qi, P. (2020). A Survey of Internet of Things (IoT) for Geohazard Prevention: Applications, Technologies, and Challenges. *IEEE Internet of Things Journal*, *7*(5), 4371–4386. doi:10.1109/JIOT.2019.2952593

Mosavi, A., Ozturk, P., & Chau, K. (2018). Flood prediction using machine learning models: Literature review. *Water (Basel)*, *10*(11), 1536. doi:10.3390/w10111536

Mukherjee, S., Nateghi, R., & Hastak, M. (2018). A multi-hazard approach to assess sev.re weather-induced major power outage risks in the us. *Reliability Engineering & System Safety*, *175*, 283–305. doi:10.1016/j.ress.2018.03.015

Mulia, I. E., Hirobe, T., Inazu, D., Endoh, T., Niwa, Y., Gusman, A. R., Tatehata, H., Waseda, T., & Hibiya, T. (2020). Advanced tsunami detection and forecasting by radar on unconventional airborne observing platforms. *Scientific Reports*, *10*(1), 2412. doi:10.1038/s41598-020-59239-1 PMID:32051457

Munawar, S., Hafiz, F. U., Hammad, A., & Ali, T. H. (2019). *After the Flood: A Novel Application of Image Processing and Machine Learning for Post-Flood Disaster Management Construction Engineering and Management at NUST Pakistan View Project Smart City Management: Applications of Disruptive Technologies View Proj*. Research Gate. https://www.researchgate.net/publication/337773028

Murray, V., Abrahams, J., Chadi, A., Kanza, A., Lucille, A., Djillali, B., Torres, B., & Hun, C. A., Cox, C., Douris, S., Lucy, F., Urbano, P., Qunli, H., John, H., Simon, H., Wirya, K., Lidia, M., Nick, M., Luiz Leal, M., & Natalie, W. (2021). Hazard Information Profiles: Supplement to UNDRR-ISC Hazard Definition & Classification Review: Technical Report. Geneva, Switzerland, United Nations Office for Disaster Risk Reduction; Paris, France, International Science Council. Doi:10.24948/2021.05

Murthy, R. S. (2014). Mental health of survivors of 1984 Bhopal disaster: A continuing challenge. *Industrial Psychiatry Journal*, *23*(2), 86. doi:10.4103/0972-6748.151668 PMID:25788796

Nagendra, N. P., Narayanamurthy, G., & Moser, R. (2020). Management of humanitarian relief operations using satellite big data analytics: The case of Kerala floods. *Annals of Operations Research*, 1–26.

Najafi, Z., Pourghasemi, H. R., Ghanbarian, G., & Fallah Shamsi, S. R. (2022). Chapter 39 - identification of land subsidence prone areas and their mapping using machine learning algorithms. Computers in earth and environmental sciences.

Nan, Z., Hong, H., Jihong, X., & Yuntao, L. (2013). Research on post disaster psychological intervention and reconstruction model. In *IEEE Conference Anthology*. (pp. 1-4). IEEE.

Naveen, D. M. N., Roopesh, D., Reddy, J. K., & Raju, P. K. (2022). Landslide detection using machine learning algorithms. *Journal of Algebraic Statistics*, *13*(3), 2822–2828. https://publishoa.com

Nawaz Ikram, M., Basharat, M., Ali, A., Usmani, N. A., Gardezi, S. A. H., Hussain, M. L., & Riaz, M. T. (2021). Comparison of landslide susceptibility models and their robustness analysis: A case study from the NW Himalayas, Pakistan. *Geocarto International*. doi:10.1080/10106049.2021.2017010

Compilation of References

Neves, L. C., Ngo, T. Q., Dam, N. D., Al-Ansari, N., Amiri, M., Phong, T. V., Prakash, I., Le, H. V., Nguyen, H. B. T., & Pham, B. T. (2021). Landslide Susceptibility Mapping Using Single Machine Learning Models: A Case Study from Pithoragarh District, India. *Advances in Civil Engineering*, *9934732*, 1–19. doi:10.1155/2021/9934732

Newnham, E. A., Mergelsberg, E. L. P., Chen, Y., Kim, Y., Gibbs, L., Dzidic, P. L., DaSilva, M. I., Chan, E. Y. Y., Shimomura, K., Narita, Z., Huang, Z., & Leaning, J. (2022). Long term mental health trajectories after disasters and pandemics: A multilingual systematic review of prevalence, risk and protective factors. *Clinical Psychology Review*, *97*, 102203. doi:10.1016/j.cpr.2022.102203 PMID:36162175

Nex, F., Duarte, D., Steenbeek, A., & Kerle, N. (2019). Towards Real-Time Building Damage Mapping with Low-Cost UAV Solutions. *Remote Sensing (Basel)*, *11*(3), 287. doi:10.3390/rs11030287

Nhu, V. H., Mohammadi, A., Shahabi, H., Ahmad, B. B., Al-Ansari, N., Shirzadi, A., Clague, J. J., Jaafari, A., Chen, W., & Nguyen, H. (2020). Landslide Susceptibility Mapping Using Machine Learning Algorithms and Remote Sensing Data in a Tropical Environment. *International Journal of Environmental Research and Public Health*, *17*(14), 4933. doi:10.3390/ijerph17144933 PMID:32650595

NIMHANS. (2020). *Centre for PSS in Disaster Management*. National Institute of Mental Health and Nurosciences. https://nimhans.ac.in/centre-for-pss-in-disaster-management

Novia, K., Hariyanti, T., & Yuliatun, L. (2020). The Impact of Natural Disaster on Mental Health of Victims Lives: Systematic Review. *The International Journal of Science in Society*, *2*, 3.

O'Brien, G. (2006). *Climate change and disaster management*. Disasters-Wiley. doi:10.1111/j.1467-9523.2006.00307.x

OchoaK. S. (2021). A Machine learning approach for rapid disaster response based on multi-modal data. The case of housing & shelter needs. arXiv:2108.00887

Ojo, O. S., & Ogunjo, S. T. (2022). Machine learning models for prediction of rainfall over Nigeria. *Scientific African*, *16*, e01246. doi:10.1016/j.sciaf.2022.e01246

Okal, E. A., & Borrero, J. C. (2019). Predict tsunami size using deep neural networks. *Geophysical Research Letters*, *46*(14), 8297–8306. doi:10.1029/2019GL082153

Omira, R., Tkalich, P., & Fadli, F. (2017). Tsunami early warning system using deep neural networks and ocean bottom sensors. *Ocean Engineering*, *137*, 171–178.

Oyounalsoud, S., Abdallah, M., Yilmaz, A. G., Siddique, M., & Atabay, S. (2023). A new meteorological drought index based on fuzzy logic: Development and comparative assessment with conventional drought indices. *Journal of Hydrology (Amsterdam)*, *619*, 129306. doi:10.1016/j.jhydrol.2023.129306

Pa Tun, P. (2018). Flood Forecasting System for the Central Region of Myanmar. *IEEE 7th Global Conference on Consumer Electronics (GCCE 2018)*. IEEE.

Pan, X. (2022). GNSS TEC-Based Earthquake Ionospheric Perturbation Detection Using a Novel Deep Learning Framework. *IEEE journal, 15*.

Park, K., & Lee, E. H. (2024). Urban flood vulnerability analysis and prediction based on the land use using Deep Neural Network. *International Journal of Disaster Risk Reduction*, *101*(1), 104231. doi:10.1016/j.ijdrr.2023.104231

Parmar, A., Mistree, K., & Sompura, M. (2017). Machine Learning Techniques For Rainfall Prediction: A Review Machine Learning View Project Rainfall Prediction Using ANN View Project Machine Learning Techniques For Rainfall Prediction: A Review. *International Conference on Innovations in information Embedded and Communication Systems*.

Patwary, M. M., Ashraf, S., Swed, S., Beaglehole, B., & Shoib, S. (2023). Natural disaster and mental health of emergency rescue workers: Lessons learned from Turkey–Syria earthquake. *Annals of Work Exposures and Health*, *67*(80), 1018–1021. doi:10.1093/annweh/wxad043 PMID:37471243

Peek L (2008). Children and disasters: Understanding vulnerability, developing capacities, and promoting resilience- An introduction. *Children Youth and Environments, 18*(1), 1-29.

Pekar, V., Binner, J., Najafi, H., Hale, C., & Schmidt, V. (2020). Early detection of heterogeneous disaster events using social media. *Journal of the Association for Information Science and Technology*, *71*(1), 43–54. doi:10.1002/asi.24208

Perez, J. (2020). Tsunami wave height prediction using convolutional neural networks. *Journal of Coastal Research*.

Pham, B. T., Le, L. M., Bui, K. T., Le, V. M., Ly, H. B., & Prakash, I. (2020). Development of advanced artificial intelligent models for daily rainfall prediction. *Atmospheric Research*, *237*, 104845. doi:10.1016/j.atmosres.2020.104845

Pham, B. T., Tien Bui, D., & Nguyen, D. B. (2016). Landslide susceptibility mapping using GIS-based statistical models and remote sensing data in tropical environment. *Geocarto International*. doi:10.1080/10106049.2015.1086027

Pimentel, D., Berger, B., Filiberto, D., Newton, M., Wolfe, B., Karabunakis, E., Clark, S., Poom, E., Abbett, E., & Nandagopal, S. (2004). Water Resources: Agricultural and environmental issues. *Bioscience*, *54*(1), 909–918. doi:10.1641/0006-3568(2004)054[0909:WRAAEI]2.0.CO;2

Poslad, S., Middleton, S. E., Chaves, F., Tao, R., Necmioglu, O., & Bügel, U. (2015). A Semantic IoT Early Warning System for Natural Environment Crisis Management. *IEEE Transactions on Emerging Topics in Computing*, *3*(2), 246–257. doi:10.1109/TETC.2015.2432742

Pourghasemi, H. R., Gayen, A., Panahi, M., Rezaie, F., & Blaschke, T. (2019). Assessment and Mapping of Multiple Hazards Probability in Iran. journal Science of the Total Environment, 692, 556-571.

Prabhakar, M., Sankaranarayanan, S., Prabhakar, M., Satish, S., Jain, P., Ramprasad, A., & Krishnan, A. (2019). Flood prediction based on weather parameters using deep learning. *Journal of Water and Climate Change*, *11*, 1766–1783.

Pradhan. (2010). Demonstrate the application of remote sensing data and GIS in landslide hazard analysis through spatial-based statistical models. *Arabian Journal of Geosciences, 3*(3), 319-326.

Prasad, P., Loveson, V. J., Das, B., & Kotha, M. (2021). Novel ensemble machine learning models in flood susceptibility mapping. *Geocarto International*, *26*, 1892209.

Pravin, R. (2023). Expedite Quantification of Landslides Using Wireless Sensors and Artificial Intelligence for Data Controlling Practices. Computational Intelligence and Neuroscience.

Presa-Reyes, M., & Chen, S. C. (2020). *Assessing Building Damage by Learning the Deep Feature Correspondence of before and after Aerial Images*. In *Proceedings of the 2020 IEEE Conference on Multimedia Information Processing and Retrieval (MIPR)*, Shenzhen, China. 10.1109/MIPR49039.2020.00017

Priyanka, P., Kumar, P., Kala, U., & Dutt, V. (2023, October). *Enhancing Landslide Prediction in the Himalayan Region Using Machine Learning Models and Antecedent Rainfall Data: A Case Study of Kamand Valley, Himachal Pradesh, India*. Paper presented at the 9th International Congress on Information and Communication Technology (ICICT 2024), London, UK.

Priyanka, R. (2015). A Survey on Infrequent Weighted Item set Mining Approaches [IJARCET]. *International Journal of Advanced Research in Computer Engineering and Technology*, *4*(1), 2278–1323.

Puliafito, C., Mingozzi, E., Longo, F., Puliafito, A., & Rana, O. (2019). Fog computing for the internet of things: A survey. [TOIT]. *ACM Transactions on Internet Technology*, *19*(2), 1–41. doi:10.1145/3301443

PuntoporPunto. (2018). *Mapa: Cortes de agua en la CDMX [Map: Water cuts in Mexico city]*. Puntopor Punto. https://www.puntoporpunto.com/multimedia/fotos/mapa-cortes-de-agua-en-la-cdmx/

Pura, T., Peri, G,. A. G,., & Hameed, A. A. (2023). Earthquake Prediction for the Düzce Province in the Marmara Region Using Artificial Intelligence. *Applied Sciences (Basel, Switzerland)*, *13*(15), 8642. doi:10.3390/app13158642

Qin, R., Khakzad, N., & Zhu, J. (2020). An overview of the impact of Hurricane Harvey on chemical and process facilities in Texas. *International Journal of Disaster Risk Reduction*, *45*, 101453. doi:10.1016/j.ijdrr.2019.101453

Rahman, M. A. (2020). Improvement of rainfall prediction model by using fuzzy logic. *American Journal of Climate Change*, *9*(4), 391–399. doi:10.4236/ajcc.2020.94024

Ramos, R. (2023). *Aumentaron 100% los recortes de agua en la CDMX* [Water cuts increased 100% in Mexico City]. https://www.eleconomista.com.mx/politica/Aumentaron-100-los-recortes-de-agua-en-la-CDMX-20231220-0123.html

Rangra, A., & Sehgal, V. (2022). Natural disasters management using social internet of things. *Multimedia Tools and Applications*, *81*(24), 1–15. doi:10.1007/s11042-021-11486-8

Rasouli, K., Hsieh, W. W., & Cannon, A. J. (2012). Daily streamflow forecasting by machine learning methods with weather and climate inputs. *Journal of Hydrology (Amsterdam)*, *414*, 284–293. doi:10.1016/j.jhydrol.2011.10.039

Rathnayake, N., Rathnayake, U., Chathuranika, I., Dang, T. L., & Hoshino, Y. (2023). Cascade-ANFIS to simulate nonlinear rainfall-runoff relationship. *Applied Soft Computing*, *147*, 110722. doi:10.1016/j.asoc.2023.110722

Ratnasari, R. N., Taniokal, Y., Yamanaka, Y., & Mulia, I. E. (2023, September 6). Development of early warning system for tsunamis accompanied by collapse of Anak Krakatau volcano, Indonesia. *Frontiers in Earth Science (Lausanne)*, *11*, 1213493. doi:10.3389/feart.2023.1213493

Ray, P. P., Mukherjee, M., & Shu, L. (2017). Internet of Things for Disaster Management: State-of-the-Art and Prospects. *IEEE Access : Practical Innovations, Open Solutions*, *5*, 18818–18835. doi:10.1109/ACCESS.2017.2752174

Ream, S. (2020). Launching our open data program for disaster response. *DigitalGlobe Blog*. http://blog.digitalglobe.com/news/launching-our-opendata-program-for-disaster-response/.

Reichenbach, P., Rossi, M., Malamud, B. D., Mihir, M., & Guzzetti, F. (2018). A review of statistically-based landslide susceptibility models. *Earth-Science Reviews*, *180*, 60–91. doi:10.1016/j.earscirev.2018.03.001

Ren, H., & Hou, Z. J. (2021). Analysis of weather and climate extremes impact on power system outage. In *IEEE Power Energy Society General Meeting (PESGM)*. IEEE. doi:10.1109/PESGM46819.2021.9637938

Resch, B., Usländer, F., & Havas, C. (2018). Combining machine-learning topic models and spatiotemporal analysis of social media data for disaster footprint and damage assessment. *Cartography and Geographic Information Science*, *45*(4), 362–376. doi:10.1080/15230406.2017.1356242

Reynard, D., & Shirgaokar, M. (2019). Harnessing the power of machine learning: Can Twitter data be useful in guiding resource allocation decisions during a natural disaster? *Transportation Research Part D, Transport and Environment*, *77*, 449–463. doi:10.1016/j.trd.2019.03.002

Robertson, B. W., Johnson, M., Murthy, D., Smith, W. R., & Stephens, K. K. (2019). Using a combination of human insights and 'deep learning' for real-time disaster communication. *Progress in Disaster Science*, *2*, 100030. doi:10.1016/j.pdisas.2019.100030

Rose, A., & Liao, S. Y. (2005). Modeling regional economic resilience to disasters: A computable general equilibrium analysis of water service disruptions. *Journal of Regional Science*, *45*(1), 75–112. doi:10.1111/j.0022-4146.2005.00365.x

Rosso, I., Mazloff, M.R., Talley, L.D., Purkey, S.G., Freeman, N.M., & Maze, G. (2020). Water mass and biogeochemical variability in the Kerguelen sector of the Southern Ocean: A machine learning approach for a mixing hot spot. *Journal of Geophysical Research: Oceans 125*(3), e2019JC015877.

Ross, T. J. (1994). *Fuzzy logic with engineering applications* (2nd ed.). John Wiley & sons Ltd.

Ruidas, D., Pal, S. C., Towfiqul Islam, A. R. M., & Saha, A. (2023). Hydrogeochemical evaluation of groundwater aquifers and associated health hazard risk mapping using ensemble data driven model in a water scares plateau region of eastern India. *Exposure and Health*, *15*(1), 113–131. doi:10.1007/s12403-022-00480-6

Saeed Sy, A., & Gargano, S. P. (2022). Natural disasters and mental health. *International Review of Psychiatry (Abingdon, England)*, *34*(1), 16–25. doi:10.1080/09540261.2022.2037524 PMID:35584023

Safar, N. Z. M., Ramli, A., Mahdin, H., Nzdi, D., & Khalif, K. M. N. (2019). Rain prediction using fuzzy rule based system in North-West Malaysia. *Indonesian Journal of Electrical Engineering and Computer Science*, *14*(3), 1572–1581.

Safran, E. B., Nilsen, E., Drake, P., & Sebok, B. (2024). Effects of video game play, avatar choice, and avatar power on motivation to prepare for earthquakes. *International Journal of Disaster Risk Reduction*, *101*(1), 104184. doi:10.1016/j.ijdrr.2023.104184

Saha, S., Roy, J., Hembram, T. K., Pradhan, B., Dikshit, A., Abdul Maulud, K. N., & Alamri, A. M. (2021). Comparison between Deep Learning and Tree-Based Machine Learning Approaches for Landslide Susceptibility Mapping. *Water*, *13*(19), 2664. MDPI AG. doi:10.3390/w13192664

Saha, S., Bera, B., Shit, P. K., Sengupta, D., Bhattacharjee, S., Sengupta, N., Majumdar, P., & Adhikary, P. P. (2023). Modelling and predicting of landslide in Western Arunachal Himalaya, India. *Geosystems and Geoenvironment*, *2*(2), 100158. doi:10.1016/j.geogeo.2022.100158

Saha, S., Majumdar, P., & Bera, B. (2023a). Deep learning and benchmark machine learning based landslide susceptibility investigation, Garhwal Himalaya (India). *Quaternary Science Advances*, *10*, 100075. doi:10.1016/j.qsa.2023.100075

Sahota, N. (2023). AI in Disaster management. *Neil Sahora*. https://www.neilsahota.com/ai-in-disaster-management-ais-role-in-disaster-risk-reduction/

Samarakkody, A., Amaratunga, D., & Haigh, R. (2023). Technological Innovations for Enhancing Disaster Resilience in Smart Cities: A Comprehensive Urban Scholar's Analysis. *Sustainability (Basel)*, *15*(15), 12036. doi:10.3390/su151512036

Santos-Reyes, J. (2024). Awareness and risk perception of a multi-hazard megacity: The case of adolescent students. *Safety Science*, *171*, 106382. doi:10.1016/j.ssci.2023.106382

Santos-Reyes, J., & Beard, A. N. (2002). Assessing Safety Management Systems. *Journal of Loss Prevention in the Process Industries*, *15*(2), 77–95. doi:10.1016/S0950-4230(01)00066-3

Saravanan, S., Abijith, D., Reddy, N. M., Kss, P., Janardhanam, N., Sathiyamurthi, S., & Sivakumar, V. (2023). Flood susceptibility mapping using machine learning boosting algorithms techniques in Idukki district of Kerala India. *Urban Climate*, *49*, 101503. doi:10.1016/j.uclim.2023.101503

Saravi, S. (2019). *Use of Artificial Intelligence to Improve Resilience and Preparedness Against Adverse Flood Events, Special Issue Flood Risk and Resilience*. MDPI.

Sathya, D., Siddique Ibrahim, S. P., & Jagadeesan, D. (2023). Wearable Sensors and AI Algorithms for Monitoring Maternal Health. In *Technological Tools for Predicting Pregnancy Complications* (pp. 66–87). IGI Global. doi:10.4018/979-8-3693-1718-1.ch005

Satriano, C., Király, E., & van der Laan, J. W. (2020). Automate tsunami source characterization using machine learning. *Geophysical Research Letters, 47*(22), e2020GL090169. Doi:10.1029/2020GL090169

Scardino, G. (2021). Insights on the origin of multiple tsunami events affected the archaeological site of Ognina (southeastern Sicily, Italy). *Quaternary International*. doi:10.1016/j.quaint.2021.09.013

Scawthorn, C., Flores, P., Blais, N., Seligson, H., Tate, E., Chang, S., Mifflin, E., Thomas, W., Murphy, J., Jones, C., & Lawrence, M. (2006). Flood Loss Estimation Methodology. II. Damage and Loss Assessment. *Natural Hazards Review, 7*(2), 72–81. doi:10.1061/(ASCE)1527-6988(2006)7:2(72)

Schmidhuber, J. (2015). Deep Learning in neural networks: An overview. [Google Scholar] [CrossRef]. *Neural Networks, 61*, 85–117. doi:10.1016/j.neunet.2014.09.003 PMID:25462637

Scicchitano, G., Gambino, S., Scardino, G., Barreca, G., Gross, F., Mastronuzzi, G., & Monaco, C. (2022). The enigmatic 1693 AD tsunami in the eastern Mediterranean Sea: new insights on the triggering mechanisms and propagation dynamics.

Senanayake, S., Pradhan, B., Wedathanthirige, H., Alamri, A., & Park, H. J. (2024). Monitoring soil erosion in support of achieving SDGs: A special focus on rainfall variation and farming systems vulnerability. *Catena, 234*, 107537. doi:10.1016/j.catena.2023.107537

Sethi, P., & Sarangi, S. R. (2017). Internet of Things: Architectures, Protocols, and Applications. *Journal of Electrical and Computer Engineering, 2017*, 9324035. doi:10.1155/2017/9324035

Shabariram, C. P. (2017). International Conference on Computer Communication and Informatics (ICCCI -2017), Coimbatore, India.

Shahfahad, N., Naikoo, M. W., Talukdar, S., Das, T., & Rahman, A. (2022). Identification of homogenous rainfall regions with trend analysis using fuzzy logic and clustering approach coupled with advanced trend analysis techniques in Mumbai city. *Urban Climate, 46*, 101306. doi:10.1016/j.uclim.2022.101306

Shah, S. A., Ben Yahia, S., Seker, D. Z., Rathore, M. M., Hameed, S., Ben Yahia, S., & Draheim, D. (2019). *Towards Disaster Resilient Smart Cities: Can Internet of Things and Big Data Analytics Be the Game Changers?* IEEE.

Shanmugam, G., & Wang, Y. (2015). The landslide problem. *Journal of Palaeogeography, 4*(2), 109–166. doi:10.3724/SP.J.1261.2015.00071

Shano, L., Raghuvanshi, T. K., & Meten, M. (2020). Landslide susceptibility evaluation and hazard zonation techniques – a review. *Geoenvironmental Disasters, 7*(1), 18. doi:10.1186/s40677-020-00152-0

Shan, Z., Wu, H., Ni, W., Sun, M., Wang, K., Zhao, L., Liu, Y. L. A., Xie, W., Zheng, X., & Guo, X. (2022). Recent Technological and Methodological Advances for the Investigation of Submarine Landslides. MDPI. *Journal of Marine Science and Engineering, 10*(11), 1728. doi:10.3390/jmse10111728

Shekar, P. R., & Mathew, A. (2023). Assessing groundwater potential zones and artificial recharge sites in the monsoon-fed Merredu river basin, India: An integrated approach using GIS, AHP, and Fuzzy-AHP. *Groundwater for Sustainable Development, 23*, 100994. doi:10.1016/j.gsd.2023.100994

Sidle, R. C., Gallina, J., & Gomi, T. (2017). The continuum of chronic to episodic natural hazards: Implications and strategies for community and landscape planning. *Landscape and Urban Planning, 167*, 189–197. doi:10.1016/j.landurbplan.2017.05.017

Silalahi, F. E. S., Pamela, Arifianti, Y., & Hidayat, F. (2019). Landslide susceptibility assessment using frequency ratio model in Bogor, West Java, Indonesia. *Geoscience Letters*, *6*(1), 10. doi:10.1186/s40562-019-0140-4

Silove, D., Ventevogel, P., & Rees, S. (2017). The contemporary refugee crisis: An overview of mental health challenges. *World Psychiatry; Official Journal of the World Psychiatric Association (WPA)*, *16*(2), 130–139. doi:10.1002/wps.20438 PMID:28498581

Singla, M. K., Kar, H. D., & Nijhawan, P. (2019). Rain prediction using fuzzy logic. *International Journal of Engineering and Advanced Technology*, *9*(1), 2796–2799.

Sit, M. A., Koylu, C., & Demir, I. (2019). Identifying disaster-related tweets and their semantic, spatial and temporal context using deep learning, natural language processing and spatial analysis: A case study of Hurricane Irma. *International Journal of Digital Earth*, *12*(11), 1205–1229. doi:10.1080/17538947.2018.1563219

Song, X., Shabasaki, R., Yuan, N. J., Xie, X., Li, T., & Adachi, R. (2017). DeepMob: Learning Deep Knowledge of Human Emergency Behaviour and Mobility from Big and Heterogeneous Data. *ACM Transactions on Information Systems*, *35*(4), 1–19. doi:10.1145/3057280

Stanly, M. (2023, May 25). *An early warning system using AI can help predict potential tsunami risks*.

Strauss, J., & Allen, R. (2016). Benefits and Costs of Earthquake Early Warning. *Seismological Research Letters*, *87*(3), 765–772. doi:10.1785/0220150149

Sundram, S., Karim, M. E., Ladrido-Ignacio, L., Maramis, A., Mufti, K. A., Nagaraja, D., Shinfuku, N., Somasundaram, D., Udomratn, P., Yizhuang, Z., Ahsan, A., Chaudhry, H. R., Chowdhury, S., D'Souza, R., Dongfeng, Z., Firoz, A. H. M., Hamid, M. A., Indradjaya, S., Math, S. B., & Wahab, M. A. (2008). Psychosocial responses to disaster: An Asian perspective. *Asian Journal of Psychiatry*, *1*(1), 7–14. doi:10.1016/j.ajp.2008.07.004 PMID:23050979

Sun, M., Yu, F. U., Chongjing, L., & Jiang, X. (2018). *Deep learning application in marine big data mining*. Science & Technology Review.

Sun, W., Bocchini, P., & Davison, B. D. (2020). Applications of artificial intelligence for disaster management. *Natural Hazards*, *103*(3), 2631–2689. doi:10.1007/s11069-020-04124-3

Syifa, M., Kadavi, P. R., & Lee, C.-W. (2019). An Artificial Intelligence Application for Post-Earthquake Damage Mapping in Palu, CentralSulawesi, Indonesia. *Sensors (Basel)*, *19*(3), 542. doi:10.3390/s19030542 PMID:30696050

Tabbakhha, M., & Astaneh-Asl, A. (2022). Analysis of the collapsed and replaced Tex-Wash bridges exposed to severe floods. *International Journal of Earthquake and Impact Engineering*, *4*(1), 30. doi:10.1504/IJEIE.2022.122821

Tang, H., Cheng, T. C. E., Elalouf, A., & Levner, E. (2014). Efficient computation of evacuation routes on a three-dimensional geometric network. *Computers & Industrial Engineering*, *76*, 231–242. doi:10.1016/j.cie.2014.08.003

Tanyu, B. F., Abbaspour, A., Alimohammadlou, Y., & Tecuci, G. (2021). Landslide Susceptibility Analyses Using Random Forest, C4.5, and C5.0 with Balanced and Unbalanced Datasets. *Catena*, *203*, 105355. https://linkinghub.elsevier.com/retrieve/pii/S0341816221002149. doi:10.1016/j.catena.2021.105355

Tao, Z., Shu, Y., Yang, X., Peng, Y., Chen, Q., & Zhang, H. (2020). Physical model test study on shear strength characteristics of slope sliding surface in Nanfen open-pit mine. *International Journal of Mining Science and Technology*, *30*(3), 421–429. doi:10.1016/j.ijmst.2020.05.006

Tapsell, S.M., Penning-Rowsell, E.C., Tunstall, S.M., & Wilson, T.L. (2002). Vulnerability to flooding:health and social dimensions. Philosophical transactions of the royal society of London. *Series A: Mathematical, Physical and Engineering Sciences, 24*(360).

Compilation of References

Tena-Colunga, A. (2021). Conditions of structural irregularity. Relationships with observed earthquake damage in Mexico City in 2017. *Soil Dynamics and Earthquake Engineering*, *143*, 106630. doi:10.1016/j.soildyn.2021.106630

The National Emergency Management Agency (NEMA) in Seoul. (2012). Development of Active Fault Map and Seismic Risk Map. NEMA.

Theodore, B. (2007). Active Learning with Support Vector Machines for Tornado Prediction, Home Computational Science – ICCS 2007. *7th International Conference*, Beijing China.

Tian, Y., Zhang, Y., & Fujita, K. (2019). Earthquake-triggered tsunami forecast using deep learning. *Natural Hazards*, *99*(3), 1509–1525.

Tiu, E. S. K., Huang, Y. F., Ng, J. L., AlDahoul, N., Ahmed, A. N., & Elshafie, A. (2022). An Evaluation of Various Data Pre-Processing Techniques with Machine Learning Models for Water Level Prediction. *Natural Hazards*, *110*(1), 121–153. https://link.springer.com/10.1007/s11069-021-04939-8. doi:10.1007/s11069-021-04939-8

Trafalis, T. B., Adrianto, I., Richman, M. B., & Lakshmivarahan, S. (2014). Machine-learning classifiers for imbalanced tornado data. *Computational Management Science*, *11*(4), 403–418. doi:10.1007/s10287-013-0174-6

Triantafyllou, I., Papadopoulos, G. A., & Lekkas, E. (2020). Impact on built and natural environment of the strong earthquakes of April 23, 1933, and July 20, 2017, in the southeast Aegean Sea, eastern Mediterranean. *Natural Hazards*, *100*(2), 671–695. doi:10.1007/s11069-019-03832-9

Tufail, S., Riggs, H., Tariq, M., & Sarwat, A. I. (2023). Advancements and Challenges in Machine Learning: A Comprehensive Review of Models, Libraries, Applications, and Algorithms. *Electronics (Basel)*, *12*(8), 1789. https://www.mdpi.com/2079-9292/12/8/1789. doi:10.3390/electronics12081789

Tunstall, S., Tapsell, S., Green, C., Floyd, P., & George, C. (2006). The health effects of flooding: social research results from England and Wales. *Journal of water and health, 4*(3), 365-80.

Turner, A. K., & Schuster, R. L. (1996). *Landslides: Investigation and Mitigation. Special Report 247*. Transportation Research Board, The National Academies Press, Washington DC.

Twister. (n.d.). In Merriam-Webster.com.

UNDRR. (2009). *UNISDR terminology on disaster risk reduction*. Geneva, Switzerland. https://www.unisdr.org/files/7817_UNISDRTerminologyEnglish.pdf

UNESCO. (n.d.). *Applying AI Based Models to predict tsunamis*. UNESCO. https://www.unesco.org/en/articles/applying-ai-based-models-predict-tsunamis

UNISDR. (2006). *Global Survey of Early Warning Systems*. United Nations International Strategy for Disaster Reduction Geneva.

United Nations Office for Disaster Risk Reduction (UNDRR). (2009). *UNISDR Terminology on Disaster Risk Reduction*. UNISDR: Geneva, Switzerland. https://www.unisdr.org/files/7817_UNISDRTerminologyEnglish.pdf

United Nations Office for Disaster Risk Reduction (UNDRR). (2019). *Sendai framework for disaster risk reduction*. United Nations Disaster Risk Reduction Website. https://www.unisdr.org/we/coordinate/sendai-framework.

University of Sheffield. (n.d.). *Using AI to reduce urban flooding*. University of Sheffield. https://www.sheffield.ac.uk/engineering/about/partnerships/using-artificial-intelligence-reduce-urban-flooding

UN-SDG (UN-Sustainable Development Goals). (2023). *Sustainable development goals*. UN. https://www.un.org/sustainabledevelopment/

Valade, S., Ley, A., Massimetti, F., D'Hondt, O., Laiolo, M., Coppola, D., Loibl, D., Hellwich, O., & Walter, T. R. (2019). Towards Global Volcano Monitoring Using Multisensor Sentinel Missions and Artificial Intelligence: The MOUNTS Monitoring System. *Remote Sensing (Basel)*, *11*(13), 1528. doi:10.3390/rs11131528

Van Wassenhove, L. N. (2006). Blackett memorial lecture humanitarian aid logistics: Supply chain management in high gear. *The Journal of the Operational Research Society*, *57*(5), 475–489. doi:10.1057/palgrave.jors.2602125

Vetrivel, A., Gerke, M., Kerle, N., Nex, F., & Vosselman, G. (2018). Disaster damage detection through synergistic use of deep learningand 3D point cloud features derived from very high resolution oblique aerial images, and multiple-kernel-learning. *ISPRS Journal of Photogrammetry and Remote Sensing*, *140*, 45–59. doi:10.1016/j.isprsjprs.2017.03.001

Vogt, J. V., & Somma, F. (2000). *Drought and Drought Mitigation in Europe - Advances in Natural and Technological Hazards Research 14*. Kluwer Academic Publishers. doi:10.1007/978-94-015-9472-1

Wachinger G, Renn O, Bianchizza C, Coates T, De Marchi B, Domènech L, Jakobson I, Kuhlicke C, Lemkow L, Pellizzoni L(2010). Risk perception and natural hazards. *WP3-Report of the CapHaz-Net Projekt*.

Wachinger, G., Renn, O., Begg, C., & Kuhlicke, C. (2013). The risk perception paradox-implications for governance and communication of natural hazards. *Risk Analysis*, *33*(6), 1049–1065. doi:10.1111/j.1539-6924.2012.01942.x PMID:23278120

Wallemacq, P. (2018). *Economic Losses; Poverty & Disasters*. Centre for Research on the Epidemiology of Disasters.

Wang, G. & Sassa, K. (2003). Pore-pressure generation and movement of rainfall-induced landslides: effects of grain size and fine-particle content. *Engineering geology, 69*(1-2)109-25.

Wang, Y. (2022). Real-time tsunami forecast using High-Frequency (HF) radar data assimilation. *Journal of Oceanographic Engineering*.

Wang, Y., & Satake, K. (2021, March 10). Real-time tsunami data assimilation of S-Net pressure gauge records during the 2016 Fukushima earthquake. *Seismological Research Letters*, *92*(4), 2145–2155. doi:10.1785/0220200447

Watts, J. (2015). Mexico City's water crisis-from source to sewer. *The Guardian*. https://www.theguardian.com/cities/2015/nov/12/mexico-city-water-crisis-source-sewer

WEF. (2023). *Successful Pilot Shows how AI can Fight Wildfires*. WEF. https://www.weforum.org/press/2023/01/successful-pilot-shows-how-artificial-intelligence-can-fight-wildfires/

Wen-Bing, J. (2024). Implementing advanced techniques for urban mountain torrent surveillance and early warning using rainfall predictive analysis. *Urban Climate*, *53*, 101782. doi:10.1016/j.uclim.2023.101782

Widiasari, I. R., & Nugroho, L. E. (2017). Deep learning multilayer perceptron (MLP) for flood prediction model using wireless sensor network based hydrology time series data mining. *2017 International Conference on Innovative and Creative Information Technology (ICITech)*. IEEE: New York, NY, USA. 10.1109/INNOCIT.2017.8319150

Wilhite, D. A., Botterill, L., & Monnik, K. (2005a). National Drought Policy: Lessons Learned from Australia, South Africa, and the Unit ed States. In: Wilhite, D. (ed.). Drought and water crises: science, technology, and management issues (137-172). CRC Press.

Wilhite, D. A., Hayes, M. J., & Knutson, C. L. (2005b). Drought preparedness planning: building institutional capacity. In: Wilhite, D. (ed.),2005. Drought and water crises: science, technology, and management issues (93-121), CRC Press.

World Health Organization. (2019). *Definitions: emergencies*. World Health Organization Website.

Compilation of References

Wubalem, A. (2022). *Landslide Inventory, Susceptibility, Hazard and Risk Mapping*. IntechOpen., doi:10.5772/intechopen.100504

Wu, Y., Hou, G., & Chen, S. (2021). Postearthquake resilience assessment and long-term restoration prioritization of transportation network. *Reliability Engineering & System Safety*, *211*, 107612. doi:10.1016/j.ress.2021.107612

Xia, L., Shen, J., Zhang, T., Dang, G., & Wang, T. (2023). GIS-based landslide susceptibility modeling using data mining techniques. *Frontiers in Earth Science (Lausanne)*, *11*, 1187384. doi:10.3389/feart.2023.1187384

Xu, X.-Y., Shao, M., Chen, P.-L., & Wang, Q.-G. (2022). Tropical Cyclone Intensity Prediction Using Deep Convolutional Neural Network. *Atmosphere (Basel)*, *13*(5), 783. https://www.mdpi.com/2073-4433/13/5/783. doi:10.3390/atmos13050783

Yang, L., & Cervone, G. (2019). Analysis of remote sensing imagery for disaster assessment using deep learning: A case study of flooding event. *Soft Computing*, *23*(24), 13393–13408. doi:10.1007/s00500-019-03878-8

Yang, Y., Tang, W., Liu, Y., Xin, Y., & Wu, Q. (2018). Quantitative resilience assessment for power transmission systems under typhoon weather. *IEEE Access : Practical Innovations, Open Solutions*, *6*, 40747–40756. doi:10.1109/ACCESS.2018.2858860

Yao, C., Ye, J., He, Z., Bastola, S., Zhang, K., & Li, Z. (2019). Evaluation of flood prediction capability of the distributed Grid-Xinanjiang model driven by weather research and forecasting precipitation. *Journal of Flood Risk Management*, *12*(S1), 12544. doi:10.1111/jfr3.12544

Yesilnacar, E., & Topal, T. (2005). Landslide susceptibility mapping: A comparison of logistic regression and neural networks methods in a medium scale study, Hendek region (Turkey). *Engineering Geology*, *79*(3–4), 251–266. doi:10.1016/j.enggeo.2005.02.002

Youssef, K., Shao, K., Moon, S., & Bouchard, L.-S. (2023). Landslide susceptibility modeling by interpretable neural network. *Communications Earth & Environment*, *4*(1), 162. doi:10.1038/s43247-023-00806-5

Yuan, J., Wang, L., Wu, P., Gao, C., & Sun, L. (2018). Detection of wildfires along transmission lines using deep time and space features. *Pattern Recognition and Image Analysis*, *28*(4), 805–812. doi:10.1134/S1054661818040168

Yuen, D. A., Scruggs, M. A., Spera, F. J., Zheng, Y., Hu, H., McNutt, S. R., Thompson, G., Mandli, K., Kellerf, B. R., Wei, S. S., Peng, Z., Zhou, Z., Mulargia, F., & Tanioka, Y. (2022). *Under the surface: Pressure-induced planetary-scale waves, volcanic lightning, and gaseous clouds caused by the submarine eruption of Hunga Tonga-Hunga Ha'apai volcano*. Earthquake Research Advances.

Yu, J., Zhao, Q., & Chin, C. S. (2019). Extracting Typhoon Disaster Information from VGI Based on Machine Learning. MDPI. *Journal of Marine Science and Engineering*, *7*(9), 318. doi:10.3390/jmse7090318

Yu, M., Yang, C., & Li, Y. (2018). Big data in natural disaster management: A review. *Geosciences*, *8*(5), 165. doi:10.3390/geosciences8050165

Zahran, B., Ayyoub, B., Abu-Ain, W., Hadi, W., & Al-Hawary, S. (2023). A fuzzy based model for rainfall prediction. *International Journal of Data and Network Science*, *7*(1), 97–106. doi:10.5267/j.ijdns.2022.12.001

Zambrano, A. M., Calderón, X., Zambrano, O. M., Esteve, M., & Jaramillo, S. (2017). *Palau C*. Community Early Warning Systems. Wireless Public Safety Networks.

Zengaffinen, T., Løvholt, F., Pedersen, G. K., & Muhari, A. (2020). Modelling 2018 Anak Krakatoa flank collapse and tsunami: Effect of landslide failure mechanism and dynamics on tsunami generation. *Pure and Applied Geophysics*, *177*(6), 2493–2516. doi:10.1007/s00024-020-02489-x

Zhang, X., Zhang, M. & Tian, X. (2021). Real-time earthquake early warning with deep learning: Application to the 2016 M 6.0 Central Apennines, Italy earthquake. *Geophysical Research Letters*, *48*(5), p.2020GL089394.

Zhang, Q., Xu, J., Xu, L., & Guo, H. (2016). *Deep convolutional neural networks for forest fire detection*. Atlantis Press. doi:10.2991/ifmeita-16.2016.105

Zhang, T., Lin, W., Lin, Y., Zhang, M., Yu, H., Cao, K., & Xue, W. (2019). Prediction of Tropical Cyclone Genesis from Mesoscale Convective Systems Using Machine Learning. *Weather and Forecasting*, *34*(4), 1035–1049. doi:10.1175/WAF-D-18-0201.1

Zhen. (2022). A Review on the Application of Machine Learning Methods in Tropical Cyclone Forecasting, Front. Earth Sci. *Atmospheric Science*, *10*.

Zheng, X., Jia, J., Guo, S., Chen, J., Sun, L., Xiong, Y., & Xu, W. (2021). Full Parameter Time Complexity (FPTC): A Method to Evaluate the Running Time of Machine Learning Classifiers for Land Use/Land Cover Classification. *IEEE Journal of Selected Topics in Applied Earth Observations and Remote Sensing*, *14*, 2222–2235. https://ieeexplore.ieee.org/document/9317826/. doi:10.1109/JSTARS.2021.3050166

Zhou, L., Pan, S., Wang, J., & Vasilakos, A. V. (2017). Machine learning on big data: Opportunities and challenges. *Neurocomputing*, *237*, 350–361. doi:10.1016/j.neucom.2017.01.026

Zhou, X., Wen, H., Zhang, Y., Xu, J., & Zhang, W. (2021). Landslide susceptibility mapping using hybrid random forest with GeoDetector and RFE for factor optimization. *Geoscience Frontiers*, *12*(5), 101211. doi:10.1016/j.gsf.2021.101211

Zia, T. (2023). *AI and earthquake prediction*. Techopedia. https://www.techopedia.com/ai-and-earthquake-prediction

Zimmermann, H. J. (2010). Fuzzy set theory. *Wiley Interdisciplinary Reviews: Computational Statistics*, *2*(3), 317–332. doi:10.1002/wics.82

About the Contributors

D. Satishkumar is an Associate Professor in the Department of Computer Science and Engineering at Nehru Institute of Technology, Coimbatore, Tamilnadu, India-641105, where he has been since 2019. From 2019 to 2021 he served as Department Research Coordinator. From 2012 to 2016 he served as Assistant Professor of Department of Computer Science and Engineering in Nehru institute of Technology, Inc. During 2003-2007 he was a Lecturer at the KCG College of technology, Chennai, Tamilnadu, India, and in 2007-2010 he was faculty at Coimbatore Institute of Engineering and Technology, Coimbatore, Tamilnadu, India, in 2010-2012 he was faculty at Kalaignar karunanidhi Institute of Technology, Coimbatore, Tamilnadu, India. He received a B.E. from Bharathiar University in 2002, and an M.E. from the Manonmaniam sundharnar University, Tamilnadu, India. He received his Ph.D. in Computer Science and Engineering from the Anna University in 2015.

Yunue Garza-Pimentel is a PhD student at SEPI-ESIME, Zac., Instituto Politecnico Nacional, Mexico. Her research interest are associated with natural hazards risk by employing IA techniques.

J. Mangaiyarkkarasi is currently working as an Associate Professor of Physics in NMSS Vellaichamy Nadar College, Nagamalai, Madurai- 625 019, Tamil Nadu, India. She has 23 years of teaching experience. Her major research interest includes synthesis of ceramic materials, powder X-ray analysis and electron density studies. She has published 10 research papers in the refereed International journals and three book chapters. She has prepared study materials (UG& PG Physics) for Madurai Kamaraj University Distance Education Course.

Sivasankari Jothiraj received the B.E. degree in Electronics and Communication Engineering from Annamalai University, Tamilnadu, India, in 2008, the M.E. degree in Communication Systems from Anna University, Tamilnadu, India, in 2011, and obtained Ph.D Degree under the faculty of Information and Communication Engineering from Anna University Chennai. She has been working as an Assistant Professor in the Department of Electronics and Communication Engineering at Velammal College of Engineering and Technology, Madurai, Tamilnadu, India. Her research interests span the areas of cognitive radio networks, energy efficiency, Compressive sensing and network security and underwater image processing.

K.V. Shiny was born in Nagercoil, Tamil Nadu State, India, She received her B.E degree in Computer Science and Engineering from Anna University, Tamil Nadu, India in the year 2011. She received her M.E degree in Computer Science and Engineering from Anna University, Tamil Nadu, India in the year 2013. She has been awarded with one international award and two national awards for her research excellence. Presently she is an Assistant Professor in the Department of Computer Science and Engineering. She has 8 years of teaching and research experience. She has published/Presented more than 15 technical papers in SCIe/International/National journals and conferences.

Mary Mariyal. P is currently doing her B.E Artificial Intelligence & Data Science in V.S.B College of Engineering Technical Campus, Coimbatore. Her Research area includes Computer Networks and Artificial Intelligence.

N. Suresh Kumar, Principal and Professor in ECE Department of Velammal College of Engineering and Technology, Madurai, obtained his B.E from Thiagarajar College of Engineering, Madurai, M.E from AlagappaChettiar College of Engineering, Karaikudi and Ph.D from Madurai Kamaraj University. He has more than 33 years of Teaching and Research Experience. He has a significant contribution in carrying out several research projects in EMI/EMC, he has published and presented in many papers in journals and conferences, He is a life member of IEEE, ISTE, IETE and IE.

P. Rajeswari, Associate Professor of ECE Department of Velammal College of Engineering & Technology, Madurai, obtained her B.E., degree from Madurai Kamaraj University, Madurai and M.E. degree from Anna University, Chennai. She has more than 18 years of Teaching experience. Completed Ph.D. in Anna University, Chennai in EMI/EMC. She has published and presented many research papers in journals and international conferences. Her area of research includes EMI/EMC and Wireless communication. She has a significant contribution in carrying out several research projects in Electromagnetic interference and Compatibility, She is a life member of ISTE, IETE and Society of EMC Engineers (India).

P. Venkadesh M.E, Ph.D., is currently working as a Professor in the Department of Artificial Intelligence & Data Science in V.S.B College of Engineering Technical Campus, Coimbatore, TamilNadu, India . He has a teaching experience of more than 20 years and had published more than 20 research papers in SCI/Scopus indexed journals and 4 Patents. He received his M.E Degree in Computer Science & Engineering from Sathyabama University, Chennai, TamilNadu, India in 2007. He completed his Ph.D at Noorul Islam Centre for Higher Education in 2017 under the area of Network Security and guiding five research scholars. His research area includes Network Security, Image Processing, Wireless Communications and Cloud Computing

Yazhini S. is pursuing her B.E CSE in V.S.B College of Engineering Technical Campus, Coimbatore. Her research area includes Machine Learning, Deep Learning etc.

S.V. Divya M.E, Ph.D., is currently working as a Professor in the Department of Computer Science & Engineering in V.S.B College of Engineering Technical Campus, Coimbatore, TamilNadu, India . She has the teaching experience of more than 16 years and had published more than 15 research papers in SCI/Scopus indexed journals and 2 Patents. She received her B.Tech Degree and M.E Degree in 2005 and 2007 respectively. She received her Ph.D in Computer Science and Engineering at Noorul Islam Centre for Higher Education in 2017 under the area of Cloud Computing and guiding four research scholars. Her research area includes Wireless Communications, Cloud Computing, Big Data and Cyber Security.

About the Contributors

Jaime Santos-Reyes is a lecturer at the National Polytechnic Institute, Mexico, whose main research interests are seismic risk, safety management systems, critical infrastructures modelling, accident and risk analysis, reliability engineering. He obtained a PhD from Heriot-Watt University, UK, in 2001. He has spent 3 years working as a research associate at Heriot-Watt University, Edinburgh, Scotland, UK.

Sanjay Tyagi completed his Masters degree and Ph.D. degree from Kurukshetra University. The author is currently working with Kurukshetra University, India for more than 31 years. His area of research includes Software Testing, Cloud Computing, Information Systems, MANETs & Machine Learning. He has successfully guided five research scholars to Ph.D. Currently, four research scholars (Ph.D.) are working under his guidance. He has more than 90 research publications to his credit. He has attended more than 100 International and National Conferences / Seminars / Workshops. He is on the review panel of various International and National Journals & Conferences. He has been the member of technical programme committees / organizing committees of various International and National Conferences.

Keerthana S. is currently doing her B.E Artificial Intelligence & Data Science in V.S.B College of Engineering Technical Campus, Coimbatore. Her Research area includes Computer Networks and Artificial Intelligence.

Index

A

Algorithms 2, 7-8, 10-11, 15, 21, 24-25, 28, 31, 34-36, 39, 41-53, 56-62, 65-67, 74-75, 77, 84, 91, 118, 122, 124-126, 130, 133-137, 141-142, 148, 150-151, 153, 158, 168-170, 175-186, 189, 193, 195, 201, 205, 208, 212-213, 215-216, 218, 221, 239, 242-244, 246-247, 254-256, 260-261, 271, 274-276, 283-286, 288-290, 294, 298

Artificial intelligence (AI) 2, 7, 24, 40-42, 63, 75, 83-84, 130, 133-136, 138-143, 146-147, 150, 170-171, 175-177, 179, 181-182, 184-185, 190, 195, 200, 204, 210-213, 237-238, 240, 242-244, 247, 249, 274-276, 284-286, 289

Artificial Neural Networks (ANN) 10, 48, 80-85, 87, 147, 153, 160, 208-210, 212-213, 215, 218, 244

B

Big Data 81, 95, 134-135

C

catastrophe prediction 34, 137, 143, 249
Climate change 3-4, 99, 113, 130, 136, 138-139, 143, 191, 228, 239, 274-275
Cloud Computing 190, 194
Convolutional Neural Network 15, 126, 247
culturally sensitive 170-172

D

Data analytics 39, 81, 83, 182, 274
data driven research 130
data mining 25, 28, 31, 33-34, 149-150
Data Sources 15, 27, 45, 47-50, 52, 56, 60-61, 63, 87, 94, 124, 168, 170, 182, 190, 211, 243, 269, 271
decision trees 21, 28, 46, 48, 52, 61, 70, 74, 83-84, 125, 158-159, 162, 294, 299

Deep Learning 10, 17, 36, 39, 46, 56, 100, 123, 125, 141, 151, 194-195, 244, 246-247, 255-256, 261, 269, 271-272, 274, 283-290
Depth 3, 68, 118, 126, 161, 199, 203, 262, 280, 293, 295, 298, 300-305
Disaster management 1-2, 4-7, 10, 13-19, 21, 24-25, 27-36, 40-42, 44-45, 47, 49-51, 53, 57-61, 65-66, 75, 77-78, 81, 83, 87, 89, 93-94, 99, 113, 122, 137, 150, 176-177, 180-186, 188, 190-191, 205, 208-213, 215, 218, 220-223, 229, 237-238, 254-257, 260-262, 268-272, 275, 285, 287-289
Disaster prediction 24, 27, 34, 36, 39, 47, 80-88, 90, 92-96, 118, 122, 124-125, 189, 192, 194, 200, 204-205, 238, 249, 276, 286, 289
Disaster Recovery 3
disaster relief 133-134, 136, 239

E

Early Warning System (EWS) 2, 7, 10, 13, 21, 25, 32-34, 39-41, 45-46, 48, 61, 63, 85, 94-95, 135-136, 138, 140, 146-147, 155-156, 170, 176, 180-181, 184, 186, 189-190, 192, 199, 201, 208-213, 215, 218-219, 221-222, 254-255, 261, 263, 271, 283, 286, 290, 294, 301
Earthquakes 1-3, 13-14, 16, 24-25, 27, 31, 39-41, 46, 49-53, 55, 57, 65-67, 74-75, 77, 81, 83, 85-86, 89, 94, 119-121, 129, 133-136, 138, 140-141, 143, 155, 176, 178-181, 184, 189, 191-192, 197, 200-201, 203, 205, 228, 231, 238, 240-241, 246-247, 254-255, 262, 269, 274-276, 278-281, 286, 293-294, 301-303, 305
Emergency Response 14-15, 24, 41-42, 60, 85, 94, 137, 140, 170, 205, 239, 283

F

Feature Selection 63, 124, 157-158, 298
Flood 1-3, 24, 42, 46, 48-49, 53, 66, 75, 77, 84-86,

Index

95, 134, 136, 140-141, 184, 194-195, 198, 228, 238-240, 274, 280
FOG Computing 194
Fuzzy logic 99, 105, 107, 113, 244-245
fuzzy ruled-based 113

G

Gradient Boosting Regressor 293-294, 296, 299-301, 304-305

H

human intuition 208-209, 212-213, 221

I

Image Analysis 1, 14, 18, 47, 59, 125, 177, 264
Image Formation 125, 130
Internet of Things (IoT) 46, 49, 140-141, 169, 189-191, 194, 201, 204-205, 240, 242, 290

K

K-Means Clustering 25, 28, 44, 60-61, 65-66

L

landslide prediction 84, 146-150, 152-153, 156-157, 159-161, 168-169, 171-172, 184, 202, 243
landslide susceptibility 25, 85, 95, 147-151, 153-159, 161, 163, 169, 242
Logistic regression 28, 41, 43, 74-77, 148, 159

M

Machine learning 1-2, 7-10, 21, 24-25, 28, 31, 33-36, 39-40, 42-47, 49-51, 53, 55-63, 65-69, 74-78, 81, 83-84, 94-96, 100, 118, 122-126, 130, 135-136, 142-143, 146-148, 150-153, 157-158, 168-172, 181-182, 184-186, 195, 204-205, 208, 211-213, 218, 221, 237-239, 243, 245-247, 249, 254-256, 261, 264-267, 269, 271-272, 274, 287, 289, 294, 298
Machine learning algorithms 2, 8, 10, 24-25, 28, 31, 34-36, 43-45, 59-60, 65, 67, 75, 84, 118, 122, 126, 130, 148, 150, 153, 158, 168, 170, 181-182, 184-185, 205, 208, 212, 218, 221, 239, 254-255, 298
Magnitude 57, 67-72, 83, 85, 90, 141, 157, 191, 197, 199, 240, 247, 274, 277-278, 293, 298-301, 303-305

membership function 105-107, 111
mending 238

N

Naive Bayes 65-66, 69, 149, 163
Natural disasters 1-2, 15, 17, 21, 24-25, 36, 39, 41, 47, 61, 63, 65-67, 75, 78, 80-90, 92-96, 119, 130, 134-143, 176-181, 183-184, 186, 189, 191-192, 194, 205, 209-210, 213, 227-229, 238-240, 249, 254-255, 261-262, 269, 274-275, 279, 285-286, 289-290, 302
natural hazards 27, 75, 103, 294
Neural Networks 10-15, 17, 19, 21, 25, 36, 39, 41, 43-44, 46, 48, 50, 56, 60, 65-66, 80-85, 87, 89-90, 100, 126, 147, 153, 160, 208-210, 212-215, 218, 242, 244-246, 256, 264, 269, 294

O

Oceanographic data 118, 124, 130

P

Performance Metrics 270-271, 300-301, 305
Prediction of Earthquakes 133
Predictive modeling 13, 34-36, 46-47, 59, 81-84, 87, 95, 134, 150, 186, 211, 221, 284, 288, 294, 301-302
Predictive models 13, 34, 39, 46, 59, 66-67, 75, 80-82, 84-86, 94, 136, 147, 150, 152, 181, 183, 254, 293, 305
prevention 1-2, 24, 42, 66, 136-139, 190, 272

R

rainfall prediction 99-101, 113
Random Forest methods 65
reaction 34-35, 44-45, 138, 232, 237-238, 275, 284
recuperation 227
Remote Sensing 1, 35, 39, 42, 50, 58-59, 138-139, 146-153, 205, 242, 254, 261, 264, 269, 283, 290
Resilience 3, 5-7, 19, 21, 27, 34-36, 40-42, 47, 52, 66-67, 81, 147, 156, 171-172, 176, 181, 185-186, 208-211, 213, 218, 221, 227-228, 233, 239-240, 254-255, 261, 263, 271-272, 275, 284-285, 302
Resource Allocation 2, 5, 13, 15-17, 21, 24, 33-34, 36, 39, 41, 45, 52, 58, 60-62, 81, 84-85, 94-95, 140, 170, 177, 179-182, 185-186, 260, 264, 283-285, 287-289

S

satellite imagery 13-14, 18, 25, 29, 34, 39, 41, 47-51, 56, 59-60, 81, 87, 95, 124, 138, 141-142, 150, 152, 170, 183-185, 246, 254, 261, 264, 269, 272, 283, 289
Sentiment analysis 47, 50-51, 255, 260
Smart Cities 42, 185
Support Vector Machines (SVM) 25, 48, 60, 65, 69, 76, 83, 152, 161, 245, 304
Sustainable Development 3, 7, 42, 100, 112, 154, 156, 190

T

Timestamp Conversion 298
Tsunami prediction 203, 212

U

Underwater disasters 118-122, 124-125, 129-130

V

Volcanic Eruptions 66, 119-120, 133-135, 142, 203, 247-248, 279

W

Warning system 53, 55, 122, 168, 189-190, 212, 215-217, 242, 247
Wearable Sensors 175-180, 184, 186

Publishing Tomorrow's Research Today

Uncover Current Insights and Future Trends in
Business & Management
with IGI Global's Cutting-Edge Recommended Books

Print Only, E-Book Only, or Print + E-Book.
Order direct through IGI Global's Online Bookstore at **www.igi-global.com** or through your preferred provider.

ISBN: 9798369306444
© 2023; 436 pp.
List Price: US$ **230**

ISBN: 9798369300084
© 2023; 358 pp.
List Price: US$ **250**

ISBN: 9781668458594
© 2023; 366 pp.
List Price: US$ **240**

ISBN: 9781668486344
© 2023; 256 pp.
List Price: US$ **280**

ISBN: 9781668493243
© 2024; 318 pp.
List Price: US$ **250**

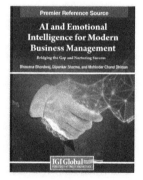

ISBN: 9798369304181
© 2023; 415 pp.
List Price: US$ **250**

Do you want to stay current on the latest research trends, product announcements, news, and special offers?
Join IGI Global's mailing list to receive customized recommendations, exclusive discounts, and more.
Sign up at: **www.igi-global.com/newsletters**.

Scan the QR Code here to
view more related titles in Business & Management.

www.igi-global.com   Sign up at www.igi-global.com/newsletters   facebook.com/igiglobal   twitter.com/igiglobal   linkedin.com/igiglobal

Ensure Quality Research is Introduced to the Academic Community

Become a Reviewer for IGI Global Authored Book Projects

 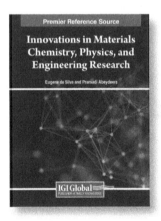 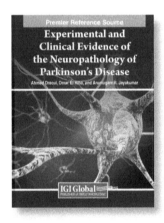 

The overall success of an authored book project is dependent on quality and timely manuscript evaluations.

Applications and Inquiries may be sent to:
development@igi-global.com

Applicants must have a doctorate (or equivalent degree) as well as publishing, research, and reviewing experience. Authored Book Evaluators are appointed for one-year terms and are expected to complete at least three evaluations per term. Upon successful completion of this term, evaluators can be considered for an additional term.

If you have a colleague that may be interested in this opportunity, we encourage you to share this information with them.

Recommended Titles from our e-Book Collection

Innovation Capabilities and Entrepreneurial Opportunities of Smart Working
ISBN: 9781799887973

Advanced Applications of Generative AI and Natural Language Processing Models
ISBN: 9798369305027

Using Influencer Marketing as a Digital Business Strategy
ISBN: 9798369305515

Human-Centered Approaches in Industry 5.0
ISBN: 9798369326473

Modeling and Monitoring Extreme Hydrometeorological Events
ISBN: 9781668487716

Data-Driven Intelligent Business Sustainability
ISBN: 9798369300497

Information Logistics for Organizational Empowerment and Effective Supply Chain Management
ISBN: 9798369301593

Data Envelopment Analysis (DEA) Methods for Maximizing Efficiency
ISBN: 9798369302552

Request More Information, or Recommend the IGI Global e-Book Collection to Your Institution's Librarian

For More Information or to Request a Free Trial, Contact IGI Global's e-Collections Team: eresources@igi-global.com | 1-866-342-6657 ext. 100 | 717-533-8845 ext. 100

Are You Ready to Publish Your Research?

IGI Global
Publishing Tomorrow's Research Today

IGI Global offers book authorship and editorship opportunities across three major subject areas, including Business, STM, and Education.

Benefits of Publishing with IGI Global:

- Free one-on-one editorial and promotional support.
- Expedited publishing timelines that can take your book from start to finish in less than one (1) year.
- Choose from a variety of formats, including Edited and Authored References, Handbooks of Research, Encyclopedias, and Research Insights.
- Utilize IGI Global's eEditorial Discovery® submission system in support of conducting the submission and double-blind peer review process.
- IGI Global maintains a strict adherence to ethical practices due in part to our full membership with the Committee on Publication Ethics (COPE).
- Indexing potential in prestigious indices such as Scopus®, Web of Science™, PsycINFO®, and ERIC – Education Resources Information Center.
- Ability to connect your ORCID iD to your IGI Global publications.
- Earn honorariums and royalties on your full book publications as well as complimentary content and exclusive discounts.

Join Your Colleagues from Prestigious Institutions, Including:

Australian National University
Massachusetts Institute of Technology
Johns Hopkins University
Tsinghua University
Harvard University
Columbia University in the City of New York

Learn More at: www.igi-global.com/publish
or Contact IGI Global's Aquisitions Team at: acquisition@igi-global.com

Printed in the USA
CPSIA information can be obtained
at www.ICGtesting.com
CBHW081651290924
15102CB00021B/127